ALMANAC
of the
50 STATES

Basic Data Profiles
with
Comparative Tables

1996 EDITION

Edith R. Hornor
Editor

information
publications

ISSN 0887-0519
ISBN 0-931845-46-7(paper)
ISBN 0-931845-47-5 (library)

Information Publications
3790 El Camino Real, #162
Palo Alto, CA 94306
415-965-4449

2/96

ALMANAC
of the
50 STATES

Basic Data Profiles
with
Comparative Tables

Table of Contents

Introduction

The <u>Almanac of the Fifty States</u> has been created in order to provide a comprehensive, easy to use, state statistical reference book. It presents a general overview of every state, along with tables of comparative ranking.

The book is divided into two parts. The first, State Profiles, is comprised of 52 individual profile sections: one for each of the 50 states, one for the District of Columbia, and one for the US in summary. Each of these profiles is eight pages long, each utilizes the same format organized into 13 subject categories, and each has been compiled from the same sources of information. The result is a set of basic data profiles which are readable, understandable, and provide a strong basis for comparative analysis.

The individual profiles are the heart of the book. Information selected for the profiles has been chosen to include those items which have the greatest general appeal to the broadest cross-section of users. The information comes from the latest reports of federal government agencies, augmented with data from business and trade organizations. No new surveys or original material is included, as the objective is to provide the most vital and significant information about each state, from the most reliable and respected collectors of data. A complete review of the profiles is provided below.

The second part of the book, Comparative Tables, is composed of tables of ranking. The 54 tables each list the states in rank order for a selected characteristic chosen from the state profiles. The purpose here has been to provide straightforward tabular data on how states compare in regard to a given characteristic.

The overall goal of the <u>Almanac of the 50 States</u> is to bring together into a single volume a wide variety of diverse information and present it, state by state, in a clear, comprehensible format. It is not intended as a detailed research tool, but rather as a ready reference source, the first place to turn to answer basic questions about the states.

For readers requiring more depth of coverage or a different focus, it goes without saying that the full range of federal government resources should be examined. Not only <u>Statistical Abstract</u> (and its supplements <u>City and County Data Book</u>, and <u>State and Metropolitan Area Data Book</u>), but the annual reports and serial publications of individual departments and agencies merit attention as well. The federal government is the largest publishing enterprise in the United States, and once the initial hurdle of access is overcome, the researcher is well rewarded: its materials cover a wider range of topics in greater depth and detail than could be imagined.

Additionally, the publications of various trade and professional associations are an excellent source of state information. Most of these organizations produce monographs and annual reports which provide statistical information that is not available elsewhere. Such publications have been useful in compiling this book, and the most pertinent of proprietary information has been reprinted here with permission.

Finally, state governments themselves are publishers of note. Frequently they bring together and make available valuable information on a state and regional level. Most of their material is collected and made available by the respective state libraries.

In order to continue to meet its goals, Almanac of the 50 States is revised and updated on an annual basis. The best suggestions for improvement in a ready-reference source such as this come from the regular users of the work. Therefore, your comments and ideas are actively solicited. If your know how this book can become more useful to you, please contact us.

The Editors
Almanac of the 50 States
Information Publications
3790 El Camino Real, #162
Palo Alto, CA 94306

The profiles

All information in the profiles has been selected from federal government reports and publications, or from materials published by business and trade organizations. The use of such sources ensures an internal consistency and reliability of data that just would not have been available otherwise. Additionally, it enables the users of this book to go back to the more detailed original source materials and use the two in combination.

To enhance this consistency, all headings and terms used in the profiles have been carried over as they appear in the original sources. Those unfamiliar with government terminology may at times be puzzled by either the meaning of a specific term , or why the data was gathered in a certain way. Unclear terms are defined (as the data collection agency uses them) in the next section, The Categories, Headings & Terms. Additionally, the source of origin for each item of information is presented. This allows readers to refer to the original sources themselves which often contain more detailed definitions, and fuller explanations of data collection procedures.

In preparing the format for the profiles, the design has been structured to enable each profile to stand alone. The headings are clear, abbreviations have been avoided (with the exception of "$mil" for millions of dollars) and indents have been used to indicate subgroups of the main heading. However, because of the ease of reading, users are cautioned to keep in mind the wording of a heading, and to note whether a dollar amount, median (midway point), mean (average), or percent is being provided. Additionally, it should be pointed out that not all subgroups add to the total shown. This may be due to rounding, or the fact that only selected subgroups are displayed.

The Categories, Headings & Terms

A review of the 13 categories which make up each of the profiles appears below. In addition to citing the source of origin, the paragraphs contain a brief identification of terms and some background methodology on the data collection.

State Summary

All information in this box is taken from the other 12 categories, and individual sources are identified below.

Geography & Environment

General coastline data represents the length of the outline of the coast. Tidal shoreline data represents the shoreline of the outer coast, off-shore islands, sounds, bays, rivers, and creeks to the head of the tidewater. The original source of this information is The Coastline of the United State, 1975.

National parks information comes from State and Metropolitan Area Data Book. All other items in this section are from Statistical Abstract.

Demographics & Characteristics of the Population

All 1970, 1980, and 1990 items are from the 1970, 1980, and 1990 Censuses of Population, respectively, conducted by the Bureau of the Census.

Metropolitan area population data comes from the Bureau of the Census. The metropolitan area population consists of all persons living in Metropolitan Areas (MAs) in the state. An MA is defined by the Bureau of the Census by fairly complicated criteria, but basically consists of a large population nucleus, together with adjacent communities which have a high degree of economic and social integration with that nucleus. Each MA must include at least: (a) one place with 50,000 or more inhabitants, or (b) a Census Bureau-defined urbanized area and a total MA population of at least 100,000 (75,000 in New England). Non-metropolitan area population is everyone not included in metropolitan area population of the state.

Change in population was calculated from Bureau of the Census data.

Racial statistics are provided, although they are a highly sensitive subject. It is important to recognize that the breakdown represents the self-identification of respondents in regard to pre-set census categories. It does not in any way denote any scientific of biological notion of race. Hispanic origin is not racial group as defined by the Bureau, and persons may be of any race and be of Hispanic origin as well. There is a fairly lengthy discussion of the issues surrounding racial categories in the introductory and explanatory sections of the 1990 Census.

A household is defined as the person or persons occupying a housing unit. A housing unit is defined below, under Housing & Construction. Briefly, a housing unit is a separate set of living quarters such as a house, apartment, mobile home, etc. A family is a type of household and consists of a householder and one or more other persons living in the same household who are related to the householder by birth, marriage, or adoption. Married couples, and female heads of household with dependent children and no husband present, are subgroups, or types of families.

The 1994 population estimates are from the Bureau of the Census P-25 series reports. Population and age distribution projections are from Statistical Abstract.

Immigration and naturalization data is from the Statistical Yearbook, 1992, a publication of the US Immigration and Naturalization Service.

Vital Statistics & Health

Birth, death, marriage, and divorce data comes from the Monthly Vital Statistics Report, a publication of the Department of Health & Human Services.

Abortion information comes from Family Planning Perspectives, a publication of the Alan Guttmacher Institute, and is reprinted here with permission.

Data for physicians and dentists are counts of active, non-federally employed practitioners. Physicians exclude doctors of osteopathy. This information comes from the Health Resources and Services Administration, Department of Health and Human Services.

Adoption information comes from the Adoption Fact Book, a publication of the National Committee for Adoption. Inc., and is used here with permission. A related adoption is one in which the person adopted is related to the adopter (an uncle, grandmother, etc.).

Average lifetime data comes from Statistical Abstract.

Hospital data comes from Statistical Abstract. Data reflects AHA member hospitals only. The average daily census refers to the average total number of in-patients receiving treatment each day, excluding newborns. The occupancy rate is the ratio of the average daily census to every 100 beds. Cost per day and cost per stay represent cost to hospital per day and per stay.

Education

Educational attainment data comes from the 1990 Census of Population.

All other education data (with the exception of finance data) is from Digest of Education Statistics 1995, compiled by the National Center for Educational Statistics, U.S. Department of Education. Finance data was taken from Statistical Abstract, 1994.

Social Insurance & Welfare Programs

All items here have been obtained from Statistical Abstract and its supplements. It should be noted that detail is provided for three major Social Security programs: those for the retired; for the survivors of enrollees; and for the disabled covered under the program. The original source of Social Security information is the Social Security Administration's Bulletin and the Bulletin's Annual Statistical Supplement. Medicare and Medicaid data are produced by the U.S. Health Care Financing Administration and are also from Statistical Abstract.

Housing & Construction

The Bureau of the Census conducts a decennial Census of Housing which is almost as extensive as its Census of Population. The selection of housing information here, taken from the 1990 Census of Housing, represents just a small portion of what is available.

The Bureau defines some key terms as follows: a housing unit is house, apartment, mobile home or trailer, group of rooms, or single room occupied as separate living quarter or, if vacant, intended as a separate living quarter. Separate living quarters are those in which occupants live and eat separately from any other persons in the building and which have direct access from the outside of the building or from a common hall.

Data for new privately owned housing units comes from Construction Reports, an annual publication of the Bureau of the Census, and from Statistical Abstract.

Government and Elections

Names of State officials and current party in majority have been obtained from telephone confirmations from the office of the Governor or Secretary of State of the respective states. Information about the governorship and legislative structure of each state was obtained from respective legislative manuals and annual election reports.

State employees is from Public Employment, 1992, an annual publication of the Bureau of the Census. Figures represent October, 1992, totals for full and part-time employees, along with October payroll data.

Information on local governments comes from the 1992 Census of Governments (conducted by the Bureau of the Census). Readers are cautioned that the data provided concerns governmental units as opposed to geographic entities. For example, in Connecticut there are eight counties, but no county governments, hence a zero appears in the county space in the Connecticut profile.

Voting age population and registration information comes from Statistical Abstract, and is unpublished data from the Bureau of the Census.

Information on women holding public offices comes from press releases provided by the Center for American Women and Politics at the Eagleton Institute of Rutgers University, and is reprinted with permission.

Data concerning black elected officials are from the Joint Center for Political & Economic Studies, Washington, DC, reprinted in Statistical Abstract.

Hispanic public officials information is from the National Association of Latino Elected and Appointed Officials, Washington, DC, reprinted in Statistical Abstract.

Governmental Finance

Revenue, expenditure and debt information comes from Governmental Finance in 1991-92. Federal aid information comes from Federal Expenditures by State for Fiscal Year 1994. Both are publications of the Bureau of the Census.

Crime, Law Enforcement & Courts

Information on crime, crime rates, police agencies, and arrests comes from Crime in the US. Information on prisoners and number of persons under sentence of death comes from Sourcebook of Criminal Justice Statistics, 1994. These sources are publications of the Department of Justice. Readers are cautioned that crime information is based on crimes known to police.

State court information comes from the legislative manuals of the respective states.

Labor & Income

All civilian labor force data comes from Geographic Profiles of Employment and Unemployment, 1994, a Department of Labor publication.

The civilian labor force includes all civilians who are either employed or unemployed. Generally, employed persons are those who: 1) did any work as a paid employee; or 2) worked 15 hours or more as an unpaid employee in a family enterprise; or 3) had jobs but were not working due to illness, vacation, etc. Unemployed persons are those who: 1) had no paid employment and were both available for and looking for work; or 2) were waiting to be recalled to a job; or 3) were waiting to report to a new job. A full-time employee is one who works at least 35 hours per week.

Unemployed persons are grouped into four categories: a job loser is someone whose employment has ended involuntarily; a job leaver is someone whose employment ended voluntarily; a reentrant is someone who has previously worked, but was out of the labor force prior to seeking employment; and a new entrant is someone who has never worked before and is now seeking employment.

Hours and earnings data comes from Employment & Earnings, May, 1995, a monthly publication of the Department of Labor.

Average annual pay comes from NEWS, a bulletin put out by the Bureau of Labor Statistics, and includes the pay of workers who are covered by state unemployment insurance laws, and federal civilian workers covered by federal unemployment. This represents approximately 89% of total civilian employment. It excludes members of the armed forces, elected officials in most states, railroad employees, most self-employed persons, and some others. Pay includes bonuses, the cash value of meals and lodging, and tips and other gratuities.

Labor union membership comes from Statistical Abstract.

Household income and poverty information comes from the 1993 P-60 Series of the U.S. Bureau of the Census.

Personal income figures come from Survey of Current Business, a monthly publication of the Department of Commerce.

Federal tax data are from Statistics of Income Bulletin, a quarterly report of the Internal Revenue Service.

Economy, Business, Industry & Agriculture

Fortune 500 companies come from a count of listed corporations found in the annual directory issue of this magazine.

Business incorporation and failure data comes from proprietary information compiled by Dun & Bradstreet. It is reprinted here with permission.

Business firm ownership is from the U.S. Bureau of the Census.

Gross state product is taken from Survey of Current Business, a publication of the Department of Commerce, Bureau of Economic Analysis.

Establishment and payroll data are from the latest available edition of County Business Patterns, a 52 volume report issued annually by the Bureau of the Census.

Agricultural data comes from the Department of Agriculture, and was republished in Statistical Abstract.

Data on federal economic activity comes from Federal Expenditures by State for Fiscal Year 1994, a publication of the Bureau of the Census, reprinted in Statistical Abstract.

Department of Defense information comes from the department and was reprinted in Statistical Abstract.

Fishing data are from Fishery Statistics of the United States, a publication of the National Oceanic and Atmospheric Administration, reprinted in Statistical Abstract.

Mining information is from the U.S. Bureau of Mines; construction information is from the Dodge Reports (McGraw Hill); manufacturing data are from the 1992 Annual Survey of Manufactures; finance information originates with the Federal Deposit Insurance Corporation and the Federal Home Loan Bank Board. Retail trade comes from the 1992 Economic Census. Wholesale trade and service industry information comes from the 1992 Economic Census.

Communication, Energy & Transportation

The count of daily newspapers is from <u>Statistical Abstract</u>.

Information on radio and TV stations and cable television households was obtained from <u>State and Metropolitan Area Data Book</u>, 1991.

All energy information comes from <u>State Energy Data Report</u>, and <u>Electric Power Annual</u>, both published by the U.S. Energy Information Administration and reprinted from <u>Statistical Abstract</u>.

All transportation information comes from <u>Highway Statistics</u>, 1994, an annual publication of the Department of Transportation.

The Profiles

Alabama 1

STATE SUMMARY

Capital City .Montgomery

Governor . . . . .Forrest "Fob" James

Address . . . . STATE CAPITOL
MONTGOMERY, AL 31630
205 242-7200

Admitted as a state 1819

Area (square miles) 52,423

Population, 1980 .3,893,800

Population, 1990 .4,040,587

Population, 1994 (est.) 4,219,000

Persons per square mile, 1994 . . . . 83.1

Largest city . . . . Birmingham
population, 1990 226,000

Personal income per capita, 1994
(in current dollars) $18,010

Gross state product ($mil), 1991 73,956

Leading industries, 1992 (by payroll)
MANUFACTURING
SERVICE INDUSTRIES
RETAIL TRADE

Leading agricultural commodities, 1993
BROILERS
CATTLE
GREENHOUSE
PEANUTS

GEOGRAPHY & ENVIRONMENT

Area (square miles)
total 52,423
land 50,750
water (includes territorial water) 1,673

Federally owned land, 1991 . . . . 3.3%

Highest point
name . . . . Cheaha Mountain
elevation (feet) 2,405

Lowest point
name . . . . .Gulf of Mexico
elevation (feet) .sea level

General coastline (miles) 53

Tidal shoreline (miles) 607

Capital city . . . . .Montgomery
population, 1990 187,000

Largest city . . . . Birmingham
population, 1990 226,000

Number of cities with over 100,000 population
1980 4

Number of cities with over 100,000 population
1990 4

State parks and Recreation areas, 1991
area (acres) 50,000
number of visitors 6,084,000
revenues $22,505,000

National forest land, 1992 (acres) 1,288,000

National park acreage, 1984 6,600

DEMOGRAPHICS & CHARACTERISTICS OF THE POPULATION

Population
1970 3,444,354
1980 3,893,800
1990 4,040,587
1994 (est.) 4,219,000
2000 (revised projection) 4,485,000
2010 (revised projection) 4,856,000

Metropolitan area population
1970 2,169,000
1980 2,462,000
1992 2,788,000

Non-metropolitan area population
1970 1,275,000
1980 1,432,000
1992 1,349,000

Change in population, 1980-90
number 146,787
percent 3.77%

Persons per square mile, 1994 . . . . 83.1

Age distribution, 1980
under 5 years 7.6%
5 to 17 years 22.2%
65 and over 11.3%

Age distribution, 1990
under 5 years 7.0%
5 to 17 years 19.1%
65 and over 12.9%

3

Alabama 2

Age distribution, 2000 (projected)
under 5 years 6.2%
5 to 17 years 18.9%
65 and over 13.2%

Persons by age, 1990
under 5 years 283,295
5 to 17 years 775,493
65 and over 522,989

Median age, 1990 .... 33.00

Race, 1990
White 2,975,797
Black 1,020,705
American Indian 16,312
Chinese 3,929
Filipino 1,816
Japanese 2,028
Asian Indian 4,348
Korean 3,454
Vietnamese 2,274
all other 9,730

Race, 2010 (projected)
White 3,529,000
Black 1,243,000

Persons of Hispanic origin, 1990
total 24,629
Mexican 9,509
Puerto Rican 3,553
Cuban 1,463
Other Hispanic 10,104

Persons by sex, 1990
male 1,936,162
female 2,104,425

Marital status, 1990
males
15 years & older 1,488,017
single 406,140
married 925,748
separated 26,921
widowed 40,619
divorced 115,510
females
15 years & older 1,676,275
single 348,728
married 933,898
separated 41,081

widowed 235,648
divorced 158,001

Households & families, 1990
households 1,506,790
persons per household 2.62
families 1,103,835
married couples 858,327
female householder, no husband
present 201,220
one person households 358,078
households, 1994 1,583,000
persons per household, 1994 .... 2.61

Nativity, 1990
number of persons born in state 3,067,607
percent of total residents 75.9%

Immigration & naturalization, 1993
immigrants admitted 2,298
persons naturalized 719
refugees granted resident status 118

VITAL STATISTICS & HEALTH

Births
1992 63,021
with low birth weight 8.5%
to teenage mothers 18.2%
to unmarried mothers 32.6%
1993 63,332
1994 60,745

Abortions, 1992
total 17,000
rate (per 1,000 women age 15-44) 18.2
rate per 1,000 live births 277

Adoptions, 1986
total 2,480
related 76.5%

Deaths
1992 39,630
1993 41,540
1994 42,138

Infant deaths
1992 683
1993 629
1994 601

Average lifetime, 1979-1981
both sexes .... 72.53 years
  men .... 68.28 years
  women .... 76.79 years

Marriages
1992 40,486
1993 39,476
1994 40,179

Divorces
1992 27,009
1993 27,047
1994 26,116

Physicians, 1993
total 7,068
rate (per 1,000 persons) 1.70

Dentists, 1992
total 1,776
rate (per 1,000 persons) 0.43

Hospitals, 1993
number 116
beds (x 1,000) 18.5
average daily census (x 1,000) 11.3
occupancy rate 60.7%
personnel (x 1,000) 66.0
average cost per day to hospital $775
average cost per stay to hospital $5,229

EDUCATION

Educational attainment of all persons
25 years and older, 1990
less than 9th grade 348,848
high school graduates 749,591
bachelor's degree 258,231
graduate or professional degree 140,997

Public school enrollment, Fall, 1993
total 734,469
  Kindergarten through grade 8 535,818
  grades 9 through 12 198,651

Public School Teachers
total, 1994 43,002
  elementary 23,929
  secondary 19,073
salaries, 1994
  beginning $22,500
  average $28,659

State receipts & expenditures for public
schools, 1993
receipts ($mil) 2,716
expenditures
  total ($mil) 2,865
  per capita $692
  per pupil $3,779

Graduating high school seniors,
public high schools, 1995 (est) 37,091

SAT scores, 1994
verbal 482
math 529

Institutions of higher education, 1995
total 80
  public 53
  private 27

Enrollment in institutions of higher
education, Fall, 1993
total 233,525
full-time men 71,148
full-time women 82,841
part-time men 33,714
part-time women 45,822

Minority enrollment in institutions of higher
education, Fall, 1993
Black, non-Hispanic 52,113
Hispanic 1,548
Asian/Pacific Islander 2,094

Earned degrees conferred, 1993
Bachelor's 20,525
First professional 866
Master's 5,636
Doctor's 406

SOCIAL INSURANCE & WELFARE PROGRAMS

Social Security beneficiaries & benefits, 1993
beneficiaries
total 752,000
  retired and dependents 472,000
  survivors 157,000
  disabled & dependents 124,000
annual benefit payments ($mil)
total $4,949
  retired and dependents 3,020
  survivors 1,175
  disabled & dependents 755

Alabama 4

Medicare, 1993
enrollment (x1,000) 618
payments ($mil) 2,461

Medicaid, 1993
recipients (x1,000) 522
payments ($mil) 1,192

Federal public aid, 1993
recipients as a percent of population 7.0%
Aid to Families with Dependent Children
    recipients (x1,000) 135
average monthly payment $154
Supplemental Security Income
    total recipients (x1,000) 156

Food Stamp Program
    participants, 1994 (x1,000) 551

HOUSING & CONSTRUCTION

Total housing units, 1990 1,670,379
    year round housing units 1,634,475
    vacant 163,589

New privately owned housing units authorized, 1994
number (x1,000) 19.1
value ($mil) 1,357

New privately owned housing units started, 1994 (x1,000) 24.1

Existing home sales, 1994 (x1,000) 77.4

GOVERNMENT & ELECTIONS

State officials, 1996
Governor (name/party/term expires)
FORREST "FOB" JAMES
Republican - 1999
Lt. Governor .... Don Siegelman
Sec. of State .... Billy Joe Camp
Atty. General .... Jeff Sessions
Chf. Justice .... E.C. Hornsby

Governorship
minimum age 30
length of term .... 4 years
number of consecutive
    terms permitted 2
who succeeds .... Lt. Governor

State legislature
name .... Legislature
    upper chamber
        name .... Senate
        number of members 35
        length of term .... 4 years
        party in majority, 1996 .... Democratic
    lower chamber
        name .... House of Representatives
        number of members 105
        length of term .... 4 years
        party in majority, 1996 .... Democratic

State employees October, 1992
total 94,907
October payroll ($1,000) 176,929

Local governments, 1992
total 1,134
    county 67
    municipal 440
    township 0
    school districts 129
    special districts 497

Voting, November, 1994
voting age population 3,136,000
    registered 70.6%
    voted 45.8%

Vote for president
1988
    Bush 809,663
    Dukakis 547,347
1992
    Clinton 679,416
    Bush 797,148
    Perot 180,108

Federal representation, 1996 (104th Congress)
Senators (name/party/term expires)

HOWELL T. HEFLIN
Democrat - 1997
RICHARD SHELBY
Democrat - 1999

Representatives, total 7
    Democrats 4
    Republicans 3
    other 0

Alabama 5

Women holding public office
U.S. Congress, 1995 0
statewide elected office, 1995 3
state legislature, 1995 5

Black elected officials, 1993
total 699
  US and state legislatures 23
  city/county/regional offices 529
  judicial/law enforcement 58
  education/school boards 89

Hispanic public officials, 1994
total ....NA
  state executives & legislators ....NA
  city/county/regional offices ....NA
  judicial/law enforcement ....NA
  education/school boards ....NA

GOVERNMENTAL FINANCE

State & local government revenues, (selected items), 1991-92 ($per capita)
total $3,873.61
  total general revenues 3,139.06
    from federal government 716.32
    from own sources 2,422.73
    from taxes 1,452.06
      from property taxes 176.15
      from all other taxes 1,094.42
    from charges & misc. 970.69

State & local government expenditures, (selected items), 1991-92 ($per capita)
total $3,690.33
  total direct general expenditures 3,146.44
    education 1,043.66
    libraries 8.34
    public welfare 461.96
    health & hospitals 572.54
    highways 225.69
    police protection 95.76
    fire protection 38.09
    correction 60.02
    housing & comm. development 45.56
    natural resources & parks 84.43
    interest on general debt 164.16

State & local debt, 1992 ($per capita) 2,719.39

Federal aid grants to state & local government, 1994 ($per capita total & selected items)
per capita total 760.70
  compensatory education 29.74
  waste treatment facilities 5.68
  medicaid 305.14
  housing assistance 40.04
  job training 13.17
  highway trust fund 64.49

CRIME, LAW ENFORCEMENT & COURTS

Crime, 1994 (all rates per 100,000 persons)
total crimes 206,859
overall crime rate 4,903.0
  property crimes 178,015
    burglaries 44,064
    larcenies 119,951
    motor vehicle thefts 14,000
  property crime rate 4,219.4
  violent crimes 28,844
    murders 501
    forcible rapes 1,487
    robberies 7,223
    aggravated assaults 19,633
  violent crime rate 683.7

Number of police agencies, 1994 260

Arrests, 1994
total 199,303
  persons under 18 years of age 17,018

Prisoners under state & federal jurisdiction, 1994
total 19,573
percent change, 1993-94 .... 5.1%
sentenced to more than one year
  total 19,074
  rate per 100,000 residents 450

Persons under sentence of death, 4/20/95 135

State's highest court
name .... Supreme Court
number of members 9
length of term .... 6 years
intermediate appeals court? .... yes

Alabama 6

LABOR & INCOME

Civilian labor force, 1994
total 2,031,000
men 1,093,000
women 938,000
persons 16-19 years 121,000
white 1,545,000
black 464,000

Civilian labor force as a percent of civilian non-institutional population, 1994
total 62.9%
men 72.1%
women 54.8%
persons 16-19 years 47.5%
white 64.2%
black 58.5%

Employment, 1994
total 1,909,000
men 1,041,000
women 868,000
persons 16-19 years 94,000
white 1,478,000
black 410,000

Full-time/part-time labor force, 1994
full-time labor force 1,690,000
  working part-time for
    ecomonic reasons 26,000
part-time labor force 341,000

Unemployment rate, 1994
total 6.0%
men 4.7%
women 7.5%
persons 16-19 years 21.9%
white 4.3%
black 11.6%

Unemployed by reason for unemployment (as a percent of total unemployment), 1994
job losers or completed temp jobs 45.8%
job leavers 8.5%
reentrants 34.1%
new entrants 11.5%

Civilian labor force, by occupation, 1994
executive/administrative/
  managerial 208,000
professional/specialty 242,000
technicians & related support 55,000
sales 233,000
adminstrative support/clerical 278,000
service occupations 251,000
precision production/craft/repair 276,000
machine operators/assemblers 208,000
transportation/material moving 109,000
handlers/helpers/laborers 88,000
farming/forestry/fishing 68,000

Civilian labor force, by industry, 1994
construction 110,000
manufacturing 440,000
transportation/communication 107,000
wholesale/retail trade 384,000
finance/real estate/insurance 81,000
services 354,000
government 311,000
agriculture 58,000

Average annual pay, 1994 (prelim.) $23,616
change in average annual pay,
  1993-1994 .... 3.6%

Hours and earnings of production workers on manufacturing payrolls, 1994
average weekly hours 41.9
average hourly earnings $10.75
average weekly earnings $450.43

Labor union membership, 1994 236,100

Household income (in constant 1993 dollars)
median household income, 1992 .... $26,581
median household income, 1993 .... $25,082

Poverty
persons below poverty level, 1992 .... 17.3%
persons below poverty level, 1993 .... 17.4%

Personal income ($per capita)
1994
  in current dollars 18,010
  in constant (1987) dollars 13,929
1995 (projected)
  in constant (1982) dollars 11,453
2000 (projected)
  in constant (1982) dollars 12,247

Federal income tax returns, 1993
returns filed 1,760,213
adjusted gross income ($1000) 49,377,846
total income tax paid ($1000) 6,448,324

ECONOMY, BUSINESS, INDUSTRY & AGRICULTURE

Fortune 500 companies, 1994 1

Business incorporations, 1994
total 7,169
change, 1993-94 .... -0.1%

Business failures, 1994
total 669
rate per 10,000 concerns 58
change, 1993-94 .... -20.3%

Business firm ownership
Hispanic owned firms, 1987 397
black owned firms, 1987 10,085
women owned firms, 1987 48,000
foreign owned firms, 1982 154

Gross state product, 1991 ($mil)
total $73,956
  agriculture services, forestry, fisheries ... 2,076
  mining 1,289
  construction 2,609
  manufacturing—durable goods 7,969
  manufacturing—nondurable goods 8,242
  transportation, communication &
    public utilities 7,129
  wholesale trade 4,351
  retail trade 6,869
  finance/real estate/insurance 10,404
  services 11,137
  federal, state & local government 11,881

Establishments, by major industry group, 1992
total 89,869
  agriculture 1,257
  mining 337
  construction 7,901
  manufacturing 6,471
  transportation 4,023
  wholesale trade 6,972
  retail trade 24,668
  finance/real estate/insurance 7,621
  service industries 29,310
  unclassified 1,309

Payroll, by major industry group, 1992
total ($1,000) $28,731,563
  agriculture 119,878
  mining 407,160
  construction 1,683,236
  manufacturing 9,212,316
  transportation 2,249,863
  wholesale trade 2,033,006
  retail trade 3,303,989
  finance/real estate/insurance 1,876,879
  service industries 7,824,463
  unclassified 20,773

Agriculture
number of farms, 1994 46,000
farm acreage, 1994 10,000,000
acres per farm, 1994 217
value of farms, 1994 ($mil) 9,637
farm income, 1993 ($mil)
  gross farm income 3,491
  net farm income 1,093
  debt/asset ratio 13.6%
farm marketings, 1993 ($mil)
  total $2,910
    crops 727
    livestock 2,184
  government payments 137
farm marketings in order of marketing
receipts, 1993
    1) Broilers
    2) Cattle
    3) Eggs
    4) Greenhouse

Federal economic activity
($mil, except per capita)
expenditures, 1994
  total $22,280
  per capita $5,281
  defense $4,058
  non-defense $18,222
defense department, 1994
  contract awards ($mil) $1,673
  payroll ($mil) $2,320
  civilian employees (x1,000) 24.3
  military personnel (x1,000) 16.7

Fishing, 1992
catch (millions of pounds) 24
value ($mil) 36

Mining, 1994 ($mil)
total non-fuel mineral production $576

Alabama 8

principal non-fuel minerals in order of value, 1994
1) Stone
2) Cement
3) Lime

Construction, 1994 ($mil)
total contracts (including
  non-building) $4,165
    residential 1,861
    non-residential 1,432

Manufacturing, 1992
total establishments 6,436
employees, total (x1,000) 380
payroll ($mil) 9,217
production workers (x1,000) 284
value added ($mil) 23,653
value of shipments ($mil) 52,708

Finance
commercial banks, 1994
  number 214
    assets ($bil) 46.9
    deposits ($bil) 37.4
    closed or assisted 0
    deposits ($bil) .... NA
savings and loan associations, 1991
  non-current real estate loans 4.05%
  net income after taxes ($mil) .... -39
  return on assets .... -0.54%

Retail trade, 1992
establishments (x1,000) 24.1
sales ($mil) 27,734
annual payroll ($mil) 2,989
paid employees (x1,000) 270

Wholesale trade, 1992
establishments 7,066
sales ($bil) 32.0
annual payroll ($mil) 1,951
paid employees (x1,000) 80.1

Service industries, 1992
establishments (x1,000) (non-exempt firms) 23.0
receipts ($mil) (non-exempt firms) 13,649
annual payroll ($mil) 5,162
paid employees (x1,000) (non-exempt firms) . 248

COMMUNICATION, ENERGY & TRANSPORTATION

Communication
daily newspapers, 1993 26
broadcast stations, 1990
  radio: commercial, educational 274
  television: commercial, noncommercial 37
cable TV households, 1988 784,000

Energy
consumption estimates, 1992
total (trillion Btu) 1,653
per capita (million Btu) 399.6
by source of production (trillion Btu)
  coal 771
  natural gas 287
  petroleum 538
  nuclear electric power 207
  hydroelectric power 106
by end-use sector (trillion Btu)
  residential 286
  commercial 159
  industrial 784
  transportation 425
electrical energy
  production, 1993 (billion kWh) 94.1
  net summer capability, 1993 (million kW) . 20.0
gas utilities, 1993
  customers 780,000
  sales (trillion Btu) 113
  revenues ($mil) 633
nuclear plants, 1993 5

Transportation, 1994
public road & street mileage
total 93,032
  urban 20,069
  rural 72,963
  interstate 904
vehicle miles of travel (mil) 48,956
total motor vehicle registrations 3,176,560
  automobiles 1,947,961
licensed drivers 2,860,724
  per 1,000 driving age population 877
deaths from motor vehicle
  accidents 1,083

Alaska 1

STATE SUMMARY

Capital City ....Juneau

Governor .... Tony Knowles

Address ....STATE CAPITOL
JUNEAU, AK 99811
907 465-3500

Admitted as a state 1959

Area (square miles) 656,424

Population, 1980 401,851

Population, 1990 550,043

Population, 1994 (est.) 606,000

Persons per square mile, 1994 .... 1.1

Largest city .... Anchorage
population, 1990 226,000

Personal income per capita, 1994
(in current dollars) $23,788

Gross state product ($mil), 1991 26,212

Leading industries, 1992 (by payroll)
SERVICE INDUSTRIES
TRANSPORTATION
RETAIL TRADE

Leading agricultural commodities, 1993
GREENHOUSE
DAIRY PRODUCTS
POTATOES
HAY

GEOGRAPHY & ENVIRONMENT

Area (square miles)
total 656,424
land 570,374
water (includes territorial water) 86,051

Federally owned land, 1991 .... 67.9%

Highest point
name ....Mt. McKinley
elevation (feet) 20,320

Lowest point
name .... Pacific Ocean
elevation (feet) ....sea level

General coastline (miles) 6,568

Tidal shoreline (miles) 33,904

Capital city ....Juneau
population, 1990 26,800

Largest city .... Anchorage
population, 1990 226,000

Number of cities with over 100,000 population
1980 1

Number of cities with over 100,000 population
1990 1

State parks and Recreation areas, 1991
area (acres) 3,169,000
number of visitors 6,815,000
revenues $853,000

National forest land, 1992 (acres) 24,345,000

National park acreage, 1984 52,106,400

DEMOGRAPHICS & CHARACTERISTICS OF THE POPULATION

Population
1970 302,583
1980 401,851
1990 550,043
1994 (est.) 606,000
2000 (revised projection) 699,000
2010 (revised projection) 781,000

Metropolitan area population
1970 126,000
1980 174,000
1992 246,000

Non-metropolitan area population
1970 176,000
1980 227,000
1992 342,000

Change in population, 1980-90
number 148,192
percent 36.88%

Persons per square mile, 1994 .... 1.1

Age distribution, 1980
under 5 years 7.9%
5 to 17 years 21.3%
65 and over 11.3%

Age distribution, 1990
under 5 years 10.0%
5 to 17 years 21.3%
65 and over 4.1%

11

Alaska 2

Age distribution, 2000 (projected)
under 5 years 8.5%
5 to 17 years 20.6%
65 and over 4.2%

Persons by age, 1990
under 5 years 54,897
5 to 17 years 117,447
65 and over 22,369

Median age, 1990 .... *29.40*

Race, 1990
White 415,492
Black 22,451
American Indian 31,245
Chinese 1,342
Filipino 7,976
Japanese 2,066
Asian Indian 472
Korean 4,163
Vietnamese 582
all other 9,801

Race, 2010 (projected)
White 543,000
Black 29,000

Persons of Hispanic origin, 1990
total 17,803
Mexican 9,321
Puerto Rican 1,938
Cuban 277
Other Hispanic 6,267

Persons by sex, 1990
male 289,867
female 260,176

Marital status, 1990
males
15 years & older 212,540
single 67,827
married 119,985
separated 4,146
widowed 2,541
divorced 22,187
females
15 years & older 187,691
single 40,938
married 115,317
separated 4,455

widowed 9,082
divorced 22,354

Households & families, 1990
households 188,915
persons per household 2.80
families 132,837
married couples 106,079
female householder, no husband
present 18,229
one person households 41,826
households, 1994 208,000
persons per household, 1994 .... 2.81

Nativity, 1990
number of persons born in state 186,887
percent of total residents 34.0%

Immigration & naturalization, 1993
immigrants admitted 1,286
persons naturalized 530
refugees granted resident status 62

VITAL STATISTICS & HEALTH

Births
1992 11,706
with low birth weight 4.9%
to teenage mothers 10.9%
to unmarried mothers 27.4%
1993 10,555
1994 12,079

Abortions, 1992
total 2,000
rate (per 1,000 women age 15-44) 16.5
rate per 1,000 live births 222

Adoptions, 1986
total 662
related 48.6%

Deaths
1992 2,225
1993 2,247
1994 2,431

Infant deaths
1992 100
1993 79
1994 71

Alaska 3

Average lifetime, 1979-1981
both sexes . . . . 72.24 years
  men . . . . 68.71 years
  women . . . . 76.87 years

Marriages
1992 5,735
1993 5,515
1994 5,560

Divorces
1992 3,678
1993 3,193
1994 3,354

Physicians, 1993
total 818
rate (per 1,000 persons) 1.42

Dentists, 1992
total 317
rate (per 1,000 persons) 0.56

Hospitals, 1993
number 16
beds (x 1,000) 1.3
average daily census (x 1,000) 0.7
occupancy rate 52.9%
personnel (x 1,000) 4.5
average cost per day to hospital $1,136
average cost per stay to hospital $7,594

EDUCATION

*Educational attainment of all persons
25 years and older, 1990*
less than 9th grade 16,621
high school graduates 92,925
bachelor's degree 48,617
graduate or professional degree 25,880

Public school enrollment, Fall, 1993
total 125,948
  Kindergarten through grade 8 93,601
  grades 9 through 12 32,347

Public School Teachers
total, 1994 7,193
  elementary 4,702
  secondary 2,491
salaries, 1994
  beginning $31,800
  average $47,902

*State receipts & expenditures for public
schools, 1993*
receipts ($mil) 1,082
expenditures
  total ($mil) 1,058
  per capita $1,800
  per pupil $9,290

*Graduating high school seniors,
public high schools, 1995 (est)* 5,945

SAT scores, 1994
verbal 434
math 477

Institutions of higher education, 1995
total 9
  public 4
  private 5

*Enrollment in institutions of higher
education, Fall, 1993*
total 30,638
full-time men 5,566
full-time women 6,651
part-time men 6,784
part-time women 11,637

*Minority enrollment in institutions of higher
education, Fall, 1993*
Black, non-Hispanic 1,306
Hispanic 791
Asian/Pacific Islander 832

Earned degrees conferred, 1993
Bachelor's 1,260
First professional . . . . NA
Master's 363
Doctor's 10

SOCIAL INSURANCE &
WELFARE PROGRAMS

Social Security beneficiaries & benefits, 1993
beneficiaries
total 39,000
  retired and dependents 25,000
  survivors 8,000
  disabled & dependents 6,000
annual benefit payments ($mil)
total $271
  retired and dependents 174
  survivors 59
  disabled & dependents 38

Alaska 4

Medicare, 1993
enrollment (x1,000) 30
payments ($mil) 97

Medicaid, 1993
recipients (x1,000) 65
payments ($mil) 217

Federal public aid, 1993
recipients as a percent of population 7.2%
Aid to Families with Dependent Children
   recipients (x1,000) 37
average monthly payment $748
Supplemental Security Income
   total recipients (x1,000) 6

Food Stamp Program
   participants, 1994 (x1,000) 46

HOUSING & CONSTRUCTION

Total housing units, 1990 232,608
   year round housing units 215,418
   vacant 43,693

New privately owned housing units
   authorized, 1994
number (x1,000) 2.1
value ($mil) 230

New privately owned housing units
   started, 1994 (x1,000) 2.2

Existing home sales, 1994 (x1,000) . . . . NA

GOVERNMENT & ELECTIONS

State officials, 1996
   Governor (name/party/term expires)
         TONY KNOWLES
         Democrat - 1998
Lt. Governor . . . . Fran Ulmer
Sec. of State . . . . (no secretary of state)
Atty. General . . . . Bruce Botelho
Chf. Justice . . . . Jay Rabinowitz

Governorship
minimum age 30
length of term . . . . 4 years
number of consecutive
   terms permitted 2
who succeeds . . . . Lt. Governor

State legislature
name . . . . Legislature
   upper chamber
      name . . . . Senate
      number of members 20
      length of term . . . . 4 years
      party in majority, 1996 . . . . Republican
   lower chamber
      name . . . . House of Representatives
      number of members 38
      length of term . . . . 2 years
      party in majority, 1996 . . . . Democratic

State employees October, 1992
total 27,485
October payroll ($1,000) 76,792

Local governments, 1992
total 176
   county 12
   municipal 149
   township 0
   school districts 0
   special districts 14

Voting, November, 1994
voting age population 393,000
   registered 71.7%
   voted 59.1%

Vote for president
1988
   Bush 102,381
   Dukakis 62,205
1992
   Clinton 62,596
   Bush 80,691
   Perot 54,074

Federal representation, 1996 (104th Congress)
Senators (name/party/term expires)

         TED STEVENS
        Republican - 1997
     FRANK H. MURKOWSKI
        Republican - 1999

Representatives, total 1
   Democrats 0
   Republicans 1
   other 0

Alaska 5

Women holding public office
U.S. Congress, 1995 0
statewide elected office, 1995 1
state legislature, 1995 14

Black elected officials, 1993
total 3
US and state legislatures 1
city/county/regional offices 2
judicial/law enforcement 0
education/school boards 0

Hispanic public officials, 1994
total 1
state executives & legislators 1
city/county/regional offices 0
judicial/law enforcement 0
education/school boards 0

GOVERNMENTAL FINANCE

State & local government revenues, (selected items), 1991-92 ($per capita)
total $13,862.86
total general revenues 11,790.62
from federal government 1,489.75
from own sources 10,300.86
from taxes 3,955.72
from property taxes 1,103.16
from all other taxes 693.90
from charges & misc. 6,345.15

State & local government expenditures, (selected items), 1991-92 ($per capita)
total $11,737.45
total direct general expenditures 10,188.1
education 2,393.99
libraries 36.12
public welfare 742.84
health & hospitals 385.97
highways 1,073.88
police protection 223.54
fire protection 83.23
correction 231.91
housing & comm. development 161.85
natural resources & parks 509.95
interest on general debt 1,272.42

State & local debt, 1992 ($per capita) . . . 15,762.71

Federal aid grants to state & local government, 1994 ($per capita total & selected items)
per capita total 1,754.71
compensatory education 39.22
waste treatment facilities 14.53
medicaid 290.34
housing assistance 145.07
job training 16.27
highway trust fund 370.49

CRIME, LAW ENFORCEMENT & COURTS

Crime, 1994 (all rates per 100,000 persons)
total crimes 34,591
overall crime rate 5,708.1
property crimes 29,947
burglaries 4,848
larcenies 21,824
motor vehicle thefts 3,275
property crime rate 4,941.7
violent crimes 4,644
murders 38
forcible rapes 418
robberies 886
aggravated assaults 3,302
violent crime rate 766.3

Number of police agencies, 1994 25

Arrests, 1994
total 38,417
persons under 18 years of age 6,737

Prisoners under state & federal jurisdiction, 1994
total 3,292
percent change, 1993-94 . . . . 7.3%
sentenced to more than one year
total 1,934
rate per 100,000 residents 317

Persons under sentence of death, 4/20/95 . . . .NA

State's highest court
name . . . . Supreme Court
number of members 5
length of term . . . . 10 years
intermediate appeals court? . . . . yes

15

Alaska 6

LABOR & INCOME

Civilian labor force, 1994

total 305,000
men 165,000
women 140,000
persons 16-19 years 15,000
white 255,000
black .... NA

*Civilian labor force as a percent of
civilian non-institutional population, 1994*

total 74.2%
men 81.2%
women 67.5%
persons 16-19 years 49.0%
white 77.3%
black .... NA%

Employment, 1994

total 282,000
men 150,000
women 132,000
persons 16-19 years 12,000
white 238,000
black .... NA

Full-time/part-time labor force, 1994

full-time labor force 250,000
working part-time for
ecomonic reasons 5,000
part-time labor force 55,000

Unemployment rate, 1994

total 7.8%
men 9.1%
women 6.2%
persons 16-19 years 19.4%
white 6.5%
black .... NA%

*Unemployed by reason for unemployment
(as a percent of total unemployment), 1994*

job losers or completed temp jobs 48.5%
job leavers 10.4%
reentrants 39.1%
new entrants 2.1%

Civilian labor force, by occupation, 1994

executive/administrative/
managerial 47,000
professional/specialty 44,000
technicians & related support 11,000

sales 32,000
adminstrative support/clerical 51,000
service occupations 45,000
precision production/craft/repair 32,000
machine operators/assemblers ....NA
transportation/material moving 13,000
handlers/helpers/laborers 15,000
farming/forestry/fishing ....NA

Civilian labor force, by industry, 1994

construction 16,000
manufacturing 12,000
transportation/communication 25,000
wholesale/retail trade 54,000
finance/real estate/insurance 12,000
services 58,000
government 85,000
agriculture ....NA

Average annual pay, 1994 (prelim.) $32,657
change in average annual pay,
1993-1994 .... 1.0%

*Hours and earnings of production workers
on manufacturing payrolls, 1994*

average weekly hours 47.4
average hourly earnings $10.96
average weekly earnings $519.50

Labor union membership, 1994 47,100

Household income (in constant 1993 dollars)
median household income, 1992 .... $43,053
median household income, 1993 .... $42,931

Poverty
persons below poverty level, 1992 .... 10.2%
persons below poverty level, 1993 .... 9.1%

Personal income ($per capita)
1994
in current dollars 23,788
in constant (1987) dollars 18,398
1995 (projected)
in constant (1982) dollars 16,075
2000 (projected)
in constant (1982) dollars 16,765

Federal income tax returns, 1993
returns filed 350,473
adjusted gross income ($1000) 10,025,224
total income tax paid ($1000) 1,550,753

Alaska 7

ECONOMY, BUSINESS, INDUSTRY & AGRICULTURE

Fortune 500 companies, 1994 0

Business incorporations, 1994
total 1,428
change, 1993-94 . . . . -0.6%

Business failures, 1994
total 111
rate per 10,000 concerns 52
change, 1993-94 . . . . 2.8%

Business firm ownership
Hispanic owned firms, 1987 502
black owned firms, 1987 507
women owned firms, 1987 14,000
foreign owned firms, 1982 46

Gross state product, 1991 ($mil)
total $26,212
    agriculture services, forestry, fisheries 637
    mining 8,942
    construction 892
    manufacturing—durable goods 293
    manufacturing—nondurable goods 834
    transportation, communication &
        public utilities 3,090
    wholesale trade 507
    retail trade 1,347
    finance/real estate/insurance 3,421
    services 2,254
    federal, state & local government 3,995

Establishments, by major industry group, 1992
total 16,001
    agriculture 351
    mining 170
    construction 1,714
    manufacturing 521
    transportation 1,325
    wholesale trade 877
    retail trade 3,782
    finance/real estate/insurance 1,102
    service industries 5,832
    unclassified 327

Payroll, by major industry group, 1992
total ($1,000) $5,347,750
    agriculture 55,986

    mining 686,814
    construction 551,822
    manufacturing 411,316
    transportation 791,160
    wholesale trade 310,307
    retail trade 719,371
    finance/real estate/insurance 278,466
    service industries 1,538,146
    unclassified 4,362

Agriculture
number of farms, 1994 1,000
farm acreage, 1994 1,000,000
acres per farm, 1994 1,788
value of farms, 1994 ($mil) . . . . NA
farm income, 1993 ($mil)
    gross farm income 35
    net farm income 7
    debt/asset ratio 7.7%
farm marketings, 1993 ($mil)
    total $27
    crops 21
    livestock 6
government payments 2
farm marketings in order of marketing receipts, 1993
    1) Greenhouse
    2) Dairy products
    3) Potatoes
    4) Hay

Federal economic activity ($mil, except per capita)
expenditures, 1994
    total $4,640
    per capita $7,656
    defense $1,567
    non-defense $3,072
defense department, 1994
    contract awards ($mil) $627
    payroll ($mil) $923
    civilian employees (x1,000) 4.7
    military personnel (x1,000) 19.0

Fishing, 1992
catch (millions of pounds) 5,638
value ($mil) 1,578

Mining, 1994 ($mil)
total non-fuel mineral production $429

17

Alaska 8

principal non-fuel minerals in order of value, 1994
1) Zinc
2) Gold
3) Sand and gravel

Construction, 1994 ($mil)
total contracts (including
   non-building) $883
     residential 226
     non-residential 299

Manufacturing, 1992
total establishments 513
employees, total (x1,000) 16
payroll ($mil) 426
production workers (x1,000) 12
value added ($mil) 1,347
value of shipments ($mil) 3,678

Finance
commercial banks, 1994
   number 8
     assets ($bil) 5.0
     deposits ($bil) 3.8
   closed or assisted 0
     deposits ($bil) .... NA
savings and loan associations, 1991
   non-current real estate loans 0.53%
   net income after taxes ($mil) .... -2
   return on assets .... -2.01%

Retail trade, 1992
establishments (x1,000) 3.7
sales ($mil) 4,982
annual payroll ($mil) 671
paid employees (x1,000) 39

Wholesale trade, 1992
establishments 908
sales ($bil) 3.6
annual payroll ($mil) 290
paid employees (x1,000) 8.5

Service industries, 1992
establishments (x1,000) (non-exempt firms) . 4.5
receipts ($mil) (non-exempt firms) 2,382
annual payroll ($mil) 884
paid employees (x1,000) (non-exempt firms) .. 32

COMMUNICATION, ENERGY & TRANSPORTATION

Communication
daily newspapers, 1993 7
broadcast stations, 1990
   radio: commercial, educational 82
   television: commercial, noncommercial 14
cable TV households, 1988 61,000

Energy
consumption estimates, 1992
   total (trillion Btu) 612
   per capita (million Btu) 1,040.4
by source of production (trillion Btu)
   coal 13
   natural gas 384
   petroleum 206
   nuclear electric power 0
   hydroelectric power 10
by end-use sector (trillion Btu)
   residential 46
   commercial 59
   industrial 358
   transportation 149
electrical energy
   production, 1993 (billion kWh) 4.6
   net summer capability, 1993 (million kW) .. 1.7
gas utilities, 1993
   customers .... NA
   sales (trillion Btu) .... NA
   revenues ($mil) .... NA
nuclear plants, 1993 0

Transportation, 1994
public road & street mileage
   total 14,325
   urban 1,782
   rural 12,543
   interstate 1,086
vehicle miles of travel (mil) 4,150
total motor vehicle registrations 533,496
   automobiles 300,420
licensed drivers 435,677
   per 1,000 driving age population 1,006
deaths from motor vehicle
   accidents 85

Arizona 1

STATE SUMMARY

Capital City . . . . Phoenix

Governor . . . . Fife Symington

Address . . . . STATE CAPITOL
PHOENIX, AZ 85007
602 542-4331

Admitted as a state 1912

Area (square miles) 114,006

Population, 1980 2,718,215

Population, 1990 3,665,228

Population, 1994 (est.) 4,075,000

Persons per square mile, 1994 . . . . 35.9

Largest city . . . . Phoenix
  population, 1990 983,000

Personal income per capita, 1994
  (in current dollars) $19,001

Gross state product ($mil), 1991 69,767

Leading industries, 1992 (by payroll)
SERVICE INDUSTRIES
MANUFACTURING
RETAIL TRADE

Leading agricultural commodities, 1993
CATTLE
COTTON
DAIRY PRODUCTS
HAY

GEOGRAPHY & ENVIRONMENT

Area (square miles)
total 114,006
land 113,642
water (includes territorial water) 364

Federally owned land, 1991 . . . . 47.2%

Highest point
name . . . . Humphrey's Peak
elevation (feet) 12,633

Lowest point
name . . . . Colorado River
elevation (feet) 70

General coastline (miles) 0

Tidal shoreline (miles) 0

Capital city . . . . Phoenix
population, 1990 983,000

Largest city . . . . Phoenix
population, 1990 983,000

Number of cities with over 100,000 population
1980 4

Number of cities with over 100,000 population
1990 6

State parks and Recreation areas, 1991
area (acres) 42,000
number of visitors 2,236,000
revenues $2,073,000

National forest land, 1992 (acres) 11,887,000

National park acreage, 1984 2,666,600

DEMOGRAPHICS & CHARACTERISTICS OF THE POPULATION

Population
1970 1,775,399
1980 2,718,215
1990 3,665,228
1994 (est.) 4,075,000
2000 (revised projection) 4,437,000
2010 (revised projection) 5,074,000

Metropolitan area population
1970 1,323,000
1980 2,040,000
1992 3,244,000

Non-metropolitan area population
1970 453,000
1980 678,000
1992 588,000

Change in population, 1980-90
number 947,013
percent 34.84%

Persons per square mile, 1994 . . . . 35.9

Age distribution, 1980
under 5 years 9.7%
5 to 17 years 22.8%
65 and over 2.9%

Age distribution, 1990
under 5 years 8.0%
5 to 17 years 18.7%
65 and over 13.0%

Arizona 2

Age distribution, 2000 (projected)
under 5 years 6.7%
5 to 17 years 19.0%
65 and over 14.1%

Persons by age, 1990
under 5 years 292,859
5 to 17 years 688,260
65 and over 478,774

Median age, 1990 .... 32.20

Race, 1990
White 2,963,186
Black 110,524
American Indian 203,009
Chinese 14,136
Filipino 7,904
Japanese 6,302
Asian Indian 5,663
Korean 5,863
Vietnamese 5,239
all other 342,884

Race, 2010 (projected)
White 4,379,000
Black 143,000

Persons of Hispanic origin, 1990
total 688,338
Mexican 616,195
Puerto Rican 8,256
Cuban 2,079
Other Hispanic 61,808

Persons by sex, 1990
male 1,810,691
female 1,854,537

Marital status, 1990
males
15 years & older 1,384,911
single 409,976
married 817,459
separated 24,512
widowed 32,270
divorced 125,206
females
15 years & older 1,447,361
single 313,652
married 816,198
separated 32,513

widowed 150,231
divorced 167,280

Households & families, 1990
households 1,368,843
persons per household 2.62
families 940,106
married couples 747,806
female householder, no husband
present 142,320
one person households 337,681
households, 1994 1,503,000
persons per household, 1994 .... 2.66

Nativity, 1990
number of persons born in state 1,252,645
percent of total residents 34.2%

Immigration & naturalization, 1993
immigrants admitted 9,778
persons naturalized 2,548
refugees granted resident status 973

VITAL STATISTICS & HEALTH

Births
1992 66,698
with low birth weight 6.4%
to teenage mothers 15.0%
to unmarried mothers 36.2%
1993 70,770
1994 66,143

Abortions, 1992
total 21,000
rate (per 1,000 women age 15-44) 24.1
rate per 1,000 live births 295

Adoptions, 1986
total 1,303
related 50.4%

Deaths
1992 30,659
1993 32,090
1994 34,677

Infant deaths
1992 566
1993 497
1994 567

Arizona 3

Average lifetime, 1979-1981
both sexes .... 74.30 years
men .... 70.46 years
women .... 78.34 years

Marriages
1992 36,366
1993 38,789
1994 36,711

Divorces
1992 25,645
1993 24,523
1994 23,725

Physicians, 1993
total 7,606
rate (per 1,000 persons) 1.94

Dentists, 1992
total 1,918
rate (per 1,000 persons) 0.50

Hospitals, 1993
number 60
beds (x 1,000) 9.9
average daily census (x 1,000) 5.6
occupancy rate 57.1%
personnel (x 1,000) 39.8
average cost per day to hospital $1,091
average cost per stay to hospital $5,528

EDUCATION

*Educational attainment of all persons
25 years and older, 1990*
less than 9th grade 207,509
high school graduates 601,440
bachelor's degree 306,554
graduate or professional degree 160,319

Public school enrollment, Fall, 1993
total 709,453
Kindergarten through grade 8 526,412
grades 9 through 12 183,041

Public School Teachers
total, 1994 37,493
elementary 27,188
secondary 10,305
salaries, 1994
beginning $21,825
average $31,825

*State receipts & expenditures for public
schools, 1993*
receipts ($mil) 3,784
expenditures
total ($mil) 3,508
per capita $915
per pupil $4,140

*Graduating high school seniors,
public high schools, 1995 (est)* 31,191

SAT scores, 1994
verbal 443
math 496

Institutions of higher education, 1995
total 43
public 22
private 21

*Enrollment in institutions of higher
education, Fall, 1993*
total 272,300
full-time men 64,181
full-time women 64,053
part-time men 59,430
part-time women 84,636

*Minority enrollment in institutions of higher
education, Fall, 1993*
Black, non-Hispanic 9,294
Hispanic 35,718
Asian/Pacific Islander 7,625

Earned degrees conferred, 1993
Bachelor's 15,807
First professional 436
Master's 5,694
Doctor's 690

SOCIAL INSURANCE &
WELFARE PROGRAMS

Social Security beneficiaries & benefits, 1993
beneficiaries
total 658,000
retired and dependents 481,000
survivors 97,000
disabled & dependents 80,000
annual benefit payments ($mil)
total $4,755
retired and dependents 3,377
survivors 823
disabled & dependents 555

Arizona 4

Medicare, 1993
enrollment (x1,000) 554
payments ($mil) 2,178

Medicaid, 1993
recipients (x1,000) 404
payments ($mil) 212

Federal public aid, 1993
recipients as a percent of population 6.5%
Aid to Families with Dependent Children
  recipients (x1,000) 203
average monthly payment $318
Supplemental Security Income
  total recipients (x1,000) 63

Food Stamp Program
  participants, 1994 (x1,000) 512

HOUSING & CONSTRUCTION

Total housing units, 1990 1,659,430
  year round housing units 1,562,400
  vacant 290,587

New privately owned housing units
  authorized, 1994
number (x1,000) 51.8
value ($mil) 5,075

New privately owned housing units
  started, 1994 (x1,000) 51.8

Existing home sales, 1994 (x1,000) 123.8

GOVERNMENT & ELECTIONS

State officials, 1996
  Governor (name/party/term expires)
      FIFE SYMINGTON
      Republican - 2001
Lt. Governor . . . . (no Lt. Governor)
Sec. of State . . . . Richard Mahoney
Atty. General . . . . Grant Woods
Chf. Justice . . . . Stanley Feldman

Governorship
minimum age 25
length of term . . . . 4 years
number of consecutive
  terms permitted . . . . not specified
who succeeds . . . . Sec. of State

State legislature
name . . . . Legislature
  upper chamber
    name . . . . Senate
    number of members 30
    length of term . . . . 2 years
    party in majority, 1996 . . . . Republican
  lower chamber
    name . . . . House of Representatives
    number of members 60
    length of term . . . . 2 years
    party in majority, 1996 . . . . Republican

State employees October, 1992
total 64,804
October payroll ($1,000) 121,955

Local governments, 1992
total 598
  county 15
  municipal 86
  township 0
  school districts 228
  special districts 268

Voting, November, 1994
voting age population 2,971,000
  registered 56.0%
  voted 41.6%

Vote for president
1988
  Bush 694,379
  Dukakis 447,272
1992
  Clinton 526,304
  Bush 549,284
  Perot 341,638

Federal representation, 1996 (104th Congress)
Senators (name/party/term expires)

      JON KYL
      Republican - 2001
      JOHN McCAIN
      Republican - 1999

Representatives, total 6
  Democrats 1
  Republicans 5
  other 0

Arizona 5

Women holding public office
U.S. Congress, 1995 0
statewide elected office, 1995 3
state legislature, 1995 27

Black elected officials, 1993
total 15
  US and state legislatures 4
  city/county/regional offices 3
  judicial/law enforcement 3
  education/school boards 5

Hispanic public officials, 1994
total 341
  state executives & legislators 11
  city/county/regional offices 144
  judicial/law enforcement 50
  education/school boards 136

GOVERNMENTAL FINANCE

State & local government revenues, (selected items), 1991-92 ($per capita)
total $4,307.53
  total general revenues 3,423.03
    from federal government 576.22
    from own sources 2,846.82
    from taxes 2,065.96
      from property taxes 688.29
      from all other taxes 1,280.16
    from charges & misc. 780.86

State & local government expenditures, (selected items), 1991-92 ($per capita)
total $4,242.78
  total direct general expenditures 3,586.22
    education 1,286.73
    libraries 19.00
    public welfare 502.57
    health & hospitals 197.48
    highways 282.24
    police protection 160.07
    fire protection 54.90
    correction 129.12
    housing & comm. development 39.44
    natural resources & parks 141.85
    interest on general debt 265.42

State & local debt, 1992 ($per capita) 5,048.70

Federal aid grants to state & local government, 1994 ($per capita total & selected items)
per capita total 735.14
  compensatory education 24.26
  waste treatment facilities 2.30
  medicaid 270.74
  housing assistance 37.24
  job training 15.01
  highway trust fund 66.41

CRIME, LAW ENFORCEMENT & COURTS

Crime, 1994 (all rates per 100,000 persons)
total crimes 322,926
overall crime rate 7,924.6
  property crimes 294,273
    burglaries 60,157
    larcenies 190,649
    motor vehicle thefts 43,467
  property crime rate 7,221.4
  violent crimes 28,653
    murders 426
    forcible rapes 1,465
    robberies 6,601
    aggravated assaults 20,161
  violent crime rate 703.1

Number of police agencies, 1994 85

Arrests, 1994
total 271,026
  persons under 18 years of age 64,452

Prisoners under state & federal jurisdiction, 1994
total 19,746
percent change, 1993-94 ....10.9%
  sentenced to more than one year
    total 19,005
    rate per 100,000 residents 459

Persons under sentence of death, 4/20/95 122

State's highest court
name .... Supreme Court
number of members 5
length of term ....6 years
intermediate appeals court? ....yes

23

Arizona 6

LABOR & INCOME

Civilian labor force, 1994
total 1,988,000
  men 1,089,000
  women 900,000
  persons 16-19 years 136,000
  white 1,817,000
  black . . . . NA

Civilian labor force as a percent of
civilian non-institutional population, 1994
total 65.5%
  men 74.1%
  women 57.4%
  persons 16-19 years 62.2%
  white 65.1%
  black . . . . NA%

Employment, 1994
total 1,862,000
  men 1,026,000
  women 836,000
  persons 16-19 years 108000
  white 1,710,000
  black . . . . NA

Full-time/part-time labor force, 1994
full-time labor force 1,600,000
  working part-time for
    ecomonic reasons 21,000
part-time labor force 389,000

Unemployment rate, 1994
total 6.4%
  men 5.7%
  women 7.1%
  persons 16-19 years 20.8%
  white 5.8%
  black . . . . NA%

Unemployed by reason for unemployment
(as a percent of total unemployment), 1994
job losers or completed temp jobs 40.0%
job leavers 14.4%
reentrants 34.3%
new entrants 11.3%

Civilian labor force, by occupation, 1994
executive/administrative/
  managerial 285,000
professional/specialty 259,000
technicians & related support 73,000

sales 253,000
adminstrative support/clerical 322,000
service occupations 277,000
precision production/craft/repair 239,000
machine operators/assemblers . . . . NA
transportation/material moving 72,000
handlers/helpers/laborers 77,000
farming/forestry/fishing . . . . NA

Civilian labor force, by industry, 1994
construction 129,000
manufacturing 220,000
transportation/communication 100,000
wholesale/retail trade 414,000
finance/real estate/insurance 121,000
services 442,000
government 314,000
agriculture . . . . NA

Average annual pay, 1994 (prelim.) $24,276
change in average annual pay,
  1993-1994 . . . . 3.3%

Hours and earnings of production workers
on manufacturing payrolls, 1994
average weekly hours 42.2
average hourly earnings $11.17
average weekly earnings $471.37

Labor union membership, 1994 126,700

Household income (in constant 1993 dollars)
median household income, 1992 . . . . $30,237
median household income, 1993 . . . . $30,510

Poverty
persons below poverty level, 1992 . . . . 15.8%
persons below poverty level, 1993 . . . . 15.4%

Personal income ($per capita)
1994
  in current dollars 19,001
  in constant (1987) dollars 14,695
1995 (projected)
  in constant (1982) dollars 13,105
2000 (projected)
  in constant (1982) dollars 13,926

Federal income tax returns, 1993
returns filed 1,707,024
adjusted gross income ($1000) 50,431,204
total income tax paid ($1000) 6,701,498

ECONOMY, BUSINESS, INDUSTRY & AGRICULTURE

Fortune 500 companies, 1994 3

Business incorporations, 1994
total 11,248
change, 1993-94 .... 0.7%

Business failures, 1994
total 1,405
rate per 10,000 concerns 116
change, 1993-94 .... -32.1%

Business firm ownership
Hispanic owned firms, 1987 9,845
black owned firms, 1987 1,811
women owned firms, 1987 60,600
foreign owned firms, 1982 172

Gross state product, 1991 ($mil)
total $69,767
  agriculture services, forestry, fisheries ... 1,586
  mining 978
  construction 3,259
  manufacturing — durable goods 7,389
  manufacturing — nondurable goods 1,996
  transportation, communication &
    public utilities 5,343
  wholesale trade 3,975
  retail trade 7,995
  finance/real estate/insurance 12,541
  services 14,396
  federal, state & local government 10,309

Establishments, by major industry group, 1992
total 90,745
  agriculture 1,765
  mining 231
  construction 8,572
  manufacturing 4,812
  transportation 3,296
  wholesale trade 63,501
  retail trade 22,044
  finance/real estate/insurance 9,014
  service industries 33,137
  unclassified 1,373

Payroll, by major industry group, 1992
total ($1,000) $27,846,970
  agriculture 184,002

  mining 527,059
  construction 1,944,357
  manufacturing 5,415,096
  transportation 2,320,741
  wholesale trade 2,032,123
  retail trade 3,892,437
  finance/real estate/insurance ... 2,457,842
  service industries 9,053,070
  unclassified 20,243

Agriculture
number of farms, 1994 8,000
farm acreage, 1994 36,000,000
acres per farm, 1994 4,557
value of farms, 1994 ($mil) 11,295
farm income, 1993 ($mil)
  gross farm income 2,100
  net farm income 638
  debt/asset ratio 10.6%
farm marketings, 1993 ($mil)
  total $1,922
  crops 1,037
  livestock 885
government payments 114
farm marketings in order of marketing receipts, 1993
    1) Cattle
    2) Cotton
    3) Dairy products
    4) Hay

Federal economic activity
  ($mil, except per capita)
expenditures, 1994
  total $19,011
  per capita $4,665
  defense $3,624
  non-defense $15,388
defense department, 1994
  contract awards ($mil) $1,975
  payroll ($mil) $1,642
  civilian employees (x1,000) 9.3
  military personnel (x1,000) 21.9

Fishing, 1992
catch (millions of pounds) .... NA
value ($mil) .... NA

Mining, 1994 ($mil)
total non-fuel mineral production $3,323

Arizona 8

principal non-fuel minerals in order of value, 1994
1) Copper
2) Sand and gravel
3) Cement

Construction, 1994 ($mil)
total contracts (including
  non-building) $7,981
    residential 5,281
    non-residential 1,811

Manufacturing, 1992
total establishments 4,758
employees, total (x1,000) 177
payroll ($mil) 5,420
production workers (x1,000) 99
value added ($mil) 14,960
value of shipments ($mil) 25,767

Finance
commercial banks, 1994
  number 37
    assets ($bil) 37.1
    deposits ($bil) 29.7
    closed or assisted 0
    deposits ($bil) ....NA
savings and loan associations, 1991
  non-current real estate loans 14.40%
  net income after taxes ($mil) .... -118
  return on assets ....-9.94%

Retail trade, 1992
establishments (x1,000) 21.4
sales ($mil) 29,366
annual payroll ($mil) 3,437
paid employees (x1,000) 288

Wholesale trade, 1992
establishments 6,518
sales ($bil) 28.0
annual payroll ($mil) 1,837
paid employees (x1,000) 68.8

Service industries, 1992
establishments (x1,000) (non-exempt firms) 28.7
receipts ($mil) (non-exempt firms) 16,616
annual payroll ($mil) 6,220
paid employees (x1,000) (non-exempt firms) . 299

COMMUNICATION, ENERGY & TRANSPORTATION

Communication
daily newspapers, 1993 22
broadcast stations, 1990
  radio: commercial, educational 141
  television: commercial, noncommercial 22
cable TV households, 1988 581,000

Energy
consumption estimates, 1992
total (trillion Btu) 945
per capita (million Btu) 246.5
by source of production (trillion Btu)
  coal 369
  natural gas 134
  petroleum 364
  nuclear electric power 273
  hydroelectric power 71
by end-use sector (trillion Btu)
  residential 206
  commercial 207
  industrial 194
  transportation 338
electrical energy
  production, 1993 (billion kWh) 68.0
  net summer capability, 1993 (million kW) . 15.0
gas utilities, 1993
  customers 660,000
  sales (trillion Btu) 67
  revenues ($mil) 351
nuclear plants, 1993 3

Transportation, 1994
public road & street mileage
total 54,380
  urban 16,212
  rural 38,168
  interstate 1,169
vehicle miles of travel (mil) 38,774
total motor vehicle registrations 2,813,462
  automobiles 1,849,994
licensed drivers 2,849,304
  per 1,000 driving age population 935
deaths from motor vehicle
  accidents 903

Arkansas 1

STATE SUMMARY

Capital City .... Little Rock

Governor .... Jim Guy Tucker

Address .... STATE CAPITOL
LITTLE ROCK, AR 72201
501 682-2345

Admitted as a state 1836

Area (square miles) 53,182

Population, 1980 2,286,435

Population, 1990 2,350,725

Population, 1994 (est.) 2,453,000

Persons per square mile, 1994 .... 47.1

Largest city .... Little Rock
population, 1990 176,000

Personal income per capita, 1994
(in current dollars) $16,898

Gross state product ($mil), 1991 40,561

Leading industries, 1992 (by payroll)
MANUFACTURING
SERVICE INDUSTRIES
RETAIL TRADE

Leading agricultural commodities, 1993
BROILERS
SOYBEANS
RICE
COTTON

GEOGRAPHY & ENVIRONMENT

Area (square miles)
total 53,182
land 52,075
water (includes territorial water) 1,107

Federally owned land, 1991 .... 8.2%

Highest point
name .... Magazine Mountain
elevation (feet) 2,753

Lowest point
name .... Ouachita River
elevation (feet) 55

General coastline (miles) 0

Tidal shoreline (miles) 0

Capital city .... Little Rock
population, 1990 176,000

Largest city .... Little Rock
population, 1990 176,000

Number of cities with over 100,000 population
1980 1

Number of cities with over 100,000 population
1990 1

State parks and Recreation areas, 1991
area (acres) 47,000
number of visitors 6,949,000
revenues $11,227,000

National forest land, 1992 (acres) 3,490,000

National park acreage, 1984 99,600

DEMOGRAPHICS & CHARACTERISTICS OF THE POPULATION

Population
1970 1,923,322
1980 2,286,435
1990 2,350,725
1994 (est.) 2,453,000
2000 (revised projection) 2,578,000
2010 (revised projection) 2,782,000

Metropolitan area population
1970 730,000
1980 885,000
1992 1,071,000

Non-metropolitan area population
1970 1,193,000
1980 1,401,000
1992 1,323,000

Change in population, 1980-90
number 64,290
percent 2.81%

Persons per square mile, 1994 .... 47.1

Age distribution, 1980
under 5 years 7.7%
5 to 17 years 21.7%
65 and over 13.7%

Age distribution, 1990
under 5 years 7.0%
5 to 17 years 19.4%
65 and over 14.8%

27

Arkansas 2

Age distribution, 2000 (projected)
under 5 years 6.0%
5 to 17 years 18.4%
65 and over 15.2%

Persons by age, 1990
under 5 years 164,667
5 to 17 years 456,464
65 and over 350,058

Median age, 1990 .... 33.80

Race, 1990
White 1,944,744
Black 373,912
American Indian 12,641
Chinese 1,726
Filipino 1,569
Japanese 957
Asian Indian 1,329
Korean 1,037
Vietnamese 2,348
all other 10,330

Race, 2010 (projected)
White 2,311,000
Black 412,000

Persons of Hispanic origin, 1990
total 19,876
Mexican 12,496
Puerto Rican 1,176
Cuban 494
Other Hispanic 5,710

Persons by sex, 1990
male 1,133,076
female 1,217,649

Marital status, 1990
males
15 years & older 868,546
single 209,851
married 563,189
separated 14,658
widowed 24,977
divorced 70,529
females
15 years & older 966,364
single 169,510
married 566,806
separated 20,598

widowed 139,365
divorced 90,683

Households & families, 1990
households 891,179
persons per household 2.57
families 651,555
married couples 527,358
female householder, no husband
present 98,924
one person households 213,778
households, 1994 927,000
persons per household, 1994 .... 2.58

Nativity, 1990
number of persons born in state 1,577,038
percent of total residents 67.1%

Immigration & naturalization, 1993
immigrants admitted 1,312
persons naturalized 405
refugees granted resident status 150

VITAL STATISTICS & HEALTH

Births
1992 34,967
with low birth weight 8.2%
to teenage mothers 19.4%
to unmarried mothers 31.0%
1993 34,248
1994 34,571

Abortions, 1992
total 7,000
rate (per 1,000 women age 15-44) 13.5
rate per 1,000 live births 213

Adoptions, 1986
total 1,541
related 50.4%

Deaths
1992 25,202
1993 26,371
1994 26,667

Infant deaths
1992 342
1993 324
1994 276

Average lifetime, 1979-1981
both sexes . . . . 73.72 years
  men . . . . 69.73 years
  women . . . . 77.83 years

Marriages
1992 37,326
1993 36,440
1994 38,169

Divorces
1992 18,405
1993 16,734
1994 17,458

Physicians, 1993
total 3,908
rate (per 1,000 persons) 1.62

Dentists, 1992
total 989
rate (per 1,000 persons) 0.41

Hospitals, 1993
number 87
beds (x 1,000) 11.0
average daily census (x 1,000) 6.4
occupancy rate 58.3%
personnel (x 1,000) 37.5
average cost per day to hospital $678
average cost per stay to hospital $4,585

EDUCATION

Educational attainment of all persons
* 25 years and older, 1990*
less than 9th grade 227,633
high school graduates 489,570
bachelor's degree 132,712
graduate or professional degree 66,592

Public school enrollment, Fall, 1993
total 444,271
  Kindergarten through grade 8 317,713
  grades 9 through 12 126,558

Public School Teachers
total, 1994 26,014
  elementary 13,706
  secondary 12,208
salaries, 1994
  beginning $19,694
  average $28,312

State receipts & expenditures for public
* schools, 1993*
receipts ($mil) 2,046
expenditures
  total ($mil) 1,825
  per capita $762
  per pupil $3,838

Graduating high school seniors,
* public high schools, 1995 (est)* 25,778

SAT scores, 1994
verbal 477
math 518

Institutions of higher education, 1995
total 35
  public 22
  private 13

Enrollment in institutions of higher
* education, Fall, 1993*
total 99,262
full-time men 31,427
full-time women 37,720
part-time men 11,376
part-time women 18,739

Minority enrollment in institutions of higher
* education, Fall, 1993*
Black, non-Hispanic 14,204
Hispanic 652
Asian/Pacific Islander 1,012

Earned degrees conferred, 1993
Bachelor's 8,449
First professional 449
Master's 1,836
Doctor's 120

SOCIAL INSURANCE & WELFARE PROGRAMS

Social Security beneficiaries & benefits, 1993
beneficiaries
total 489,000
  retired and dependents 315,000
  survivors 90,000
  disabled & dependents 84,000
annual benefit payments ($mil)
total $3,153
  retired and dependents 1,973
  survivors 668
  disabled & dependents 513

Arkansas 4

Medicare, 1993
enrollment (x1,000) 410
payments ($mil) 1,306

Medicaid, 1993
recipients (x1,000) 339
payments ($mil) 998

Federal public aid, 1993
recipients as a percent of population 6.6%
Aid to Families with Dependent Children
  recipients (x1,000) 70
average monthly payment $186
Supplemental Security Income
  total recipients (x1,000) 91

Food Stamp Program
  participants, 1994 (x1,000) 283

HOUSING & CONSTRUCTION

Total housing units, 1990 1,000,667
  year round housing units 982,000
  vacant 109,488

New privately owned housing units authorized, 1994
number (x1,000) 12.4
value ($mil) 795

New privately owned housing units started, 1994 (x1,000) 14.7

Existing home sales, 1994 (x1,000) 52.3

GOVERNMENT & ELECTIONS

State officials, 1996
Governor (name/party/term expires)
    JIM GUY TUCKER
    Democrat - 1998
Lt. Governor .... Mike Huckabee
Sec. of State .... Bill McCuen
Atty. General .... Winston Bryant
Chf. Justice .... Jack Holt, Jr.

Governorship
minimum age 30
length of term .... 2 years
number of consecutive
  terms permitted .... not specified
who succeeds .... Lt. Governor

State legislature
name .... General Assembly
  upper chamber
    name .... Senate
    number of members 35
    length of term .... 4 years
    party in majority, 1996 .... Democratic
  lower chamber
    name .... House of Representatives
    number of members 100
    length of term .... 2 years
    party in majority, 1996 .... Democratic

State employees October, 1992
total 53,364
October payroll ($1,000) 99,385

Local governments, 1992
total 1,473
  county 75
  municipal 489
  township 0
  school districts 324
  special districts 584

Voting, November, 1994
voting age population 1,801,000
  registered 60.0%
  voted 41.6%

Vote for president
1988
  Bush 463,574
  Dukakis 344,991
1992
  Clinton 497,585
  Bush 329,037
  Perot 97,790

Federal representation, 1996 (104th Congress)
Senators (name/party/term expires)

    DAVID H. PRYOR
    Democrat - 1997
    DALE BUMPERS
    Democrat - 1999

Representatives, total 4
  Democrats 2
  Republicans 2
  other 0

Women holding public office
U.S. Congress, 1995 1
statewide elected office, 1995 2
state legislature, 1995 17

Black elected officials, 1993
total 380
  US and state legislatures 13
  city/county/regional offices 214
  judicial/law enforcement 51
  education/school boards 102

Hispanic public officials, 1994
total 2
  state executives & legislators 1
  city/county/regional offices 0
  judicial/law enforcement 0
  education/school boards 1

GOVERNMENTAL FINANCE

State & local government revenues, (selected items), 1991-92 ($per capita)
total $3,329.85
  total general revenues 2,904.18
    from federal government 724.94
    from own sources 2,179.24
    from taxes 1,531.69
      from property taxes 263.88
      from all other taxes 1,159.56
    from charges & misc. 647.54

State & local government expenditures, (selected items), 1991-92 ($per capita)
total $3,087.87
  total direct general expenditures 2,781.87
    education 17118782
    libraries 7.28
    public welfare 496.96
    health & hospitals 230.05
    highways 266.23
    police protection 70.55
    fire protection 27.19
    correction 55.09
    housing & comm. development 33.68
    natural resources & parks 77.59
    interest on general debt 126.55

State & local debt, 1992 ($per capita) 2,117.20

Federal aid grants to state & local government, 1994 ($per capita total & selected items)
per capita total 801.60
  compensatory education 30.90
  waste treatment facilities 6.12
  medicaid 339.83
  housing assistance 40.01
  job training 13.84
  highway trust fund 75.38

CRIME, LAW ENFORCEMENT & COURTS

Crime, 1994 (all rates per 100,000 persons)
total crimes 117,713
overall crime rate 4,798.7
  property crimes 103,115
    burglaries 26,911
    larcenies 68,478
    motor vehicle thefts 7,726
  property crime rate 4,203.6
  violent crimes 14,598
    murders 294
    forcible rapes 1,028
    robberies 3,158
    aggravated assaults 10,118
  violent crime rate 595.1

Number of police agencies, 1994 184

Arrests, 1994
total 175,692
  persons under 18 years of age 18,730

Prisoners under state & federal jurisdiction, 1994
total 8,836
percent change, 1993-94 .... 2.4%
  sentenced to more than one year
    total 8,711
    rate per 100,000 residents 353

Persons under sentence of death, 4/20/95 39

State's highest court
name .... Supreme Court
number of members 7
length of term .... 8 years
intermediate appeals court? .... yes

Arkansas 6

LABOR & INCOME

Civilian labor force, 1994
total 1,207,000
  men 653,000
  women 554,000
  persons 16-19 years 83,000
  white 1,022,000
  black 166,000

Civilian labor force as a percent of
civilian non-institutional population, 1994
total 64.7%
  men 72.7%
  women 57.3%
  persons 16-19 years 54.1%
  white 65.2%
  black 61.1%

Employment, 1994
total 1,142,000
  men 622,000
  women 520,000
  persons 16-19 years 70,000
  white 976,000
  black 148,000

Full-time/part-time labor force, 1994
full-time labor force 1,002,000
  working part-time for
    ecomonic reasons 16,000
part-time labor force 204,000

Unemployment rate, 1994
total 5.3%
  men 4.7%
  women 6.1%
  persons 16-19 years 15.8%
  white 4.4%
  black 11.1%

Unemployed by reason for unemployment
(as a percent of total unemployment), 1994
job losers or completed temp jobs 45.1%
job leavers 14.1%
reentrants 36.0%
new entrants 4.9%

Civilian labor force, by occupation, 1994
executive/administrative/
  managerial 119,000
professional/specialty 126,000
technicians & related support 35,000
sales 133,000
adminstrative support/clerical 162,000
service occupations 152,000
precision production/craft/repair 146,000
machine operators/assemblers 128,000
transportation/material moving 70,000
handlers/helpers/laborers 70,000
farming/forestry/fishing 62,000

Civilian labor force, by industry, 1994
construction 52,000
manufacturing 269,000
transportation/communication 62,000
wholesale/retail trade 229,000
finance/real estate/insurance 58,000
services 212,000
government 162,000
agriculture 57,000

Average annual pay, 1994 (prelim.) $20,898
change in average annual pay,
  1993-1994 .... 2.8%

Hours and earnings of production workers
on manufacturing payrolls, 1994
average weekly hours 41.8
average hourly earnings $9.65
average weekly earnings $403.37

Labor union membership, 1994 77,100

Household income (in constant 1993 dollars)
median household income, 1992 .... $24,597
median household income, 1993 .... $23,039

Poverty
persons below poverty level, 1992 .... 17.5%
persons below poverty level, 1993 .... 20.0%

Personal income ($per capita)
1994
  in current dollars 16,898
  in constant (1987) dollars 13,069
1995 (projected)
  in constant (1982) dollars 10,858
2000 (projected)
  in constant (1982) dollars 11,594

Federal income tax returns, 1993
returns filed 994,988
adjusted gross income ($1000) 25,664,608
total income tax paid ($1000) 3,249,651

Arkansas 7

ECONOMY, BUSINESS, INDUSTRY & AGRICULTURE

Fortune 500 companies, 1994 5

Business incorporations, 1994
total 5,867
change, 1993-94 ....8.4%

Business failures, 1994
total 365
rate per 10,000 concerns 46
change, 1993-94 ....96.2%

Business firm ownership
Hispanic owned firms, 1987 324
black owned firms, 1987 4,392
women owned firms, 1987 35,500
foreign owned firms, 1982 96

Gross state product, 1991 ($mil)
total $40,561
  agriculture services, forestry, fisheries ...1,721
  mining 385
  construction 1,323
  manufacturing—durable goods 4,873
  manufacturing—nondurable goods 5,024
  transportation, communication &
    public utilities 4,699
  wholesale trade 2,269
  retail trade 4,315
  finance/real estate/insurance 5,518
  services 5,691
  federal, state & local government 4,743

Establishments, by major industry group, 1992
total 55,785
  agriculture 874
  mining 323
  construction 4,568
  manufacturing 3,935
  transportation 3,076
  wholesale trade 4,213
  retail trade 15,233
  finance/real estate/insurance 4,558
  service industries 18,159
  unclassified 846

Payroll, by major industry group, 1992
total ($1,000) $14,793,374
  agriculture 84,549

  mining 82,147
  construction 672,460
  manufacturing 4,917,384
  transportation 1,343,283
  wholesale trade 1,065,379
  retail trade 1,992,320
  finance/real estate/insurance 904,583
  service industries 3,719,344
  unclassified 11,925

Agriculture
number of farms, 1994 44,000
farm acreage, 1994 15,000,000
acres per farm, 1994 350
value of farms, 1994 ($mil) 12,312
farm income, 1993 ($mil)
  gross farm income 5,457
  net farm income 1,051
  debt/asset ratio 21.2%
farm marketings, 1993 ($mil)
total $4,382
  crops 1,480
  livestock 2,902
government payments 705
farm marketings in order of marketing receipts, 1993
    1) Broilers
    2) Soybeans
    3) Cotton
    4) Cattle

Federal economic activity ($mil, except per capita)
expenditures, 1994
  total $11,376
  per capita $4,638
  defense $1,072
  non-defense $10,305
defense department, 1994
  contract awards ($mil) $374
  payroll ($mil) $701
  civilian employees (x1,000) 4.2
  military personnel (x1,000) 5.9

Fishing, 1992
catch (millions of pounds) ....NA
value ($mil) ....NA

Mining, 1994 ($mil)
total non-fuel mineral production $392

Arkansas 8

principal non-fuel minerals in order of value, 1994
   1) Bromine
   2) Stone
   3) Sand and gravel

Construction, 1994 ($mil)
total contracts (including
   non-building) $2,735
      residential 1,228
      non-residential 829

Manufacturing, 1992
total establishments 3,913
employees, total (x1,000) 227
payroll ($mil) 4,878
production workers (x1,000) 179
value added ($mil) 14,204
value of shipments ($mil) 34,050

Finance
commercial banks, 1994
   number 257
      assets ($bil) 26.0
      deposits ($bil) 22.8
      closed or assisted 0
      deposits ($bil) .... NA
savings and loan associations, 1991
   non-current real estate loans 2.04%
   net income after taxes ($mil) .... -48
   return on assets ....-1.51%

Retail trade, 1992
establishments (x1,000) 14.9
sales ($mil) 15,925
annual payroll ($mil) 1,633
paid employees (x1,000) 152

Wholesale trade, 1992
establishments 4,296
sales ($bil) 18.1
annual payroll ($mil) 989
paid employees (x1,000) 43.9

Service industries, 1992
establishments (x1,000) (non-exempt firms) 14.0
receipts ($mil) (non-exempt firms) 6,007
annual payroll ($mil) 2,250
paid employees (x1,000) (non-exempt firms) . 133

COMMUNICATION, ENERGY & TRANSPORTATION

Communication
daily newspapers, 1993 32
broadcast stations, 1990
   radio: commercial, educational 228
   television: commercial, noncommercial 20
cable TV households, 1988 469,000

Energy
consumption estimates, 1992
total (trillion Btu) 796
per capita (million Btu) 332.5
by source of production (trillion Btu)
   coal 221
   natural gas 227
   petroleum 286
   nuclear electric power 121
   hydroelectric power 35
by end-use sector (trillion Btu)
   residential 157
   commercial 101
   industrial 307
   transportation 231
electrical energy
   production, 1993 (billion kWh) 38.0
   net summer capability, 1993 (million kW) .. 9.7
gas utilities, 1993
   customers 578,000
   sales (trillion Btu) 90
   revenues ($mil) 419
nuclear plants, 1993 2

Transportation, 1994
public road & street mileage
total 77,216
   urban 7,677
   rural 69,539
   interstate 543
vehicle miles of travel (mil) 24,948
total motor vehicle registrations 1,566,838
   automobiles 775,142
licensed drivers 1,768,394
   per 1,000 driving age population 938
deaths from motor vehicle
   accidents 610

California 1

STATE SUMMARY

Capital City .... Sacramento

Governor .... Pete Wilson

Address .... STATE CAPITOL
        SACRAMENTO, CA 95814
        916 445-2841

Admitted as a state 1850

Area (square miles) 163,707

Population, 1980 23,667,902

Population, 1990 29,760,021

Population, 1994 (est.) 31,431,000

Persons per square mile, 1994 .... 201.5

Largest city .... Los Angeles
    population, 1990 3,485,000

Personal income per capita, 1994
    (in current dollars) $22,493

Gross state product ($mil), 1991 763,577

Leading industries, 1992 (by payroll)
        SERVICE INDUSTRIES
        MANUFACTURING
        RETAIL TRADE

Leading agricultural commodities, 1993
        DAIRY PRODUCTS
        GREENHOUSE
        GRAPES
        CATTLE

GEOGRAPHY & ENVIRONMENT

Area (square miles)
total 163,707
    land 155,973
    water (includes territorial water) 7,734

Federally owned land, 1991 .... 44.6%

Highest point
name .... Mt. Whitney
elevation (feet) 14,494

Lowest point
name .... Death Valley
elevation (feet) .... -282

General coastline (miles) 840

Tidal shoreline (miles) 3,427

Capital city .... Sacramento
population, 1990 369,000

Largest city .... Los Angeles
population, 1990 3,485,000

Number of cities with over 100,000 population
1980 26

Number of cities with over 100,000 population
1990 43

State parks and Recreation areas, 1991
area (acres) 1,314,000
number of visitors 70,444,000
revenues $70,211,000

National forest land, 1992 (acres) 24,401,000

National park acreage, 1984 4,510,700

DEMOGRAPHICS & CHARACTERISTICS OF THE POPULATION

Population
1970 19,971,069
1980 23,667,902
1990 29,760,021
1994 (est.) 31,431,000
2000 (revised projection) 34,888,000
2010 (revised projection) 41,085,000

Metropolitan area population
1970 19,241,000
1980 22,689,000
1992 29,875,000

Non-metropolitan area population
1970 730,000
1980 979,000
1992 1,021,000

Change in population, 1980-90
number 6,092,119
percent 25.74%

Persons per square mile, 1994 .... 201.5

Age distribution, 1980
under 5 years 7.2%
5 to 17 years 19.8%
65 and over 10.2%

Age distribution, 1990
under 5 years 8.1%
5 to 17 years 17.9%
65 and over 10.5%

California 2

Age distribution, 2000 (projected)
under 5 years 6.7%
5 to 17 years 18.4%
65 and over 11.4%

Persons by age, 1990
under 5 years 2,397,715
5 to 17 years 5,353,010
65 and over 3,135,552

Median age, 1990 .... *31.50*

Race, 1990
White 20,524,327
Black 2,208,801
American Indian 236,078
Chinese 704,850
Filipino 731,685
Japanese 312,989
Asian Indian 159,973
Korean 259,941
Vietnamese 280,223
all other 4,335,068

Race, 2010 (projected)
White 30,357,000
Black 3,245,000

Persons of Hispanic origin, 1990
total 7,687,938
Mexican 6,118,996
Puerto Rican 126,417
Cuban 71,977
Other Hispanic 1,370,548

Persons by sex, 1990
male 14,897,627
female 14,862,394

Marital status, 1990
males
15 years & older 11,518,004
single 4,034,185
married 6,348,675
separated 252,628
widowed 237,667
divorced 897,477
females
15 years & older 11,642,977
single 2,939,043
married 6,274,255
separated 359,727

widowed 1,148,050
divorced 1,281,629

Households & families, 1990
households 10,381,206
persons per household 2.79
families 7,139,394
married couples 5,469,522
female householder, no husband
present 1,192,180
one person households 2,429,867
households, 1994 10,850,000
persons per household, 1994 .... 2.83

Nativity, 1990
number of persons born in state 13,797,065
percent of total residents 46.4%

Immigration & naturalization, 1993
immigrants admitted 260,090
persons naturalized 68,100
refugees granted resident status 39,516

VITAL STATISTICS & HEALTH

Births
1992 601,028
with low birth weight 5.9%
to teenage mothers 11.8%
to unmarried mothers 34.3%
1993 589,685
1994 581,763

Abortions, 1992
total 304,000
rate (per 1,000 women age 15-44) 42.1
rate per 1,000 live births 519

Adoptions, 1986
total 5,069
related 21.6%

Deaths
1992 215,206
1993 217,559
1994 224,082

Infant deaths
1992 4,168
1993 3,925
1994 3,884

Average lifetime, 1979-1981
both sexes . . . . 74.57 years
  men . . . . 71.09 years
  women . . . . 78.02 years

Marriages
1992 . . . . NA
1993 203,897
1994 202,827

Divorces
1992 . . . . NA
1993 . . . . NA
1994 . . . . NA

Physicians, 1993
total 74,165
rate (per 1,000 persons) 2.40

Dentists, 1992
total 20,751
rate (per 1,000 persons) 0.68

Hospitals, 1993
number 429
beds (x 1,000) 77.7
average daily census (x 1,000) 47.6
occupancy rate 61.2%
personnel (x 1,000) 320.5
average cost per day to hospital $1,221
average cost per stay to hospital $6,918

EDUCATION

Educational attainment of all persons
  25 years and older, 1990
less than 9th grade 2,085,905
high school graduates 4,167,897
bachelor's degree 2,858,107
graduate or professional degree 1,508,567

Public school enrollment, Fall, 1993
total 5,328,558
  Kindergarten through grade 8 3,904,471
  grades 9 through 12 1,424,087

Public School Teachers
total, 1994 221,779
  elementary 142,436
  secondary 56,384
salaries, 1994
  beginning $25,500
  average $40,636

State receipts & expenditures for public
  schools, 1993
receipts ($mil) 28,862
expenditures
  total ($mil) 28,387
  per capita $919
  per pupil $4,608

Graduating high school seniors,
  public high schools, 1995 (est) 262,000

SAT scores, 1994
verbal 413
math 482

Institutions of higher education, 1995
total 336
  public 138
  private 198

Enrollment in institutions of higher
  education, Fall, 1993
total 1,836,349
full-time men 406,101
full-time women 435,586
part-time men 432,747
part-time women 561,915

Minority enrollment in institutions of higher
  education, Fall, 1993
Black, non-Hispanic 133,532
Hispanic 322,898
Asian/Pacific Islander 292,064

Earned degrees conferred, 1993
Bachelor's 111,010
First professional 9,195
Master's 37,046
Doctor's 4,987

SOCIAL INSURANCE & WELFARE PROGRAMS

Social Security beneficiaries & benefits, 1993
beneficiaries
total 3,891,000
  retired and dependents 2,814,000
  survivors 618,000
  disabled & dependents 460,000
annual benefit payments ($mil)
total $28,405
  retired and dependents 19,953
  survivors 5,302
  disabled & dependents 3,151

California 4

Medicare, 1993
enrollment (x1,000) 3,504
payments ($mil) 16,488

Medicaid, 1993
recipients (x1,000) 4,834
payments ($mil) 9,650

Federal public aid, 1993
recipients as a percent of population 11.2%
Aid to Families with Dependent Children
    recipients (x1,000) 2,597
    average monthly payment $568
Supplemental Security Income
    total recipients (x1,000) 994

Food Stamp Program
participants, 1994 (x1,000) 3,155

HOUSING & CONSTRUCTION

Total housing units, 1990 11,182,882
    year round housing units 10,984,446
    vacant 801,676

New privately owned housing units authorized, 1994
number (x1,000) 97.0
value ($mil) 11,937

New privately owned housing units started, 1994 (x1,000) 101.2

Existing home sales, 1994 (x1,000) 482.8

GOVERNMENT & ELECTIONS

State officials, 1996
Governor (name/party/term expires)
PETE WILSON
Republican - 1999
Lt. Governor . . . . Gray Davis
Sec. of State . . . . Bill Jones
Atty. General . . . . Dan Lungren
Chf. Justice . . . . .Malcolm Lucas

Governorship
minimum age 18
length of term . . . . 4 years
number of consecutive
    terms permitted . . . . not specified
who succeeds . . . . Lt. Governor

State legislature
name . . . . Legislature
upper chamber
    name . . . . Senate
    number of members 40
    length of term . . . . 4 years
    party in majority, 1996 . . . . .Democratic
lower chamber
    name . . . . Assembly
    number of members 80
    length of term . . . . 2 years
    party in majority, 1996 . . . . 50/50

State employees October, 1992
total 385,807
October payroll ($1,000) 1,062,204

Local governments, 1992
total 4,495
    county 57
    municipal 460
    township 0
    school districts 1,080
    special districts 2,897

Voting, November, 1994
voting age population 22,639,000
    registered 54.2%
    voted 45.0%

Vote for president
1988
    Bush 4,756,490
    Dukakis 4,448,393
1992
    Clinton 4,815,039
    Bush 3,341,726
    Perot 2,147,409

Federal representation, 1996 (104th Congress)
Senators (name/party/term expires)

BARBARA BOXER
Democrat - 1999
DIANNE FEINSTEIN
Democrat - 2001

Representatives, total 52
    Democrats 27
    Republicans 25
    other 0

California 5

Women holding public office
U.S. Congress, 1995 11
statewide elected office, 1995 2
state legislature, 1995 25

Black elected officials, 1993
total 273
  US and state legislatures 13
  city/county/regional offices 72
  judicial/law enforcement 82
  education/school boards 106

Hispanic public officials, 1994
total 796
  state executives & legislators 16
  city/county/regional offices 349
  judicial/law enforcement 50
  education/school boards 381

GOVERNMENTAL FINANCE

State & local government revenues, (selected items), 1991-92 ($per capita)
total $5,348.17
  total general revenues 4,210.59
    from federal government 796.97
    from own sources 3,413.62
    from taxes 2,372.41
      from property taxes 678.54
      from all other taxes 1,541.26
    from charges & misc. 1,041.21

State & local government expenditures, (selected items), 1991-92 ($per capita)
total $5,353.98
  total direct general expenditures 4,282.15
    education 1,295.19
    libraries 20.14
    public welfare 664.72
    health & hospitals 431.18
    highways 204.87
    police protection 193.84
    fire protection 80.37
    correction 163.04
    housing & comm. development 111.90
    natural resources & parks 169.09
    interest on general debt 193.26

State & local debt, 1992 ($per capita) 3,757.76

Federal aid grants to state & local government, 1994 ($per capita total & selected items)
per capita total 834.17
  compensatory education 24.71
  waste treatment facilities 4.58
  medicaid 250.11
  housing assistance 50.07
  job training 14.33
  highway trust fund 64.11

CRIME, LAW ENFORCEMENT & COURTS

Crime, 1994 (all rates per 100,000 persons)
total crimes 1,940,497
overall crime rate 6,173.8
  property crimes 1,622,102
    burglaries 384,257
    larcenies 929,640
    motor vehicle thefts 308,205
  property crime rate 5,160.8
  violent crimes 318,395
    murders 3,703
    forcible rapes 10,984
    robberies 112,160
    aggravated assaults 191,548
  violent crime rate 1,013.0

Number of police agencies, 1994 701

Arrests, 1994
total 1,616,563
  persons under 18 years of age 257,389

Prisoners under state & federal jurisdiction, 1994
total 125,605
percent change, 1993-94 .... 4.7%
  sentenced to more than one year
    total 121,084
    rate per 100,000 residents 384

Persons under sentence of death, 4/20/95 407

State's highest court
name .... Supreme Court
number of members 7
length of term .... 12 years
intermediate appeals court? .... yes

California 6

LABOR & INCOME

Civilian labor force, 1994
total 15,471,000
  men 8,651,000
  women 6,819,000
  persons 16-19 years 799,000
  white 12,845,000
  black 866,000

Civilian labor force as a percent of
civilian non-institutional population, 1994
total 65.9%
  men 75.4%
  women 56.9%
  persons 16-19 years 46.2%
  white 66.4%
  black 63.5%

Employment, 1994
total 14,141,000
  men 7,898,000
  women 6,243,000
  persons 16-19 years 617,000
  white 11,794,000
  black 739,000

Full-time/part-time labor force, 1994
full-time labor force 12,443,000
  working part-time for
    ecomonic reasons 225,000
part-time labor force 3,027,000

Unemployment rate, 1994
total 8.6%
  men 8.7%
  women 8.4%
  persons 16-19 years 22.8%
  white 8.2%
  black 14.6%

Unemployed by reason for unemployment
(as a percent of total unemployment), 1994
job losers or completed temp jobs 51.0%
job leavers 7.5%
reentrants 33.5%
new entrants 8.0%

Civilian labor force, by occupation, 1994
executive/administrative/
  managerial 2,191,000
professional/specialty 2,125,000
technicians & related support 437,000

sales 1,880,000
adminstrative support/clerical 2,366,000
service occupations 2,130,000
precision production/craft/repair 1,581,000
machine operators/assemblers 844,000
transportation/material moving 571,000
handlers/helpers/laborers 656,000
farming/forestry/fishing 576,000

Civilian labor force, by industry, 1994
construction 661,000
manufacturing 2,212,000
transportation/communication 809,000
wholesale/retail trade 2,955,000
finance/real estate/insurance 903,000
services 3,417,000
government 2,124,000
agriculture 543,000

Average annual pay, 1994 (prelim.) $29,878
change in average annual pay,
  1993-1994 . . . . 1.4%

Hours and earnings of production workers
on manufacturing payrolls, 1994
average weekly hours 41.4
average hourly earnings $12.44
average weekly earnings $515.02

Labor union membership, 1994 2,185,100

Household income (in constant 1993 dollars)
median household income, 1992 . . . . $35,948
median household income, 1993 . . . . $34,073

Poverty
persons below poverty level, 1992 . . . . 16.4%
persons below poverty level, 1993 . . . . 18.2%

Personal income ($per capita)
1994
  in current dollars 22,493
  in constant (1987) dollars 17,396
1995 (projected)
  in constant (1982) dollars 16,241
2000 (projected)
  in constant (1982) dollars 17,113

Federal income tax returns, 1993
returns filed 13,218,412
adjusted gross income ($1000) 451,175,269
total income tax paid ($1000) 63,907,920

California 7

ECONOMY, BUSINESS, INDUSTRY & AGRICULTURE

Fortune 500 companies, 1994 51

Business incorporations, 1994
total 42,871
change, 1993-94 .... 7.0%

Business failures, 1994
total 16,803
rate per 10,000 concerns 163
change, 1993-94 .... -14.9%

Business firm ownership
Hispanic owned firms, 1987 132,212
black owned firms, 1987 47,728
women owned firms, 1987 559,800
foreign owned firms, 1982 942

Gross state product, 1991 ($mil)
total $763,577
  agriculture services, forestry, fisheries .. 15,672
  mining 4,834
  construction 32,646
  manufacturing—durable goods 72,282
  manufacturing—nondurable goods 42,524
  transportation, communication &
    public utilities 53,642
  wholesale trade 49,214
  retail trade 74,353
  finance/real estate/insurance 160,441
  services 167,102
  federal, state & local government 90,866

Establishments, by major industry group, 1992
total 746,789
  agriculture 11,935
  mining 1,176
  construction 66,277
  manufacturing 51,715
  transportation 26,517
  wholesale trade 58,365
  retail trade 166,032
  finance/real estate/insurance 76,741
  service industries 277,928
  unclassified 10,103

Payroll, by major industry group, 1992
total ($1,000) $290,374,778
  agriculture 1,694,225

  mining 1,522,730
  construction 15,134,676
  manufacturing 66,384,964
  transportation 20,651,661
  wholesale trade 25,686,776
  retail trade 32,795,360
  finance/real estate/insurance 27,862,833
  service industries 98,425,770
  unclassified 215,783

Agriculture
number of farms, 1994 76,000
farm acreage, 1994 30,000,000
acres per farm, 1994 388
value of farms, 1994 ($mil) 51,153
farm income, 1993 ($mil)
  gross farm income 21,533
  net farm income 5,235
  debt/asset ratio 20.3%
farm marketings, 1993 ($mil)
total $19,850
  crops 14,604
  livestock 5,246
government payments 522
farm marketings in order of marketing
receipts, 1993
  1) Dairy products
  2) Greenhouse
  3) Grapes
  4) Cattle

Federal economic activity ($mil, except per capita)
expenditures, 1994
  total $155,391
  per capita $4,944
  defense $36,198
  non-defense $119,192
defense department, 1994
  contract awards ($mil) $22,573
  payroll ($mil) $13,467
  civilian employees (x1,000) 99.9
  military personnel (x1,000) 143.2

Fishing, 1992
catch (millions of pounds) 302
value ($mil) 136

Mining, 1994 ($mil)
total non-fuel mineral production $2,497

California 8

principal non-fuel minerals in order of value, 1994
1) Cement
2) Sand and gravel
3) Gold

Construction, 1994 ($mil)
total contracts (including
non-building) $30,412
residential 12,275
non-residential 10,914

Manufacturing, 1992
total establishments 50,513
employees, total (x1,000) 1,960
payroll ($mil) 65,766
production workers (x1,000) 1,117
value added ($mil) 158,240
value of shipments ($mil) 305,805

Finance
commercial banks, 1994
number 425
assets ($bil) 328.5
deposits ($bil) 267.0
closed or assisted 8
deposits ($bil) 0.7
savings and loan associations, 1991
non-current real estate loans 3.59%
net income after taxes ($mil) .... -249
return on assets .... -0.08%

Retail trade, 1992
establishments (x1,000) 162.1
sales ($mil) 224,593
annual payroll ($mil) 28,064
paid employees (x1,000) 2,051

Wholesale trade, 1992
establishments 58,437
sales ($bil) 432.9
annual payroll ($mil) 23,537
paid employees (x1,000) 731.6

Service industries, 1992
establishments (x1,000) (non-exempt firms) 244.5
receipts ($mil) (non-exempt firms) 198,432
annual payroll ($mil) 71,824
paid employees (x1,000) (non-exempt firms) 2,646

COMMUNICATION, ENERGY & TRANSPORTATION

Communication
daily newspapers, 1993 104
broadcast stations, 1990
radio: commercial, educational 627
television: commercial, noncommercial 92
cable TV households, 1988 5,115,000

Energy
consumption estimates, 1992
total (trillion Btu) 7,092
per capita (million Btu) 229.6
by source of production (trillion Btu)
coal 65
natural gas 2,090
petroleum 3,243
nuclear electric power 376
hydroelectric power 244
by end-use sector (trillion Btu)
residential 1,240
commercial 1,256
industrial 1,915
transportation 2,681
electrical energy
production, 1993 (billion kWh) 125.8
net summer capability, 1993 (million kW) . 44.3
gas utilities, 1993
customers .... NA
sales (trillion Btu) .... NA
revenues ($mil) .... NA
nuclear plants, 1993 4

Transportation, 1994
public road & street mileage
total 169,047
urban 81,117
rural 87,930
interstate 2,427
vehicle miles of travel (mil) 271,943
total motor vehicle registrations 22,338,875
automobiles 14,742,557
licensed drivers 20,156,177
per 1,000 driving age population 856
deaths from motor vehicle
accidents 4,226

42

STATE SUMMARY

Capital City .... Denver

Governor .... Roy Romer

Address .... STATE CAPITOL
DENVER, CO 80203
303 866-2471

Admitted as a state 1876

Area (square miles) 104,100

Population, 1980 2,889,964

Population, 1990 3,294,394

Population, 1994 (est.) 3,656,000

Persons per square mile, 1994 .... 35.2

Largest city .... Denver
population, 1990 468,000

Personal income per capita, 1994
(in current dollars) $22,333

Gross state product ($mil), 1991 76,921

Leading industries, 1992 (by payroll)
SERVICE INDUSTRIES
MANUFACTURING
RETAIL TRADE

Leading agricultural commodities, 1993
CATTLE
CORN
WHEAT
DAIRY PRODUCTS

GEOGRAPHY & ENVIRONMENT

Area (square miles)
total 104,100
  land 103,730
  water (includes territorial water) 371

Federally owned land, 1991 .... 36.3%

Highest point
name .... Mt. Elbert
elevation (feet) 14,433

Lowest point
name .... Arkansas River
elevation (feet) 3,350

General coastline (miles) 0

Tidal shoreline (miles) 0

Capital city .... Denver
population, 1990 468,000

Largest city .... Denver
population, 1990 468,000

Number of cities with over 100,000 population
1980 5

Number of cities with over 100,000 population
1990 4

State parks and Recreation areas, 1991
area (acres) 307,000
number of visitors 8,653,000
revenues $10,854,000

National forest land, 1992 (acres) 16,037,000

National park acreage, 1984 588,200

DEMOGRAPHICS & CHARACTERISTICS OF THE POPULATION

Population
1970 2,209,596
1980 2,889,964
1990 3,294,394
1994 (est.) 3,656,000
2000 (revised projection) 4,059,000
2010 (revised projection) 4,494,000

Metropolitan area population
1970 1,772,000
1980 2,326,000
1992 2,832,000

Non-metropolitan area population
1970 438,000
1980 563,000
1992 632,000

Change in population, 1980-90
number 404,430
percent 13.99%

Persons per square mile, 1994 .... 35.2

Age distribution, 1980
under 5 years 7.5%
5 to 17 years 20.5%
65 and over 8.6%

Age distribution, 1990
under 5 years 7.7%
5 to 17 years 18.4%
65 and over 10.0%

Colorado 2

Age distribution, 2000 (projected)
under 5 years 6.2%
5 to 17 years 18.0%
65 and over 10.2%

Persons by age, 1990
under 5 years 252,893
5 to 17 years 608,373
65 and over 329,443

Median age, 1990 . . . . *32.50*

Race, 1990
White 2,905,474
Black 133,146
American Indian 27,271
Chinese 8,695
Filipino 5,426
Japanese 11,402
Asian Indian 3,836
Korean 11,339
Vietnamese 7,210
all other 180,090

Race, 2010 (projected)
White 4,090,000
Black 200,000

Persons of Hispanic origin, 1990
total . . . . : 424,302
Mexican 282,478
Puerto Rican 7,225
Cuban 2,058
Other Hispanic 132,541

Persons by sex, 1990
male 1,631,295
female 1,663,099

Marital status, 1990
males
15 years & older 1,255,439
single 373,157
married 742,483
separated 22,645
widowed 23,473
divorced 116,326
females
15 years & older 1,305,576
single 287,612
married 743,243
separated 29,520

widowed 118,193
divorced 156,528

Households & families, 1990
households 1,282,489
persons per household 2.51
families 854,214
married couples 690,292
female householder, no husband
present 124,569
one person households 340,962
households, 1994 1,417,000
persons per household, 1994 . . . . 2.52

Nativity, 1990
number of persons born in state 1,427,412
percent of total residents 43.3%

Immigration & naturalization, 1993
immigrants admitted 6,650
persons naturalized 2,732
refugees granted resident status 1,106

VITAL STATISTICS & HEALTH

Births
1992 54,586
with low birth weight 8.5%
to teenage mothers 12.0%
to unmarried mothers 23.8%
1993 54,817
1994 54,144

Abortions, 1992
total 20,000
rate (per 1,000 women age 15-44) 23.6
rate per 1,000 live births 362

Adoptions, 1986
total 2,036
related 62.2%

Deaths
1992 22,528
1993 23,722
1994 24,416

Infant deaths
1992 396
1993 413
1994 358

Average lifetime, 1979-1981
both sexes .... 75.30 years
men .... 71.78 years
women .... 78.80 years

Marriages
1992 33,672
1993 34,036
1994 34,367

Divorces
1992 19,508
1993 19,138
1994 18,795

Physicians, 1993
total 7,830
rate (per 1,000 persons) 2.22

Dentists, 1992
total 2,451
rate (per 1,000 persons) 0.71

Hospitals, 1993
number 72
beds (x 1,000) 10.3
average daily census (x 1,000) 6.0
occupancy rate 58.6%
personnel (x 1,000) 42.2
average cost per day to hospital $961
average cost per stay to hospital $6,212

EDUCATION

*Educational attainment of all persons
25 years and older, 1990*
less than 9th grade 118,252
high school graduates 558,312
bachelor's degree 379,150
graduate or professional degree 189,106

Public school enrollment, Fall, 1993
total 625,062
Kindergarten through grade 8 459,930
grades 9 through 12 165,132

Public School Teachers
total, 1994 33,661
elementary 17,439
secondary 16,222
salaries, 1994
beginning $20,091
average $33,826

*State receipts & expenditures for public
schools, 1993*
receipts ($mil) 3,435
expenditures
total ($mil) 3,375
per capita $974
per pupil $4,969

*Graduating high school seniors,
public high schools, 1995 (est) 33,088*

SAT scores, 1994
verbal 456
math 513

Institutions of higher education, 1995
total 61
public 29
private 32

*Enrollment in institutions of higher
education, Fall, 1993*
total 239,805
full-time men 63,284
full-time women 63,610
part-time men 48,383
part-time women 64,528

*Minority enrollment in institutions of higher
education, Fall, 1993*
Black, non-Hispanic 7,820
Hispanic 20,622
Asian/Pacific Islander 7,135

Earned degrees conferred, 1993
Bachelor's 18,925
First professional 813
Master's 6,391
Doctor's 768

SOCIAL INSURANCE &
WELFARE PROGRAMS

Social Security beneficiaries & benefits, 1993
beneficiaries
total 469,000
retired and dependents 326,000
survivors 77,000
disabled & dependents 66,000
annual benefit payments ($mil)
total $3,279
retired and dependents 2,191
survivors 652
disabled & dependents 436

Colorado 4

Medicare, 1993
enrollment (x1,000) 396
payments ($mil) 1,430

Medicaid, 1993
recipients (x1,000) 281
payments ($mil) 911

Federal public aid, 1993
recipients as a percent of population 4.8%
Aid to Families with Dependent Children
   recipients (x1,000) 126
average monthly payment $319
Supplemental Security Income
   total recipients (x1,000) 51

Food Stamp Program
   participants, 1994 (x1,000) 268

HOUSING & CONSTRUCTION

Total housing units, 1990 1,477,349
   year round housing units 1,412,728
   vacant 194,860

New privately owned housing units authorized, 1994
number (x1,000) 37.2
value ($mil) 3,906

New privately owned housing units started, 1994 (x1,000) 38.2

Existing home sales, 1994 (x1,000) 80.6

GOVERNMENT & ELECTIONS

State officials, 1996
   Governor (name/party/term expires)
ROY ROMER
Democrat - 1999

Lt. Governor . . . . .Mike Callihan
Sec. of State . . . . Natalie Meyer
Atty. General . . . . Gail Norton
Chf. Justice .Louis Rovira

Governorship
minimum age 30
length of term . . . . 4 years
number of consecutive
   terms permitted . . . . not specified
who succeeds . . . . Lt. Governor

State legislature
name . . . . .General Assembly
   upper chamber
      name . . . . Senate
      number of members 35
      length of term . . . . 4 years
      party in majority, 1996 . . . . Republican
   lower chamber
      name . . . . House of Representatives
      number of members 65
      length of term . . . . 2 years
      party in majority, 1996 . . . . .Democratic

State employees October, 1992
total 72,424
October payroll ($1,000) 165,021

Local governments, 1992
total 1,826
   county 62
   municipal 266
   township 0
   school districts 180
   special districts 1,317

Voting, November, 1994
voting age population 2,703,000
   registered 64.3%
   voted 46.4%

Vote for president
1988
   Bush 727,633
   Dukakis 621,093
1992
   Clinton 626,207
   Bush 557,528
   Perot 362,304

Federal representation, 1996 (104th Congress)
Senators (name/party/term expires)

HANK BROWN
Republican - 1997
BEN NIGHTHORSE CAMPBELL
Democrat - 1999

Representatives, total 6
   Democrats 2
   Republicans 4
   other 0

Colorado 5

Women holding public office
U.S. Congress, 1995 1
statewide elected office, 1995 3
state legislature, 1995 31

Black elected officials, 1993
total 20
  US and state legislatures 4
  city/county/regional offices 4
  judicial/law enforcement 10
  education/school boards 2

Hispanic public officials, 1994
total 201
  state executives & legislators 9
  city/county/regional offices 140
  judicial/law enforcement 10
  education/school boards 42

GOVERNMENTAL FINANCE

State & local government revenues, (selected items), 1991-92 ($per capita)
total $4,724.33
  total general revenues 3,779.49
    from federal government 617.63
    from own sources 3,161.86
    from taxes 2,076.85
      from property taxes 691.82
      from all other taxes 1,263.19
    from charges & misc. 1,085.01

State & local government expenditures, (selected items), 1991-92 ($per capita)
total $4,480.63
  total direct general expenditures 3,798.53
    education 1,384.67
    libraries 26.42
    public welfare 450.51
    health & hospitals 251.15
    highways 306.86
    police protection 136.74
    fire protection 58.17
    correction 114.86
    housing & comm. development 53.28
    natural resources & parks 150.77
    interest on general debt 272.77

State & local debt, 1992 ($per capita) 4,693.14

Federal aid grants to state & local government, 1994 ($per capita total & selected items)
per capita total 575.08
  compensatory education 17.89
  waste treatment facilities 1.86
  medicaid 177.43
  housing assistance 39.95
  job training 10.10
  highway trust fund 70.18

CRIME, LAW ENFORCEMENT & COURTS

Crime, 1994 (all rates per 100,000 persons)
total crimes 194,440
overall crime rate 5,318.4
  property crimes 175,808
    burglaries 33,843
    larcenies 127,600
    motor vehicle thefts 14,365
  property crime rate 4,808.8
  violent crimes 18,632
    murders 199
    forcible rapes 1,579
    robberies 3,910
    aggravated assaults 12,944
  violent crime rate 509.6

Number of police agencies, 1994 97

Arrests, 1994
total 217,438
  persons under 18 years of age 51,163

Prisoners under state & federal jurisdiction, 1994
total 10,717
percent change, 1993-94 .... 13.3%
  sentenced to more than one year
    total 10,717
    rate per 100,000 residents 289

Persons under sentence of death, 4/20/95 3

State's highest court
name .... Supreme Court
number of members 7
length of term .... 10 years
intermediate appeals court? .... yes

47

Colorado 6

LABOR & INCOME

Civilian labor force, 1994
total 1,996,000
  men 1,081,000
  women 915,000
  persons 16-19 years 105,000
  white 1,814,000
  black 78,000

Civilian labor force as a percent of civilian non-institutional population, 1994
total 72.5%
  men 79.4%
  women 65.7%
  persons 16-19 years 61.6%
  white 73.0%
  black 67.4%

Employment, 1994
total 1,912,000
  men 1,034,000
  women 878,000
  persons 16-19 years 92,000
  white 1,742,000
  black 71,000

Full-time/part-time labor force, 1994
full-time labor force 1,603,000
  working part-time for
    ecomonic reasons 19,000
part-time labor force 393,000

Unemployment rate, 1994
total 4.2%
  men 4.4%
  women 4.0%
  persons 16-19 years 11.8%
  white 3.9%
  black 8.6%

Unemployed by reason for unemployment (as a percent of total unemployment), 1994
job losers or completed temp jobs 43.1%
job leavers 15.1%
reentrants 39.0%
new entrants 2.9%

Civilian labor force, by occupation, 1994
executive/administrative/
  managerial 294,000
professional/specialty 317,000
technicians & related support 74,000
sales 280,000
adminstrative support/clerical 300,000
service occupations 261,000
precision production/craft/repair 198,000
machine operators/assemblers 68,000
transportation/material moving 82,000
handlers/helpers/laborers 72,000
farming/forestry/fishing ....NA

Civilian labor force, by industry, 1994
construction 108,000
manufacturing 240,000
transportation/communication 129,000
wholesale/retail trade 404,000
finance/real estate/insurance 122,000
services 460,000
government 283,000
agriculture ....NA

Average annual pay, 1994 (prelim.) $26,164
change in average annual pay,
  1993-1994 .... 1.9%

Hours and earnings of production workers on manufacturing payrolls, 1994
average weekly hours 41.3
average hourly earnings $12.27
average weekly earnings $506.75

Labor union membership, 1994 179,100

Household income (in constant 1993 dollars)
median household income, 1992 .... $33,456
median household income, 1993 .... $34,488

Poverty
persons below poverty level, 1992 .... 10.8%
persons below poverty level, 1993 .... 9.9%

Personal income ($per capita)
1994
  in current dollars 22,333
  in constant (1987) dollars 17,272
1995 (projected)
  in constant (1982) dollars 14,418
2000 (projected)
  in constant (1982) dollars 15,311

Federal income tax returns, 1993
returns filed 1,688,397
adjusted gross income ($1000) 55,892,623
total income tax paid ($1000) 8,136,012

ECONOMY, BUSINESS, INDUSTRY & AGRICULTURE

Fortune 500 companies, 1994 4

Business incorporations, 1994
total 15,187
change, 1993-94 .... -1.7%

Business failures, 1994
total 1,311
rate per 10,000 concerns 91
change, 1993-94 .... -15.3%

Business firm ownership
Hispanic owned firms, 1987 9,516
black owned firms, 1987 2,871
women owned firms, 1987 89,400
foreign owned firms, 1982 237

Gross state product, 1991 ($mil)
total $76,921
  agriculture services, forestry, fisheries ... 1,756
  mining 1,332
  construction 3,339
  manufacturing—durable goods 5,636
  manufacturing—nondurable goods 4,291
  transportation, communication &
    public utilities 7,764
  wholesale trade 4,890
  retail trade 7,877
  finance/real estate/insurance 12,994
  services 15,953
  federal, state & local government 11,088

Establishments, by major industry group, 1992
total 103,959
  agriculture 1,685
  mining 1,089
  construction 10,014
  manufacturing 5,357
  transportation 4,000
  wholesale trade 7,614
  retail trade 23,530
  finance/real estate/insurance 10,702
  service industries 38,448
  unclassified 1,520

Payroll, by major industry group, 1992
total ($1,000) $31,918,920
  agriculture 146,852

  mining 817,328
  construction 2,091,923
  manufacturing 5,939,817
  transportation 2,985,130
  wholesale trade 2,695,621
  retail trade 3,917,661
  finance/real estate/insurance 2,987,713
  service industries 10,313,435
  unclassified 23,440

Agriculture
number of farms, 1994 25,000
farm acreage, 1994 33,000,000
acres per farm, 1994 1,292
value of farms, 1994 ($mil) 14,104
farm income, 1993 ($mil)
  gross farm income 4,689
  net farm income 996
  debt/asset ratio 16.8%
farm marketings, 1993 ($mil)
  total $4,083
    crops 1,204
    livestock 2,879
  government payments 250
farm marketings in order of marketing receipts, 1993
  1) Cattle
  2) Wheat
  3) Corn
  4) Dairy products

Federal economic activity
($mil, except per capita)
expenditures, 1994
  total $18,989
  per capita $5,194
  defense $4,897
  non-defense $14,092
defense department, 1994
  contract awards ($mil) $2,620
  payroll ($mil) $2,298
  civilian employees (x1,000) 13.3
  military personnel (x1,000) 34.2

Fishing, 1992
catch (millions of pounds) .... NA
value ($mil) .... NA

Mining, 1994 ($mil)
total non-fuel mineral production $440

Colorado 8

principal non-fuel minerals in order of value, 1994
  1) Sand and gravel
  2) Cement
  3) Gold

Construction, 1994 ($mil)
total contracts (including
  non-building) $6,415
  residential 3,893
  non-residential 1,548

Manufacturing, 1992
total establishments 5,295
employees, total (x1,000) 184
payroll ($mil) 5,926
production workers (x1,000) 107
value added ($mil) 15,300
value of shipments ($mil) 29,220

Finance
commercial banks, 1994
  number 322
  assets ($bil) 34.4
  deposits ($bil) 30.0
  closed or assisted 0
  deposits ($bil) .... NA
savings and loan associations, 1991
  non-current real estate loans 1.96%
  net income after taxes ($mil) 12
  return on assets .... +0.13%

Retail trade, 1992
establishments (x1,000) 22.9
sales ($mil) 28,533
annual payroll ($mil) 3,488
paid employees (x1,000) 283

Wholesale trade, 1992
establishments 7,554
sales ($bil) 46.9
annual payroll ($mil) 2,478
paid employees (x1,000) 84.0

Service industries, 1992
establishments (x1,000) (non-exempt firms) 32.9
receipts ($mil) (non-exempt firms) 18,810
annual payroll ($mil) 7,183
paid employees (x1,000) (non-exempt firms) . 319

COMMUNICATION, ENERGY & TRANSPORTATION

Communication
daily newspapers, 1993 28
broadcast stations, 1990
  radio: commercial, educational 192
  television: commercial, noncommercial 22
cable TV households, 1988 637,000

Energy
consumption estimates, 1992
total (trillion Btu) 959
per capita (million Btu) 276.8
by source of production (trillion Btu)
  coal 332
  natural gas 259
  petroleum 349
  nuclear electric power 0
  hydroelectric power 16
by end-use sector (trillion Btu)
  residential 213
  commercial 233
  industrial 233
  transportation 280
electrical energy
  production, 1993 (billion kWh) 32.7
  net summer capability, 1993 (million kW) .. 6.6
gas utilities, 1993
  customers 1,176,000
  sales (trillion Btu) 184
  revenues ($mil) 785
nuclear plants, 1993 0

Transportation, 1994
public road & street mileage
total 84,195
  urban 13,324
  rural 70,871
  interstate 954
vehicle miles of travel (mil) 33,705
total motor vehicle registrations 2,749,858
  automobiles 1,651,591
licensed drivers 2,732,682
  per 1,000 driving age population 981
deaths from motor vehicle
  accidents 585

Connecticut 1

STATE SUMMARY

Capital City .... Hartford

Governor .... John Rowland

Address .... STATE CAPITOL
 HARTFORD, CT 06106
 203 566-4840

Admitted as a state 1788

Area (square miles) 5,544

Population, 1980 3,107,576

Population, 1990 3,287,116

Population, 1994 (est.) 3,275,000

Persons per square mile, 1994 .... 676.0

Largest city .... Bridgeport
 population, 1990 142,000

Personal income per capita, 1994
 (in current dollars) $29,402

Gross state product ($mil), 1991 96,384

Leading industries, 1992 (by payroll)
 MANUFACTURING
 SERVICE INDUSTRIES
 FINANCE, REAL ESTATE &
 INSURANCE

Leading agricultural commodities, 1993
 GREENHOUSE
 DAIRY PRODUCTS
 EGGS
 TOBACCO

GEOGRAPHY & ENVIRONMENT

Area (square miles)
total 5,544
 land 4,845
 water (includes territorial water) 698

Federally owned land, 1991 .... 0.2%

Highest point
name .... Mt. Frissell (south slope)
elevation (feet) 2,380

Lowest point
name .... Long Island Sound
elevation (feet) .... sea level

General coastline (miles) 0

Tidal shoreline (miles) 618

Capital city .... Hartford
population, 1990 140,000

Largest city .... Bridgeport
population, 1990 142,000

Number of cities with over 100,000 population
 1980 4

Number of cities with over 100,000 population
 1990 5

State parks and Recreation areas, 1991
area (acres) 172,000
number of visitors 6,743,000
revenues $3,327,000

National forest land, 1992 (acres) 500

National park acreage, 1984 3,300

DEMOGRAPHICS & CHARACTERISTICS OF THE POPULATION

Population
1970 3,032,217
1980 3,107,576
1990 3,287,116
1994 (est.) 3,275,000
2000 (revised projection) 3,271,000
2010 (revised projection) 3,412,000

Metropolitan area population
1970 2,819,000
1980 2,879,000
1992 3,138,000

Non-metropolitan area population
1970 213,000
1980 228,000
1992 141,000

Change in population, 1980-90
number 179,540
percent 5.78%

Persons per square mile, 1994 .... 676.0

Age distribution, 1980
under 5 years 6.0%
5 to 17 years 20.5%
65 and over 11.7%

Age distribution, 1990
under 5 years 7.0%
5 to 17 years 15.8%
65 and over 13.5%

Connecticut 2

Age distribution, 2000 (projected)
under 5 years 5.5%
5 to 17 years 17.1%
65 and over 14.1%

Persons by age, 1990
under 5 years 228,356
5 to 17 years 521,225
65 and over 445,907

Median age, 1990 .... *34.40*

Race, 1990
White 2,859,353
Black 274,269
American Indian 6,472
Chinese 11,082
Filipino 5,160
Japanese 3,811
Asian Indian 11,755
Korean 5,126
Vietnamese 4,085
all other 105,821

Race, 2010 (projected)
White 2,960,000
Black 347,000

Persons of Hispanic origin, 1990
total 213,116
Mexican 8,393
Puerto Rican 146,842
Cuban 6,386
Other Hispanic 51,495

Persons by sex, 1990
male 1,592,873
female 1,694,243

Marital status, 1990
males
15 years & older 1,269,569
single 412,921
married 739,187
separated 17,931
widowed 33,892
divorced 83,569
females
15 years & older 1,385,814
single 357,734
married 742,707
separated 27,542

widowed 163,081
divorced 122,292

Households & families, 1990
households 1,230,479
persons per household 2.59
families 864,493
married couples 684,660
female householder, no husband
present 140,385
one person households 297,161
households, 1994 1,222,000
persons per household, 1994 .... 2.60

Nativity, 1990
number of persons born in state 1,874,080
percent of total residents 57.0%

Immigration & naturalization, 1993
immigrants admitted 10,966
persons naturalized 6,125
refugees granted resident status 1,116

VITAL STATISTICS & HEALTH

Births
1992 47,335
with low birth weight 6.9%
to teenage mothers 8.0%
to unmarried mothers 28.7%
1993 45,821
1994 42,108

Abortions, 1992
total 20,000
rate (per 1,000 women age 15-44) 26.2
rate per 1,000 live births 444

Adoptions, 1986
total 975
related 51.3%

Deaths
1992 28,295
1993 29,057
1994 28,552

Infant deaths
1992 354
1993 327
1994 .... NA

Connecticut 3

Average lifetime, 1979-1981
both sexes .... 75.12 years
men .... 71.51 years
women .... 78.57 years

Marriages
1992 28,944
1993 22,791
1994 21,888

Divorces
1992 10,081
1993 10,199
1994 9,095

Physicians, 1993
total 10,482
rate (per 1,000 persons) 3.21

Dentists, 1992
total 2,635
rate (per 1,000 persons) 0.81

Hospitals, 1993
number 35
beds (x 1,000) 9.2
average daily census (x 1,000) 6.9
occupancy rate 74.4%
personnel (x 1,000) 44.8
average cost per day to hospital $1,058
average cost per stay to hospital $7,478

EDUCATION

*Educational attainment of all persons
25 years and older, 1990*
less than 9th grade 185,213
high school graduates 648,366
bachelor's degree 356,289
graduate or professional degree 241,404

Public school enrollment, Fall, 1993
total 496,298
  Kindergarten through grade 8 368,632
  grades 9 through 12 127,666

Public School Teachers
total, 1994 34,526
  elementary 20,132
  secondary 9,345
salaries, 1994
  beginning $28,052
  average $50,389

*State receipts & expenditures for public
schools, 1993*
receipts ($mil) 4,107
expenditures
  total ($mil) 4,107
  per capita $1,252
  per pupil $8,188

*Graduating high school seniors,
public high schools, 1995 (est)* 26,800

SAT scores, 1994
verbal 426
math 472

Institutions of higher education, 1995
total 43
  public 19
  private 24

*Enrollment in institutions of higher
education, Fall, 1993*
total 162,300
full-time men 39,634
full-time women 42,464
part-time men 31,570
part-time women 48,632

*Minority enrollment in institutions of higher
education, Fall, 1993*
Black, non-Hispanic 11,419
Hispanic 6,939
Asian/Pacific Islander 5,032

Earned degrees conferred, 1993
Bachelor's 14,931
First professional 679
Master's 6,590
Doctor's 630

SOCIAL INSURANCE & WELFARE PROGRAMS

Social Security beneficiaries & benefits, 1993
beneficiaries
total 553,000
  retired and dependents 424,000
  survivors 78,000
  disabled & dependents 51,000
annual benefit payments ($mil)
total $4,396
  retired and dependents 3,308
  survivors 733
  disabled & dependents 355

53

Connecticut 4

Medicare, 1993
enrollment (x1,000) 491
payments ($mil) 2,053

Medicaid, 1993
recipients (x1,000) 334
payments ($mil) 1,825

Federal public aid, 1993
recipients as a percent of population 6.2%
Aid to Families with Dependent Children
recipients (x1,000) 163
average monthly payment $560
Supplemental Security Income
total recipients (x1,000) 40

Food Stamp Program
participants, 1994 (x1,000) 223

HOUSING & CONSTRUCTION

Total housing units, 1990 1,320,850
year round housing units 1,300,375
vacant 90,371

New privately owned housing units
authorized, 1994
number (x1,000) 9.5
value ($mil) 1,030

New privately owned housing units
started, 1994 (x1,000) 9.4

Existing home sales, 1994 (x1,000) 49.8

GOVERNMENT & ELECTIONS

State officials, 1996
Governor (name/party/term expires)
JOHN ROWLAND
Republican - 1999
Lt. Governor ....Eunice Groark
Sec. of State ....Pauline Kezer
Atty. General .... Richard Blumenthal
Chf. Justice .... Ellen Ash Peters

Governorship
minimum age 30
length of term ....4 years
number of consecutive
terms permitted ....not specified
who succeeds .... Lt. Governor

State legislature
name ....General Assembly
upper chamber
name ....Senate
number of members 36
length of term ....2 years
party in majority, 1996 ....Republican
lower chamber
name .... House of Representatives
number of members 151
length of term ....2 years
party in majority, 1996 ....Democratic

State employees October, 1992
total 63,843
October payroll ($1,000) 174,518

Local governments, 1992
total 575
county 0
municipal 30
township 149
school districts 17
special districts 378

Voting, November, 1994
voting age population 2,431,000
registered 68.4%
voted 51.3%

Vote for president
1988
Bush 747,082
Dukakis 674,873
1992
Clinton 682,406
Bush 576,777
Perot 347,407

Federal representation, 1996 (104th Congress)
Senators (name/party/term expires)

JOE LIEBERMAN
Democrat - 2001
CHRISTOPHER J. DODD
Democrat - 1999

Representatives, total 6
Democrats 3
Republicans 3
other 0

Connecticut 5

Women holding public office
U.S. Congress, 1995 3
statewide elected office, 1995 2
state legislature, 1995 50

Black elected officials, 1993
total 62
  US and state legislatures 14
  city/county/regional offices 38
  judicial/law enforcement 2
  education/school boards 8

Hispanic public officials, 1994
total 26
  state executives & legislators 12
  city/county/regional offices 9
  judicial/law enforcement 0
  education/school boards 5

GOVERNMENTAL FINANCE

State & local government revenues, (selected items), 1991-92 ($per capita)
total $5,249.92
  total general revenues 4,569.63
    from federal government 751.18
    from own sources 3,818.45
    from taxes 3,049.34
      from property taxes 1,193.64
      from all other taxes 1,681.22
    from charges & misc. 769.11

State & local government expenditures, (selected items), 1991-92 ($per capita)
total $5,237.07
  total direct general expenditures 4,577.45
    education 1,406.29
    libraries 25.91
    public welfare 753.07
    health & hospitals 346.41
    highways 328.15
    police protection 141.58
    fire protection 82.75
    correction 127.87
    housing & comm. development 99.36
    natural resources & parks 68.51
    interest on general debt 281.04

State & local debt, 1992 ($per capita) 4,752.04

Federal aid grants to state & local government, 1994 ($per capita total & selected items)
per capita total 924.48
  compensatory education 18.29
  waste treatment facilities 7.30
  medicaid 358.80
  housing assistance 79.27
  job training 12.63
  highway trust fund 120.14

CRIME, LAW ENFORCEMENT & COURTS

Crime, 1994 (all rates per 100,000 persons)
total crimes 148,946
overall crime rate 4,548.0
  property crimes 134,030
    burglaries 29,142
    larcenies 84,721
    motor vehicle thefts 20,167
  property crime rate 4,092.5
  violent crimes 14,916
    murders 215
    forcible rapes 806
    robberies 6,150
    aggravated assaults 7,745
  violent crime rate 455.5

Number of police agencies, 1994 98

Arrests, 1994
total 182,873
  persons under 18 years of age 32,154

Prisoners under state & federal jurisdiction, 1994
total 14,380
percent change, 1993-94 . . . . 5.0%
  sentenced to more than one year
    total 10,500
    rate per 100,000 residents 321

Persons under sentence of death, 4/20/95 5

State's highest court
name . . . . Supreme Court
number of members 6
length of term . . . . 8 years
intermediate appeals court? . . . . yes

Connecticut 6

LABOR & INCOME

Civilian labor force, 1994
total	1,726,000
men	908,000
women	818,000
persons 16-19 years	107,000
white	1,578,000
black	118,000

Civilian labor force as a percent of civilian non-institutional population, 1994
total	68.8%
men	76.9%
women	61.5%
persons 16-19 years	54.7%
white	68.8%
black	68.9%

Employment, 1994
total	1,630,000
men	860,000
women	769,000
persons 16-19 years	96,000
white	1,497,000
black	104,000

Full-time/part-time labor force, 1994
full-time labor force	1,370,000
working part-time for ecomonic reasons	13,000
part-time labor force	356,000

Unemployment rate, 1994
total	5.6%
men	5.3%
women	5.9%
persons 16-19 years	10.4%
white	5.2%
black	12.2%

Unemployed by reason for unemployment (as a percent of total unemployment), 1994
job losers or completed temp jobs	57.2%
job leavers	7.5%
reentrants	28.9%
new entrants	6.7%

Civilian labor force, by occupation, 1994
executive/administrative/managerial	243,000
professional/specialty	276,000
technicians & related support	NA
sales	216,000
adminstrative support/clerical	265,000
service occupations	228,000
precision production/craft/repair	195,000
machine operators/assemblers	89,000
transportation/material moving	64,000
handlers/helpers/laborers	64,000
farming/forestry/fishing	NA

Civilian labor force, by industry, 1994
construction	64,000
manufacturing	306,000
transportation/communication	84,000
wholesale/retail trade	307,000
finance/real estate/insurance	150,000
services	432,000
government	219,000
agriculture	NA

Average annual pay, 1994 (prelim.) $33,811
change in average annual pay, 1993-1994 ...... 1.9%

Hours and earnings of production workers on manufacturing payrolls, 1994
average weekly hours	42.8
average hourly earnings	$13.53
average weekly earnings	$579.08

Labor union membership, 1994 290,100

Household income (in constant 1993 dollars)
median household income, 1992	$42,064
median household income, 1993	$39,516

Poverty
persons below poverty level, 1992	9.8%
persons below poverty level, 1993	8.5%

Personal income ($per capita)
1994
in current dollars	29,402
in constant (1987) dollars	22,739
1995 (projected)
in constant (1982) dollars	19,625
2000 (projected)
in constant (1982) dollars	20,503

Federal income tax returns, 1993
returns filed	1,552,730
adjusted gross income ($1000)	67,654,719
total income tax paid ($1000)	11,443,060

ECONOMY, BUSINESS, INDUSTRY & AGRICULTURE

Fortune 500 companies, 1994 23

Business incorporations, 1994
total 6,911
change, 1993-94 .... -8.1%

Business failures, 1994
total 573
rate per 10,000 concerns 44
change, 1993-94 .... -48.1%

Business firm ownership
Hispanic owned firms, 1987 2,235
black owned firms, 1987 4,061
women owned firms, 1987 60,900
foreign owned firms, 1982 231

Gross state product, 1991 ($mil)
total $96,384
agriculture services, forestry, fisheries 682
mining 60
construction 3,166
manufacturing—durable goods 13,622
manufacturing—nondurable goods 5,908
transportation, communication &
   public utilities 6,909
wholesale trade 6,663
retail trade 8,713
finance/real estate/insurance 23,010
services 18,915
federal, state & local government 8,735

Establishments, by major industry group, 1992
total 90,238
agriculture 1,802
mining 98
construction 8,994
manufacturing 6,321
transportation 2,962
wholesale trade 6,196
retail trade 21,584
finance/real estate/insurance 8,382
service industries 32,916
unclassified 983

Payroll, by major industry group, 1992
total ($1,000) $43,257,420
agriculture 153,829

mining 71,135
construction 1,915,258
manufacturing 12,472,629
transportation 2,395,705
wholesale trade 3,669,682
retail trade 4,048,082
finance/real estate/insurance 6,240,461
service industries 12,271,287
unclassified 19,352

Agriculture
number of farms, 1994 4,000
farm acreage, 1994 500,000
acres per farm, 1994 108
value of farms, 1994 ($mil) 1,921
farm income, 1993 ($mil)
gross farm income 565
net farm income 216
debt/asset ratio 6.0%
farm marketings, 1993 ($mil)
total $521
   crops 263
   livestock 258
government payments 3
farm marketings in order of marketing
receipts, 1993
   1) Greenhouse
   2) Eggs
   3) Dairy products
   4) Aquaculture

Federal economic activity
   ($mil, except per capita)
expenditures, 1994
   total $16,591
   per capita $5,066
   defense $3,042
   non-defense $13,548
defense department, 1994
   contract awards ($mil) $2,450
   payroll ($mil) $621
   civilian employees (x1,000) 4.2
   military personnel (x1,000) 5.6

Fishing, 1992
catch (millions of pounds) 20
value ($mil) 63

Mining, 1994 ($mil)
total non-fuel mineral production $97

Connecticut 8

principal non-fuel minerals in order of value, 1994
  1) Stone
  2) Sand and gravel
  3) Sand and gravel

Construction, 1994 ($mil)
total contracts (including
  non-building) $3,027
    residential 1,175
    non-residential 1,052

Manufacturing, 1992
total establishments 6,283
employees, total (x1,000) 326
payroll ($mil) 12,411
production workers (x1,000) 171
value added ($mil) 24,677
value of shipments ($mil) 40,778

Finance
commercial banks, 1994
  number 46
    assets ($bil) 32.9
    deposits ($bil) 23.6
    closed or assisted 2
    deposits ($bil) 0.3
savings and loan associations, 1991
    non-current real estate loans 4.45%
    net income after taxes ($mil) .... -36
    return on assets .... -1.70%

Retail trade, 1992
establishments (x1,000) 21.0
sales ($mil) 27,754
annual payroll ($mil) 3,464
paid employees (x1,000) 241

Wholesale trade, 1992
establishments 6,262
sales ($bil) 78.3
annual payroll ($mil) 3,200
paid employees (x1,000) 77.1

Service industries, 1992
establishments (x1,000) (non-exempt firms) 27.4
receipts ($mil) (non-exempt firms) 19,102
annual payroll ($mil) 7,551
paid employees (x1,000) (non-exempt firms) . 273

COMMUNICATION, ENERGY & TRANSPORTATION

Communication
daily newspapers, 1993 19
broadcast stations, 1990
  radio: commercial, educational 92
  television: commercial, noncommercial 12
cable TV households, 1988 862,000

Energy
consumption estimates, 1992
total (trillion Btu) 762
per capita (million Btu) 232.3
by source of production (trillion Btu)
  coal 22
  natural gas 114
  petroleum 414
  nuclear electric power 179
  hydroelectric power 14
by end-use sector (trillion Btu)
  residential 240
  commercial 179
  industrial 137
  transportation 206
electrical energy
  production, 1993 (billion kWh) 28.7
  net summer capability, 1993 (million kW) .. 6.8
gas utilities, 1993
  customers 477,000
  sales (trillion Btu) 98
  revenues ($mil) 725
nuclear plants, 1993 4

Transportation, 1994
public road & street mileage
total 20,384
  urban 11,555
  rural 8,829
  interstate 346
vehicle miles of travel (mil) 27,138
total motor vehicle registrations 2,599,489
  automobiles 2,046,422
licensed drivers 2,318,543
  per 1,000 driving age population 904
deaths from motor vehicle
  accidents 310

58

STATE SUMMARY

Capital City .... Dover

Governor .... Thomas Carper

Address .... LEGISLATIVE HALL
DOVER, DE 19901
302 739-4111

Admitted as a state 1787

Area (square miles) 2,489

Population, 1980 594,338

Population, 1990 666,168

Population, 1994 (est.) 706,000

Persons per square mile, 1994 .... 361.3

Largest city .... Wilmington
population, 1990 71,500

Personal income per capita, 1994
(in current dollars) $22,828

Gross state product ($mil), 1991 21,274

Leading industries, 1992 (by payroll)
MANUFACTURING
SERVICE INDUSTRIES
FINANCE, REAL ESTATE &,
INSURANCE

Leading agricultural commodities, 1993
BROILERS
SOYBEANS
CORN
GREENHOUSE

GEOGRAPHY & ENVIRONMENT

Area (square miles)
total 2,489
land 1,955
water (includes territorial water) 535

Federally owned land, 1991 .... 2.2%

Highest point
name .... Ebright Road (New Castle County)
elevation (feet) 442

Lowest point
name .... Atlantic Ocean
elevation (feet) .... sea level

General coastline (miles) 28

Tidal shoreline (miles) 381

Capital city .... Dover
population, 1990 27,600

Largest city .... Wilmington
population, 1990 71,500

Number of cities with over 100,000 population
1980 0

Number of cities with over 100,000 population
1990 0

State parks and Recreation areas, 1991
area (acres) 13,000
number of visitors 3,212,000
revenues $3,889,000

National forest land, 1992 (acres) 0

National park acreage, 1984 .... NA

DEMOGRAPHICS & CHARACTERISTICS OF THE POPULATION

Population
1970 548,107
1980 594,338
1990 666,168
1994 (est.) 706,000
2000 (revised projection) 759,000
2010 (revised projection) 815,000

Metropolitan area population
1970 386,000
1980 398,000
1992 571,000

Non-metropolitan area population
1970 162,000
1980 196,000
1992 120,000

Change in population, 1980-90
number 71,830
percent 12.09%

Persons per square mile, 1994 .... 361.3

Age distribution, 1980
under 5 years 6.9%
5 to 17 years 21.1%
65 and over 10.0%

Age distribution, 1990
under 5 years 7.3%
5 to 17 years 17.1%
65 and over 12.1%

Delaware 2

Age distribution, 2000 (projected)
under 5 years 6.4%
5 to 17 years 17.9%
65 and over 13.2%

Persons by age, 1990
under 5 years 48,824
5 to 17 years 114,517
65 and over 80,735

Median age, 1990 .... 32.90

Race, 1990
White 535,094
Black 112,460
American Indian 1,982
Chinese 2,301
Filipino 1,321
Japanese 690
Asian Indian 2,183
Korean 1,229
Vietnamese 348
all other 8,523

Race, 2010 (projected)
White 603,000
Black 181,000

Persons of Hispanic origin, 1990
total 15,820
  Mexican 3,083
  Puerto Rican 8,257
  Cuban 728
  Other Hispanic 3,752

Persons by sex, 1990
male.............................. 322,968
female 343,200

Marital status, 1990
males
  15 years & older 251,905
  single 76,997
  married 149,973
    separated 5,339
    widowed 6,760
    divorced 18,175
females
  15 years & older 275,435
  single 68,503
  married 150,309
    separated 7,048

  widowed 31,351
  divorced 25,272

Households & families, 1990
households 247,497
persons per household 2.61
  families 175,867
    married couples 137,983
    female householder, no husband
      present 29,319
    one person households 57,451
households, 1994 264,000
persons per household, 1994 .... 2.59

Nativity, 1990
number of persons born in state 334,209
percent of total residents 50.2%

Immigration & naturalization, 1993
immigrants admitted 1,132
persons naturalized 423
refugees granted resident status 47

VITAL STATISTICS & HEALTH

Births
1992 10,902
  with low birth weight 7.6%
  to teenage mothers 12.4%
  to unmarried mothers 32.6%
1993 10,555
1994 10,361

Abortions, 1992
total 6,000
rate (per 1,000 women age 15-44) 35.2
rate per 1,000 live births 502

Adoptions, 1986
total 186
  related 47.3%

Deaths
1992 5,937
1993 6,116
1994 6,185

Infant deaths
1992 106
1993 88
1994 73

Average lifetime, 1979-1981
both sexes .... 73.21 years
  men .... 69.56 years
  women .... 76.78 years

Marriages
1992 5,059
1993 5,015
1994 5,066

Divorces
1992 3,400
1993 3,120
1994 3,385

Physicians, 1993
total 1,453
rate (per 1,000 persons) 2.09

Dentists, 1992
total 320
rate (per 1,000 persons) 0.47

Hospitals, 1993
number 8
beds (x 1,000) 2.2
average daily census (x 1,000) 1.5
occupancy rate 70.9%
personnel (x 1,000) 10.9
average cost per day to hospital $1,028
average cost per stay to hospital $7,307

EDUCATION

*Educational attainment of all persons
25 years and older, 1990*
less than 9th grade 31,009
high school graduates 140,030
bachelor's degree 58,615
graduate or professional degree 33,107

Public school enrollment, Fall, 1993
total 105,547
  Kindergarten through grade 8 76,617
  grades 9 through 12 28,930

Public School Teachers
total, 1994 6,380
  elementary 3,259
  secondary 3,121
salaries, 1994
  beginning $22,795
  average $37,469

*State receipts & expenditures for public
schools, 1993*
receipts ($mil) 698
expenditures
  total ($mil) 673
  per capita $974
  per pupil $6,420

*Graduating high school seniors,
public high schools, 1995 (est)* 5,215

SAT scores, 1994
verbal 428
math 464

Institutions of higher education, 1995
total 9
  public 5
  private 4

*Enrollment in institutions of higher
education, Fall, 1993*
total 43,528
full-time men 11,497
full-time women 14,338
part-time men 7,258
part-time women 10,435

*Minority enrollment in institutions of higher
education, Fall, 1993*
Black, non-Hispanic 5,456
Hispanic 661
Asian/Pacific Islander 948

Earned degrees conferred, 1993
Bachelor's 4,119
First professional 550
Master's 954
Doctor's 144

SOCIAL INSURANCE & WELFARE PROGRAMS

Social Security beneficiaries & benefits, 1993
beneficiaries
total 115,000
  retired and dependents 85,000
  survivors 18,000
  disabled & dependents 13,000
annual benefit payments ($mil)
total $864
  retired and dependents 616
  survivors 160
  disabled & dependents 88

Delaware 4

Medicare, 1993
enrollment (x1,000) 96
payments ($mil) 368

Medicaid, 1993
recipients (x1,000) 69
payments ($mil) 252

Federal public aid, 1993
recipients as a percent of population 5.3%
Aid to Families with Dependent Children
  recipients (x1,000) 28
average monthly payment $291
Supplemental Security Income
  total recipients (x1,000) 10

Food Stamp Program
  participants, 1994 (x1,000) 59

HOUSING & CONSTRUCTION

Total housing units, 1990 289,919
  year round housing units 270,554
  vacant 42,422

New privately owned housing units
  authorized, 1994
number (x1,000) 5.0
value ($mil) 337

New privately owned housing units
  started, 1994 (x1,000) 6.2

Existing home sales, 1994 (x1,000) 10.4

GOVERNMENT & ELECTIONS

State officials, 1996
  Governor (name/party/term expires)
    THOMAS CARPER
    Democrat - 1997
Lt. Governor .... Ruth Ann Minner
Sec. of State .... William Quillen
Atty. General .... M. Jane Brady
Chf. Justice .... Norman Veasey

Governorship
minimum age 30
length of term .... 4 years
number of consecutive
  terms permitted ..2 max. (not nec. consecutive)
who succeeds .... Lt. Governor

State legislature
name .... General Assembly
  upper chamber
    name .... Senate
    number of members 21
    length of term .... 4 years
    party in majority, 1996 .... Republican
  lower chamber
    name .... House of Representatives
    number of members 41
    length of term .... 2 years
    party in majority, 1996 .... Democratic

State employees October, 1992
total 24,385
October payroll ($1,000) 49,451

Local governments, 1992
total 281
  county 3
  municipal 57
  township 0
  school districts 19
  special districts 201

Voting, November, 1994
voting age population 528,000
  registered 58.7%
  voted 41.2%

Vote for president
1988
  Bush 130,581
  Dukakis 99,479
1992
  Clinton 125,997
  Bush 102,436
  Perot 59,061

Federal representation, 1996 (104th Congress)
Senators (name/party/term expires)

WILLIAM V. ROTH, JR.
Republican - 2001
JOSEPH R. BIDEN, JR.
Democrat - 1997

Representatives, total 1
  Democrats 0
  Republicans 1
  other 0

Delaware 5

Women holding public office
U.S. Congress, 1995 0
statewide elected office, 1995 4
state legislature, 1995 13

Black elected officials, 1993
total 23
  US and state legislatures 3
  city/county/regional offices 14
  judicial/law enforcement 0
  education/school boards 6

Hispanic public officials, 1994
total 1
  state executives & legislators 0
  city/county/regional offices 1
  judicial/law enforcement 0
  education/school boards 0

GOVERNMENTAL FINANCE

State & local government revenues, (selected
items), 1991-92 ($per capita)
total $5,169.63
  total general revenues 4,436.89
    from federal government 643.38
    from own sources 3,793.51
    from taxes 2,379.23
      from property taxes 335.77
      from all other taxes 1,249.90
    from charges & misc. 1,414.29

State & local government expenditures, (selected
items), 1991-92 ($per capita)
total $4,813.22
  total direct general expenditures 4,305.76
  education 1,605.28
  libraries 11.13
  public welfare 430.01
  health & hospitals 232.12
  highways 401.00
  police protection 143.66
  fire protection 19.88
  correction 160.50
  housing & comm. development 93.74
  natural resources & parks 106.33
  interest on general debt 425.80

State & local debt, 1992 ($per capita) 6,700.65

Federal aid grants to state & local government,
1994 ($per capita total & selected items)
per capita total 668.77
  compensatory education 22.33
  waste treatment facilities 12.91
  medicaid 216.12
  housing assistance 31.88
  job training 10.90
  highway trust fund 75.64

CRIME, LAW ENFORCEMENT & COURTS

Crime, 1994 (all rates per 100,000 persons)
total crimes 29,282
overall crime rate 4,147.6
  property crimes 25,321
    burglaries 5,580
    larcenies 17,270
    motor vehicle thefts 2,471
  property crime rate 3,586.5
  violent crimes 3,961
    murders 33
    forcible rapes 534
    robberies 889
    aggravated assaults 2,505
  violent crime rate 561.0

Number of police agencies, 1994 3

Arrests, 1994
total 9,729
  persons under 18 years of age 1,796

Prisoners under state & federal jurisdiction, 1994
total 4,411
percent change, 1993-94 . . . . 4.8%
sentenced to more than one year
  total 2,788
  rate per 100,000 residents 393

Persons under sentence of death, 4/20/95 14

State's highest court
name . . . . Supreme Court
number of members 5
length of term . . . . 12 years
intermediate appeals court? . . . . no

Delaware 6

LABOR & INCOME

Civilian labor force, 1994
total 384,000
men 211,000
women 173,000
persons 16-19 years 24,000
white 306,000
black 66,000

Civilian labor force as a percent of civilian non-institutional population, 1994
total 70.8%
men 78.3%
women 63.4%
persons 16-19 years 63.6%
white 70.7%
black 70.9%

Employment, 1994
total 365,000
men 201,000
women 164,000
persons 16-19 years 22,000
white 294,000
black 59,000

Full-time/part-time labor force, 1994
full-time labor force 313,000
working part-time for
ecomonic reasons 4,000
part-time labor force 70,000

Unemployment rate, 1994
total 4.9%
men 4.5%
women 5.3%
persons 16-19 years 9.8%
white 3.9%
black 9.5%

Unemployed by reason for unemployment (as a percent of total unemployment), 1994
job losers or completed temp jobs 50.8%
job leavers 13.1%
reentrants 32.5%
new entrants 3.7%

Civilian labor force, by occupation, 1994
executive/administrative/
managerial 51,000
professional/specialty 52,000
technicians & related support 11,000

sales 46,000
adminstrative support/clerical 63,000
service occupations 58,000
precision production/craft/repair 43,000
machine operators/assemblers 19,000
transportation/material moving 17,000
handlers/helpers/laborers 15,000
farming/forestry/fishing ....NA

Civilian labor force, by industry, 1994
construction 23,000
manufacturing 68,000
transportation/communication 14,000
wholesale/retail trade 78,000
finance/real estate/insurance 34,000
services 94,000
government 44,000
agriculture ....NA

Average annual pay, 1994 (prelim.) $27,950
change in average annual pay,
1993-1994 .... 3.0%

Hours and earnings of production workers on manufacturing payrolls, 1994
average weekly hours 42.8
average hourly earnings $13.90
average weekly earnings $594.92

Labor union membership, 1994 39,900

Household income (in constant 1993 dollars)
median household income, 1992 .... $36,746
median household income, 1993 .... $36,064

Poverty
persons below poverty level, 1992 .... 7.8%
persons below poverty level, 1993 .... 10.2%

Personal income ($per capita)
1994
in current dollars 22,828
in constant (1987) dollars 17,655
1995 (projected)
in constant (1982) dollars 15,033
2000 (projected)
in constant (1982) dollars 15,747

Federal income tax returns, 1993
returns filed 330,809
adjusted gross income ($1000) 11,423,905
total income tax paid ($1000) 1,572,621

ECONOMY, BUSINESS, INDUSTRY & AGRICULTURE

Fortune 500 companies, 1994 3

Business incorporations, 1994
total 44,762
change, 1993-94 .... 14.4%

Business failures, 1994
total 88
rate per 10,000 concerns 41
change, 1993-94 .... -36.2%

Business firm ownership
Hispanic owned firms, 1987 184
black owned firms, 1987 1,399
women owned firms, 1987 9,700
foreign owned firms, 1982 65

Gross state product, 1991 ($mil)
total $21,274
  agriculture services, forestry, fisheries 261
  mining 6
  construction 847
  manufacturing—durable goods 904
  manufacturing—nondurable goods 3,946
  transportation, communication &
    public utilities 1,161
  wholesale trade 789
  retail trade 1,358
  finance/real estate/insurance 7,323
  services 2,784
  federal, state & local government 1,896

Establishments, by major industry group, 1992
total 19,718
  agriculture 300
  mining 15
  construction 2,172
  manufacturing 744
  transportation 796
  wholesale trade 1,085
  retail trade 4,922
  finance/real estate/insurance 2,885
  service industries 6,474
  unclassified 325

Payroll, by major industry group, 1992
total ($1,000) $8,271,138
  agriculture 26,851

  mining 2,194
  construction 455,598
  manufacturing 2,795,943
  transportation 410,023
  wholesale trade 714,841
  retail trade 805,383
  finance/real estate/insurance 1,052,791
  service industries 1,999,362
  unclassified 8,152

Agriculture
number of farms, 1994 3,000
farm acreage, 1994 1,000,000
acres per farm, 1994 220
value of farms, 1994 ($mil) 1,452
farm income, 1993 ($mil)
  gross farm income 684
  net farm income 107
  debt/asset ratio 21.6%
farm marketings, 1993 ($mil)
total $622
  crops 159
  livestock 463
government payments 6
farm marketings in order of marketing
receipts, 1993
  1) Broilers
  2) Soybeans
  3) Corn
  4) Greenhouse

Federal economic activity
  ($mil, except per capita)
expenditures, 1994
  total $2,950
  per capita $4,179
  defense $398
  non-defense $2,552
defense department, 1994
  contract awards ($mil) $108
  payroll ($mil) $285
  civilian employees (x1,000) 1.6
  military personnel (x1,000) 4.6

Fishing, 1992
catch (millions of pounds) 7
value ($mil) 4

Mining, 1994 ($mil)
total non-fuel mineral production $9

Delaware 8

principal non-fuel minerals in order of value, 1994
1) Magnesium compounds
2) Sand and gravel
3) Sand and gravel

Construction, 1994 ($mil)
total contracts (including
  non-building) $705
    residential 339
    non-residential 228

Manufacturing, 1992
total establishments 736
employees, total (x1,000) 67
payroll ($mil) 2,770
production workers (x1,000) 31
value added ($mil) 4,881
value of shipments ($mil) 13,000

Finance
commercial banks, 1994
  number 36
    assets ($bil) 85.8
    deposits ($bil) 34.9
  closed or assisted 0
    deposits ($bil) .... NA
savings and loan associations, 1991
  non-current real estate loans 2.59%
  net income after taxes ($mil) 18
  return on assets .... +2.96%

Retail trade, 1992
establishments (x1,000) 4.9
sales ($mil) 6,492
annual payroll ($mil) 763
paid employees (x1,000) 60

Wholesale trade, 1992
establishments 1,088
sales ($bil) 12.3
annual payroll ($mil) 674
paid employees (x1,000) 16.1

Service industries, 1992
establishments (x1,000) (non-exempt firms) . 5.3
receipts ($mil) (non-exempt firms) 2,823
annual payroll ($mil) 1,170
paid employees (x1,000) (non-exempt firms) ..54

COMMUNICATION, ENERGY & TRANSPORTATION

Communication
daily newspapers, 1993 3
broadcast stations, 1990
  radio: commercial, educational 21
  television: commercial, noncommercial 3
cable TV households, 1988 163,000

Energy
consumption estimates, 1992
total (trillion Btu) 241
per capita (million Btu) 348.2
by source of production (trillion Btu)
  coal 46
  natural gas 41
  petroleum 141
  nuclear electric power 0
  hydroelectric power 0
by end-use sector (trillion Btu)
  residential 47
  commercial 35
  industrial 93
  transportation 65
electrical energy
  production, 1993 (billion kWh) 8.3
  net summer capability, 1993 (million kW) .. 2.3
gas utilities, 1993
  customers 106,000
  sales (trillion Btu) 23
  revenues ($mil) 117
nuclear plants, 1993 0

Transportation, 1994
public road & street mileage
total 5,592
  urban 1,907
  rural 3,685
  interstate 41
vehicle miles of travel (mil) 7,025
total motor vehicle registrations 578,036
  automobiles 404,129
licensed drivers 513,406
  per 1,000 driving age population 935
deaths from motor vehicle
  accidents 112

STATE SUMMARY

Capital City .... Washington, DC

Governor .... Marion Barry (mayor)

Address .... DISTRICT BUILDING
WASHINGTON, DC 20002
202 727-1000

Admitted as a state .... NA

Area (square miles) 68

Population, 1980 638,333

Population, 1990 606,900

Population, 1994 (est.) 570,000

Persons per square mile, 1994 .... 9,347.1

Largest city .... Washington, DC
population, 1990 607,000

Personal income per capita, 1994
(in current dollars) $31,136

Gross state product ($mil), 1991 38,160

Leading industries, 1992 (by payroll)
SERVICE INDUSTRIES
FINANCE, REAL ESTATE, &
INSURANCE
TRANSPORTATION

Leading agricultural commodities, 1993
NA
NA
NA
NA

GEOGRAPHY & ENVIRONMENT

Area (square miles)
total 68
land 61
water (includes territorial water) 7

Federally owned land, 1991 .... 26.1%

Highest point
name .... Tenleytown
elevation (feet) 410

Lowest point
name .... Potomac River
elevation (feet) .... sea level

General coastline (miles) 0

Tidal shoreline (miles) 0

Capital city .... Washington, DC
population, 1990 607,000

Largest city .... Washington, DC
population, 1990 607,000

Number of cities with over 100,000 population
1980 .... NA

Number of cities with over 100,000 population
1990 .... NA

State parks and Recreation areas, 1991
area (acres) .... NA
number of visitors .... NA
revenues .... $NA

National forest land, 1992 (acres) 0

National park acreage, 1984 6,900

DEMOGRAPHICS & CHARACTERISTICS OF THE POPULATION

Population
1970 756,668
1980 638,333
1990 606,900
1994 (est.) 570,000
2000 (revised projection) 537,000
2010 (revised projection) 577,000

Metropolitan area population
1970 757,000
1980 638,000
1992 585,000

Non-metropolitan area population
1970 .... NA
1980 .... NA
1992 .... NA

Change in population, 1980-90
number .... -31,433
percent .... -4.92%

Persons per square mile, 1994 .... 9,347.1

Age distribution, 1980
under 5 years 5.4%
5 to 17 years 17.1%
65 and over 11.6%

Age distribution, 1990
under 5 years 6.2%
5 to 17 years 13.1%
65 and over 12.8%

District of Columbia 2

Age distribution, 2000 (projected)
under 5 years 4.4%
5 to 17 years 13.0%
65 and over 13.0%

Persons by age, 1990
under 5 years 37,351
5 to 17 years 79,741
65 and over 77,847

Median age, 1990 .... 33.50

Race, 1990
White 179,667
Black 399,604
American Indian 1,432
Chinese 3,144
Filipino 2,082
Japanese 1,029
Asian Indian 1,601
Korean 814
Vietnamese 747
all other 16,746

Race, 2010 (projected)
White 195,000
Black 365,000

Persons of Hispanic origin, 1990
total 32,710
  Mexican 2,981
  Puerto Rican 2,204
  Cuban 1,241
  Other Hispanic 26,284

Persons by sex, 1990
male 282,970
female 323,930

Marital status, 1990
males
  15 years & older 232,989
  single 118,273
  married 87,306
    separated 12,860
    widowed 8,428
    divorced 18,982
females
  15 years & older 275,245
  single 123,762
  married 88,488
    separated 16,721

widowed 35,180
divorced 27,815

Households & families, 1990
households 249,634
persons per household 2.26
  families 122,087
    married couples 63,110
    female householder, no husband
      present 48,575
    one person households 103,626
households, 1994 237,000
persons per household, 1994 .... 2.24

Nativity, 1990
number of persons born in state 238,728
percent of total residents 39.3%

Immigration & naturalization, 1993
immigrants admitted 3,608
persons naturalized 773
refugees granted resident status 355

VITAL STATISTICS & HEALTH

Births
1992 10,052
  with low birth weight 14.3%
  to teenage mothers 16.3%
  to unmarried mothers 66.9%
1993 9,780
1994 9,440

Abortions, 1992
total 21,000
rate (per 1,000 women age 15-44) 138.4
rate per 1,000 live births 1,104

Adoptions, 1986
total 326
  related 50.3%

Deaths
1992 6,578
1993 6,713
1994 6,445

Infant deaths
1992 187
1993 181
1994 168

Average lifetime, 1979-1981
both sexes . . . . 69.20 years
men . . . . 64.55 years
women . . . . 73.70 years

Marriages
1992 3,973
1993 3,029
1994 3,616

Divorces
1992 2,655
1993 1,941
1994 2,244

Physicians, 1993
total 3,814
rate (per 1,000 persons) 6.67

Dentists, 1992
total 750
rate (per 1,000 persons) 1.29

Hospitals, 1993
number 11
beds (x 1,000) 4.2
average daily census (x 1,000) 3.1
occupancy rate 73.2%
personnel (x 1,000) 20.1
average cost per day to hospital $1,201
average cost per stay to hospital $8,594

EDUCATION

*Educational attainment of all persons
25 years and older, 1990*
less than 9th grade 39,107
high school graduates 86,756
bachelor's degree 65,892
graduate or professional degree 70,393

Public school enrollment, Fall, 1993
total 80,678
Kindergarten through grade 8 61,434
grades 9 through 12 19,244

Public School Teachers
total, 1994 6,056
elementary 3,353
secondary 2,259
salaries, 1994
beginning $25,825
average $43,014

*State receipts & expenditures for public
schools, 1993*
receipts ($mil) 622
expenditures
total ($mil) 621
per capita $1,061
per pupil $7,998

*Graduating high school seniors,
public high schools, 1995 (est)* 3,120

SAT scores, 1994
verbal 406
math 443

Institutions of higher education, 1995
total 19
public 2
private 17

*Enrollment in institutions of higher
education, Fall, 1993*
total 81,916
full-time men 23,544
full-time women 26,983
part-time men 14,146
part-time women 17,243

*Minority enrollment in institutions of higher
education, Fall, 1993*
Black, non-Hispanic 24,850
Hispanic 2,886
Asian/Pacific Islander 4,144

Earned degrees conferred, 1993
Bachelor's 8,095
First professional 2,321
Master's 6,059
Doctor's 562

SOCIAL INSURANCE &
WELFARE PROGRAMS

Social Security beneficiaries & benefits, 1993
beneficiaries
total 79,000
retired and dependents 55,000
survivors 15,000
disabled & dependents 9,000
annual benefit payments ($mil)
total $495
retired and dependents 333
survivors 105
disabled & dependents 57

District of Columbia 4

Medicare, 1993
enrollment (x1,000) 78
payments ($mil) 1,112

Medicaid, 1993
recipients (x1,000) 120
payments ($mil) 555

Federal public aid, 1993
recipients as a percent of population 15.0%
Aid to Families with Dependent Children
   recipients (x1,000) 74
average monthly payment $383
Supplemental Security Income
   total recipients (x1,000) 19

Food Stamp Program
  participants, 1994 (x1,000) 91

HOUSING & CONSTRUCTION

Total housing units, 1990 278,489
  year round housing units 276,826
  vacant 28,855

New privately owned housing units
authorized, 1994
number (x1,000) 0.2
value ($mil) 18

New privately owned housing units
  started, 1994 (x1,000) 0.3

Existing home sales, 1994 (x1,000) 12.3

GOVERNMENT & ELECTIONS

State officials, 1996
  Governor (name/party/term expires)
     MARION BARRY (MAYOR)
     Democrat - 2000

Lt. Governor ....
Sec. of State ....
Atty. General ....
Chf. Justice ....

Governorship
minimum age ....
length of term ....
number of consecutive
  terms permitted ....
who succeeds ....

State legislature
name ....
  upper chamber
    name ....
    number of members ....
    length of term ....
    party in majority, 1996 ....
  lower chamber
    name ....
    number of members ....
    length of term ....
    party in majority, 1996 ....

State employees October, 1992
total 56,419
October payroll ($1,000) 171,441

Local governments, 1992
total 2
  county 0
  municipal 1
  township 0
  school districts 0
  special districts 1

Voting, November, 1994
voting age population 440,000
  registered 66.9%
  voted 55.6%

Vote for president
1988
  Bush 25,732
  Dukakis 153,100
1992
  Clinton 186,301
  Bush 19,813
  Perot 9,284

Federal representation, 1996 (104th Congress)
Senators (name/party/term expires)

Representatives, total 1
  Democrats 0
  Republicans 0
  other 1

District of Columbia 5

Women holding public office
U.S. Congress, 1995 1
statewide elected office, 1995 0
state legislature, 1995 0

Black elected officials, 1993
total 198
US and state legislatures 4
city/county/regional offices 185
judicial/law enforcement 0
education/school boards 9

Hispanic public officials, 1994
total 1
state executives & legislators 0
city/county/regional offices 0
judicial/law enforcement 1
education/school boards 0

GOVERNMENTAL FINANCE

State & local government revenues, (selected items), 1991-92 ($per capita)
total $9,151.60
total general revenues 8,054.38
from federal government 3,036.23
from own sources 6,018.15
from taxes 4,113.92
from property taxes 1,544.14
from all other taxes 2,371.81
from charges & misc. 904.22

State & local government expenditures, (selected items), 1991-92 ($per capita)
total $9,953.85
total direct general expenditures 7,561.24
education 1,269.90
libraries 37.34
public welfare 1,490.67
health & hospitals 914.79
highways 207.94
police protection 466.24
fire protection 165.54
correction 544.13
housing & comm. development 374.21
natural resources & parks 102.39
interest on general debt 403.83

State & local debt, 1992 ($per capita) 8,136.47

Federal aid grants to state & local government, 1994 ($per capita total & selected items)
per capita total 3,897.85
compensatory education 45.08
waste treatment facilities 29.26
medicaid 693.49
housing assistance 130.42
job training 18.46
highway trust fund 126.70

CRIME, LAW ENFORCEMENT & COURTS

Crime, 1994 (all rates per 100,000 persons)
total crimes 63,186
overall crime rate 11,085.3
property crimes 48,009
burglaries 10,037
larcenies 29,711
motor vehicle thefts 8,261
property crime rate 8,422.6
violent crimes 15,177
murders 399
forcible rapes 249
robberies 6,311
aggravated assaults 8,218
violent crime rate 2,622.6

Number of police agencies, 1994 1

Arrests, 1994
total 48,502
persons under 18 years of age 3,733

Prisoners under state & federal jurisdiction, 1994
total 10,943
percent change, 1993-94 .... 0.9%
sentenced to more than one year
total 8,962
rate per 100,000 residents 1,583

Persons under sentence of death, 4/20/95 ....NA

State's highest court
name .... Court of Appeals
number of members 9
length of term .... 15 years
intermediate appeals court? .... no

District of Columbia 6

LABOR & INCOME

Civilian labor force, 1994
total 314,000
  men 162,000
  women 153,000
  persons 16-19 years 8,000
  white 131,000
  black........................... 172,000

Civilian labor force as a percent of
civilian non-institutional population, 1994
total 67.0%
  men 74.0%
  women 60.9%
  persons 16-19 years 32.4%
  white 79.6%
  black........................... 59.1%

Employment, 1994
total 289,000
  men 148,000
  women 140,000
  persons 16-19 years 6,000
  white 126,000
  black........................... 151,000

Full-time/part-time labor force, 1994
full-time labor force 273,000
  working part-time for
    ecomonic reasons 2,000
part-time labor force 41,000

Unemployment rate, 1994
total 8.2%
  men 8.3%
  women 8.0%
  persons 16-19 years 31.0%
  white 3.5%
  black........................... 12.0%

Unemployed by reason for unemployment
(as a percent of total unemployment), 1994
job losers or completed temp jobs 47.3%
job leavers 6.5%
reentrants 42.5%
new entrants 3.6%

Civilian labor force, by occupation, 1994
executive/administrative/
  managerial 53,000
professional/specialty 74,000
technicians & related support 13,000

sales 22,000
adminstrative support/clerical 51,000
service occupations 59,000
precision production/craft/repair 16,000
machine operators/assemblers ....NA
transportation/material moving 10,000
handlers/helpers/laborers 9,000
farming/forestry/fishing ....NA

Civilian labor force, by industry, 1994
construction 9,000
manufacturing 9,000
transportation/communication 16,000
wholesale/retail trade 41,000
finance/real estate/insurance 17,000
services 107,000
government 95,000
agriculture ....NA

Average annual pay, 1994 (prelim.) $40,919
change in average annual pay,
  1993-1994 .... 4.4%

Hours and earnings of production workers
on manufacturing payrolls, 1994
average weekly hours 39.7
average hourly earnings $13.46
average weekly earnings $534.36

Labor union membership, 1994 44,200

Household income (in constant 1993 dollars)
median household income, 1992 .... $31,152
median household income, 1993 .... $27,304

Poverty
persons below poverty level, 1992 .... 20.3%
persons below poverty level, 1993 .... 26.4%

Personal income ($per capita)
1994
  in current dollars 31,136
  in constant (1987) dollars 24,080
1995 (projected)
  in constant (1982) dollars 18,801
2000 (projected)
  in constant (1982) dollars 19,823

Federal income tax returns, 1993
returns filed 289,362
adjusted gross income ($1000) 10,235,729
total income tax paid ($1000) 1,620,314

District of Columbia 7

ECONOMY, BUSINESS, INDUSTRY & AGRICULTURE

Fortune 500 companies, 1994 5

Business incorporations, 1994
total 2,256
change, 1993-94 .... 0.0%

Business failures, 1994
total 167
rate per 10,000 concerns 57
change, 1993-94 .... -15.2%

Business firm ownership
Hispanic owned firms, 1987 762
black owned firms, 1987 8,275
women owned firms, 1987 11,000
foreign owned firms, 1982 101

Gross state product, 1991 ($mil)
total $38,160
  agriculture services, forestry, fisheries 11
  mining 11
  construction 512
  manufacturing—durable goods 143
  manufacturing—nondurable goods 1,058
  transportation, communication &
    public utilities 2,242
  wholesale trade 639
  retail trade 1,482
  finance/real estate/insurance 4,701
  services 12,909
  federal, state & local government 14,452

Establishments, by major industry
  group, 1992
total 19,499
  agriculture 48
  mining 18
  construction 359
  manufacturing 456
  transportation 767
  wholesale trade 491
  retail trade 3,898
  finance/real estate/insurance 2,363
  service industries 10,804
  unclassified 295

Payroll, by major industry group, 1992
total ($1,000) $12,992,874
  agriculture 9,551

  mining 7,333
  construction 220,672
  manufacturing 592,936
  transportation 826,213
  wholesale trade 317,354
  retail trade 726,226
  finance/real estate/insurance 1,282,618
  service industries 8,999,268
  unclassified 10,703

Agriculture
number of farms, 1994 .... NA
farm acreage, 1994 .... NA
acres per farm, 1994 .... NA
value of farms, 1994 ($mil) .... NA
farm income, 1993 ($mil)
  gross farm income .... NA
  net farm income .... NA
  debt/asset ratio .... NA%
farm marketings, 1993 ($mil)
  total .... $NA
  crops .... NA
  livestock .... NA
  government payments .... NA
farm marketings in order of marketing
  receipts, 1993
    1) NA
    2) NA
    3) NA
    4) NA

Federal economic activity
  ($mil, except per capita)
expenditures, 1994
  total $21,766
  per capita $38,186
  defense $2,308
  non-defense $19,458
defense department, 1994
  contract awards ($mil) $1,096
  payroll ($mil) $1,251
  civilian employees (x1,000) 15.8
  military personnel (x1,000) 13.8

Fishing, 1992
catch (millions of pounds) .... NA
value ($mil) .... NA

Mining, 1994 ($mil)
total non-fuel mineral production .... $NA

District of Columbia 8

principal non-fuel minerals in order of value, 1994
- 1) NA
- 2) NA
- 3) NA

Construction, 1994 ($mil)
total contracts (including
    non-building) $859
        residential 49
        non-residential 575

Manufacturing, 1992
total establishments 458
employees, total (x1,000) 13
payroll ($mil) 553
production workers (x1,000) 4
value added ($mil) 1,570
value of shipments ($mil) 2,008

Finance
commercial banks, 1994
    number 18
      assets ($bil) 13.3
      deposits ($bil) 9.8
    closed or assisted 0
      deposits ($bil) .... NA
savings and loan associations, 1991
    non-current real estate loans 2.36%
    net income after taxes ($mil) 1
    return on assets .... +0.19%

Retail trade, 1992
establishments (x1,000) 3.8
sales ($mil) 3,587
annual payroll ($mil) 642
paid employees (x1,000) 47

Wholesale trade, 1992
establishments 499
sales ($bil) 3.3
annual payroll ($mil) 231
paid employees (x1,000) 6.6

Service industries, 1992
establishments (x1,000) (non-exempt firms) . 7.4
receipts ($mil) (non-exempt firms) 11,238
annual payroll ($mil) 4,299
paid employees (x1,000) (non-exempt firms) . 121

COMMUNICATION, ENERGY & TRANSPORTATION

Communication
daily newspapers, 1993 2
broadcast stations, 1990
    radio: commercial, educational 20
    television: commercial, noncommercial 8
cable TV households, 1988 19,000

Energy
consumption estimates, 1992
total (trillion Btu) 174
per capita (million Btu) 297.3
by source of production (trillion Btu)
    coal 1
    natural gas 33
    petroleum 34
    nuclear electric power 0
    hydroelectric power 0
by end-use sector (trillion Btu)
    residential 34
    commercial 80
    industrial 33
    transportation 27
electrical energy
    production, 1993 (billion kWh) 0.2
    net summer capability, 1993 (million kW) .. 0.8
gas utilities, 1993
    customers 147,000
    sales (trillion Btu) 33
    revenues ($mil) 234
nuclear plants, 1993 0

Transportation, 1994
public road & street mileage
total 1,104
    urban 1,104
    rural 0
    interstate 12
vehicle miles of travel (mil) 3,448
total motor vehicle registrations 248,795
    automobiles 211,378
licensed drivers 361,854
    per 1,000 driving age population 783
deaths from motor vehicle
    accidents 69

Florida 1

STATE SUMMARY

Capital City . . . . Tallahassee

Governor . . . . Lawton Chiles

Address . . . . THE CAPITOL
TALLAHASSEE, FL 32301
904 488-4441

Admitted as a state 1845

Area (square miles) 65,758

Population, 1980 9,746,324

Population, 1990 12,937,926

Population, 1994 (est.) 13,953,000

Persons per square mile, 1994 . . . . 258.4

Largest city . . . . Jacksonville
population, 1990 635,000

Personal income per capita, 1994
(in current dollars) $21,677

Gross state product ($mil), 1991 255,129

Leading industries, 1992 (by payroll)
SERVICE INDUSTRIES
RETAIL TRADE
MANUFACTURING

Leading agricultural commodities, 1993
ORANGES
GREENHOUSE
TOMATOES
CANE/SUGAR

GEOGRAPHY & ENVIRONMENT

Area (square miles)
total 65,758
land 53,997
water (includes territorial water) 11,761

Federally owned land, 1991 . . . . 9.0%

Highest point
name . . . . . Sec. 30 TGN R20W (Walton County)
elevation (feet) 345

Lowest point
name . . . . Atlantic Ocean
elevation (feet) . . . . sea level

General coastline (miles) 1,650

Tidal shoreline (miles) 8,426

Capital city . . . . Tallahassee
population, 1990 125,000

Largest city . . . . Jacksonville
population, 1990 635,000

Number of cities with over 100,000 population
1980 9

Number of cities with over 100,000 population
1990 9

State parks and Recreation areas, 1991
area (acres) 444,000
number of visitors 13,087,000
revenues $16,248,000

National forest land, 1992 (acres) 1,254,000

National park acreage, 1984 2,145,100

DEMOGRAPHICS & CHARACTERISTICS OF THE POPULATION

Population
1970 6,791,418
1980 9,746,324
1990 12,937,926
1994 (est.) 13,953,000
2000 (revised projection) 15,313,000
2010 (revised projection) 17,372,000

Metropolitan area population
1970 6,213,000
1980 8,885,000
1992 12,532,000

Non-metropolitan area population
1970 578,000
1980 862,000
1992 950,000

Change in population, 1980-90
number 3,191,602
percent 32.75%

Persons per square mile, 1994 . . . . 258.4

Age distribution, 1980
under 5 years 5.9%
5 to 17 years 18.3%
65 and over 17.3%

Age distribution, 1990
under 5 years 6.6%
5 to 17 years 15.5%
65 and over 18.3%

Florida 2

Age distribution, 2000 (projected)
under 5 years 5.2%
5 to 17 years 15.7%
65 and over 19.9%

Persons by age, 1990
under 5 years 849,596
5 to 17 years 2,016,641
65 and over 2,369,431

Median age, 1990 .... 36.40

Race, 1990
White 10,749,285
Black 1,759,534
American Indian 35,461
Chinese 30,737
Filipino 31,945
Japanese 8,505
Asian Indian 31,457
Korean 12,404
Vietnamese 16,346
all other 261,378

Race, 2010 (projected)
White 13,981,000
Black 2,906,000

Persons of Hispanic origin, 1990
total 1,574,143
Mexican 161,499
Puerto Rican 247,010
Cuban 674,052
Other Hispanic 491,582

Persons by sex, 1990
male 6,261,719
female 6,676,207

Marital status, 1990
males
15 years & older 5,027,000
single 1,336,469
married 3,082,684
separated 104,624
widowed 156,680
divorced 451,167
females
15 years & older 5,498,857
single 1,046,893
married 3,084,722
separated 138,290

widowed 758,011
divorced 609,231

Households & families, 1990
households 5,134,869
persons per household 2.46
families 3,511,825
married couples 2,791,734
female householder, no husband
present 548,556
one person households 1,309,954
households, 1994 5,456,000
persons per household, 1994 .... 2.50

Nativity, 1990
number of persons born in state 3,940,240
percent of total residents 30.5%

Immigration & naturalization, 1993
immigrants admitted 61,423
persons naturalized 26,628
refugees granted resident status 14,344

VITAL STATISTICS & HEALTH

Births
1992 192,291
with low birth weight 7.4%
to teenage mothers 13.5%
to unmarried mothers 34.2%
1993 193,087
1994 191,003

Abortions, 1992
total 85,000
rate (per 1,000 women age 15-44) 30.0
rate per 1,000 live births 438

Adoptions, 1986
total 7,683
related 50.4%

Deaths
1992 140,401
1993 146,309
1994 148,414

Infant deaths
1992 1,743
1993 1,674
1994 1,553

Average lifetime, 1979-1981
both sexes .... 74.00 years
  men .... 70.08 years
  women .... 77.98 years

Marriages
1992 138,129
1993 142,937
1994 144,548

Divorces
1992 84,074
1993 83,581
1994 82,963

Physicians, 1993
total 29,209
rate (per 1,000 persons) 2.15

Dentists, 1992
total 7,079
rate (per 1,000 persons) 0.53

Hospitals, 1993
number 223
beds (x 1,000) 51.3
average daily census (x 1,000) 31.0
occupancy rate 60.4%
personnel (x 1,000) 193.6
average cost per day to hospital $940
average cost per stay to hospital $6,169

EDUCATION

*Educational attainment of all persons
  25 years and older, 1990*
less than 9th grade 842,811
high school graduates 2,679,285
bachelor's degree 1,062,649
graduate or professional degree 561,756

Public school enrollment, Fall, 1993
total 2,040,763
  Kindergarten through grade 8 1,515,194
  grades 9 through 12 525,569

Public School Teachers
total, 1994 110,653
  elementary 48,139
  secondary 40,876
salaries, 1994
  beginning $23,171
  average $31,944

*State receipts & expenditures for public
  schools, 1993*
receipts ($mil) 12,032
expenditures
  total ($mil) 11,645
  per capita $864
  per pupil $5,303

*Graduating high school seniors,
  public high schools, 1995 (est)* 90,311

SAT scores, 1994
verbal 413
math 466

Institutions of higher education, 1995
total 111
  public 38
  private 73

*Enrollment in institutions of higher
  education, Fall, 1993*
total 623,403
full-time men 141,429
full-time women 155,591
part-time men 135,506
part-time women 190,877

*Minority enrollment in institutions of higher
  education, Fall, 1993*
Black, non-Hispanic 75,424
Hispanic 77,292
Asian/Pacific Islander 16,572

Earned degrees conferred, 1993
Bachelor's 43,212
First professional 2,322
Master's 13,145
Doctor's 1,661

SOCIAL INSURANCE &
WELFARE PROGRAMS

Social Security beneficiaries & benefits, 1993
beneficiaries
total 2,866,000
  retired and dependents 2,178,000
  survivors 413,000
  disabled & dependents 274,000
annual benefit payments ($mil)
total $20,685
  retired and dependents 15,223
  survivors 3,575
  disabled & dependents 1,886

Florida 4

Medicare, 1993
enrollment (x1,000) 2,494
payments ($mil) 11,722

Medicaid, 1993
recipients (x1,000) 1,745
payments ($mil) 4,131

Federal public aid, 1993
recipients as a percent of population 7.0%
Aid to Families with Dependent Children
  recipients (x1,000) 692
average monthly payment $275
Supplemental Security Income
  total recipients (x1,000) 293

Food Stamp Program
  participants, 1994 (x1,000) 1,474

HOUSING & CONSTRUCTION

Total housing units, 1990 6,100,262
  year round housing units 5,679,259
  vacant 965,393

*New privately owned housing units
authorized, 1994*
number (x1,000) 128.6
value ($mil) 11,076

*New privately owned housing units
started, 1994 (x1,000)* 130.8

Existing home sales, 1994 (x1,000) 229.7

GOVERNMENT & ELECTIONS

State officials, 1996
  Governor (name/party/term expires)
       LAWTON CHILES
       Democrat - 1999
Lt. Governor . . . . .Buddy McKay
Sec. of State . . . . .Jim Smith
Atty. General . . . . Robert Butterworth
Chf. Justice . . . . Rosemary Barkett

Governorship
minimum age 30
length of term . . . . 4 years
number of consecutive
  terms permitted 2
who succeeds . . . . Lt. Governor

State legislature
name . . . . Legislature
  upper chamber
       name . . . . Senate
       number of members 40
       length of term . . . . 4 years
       party in majority, 1996 . . . . Republican
  lower chamber
       name . . . . House of Representatives
       number of members 120
       length of term . . . . 2 years
       party in majority, 1996 . . . . .Democratic

State employees October, 1992
total 187,813
October payroll ($1,000) 354,591

Local governments, 1992
total 1,041
  county 66
  municipal 390
  township 0
  school districts 95
  special districts 489

Voting, November, 1994
voting age population 10,582,000
  registered 55.5%
  voted 42.3%

Vote for president
1988
  Bush 2,538,994
  Dukakis 1,632,086
1992
  Clinton 2,051,845
  Bush 2,137,752
  Perot 1,041,607

Federal representation, 1996 (104th Congress)
Senators (name/party/term expires)

       CONNIE MACK, III
       Republican - 2001
       BOB GRAHAM
       Democrat - 1999

Representatives, total 23
  Democrats 8
  Republicans 15
  other 0

Florida 5

Women holding public office
U.S. Congress, 1995 5
statewide elected office, 1995 1
state legislature, 1995 31

Black elected officials, 1993
total 200
  US and state legislatures 22
  city/county/regional offices 133
  judicial/law enforcement 28
  education/school boards 17

Hispanic public officials, 1994
total 64
  state executives & legislators 16
  city/county/regional offices 33
  judicial/law enforcement 12
  education/school boards 3

GOVERNMENTAL FINANCE

State & local government revenues, (selected items), 1991-92 ($per capita)
total $4,109.25
  total general revenues 3,462.67
    from federal government 478.62
    from own sources 2,964.06
    from taxes 1,952.19
      from property taxes 749.31
      from all other taxes 1,033.05
    from charges & misc. 1,031.87

State & local government expenditures, (selected items), 1991-92 ($per capita)
total $4,068.95
  total direct general expenditures 3,559.81
  education 1,107.46
  libraries 16.92
  public welfare 415.14
  health & hospitals 344.15
  highways 254.04
  police protection 172.58
  fire protection 67.49
  correction 141.87
  housing & comm. development 46.45
  natural resources & parks 170.74
  interest on general debt 233.69

State & local debt, 1992 ($per capita) 4,117.87

Federal aid grants to state & local government, 1994 ($per capita total & selected items)
per capita total 574.65
  compensatory education 21.29
  waste treatment facilities 5.78
  medicaid 211.09
  housing assistance 33.97
  job training 13.81
  highway trust fund 56.95

CRIME, LAW ENFORCEMENT & COURTS

Crime, 1994 (all rates per 100,000 persons)
total crimes 1,151,121
overall crime rate 8,250.0
  property crimes 991,105
    burglaries 237,341
    larcenies 626,578
    motor vehicle thefts 127,186
  property crime rate 7,103.2
  violent crimes 160,016
    murders 1,165
    forcible rapes 7,301
    robberies 45,871
    aggravated assaults 105,679
  violent crime rate 1,146.8

Number of police agencies, 1994 616

Arrests, 1994
total 756,362
  persons under 18 years of age 154,569

Prisoners under state & federal jurisdiction, 1994
total 57,139
percent change, 1993-94 . . . . 7.7%
  sentenced to more than one year
    total 57,129
    rate per 100,000 residents 406

Persons under sentence of death, 4/20/95 342

State's highest court
name . . . . Supreme Court
number of members 7
length of term . . . . 6 years
intermediate appeals court? . . . . yes

79

Florida 6

LABOR & INCOME

Civilian labor force, 1994
total 6,824,000
  men 3,660,000
  women 3,164,000
  persons 16-19 years 353,000
  white 5,667,000
  black 998,000

Civilian labor force as a percent of
civilian non-institutional population, 1994
total 62.6%
  men 70.7%
  women 55.4%
  persons 16-19 years 52.7%
  white 62.0%
  black 66.7%

Employment, 1994
total 6,376,000
  men 3,430,000
  women 2,945,000
  persons 16-19 years 281,000
  white 5,351,000
  black 881,000

Full-time/part-time labor force, 1994
full-time labor force 5,612,000
  working part-time for
    ecomonic reasons 80,000
part-time labor force 1,211,000

Unemployment rate, 1994
total 6.6%
  men 6.3%
  women 6.9%
  persons 16-19 years 20.4%
  white 5.6%
  black 11.7%

Unemployed by reason for unemployment
(as a percent of total unemployment), 1994
job losers or completed temp jobs 46.9%
job leavers 10.4%
reentrants 34.3%
new entrants 8.4%

Civilian labor force, by occupation, 1994
executive/administrative/
  managerial 927,000
professional/specialty 861,000
technicians & related support 191,000
sales 964,000
adminstrative support/clerical 1,049,000
service occupations 1,068,000
precision production/craft/repair 738,000
machine operators/assemblers 234,000
transportation/material moving 265,000
handlers/helpers/laborers 268,000
farming/forestry/fishing 219,000

Civilian labor force, by industry, 1994
construction 395,000
manufacturing 584,000
transportation/communication 391,000
wholesale/retail trade 1,537,000
finance/real estate/insurance 480,000
services 1,795,000
government 913,000
agriculture 187,000

Average annual pay, 1994 (prelim.) $23,925
change in average annual pay,
  1993-1994 .... 1.5%

Hours and earnings of production workers
on manufacturing payrolls, 1994
average weekly hours 41.4
average hourly earnings $9.97
average weekly earnings $412.76

Labor union membership, 1994 452,000

Household income (in constant 1993 dollars)
median household income, 1992 .... $28,168
median household income, 1993 .... $28,550

Poverty
persons below poverty level, 1992 .... 15.6%
persons below poverty level, 1993 .... 17.8%

Personal income ($per capita)
1994
  in current dollars 21,677
  in constant (1987) dollars 16,765
1995 (projected)
  in constant (1982) dollars 14,583
2000 (projected)
  in constant (1982) dollars 15,496

Federal income tax returns, 1993
returns filed 6,282,136
adjusted gross income ($1000) 193,995,295
total income tax paid ($1000) 29,539,064

Florida 7

ECONOMY, BUSINESS, INDUSTRY & AGRICULTURE

Fortune 500 companies, 1994 12

Business incorporations, 1994
total 93,388
change, 1993-94 .... 6.1%

Business failures, 1994
total 3,605
rate per 10,000 concerns 76
change, 1993-94 .... -29.2%

Business firm ownership
Hispanic owned firms, 1987 64,413
black owned firms, 1987 25,527
women owned firms, 1987 221,400
foreign owned firms, 1982 421

Gross state product, 1991 ($mil)
total $255,129
  agriculture services, forestry, fisheries ... 6,581
  mining 750
  construction 11,570
  manufacturing—durable goods 13,114
  manufacturing—nondurable goods 9,949
  transportation, communication &
    public utilities 24,166
  wholesale trade 17,327
  retail trade 29,482
  finance/real estate/insurance 50,631
  services 57,679
  federal, state & local government 33,881

Establishments, by major industry group, 1992
total 376,028
  agriculture 7,555
  mining 291
  construction 35,186
  manufacturing 16,719
  transportation 13,727
  wholesale trade 29,470
  retail trade 90,115
  finance/real estate/insurance 39,400
  service industries 135,700
  unclassified 7,865

Payroll, by major industry group, 1992
total ($1,000) $98,373,011
  agriculture 715,856
  mining 261,318
  construction 5,750,719
  manufacturing 12,964,515
  transportation 8,239,492
  wholesale trade 7,762,488
  retail trade 14,906,765
  finance/real estate/insurance 10,116,713
  service industries 37,511,420
  unclassified 143,725

Agriculture
number of farms, 1994 39,000
farm acreage, 1994 10,000,000
acres per farm, 1994 264
value of farms, 1994 ($mil) 22,709
farm income, 1993 ($mil)
  gross farm income 6,070
  net farm income 2,224
  debt/asset ratio 15.1%
farm marketings, 1993 ($mil)
  total $5,750
  crops 4,548
  livestock 1,202
government payments 111
farm marketings in order of marketing receipts, 1993
  1) Greenhouse
  2) Oranges
  3) Tomatoes
  4) Sugar

Federal economic activity ($mil, except per capita)
expenditures, 1994
  total $71,092
  per capita $5,095
  defense $12,138
  non-defense $58,954
defense department, 1994
  contract awards ($mil) $5,910
  payroll ($mil) $6,164
  civilian employees (x1,000) 30.3
  military personnel (x1,000) 60.8

Fishing, 1992
catch (millions of pounds) 152
value ($mil) 155

Mining, 1994 ($mil)
total non-fuel mineral production $1,468

81

Florida 8

principal non-fuel minerals in order of value, 1994
- 1) Phosphate rock
- 2) Stone
- 3) Cement

Construction, 1994 ($mil)
total contracts (including
  non-building) $21,927
    residential 11,596
    non-residential 6,582

Manufacturing, 1992
total establishments 16,396
employees, total (x1,000) 474
payroll ($mil) 13,018
production workers (x1,000) 289
value added ($mil) 33,081
value of shipments ($mil) 64,320

Finance
commercial banks, 1994
  number 375
    assets ($bil) 150.2
    deposits ($bil) 123.4
  closed or assisted 0
    deposits ($bil) .... NA
savings and loan associations, 1991
  non-current real estate loans 4.27%
  net income after taxes ($mil) .... -234
  return on assets .... -0.43%

Retail trade, 1992
establishments (x1,000) 87.7
sales ($mil) 118,742
annual payroll ($mil) 13,276
paid employees (x1,000) 1,102

Wholesale trade, 1992
establishments 30,137
sales ($bil) 132.6
annual payroll ($mil) 7,485
paid employees (x1,000) 280.9

Service industries, 1992
establishments (x1,000) (non-exempt firms) 120.0
receipts ($mil) (non-exempt firms) 74,347
annual payroll ($mil) 27,658
paid employees (x1,000) (non-exempt firms) 1,274

COMMUNICATION, ENERGY & TRANSPORTATION

Communication
daily newspapers, 1993 40
broadcast stations, 1990
  radio: commercial, educational 428
  television: commercial, noncommercial 67
cable TV households, 1988 2,854,000

Energy
consumption estimates, 1992
total (trillion Btu) 3,066
per capita (million Btu) 227.4
by source of production (trillion Btu)
  coal 653
  natural gas 370
  petroleum 1,577
  nuclear electric power 268
  hydroelectric power 2
by end-use sector (trillion Btu)
  residential 821
  commercial 695
  industrial 438
  transportation 1,112
electrical energy
  production, 1993 (billion kWh) 140.1
  net summer capability, 1993 (million kW) . 34.8
gas utilities, 1993
  customers 581,000
  sales (trillion Btu) 87
  revenues ($mil) 502
nuclear plants, 1993 5

Transportation, 1994
public road & street mileage
total 113,478
  urban 48,394
  rural 65,084
  interstate 1,472
vehicle miles of travel (mil) 121,989
total motor vehicle registrations 10,251,810
  automobiles 7,519,206
licensed drivers 11,005,438
  per 1,000 driving age population .... 999 ·
deaths from motor vehicle
  accidents 2,687

Georgia 1

STATE SUMMARY

Capital City .... Atlanta

Governor .... Zell Miller

Address .... STATE CAPITOL
ATLANTA, GA 30334
404 656-1776

Admitted as a state 1788

Area (square miles) 59,441

Population, 1980 5,463,105

Population, 1990 6,478,216

Population, 1994 (est.) 7,055,000

Persons per square mile, 1994 .... 121.8

Largest city .... Atlanta
population, 1990 394,000

Personal income per capita, 1994
(in current dollars) $20,251

Gross state product ($mil), 1991 143,643

Leading industries, 1992 (by payroll)
SERVICE INDUSTRIES
MANUFACTURING
RETAIL TRADE

Leading agricultural commodities, 1993
BROILERS
PEANUTS
CATTLE
EGGS

GEOGRAPHY & ENVIRONMENT

Area (square miles)
total 59,441
land 57,919
water (includes territorial water) 1,522

Federally owned land, 1991 .... 4.0%

Highest point
name .... Brasstown Bald
elevation (feet) 4,784

Lowest point
name .... Atlantic Ocean
elevation (feet) .... sea level

General coastline (miles) 100

Tidal shoreline (miles) 2,344

Capital city .... Atlanta
population, 1990 394,000

Largest city .... Atlanta
population, 1990 394,000

Number of cities with over 100,000 population
1980 4

Number of cities with over 100,000 population
1990 4

State parks and Recreation areas, 1991
area (acres) 57,000
number of visitors 16,262,000
revenues $14,811,000

National forest land, 1992 (acres) 1,846,000

National park acreage, 1984 40,100

DEMOGRAPHICS & CHARACTERISTICS OF THE POPULATION

Population
1970 4,587,930
1980 5,463,105
1990 6,478,216
1994 (est.) 7,055,000
2000 (revised projection) 7,637,000
2010 (revised projection) 8,553,000

Metropolitan area population
1970 2,807,000
1980 3,403,000
1992 4,587,000

Non-metropolitan area population
1970 1,781,000
1980 2,060,000
1992 2,186,000

Change in population, 1980-90
number 1,015,111
percent 18.58%

Persons per square mile, 1994 .... 121.8

Age distribution, 1980
under 5 years 7.6%
5 to 17 years 22.5%
65 and over 9.5%

Age distribution, 1990
under 5 years 7.7%
5 to 17 years 19.0%
65 and over 10.1%

Georgia 2

Age distribution, 2000 (projected)

Age distribution, 2000 (projected)
under 5 years 6.6%
5 to 17 years 19.1%
65 and over 10.4%

Persons by age, 1990
under 5 years 495,535
5 to 17 years 1,231,768
65 and over 654,270

Median age, 1990 .... *31.60*

Race, 1990
White 4,600,148
Black 1,746,565
American Indian 12,926
Chinese 12,657
Filipino 5,848
Japanese 6,372
Asian Indian 13,926
Korean 15,275
Vietnamese 7,801
all other 56,276

Race, 2010 (projected)
White 5,857,000
Black 2,485,000

Persons of Hispanic origin, 1990
total 108,922
  Mexican 49,182
  Puerto Rican 17,443
  Cuban 7,818
  Other Hispanic 34,479

Persons by sex, 1990
male 3,144,503
female 3,333,713

Marital status, 1990
males
  15 years & older 2,404,921
    single 716,125
    married 1,439,894
      separated 54,170
      widowed 52,429
      divorced 196,473
females
  15 years & older 2,627,194
    single 601,461
    married 1,447,597
      separated 81,530

widowed 306,707
divorced 271,429

Households & families, 1990
households 2,366,615
persons per household 2.66
  families 1,713,072
    married couples 1,306,756
    female householder, no husband
      present 329,641
    one person households 537,702
households, 1994 2,581,000
persons per household, 1994 .... 2.67

Nativity, 1990
number of persons born in state 4,179,861
percent of total residents 64.5%

Immigration & naturalization, 1993
immigrants admitted 10,213
persons naturalized 4,185
refugees granted resident status 1,765

VITAL STATISTICS & HEALTH

Births
1992 111,397
  with low birth weight 8.5%
  to teenage mothers 16.2%
  to unmarried mothers 35.0%
1993 112,400
1994 108,908

Abortions, 1992
total 40,000
rate (per 1,000 women age 15-44) 24.0
rate per 1,000 live births 350

Adoptions, 1986
total 2,732
  related 65.0%

Deaths
1992 53,288
1993 55,851
1994 56,377

Infant deaths
1992 1,163
1993 1,140
1994 1,057

Average lifetime, 1979-1981
both sexes . . . . 72.22 years
  men . . . . 68.01 years
  women . . . . 76.35 years

Marriages
1992 63,417
1993 61,577
1994 62,879

Divorces
1992 39,586
1993 38,349
1994 37,001

Physicians, 1993
total 12,456
rate (per 1,000 persons) 1.82

Dentists, 1992
total 3,165
rate (per 1,000 persons) 0.47

Hospitals, 1993
number 159
beds (x 1,000) 26.5
average daily census (x 1,000) 16.8
occupancy rate 63.4%
personnel (x 1,000) 97.7
average cost per day to hospital $775
average cost per stay to hospital $5,554

EDUCATION

Educational attainment of all persons
25 years and older, 1990
less than 9th grade 483,755
high school graduates 1,192,935
bachelor's degree 519,613
graduate or professional degree 257,545

Public school enrollment, Fall, 1993
total 1,235,304
  Kindergarten through grade 8 910,425
  grades 9 through 12 324,879

Public School Teachers
total, 1994 75,602
  elementary 54,863
  secondary 20,739
salaries, 1994
  beginning $21,885
  average $29,214

State receipts & expenditures for public
schools, 1993
receipts ($mil) 5,767
expenditures
  total ($mil) 5,646
  per capita $834
  per pupil $4,544

Graduating high school seniors,
public high schools, 1995 (est) 57,778

SAT scores, 1994
verbal 398
math 446

Institutions of higher education, 1995
total 119
  public 72
  private 47

Enrollment in institutions of higher
education, Fall, 1993
total 302,844
full-time men 92,115
full-time women 107,003
part-time men 41,417
part-time women 62,309

Minority enrollment in institutions of higher
education, Fall, 1993
Black, non-Hispanic 70,987
Hispanic 4,269
Asian/Pacific Islander 6,534

Earned degrees conferred, 1993
Bachelor's 25,390
First professional 1,949
Master's 7,958
Doctor's 899

SOCIAL INSURANCE &
WELFARE PROGRAMS

Social Security beneficiaries & benefits, 1993
beneficiaries
total 964,000
  retired and dependents 613,000
  survivors 186,000
  disabled & dependents 165,000
annual benefit payments ($mil)
total $6,449
  retired and dependents 4,021
  survivors 1,391
  disabled & dependents 1,037

Georgia 4

Medicare, 1993
enrollment (x1,000) 791
payments ($mil) 3,302

Medicaid, 1993
recipients (x1,000) 955
payments ($mil) 2,441

Federal public aid, 1993
recipients as a percent of population 8.4%
Aid to Families with Dependent Children
  recipients (x1,000) 394
average monthly payment $255
Supplemental Security Income
  total recipients (x1,000) 187

Food Stamp Program
  participants, 1994 (x1,000) 830

HOUSING & CONSTRUCTION

Total housing units, 1990 2,638,418
  year round housing units 2,604,164
  vacant 271,803

*New privately owned housing units
authorized, 1994*
number (x1,000) 64.9
value ($mil) 5,095

*New privately owned housing units
started, 1994* (x1,000) 62.4

Existing home sales, 1994 (x1,000) . . . . NA

GOVERNMENT & ELECTIONS

State officials, 1996
  Governor (name/party/term expires)
                ZELL MILLER
                Democrat - 1999
Lt. Governor . . . . Pierre Howard
Sec. of State . . . . Max Cleland
Atty. General . . . . Michael J. Bowers
Chf. Justice . . . . Harold Clark

Governorship
minimum age 30
length of term . . . . 4 years
number of consecutive
  terms permitted 2
who succeeds . . . . Lt. Governor

State legislature
name . . . . General Assembly
  upper chamber
    name . . . . Senate
    number of members 56
    length of term . . . . 2 years
    party in majority, 1996 . . . . Democratic
  lower chamber
    name . . . . House of Representatives
    number of members 180
    length of term . . . . 2 years
    party in majority, 1996 . . . . Democratic

State employees October, 1992
total 127,075
October payroll ($1,000) 233,831

Local governments, 1992
total 1,321
  county 157
  municipal 536
  township 0
  school districts 185
  special districts 442

Voting, November, 1994
voting age population 5,105,000
  registered 54.9%
  voted 35.4%

Vote for president
1988
  Bush 1,070,089
  Dukakis 715,635
1992
  Clinton 1,000,745
  Bush 987,337
  Perot 307,001

Federal representation, 1996 (104th Congress)
Senators (name/party/term expires)

                SAM NUNN
                Democrat - 1997
            PAUL CLOVERDELL
            Republican - 1999

Representatives, total 11
  Democrats 4
  Republicans 7
  other 0

Women holding public office
U.S. Congress, 1995 1
statewide elected office, 1995 1
state legislature, 1995 43

Black elected officials, 1993
total 545
　US and state legislatures 43
　city/county/regional offices 371
　judicial/law enforcement 32
　education/school boards 99

Hispanic public officials, 1994
total .... NA
　state executives & legislators .... NA
　city/county/regional offices .... NA
　judicial/law enforcement .... NA
　education/school boards .... NA

GOVERNMENTAL FINANCE

State & local government revenues, (selected items), 1991-92 ($per capita)
total $4,049.46
　total general revenues 3,378.81
　　from federal government 640.42
　　from own sources 2,738.39
　　from taxes 1,867.64
　　　from property taxes 552.61
　　　from all other taxes 1,247.13
　　from charges & misc. 870.75

State & local government expenditures, (selected items), 1991-92 ($per capita)
total $3,937.96
　total direct general expenditures 3,374.98
　　education 1,105.07
　　libraries 10.93
　　public welfare 506.40
　　health & hospitals 540.74
　　highways 208.39
　　police protection 107.37
　　fire protection 47.98
　　correction 120.92
　　housing & comm. development 52.33
　　natural resources & parks 107.20
　　interest on general debt 128.67

State & local debt, 1992 ($per capita) 3,126.28

Federal aid grants to state & local government, 1994 ($per capita total & selected items)
per capita total 712.74
　compensatory education 24.42
　waste treatment facilities 2.71
　medicaid 294.80
　housing assistance 39.76
　job training 8.59
　highway trust fund 54.44

CRIME, LAW ENFORCEMENT & COURTS

Crime, 1994 (all rates per 100,000 persons)
total crimes 424,029
overall crime rate 6,010.3
　property crimes 376,926
　　burglaries 81,406
　　larcenies 256,208
　　motor vehicle thefts 39,312
　property crime rate 5,342.7
　violent crimes 47,103
　　murders 703
　　forcible rapes 2,448
　　robberies 15,703
　　aggravated assaults 28,249
　violent crime rate 667.7

Number of police agencies, 1994 300

Arrests, 1994
total 286,256
　persons under 18 years of age 37,514

Prisoners under state & federal jurisdiction, 1994
total 33,425
percent change, 1993-94 .... 20.3%
　sentenced to more than one year
　　total 32,523
　　rate per 100,000 residents 456

Persons under sentence of death, 4/20/95 104

State's highest court
name .... Supreme Court
number of members 7
length of term .... 6 years
intermediate appeals court? .... yes

Georgia 6

LABOR & INCOME

Civilian labor force, 1994
total 3,566,000
  men 1,890,000
  women 1,676,000
  persons 16-19 years 175,000
  white 2,417,000
  black 1,088,000

Civilian labor force as a percent of
civilian non-institutional population, 1994
total 67.6%
  men 76.0%
  women 60.1%
  persons 16-19 years 46.6%
  white 67.4%
  black 68.4%

Employment, 1994
total 3,381,000
  men 1,795,000
  women 1,586,000
  persons 16-19 years 143,000
  white 2,330,000
  black 993,000

Full-time/part-time labor force, 1994
full-time labor force 3,038,000
  working part-time for
   ecomonic reasons 38,000
part-time labor force 528,000

Unemployment rate, 1994
total 5.2%
  men 5.0%
  women 5.4%
  persons 16-19 years 18.6%
  white 3.6%
  black 8.7%

Unemployed by reason for unemployment
(as a percent of total unemployment), 1994
job losers or completed temp jobs 39.0%
job leavers 11.1%
reentrants 40.0%
new entrants 9.9%

Civilian labor force, by occupation, 1994
executive/administrative/
  managerial 477,000
professional/specialty 477,000
technicians & related support 81,000

sales 447,000
adminstrative support/clerical 494,000
service occupations 457,000
precision production/craft/repair 415,000
machine operators/assemblers 267,000
transportation/material moving 150,000
handlers/helpers/laborers 199,000
farming/forestry/fishing 81,000

Civilian labor force, by industry, 1994
construction 175,000
manufacturing 636,000
transportation/communication 223,000
wholesale/retail trade 672,000
finance/real estate/insurance 195,000
services 764,000
government 552,000
agriculture 75,000

Average annual pay, 1994 (prelim.) $25,306
change in average annual pay,
  1993-1994 . . . . 1.8%

Hours and earnings of production workers
on manufacturing payrolls, 1994
average weekly hours 42.4
average hourly earnings $10.35
average weekly earnings $438.84

Labor union membership, 1994 244,100

Household income (in constant 1993 dollars)
median household income, 1992 . . . . $29,659
median household income, 1993 . . . . $31,663

Poverty
persons below poverty level, 1992 . . . . 17.7%
persons below poverty level, 1993 . . . . 13.5%

Personal income ($per capita)
1994
  in current dollars 20,251
  in constant (1987) dollars 15,662
1995 (projected)
  in constant (1982) dollars 13,450
2000 (projected)
  in constant (1982) dollars 14,297

Federal income tax returns, 1993
returns filed 3,022,938
adjusted gross income ($1000) 94,470,361
total income tax paid ($1000) 12,946,742

Georgia 7

ECONOMY, BUSINESS, INDUSTRY & AGRICULTURE

Fortune 500 companies, 1994 15

Business incorporations, 1994
total 24,707
change, 1993-94 .... 7.0%

Business failures, 1994
total 1,958
rate per 10,000 concerns 99
change, 1993-94 .... -16.9%

Business firm ownership
Hispanic owned firms, 1987 1,931
black owned firms, 1987 21,283
women owned firms, 1987 88,100
foreign owned firms, 1982 449

Gross state product, 1991 ($mil)
total $143,643
  agriculture services, forestry, fisheries ... 2,841
  mining 653
  construction 5,497
  manufacturing – durable goods 9,710
  manufacturing – nondurable goods 16,393
  transportation, communication &
    public utilities 15,939
  wholesale trade 13,270
  retail trade 13,309
  finance/real estate/insurance 22,895
  services 24,164
  federal, state & local government 18,974

Establishments, by major industry group, 1992
total 163,330
  agriculture 2,380
  mining 205
  construction 14,125
  manufacturing 9,898
  transportation 6,531
  wholesale trade 14,699
  retail trade 41,920
  finance/real estate/insurance 14,969
  service industries 55,522
  unclassified 3,081

Payroll, by major industry group, 1992
total ($1,000) $58,908,142
  agriculture 244,285

mining 241,624
construction 2,808,744
manufacturing 14,565,722
transportation 6,309,186
wholesale trade 6,166,634
retail trade 6,786,827
finance/real estate/insurance 5,317,231
service industries 16,394,589
unclassified 73,300

Agriculture
number of farms, 1994 43,000
farm acreage, 1994 12,000,000
acres per farm, 1994 281
value of farms, 1994 ($mil) 11,893
farm income, 1993 ($mil)
  gross farm income 4,876
  net farm income 1,532
  debt/asset ratio 18.9%
farm marketings, 1993 ($mil)
  total $4,211
  crops 1,639
  livestock 2,572
government payments 226
farm marketings in order of marketing receipts, 1993
  1) Broilers
  2) Peanuts
  3) Cattle
  4) Eggs

Federal economic activity
  ($mil, except per capita)
expenditures, 1994
  total $32,067
  per capita $4,545
  defense $8,463
  non-defense $23,604
defense department, 1994
  contract awards ($mil) $4,121
  payroll ($mil) $4,273
  civilian employees (x1,000) 35.0
  military personnel (x1,000) 61.8

Fishing, 1992
catch (millions of pounds) 18
value ($mil) 23

Mining, 1994 ($mil)
total non-fuel mineral production $1,535

Georgia 8

principal non-fuel minerals in order of value, 1994
1) Clay
2) Stone
3) Cement

Construction, 1994 ($mil)
total contracts (including
  non-building) $10,623
  residential 5,868
  non-residential 3,023

Manufacturing, 1992
total establishments 9,767
employees, total (x1,000) 556
payroll ($mil) 14,278
production workers (x1,000) 394
value added ($mil) 41,038
value of shipments ($mil) 90,999

Finance
commercial banks, 1994
  number 399
  assets ($bil) 90.1
  deposits ($bil) 63.3
  closed or assisted 0
  deposits ($bil) ....NA
savings and loan associations, 1991
  non-current real estate loans 2.02%
  net income after taxes ($mil) 21
  return on assets .... +0.12%

Retail trade, 1992
establishments (x1,000) 40.9
sales ($mil) 49,940
annual payroll ($mil) 5,809
paid employees (x1,000) 509

Wholesale trade, 1992
establishments 14,608
sales ($bil) 113.8
annual payroll ($mil) 5,329
paid employees (x1,000) 179.4

Service industries, 1992
establishments (x1,000) (non-exempt firms) 46.9
receipts ($mil) (non-exempt firms) 30,802
annual payroll ($mil) 11,409
paid employees (x1,000) (non-exempt firms) . 502

COMMUNICATION, ENERGY & TRANSPORTATION

Communication
daily newspapers, 1993 34
broadcast stations, 1990
  radio: commercial, educational 358
  television: commercial, noncommercial 39
cable TV households, 1988 1,148,000

Energy
consumption estimates, 1992
total (trillion Btu) 2,095
per capita (million Btu) 309.3
by source of production (trillion Btu)
  coal 616
  natural gas 352
  petroleum 808
  nuclear electric power 299
  hydroelectric power 56
by end-use sector (trillion Btu)
  residential 454
  commercial 330
  industrial 640
  transportation 671
electrical energy
  production, 1993 (billion kWh) 95.7
  net summer capability, 1993 (million kW) . 21.5
gas utilities, 1993
  customers 1,527,000
  sales (trillion Btu) 332
  revenues ($mil) 1,269
nuclear plants, 1993 4

Transportation, 1994
public road & street mileage
total 111,252
  urban 26,396
  rural 84,856
  interstate 1,242
vehicle miles of travel (mil) 82,822
total motor vehicle registrations 5,969,702
  automobiles 4,167,597
licensed drivers 4,816,618
  per 1,000 driving age population 898
deaths from motor vehicle
  accidents 1,426

STATE SUMMARY

Capital City . . . . .Honolulu

Governor .Ben Cayetano

Address . . . . . . .STATE CAPITOL
HONOLULU, HI 96813
808 586-0034

Admitted as a state 1959

Area (square miles) 10,932

Population, 1980 964,691

Population, 1990 1,108,229

Population, 1994 (est.) 1,179,000

Persons per square mile, 1994 . . . . 183.5

Largest city . . . . .Honolulu
population, 1990 365,000

Personal income per capita, 1994
(in current dollars) $24,057

Gross state product ($mil), 1991 30,802

Leading industries, 1992 (by payroll)
SERVICE INDUSTRIES
RETAIL TRADE
TRANSPORTATION

Leading agricultural commodities, 1993
CANE/SUGAR
PINEAPPLES
GREENHOUSE
NUTS

GEOGRAPHY & ENVIRONMENT

Area (square miles)
total 10,932
  land 6,423
  water (includes territorial water) 4,508

Federally owned land, 1991 . . . . 15.5%

Highest point
name . . . . .Mauna Kea
elevation (feet) 13,796

Lowest point
name . . . . Pacific Ocean
elevation (feet) .sea level

General coastline (miles) 750

Tidal shoreline (miles) 1,052

Capital city . . . . Honolulu
population, 1990 365,000

Largest city . . . . Honolulu
population, 1990 365,000

Number of cities with over 100,000 population
1980 1

Number of cities with over 100,000 population
1990 1

State parks and Recreation areas, 1991
area (acres) 25,000
number of visitors 19,112,000
revenues $1,231,000

National forest land, 1992 (acres) 500

National park acreage, 1984 245,000

DEMOGRAPHICS & CHARACTERISTICS OF THE POPULATION

Population
1970 769,913
1980 964,691
1990 1,108,229
1994 (est.) 1,179,000
2000 (revised projection) 1,327,000
2010 (revised projection) 1,551,000

Metropolitan area population
1970 631,000
1980 763,000
1992 863,000

Non-metropolitan area population
1970 139,000
1980 202,000
1992 293,000

Change in population, 1980-90
number 143,538
percent 14.88%

Persons per square mile, 1994 . . . . 183.5

Age distribution, 1980
under 5 years 8.1%
5 to 17 years 20.5%
65 and over 7.9%

Age distribution, 1990
under 5 years 7.5%
5 to 17 years 17.7%
65 and over 11.2%

Hawaii 2

Age distribution, 2000 (projected)
under 5 years 5.5%
5 to 17 years 16.5%
65 and over 13.1%

Persons by age, 1990
under 5 years 83,223
5 to 17 years 196,903
65 and over 125,005

Median age, 1990 .... *32.60*

Race, 1990
White 369,616
Black 27,195
American Indian 4,738
Chinese 68,804
Filipino 168,682
Japanese 247,486
Asian Indian 1,015
Korean 24,454
Vietnamese 5,468
all other 190,410

Race, 2010 (projected)
White 745,000
Black 50,000

Persons of Hispanic origin, 1990
total 81,390
Mexican 14,367
Puerto Rican 25,778
Cuban 558
Other Hispanic 40,687

Persons by sex, 1990
male 563,891
female 544,338

Marital status, 1990
males
15 years & older 441,420
single 152,188
married 248,386
separated 6,425
widowed 9,053
divorced 31,793
females
15 years & older 428,783
single 106,715
married 244,799
separated 7,539

widowed 38,530
divorced 38,739

Households & families, 1990
households 356,267
persons per household 3.01
families 263,456
married couples 210,468
female householder, no husband
present 37,409
one person households 68,985
households, 1994 381,000
persons per household, 1994 .... 2.99

Nativity, 1990
number of persons born in state 621,992
percent of total residents 56.1%

Immigration & naturalization, 1993
immigrants admitted 8,528
persons naturalized 4,960
refugees granted resident status 241

VITAL STATISTICS & HEALTH

Births
1992 19,910
with low birth weight 7.2%
to teenage mothers 10.0%
to unmarried mothers 26.2%
1993 19,589
1994 19,244

Abortions, 1992
total 12,000
rate (per 1,000 women age 15-44) 46.0
rate per 1,000 live births 617

Adoptions, 1986
total 276
related 69.6%

Deaths
1992 6,909
1993 7,280
1994 7,236

Infant deaths
1992 132
1993 132
1994 126

Hawaii 3

Average lifetime, 1979-1981
both sexes . . . . 77.02 years
  men . . . . 74.08 years
  women . . . . 80.33 years

Marriages
1992 17,643
1993 17,494
1994 17,927

Divorces
1992 5,012
1993 4,876
1994 4,979

Physicians, 1993
total 2,728
rate (per 1,000 persons) 2.44

Dentists, 1992
total 920
rate (per 1,000 persons) 0.83

Hospitals, 1993
number 20
beds (x 1,000) 2.9
average daily census (x 1,000) 2.4
occupancy rate 83.1%
personnel (x 1,000) 13.9
average cost per day to hospital $823
average cost per stay to hospital $7,633

EDUCATION

*Educational attainment of all persons
  25 years and older, 1990*
less than 9th grade 71,806
high school graduates 203,893
bachelor's degree 111,837
graduate or professional degree 50,587

Public school enrollment, Fall, 1993
total 180,430
  Kindergarten through grade 8 131,658
  grades 9 through 12 48,772

Public School Teachers
total, 1994 10,111
  elementary 5,739
  secondary 4,328
salaries, 1994
  beginning $25,100
  average $36,564

*State receipts & expenditures for public
  schools, 1993*
receipts ($mil) 1,084
expenditures
  total ($mil) 1,077
  per capita $932
  per pupil $5,806

*Graduating high school seniors,
  public high schools, 1995 (est)* 9,949

SAT scores, 1994
verbal 401
math 480

Institutions of higher education, 1995
total 16
  public 10
  private 6

*Enrollment in institutions of higher
  education, Fall, 1993*
total 62,871
full-time men 15,898
full-time women 18,564
part-time men 12,539
part-time women 15,870

*Minority enrollment in institutions of higher
  education, Fall, 1993*
Black, non-Hispanic 1,613
Hispanic 1,443
Asian/Pacific Islander 36,776

Earned degrees conferred, 1993
Bachelor's 4,186
First professional 176
Master's 1,383
Doctor's 168

SOCIAL INSURANCE & WELFARE PROGRAMS

Social Security beneficiaries & benefits, 1993
beneficiaries
total 158,000
  retired and dependents 125,000
  survivors 21,000
  disabled & dependents 12,000
annual benefit payments ($mil)
total $1,106
  retired and dependents 852
  survivors 171
  disabled & dependents 83

Hawaii 4

Medicare, 1993
enrollment (x1,000) 141
payments ($mil) 473

Medicaid, 1993
recipients (x1,000) 110
payments ($mil) 293

Federal public aid, 1993
recipients as a percent of population 6.3%
Aid to Families with Dependent Children
recipients (x1,000) 60
average monthly payment $654
Supplemental Security Income
total recipients (x1,000) 17

Food Stamp Program
participants, 1994 (x1,000) 115

HOUSING & CONSTRUCTION

Total housing units, 1990 389,810
year round housing units 376,922
vacant 33,543

New privately owned housing units
authorized, 1994
number (x1,000) 7.3
value ($mil) 801

New privately owned housing units
started, 1994 (x1,000) 7.8

Existing home sales, 1994 (x1,000) 13.1

GOVERNMENT & ELECTIONS

State officials, 1996
Governor (name/party/term expires)
BEN CAYETANO
Democrat - 1998
Lt. Governor . . . . .Mazie Hirono
Sec. of State . . . . (no sec. of state)
Atty. General . . . . .Robert Marks
Chf. Justice . . . . .Ronald Moon

Governorship
minimum age 30
length of term . . . . 4 years
number of consecutive
terms permitted 2
who succeeds . . . . Lt. Governor

State legislature
name . . . . Legislature
upper chamber
name . . . . Senate
number of members 25
length of term . . . . 4 years
party in majority, 1996 . . . . .Democratic
lower chamber
name . . . . House of Representatives
number of members 51
length of term . . . . 2 years
party in majority, 1996 . . . . .Democratic

State employees October, 1992
total 61,786
October payroll ($1,000) 130,808

Local governments, 1992
total 21
county 3
municipal 1
township 0
school districts 0
special districts 16

Voting, November, 1994
voting age population 833,000
registered 51.5%
voted 46.0%

Vote for president
1988
Bush 158,625
Dukakis 192,364
1992
Clinton 179,310
Bush 136,822
Perot 53,003

Federal representation, 1996 (104th Congress)
Senators (name/party/term expires)

DANIEL AKATA
Democrat - 2001
DANIEL K. INOUYE
Democrat - 1999

Representatives, total 2
Democrats 2
Republicans 0
other 0

Hawaii 5

Women holding public office
U.S. Congress, 1995 1
statewide elected office, 1995 1
state legislature, 1995 16

Black elected officials, 1993
total 0
  US and state legislatures 0
  city/county/regional offices 0
  judicial/law enforcement 0
  education/school boards 0

Hispanic public officials, 1994
total 2
  state executives & legislators 2
  city/county/regional offices 0
  judicial/law enforcement 0
  education/school boards 0

GOVERNMENTAL FINANCE

State & local government revenues, (selected items), 1991-92 ($per capita)
total $5,746.25
  total general revenues 4,992.54
    from federal government 827.63
    from own sources 4,164.91
    from taxes 2,988.85
      from property taxes 490.27
      from all other taxes 2,388.87
    from charges & misc. 1,176.07

State & local government expenditures, (selected items), 1991-92 ($per capita)
total $5,889.41
  total direct general expenditures 5,317.89
  education 1,184.51
  libraries 32.83
  public welfare 527.68
  health & hospitals 358.18
  highways 381.22
  police protection 146.48
  fire protection 58.33
  correction 92.21
  housing & comm. development 189.80
  natural resources & parks 309.76
  interest on general debt 312.40

State & local debt, 1992 ($per capita) 5,328.96
Federal aid grants to state & local government, 1994 ($per capita total & selected items)
per capita total 922.82
  compensatory education 15.58
  waste treatment facilities 6.06
  medicaid 205.86
  housing assistance 74.91
  job training 14.17
  highway trust fund 187.91

CRIME, LAW ENFORCEMENT & COURTS
Crime, 1994 (all rates per 100,000 persons)
total crimes 78,763
overall crime rate 6,680.5
  property crimes 75,672
    burglaries 14,029
    larcenies 55,260
    motor vehicle thefts 6,383
  property crime rate 6,418.3
  violent crimes 3,091
    murders 50
    forcible rapes 359
    robberies 1,221
    aggravated assaults 1,461
  violent crime rate 262.2

Number of police agencies, 1994 5

Arrests, 1994
total 68,990
  persons under 18 years of age 20,648

Prisoners under state & federal jurisdiction, 1994
total 3,333
percent change, 1993-94 ....6.5%
  sentenced to more than one year
    total 2,392
    rate per 100,000 residents 202

Persons under sentence of death, 4/20/95 ....NA
State's highest court
name ....Supreme Court
number of members 5
length of term ....10 years
intermediate appeals court? ....yes

Hawaii 6

LABOR & INCOME

Civilian labor force, 1994
total 583,000
  men 298,000
  women 284,000
  persons 16-19 years 26,000
  white 204,000
  black .... NA

Civilian labor force as a percent of
civilian non-institutional population, 1994
total 68.1%
  men 74.1%
  women 62.8%
  persons 16-19 years 47.3%
  white 70.2%
  black .... NA%

Employment, 1994
total 547,000
  men 277,000
  women 270,000
  persons 16-19 years 22,000
  white 190,000
  black .... NA

Full-time/part-time labor force, 1994
full-time labor force 476,000
  working part-time for
    ecomonic reasons 6,000
part-time labor force 107,000

Unemployment rate, 1994
total 6.1%
  men 7.1%
  women 5.0%
  persons 16-19 years 16.9%
  white 6.7%
  black.............................. NA%

Unemployed by reason for unemployment
(as a percent of total unemployment), 1994
job losers or completed temp jobs 48.2%
job leavers 14.3%
reentrants 30.2%
new entrants 7.3%

Civilian labor force, by occupation, 1994
executive/administrative/
  managerial 82,000
professional/specialty 76,000
technicians & related support 17,000

sales 75,000
adminstrative support/clerical 87,000
service occupations 107,000
precision production/craft/repair 58,000
machine operators/assemblers ....NA
transportation/material moving 22,000
handlers/helpers/laborers 24,000
farming/forestry/fishing 22,000

Civilian labor force, by industry, 1994
construction 35,000
manufacturing 17,000
transportation/communication 40,000
wholesale/retail trade 122,000
finance/real estate/insurance 40,000
services 149,000
government 109,000
agriculture 16,000

Average annual pay, 1994 (prelim.) $26,746
change in average annual pay,
  1993-1994 .... 1.6%

Hours and earnings of production workers
on manufacturing payrolls, 1994
average weekly hours 38.3
average hourly earnings $12.22
average weekly earnings $468.03

Labor union membership, 1994 135,200

Household income (in constant 1993 dollars)
median household income, 1992 .... $43,374
median household income, 1993 .... $42,662

Poverty
persons below poverty level, 1992 .... 11.2%
persons below poverty level, 1993 .... 8.0%

Personal income ($per capita)
1994
  in current dollars 24,057
  in constant (1987) dollars 18,606
1995 (projected)
  in constant (1982) dollars 14,477
2000 (projected)
  in constant (1982) dollars 15,219

Federal income tax returns, 1993
returns filed 556,041
adjusted gross income ($1000) 18,519,252
total income tax paid ($1000) 2,506,998

ECONOMY, BUSINESS, INDUSTRY & AGRICULTURE

Fortune 500 companies, 1994 0

Business incorporations, 1994
total 3,792
change, 1993-94 .... 0.0%

Business failures, 1994
total 258
rate per 10,000 concerns 77
change, 1993-94 .... -15.7%

Business firm ownership
Hispanic owned firms, 1987 1,226
black owned firms, 1987 399
women owned firms, 1987 21,700
foreign owned firms, 1982 100

Gross state product, 1991 ($mil)
total $30,802
  agriculture services, forestry, fisheries 527
  mining 26
  construction 2,000
  manufacturing—durable goods 262
  manufacturing—nondurable goods 933
  transportation, communication &
    public utilities 3,077
  wholesale trade 1,272
  retail trade 3,889
  finance/real estate/insurance 5,795
  services 6,829
  federal, state & local government 6,192

Establishments, by major industry group, 1992
total 30,467
  agriculture 335
  mining 12
  construction 2,564
  manufacturing 1,030
  transportation 1,590
  wholesale trade 2,168
  retail trade 8,079
  finance/real estate/insurance 3,983
  service industries 10,273
  unclassified 433

Payroll, by major industry group, 1992
total ($1,000) $10,470,074
  agriculture 58,005
  mining 10,494
  construction 1,201,192
  manufacturing 559,966
  transportation 1,271,484
  wholesale trade 646,027
  retail trade 1,721,074
  finance/real estate/insurance 1,122,515
  service industries 3,870,336
  unclassified 8,981

Agriculture
number of farms, 1994 4,000
farm acreage, 1994 2,000,000
acres per farm, 1994 389
value of farms, 1994 ($mil) .... NA
farm income, 1993 ($mil)
  gross farm income 519
  net farm income 29
  debt/asset ratio 7.9%
farm marketings, 1993 ($mil)
  total $492
  crops 406
  livestock 85
government payments 3
farm marketings in order of marketing receipts, 1993
  1) Sugar
  2) Pineapples
  3) Greenhouse
  4) Nuts

Federal economic activity
  ($mil, except per capita)
expenditures, 1994
  total $7,603
  per capita $6,449
  defense $3,196
  non-defense $4,407
defense department, 1994
  contract awards ($mil) $803
  payroll ($mil) $2,417
  civilian employees (x1,000) 17.0
  military personnel (x1,000) 42.2

Fishing, 1992
catch (millions of pounds) 28
value ($mil) 70

Mining, 1994 ($mil)
total non-fuel mineral production $137

Hawaii 8

principal non-fuel minerals in order of value, 1994
1) Stone
2) Cement
3) Sand and gravel

Construction, 1994 ($mil)
total contracts (including
  non-building) $2,156
    residential 908
    non-residential 823

Manufacturing, 1992
total establishments 1,018
employees, total (x1,000) 21
payroll ($mil) 556
production workers (x1,000) 13
value added ($mil) 1,526
value of shipments ($mil) 3,790

Finance
commercial banks, 1994
  number 17
    assets ($bil) 22.3
    deposits ($bil) 14.3
  closed or assisted 0
    deposits ($bil) .... NA
savings and loan associations, 1991
  non-current real estate loans 0.66%
  net income after taxes ($mil) 68
  return on assets .... +0.92%

Retail trade, 1992
establishments (x1,000) 7.8
sales ($mil) 11,250
annual payroll ($mil) 1,481
paid employees (x1,000) 110

Wholesale trade, 1992
establishments 2,202
sales ($bil) 8.0
annual payroll ($mil) 625
paid employees (x1,000) 23.3

Service industries, 1992
establishments (x1,000) (non-exempt firms) . 8.5
receipts ($mil) (non-exempt firms) 7,291
annual payroll ($mil) 2,654
paid employees (x1,000) (non-exempt firms) . 118

COMMUNICATION, ENERGY & TRANSPORTATION

Communication
daily newspapers, 1993 6
broadcast stations, 1990
  radio: commercial, educational 54
  television: commercial, noncommercial 21
cable TV households, 1988 271,000

Energy
consumption estimates, 1992
total (trillion Btu) 263
per capita (million Btu) 227.6
by source of production (trillion Btu)
  coal 1
  natural gas 3
  petroleum 258
  nuclear electric power 0
  hydroelectric power 1
by end-use sector (trillion Btu)
  residential 23
  commercial 33
  industrial 64
  transportation 143
electrical energy
  production, 1993 (billion kWh) 6.1
  net summer capability, 1993 (million kW) .. 1.6
gas utilities, 1993
  customers .... NA
  sales (trillion Btu) .... NA
  revenues ($mil) .... NA
nuclear plants, 1993 0

Transportation, 1994
public road & street mileage
total 4,106
  urban 1,813
  rural 2,293
  interstate 43
vehicle miles of travel (mil) 7,935
total motor vehicle registrations 778,876
  automobiles 509,220
licensed drivers 745,392
  per 1,000 driving age population 824
deaths from motor vehicle
  accidents 122

Idaho 1

STATE SUMMARY

Capital City . . . . Boise

Governor . . . . Phil Batt

Address . . . . STATE CAPITOL
BOISE, ID 83720
208 334-2100

Admitted as a state 1890

Area (square miles) 83,574

Population, 1980 943,935

Population, 1990 1,006,749

Population, 1994 (est.) 1,133,000

Persons per square mile, 1994 . . . . 13.7

Largest city . . . . Boise
population, 1990 126,000

Personal income per capita, 1994
(in current dollars) $18,231

Gross state product ($mil), 1991 19,047

Leading industries, 1992 (by payroll)
MANUFACTURING
SERVICE INDUSTRIES
RETAIL TRADE

Leading agricultural commodities, 1993
CATTLE
POTATOES
DAIRY PRODUCTS
WHEAT

GEOGRAPHY & ENVIRONMENT

Area (square miles)
total 83,574
  land 82,751
  water (includes territorial water) 823

Federally owned land, 1991 . . . . 61.7%

Highest point
name . . . . Borah Peak
elevation (feet) 12,662

Lowest point
name . . . . Snake River
elevation (feet) 710

General coastline (miles) 0

Tidal shoreline (miles) 0

Capital city . . . . Boise
population, 1990 126,000

Largest city . . . . Boise
population, 1990 126,000

Number of cities with over 100,000 population
  1980 1

Number of cities with over 100,000 population
  1990 1

State parks and Recreation areas, 1991
area (acres) 42,000
number of visitors 2,500,000
revenues $1,651,000

National forest land, 1992 (acres) 21,674,000

National park acreage, 1984 86,900

DEMOGRAPHICS & CHARACTERISTICS OF THE POPULATION

Population
1970 713,015
1980 943,935
1990 1,006,749
1994 (est.) 1,133,000
2000 (revised projection) 1,290,000
2010 (revised projection) 1,454,000

Metropolitan area population
1970 112,000
1980 173,000
1992 320,000

Non-metropolitan area population
1970 601,000
1980 771,000
1992 746,000

Change in population, 1980-90
number 62,814
percent 6.65%

Persons per square mile, 1994 . . . . 13.7

Age distribution, 1980
under 5 years 9.9%
5 to 17 years 22.6%
65 and over 9.9%

Age distribution, 1990
under 5 years 8.0%
5 to 17 years 22.6%
65 and over 12.0%

Idaho 2

Age distribution, 2000 (projected)
under 5 years 7.3%
5 to 17 years 20.4%
65 and over 11.5%

Persons by age, 1990
under 5 years 80,193
5 to 17 years 228,212
65 and over 121,265

Median age, 1990 ....*31.50*

Race, 1990
White 950,451
Black 3,370
American Indian 13,594
Chinese 1,420
Filipino 1,083
Japanese 2,719
Asian Indian 473
Korean 935
Vietnamese 600
all other 31,918

Race, 2010 (projected)
White 1,392,000
Black 8,000

Persons of Hispanic origin, 1990
total 52,927
  Mexican 43,213
  Puerto Rican 665
  Cuban 164
  Other Hispanic 8,885

Persons by sex, 1990
male 500,956
female 505,793

Marital status, 1990
males
  15 years & older 367,363
  single 91,380
  married 237,525
  separated 4,284
  widowed 7,312
  divorced 31,146
females
  15 years & older 378,964
  single 66,935
  married 236,258
  separated 5,397

widowed 38,831
divorced 36,940

Households & families, 1990
households 360,723
persons per household 2.73
  families 263,194
  married couples 224,198
  female householder, no husband
    present 28,883
  one person households 80,800
households, 1994 405,000
persons per household, 1994 .... 2.75

Nativity, 1990
number of persons born in state 508,992
percent of total residents 50.6%

Immigration & naturalization, 1993
immigrants admitted 1,270
persons naturalized 255
refugees granted resident status 146

VITAL STATISTICS & HEALTH

Births
1992 17,475
  with low birth weight 5.5%
  to teenage mothers 13.0%
  to unmarried mothers 18.3%
1993 17,162
1994 17,358

Abortions, 1992
total 2,000
rate (per 1,000 women age 15-44) 7.2
rate per 1,000 live births 97

Adoptions, 1986
total 330
  related 16.1%

Deaths
1992 8,063
1993 8,345
1994 8,552

Infant deaths
1992 144
1993 128
1994 127

Idaho 3

Average lifetime, 1979-1981
both sexes . . . . 75.19 years
  men . . . . 71.52 years
  women . . . . 79.15 years

Marriages
1992 14,457
1993 13,966
1994 15,234

Divorces
1992 6,700
1993 6,928
1994 7,075

Physicians, 1993
total 1,428
rate (per 1,000 persons) 1.31

Dentists, 1992
total 567
rate (per 1,000 persons) 0.53

Hospitals, 1993
number 41
beds (x 1,000) 3.4
average daily census (x 1,000) 1.9
occupancy rate 55.4%
personnel (x 1,000) 11.4
average cost per day to hospital $659
average cost per stay to hospital $4,635

EDUCATION

Educational attainment of all persons 25 years and older, 1990
less than 9th grade 44,219
high school graduates 182,892
bachelor's degree 74,443
graduate or professional degree 31,692

Public school enrollment, Fall, 1993
total 236,774
  Kindergarten through grade 8 166,999
  grades 9 through 12 69,775

Public School Teachers
total, 1994 12,007
  elementary 6,185
  secondary 5,642
salaries, 1994
  beginning $18,700
  average $27,756

State receipts & expenditures for public schools, 1993
receipts ($mil) 997
expenditures
  total ($mil) 957
  per capita $898
  per pupil $4,025

Graduating high school seniors, public high schools, 1995 (est) 13,900

SAT scores, 1994
verbal 461
math 508

Institutions of higher education, 1995
total 11
  public 6
  private 5

Enrollment in institutions of higher education, Fall, 1993
total 58,768
full-time men 19,469
full-time women 20,463
part-time men 7,674
part-time women 11,162

Minority enrollment in institutions of higher education, Fall, 1993
Black, non-Hispanic 390
Hispanic 1,468
Asian/Pacific Islander 883

Earned degrees conferred, 1993
Bachelor's 3,923
First professional 146
Master's 1,005
Doctor's 65

SOCIAL INSURANCE & WELFARE PROGRAMS

Social Security beneficiaries & benefits, 1993
beneficiaries
total 170,000
  retired and dependents 123,000
  survivors 27,000
  disabled & dependents 20,000
annual benefit payments ($mil)
total $1,183
  retired and dependents 828
  survivors 230
  disabled & dependents 125

Idaho 4

Medicare, 1993
enrollment (x1,000) 142
payments ($mil) 342

Medicaid, 1993
recipients (x1,000) 100
payments ($mil) 301

Federal public aid, 1993
recipients as a percent of population 3.2%
Aid to Families with Dependent Children
  recipients (x1,000) 23
average monthly payment $307
Supplemental Security Income
  total recipients (x1,000) 14

Food Stamp Program
participants, 1994 (x1,000) 82

HOUSING & CONSTRUCTION

Total housing units, 1990 413,327
  year round housing units 387,985
  vacant 52,604

New privately owned housing units authorized, 1994
number (x1,000) 12.6
value ($mil) 1,043

New privately owned housing units started, 1994 (x1,000) 14.2

Existing home sales, 1994 (x1,000) 23.1

GOVERNMENT & ELECTIONS

State officials, 1996
Governor (name/party/term expires)
PHIL BATT
Republican - 1999
Lt. Governor . . . . C.L. Otter
Sec. of State . . . . Pete T. Cenarrusa
Atty. General . . . . Alan Lance
Chf. Justice . . . . Charles McDevitt

Governorship
minimum age 30
length of term . . . . 4 years
number of consecutive
  terms permitted . . . . not specified
who succeeds . . . . Lt. Governor

State legislature
name . . . . Legislature
  upper chamber
    name . . . . Senate
    number of members 35
    length of term . . . . 2 years
    party in majority, 1996 . . . . Republican
  lower chamber
    name . . . . House of Representatives
    number of members 70
    length of term . . . . 2 years
    party in majority, 1996 . . . . Republican

State employees October, 1992
total 25,586
October payroll ($1,000) 43,387

Local governments, 1992
total 1,105
  county 44
  municipal 199
  township 0
  school districts 116
  special districts 745

Voting, November, 1994
voting age population 798,000
  registered 63.0%
  voted 50.7%

Vote for president
1988
  Bush 253,467
  Dukakis 147,420
1992
  Clinton 136,734
  Bush 202,421
  Perot 130,282

Federal representation, 1996 (104th Congress)
Senators (name/party/term expires)

LARRY CRAIG
Republican - 1997
DIRK KEMPTHORNE
Republican - 1999

Representatives, total 2
  Democrats 0
  Republicans 2
  other 0

Women holding public office
U.S. Congress, 1995 1
statewide elected office, 1995 2
state legislature, 1995 30

Black elected officials, 1993
total 0
  US and state legislatures 0
  city/county/regional offices 0
  judicial/law enforcement 0
  education/school boards 0

Hispanic public officials, 1994
total 2
  state executives & legislators 1
  city/county/regional offices 1
  judicial/law enforcement 0
  education/school boards 0

GOVERNMENTAL FINANCE

State & local government revenues, (selected items), 1991-92 ($per capita)
total $3,859.15
  total general revenues 3,307.34
    from federal government 642.83
    from own sources 2,664.51
      from taxes 1,826.43
        from property taxes 458.12
        from all other taxes 1,221.02
      from charges & misc. 838.08

State & local government expenditures, (selected items), 1991-92 ($per capita)
total $3,510.53
  total direct general expenditures 3,142.86
    education 1,200.03
    libraries 13.55
    public welfare 367.23
    health & hospitals 273.68
    highways 326.31
    police protection 107.88
    fire protection 37.96
    correction 68.88
    housing & comm. development 22.61
    natural resources & parks 162.76
    interest on general debt 126.84

State & local debt, 1992 ($per capita) 1,846.91

Federal aid grants to state & local government, 1994 ($per capita total & selected items)
per capita total 686.46
  compensatory education 21.75
  waste treatment facilities 8.92
  medicaid 207.11
  housing assistance 32.92
  job training 9.89
  highway trust fund 101.60

CRIME, LAW ENFORCEMENT & COURTS

Crime, 1994 (all rates per 100,000 persons)
total crimes 46,192
overall crime rate 4,077.0
  property crimes 42,954
    burglaries 8,147
    larcenies 32,597
    motor vehicle thefts 2,210
  property crime rate 3,791.2
  violent crimes 3,238
    murders 40
    forcible rapes 316
    robberies 209
    aggravated assaults 2,673
  violent crime rate 285.8

Number of police agencies, 1994 102

Arrests, 1994
total 63,762
  persons under 18 years of age 20,034

Prisoners under state & federal jurisdiction, 1994
total 2,964
  percent change, 1993-94 . . . . 13.7%
  sentenced to more than one year
    total 2,964
    rate per 100,000 residents 258

Persons under sentence of death, 4/20/95 20

State's highest court
name . . . . Supreme Court
number of members 5
length of term . . . . 6 years
intermediate appeals court? . . . . yes

Idaho 6

LABOR & INCOME

Civilian labor force, 1994
total 591,000
  men 325,000
  women 265,000
  persons 16-19 years 51,000
  white 576,000
  black .... NA

Civilian labor force as a percent of
civilian non-institutional population, 1994
total 71.2%
  men 79.2%
  women 63.3%
  persons 16-19 years 66.4%
  white 71.2%
  black .... NA%

Employment, 1994
total 558,000
  men 307,000
  women 250,000
  persons 16-19 years 42,000
  white 545,000
  black .... NA

Full-time/part-time labor force, 1994
full-time labor force 468,000
  working part-time for
    ecomonic reasons 10,000
part-time labor force 122,000

Unemployment rate, 1994
total 5.6%
  men 5.6%
  women 5.6%
  persons 16-19 years 17.2%
  white 5.4%
  black .... NA%

Unemployed by reason for unemployment
(as a percent of total unemployment), 1994
job losers or completed temp jobs 43.2%
job leavers 13.5%
reentrants 37.9%
new entrants 5.4%

Civilian labor force, by occupation, 1994
executive/administrative/
  managerial 64,000
professional/specialty 77,000
technicians & related support 16,000

sales 66,000
adminstrative support/clerical 80,000
service occupations 84,000
precision production/craft/repair 71,000
machine operators/assemblers 34,000
transportation/material moving 28,000
handlers/helpers/laborers 25,000
farming/forestry/fishing 44,000

Civilian labor force, by industry, 1994
construction 36,000
manufacturing 88,000
transportation/communication 25,000
wholesale/retail trade 117,000
finance/real estate/insurance 24,000
services 97,000
government 95,000
agriculture 41,000

Average annual pay, 1994 (prelim.) $21,938
change in average annual pay,
  1993-1994 .... 3.5%

Hours and earnings of production workers
on manufacturing payrolls, 1994
average weekly hours 40.0
average hourly earnings $11.88
average weekly earnings $475.20

Labor union membership, 1994 38,700

Household income (in constant 1993 dollars)
median household income, 1992 .... $28,533
median household income, 1993 .... $31,010

Poverty
persons below poverty level, 1992 .... 15.2%
persons below poverty level, 1993 .... 13.1%

Personal income ($per capita)
1994
  in current dollars 18,231
  in constant (1987) dollars 14,100
1995 (projected)
  in constant (1982) dollars 11,325
2000 (projected)
  in constant (1982) dollars 12,181

Federal income tax returns, 1993
returns filed 468,361
adjusted gross income ($1000) 13,271,689
total income tax paid ($1000) 1,719,483

ECONOMY, BUSINESS, INDUSTRY & AGRICULTURE

Fortune 500 companies, 1994 3

Business incorporations, 1994
total 2,530
change, 1993-94 .... 0.8%

Business failures, 1994
total 277
rate per 10,000 concerns 68
change, 1993-94 .... -21.1%

Business firm ownership
Hispanic owned firms, 1987 974
black owned firms, 1987 94
women owned firms, 1987 19,000
foreign owned firms, 1982 46

Gross state product, 1991 ($mil)
total $19,047
   agriculture services, forestry, fisheries ... 1,602
   mining 175
   construction 890
   manufacturing—durable goods 1,973
   manufacturing—nondurable goods 1,411
   transportation, communication &
     public utilities 1,612
   wholesale trade 1,075
   retail trade 1,977
   finance/real estate/insurance 3,019
   services 2,871
   federal, state & local government 2,441

Establishments, by major industry group, 1992
total 28,914
   agriculture 590
   mining 123
   construction 3,635
   manufacturing 1,850
   transportation 1,529
   wholesale trade 2,260
   retail trade 7,188
   finance/real estate/insurance 2,420
   service industries 8,898
   unclassified 421

Payroll, by major industry group, 1992
total ($1,000) $6,592,618
   agriculture 53,600

   mining 114,227
   construction 541,021
   manufacturing 1,775,153
   transportation 437,392
   wholesale trade 527,578
   retail trade 968,446
   finance/real estate/insurance 401,777
   service industries 1,768,692
   unclassified 4,732

Agriculture
number of farms, 1994 21,000
farm acreage, 1994 14,000,000
acres per farm, 1994 659
value of farms, 1994 ($mil) 10,587
farm income, 1993 ($mil)
   gross farm income 3,314
   net farm income 1,072
   debt/asset ratio 19.6%
farm marketings, 1993 ($mil)
total $2,847
   crops 1,680
   livestock 1,167
government payments 159
farm marketings in order of marketing receipts, 1993
   1) Cattle
   2) Potatoes
   3) Dairy products
   4) Wheat

Federal economic activity ($mil, except per capita)
expenditures, 1994
   total $4,965
   per capita $4,382
   defense $401
   non-defense $4,564
defense department, 1994
   contract awards ($mil) $66
   payroll ($mil) $315
   civilian employees (x1,000) 1.5
   military personnel (x1,000) 4.3

Fishing, 1992
catch (millions of pounds) ....NA
value ($mil) ....NA

Mining, 1994 ($mil)
total non-fuel mineral production $343

Idaho 8

principal non-fuel minerals in order of value, 1994
1) Phosphate rock
2) Gold
3) Sand and gravel

Construction, 1994 ($mil)
total contracts (including
non-building) $1,790
   residential 1,043
   non-residential 494

Manufacturing, 1992
total establishments 1,838
employees, total (x1,000) 66
payroll ($mil) 1,769
production workers (x1,000) 46
value added ($mil) 4,465
value of shipments ($mil) 10,557

Finance
commercial banks, 1994
   number 21
   assets ($bil) 10.9
   deposits ($bil) 8.3
   closed or assisted 0
   deposits ($bil) .... NA
savings and loan associations, 1991
   non-current real estate loans 2.93%
   net income after taxes ($mil) 4
   return on assets .... +0.60%

Retail trade, 1992
establishments (x1,000) 7.0
sales ($mil) 7,727
annual payroll ($mil) 846
paid employees (x1,000) 74

Wholesale trade, 1992·
establishments 2,288
sales ($bil) 8.9
annual payroll ($mil) 528
paid employees (x1,000) 24.9

Service industries, 1992
establishments (x1,000) (non-exempt firms) . 7.3
receipts ($mil) (non-exempt firms) 3,440
annual payroll ($mil) 1,305
paid employees (x1,000) (non-exempt firms) .. 64

COMMUNICATION, ENERGY & TRANSPORTATION

Communication
daily newspapers, 1993 12
broadcast stations, 1990
   radio: commercial, educational 96
   television: commercial, noncommercial 12
cable TV households, 1988 165,000

Energy
consumption estimates, 1992
   total (trillion Btu) 387
   per capita (million Btu) 362.7
by source of production (trillion Btu)
   coal 10
   natural gas 50
   petroleum 123
   nuclear electric power 0
   hydroelectric power 67
by end-use sector (trillion Btu)
   residential 76
   commercial 75
   industrial 145
   transportation 91
electrical energy
   production, 1993 (billion kWh) 9.0
   net summer capability, 1993 (million kW) .. 2.3
gas utilities, 1993
   customers 168,000
   sales (trillion Btu) 23
   revenues ($mil) 110
nuclear plants, 1993 0

Transportation, 1994
public road & street mileage
total 59,897
   urban 3,462
   rural 56,435
   interstate 611
vehicle miles of travel (mil) 11,652
total motor vehicle registrations 1,034,729
   automobiles 545,163
licensed drivers 800,513
   per 1,000 driving age population 960
deaths from motor vehicle
accidents 249

Illinois 1

STATE SUMMARY

Capital City .... Springfield

Governor .... Jim Edgar

Address .... STATE CAPITOL
SPRINGFIELD, IL 62706
217 782-6830

Admitted as a state 1818

Area (square miles) 57,918

Population, 1980 11,426,518

Population, 1990 11,430,602

Population, 1994 (est.) 11,752,000

Persons per square mile, 1994 .... 211.4

Largest city .... Chicago
population, 1990 2,784,000

Personal income per capita, 1994
(in current dollars) $23,784

Gross state product ($mil), 1991 279,283

Leading industries, 1992 (by payroll)
SERVICE INDUSTRIES
MANUFACTURING
FINANCE, REAL ESTATE &
INSURANCE

Leading agricultural commodities, 1993
CORN
SOYBEANS
HOGS
CATTLE

GEOGRAPHY & ENVIRONMENT

Area (square miles)
total 57,918
land 55,593
water (includes territorial water) 2,325

Federally owned land, 1991 .... 2.7%

Highest point
name .... Charles Mound
elevation (feet) 1,235

Lowest point
name .... Mississippi River
elevation (feet) 279

General coastline (miles) 0

Tidal shoreline (miles) 0

Capital city .... Springfield
population, 1990 105,000

Largest city .... Chicago
population, 1990 2,784,000

Number of cities with over 100,000 population
1980 4

Number of cities with over 100,000 population
1990 4

State parks and Recreation areas, 1991
area (acres) 405,000
number of visitors 34,594,000
revenues $3,058,000

National forest land, 1992 (acres) 840,000

National park acreage, 1984 .... NA

DEMOGRAPHICS & CHARACTERISTICS OF THE POPULATION

Population
1970 11,110,285
1980 11,426,518
1990 11,430,602
1994 (est.) 11,752,000
2000 (revised projection) 12,168,000
2010 (revised projection) 12,652,000

Metropolitan area population
1970 9,125,000
1980 9,339,000
1992 9,757,000

Non-metropolitan area population
1970 1,986,000
1980 2,088,000
1992 1,856,000

Change in population, 1980-90
number 4,084
percent 0.04%

Persons per square mile, 1994 .... 211.4

Age distribution, 1980
under 5 years 7.4%
5 to 17 years 21.0%
65 and over 11.0%

Age distribution, 1990
under 5 years 7.4%
5 to 17 years 18.3%
65 and over 12.5%

Illinois 2

Age distribution, 2000 (projected)
under 5 years 6.6%
5 to 17 years 18.8%
65 and over 12.5%

Persons by age, 1990
under 5 years 848,141
5 to 17 years 2,098,225
65 and over 1,436,545

Median age, 1990 .... *32.80*

Race, 1990
White 8,952,978
Black 1,694,273
American Indian 20,970
Chinese 49,936
Filipino 64,224
Japanese 21,831
Asian Indian 64,200
Korean 41,506
Vietnamese 10,309
all other 509,509

Race, 2010 (projected)
White 9,801,000
Black 2,181,000

Persons of Hispanic origin, 1990
total 904,446
  Mexican 623,688
  Puerto Rican 146,059
  Cuban 18,204
  Other Hispanic 116,495

Persons by sex, 1990
male 5,552,233
female 5,878,369

Marital status, 1990
males
  15 years & older 4,282,894
    single 1,395,167
    married 2,474,607
    separated 73,642
    widowed 114,145
    divorced 298,975
females
  15 years & older 4,666,480
    single 1,184,564
    married 2,477,596
    separated 106,037

widowed 581,341
divorced 422,979

Households & families, 1990
households 4,202,240
persons per household 2.65
  families 2,924,880
    married couples 2,271,962
    female householder, no husband
      present 505,745
    one person households 1,081,113
households, 1994 4,308,000
persons per household, 1994 .... 2.66

Nativity, 1990
number of persons born in state 7,897,755
percent of total residents 69.1%

Immigration & naturalization, 1993
immigrants admitted 46,744
persons naturalized 17,394
refugees granted resident status 3,906

VITAL STATISTICS & HEALTH

Births
1992 192,483
  with low birth weight 7.7%
  to teenage mothers 12.9%
  to unmarried mothers 33.4%
1993 191,042
1994 189,228

Abortions, 1992
total 68,000
rate (per 1,000 women age 15-44) 25.4
rate per 1,000 live births 361

Adoptions, 1986
total 5,430
  related 19.4%

Deaths
1992 101,590
1993 107,563
1994 107,611

Infant deaths
1992 1,922
1993 1,975
1994 1,725

Average lifetime, 1979-1981
both sexes .... 73.37 years
men .... 69.55 years
women .... 77.13 years

Marriages
1992 93,500
1993 91,579
1994 92,719

Divorces
1992 43,612
1993 43,228
1994 43,398

Physicians, 1993
total 26,804
rate (per 1,000 persons) 2.30

Dentists, 1992
total 8,066
rate (per 1,000 persons) 0.70

Hospitals, 1993
number 208
beds (x 1,000) 44.1
average daily census (x 1,000) 28.0
occupancy rate 63.5%
personnel (x 1,000) 180.0
average cost per day to hospital $912
average cost per stay to hospital $6,318

EDUCATION

*Educational attainment of all persons
25 years and older, 1990*
less than 9th grade 750,932
high school graduates 2,187,342
bachelor's degree 989,808
graduate or professional degree 545,188

Public school enrollment, Fall, 1993
total 1,893,078
Kindergarten through grade 8 1,356,329
grades 9 through 12 536,749

Public School Teachers
total, 1994 110,874
elementary 65,188
secondary 28,207
salaries, 1994
beginning $25,171
average $39,416

*State receipts & expenditures for public
schools, 1993*
receipts ($mil) 11,010
expenditures
total ($mil) 10,043
per capita $865
per pupil $5,191

*Graduating high school seniors,
public high schools, 1995 (est)* 105,829

SAT scores, 1994
verbal 478
math 546

Institutions of higher education, 1995
total 167
public 61
private 106

*Enrollment in institutions of higher
education, Fall, 1993*
total 734,089
full-time men 181,736
full-time women 191,806
part-time men 146,735
part-time women 213,812

*Minority enrollment in institutions of higher
education, Fall, 1993*
Black, non-Hispanic 91,130
Hispanic 55,721
Asian/Pacific Islander 37,525

Earned degrees conferred, 1993
Bachelor's 51,482
First professional 4,410
Master's 22,440
Doctor's 2,601

SOCIAL INSURANCE &
WELFARE PROGRAMS

Social Security beneficiaries & benefits, 1993
beneficiaries
total 1,815,000
retired and dependents 1,298,000
survivors 318,000
disabled & dependents 200,000
annual benefit payments ($mil)
total $13,940
retired and dependents 9,668
survivors 2,879
disabled & dependents 1,393

Illinois 4

Medicare, 1993
enrollment (x1,000) 1,593
payments ($mil) 6,136

Medicaid, 1993
recipients (x1,000) 1,396
payments ($mil) 4,625

Federal public aid, 1993
recipients as a percent of population 7.9%
Aid to Families with Dependent Children
    recipients (x1,000) 709
average monthly payment $324
Supplemental Security Income
    total recipients (x1,000) 245

Food Stamp Program
participants, 1994 (x1,000) 1,189

HOUSING & CONSTRUCTION

Total housing units, 1990 4,506,275
    year round housing units 4,481,012
    vacant 304,035

New privately owned housing units
authorized, 1994
number (x1,000) 49.3
value ($mil) 5,012

New privately owned housing units
started, 1994 (x1,000) 48.2

Existing home sales, 1994 (x1,000) 188.4

GOVERNMENT & ELECTIONS

State officials, 1996
Governor (name/party/term expires)
JIM EDGAR
Republican - 1999
Lt. Governor .... Bob Kustra
Sec. of State .... George Ryan
Atty. General .... Roland Burris
Chf. Justice .... Michael Bilandic

Governorship
minimum age 25
length of term .... 4 years
number of consecutive
    terms permitted .... not specified
who succeeds .... Lt. Governor

State legislature
name .... General Assembly
    upper chamber
        name .... Senate
        number of members 59
        length of term .... 4 years
        party in majority, 1996 .... Republican
    lower chamber
        name .... House of Representatives
        number of members 118
        length of term .... 2 years
        party in majority, 1996 .... Republican

State employees October, 1992
total 164,182
October payroll ($1,000) 346,998

Local governments, 1992
total 6,810
    county 102
    municipal 1,282
    township 1,433
    school districts 997
    special districts 2,995

Voting, November, 1994
voting age population 8,561,000
    registered 63.0%
    voted 42.8%

Vote for president
1988
    Bush 2,298,648
    Dukakis 2,180,657
1992
    Clinton 2,401,611
    Bush 1,721,437
    Perot 834,152

Federal representation, 1996 (104th Congress)
Senators (name/party/term expires)

PAUL SIMON
Democrat - 1997
CAROL MOSELEY BRAUN
Democrat - 1999

Representatives, total 20
    Democrats 10
    Republicans 10
    other 0

Women holding public office
U.S. Congress, 1995 2
statewide elected office, 1995 2
state legislature, 1995 42

Black elected officials, 1993
total 465
  US and state legislatures 25
  city/county/regional offices 282
  judicial/law enforcement 37
  education/school boards 121

Hispanic public officials, 1994
total 881
  state executives & legislators 7
  city/county/regional offices 26
  judicial/law enforcement 3
  education/school boards 845

GOVERNMENTAL FINANCE

State & local government revenues, (selected items), 1991-92 ($per capita)
total $4,161.18
  total general revenues 3,536.07
    from federal government 583.51
    from own sources 2,952.55
    from taxes 2,218.60
      from property taxes 854.16
      from all other taxes 1,255.82
    from charges & misc. 733.95

State & local government expenditures, (selected items), 1991-92 ($per capita)
total $4,052.78
  total direct general expenditures 3,493.14
    education 1,156.30
    libraries 24.96
    public welfare 537.34
    health & hospitals 228.44
    highways 309.09
    police protection 149.17
    fire protection 63.40
    correction 81.00
    housing & comm. development 52.05
    natural resources & parks 129.06
    interest on general debt 210.89

State & local debt, 1992 ($per capita) 3,515.39

Federal aid grants to state & local government, 1994 ($per capita total & selected items)
per capita total 723.75
  compensatory education 24.70
  waste treatment facilities 9.01
  medicaid 236.60
  housing assistance 63.83
  job training 13.86
  highway trust fund 61.99

CRIME, LAW ENFORCEMENT & COURTS

Crime, 1994 (all rates per 100,000 persons)
total crimes 661,150
overall crime rate 5,625.9
  property crimes 548,222
    burglaries 118,116
    larcenies 363,888
    motor vehicle thefts 66,218
  property crime rate 4,664.9
  violent crimes 112,928
    murders 1,378
    forcible rapes 3,913
    robberies 43,788
    aggravated assaults 63,849
  violent crime rate 960.9

Number of police agencies, 1994 37

Arrests, 1994
total 83,693
  persons under 18 years of age 19,671

Prisoners under state & federal jurisdiction, 1994
total 36,531
percent change, 1993-94 .... 5.9%
  sentenced to more than one year
    total 36,531
    rate per 100,000 residents 310

Persons under sentence of death, 4/20/95 161

State's highest court
name .... Supreme Court
number of members 7
length of term .... 10 years
intermediate appeals court? .... yes

Illinois 6

LABOR & INCOME

Civilian labor force, 1994

total	6,000,000
men	3,224,000
women	2,775,000
persons 16-19 years	362,000
white	5,026,000
black	739,000

Civilian labor force as a percent of civilian non-institutional population, 1994

total	67.7%
men	76.5%
women	59.7%
persons 16-19 years	55.5%
white	68.9%
black	60.1%

Employment, 1994

total	5,660,000
men	3,037,000
women	2,623,000
persons 16-19 years	309,000
white	4,806,000
black	636,000

Full-time/part-time labor force, 1994

full-time labor force	4,878,000
working part-time for ecomonic reasons	48,000
part-time labor force	1,122,000

Unemployment rate, 1994

total	5.7%
men	5.8%
women	5.5%
persons 16-19 years	14.6%
white	4.4%
black	14.0%

Unemployed by reason for unemployment (as a percent of total unemployment), 1994

job losers or completed temp jobs	49.1%
job leavers	8.7%
reentrants	34.5%
new entrants	7.6%

Civilian labor force, by occupation, 1994

executive/administrative/ managerial	764,000
professional/specialty	817,000
technicians & related support	184,000
sales	711,000
adminstrative support/clerical	984,000
service occupations	794,000
precision production/craft/repair	677,000
machine operators/assemblers	412,000
transportation/material moving	230,000
handlers/helpers/laborers	286,000
farming/forestry/fishing	114,000

Civilian labor force, by industry, 1994

construction	259,000
manufacturing	1,073,000
transportation/communication	335,000
wholesale/retail trade	1,166,000
finance/real estate/insurance	434,000
services	1,447,000
government	731,000
agriculture	106,000

Average annual pay, 1994 (prelim.) $29,105
change in average annual pay, 1993-1994 ..... 2.4%

Hours and earnings of production workers on manufacturing payrolls, 1994

average weekly hours	41.9
average hourly earnings	$12.26
average weekly earnings	$513.69

Labor union membership, 1994 1,006,600

Household income (in constant 1993 dollars)

median household income, 1992	$32,496
median household income, 1993	$32,857

Poverty

persons below poverty level, 1992	15.6%
persons below poverty level, 1993	13.6%

Personal income ($per capita)

1994
in current dollars	23,784
in constant (1987) dollars	18,394

1995 (projected)
in constant (1982) dollars	15,280

2000 (projected)
in constant (1982) dollars	16,131

Federal income tax returns, 1993

returns filed	5,308,701
adjusted gross income ($1000)	186,987,904
total income tax paid ($1000)	28,529,617

Illinois 7

ECONOMY, BUSINESS, INDUSTRY & AGRICULTURE

Fortune 500 companies, 1994 40

Business incorporations, 1994
total 34,287
change, 1993-94 .... 4.7%

Business failures, 1994
total 1,749
rate per 10,000 concerns 46
change, 1993-94 .... -16.4%

Business firm ownership
Hispanic owned firms, 1987 9,636
black owned firms, 1987 19,011
women owned firms, 1987 177,100
foreign owned firms, 1982 631

Gross state product, 1991 ($mil)
total $279,283
  agriculture services, forestry, fisheries ... 3,608
  mining 1,480
  construction 11,472
  manufacturing—durable goods 27,481
  manufacturing—nondurable goods 25,834
  transportation, communication &
    public utilities 27,772
  wholesale trade 23,286
  retail trade 24,527
  finance/real estate/insurance 52,677
  services 53,888
  federal, state & local government 27,259

Establishments, by major industry group, 1992
total 280,703
  agriculture 3,662
  mining 830
  construction 25,256
  manufacturing 18,985
  transportation 12,092
  wholesale trade 24,581
  retail trade 66,469
  finance/real estate/insurance 27,858
  service industries 97,289
  unclassified 3,681

Payroll, by major industry group, 1992
total ($1,000) $122,027,562
  agriculture 437,975

  mining 686,067
  construction 6,687,724
  manufacturing 31,705,694
  transportation 9,917,776
  wholesale trade 11,954,329
  retail trade 12,158,671
  finance/real estate/insurance 13,794,881
  service industries 34,608,034
  unclassified 76,411

Agriculture
number of farms, 1994 77,000
farm acreage, 1994 28,000,000
acres per farm, 1994 368
value of farms, 1994 ($mil) 46,544
farm income, 1993 ($mil)
  gross farm income 9,161
  net farm income 1,342
  debt/asset ratio 13.8%
farm marketings, 1993 ($mil)
  total $8,082
    crops 5,835
    livestock 2,248
  government payments 851
farm marketings in order of marketing receipts, 1993
  1) Corn
  2) Soybeans
  3) Hogs
  4) Cattle

Federal economic activity ($mil, except per capita)
expenditures, 1994
  total $49,936
  per capita $4,249
  defense $3,149
  non-defense $46,788
defense department, 1994
  contract awards ($mil) $1,256
  payroll ($mil) $1,810
  civilian employees (x1,000) 16.8
  military personnel (x1,000) 27.3

Fishing, 1992
catch (millions of pounds) .... NA
value ($mil) .... NA

Mining, 1994 ($mil)
total non-fuel mineral production $770

Illinois 8

principal non-fuel minerals in order of value, 1994

1) Stone
2) Sand and gravel
3) Cement

Construction, 1994 ($mil)
total contracts (including
  non-building) $11,916
  residential 5,165
  non-residential 3,735

Manufacturing, 1992
total establishments 18,784
employees, total (x1,000) 970
payroll ($mil) 31,605
production workers (x1,000) 588
value added ($mil) 74,860
value of shipments ($mil) 158,129

Finance
commercial banks, 1994
  number 958
    assets ($bil) 212.0
    deposits ($bil) 161.2
  closed or assisted 0
    deposits ($bil) .... NA
savings and loan associations, 1991
  non-current real estate loans 1.60%
  net income after taxes ($mil) 260
  return on assets .... +0.52%

Retail trade, 1992
establishments (x1,000) 64.8
sales ($mil) 85,766
annual payroll ($mil) 10,076
paid employees (x1,000) 846

Wholesale trade, 1992
establishments 24,637
sales ($bil) 219.4
annual payroll ($mil) 10,931
paid employees (x1,000) 331.9

Service industries, 1992
establishments (x1,000) (non-exempt firms) 79.8
receipts ($mil) (non-exempt firms) 57,927
annual payroll ($mil) 22,077
paid employees (x1,000) (non-exempt firms) . 902

COMMUNICATION, ENERGY & TRANSPORTATION

Communication
daily newspapers, 1993 68
broadcast stations, 1990
  radio: commercial, educational 358
  television: commercial, noncommercial 45
cable TV households, 1988 1,911,000

Energy
consumption estimates, 1992
total (trillion Btu) 3,487
per capita (million Btu) 300.3
by source of production (trillion Btu)
  coal 693
  natural gas 1,011
  petroleum 1,143
  nuclear electric power 787
  hydroelectric power 1
by end-use sector (trillion Btu)
  residential 852
  commercial 636
  industrial 1,238
  transportation 762
electrical energy
  production, 1993 (billion kWh) 140.1
  net summer capability, 1993 (million kW) . 32.8
gas utilities, 1993
  customers 3,665,000
  sales (trillion Btu) 632
  revenues ($mil) 3,216
nuclear plants, 1993 13

Transportation, 1994
public road & street mileage
total 137,149
  urban 35,312
  rural 101,837
  interstate 2,054
vehicle miles of travel (mil) 92,316
total motor vehicle registrations 8,697,854
  automobiles 6,226,009
licensed drivers 7,502,201
  per 1,000 driving age population 835
deaths from motor vehicle
  accidents 1,554

Indiana 1

STATE SUMMARY
Capital City .... Indianapolis

Governor ....Evan Bayh

Address .... STATE HOUSE
INDIANAPOLIS, IN 46204
317 232-4567

Admitted as a state 1816

Area (square miles) 36,420

Population, 1980 5,490,224

Population, 1990 5,544,159

Population, 1994 (est.) 5,752,000

Persons per square mile, 1994 .... 160.4

Largest city .... Indianapolis
population, 1990 731,000

Personal income per capita, 1994
(in current dollars) $20,378

Gross state product ($mil), 1991 114,211

Leading industries, 1992 (by payroll)
MANUFACTURING
SERVICE INDUSTRIES
RETAIL TRADE

Leading agricultural commodities, 1993
CORN
SOYBEANS
HOGS
CATTLE

GEOGRAPHY & ENVIRONMENT
Area (square miles)
total 36,420
land 35,870
water (includes territorial water) 550

Federally owned land, 1991 .... 1.7%

Highest point
name ....Franklin Twp., Wayne County
elevation (feet) 1,257

Lowest point
name .... Ohio River
elevation (feet) 320

General coastline (miles) 0

Tidal shoreline (miles) 0

Capital city .... Indianapolis
population, 1990 731,000

Largest city .... Indianapolis
population, 1990 731,000

Number of cities with over 100,000 population
1980 5

Number of cities with over 100,000 population
1990 5

State parks and Recreation areas, 1991
area (acres) 57,000
number of visitors 10,536,000
revenues $9,011,000

National forest land, 1992 (acres) 644,000

National park acreage, 1984 9,700

DEMOGRAPHICS & CHARACTERISTICS OF THE POPULATION
Population
1970 5,195,392
1980 5,490,224
1990 5,544,159
1994 (est.) 5,752,000
2000 (revised projection) 6,045,000
2010 (revised projection) 6,286,000

Metropolitan area population
1970 3,551,000
1980 3,719,000
1992 4,052,000

Non-metropolitan area population
1970 1,644,000
1980 1,771,000
1992 1,606,000

Change in population, 1980-90
number 53,935
percent 0.98%

Persons per square mile, 1994 .... 160.4

Age distribution, 1980
under 5 years 7.6%
5 to 17 years 21.9%
65 and over 10.7%

Age distribution, 1990
under 5 years 7.2%
5 to 17 years 19.0%
65 and over 12.5%

Indiana 2

Age distribution, 2000 (projected)
under 5 years 6.4%
5 to 17 years 18.7%
65 and over 13.0%

Persons by age, 1990
under 5 years 398,656
5 to 17 years 1,057,308
65 and over 696,196

Median age, 1990 .... *32.80*

Race, 1990
White 5,020,700
Black 432,092
American Indian 12,453
Chinese 7,371
Filipino 4,754
Japanese 4,715
Asian Indian 7,095
Korean 5,475
Vietnamese 2,467
all other 46,770

Race, 2010 (projected)
White 5,587,000
Black 582,000

Persons of Hispanic origin, 1990
total 98,788
  Mexican 66,736
  Puerto Rican 14,021
  Cuban 1,853
  Other Hispanic 16,178

Persons by sex, 1990
male 2,688,281
female 2,855,878

Marital status, 1990
males
  15 years & older 2,064,662
  single 569,459
  married 1,268,941
    separated 24,707
  widowed 50,574
  divorced 175,688
females
  15 years & older 2,263,865
  single 481,644
  married 1,272,465
    separated 33,317

  widowed 274,357
  divorced 235,399

Households & families, 1990
households 2,065,355
persons per household 2.61
  families 1,480,351
    married couples 1,202,020
    female householder, no husband
      present 217,628
    one person households 496,841
households, 1994 2,161,000
persons per household, 1994 .... 2.59

Nativity, 1990
number of persons born in state 3,940,076
percent of total residents 71.1%

Immigration & naturalization, 1993
immigrants admitted 4,539
persons naturalized 1,395
refugees granted resident status 457

VITAL STATISTICS & HEALTH

Births
1992 83,832
  with low birth weight 6.7%
  to teenage mothers 14.1%
  to unmarried mothers 29.5%
1993 84,644
1994 83,381

Abortions, 1992
total 16,000
rate (per 1,000 women age 15-44) 12.0
rate per 1,000 live births 185

Adoptions, 1986
total 3,791
  related 60.6%

Deaths
1992 50,144
1993 52,210
1994 53,290

Infant deaths
1992 796
1993 790
1994 793

116

Indiana 3

Average lifetime, 1979-1981
both sexes . . . . 73.84 years
  men . . . . 70.16 years
  women . . . . 77.46 years

Marriages
1992 50,372
1993 49,764
1994 50,282

Divorces
1992 . . . . NA
1993 . . . . NA
1994 . . . . NA

Physicians, 1993
total 9,611
rate (per 1,000 persons) 1.68

Dentists, 1992
total 2,798
rate (per 1,000 persons) 0.49

Hospitals, 1993
number 115
beds (x 1,000) 21.3
average daily census (x 1,000) 12.5
occupancy rate 58.7%
personnel (x 1,000) 90.6
average cost per day to hospital $898
average cost per stay to hospital $5,677

EDUCATION

*Educational attainment of all persons
25 years and older, 1990*
less than 9th grade 297,423
high school graduates 1,333,093
bachelor's degree 321,278
graduate or professional degree 221,663

Public school enrollment, Fall, 1993
total 965,599
  Kindergarten through grade 8 679,006
  grades 9 through 12 286,593

Public School Teachers
total, 1994 55,107
  elementary 27,649
  secondary 24,948
salaries, 1994
  beginning $22,021
  average $35,741

*State receipts & expenditures for public
schools, 1993*
receipts ($mil) 5,805
expenditures
  total ($mil) 5,821
  per capita $1,029
  per pupil $5,641

*Graduating high school seniors,
public high schools, 1995 (est)* 58,969

SAT scores, 1994
verbal 410
math 466

Institutions of higher education, 1995
total 78
  public 28
  private 50

*Enrollment in institutions of higher
education, Fall, 1993*
total 294,685
full-time men 94,283
full-time women 97,858
part-time men 41,745
part-time women 60,799

*Minority enrollment in institutions of higher
education, Fall, 1993*
Black, non-Hispanic 17,539
Hispanic 5,752
Asian/Pacific Islander 4,774

Earned degrees conferred, 1993
Bachelor's 31,453
First professional 1,496
Master's 6,874
Doctor's 1,107

SOCIAL INSURANCE &
WELFARE PROGRAMS

Social Security beneficiaries & benefits, 1993
beneficiaries
total 951,000
  retired and dependents 667,000
  survivors 165,000
  disabled & dependents 120,000
annual benefit payments ($mil)
total $7,161
  retired and dependents 4,877
  survivors 1,476
  disabled & dependents 808

Indiana 4

Medicare, 1993
enrollment (x1,000) 803
payments ($mil) 2,877

Medicaid, 1993
recipients (x1,000) 565
payments ($mil) 2,354

Federal public aid, 1993
recipients as a percent of population 5.1%
Aid to Families with Dependent Children
  recipients (x1,000) 220
average monthly payment $235
Supplemental Security Income
  total recipients (x1,000) 82

Food Stamp Program
  participants, 1994 (x1,000) 521

HOUSING & CONSTRUCTION

Total housing units, 1990 2,246,046
  year round housing units 2,208,981
  vacant 180,691

New privately owned housing units authorized, 1994
number (x1,000) 34.4
value ($mil) 3,324

New privately owned housing units started, 1994 (x1,000) 41.4

Existing home sales, 1994 (x1,000) 103.3

GOVERNMENT & ELECTIONS

State officials, 1996
  Governor (name/party/term expires)
            EVAN BAYH
          Democrat - 1996
Lt. Governor .... Frank O'Bannon
Sec. of State .... Joseph Hogsett
Atty. General .... Pamela Carter
Chf. Justice .... Randall T. Shepard

Governorship
minimum age 30
length of term .... 4 years
number of consecutive
  terms permitted 2
who succeeds .... Lt. Governor

State legislature
name .... General Assembly
  upper chamber
    name .... Senate
    number of members 50
    length of term .... 4 years
    party in majority, 1996 .... Republican
  lower chamber
    name .... House of Representatives
    number of members 100
    length of term .... 2 years
    party in majority, 1996 .... Democratic

State employees October, 1992
total 115,618
October payroll ($1,000) 227,829

Local governments, 1992
total 2,976
  county 91
  municipal 566
  township 1,008
  school districts 310
  special districts 1,000

Voting, November, 1994
voting age population 4,191,000
  registered 55.6%
  voted 38.7%

Vote for president
1988
  Bush 1,280,292
  Dukakis 850,851
1992
  Clinton 837,546
  Bush 969,689
  Perot 450,107

Federal representation, 1996 (104th Congress)
Senators (name/party/term expires)

        RICHARD G. LUGAR
         Republican - 2001
           DAN COATS
         Republican - 1999

Representatives, total 10
  Democrats 4
  Republicans 6
  other 0

Indiana 5

Women holding public office
U.S. Congress, 1995 0
statewide elected office, 1995 4
state legislature, 1995 33

Black elected officials, 1993
total 72
  US and state legislatures 12
  city/county/regional offices 50
  judicial/law enforcement 4
  education/school boards 6

Hispanic public officials, 1994
total 8
  state executives & legislators 1
  city/county/regional offices 5
  judicial/law enforcement 1
  education/school boards 1

GOVERNMENTAL FINANCE

State & local government revenues, (selected items), 1991-92 ($per capita)
total $3,769.95
  total general revenues 3,365.44
    from federal government 593.12
    from own sources 2,772.33
    from taxes 1,879.88
      from property taxes 572.92
      from all other taxes 1,247.67
    from charges & misc. 892.44

State & local government expenditures, (selected items), 1991-92 ($per capita)
total $3,545.32
  total direct general expenditures 3,218.19
    education 1,304.70
    libraries 23.05
    public welfare 482.00
    health & hospitals 347.89
    highways 211.57
    police protection 76.49
    fire protection 39.85
    correction 71.20
    housing & comm. development 37.62
    natural resources & parks 63.34
    interest on general debt 123.83

State & local debt, 1992 ($per capita) 2,225.64

Federal aid grants to state & local government, 1994 ($per capita total & selected items)
per capita total 617.74
  compensatory education 17.79
  waste treatment facilities 5.39
  medicaid 276.65
  housing assistance 34.79
  job training 8.85
  highway trust fund 61.43

CRIME, LAW ENFORCEMENT & COURTS

Crime, 1994 (all rates per 100,000 persons)
total crimes 264,180
  overall crime rate 4,592.8
    property crimes 233,975
      burglaries 48,921
      larcenies 160,043
      motor vehicle thefts 25,011
    property crime rate 4,067.7
    violent crimes 30,205
      murders 453
      forcible rapes 2,046
      robberies 7,490
      aggravated assaults 20,216
    violent crime rate 525.1

Number of police agencies, 1994 108

Arrests, 1994
total 150,746
  persons under 18 years of age 38,756

Prisoners under state & federal jurisdiction, 1994
total 15,014
percent change, 1993-94 .... 3.8%
  sentenced to more than one year
    total 14,925
    rate per 100,000 residents 258

Persons under sentence of death, 4/20/95 50

State's highest court
name .... Supreme Court
number of members 5
length of term .... 10 years
intermediate appeals court? .... yes

119

Indiana 6

LABOR & INCOME

Civilian labor force, 1994
total 3,056,000
  men 1,601,000
  women 1,455,000
  persons 16-19 years 205,000
  white 2,801,000
  black 224,000

Civilian labor force as a percent of
civilian non-institutional population, 1994
total 69.9%
  men 78.3%
  women 62.5%
  persons 16-19 years 59.4%
  white 70.7%
  black 60.9%

Employment, 1994
total 2,905,000
  men 1,529,000
  women 1,377,000
  persons 16-19 years 176,000
  white 2,690,000
  black 186,000

Full-time/part-time labor force, 1994
full-time labor force 2,497,000
  working part-time for
    ecomonic reasons 27,000
part-time labor force 559,000

Unemployment rate, 1994
total 4.9%
  men 4.5%
  women 5.4%
  persons 16-19 years 14.0%
  white 4.0%
  black 17.0%

Unemployed by reason for unemployment
(as a percent of total unemployment), 1994
job losers or completed temp jobs 42.8%
job leavers 9.7%
reentrants 39.3%
new entrants 8.1%

Civilian labor force, by occupation, 1994
executive/administrative/
  managerial 325,000
professional/specialty 294,000
technicians & related support 82,000

sales 349,000
adminstrative support/clerical 430,000
service occupations 414,000
precision production/craft/repair 406,000
machine operators/assemblers 356,000
transportation/material moving 144,000
handlers/helpers/laborers 170,000
farming/forestry/fishing ....NA

Civilian labor force, by industry, 1994
construction 149,000
manufacturing 770,000
transportation/communication 143,000
wholesale/retail trade 594,000
finance/real estate/insurance 170,000
services 618,000
government 324,000
agriculture ....NA

Average annual pay, 1994 (prelim.) $24,908
change in average annual pay,
  1993-1994 .... 3.3%

Hours and earnings of production workers
on manufacturing payrolls, 1994
average weekly hours 43.2
average hourly earnings $13.56
average weekly earnings $585.79

Labor union membership, 1994 494,300

Household income (in constant 1993 dollars)
median household income, 1992 .... $29,384
median household income, 1993 .... $29,475

Poverty
persons below poverty level, 1992 .... 11.8%
persons below poverty level, 1993 .... 12.2%

Personal income ($per capita)
1994
  in current dollars 20,378
  in constant (1987) dollars 15,760
1995 (projected)
  in constant (1982) dollars 13,201
2000 (projected)
  in constant (1982) dollars 14,031

Federal income tax returns, 1993
returns filed 2,548,815
adjusted gross income ($1000) 78,734,412
total income tax paid ($1000) 10,882,796

ECONOMY, BUSINESS, INDUSTRY & AGRICULTURE

Fortune 500 companies, 1994 6

Business incorporations, 1994
total 11,987
change, 1993-94 .... 3.9%

Business failures, 1994
total 904
rate per 10,000 concerns 56
change, 1993-94 .... -17.7%

Business firm ownership
Hispanic owned firms, 1987 1,427
black owned firms, 1987 5,867
women owned firms, 1987 89,900
foreign owned firms, 1982 186

Gross state product, 1991 ($mil)
total $114,211
  agriculture services, forestry, fisheries ... 1,758
  mining 647
  construction 4,828
  manufacturing—durable goods 21,910
  manufacturing—nondurable goods 11,409
  transportation, communication &
    public utilities 10,566
  wholesale trade 6,678
  retail trade 11,415
  finance/real estate/insurance 16,637
  services 16,794
  federal, state & local government 11,567

Establishments, by major industry group, 1992
total 133,377
  agriculture 1,913
  mining 396
  construction 13,467
  manufacturing 9,363
  transportation 5,619
  wholesale trade 10,115
  retail trade 34,415
  finance/real estate/insurance 11,618
  service industries 44,918
  unclassified 1,553

Payroll, by major industry group, 1992
total ($1,000) $49,537,167
  agriculture 174,207

  mining 255,107
  construction 3,046,305
  manufacturing 19,397,596
  transportation 3,501,285
  wholesale trade 3,187,331
  retail trade 5,378,980
  finance/real estate/insurance 3,280,421
  service industries 11,297,084
  unclassified 18,851

Agriculture
number of farms, 1994 63,000
farm acreage, 1994 16,000,000
acres per farm, 1994 254
value of farms, 1994 ($mil) 23,569
farm income, 1993 ($mil)
  gross farm income 5,770
  net farm income 832
  debt/asset ratio 16.5%
farm marketings, 1993 ($mil)
  total $5,118
  crops 3,186
  livestock 1,932
government payments 379
farm marketings in order of marketing receipts, 1993
  1) Corn
  2) Soybeans
  3) Hogs
  4) Cattle

Federal economic activity
  ($mil, except per capita)
expenditures, 1994
  total $22,104
  per capita $3,843
  defense $2,470
  non-defense $19,634
defense department, 1994
  contract awards ($mil) $1,319
  payroll ($mil) $1,170
  civilian employees (x1,000) 14.3
  military personnel (x1,000) 3.8

Fishing, 1992
catch (millions of pounds) .... NA
value ($mil) .... NA

Mining, 1994 ($mil)
total non-fuel mineral production $517

Indiana 8

principal non-fuel minerals in order of value, 1994

1) Stone
2) Cement
3) Sand and gravel

Construction, 1994 ($mil)
total contracts (including
  non-building) $7,629
    residential 3,792
    non-residential 2,614

Manufacturing, 1992
total establishments 9,285
employees, total (x1,000) 619
payroll ($mil) 19,114
production workers (x1,000) 435
value added ($mil) 49,662
value of shipments ($mil) 104,871

Finance
commercial banks, 1994
  number 237
    assets ($bil) 61.5
    deposits ($bil) 49.5
  closed or assisted 0
    deposits ($bil) .... NA
savings and loan associations, 1991
  non-current real estate loans 1.12%
  net income after taxes ($mil) 112
  return on assets .... +0.84%

Retail trade, 1992
establishments (x1,000) 33.4
sales ($mil) 42,373
annual payroll ($mil) 4,772
paid employees (x1,000) 442

Wholesale trade, 1992
establishments 10,264
sales ($bil) 52.4
annual payroll ($mil) 3,052
paid employees (x1,000) 115.7

Service industries, 1992
establishments (x1,000) (non-exempt firms) 34.5
receipts ($mil) (non-exempt firms) 17,548
annual payroll ($mil) 6,742
paid employees (x1,000) (non-exempt firms) . 355

COMMUNICATION, ENERGY & TRANSPORTATION

Communication
daily newspapers, 1993 73
broadcast stations, 1990
  radio: commercial, educational 246
  television: commercial, noncommercial 37
cable TV households, 1988 1,017,000

Energy
consumption estimates, 1992
total (trillion Btu) 2,408
per capita (million Btu) 425.5
by source of production (trillion Btu)
  coal 1,297
  natural gas 489
  petroleum 808
  nuclear electric power 0
  hydroelectric power 6
by end-use sector (trillion Btu)
  residential 426
  commercial 271
  industrial 1,154
  transportation 556
electrical energy
  production, 1993 (billion kWh) 100.0
  net summer capability, 1993 (million kW) . 20.9
gas utilities, 1993
  customers 1,573,000
  sales (trillion Btu) 306
  revenues ($mil) 1,567
nuclear plants, 1993 0

Transportation, 1994
public road & street mileage
total 92,476
  urban 19,315
  rural 73,161
  interstate 1,138
vehicle miles of travel (mil) 62,108
total motor vehicle registrations 4,888,635
  automobiles 3,230,511
licensed drivers 3,860,329
  per 1,000 driving age population 868
deaths from motor vehicle
  accidents 974

STATE SUMMARY

Capital City .... Des Moines

Governor .... Terry E. Branstad

Address .... STATE CAPITOL
DES MOINES, IA 50319
515 281-5211

Admitted as a state 1846

Area (square miles) 56,276

Population, 1980 2,913,808

Population, 1990 2,776,755

Population, 1994 (est.) 2,829,000

Persons per square mile, 1994 .... 50.6

Largest city .... Des Moines
population, 1990 193,000

Personal income per capita, 1994
(in current dollars) $20,265

Gross state product ($mil), 1991 56,032

Leading industries, 1992 (by payroll)
MANUFACTURING
SERVICE INDUSTRIES
RETAIL TRADE

Leading agricultural commodities, 1993
HOGS
CORN
CATTLE
SOYBEANS

GEOGRAPHY & ENVIRONMENT

Area (square miles)
total 56,276
land 55,875
water (includes territorial water) 401

Federally owned land, 1991 .... 0.9%

Highest point
name ...... Sec. 29 T 100N R 41W (Oscealo Co.)
elevation (feet) 1,670

Lowest point
name .... Mississippi River
elevation (feet) 480

General coastline (miles) 0

Tidal shoreline (miles) 0

Capital city .... Des Moines
population, 1990 193,000

Largest city .... Des Moines
population, 1990 193,000

Number of cities with over 100,000 population
1980 2

Number of cities with over 100,000 population
1990 2

State parks and Recreation areas, 1991
area (acres) 82,000
number of visitors 12,111,000
revenues $1,571,000

National forest land, 1992 (acres) 0

National park acreage, 1984 1,700

DEMOGRAPHICS & CHARACTERISTICS OF THE POPULATION

Population
1970 2,825,368
1980 2,913,808
1990 2,776,755
1994 (est.) 2,829,000
2000 (revised projection) 2,930,000
2010 (revised projection) 2,981,000

Metropolitan area population
1970 1,154,000
1980 1,223,000
1992 1,228,000

Non-metropolitan area population
1970 1,671,000
1980 1,691,000
1992 1,575,000

Change in population, 1980-90
number .... -137,053
percent .... -4.70%

Persons per square mile, 1994 .... 50.6

Age distribution, 1980
under 5 years 7.6%
5 to 17 years 20.7%
65 and over 13.3%

Age distribution, 1990
under 5 years 7.0%
5 to 17 years 18.9%
65 and over 15.3%

Iowa 2

Age distribution, 2000 (projected)
under 5 years 6.1%
5 to 17 years 18.2%
65 and over 15.5%

Persons by age, 1990
under 5 years 193,203
5 to 17 years 525,677
65 and over 426,106

Median age, 1990 .... *34.00*

Race, 1990
White 2,683,090
Black 48,090
American Indian 7,217
Chinese 4,442
Filipino 1,607
Japanese 1,619
Asian Indian 3,021
Korean 4,618
Vietnamese 2,882
all other 20,037

Race, 2010 (projected)
White 2,841,000
Black 78,000

Persons of Hispanic origin, 1990
total 32,647
Mexican 24,386
Puerto Rican 1,270
Cuban 488
Other Hispanic 6,503

Persons by sex, 1990
male 1,344,802
female 1,431,953

Marital status, 1990
males
15 years & older 1,033,960
single 281,081
married 656,858
separated 9,933
widowed 27,309
divorced 68,712
females
15 years & older 1,136,037
single 232,630
married 658,571
separated 13,418

widowed 154,259
divorced 90,577

Households & families, 1990
households 1,064,325
persons per household 2.52
families 740,819
married couples 629,893
female householder, no husband
present 85,141
one person households 275,466
households, 1994 1,082,000
persons per household, 1994 .... 2.52

Nativity, 1990
number of persons born in state 2,154,669
percent of total residents 77.6%

Immigration & naturalization, 1993
immigrants admitted 2,626
persons naturalized 578
refugees granted resident status 654

VITAL STATISTICS & HEALTH

Births
1992 38,120
with low birth weight 5.7%
to teenage mothers 10.2%
to unmarried mothers 23.5%
1993 37,044
1994 35,926

Abortions, 1992
total 7,000
rate (per 1,000 women age 15-44) 11.4
rate per 1,000 live births 185

Adoptions, 1986
total 1,504
related 52.1%

Deaths
1992 27,002
1993 27,862
1994 26,352

Infant deaths
1992 296
1993 257
1994 253

Iowa 3

Average lifetime, 1979-1981
both sexes .... 75.81 years
　men .... 72.00 years
　women .... 79.60 years

Marriages
1992 22,088
1993 25,006
1994 22,732

Divorces
1992 10,956
1993 10,903
1994 10,930

Physicians, 1993
total 4,470
rate (per 1,000 persons) 1.59

Dentists, 1992
total 1,528
rate (per 1,000 persons) 0.54

Hospitals, 1993
number 119
beds (x 1,000) 13.4
average daily census (x 1,000) 7.7
occupancy rate 57.9%
personnel (x 1,000) 44.1
average cost per day to hospital $612
average cost per stay to hospital $4,980

EDUCATION

*Educational attainment of all persons
　25 years and older, 1990*
less than 9th grade 163,335
high school graduates 684,368
bachelor's degree 207,269
graduate or professional degree 92,123

Public school enrollment, Fall, 1993
total 498,519
　Kindergarten through grade 8 348,006
　grades 9 through 12 150,513

Public School Teachers
total, 1994 31,616
　elementary 18,321
　secondary 12,188
salaries, 1994
　beginning $20,709
　average $30,760

*State receipts & expenditures for public
　schools, 1993*
receipts ($mil) 2,616
expenditures
　total ($mil) 2,642
　per capita $943
　per pupil $5,297

*Graduating high school seniors,
　public high schools, 1995 (est)* 31,671

SAT scores, 1994
verbal 506
math 574

Institutions of higher education, 1995
total 60
　public 20
　private 40

*Enrollment in institutions of higher
　education, Fall, 1993*
total 172,797
full-time men 60,629
full-time women 61,612
part-time men 18,549
part-time women 32,007

*Minority enrollment in institutions of higher
　education, Fall, 1993*
Black, non-Hispanic 4,979
Hispanic 2,435
Asian/Pacific Islander 3,303

Earned degrees conferred, 1993
Bachelor's 17,598
First professional 1,534
Master's 3,517
Doctor's 683

SOCIAL INSURANCE & WELFARE PROGRAMS

Social Security beneficiaries & benefits, 1993
beneficiaries
total 535,000
　retired and dependents 393,000
　survivors 91,000
　disabled & dependents 52,000
annual benefit payments ($mil)
total $3,871
　retired and dependents 2,727
　survivors 805
　disabled & dependents 339

Iowa 4

Medicare, 1993
enrollment (x1,000) 469
payments ($mil) 1,305

Medicaid, 1993
recipients (x1,000) 289
payments ($mil) 896

Federal public aid, 1993
recipients as a percent of population 4.9%
Aid to Families with Dependent Children
  recipients (x1,000) 109
average monthly payment $370
Supplemental Security Income
  total recipients (x1,000) 39

Food Stamp Program
  participants, 1994 (x1,000) 196

HOUSING & CONSTRUCTION

Total housing units, 1990 1,143,669
  year round housing units 1,128,973
  vacant 79,344

New privately owned housing units authorized, 1994
number (x1,000) 12.5
value ($mil) 998

New privately owned housing units started, 1994 (x1,000) 13.6

Existing home sales, 1994 (x1,000) 54.3

GOVERNMENT & ELECTIONS

State officials, 1996
  Governor (name/party/term expires)
      TERRY E. BRANSTAD
      Republican - 1999
Lt. Governor .... Joy Corning
Sec. of State .... Paul Danny Pate
Atty. General .... Tom Miller
Chf. Justice .... Arthur A. McGirverin

Governorship
minimum age 30
length of term .... 4 years
number of consecutive
  terms permitted .... not specified
who succeeds .... Lt. Governor

State legislature
name .... General Assembly
  upper chamber
    name .... Senate
    number of members 50
    length of term .... 4 years
    party in majority, 1996 .... Democratic
  lower chamber
    name .... House of Representatives
    number of members 100
    length of term .... 2 years
    party in majority, 1996 .... Republican

State employees October, 1992
total 60,418
October payroll ($1,000) 136,016

Local governments, 1992
total 1,904
  county 99
  municipal 953
  township 0
  school districts 445
  special districts 406

Voting, November, 1994
voting age population 2,059,000
  registered 71.7%
  voted 52.5%

Vote for president
1988
  Bush 541,540
  Dukakis 667,085
1992
  Clinton 583,150
  Bush 502,806
  Perot 250,851

Federal representation, 1996 (104th Congress)
Senators (name/party/term expires)

TOM HARKIN
Democrat - 1997
CHARLES E. GRASSLEY
Republican - 1999

Representatives, total 5
  Democrats 1
  Republicans 4
  other 0

Women holding public office
U.S. Congress, 1995 0
statewide elected office, 1995 1
state legislature, 1995 27

Black elected officials, 1993
total 11
   US and state legislatures 1
   city/county/regional offices 6
   judicial/law enforcement 1
   education/school boards 3

Hispanic public officials, 1994
total .... NA
   state executives & legislators .... NA
   city/county/regional offices .... NA
   judicial/law enforcement .... NA
   education/school boards .... NA

GOVERNMENTAL FINANCE

State & local government revenues, (selected items), 1991-92 ($per capita)
total $4,153.39
   total general revenues 3,634.58
     from federal government 620.72
     from own sources 3,013.85
     from taxes 2,042.78
      from property taxes 714.99
      from all other taxes 1,159.04
     from charges & misc. 971.08

State & local government expenditures, (selected items), 1991-92 ($per capita)
total $4,009.78
   total direct general expenditures 3,642.84
   education 1,427.30
   libraries 18.91
   public welfare 500.28
   health & hospitals 389.47
   highways 443.68
   police protection 93.87
   fire protection 31.63
   correction 48.77
   housing & comm. development 25.00
   natural resources & parks 122.09
   interest on general debt 126.07

State & local debt, 1992 ($per capita) 1,926.65

Federal aid grants to state & local government, 1994 ($per capita total & selected items)
per capita total 712.36
   compensatory education 17.41
   waste treatment facilities 8.65
   medicaid 245.07
   housing assistance 32.47
   job training 12.53
   highway trust fund 87.26

CRIME, LAW ENFORCEMENT & COURTS

Crime, 1994 (all rates per 100,000 persons)
total crimes 103,389
overall crime rate 3,654.6
   property crimes 94,475
     burglaries 18,872
     larcenies 70,507
     motor vehicle thefts 5,096
   property crime rate 3,339.5
   violent crimes 8,914
     murders 47
     forcible rapes 666
     robberies 1,327
     aggravated assaults 6,874
   violent crime rate 315.1

Number of police agencies, 1994 184

Arrests, 1994
total 87,257
   persons under 18 years of age 16,940

Prisoners under state & federal jurisdiction, 1994
total 5,437
percent change, 1993-94 .... 11.0%
   sentenced to more than one year
     total 5,437
     rate per 100,000 residents 192

Persons under sentence of death, 4/20/95 .... NA

State's highest court
name .... Supreme Court
number of members 9
length of term .... 8 years
intermediate appeals court? .... yes

Iowa 6

LABOR & INCOME

Civilian labor force, 1994
total 1,565,000
  men 844,000
  women 721,000
  persons 16-19 years 106,000
  white 1,522,000
  black .... NA

Civilian labor force as a percent of
civilian non-institutional population, 1994
total 73.1%
  men 80.9%
  women 65.6%
  persons 16-19 years 68.2%
  white 73.3%
  black .... NA%

Employment, 1994
total 1,508,000
  men 811,000
  women 697,000
  persons 16-19 years 94,000
  white 1,468,000
  black .... NA

Full-time/part-time labor force, 1994
full-time labor force 1,210,000
  working part-time for
    ecomonic reasons 12,000
part-time labor force 356,000

Unemployment rate, 1994
total 3.7%
  men 3.9%
  women 3.4%
  persons 16-19 years 11.2%
  white 3.5%
  black .... NA%

Unemployed by reason for unemployment
(as a percent of total unemployment), 1994
job losers or completed temp jobs 44.6%
job leavers 10.9%
reentrants 39.3%
new entrants 5.3%

Civilian labor force, by occupation, 1994
executive/administrative/
  managerial 166,000
professional/specialty 194,000
technicians & related support 42,000

sales 182,000
adminstrative support/clerical 215,000
service occupations 223,000
precision production/craft/repair 165,000
machine operators/assemblers 110,000
transportation/material moving 71,000
handlers/helpers/laborers 62,000
farming/forestry/fishing 131,000

Civilian labor force, by industry, 1994
construction 65,000
manufacturing 252,000
transportation/communication 66,000
wholesale/retail trade 295,000
finance/real estate/insurance 81,000
services 309,000
government 218,000
agriculture 135,000

Average annual pay, 1994 (prelim.) $22,187
change in average annual pay,
  1993-1994 .... 3.5%

Hours and earnings of production workers
on manufacturing payrolls, 1994
average weekly hours 42.4
average hourly earnings $12.47
average weekly earnings $528.73

Labor union membership, 1994 161,000

Household income (in constant 1993 dollars)
median household income, 1992 .... $29,603
median household income, 1993 .... $28,663

Poverty
persons below poverty level, 1992 .... 11.5%
persons below poverty level, 1993 .... 10.3%

Personal income ($per capita)
1994
  in current dollars 20,265
  in constant (1987) dollars 15,673
1995 (projected)
  in constant (1982) dollars 12,998
2000 (projected)
  in constant (1982) dollars 13,849

Federal income tax returns, 1993
returns filed 1,256,442
adjusted gross income ($1000) 35,719,321
total income tax paid ($1000) 4,648,062

ECONOMY, BUSINESS, INDUSTRY & AGRICULTURE

Fortune 500 companies, 1994 2

Business incorporations, 1994
total 4,915
change, 1993-94 .... 2.3%

Business failures, 1994
total 473
rate per 10,000 concerns 40
change, 1993-94 .... -6.9%

Business firm ownership
Hispanic owned firms, 1987 475
black owned firms, 1987 703
women owned firms, 1987 53,600
foreign owned firms, 1982 115

Gross state product, 1991 ($mil)
total $56,032
  agriculture services, forestry, fisheries ... 3,994
  mining 99
  construction 1,844
  manufacturing—durable goods 6,747
  manufacturing—nondurable goods 6,018
  transportation, communication &
    public utilities 4,633
  wholesale trade 3,875
  retail trade 5,141
  finance/real estate/insurance 9,072
  services 8,019
  federal, state & local government 6,590

Establishments, by major industry group, 1992
total 75,971
  agriculture 1,163
  mining 197
  construction 6,874
  manufacturing 3,949
  transportation 4,066
  wholesale trade 6,820
  retail trade 20,304
  finance/real estate/insurance 6,962
  service industries 24,664
  unclassified 972

Payroll, by major industry group, 1992
total ($1,000) $20,709,355
  agriculture 112,884

  mining 53,100
  construction 1,148,593
  manufacturing 6,447,541
  transportation 1,389,523
  wholesale trade 1,736,592
  retail trade 2,615,835
  finance/real estate/insurance 1,897,425
  service industries 5,297,752
  unclassified 10,110

Agriculture
number of farms, 1994 100,000
farm acreage, 1994 33,000,000
acres per farm, 1994 332
value of farms, 1994 ($mil) 43,838
farm income, 1993 ($mil)
  gross farm income 10,221
  net farm income 462
  debt/asset ratio 18.9%
farm marketings, 1993 ($mil)
total $10,001
  crops 4,173
  livestock 5,829
government payments 1,230
farm marketings in order of marketing receipts, 1993
    1) Hogs
    2) Corn
    3) Cattle
    4) Soybeans

Federal economic activity
  ($mil, except per capita)
expenditures, 1994
  total $12,979
  per capita $4,588
  defense $564
  non-defense $12,416
defense department, 1994
  contract awards ($mil) $309
  payroll ($mil) $236
  civilian employees (x1,000) 1.4
  military personnel (x1,000) 0.4

Fishing, 1992
catch (millions of pounds) .... NA
value ($mil) .... NA

Mining, 1994 ($mil)
total non-fuel mineral production $426

Iowa 8

principal non-fuel minerals in order of value, 1994
1) Stone
2) Cement
3) Sand and gravel

Construction, 1994 ($mil)
total contracts (including
non-building) $2,705
   residential 944
   non-residential 972

Manufacturing, 1992
total establishments 3,913
employees, total (x1,000) 227
payroll ($mil) 6,484
production workers (x1,000) 158
value added ($mil) 20,502
value of shipments ($mil) 46,432

Finance
commercial banks, 1994
   number 530
   assets ($bil) 38.7
   deposits ($bil) 32.0
   closed or assisted 0
   deposits ($bil) .... NA
savings and loan associations, 1991
   non-current real estate loans 3.09%
   net income after taxes ($mil) 12
   return on assets .... +0.21%

Retail trade, 1992
establishments (x1,000) 19.7
sales ($mil) 19,960
annual payroll ($mil) 2,304
paid employees (x1,000) 226

Wholesale trade, 1992
establishments 6,971
sales ($bil) 29.4
annual payroll ($mil) 1,639
paid employees (x1,000) 69.4

Service industries, 1992
establishments (x1,000) (non-exempt firms) 17.8
receipts ($mil) (non-exempt firms) 7,711
annual payroll ($mil) 2,899
paid employees (x1,000) (non-exempt firms) . 163

COMMUNICATION, ENERGY & TRANSPORTATION

Communication
daily newspapers, 1993 39
broadcast stations, 1990
   radio: commercial, educational 210
   television: commercial, noncommercial 26
cable TV households, 1988 570,000

Energy
consumption estimates, 1992
total (trillion Btu) 927
per capita (million Btu) 330.6
by source of production (trillion Btu)
   coal 327
   natural gas 232
   petroleum 320
   nuclear electric power 36
   hydroelectric power 10
by end-use sector (trillion Btu)
   residential 203
   commercial 139
   industrial 361
   transportation 224
electrical energy
   production, 1993 (billion kWh) 31.0
   net summer capability, 1993 (million kW) .. 8.1
gas utilities, 1993
   customers 958,000
   sales (trillion Btu) 176
   revenues ($mil) 854
nuclear plants, 1993 1

Transportation, 1994
public road & street mileage
total 112,793
   urban 9,319
   rural 103,474
   interstate 785
vehicle miles of travel (mil) 25,737
total motor vehicle registrations 2,765,878
   automobiles 1,806,075
licensed drivers 1,896,518
   per 1,000 driving age population 868
deaths from motor vehicle
   accidents 478

STATE SUMMARY

Capital City .... Topeka

Governor .... Bill Graves

Address .... STATE CAPITOL
TOPEKA, KS 66612
913 296-3232

Admitted as a state 1861

Area (square miles) 82,282

Population, 1980 2,363,679

Population, 1990 2,477,574

Population, 1994 (est.) 2,554,000

Persons per square mile, 1994 .... 31.2

Largest city .... Wichita
population, 1990 304,000

Personal income per capita, 1994
(in current dollars) $20,896

Gross state product ($mil), 1991 53,281

Leading industries, 1992 (by payroll)
MANUFACTURING
SERVICE INDUSTRIES
RETAIL TRADE

Leading agricultural commodities, 1993
CATTLE
WHEAT
CORN
SORGHUM GRAIN

GEOGRAPHY & ENVIRONMENT

Area (square miles)
total 82,282
land 81,823
water (includes territorial water) 459

Federally owned land, 1991 .... 0.8%

Highest point
name .... Mt. Sunflower
elevation (feet) 4,039

Lowest point
name .... Verdigris River
elevation (feet) 679

General coastline (miles) 0

Tidal shoreline (miles) 0

Capital city .... Topeka
population, 1990 120,000

Largest city .... Wichita
population, 1990 304,000

Number of cities with over 100,000 population
1980 3

Number of cities with over 100,000 population
1990 4

State parks and Recreation areas, 1991
area (acres) 30,000
number of visitors 4,117,000
revenues $2,426,000

National forest land, 1992 (acres) 116,000

National park acreage, 1984 700

DEMOGRAPHICS & CHARACTERISTICS OF THE POPULATION

Population
1970 2,249,071
1980 2,363,679
1990 2,477,574
1994 (est.) 2,554,000
2000 (revised projection) 2,722,000
2010 (revised projection) 2,922,000

Metropolitan area population
1970 1,109,000
1980 1,184,000
1992 1,374,000

Non-metropolitan area population
1970 1,140,000
1980 1,180,000
1992 1,141,000

Change in population, 1980-90
number 113,895
percent 4.82%

Persons per square mile, 1994 .... 31.2

Age distribution, 1980
under 5 years 7.7%
5 to 17 years 19.8%
65 and over 13.0%

Age distribution, 1990
under 5 years 7.6%
5 to 17 years 19.1%
65 and over 13.8%

131

Kansas 2

Age distribution, 2000 (projected)
under 5 years 6.5%
5 to 17 years 18.4%
65 and over 14.1%

Persons by age, 1990
under 5 years 188,390
5 to 17 years 473,224
65 and over 342,571

Median age, 1990 .... 32.90

Race, 1990
White 2,231,986
Black 143,076
American Indian 21,767
Chinese 5,330
Filipino 2,548
Japanese 2,037
Asian Indian 3,956
Korean 4,016
Vietnamese 6,577
all other 56,083

Race, 2010 (projected)
White 2,588,000
Black 198,000

Persons of Hispanic origin, 1990
total 93,670
Mexican 75,798
Puerto Rican 3,570
Cuban 1,403
Other Hispanic 12,899

Persons by sex, 1990
male 1,214,645
female 1,262,929

Marital status, 1990
males
15 years & older 924,895
single 244,866
married 585,864
separated 9,846
widowed 22,096
divorced 72,069
females
15 years & older 988,835
single 189,997
married 581,241
separated 12,874

widowed 122,731
divorced 94,866

Households & families, 1990
households 944,726
persons per household 2.53
families 658,600
married couples 552,495
female householder, no husband
present 81,433
one person households 245,156
households, 1994 966,000
persons per household, 1994 .... 2.56

Nativity, 1990
number of persons born in state ... 1,519,904
percent of total residents 61.3%

Immigration & naturalization, 1993
immigrants admitted 3,225
persons naturalized 1,085
refugees granted resident status .. 623

VITAL STATISTICS & HEALTH

Births
1992 37,484
with low birth weight 6.4%
to teenage mothers 12.4%
to unmarried mothers 24.3%
1993 38,040
1994 33,272

Abortions, 1992
total 13,000
rate (per 1,000 women age 15-44) .. 22.4
rate per 1,000 live births 353

Adoptions, 1986
total 990
related 50.4%

Deaths
1992 22,160
1993 23,337
1994 23,524

Infant deaths
1992 313
1993 312
1994 293

Kansas 3

Average lifetime, 1979-1981
both sexes .... 75.31 years
  men .... 71.60 years
  women .... 78.99 years

Marriages
1992 21,703
1993 21,117
1994 20,914

Divorces
1992 13,198
1993 12,035
1994 12,093

Physicians, 1993
total 4,643
rate (per 1,000 persons) 1.85

Dentists, 1992
total 1,322
rate (per 1,000 persons) 0.53

Hospitals, 1993
number 134
beds (x 1,000) 11.3
average daily census (x 1,000) 6.1
occupancy rate 54.2%
personnel (x 1,000) 36.3
average cost per day to hospital $666
average cost per stay to hospital $5,108

EDUCATION

Educational attainment of all persons 25 years and older, 1990
less than 9th grade 120,951
high school graduates 514,177
bachelor's degree 221,016
graduate or professional degree 109,361

Public school enrollment, Fall, 1993
total 457,614
  Kindergarten through grade 8 329,708
  grades 9 through 12 127,906

Public School Teachers
total, 1994 30,283
  elementary 14,712
  secondary 12,561
salaries, 1994
  beginning $22,624
  average $31,700

State receipts & expenditures for public schools, 1993
receipts ($mil) 2,572
expenditures
  total ($mil) 2,575
  per capita $1,024
  per pupil $5,459

Graduating high school seniors, public high schools, 1995 (est) 26,090

SAT scores, 1994
verbal 494
math 550

Institutions of higher education, 1995
total 52
  public 29
  private 23

Enrollment in institutions of higher education, Fall, 1993
total 170,135
full-time men 48,178
full-time women 49,373
part-time men 27,220
part-time women 45,364

Minority enrollment in institutions of higher education, Fall, 1993
Black, non-Hispanic 7,902
Hispanic 4,314
Asian/Pacific Islander 3,434

Earned degrees conferred, 1993
Bachelor's 14,282
First professional 601
Master's 3,920
Doctor's 387

SOCIAL INSURANCE & WELFARE PROGRAMS

Social Security beneficiaries & benefits, 1993
beneficiaries
total 426,000
  retired and dependents 312,000
  survivors 73,000
  disabled & dependents 42,000
annual benefit payments ($mil)
total $3,142
  retired and dependents 2,234
  survivors 641
  disabled & dependents 267

Kansas 4

Medicare, 1993
enrollment (x1,000) 376
payments ($mil) 1,350

Medicaid, 1993
recipients (x1,000) 243
payments ($mil) 702

Federal public aid, 1993
recipients as a percent of population 4.7%
Aid to Families with Dependent Children
  recipients (x1,000) 87
average monthly payment $346
Supplemental Security Income
  total recipients (x1,000) 33

Food Stamp Program
  participants, 1994 (x1,000) 192

HOUSING & CONSTRUCTION

Total housing units, 1990 1,044,112
  year round housing units 1,036,581
  vacant 99,386

New privately owned housing units authorized, 1994
number (x1,000) 13.0
value ($mil) 1,177

New privately owned housing units started, 1994 (x1,000) 13.8

Existing home sales, 1994 (x1,000) 55.7

GOVERNMENT & ELECTIONS

State officials, 1996
  Governor (name/party/term expires)
      BILL GRAVES
      Republican - 1999
Lt. Governor . . . . Sheila Framm
Sec. of State . . . . Ron Thornburgh
Atty. General . . . . Carla Stovall
Chf. Justice . . . . Richard Holmes

Governorship
minimum age . . . . not specified
length of term . . . . 4 years
number of consecutive
  terms permitted 2
who succeeds . . . . Lt. Governor

State legislature
name . . . . Legislature
  upper chamber
      name . . . . Senate
      number of members 40
      length of term . . . . 4 years
      party in majority, 1996 . . . . Republican
  lower chamber
      name . . . . House of Representatives
      number of members 125
      length of term . . . . 2 years
      party in majority, 1996 . . . . Republican

State employees October, 1992
total 56,168
October payroll ($1,000) 100,811

Local governments, 1992
total 3,918
  county 105
  municipal 627
  township 1,355
  school districts 324
  special districts 1,506

Voting, November, 1994
voting age population 1,798,000
  registered 65.3%
  voted 50.5%

Vote for president
1988
  Bush 552,659
  Dukakis 422,056
1992
  Clinton 387,488
  Bush 445,790
  Perot 309,523

Federal representation, 1996 (104th Congress)
Senators (name/party/term expires)

      NANCY L. KASSEBAUM
      Republican - 1997
      ROBERT DOLE
      Republican - 1999

Representatives, total 4
  Democrats 0
  Republicans 4
  other 0

Kansas 5

GOVERNMENTAL FINANCE

State & local government revenues, (selected items), 1991-92 ($per capita)
total $3,975.79
  total general revenues 3,400.39
    from federal government 568.39
    from own sources 2,832.00
    from taxes 1,979.86
    from property taxes 733.67
    from all other taxes 1,105.79
    from charges & misc. 852.15

State & local government expenditures, (selected items), 1991-92 ($per capita)
total $3,849.70
  total direct general expenditures 3,429.57
    education 1,402.86
    libraries 15.70
    public welfare 364.49
    health & hospitals 295.48
    highways 376.63
    police protection 107.84
    fire protection 44.49
    correction 83.60
    housing & comm. development 20.07
    natural resources & parks 108.87
    interest on general debt 178.87

State & local debt, 1992 ($per capita) 2,869.57

Federal aid grants to state & local government, 1994 ($per capita total & selected items)
per capita total 652.48
  compensatory education 20.37
  waste treatment facilities 6.36
  medicaid 235.70
  housing assistance 25.49
  job training 7.19
  highway trust fund 84.34

CRIME, LAW ENFORCEMENT & COURTS

Crime, 1994 (all rates per 100,000 persons)
total crimes 124,987
overall crime rate 4,893.8
  property crimes 112,761
    burglaries 28,635
    larcenies 75,459
    motor vehicle thefts 8,667
  property crime rate 4,415.1
  violent crimes 12,226
    murders 149
    forcible rapes 947
    robberies 3,060
    aggravated assaults 8,070
  violent crime rate 478.7

Number of police agencies, 1994 .... NA

Arrests, 1994
total .... NA
  persons under 18 years of age .... NA

Prisoners under state & federal jurisdiction, 1994
total 6,373
percent change, 1993-94 .... 11.3%
sentenced to more than one year
  total 6,373
  rate per 100,000 residents 249

Persons under sentence of death, 4/20/95 0

State's highest court
name .... Supreme Court
number of members 7
length of term .... 6 years
intermediate appeals court? .... yes

135

Kansas 6

LABOR & INCOME

Civilian labor force, 1994

total	1,331,000
men	707,000
women	624,000
persons 16-19 years	97,000
white	1,220,000
black	79,000

Civilian labor force as a percent of civilian non-institutional population, 1994

total	70.8%
men	78.4%
women	63.8%
persons 16-19 years	64.9%
white	71.4%
black	64.6%

Employment, 1994

total	1,261,000
men	667,000
women	593,000
persons 16-19 years	82,000
white	1,164,000
black	68,000

Full-time/part-time labor force, 1994

full-time labor force	1,057,000
working part-time for ecomonic reasons	10,000
part-time labor force	273,000

Unemployment rate, 1994

total	5.3%
men	5.6%
women	5.0%
persons 16-19 years	16.1%
white	4.6%
black	14.0%

Unemployed by reason for unemployment (as a percent of total unemployment), 1994

job losers or completed temp jobs	43.1%
job leavers	9.3%
reentrants	41.8%
new entrants	5.8%

Civilian labor force, by occupation, 1994

executive/administrative/ managerial	157,000
professional/specialty	182,000
technicians & related support	36,000
sales	149,000
adminstrative support/clerical	215,000
service occupations	190,000
precision production/craft/repair	128,000
machine operators/assemblers	87,000
transportation/material moving	54,000
handlers/helpers/laborers	50,000
farming/forestry/fishing	79,000

Civilian labor force, by industry, 1994

construction	53,000
manufacturing	214,000
transportation/communication	78,000
wholesale/retail trade	246,000
finance/real estate/insurance	67,000
services	270,000
government	213,000
agriculture	80,000

Average annual pay, 1994 (prelim.) $22,900

change in average annual pay, 1993-1994	2.1%

Hours and earnings of production workers on manufacturing payrolls, 1994

average weekly hours	41.6
average hourly earnings	$12.14
average weekly earnings	$505.02

Labor union membership, 1994 106,400

Household income (in constant 1993 dollars)

median household income, 1992	$31,254
median household income, 1993	$29,770

Poverty

persons below poverty level, 1992	11.1%
persons below poverty level, 1993	13.1%

Personal income ($per capita)

1994	
in current dollars	20,896
in constant (1987) dollars	16,161
1995 (projected)	
in constant (1982) dollars	14,055
2000 (projected)	
in constant (1982) dollars	14,986

Federal income tax returns, 1993

returns filed	1,108,625
adjusted gross income ($1000)	34,461,922
total income tax paid ($1000)	4,749,185

ECONOMY, BUSINESS, INDUSTRY & AGRICULTURE

Fortune 500 companies, 1994 2

Business incorporations, 1994
total 4,273
change, 1993-94 .... -3.2%

Business failures, 1994
total 870
rate per 10,000 concerns 89
change, 1993-94 .... -18.6%

Business firm ownership
Hispanic owned firms, 1987 1,541
black owned firms, 1987 2,323
women owned firms, 1987 53,500
foreign owned firms, 1982 131

Gross state product, 1991 ($mil)
total $53,281
  agriculture services, forestry, fisheries ... 2,330
  mining 858
  construction 1,713
  manufacturing—durable goods 4,970
  manufacturing—nondurable goods 5,312
  transportation, communication &
    public utilities 6,159
  wholesale trade 3,802
  retail trade 5,067
  finance/real estate/insurance 7,997
  services 8,157
  federal, state & local government 6,916

Establishments, by major industry group, 1992
total 67,630
  agriculture 1,104
  mining 1,134
  construction 6,066
  manufacturing 3,511
  transportation 3,232
  wholesale trade 5,747
  retail trade 16,839
  finance/real estate/insurance 6,500
  service industries 22,531
  unclassified 966

Payroll, by major industry group, 1992
total ($1,000) $19,244,346
  agriculture 75,902
  mining 363,599
  construction 1,110,317
  manufacturing 5,220,325
  transportation 1,667,662
  wholesale trade 1,754,857
  retail trade 2,423,499
  finance/real estate/insurance 1,561,871
  service industries 5,055,141
  unclassified 11,173

Agriculture
number of farms, 1994 65,000
farm acreage, 1994 48,000,000
acres per farm, 1994 735
value of farms, 1994 ($mil) 25,647
farm income, 1993 ($mil)
  gross farm income 8,605
  net farm income 1,623
  debt/asset ratio 17.9%
farm marketings, 1993 ($mil)
  total $7,363
  crops 2,493
  livestock 4,870
government payments 784
farm marketings in order of marketing
receipts, 1993
    1) Cattle
    2) Wheat
    3) Corn
    4) Soybeans

Federal economic activity
  ($mil, except per capita)
expenditures, 1994
  total $12,506
  per capita $4,897
  defense $2,073
  non-defense $10,433
defense department, 1994
  contract awards ($mil) $580
  payroll ($mil) $1,266
  civilian employees (x1,000) 6.2
  military personnel (x1,000) 21.9

Fishing, 1992
catch (millions of pounds) .... NA
value ($mil) .... NA

Mining, 1994 ($mil)
total non-fuel mineral production $495

Kansas 8

principal non-fuel minerals in order of value, 1994
1) Stone
2) Salt
3) Helium

Construction, 1994 ($mil)
total contracts (including
  non-building) $3,146
    residential 1,401
    non-residential 936

Manufacturing, 1992
total establishments 3,464
employees, total (x1,000) 189
payroll ($mil) 5,261
production workers (x1,000) 126
value added ($mil) 15,156
value of shipments ($mil) 36,095

Finance
commercial banks, 1994
  number 490
    assets ($bil) 30.3
    deposits ($bil) 25.5
  closed or assisted 1
    deposits ($bil) 5
savings and loan associations, 1991
  non-current real estate loans 0.96%
  net income after taxes ($mil) 21
  return on assets .... +0.14%

Retail trade, 1992
establishments (x1,000) 16.3
sales ($mil) 17,567
annual payroll ($mil) 2,022
paid employees (x1,000) 186

Wholesale trade, 1992
establishments 5,854
sales ($bil) 34.9
annual payroll ($mil) 1,638
paid employees (x1,000) 61.8

Service industries, 1992
establishments (x1,000) (non-exempt firms) 16.9
receipts ($mil) (non-exempt firms) 8,460
annual payroll ($mil) 3,168
paid employees (x1,000) (non-exempt firms) . 162

COMMUNICATION, ENERGY & TRANSPORTATION

Communication
daily newspapers, 1993 47
broadcast stations, 1990
  radio: commercial, educational 160
  television: commercial, noncommercial 20
cable TV households, 1988 561,000

Energy
consumption estimates, 1992
total (trillion Btu) 1,014
per capita (million Btu) 402.9
by source of production (trillion Btu)
  coal 254
  natural gas 339
  petroleum 396
  nuclear electric power 91
  hydroelectric power 0
by end-use sector (trillion Btu)
  residential 170
  commercial 162
  industrial 425
  transportation 257
electrical energy
  production, 1993 (billion kWh) 36.4
  net summer capability, 1993 (million kW) .. 9.7
gas utilities, 1993
  customers 870,000
  sales (trillion Btu) 158
  revenues ($mil) 673
nuclear plants, 1993 1

Transportation, 1994
public road & street mileage
total 133,280
  urban 9,596
  rural 123,684
  interstate 872
vehicle miles of travel (mil) 24,678
total motor vehicle registrations 2,082,957
  automobiles 1,093,876
licensed drivers 1,771,566
  per 1,000 driving age population 915
deaths from motor vehicle
  accidents 442

Kentucky 1

STATE SUMMARY

Capital City . . . . Frankfort

Governor . . . . Paul Patton

Address . . . . STATE CAPITOL
FRANKFORT, KY 40601
502 564-2611

Admitted as a state 1792

Area (square miles) 40,411

Population, 1980 3,660,777

Population, 1990 3,685,296

Population, 1994 (est.) 3,827,000

Persons per square mile, 1994 . . . . 96.3

Largest city . . . . Louisville
population, 1990 269,000

Personal income per capita, 1994
(in current dollars) $17,807

Gross state product ($mil), 1991 69,839

Leading industries, 1992 (by payroll)
MANUFACTURING
SERVICE INDUSTRIES
RETAIL TRADE

Leading agricultural commodities, 1993
TOBACCO
CATTLE
HORSES
DAIRY PRODUCTS

GEOGRAPHY & ENVIRONMENT

Area (square miles)
total 40,411
land 39,732
water (includes territorial water) 679

Federally owned land, 1991 . . . . 4.2%

Highest point
name . . . . Black Mountain
elevation (feet) 4,139

Lowest point
name . . . . Mississippi River
elevation (feet) 257

General coastline (miles) 0

Tidal shoreline (miles) 0

Capital city . . . . Frankfort
population, 1990 26,000

Largest city . . . . Louisville
population, 1990 269,000

Number of cities with over 100,000 population
1980 2

Number of cities with over 100,000 population
1990 2

State parks and Recreation areas, 1991
area (acres) 42,000
number of visitors 27,272,000
revenues $37,668,000

National forest land, 1992 (acres) 2,102,000

National park acreage, 1984 79,300

DEMOGRAPHICS & CHARACTERISTICS OF THE POPULATION

Population
1970 3,220,711
1980 3,660,777
1990 3,685,296
1994 (est.) 3,827,000
2000 (revised projection) 3,989,000
2010 (revised projection) 4,160,000

Metropolitan area population
1970 1,550,000
1980 1,677,000
1992 1,820,000

Non-metropolitan area population
1970 1,671,000
1980 1,984,000
1992 1,934,000

Change in population, 1980-90
number 24,519
percent 0.67%

Persons per square mile, 1994 . . . . 96.3

Age distribution, 1980
under 5 years 7.7%
5 to 17 years 21.8%
65 and over 11.2%

Age distribution, 1990
under 5 years 6.8%
5 to 17 years 19.0%
65 and over 12.6%

Kentucky 2

Age distribution, 2000 (projected)
under 5 years 6.2%
5 to 17 years 18.0%
65 and over 13.2%

Persons by age, 1990
under 5 years 250,871
5 to 17 years 703,223
65 and over 466,845

Median age, 1990 .... *33.00*

Race, 1990
White 3,391,832
Black 262,907
American Indian 5,614
Chinese 2,736
Filipino 2,193
Japanese 2,513
Asian Indian 2,922
Korean 2,972
Vietnamese 1,506
all other 9,946

Race, 2010 (projected)
White 3,769,000
Black 345,000

Persons of Hispanic origin, 1990
total 21,984
  Mexican 8,692
  Puerto Rican 3,682
  Cuban 1,075
  Other Hispanic 8,535

Persons by sex, 1990
male 1,785,235
female 1,900,061

Marital status, 1990
males
  15 years & older 1,378,871
    single 361,278
    married 871,978
    separated 19,937
    widowed 36,071
    divorced 109,544
females
  15 years & older 1,514,810
    single 293,241
    married 873,810
    separated 28,705

widowed 200,233
divorced 147,526

Households & families, 1990
households 1,379,782
persons per household 2.60
  families 1,015,998
    married couples 816,732
    female householder, no husband
      present 159,660
    one person households 321,247
households, 1994 1,440,000
persons per household, 1994 .... 2.59

Nativity, 1990
number of persons born in state 2,851,449
percent of total residents 77.4%

Immigration & naturalization, 1993
immigrants admitted 2,182
persons naturalized 534
refugees granted resident status 286

VITAL STATISTICS & HEALTH

Births
1992 53,906
  with low birth weight 6.8%
  to teenage mothers 16.5%
  to unmarried mothers 26.3%
1993 52,256
1994 51,926

Abortions, 1992
total 10,000
rate (per 1,000 women age 15-44) 11.4
rate per 1,000 live births 191

Adoptions, 1986
total 1,040
  related 62.1%

Deaths
1992 35,341
1993 36,921
1994 37,407

Infant deaths
1992 469
1993 462
1994 401

Kentucky 3

Average lifetime, 1979-1981
both sexes .... 73.06 years
men .... 69.14 years
women .... 77.12 years

Marriages
1992 49,922
1993 45,544
1994 47,322

Divorces
1992 24,185
1993 21,840
1994 22,211

Physicians, 1993
total 6,740
rate (per 1,000 persons) 1.79

Dentists, 1992
total 2,113
rate (per 1,000 persons) 0.57

Hospitals, 1993
number 106
beds (x 1,000) 15.9
average daily census (x 1,000) 9.9
occupancy rate 62.2%
personnel (x 1,000) 58.5
average cost per day to hospital $703
average cost per stay to hospital $4,749

EDUCATION

*Educational attainment of all persons
25 years and older, 1990*
less than 9th grade 442,579
high school graduates 741,012
bachelor's degree 189,539
graduate or professional degree 128,588

Public school enrollment, Fall, 1993
total 655,265
  Kindergarten through grade 8 467,315
  grades 9 through 12 187,950

Public School Teachers
total, 1994 37,324
  elementary 26,178
  secondary 11,146
salaries, 1994
  beginning $21,257
  average $31,639

*State receipts & expenditures for public
schools, 1993*
receipts ($mil) 3,340
expenditures
  total ($mil) 3,158
  per capita $841
  per pupil $4,942

*Graduating high school seniors,
public high schools, 1995 (est)* 36,431

SAT scores, 1994
verbal 474
math 523

Institutions of higher education, 1995
total 62
  public 22
  private 40

*Enrollment in institutions of higher
education, Fall, 1993*
total 187,332
full-time men 54,597
full-time women 66,751
part-time men 23,505
part-time women 42,479

*Minority enrollment in institutions of higher
education, Fall, 1993*
Black, non-Hispanic 12,454
Hispanic 1,073
Asian/Pacific Islander 1,797

Earned degrees conferred, 1993
Bachelor's 14,396
First professional 985
Master's 4,195
Doctor's 328

SOCIAL INSURANCE &
WELFARE PROGRAMS
Social Security beneficiaries & benefits, 1993
beneficiaries
total 687,000
  retired and dependents 415,000
  survivors 140,000
  disabled & dependents 133,000
annual benefit payments ($mil)
total $4,509
  retired and dependents 2,622
  survivors 1,068
  disabled & dependents 820

Kentucky 4

Medicare, 1993
enrollment (x1,000) 565
payments ($mil) 1,959

Medicaid, 1993
recipients (x1,000) 618
payments ($mil) 1,707

Federal public aid, 1993
recipients as a percent of population 9.5%
Aid to Families with Dependent Children
recipients (x1,000) 211
average monthly payment $211
Supplemental Security Income
total recipients (x1,000) 146

Food Stamp Program
participants, 1994 (x1,000) 522

HOUSING & CONSTRUCTION

Total housing units, 1990 1,506,845
year round housing units 1,485,686
vacant 127,063

New privately owned housing units authorized, 1994
number (x1,000) 18.6
value ($mil) 1,370

New privately owned housing units started, 1994 (x1,000) 22.5

Existing home sales, 1994 (x1,000) 81.1

GOVERNMENT & ELECTIONS

State officials, 1996
Governor (name/party/term expires)
PAUL PATTON
Democrat - 2000
Lt. Governor .... Steve Henry
Sec. of State .... John Y. Brown, III
Atty. General .... Ben Chandler, III
Chf. Justice .... Robert F. Stephens

Governorship
minimum age 30
length of term .... 4 years
number of consecutive
terms permitted .... none
who succeeds .... Lt. Governor

State legislature
name .... General Assembly
upper chamber
name .... Senate
number of members 38
length of term .... 4 years
party in majority, 1996 .... Democratic
lower chamber
name .... House of Representatives
number of members 100
length of term .... 2 years
party in majority, 1996 .... Democratic

State employees October, 1992
total 85,605
October payroll ($1,000) 166,307

Local governments, 1992
total 1,345
county 119
municipal 438
township 0
school districts 177
special districts 610

Voting, November, 1994
voting age population 2,807,000
registered 62.5%
voted 34.5%

Vote for president
1988
Bush 731,446
Dukakis 579,077
1992
Clinton 662,693
Bush 614,895
Perot 203,273

Federal representation, 1996 (104th Congress)
Senators (name/party/term expires)

MITCH McCONNELL
Republican - 1997
WENDELL H. FORD
Democrat - 1999

Representatives, total 6
Democrats 4
Republicans 2
other 0

Kentucky 5

Women holding public office
U.S. Congress, 1995 0
statewide elected office, 1995 1
state legislature, 1995 11

Black elected officials, 1993
total 63
  US and state legislatures 4
  city/county/regional offices 47
  judicial/law enforcement 5
  education/school boards 7

Hispanic public officials, 1994
total ....NA
  state executives & legislators ....NA
  city/county/regional offices ....NA
  judicial/law enforcement ....NA
  education/school boards ....NA

GOVERNMENTAL FINANCE

State & local government revenues, (selected items), 1991-92 ($per capita)
total $3,837.71
  total general revenues 3,294.15
    from federal government 751.98
    from own sources 2,542.18
    from taxes 1,774.45
      from property taxes 300.18
      from all other taxes 1,257.84
    from charges & misc. 767.73

State & local government expenditures, (selected items), 1991-92 ($per capita)
total $3,653.50
  total direct general expenditures 3,219.61
  education 1,080.60
  libraries 11.50
  public welfare 647.92
  health & hospitals 219.22
  highways 286.11
  police protection 81.01
  fire protection 36.24
  correction 71.16
  housing & comm. development 31.93
  natural resources & parks 109.98
  interest on general debt 272.19

State & local debt, 1992 ($per capita) 4,232.98

Federal aid grants to state & local government, 1994 ($per capita total & selected items)
per capita total 809.03
  compensatory education 30.40
  waste treatment facilities 3.67
  medicaid 347.64
  housing assistance 47.10
  job training 12.81
  highway trust fund 62.47

CRIME, LAW ENFORCEMENT & COURTS

Crime, 1994 (all rates per 100,000 persons)
total crimes 133,890
overall crime rate 3,498.6
  property crimes 110,725
    burglaries 28,718
    larcenies 73,449
    motor vehicle thefts 8,558
  property crime rate 2,893.3
  violent crimes 23,165
    murders 244
    forcible rapes 1,350
    robberies 3,595
    aggravated assaults 17,976
  violent crime rate 605.3

Number of police agencies, 1994 378

Arrests, 1994
total 113,630
  persons under 18 years of age 11,644

Prisoners under state & federal jurisdiction, 1994
total 11,066
percent change, 1993-94 ....6.0%
  sentenced to more than one year
    total 11,066
    rate per 100,000 residents 288

Persons under sentence of death, 4/20/95 27

State's highest court
name ....Supreme Court
number of members 7
length of term ....6 years
intermediate appeals court? ....yes

143

Kentucky 6

LABOR & INCOME

Civilian labor force, 1994
total 1,825,000
  men 973,000
  women 853,000
  persons 16-19 years 106,000
  white 1,706,000
  black 101,000

Civilian labor force as a percent of civilian non-institutional population, 1994
total 62.4%
  men 70.3%
  women 55.3%
  persons 16-19 years 51.3%
  white 62.5%
  black 59.9%

Employment, 1994
total 1,727,000
  men 917,000
  women 811,000
  persons 16-19 years 88,000
  white 1,620,000
  black 90,000

Full-time/part-time labor force, 1994
full-time labor force 1,479,000
  working part-time for
    ecomonic reasons 19,000
part-time labor force 347,000

Unemployment rate, 1994
total 5.4%
  men 5.8%
  women 4.9%
  persons 16-19 years 17.5%
  white 5.0%
  black 11.2%

Unemployed by reason for unemployment (as a percent of total unemployment), 1994
job losers or completed temp jobs 40.6%
job leavers 13.0%
reentrants 36.1%
new entrants 10.3%

Civilian labor force, by occupation, 1994
executive/administrative/
  managerial 196,000
professional/specialty 217,000
technicians & related support 61,000
sales 202,000
adminstrative support/clerical 262,000
service occupations 253,000
precision production/craft/repair 230,000
machine operators/assemblers 135,000
transportation/material moving 99,000
handlers/helpers/laborers 98,000
farming/forestry/fishing 61,000

Civilian labor force, by industry, 1994
construction 87,000
manufacturing 305,000
transportation/communication 111,000
wholesale/retail trade 344,000
finance/real estate/insurance 81,000
services 372,000
government 271,000
agriculture 60,000

Average annual pay, 1994 (prelim.) $22,747
change in average annual pay,
  1993-1994 .... 2.6%

Hours and earnings of production workers on manufacturing payrolls, 1994
average weekly hours 41.3
average hourly earnings $11.82
average weekly earnings $488.17

Labor union membership, 1994 171,300

Household income (in constant 1993 dollars)
median household income, 1992 .... $24,188
median household income, 1993 .... $24,376

Poverty
persons below poverty level, 1992 .... 19.7%
persons below poverty level, 1993 .... 20.4%

Personal income ($per capita)
1994
  in current dollars 17,807
  in constant (1987) dollars 13,772
1995 (projected)
  in constant (1982) dollars 11,402
2000 (projected)
  in constant (1982) dollars 12,178

Federal income tax returns, 1993
returns filed 1,549,407
adjusted gross income ($1000) 43,119,227
total income tax paid ($1000) 5,602,738

Kentucky 7

ECONOMY, BUSINESS, INDUSTRY & AGRICULTURE

Fortune 500 companies, 1994 3

Business incorporations, 1994
total 7,688
change, 1993-94 . . . . -0.9%

Business failures, 1994
total 706
rate per 10,000 concerns 69
change, 1993-94 . . . . -16.4%

Business firm ownership
Hispanic owned firms, 1987 359
black owned firms, 1987 3,738
women owned firms, 1987 53,500
foreign owned firms, 1982 140

Gross state product, 1991 ($mil)
total $69,839
  agriculture services, forestry, fisheries . . . 2,328
  mining 2,381
  construction 2,521
  manufacturing—durable goods 8,056
  manufacturing—nondurable goods 9,114
  transportation, communication &
    public utilities 6,451
  wholesale trade 3,704
  retail trade 6,625
  finance/real estate/insurance 9,487
  services 9,834
  federal, state & local government 9,338

Establishments, by major industry group, 1992
total 81,344
  agriculture 1,067
  mining 1,083
  construction 7,543
  manufacturing 4,344
  transportation 4,058
  wholesale trade 5,880
  retail trade 22,769
  finance/real estate/insurance 6,703
  service industries 27,071
  unclassified 826

Payroll, by major industry group, 1992
total ($1,000) $25,192,993
  agriculture 104,654

  mining 1,043,260
  construction 1,380,184
  manufacturing 7,503,487
  transportation 2,129,188
  wholesale trade 1,884,212
  retail trade 3,176,969
  finance/real estate/insurance 1,600,838
  service industries 6,355,900
  unclassified 14,301

Agriculture
number of farms, 1994 89,000
farm acreage, 1994 14,000,000
acres per farm, 1994 158
value of farms, 1994 ($mil) 16,127
farm income, 1993 ($mil)
  gross farm income 3,778
  net farm income 1,135
  debt/asset ratio 14.1%
farm marketings, 1993 ($mil)
total $3,376
  crops 1,656
  livestock 1,720
government payments 97
farm marketings in order of marketing receipts, 1993
    1) Tobacco
    2) Cattle
    3) Horses
    4) Dairy products

*Federal economic activity
  ($mil, except per capita)*
expenditures, 1994
  total $17,504
  per capita $4,574
  defense $2,618
  non-defense $14,886
defense department, 1994
  contract awards ($mil) $769
  payroll ($mil) $1,902
  civilian employees (x1,000) 12.2
  military personnel (x1,000) 33.6

Fishing, 1992
catch (millions of pounds) . . . . NA
value ($mil) . . . . NA

Mining, 1994 ($mil)
total non-fuel mineral production $431

Kentucky 8

principal non-fuel minerals in order of value, 1994
1) Stone
2) Lime
3) Cement

Construction, 1994 ($mil)
total contracts (including
  non-building) $4,262
    residential 2,095
    non-residential 1,329

Manufacturing, 1992
total establishments 4,310
employees, total (x1,000) 277
payroll ($mil) 7,524
production workers (x1,000) 203
value added ($mil) 25,265
value of shipments ($mil) 60,029

Finance
commercial banks, 1994
  number 309
    assets ($bil) 45.5
    deposits ($bil) 35.1
  closed or assisted 0
    deposits ($bil) .... NA
savings and loan associations, 1991
  non-current real estate loans 1.04%
  net income after taxes ($mil) 45
  return on assets .... +0.59%

Retail trade, 1992
establishments (x1,000) 22.1
sales ($mil) 25,268
annual payroll ($mil) 2,803
paid employees (x1,000) 261

Wholesale trade, 1992
establishments 5,931
sales ($bil) 31.6
annual payroll ($mil) 1,701
paid employees (x1,000) 70.3

Service industries, 1992
establishments (x1,000) (non-exempt firms) 21.0
receipts ($mil) (non-exempt firms) 10,378
annual payroll ($mil) 3,864
paid employees (x1,000) (non-exempt firms) . 211

COMMUNICATION, ENERGY & TRANSPORTATION

Communication
daily newspapers, 1993 23
broadcast stations, 1990
  radio: commercial, educational 279
  television: commercial, noncommercial 34
cable TV households, 1988 775,000

Energy
consumption estimates, 1992
total (trillion Btu) 1,532
per capita (million Btu) 408.2
by source of production (trillion Btu)
  coal 814
  natural gas 201
  petroleum 539
  nuclear electric power 0
  hydroelectric power 39
by end-use sector (trillion Btu)
  residential 271
  commercial 180
  industrial 691
  transportation 391
electrical energy
  production, 1993 (billion kWh) 85.0
  net summer capability, 1993 (million kW) . 15.3
gas utilities, 1993
  customers 728,000
  sales (trillion Btu) 140
  revenues ($mil) 605
nuclear plants, 1993 0

Transportation, 1994
public road & street mileage
total 72,981
  urban 10,311
  rural 62,670
  interstate 762
vehicle miles of travel (mil) 39,822
total motor vehicle registrations 2,665,705
  automobiles 1,732,359
licensed drivers 2,516,408
  per 1,000 driving age population 847
deaths from motor vehicle
  accidents 778

Louisiana 1

STATE SUMMARY

Capital City .... Baton Rouge

Governor .... Mike Foster

Address .... STATE CAPITOL
BATON ROUGE, LA 70804
504 342-7015

Admitted as a state 1812

Area (square miles) 51,843

Population, 1980 4,205,900

Population, 1990 4,219,973

Population, 1994 (est.) 4,315,000

Persons per square mile, 1994 .... 99.0

Largest city .... New Orleans
population, 1990 497,000

Personal income per capita, 1994
(in current dollars) $17,651

Gross state product ($mil), 1991 95,377

Leading industries, 1992 (by payroll)
SERVICE INDUSTRIES
MANUFACTURING
RETAIL TRADE

Leading agricultural commodities, 1993
COTTON
CANE/SUGAR
SOYBEANS
RICE

GEOGRAPHY & ENVIRONMENT

Area (square miles)
total 51,843
land 43,566
water (includes territorial water) 8,277

Federally owned land, 1991 .... 2.6%

Highest point
name .... Driskill Mountain
elevation (feet) 535

Lowest point
name .... New Orleans
elevation (feet) .... -8

General coastline (miles) 397

Tidal shoreline (miles) 7,721

Capital city .... Baton Rouge
population, 1990 220,000

Largest city .... New Orleans
population, 1990 497,000

Number of cities with over 100,000 population
1980 2

Number of cities with over 100,000 population
1990 4

State parks and Recreation areas, 1991
area (acres) 39,000
number of visitors 1,107,000
revenues $1,860,000

National forest land, 1992 (acres) 1,022,000

National park acreage, 1984 6,300

DEMOGRAPHICS & CHARACTERISTICS OF THE POPULATION

Population
1970 3,644,637
1980 4,205,900
1990 4,219,973
1994 (est.) 4,315,000
2000 (revised projection) 4,478,000
2010 (revised projection) 4,808,000

Metropolitan area population
1970 2,439,000
1980 2,892,000
1992 3,210,000

Non-metropolitan area population
1970 1,205,000
1980 1,314,000
1992 1,069,000

Change in population, 1980-90
number 14,073
percent 0.33%

Persons per square mile, 1994 .... 99.0

Age distribution, 1980
under 5 years 8.6%
5 to 17 years 22.0%
65 and over 9.6%

Age distribution, 1990
under 5 years 7.9%
5 to 17 years 21.1%
65 and over 11.1%

Louisiana 2

Age distribution, 2000 (projected)
under 5 years 7.0%
5 to 17 years 20.1%
65 and over 11.4%

Persons by age, 1990
under 5 years 334,650
5 to 17 years 892,619
65 and over 468,991

Median age, 1990 .... *31.00*

Race, 1990
White 2,839,138
Black 1,299,281
American Indian 18,361
Chinese 5,430
Filipino 3,731
Japanese 1,526
Asian Indian 5,083
Korean 2,750
Vietnamese 17,598
all other 26,895

Race, 2010 (projected)
White 3,119,000
Black 1,550,000

Persons of Hispanic origin, 1990
total 93,044
  Mexican 23,452
  Puerto Rican 6,180
  Cuban 8,569
  Other Hispanic 54,843

Persons by sex, 1990
male 2,031,386
female 2,188,587

Marital status, 1990
males
  15 years & older 1,503,716
    single 464,285
    married 892,014
      separated 45,440
    widowed 42,270
    divorced 105,147
females
  15 years & older 1,680,787
    single 409,309
    married 905,705
      separated 66,061

widowed 216,577
divorced 149,196

Households & families, 1990
households 1,499,269
persons per household 2.74
  families 1,089,882
    married couples 803,282
    female householder, no husband
      present 234,129
    one person households 356,060
households, 1994 1,543,000
persons per household, 1994 .... 2.72

Nativity, 1990
number of persons born in state 3,332,542
percent of total residents 79.0%

Immigration & naturalization, 1993
immigrants admitted 3,725
persons naturalized 2,016
refugees granted resident status 660

VITAL STATISTICS & HEALTH

Births
1992 71,743
  with low birth weight 9.4%
  to teenage mothers 18.1%
  to unmarried mothers 40.2%
1993 69,819
1994 68,454

Abortions, 1992
total 14,000
rate (per 1,000 women age 15-44) 13.4
rate per 1,000 live births 195

Adoptions, 1986
total 1,683
  related 70.6%

Deaths
1992 37,446
1993 40,117
1994 40,418

Infant deaths
1992 687
1993 686
1994 652

Louisiana 3

Average lifetime, 1979-1981
both sexes .... 71.74 years
  men .... 67.64 years
  women .... 75.89 years

Marriages
1992 35,386
1993 36,179
1994 41,750

Divorces
1992 .... NA
1993 .... NA
1994 .... NA

Physicians, 1993
total 8,591
rate (per 1,000 persons) 2.01

Dentists, 1992
total 2,005
rate (per 1,000 persons) 0.47

Hospitals, 1993
number 132
beds (x 1,000) 19.1
average daily census (x 1,000) 10.9
occupancy rate 57.0%
personnel (x 1,000) 73.0
average cost per day to hospital $875
average cost per stay to hospital $5,781

EDUCATION

*Educational attainment of all persons
  25 years and older, 1990*
less than 9th grade 372,913
high school graduates 803,328
bachelor's degree 267,055
graduate or professional degree 142,068

Public school enrollment, Fall, 1993
total 800,560
  Kindergarten through grade 8 587,490
  grades 9 through 12 213,070

Public School Teachers
total, 1994 46,913
  elementary 26,556
  secondary 10,377
salaries, 1994
  beginning $18,195
  average $26,243

*State receipts & expenditures for public
  schools, 1993*
receipts ($mil) 3,789
expenditures
  total ($mil) 3,442
  per capita $804
  per pupil $4,352

*Graduating high school seniors,
  public high schools, 1995 (est)* 36,020

SAT scores, 1994
verbal 481
math 530

Institutions of higher education, 1995
total 35
  public 20
  private 15

*Enrollment in institutions of higher
  education, Fall, 1993*
total 201,987
full-time men 64,588
full-time women 77,444
part-time men 22,422
part-time women 37,533

*Minority enrollment in institutions of higher
  education, Fall, 1993*
Black, non-Hispanic 50,074
Hispanic 4,526
Asian/Pacific Islander 3,644

Earned degrees conferred, 1993
Bachelor's 17,825
First professional 1,502
Master's 4,723
Doctor's 428

SOCIAL INSURANCE & WELFARE PROGRAMS

Social Security beneficiaries & benefits, 1993
beneficiaries
total 689,000
  retired and dependents 408,000
  survivors 160,000
  disabled & dependents 121,000
annual benefit payments ($mil)
total $4,500
  retired and dependents 2,564
  survivors 1,215
  disabled & dependents 720

Louisiana 4

Medicare, 1993
enrollment (x1,000) 563
payments ($mil) 2,607

Medicaid, 1993
recipients (x1,000) 751
payments ($mil) 2,873

Federal public aid, 1993
recipients as a percent of population 9.9%
Aid to Families with Dependent Children
  recipients (x1,000) 256
average monthly payment $164
Supplemental Security Income
  total recipients (x1,000) 170

Food Stamp Program
participants, 1994 (x1,000) 756

HOUSING & CONSTRUCTION

Total housing units, 1990 1,716,241
  year round housing units 1,685,455
  vacant 216,972

New privately owned housing units authorized, 1994
number (x1,000) 14.8
value ($mil) 1,141

New privately owned housing units started, 1994 (x1,000) 15.5

Existing home sales, 1994 (x1,000) 51.4

GOVERNMENT & ELECTIONS

State officials, 1996
Governor (name/party/term expires)
MIKE FOSTER
Republican - 2000
Lt. Governor . . . . Melinda Schwegmann
Sec. of State . . . . Fox McKeithen
Atty. General . . . . Richard Ieyoub
Chf. Justice . . . . Pascal Calagero

Governorship
minimum age 25
length of term . . . . .4 years
number of consecutive
  terms permitted 2
who succeeds . . . . Lt. Governor

State legislature
name . . . . Legislature
  upper chamber
    name . . . . Senate
    number of members .39
    length of term . . . . .4 years
    party in majority, 1996 . . . . .Democratic
  lower chamber
    name . . . . House of Representatives
    number of members 105
    length of term . . . . .4 years
    party in majority, 1996 . . . . .Democratic

State employees October, 1992
total 103,048
October payroll ($1,000) 190,313

Local governments, 1992
total 461
  county 61
  municipal 301
  township 0
  school districts 66
  special districts 32

Voting, November, 1994
voting age population 3,013,000
  registered 70.6%
  voted 34.2%

Vote for president
1988
  Bush 880,830
  Dukakis 715,612
1992
  Clinton 815,530
  Bush 731,619
  Perot 210,703

Federal representation, 1996 (104th Congress)
Senators (name/party/term expires)

J. BENNET JOHNSTON, JR
Democrat - 1997
JOHN BREAUX
Democrat - 1999

Representatives, total 7
  Democrats 4
  Republicans 3
  other 0

Louisiana 5

Women holding public office
U.S. Congress, 1995 0
statewide elected office, 1995 2
state legislature, 1995 14

Black elected officials, 1993
total 636
   US and state legislatures 33
   city/county/regional offices 346
   judicial/law enforcement 104
   education/school boards 153

Hispanic public officials, 1994
total 12
   state executives & legislators 3
   city/county/regional offices 1
   judicial/law enforcement 8
   education/school boards 0

GOVERNMENTAL FINANCE

State & local government revenues, (selected items), 1991-92 ($per capita)
total $4,151.72
   total general revenues 3,662.21
    from federal government 944.91
    from own sources 2,717.31
    from taxes 1,664.23
     from property taxes 278.48
     from all other taxes 1,139.82
    from charges & misc. 1,053.07

State & local government expenditures, (selected items), 1991-92 ($per capita)
total $4,141.33
   total direct general expenditures 3,711.19
    education 1,173.52
    libraries 13.72
    public welfare 595.72
    health & hospitals 447.28
    highways 284.22
    police protection 127.73
    fire protection 44.04
    correction 82.19
    housing & comm. development 44.07
    natural resources & parks 123.14
    interest on general debt 313.14

State & local debt, 1992 ($per capita) 4,441.56

Federal aid grants to state & local government, 1994 ($per capita total & selected items)
per capita total 1,212.68
   compensatory education 41.30
   waste treatment facilities 3.11
   medicaid 754.49
   housing assistance 44.03
   job training 18.89
   highway trust fund 60.83

CRIME, LAW ENFORCEMENT & COURTS

Crime, 1994 (all rates per 100,000 persons)
total crimes 287,857
overall crime rate 6,671.1
   property crimes 245,488
    burglaries 55,188
    larcenies 164,081
    motor vehicle thefts 26,219
   property crime rate 5,689.2
   violent crimes 42,369
    murders 856
    forcible rapes 1,923
    robberies 11,530
    aggravated assaults 28,060
   violent crime rate 981.9

Number of police agencies, 1994 107

Arrests, 1994
total 189,392
   persons under 18 years of age 33,997

Prisoners under state & federal jurisdiction, 1994
total 24,092
percent change, 1993-94 . . . . 7.2%
   sentenced to more than one year
    total 22,956
    rate per 100,000 residents 530

Persons under sentence of death, 4/20/95 45

State's highest court
name . . . . Supreme Court
number of members 7
length of term . . . . 10 years
intermediate appeals court? . . . . yes

Louisiana 6

LABOR & INCOME

Civilian labor force, 1994
total 1,939,000
  men 1,042,000
  women 897,000
  persons 16-19 years 136,000
  white 1,413,000
  black 504,000

Civilian labor force as a percent of
civilian non-institutional population, 1994
total 61.2%
  men 70.1%
  women 53.3%
  persons 16-19 years 45.4%
  white 62.5%
  black 58.1%

Employment, 1994
total 1,783,000
  men 966,000
  women 817,000
  persons 16-19 years 104,000
  white 1,332,000
  black 430,000

Full-time/part-time labor force, 1994
full-time labor force 1,571,000
  working part-time for
    ecomonic reasons 23,000
part-time labor force 368,000

Unemployment rate, 1994
total 8.0%
  men 7.3%
  women 9.0%
  persons 16-19 years 24.0%
  white 5.7%
  black 14.6%

Unemployed by reason for unemployment
(as a percent of total unemployment), 1994
job losers or completed temp jobs 39.9%
job leavers 6.5%
reentrants 41.6%
new entrants 12.0%

Civilian labor force, by occupation, 1994
executive/administrative/
  managerial 228,000
professional/specialty 249,000
technicians & related support 56,000

sales 236,000
adminstrative support/clerical 277,000
service occupations 310,000
precision production/craft/repair 207,000
machine operators/assemblers 82,000
transportation/material moving 121,000
handlers/helpers/laborers 83,000
farming/forestry/fishing 70,000

Civilian labor force, by industry, 1994
construction 109,000
manufacturing 180,000
transportation/communication 123,000
wholesale/retail trade 414,000
finance/real estate/insurance 102,000
services 416,000
government 308,000
agriculture 57,000

Average annual pay, 1994 (prelim.) $23,176
change in average annual pay,
  1993-1994 .... 2.4%

Hours and earnings of production workers
on manufacturing payrolls, 1994
average weekly hours 43.4
average hourly earnings $13.13
average weekly earnings $569.84

Labor union membership, 1994 121,400

Household income (in constant 1993 dollars)
median household income, 1992 .... $26,201
median household income, 1993 .... $26,312

Poverty
persons below poverty level, 1992 .... 24.5%
persons below poverty level, 1993 .... 26.4%

Personal income ($per capita)
1994
  in current dollars 17,651
  in constant (1987) dollars 13,651
1995 (projected)
  in constant (1982) dollars 10,928
2000 (projected)
  in constant (1982) dollars 11,680

Federal income tax returns, 1993
returns filed 1,699,646
adjusted gross income ($1000) 46,472,002
total income tax paid ($1000) 6,345,386

ECONOMY, BUSINESS, INDUSTRY & AGRICULTURE

Fortune 500 companies, 1994 1

Business incorporations, 1994
total 11,328
change, 1993-94 .... 6.3%

Business failures, 1994
total 657
rate per 10,000 concerns 53
change, 1993-94 .... -1.6%

Business firm ownership
Hispanic owned firms, 1987 2,697
black owned firms, 1987 15,331
women owned firms, 1987 55,900
foreign owned firms, 1982 221

Gross state product, 1991 ($mil)
total $95,377
  agriculture services, forestry, fisheries ... 1,118
  mining 13,547
  construction 3,836
  manufacturing—durable goods 3,795
  manufacturing—nondurable goods 14,279
  transportation, communication &
    public utilities 10,258
  wholesale trade 4,819
  retail trade 7,560
  finance/real estate/insurance 13,230
  services 13,284
  federal, state & local government 9,650

Establishments, by major industry group, 1992
total 91,332
  agriculture 1,150
  mining 1,575
  construction 6,596
  manufacturing 4,065
  transportation 4,842
  wholesale trade 7,200
  retail trade 23,219
  finance/real estate/insurance 8,901
  service industries 32,530
  unclassified 1,254

Payroll, by major industry group, 1992
total ($1,000) $28,195,784
  agriculture 95,575

  mining 1,933,626
  construction 2,171,083
  manufacturing 5,447,615
  transportation 2,806,243
  wholesale trade 2,059,364
  retail trade 3,414,221
  finance/real estate/insurance 1,905,396
  service industries 8,341,402
  unclassified 21,259

Agriculture
number of farms, 1994 28,000
farm acreage, 1994 8,000,000
acres per farm, 1994 300
value of farms, 1994 ($mil) 8,366
farm income, 1993 ($mil)
  gross farm income 2,246
  net farm income 335
  debt/asset ratio 20.9%
farm marketings, 1993 ($mil)
total $1,757
  crops 1,069
  livestock 688
government payments 367
farm marketings in order of marketing receipts, 1993
  1) Cotton
  2) Sugar
  3) Cattle
  4) Soybeans

Federal economic activity ($mil, except per capita)
expenditures, 1994
  total $21,672
  per capita $5,022
  defense $3,541
  non-defense $18,131
defense department, 1994
  contract awards ($mil) $2,148
  payroll ($mil) $1,355
  civilian employees (x1,000) 8.6
  military personnel (x1,000) 20.3

Fishing, 1992
catch (millions of pounds) 1,013
value ($mil) 295

Mining, 1994 ($mil)
total non-fuel mineral production $328

153

Louisiana 8

principal non-fuel minerals in order of value, 1994
  1) Salt
  2) Sulfur
  3) Sand and gravel

Construction, 1994 ($mil)
total contracts (including
  non-building) $4,065
    residential 1,325
    non-residential 1,728

Manufacturing, 1992
total establishments 4,048
employees, total (x1,000) 179
payroll ($mil) 5,460
production workers (x1,000) 126
value added ($mil) 20,509
value of shipments ($mil) 60,940

Finance
commercial banks, 1994
  number 217
    assets ($bil) 40.1
    deposits ($bil) 34.0
  closed or assisted 0
    deposits ($bil) .... NA
savings and loan associations, 1991
  non-current real estate loans 6.45%
  net income after taxes ($mil) .... -311
  return on assets .... -3.41%

Retail trade, 1992
establishments (x1,000) 22.6
sales ($mil) 27,806
annual payroll ($mil) 3,096
paid employees (x1,000) 289

Wholesale trade, 1992
establishments 7,347
sales ($bil) 37.3
annual payroll ($mil) 1,994
paid employees (x1,000) 81.3

Service industries, 1992
establishments (x1,000) (non-exempt firms) 27.1
receipts ($mil) (non-exempt firms) 16,067
annual payroll ($mil) 5,912
paid employees (x1,000) (non-exempt firms) . 296

COMMUNICATION, ENERGY & TRANSPORTATION

Communication
daily newspapers, 1993 25
broadcast stations, 1990
  radio: commercial, educational 213
  television: commercial, noncommercial 29
cable TV households, 1988 920,000

Energy
consumption estimates, 1992
total (trillion Btu) 3,558
per capita (million Btu) 831.4
by source of production (trillion Btu)
  coal 224
  natural gas 1,614
  petroleum 1,508
  nuclear electric power 111
  hydroelectric power 0
by end-use sector (trillion Btu)
  residential 288
  commercial 211
  industrial 2,314
  transportation 745
electrical energy
  production, 1993 (billion kWh) 59.4
  net summer capability, 1993 (million kW) . 16.9
gas utilities, 1993
  customers 1,007,000
  sales (trillion Btu) 387
  revenues ($mil) 1,178
nuclear plants, 1993 2

Transportation, 1994
public road & street mileage
total 60,021
  urban 13,949
  rural 46,072
  interstate 878
vehicle miles of travel (mil) 37,430
total motor vehicle registrations 3,426,464
  automobiles 1,977,787
licensed drivers 2,594,615
  per 1,000 driving age population 806
deaths from motor vehicle
  accidents 838

Maine 1

STATE SUMMARY

Capital City .... Augusta

Governor .... Angus King

Address .... STATE HOUSE
              AUGUSTA, ME 04333
              207 287-3531

Admitted as a state 1820

Area (square miles) 35,387

Population, 1980 1,124,660

Population, 1990 1,227,928

Population, 1994 (est.) 1,240,000

Persons per square mile, 1994 .... 40.2

Largest city .... Portland
    population, 1990 64,400

Personal income per capita, 1994
    (in current dollars) $19,663

Gross state product ($mil), 1991 23,241

Leading industries, 1992 (by payroll)
           SERVICE INDUSTRIES
           MANUFACTURING
           RETAIL TRADE

Leading agricultural commodities, 1993
           POTATOES
           DAIRY PRODUCTS
           EGGS
           AQUACULTURE

GEOGRAPHY & ENVIRONMENT

Area (square miles)
total 35,387
    land 30,865
    water (includes territorial water) 4,523

Federally owned land, 1991 .... 0.8%

Highest point
name .... Mount Katahdin
elevation (feet) 5,267

Lowest point
name .... Atlantic Ocean
elevation (feet) .... sea level

General coastline (miles) 228

Tidal shoreline (miles) 3,478

Capital city .... Augusta
population, 1990 21,300

Largest city .... Portland
population, 1990 64,400

Number of cities with over 100,000 population
    1980 0

Number of cities with over 100,000 population
    1990 0

State parks and Recreation areas, 1991
area (acres) 75,000
number of visitors 2,448,000
revenues $1,310,000

National forest land, 1992 (acres) 93,000

National park acreage, 1984 41,100

DEMOGRAPHICS & CHARACTERISTICS OF THE POPULATION

Population
1970 993,722
1980 1,124,660
1990 1,227,928
1994 (est.) 1,240,000
2000 (revised projection) 1,240,000
2010 (revised projection) 1,309,000

Metropolitan area population
1970 365,000
1980 404,000
1992 441,000

Non-metropolitan area population
1970 628,000
1980 720,000
1992 795,000

Change in population, 1980-90
number 103,268
percent 9.18%

Persons per square mile, 1994 .... 40.2

Age distribution, 1980
under 5 years 7.0%
5 to 17 years 21.6%
65 and over 12.3%

Age distribution, 1990
under 5 years 7.0%
5 to 17 years 18.1%
65 and over 13.3%

155

Maine 2

Age distribution, 2000 (projected)
under 5 years 5.9%
5 to 17 years 18.4%
65 and over 13.5%

Persons by age, 1990
under 5 years 85,722
5 to 17 years 223,280
65 and over 163,373

Median age, 1990 .... *33.90*

Race, 1990
White 1,208,360
Black 5,138
American Indian 5,945
Chinese 1,262
Filipino 1,058
Japanese 590
Asian Indian 607
Korean 858
Vietnamese 642
all other 3,415

Race, 2010 (projected)
White 1,283,000
Black 5,000

Persons of Hispanic origin, 1990
total 6,829
  Mexican 2,153
  Puerto Rican 1,250
  Cuban 350
  Other Hispanic 3,076

Persons by sex, 1990
male 597,850
female 630,078

Marital status, 1990
males
  15 years & older 465,004
    single 126,930
    married 287,910
      separated 5,460
    widowed 12,311
    divorced 37,853
females
  15 years & older 504,117
    single 106,076
    married 286,893
      separated 7,413

widowed 60,977
divorced 50,171

Households & families, 1990
households 465,312
persons per household 2.56
  families 328,685
    married couples 270,565
    female householder, no husband
      present 44,360
    one person households 108,474
households, 1994 474,000
persons per household, 1994 .... 2.54

Nativity, 1990
number of persons born in state 840,930
percent of total residents 68.5%

Immigration & naturalization, 1993
immigrants admitted 838
persons naturalized 584
refugees granted resident status 131

VITAL STATISTICS & HEALTH

Births
1992 15,623
  with low birth weight 5.0%
  to teenage mothers 10.2%
  to unmarried mothers 25.3%
1993 15,027
1994 14,320

Abortions, 1992
total 4,000
rate (per 1,000 women age 15-44) 14.7
rate per 1,000 live births 282

Adoptions, 1986
total 873
  related 68.8%

Deaths
1992 10,900
1993 11,479
1994 11,386

Infant deaths
1992 89
1993 99
1994 90

Average lifetime, 1979-1981
both sexes .... 74.59 years
  men .... 70.78 years
  women .... 78.41 years

Marriages
1992 11,215
1993 10,899
1994 10,872

Divorces
1992 5,877
1993 5,282
1994 5,433

Physicians, 1993
total 2,365
rate (per 1,000 persons) 1.92

Dentists, 1992
total 590
rate (per 1,000 persons) 0.48

Hospitals, 1993
number 39
beds (x 1,000) 4.4
average daily census (x 1,000) 3.0
occupancy rate 68.0%
personnel (x 1,000) 18.5
average cost per day to hospital $738
average cost per stay to hospital $5,543

EDUCATION

*Educational attainment of all persons
  25 years and older, 1990*
less than 9th grade 70,153
high school graduates 295,074
bachelor's degree 100,788
graduate or professional degree 48,564

Public school enrollment, Fall, 1993
total 216,995
  Kindergarten through grade 8 156,528
  grades 9 through 12 60,467

Public School Teachers
total, 1994 15,344
  elementary 10,440
  secondary 4,904
salaries, 1994
  beginning $19,840
  average $30,996

*State receipts & expenditures for public
  schools, 1993*
receipts ($mil) 1,357
expenditures
  total ($mil) 1,357
  per capita $1,098
  per pupil $6,162

*Graduating high school seniors,
  public high schools, 1995 (est)* 12,996

SAT scores, 1994
verbal 420
math 463

Institutions of higher education, 1995
total 33
  public 14
  private 19

*Enrollment in institutions of higher
  education, Fall, 1993*
total 56,294
full-time men 15,523
full-time women 17,008
part-time men 8,097
part-time women 15,666

*Minority enrollment in institutions of higher
  education, Fall, 1993*
Black, non-Hispanic 464
Hispanic 255
Asian/Pacific Islander 595

Earned degrees conferred, 1993
Bachelor's 5,976
First professional 168
Master's 917
Doctor's 40

SOCIAL INSURANCE &
WELFARE PROGRAMS

Social Security beneficiaries & benefits, 1993
beneficiaries
total 228,000
  retired and dependents 161,000
  survivors 36,000
  disabled & dependents 31,000
annual benefit payments ($mil)
total $1,521
  retired and dependents 1,040
  survivors 295
  disabled & dependents 185

Maine 4

HOUSING & CONSTRUCTION

GOVERNMENT & ELECTIONS

Maine 5

Women holding public office
U.S. Congress, 1995 1
statewide elected office, 1995 0
state legislature, 1995 50

Black elected officials, 1993
total 1
  US and state legislatures 0
  city/county/regional offices 1
  judicial/law enforcement 0
  education/school boards 0

Hispanic public officials, 1994
total ....NA
  state executives & legislators ....NA
  city/county/regional offices ....NA
  judicial/law enforcement ....NA
  education/school boards ....NA

GOVERNMENTAL FINANCE

State & local government revenues, (selected items), 1991-92 ($per capita)
total $4,356.56
  total general revenues 3,804.02
    from federal government 808.87
    from own sources 2,995.35
    from taxes 2,158.63
      from property taxes 827.91
      from all other taxes 1,227.67
    from charges & misc. 836.73

State & local government expenditures, (selected items), 1991-92 ($per capita)
total $4,239.37
  total direct general expenditures 3,761.99
    education 1,297.19
    libraries 11.95
    public welfare 814.10
    health & hospitals 168.04
    highways 315.46
    police protection 79.99
    fire protection 49.39
    correction 85.58
    housing & comm. development 64.07
    natural resources & parks 96.57
    interest on general debt 215.67

State & local debt, 1992 ($per capita) 3,295.21

Federal aid grants to state & local government, 1994 ($per capita total & selected items)
per capita total 1,023.44
  compensatory education 25.95
  waste treatment facilities 8.48
  medicaid 487.21
  housing assistance 66.41
  job training 14.57
  highway trust fund 71.19

CRIME, LAW ENFORCEMENT & COURTS

Crime, 1994 (all rates per 100,000 persons)
total crimes 40,582
overall crime rate 3,272.7
  property crimes 38,971
    burglaries 8,938
    larcenies 28,257
    motor vehicle thefts 1,776
  property crime rate 3,142.8
  violent crimes 1,611
    murders 28
    forcible rapes 318
    robberies 278
    aggravated assaults 987
  violent crime rate 129.9

Number of police agencies, 1994 141

Arrests, 1994
total 46,627
  persons under 18 years of age 10,295

Prisoners under state & federal jurisdiction, 1994
total 1,537
percent change, 1993-94 ....4.6%
sentenced to more than one year
  total 1,464
  rate per 100,000 residents 118

Persons under sentence of death, 4/20/95 ....NA

State's highest court
name .... Supreme Court
number of members 7
length of term ....7 years
intermediate appeals court? ....no

159

Maine 6

LABOR & INCOME

Civilian labor force, 1994
total 613,000
  men 323,000
  women 290,000
  persons 16-19 years 38,000
  white 604,000
  black .... NA

Civilian labor force as a percent of civilian non-institutional population, 1994
total 64.3%
  men 70.3%
  women 58.6%
  persons 16-19 years 53.4%
  white 64.5%
  black .... NA%

Employment, 1994
total 567,000
  men 296,000
  women 272,000
  persons 16-19 years 31,000
  white 560,000
  black .... NA

Full-time/part-time labor force, 1994
full-time labor force 469,000
  working part-time for
    ecomonic reasons 8,000
part-time labor force 143,000

Unemployment rate, 1994
total 7.4%
  men 8.3%
  women 6.3%
  persons 16-19 years 18.3%
  white 7.3%
  black .... NA%

Unemployed by reason for unemployment (as a percent of total unemployment), 1994
job losers or completed temp jobs 54.8%
job leavers 8.0%
reentrants 33.1%
new entrants 4.2%

Civilian labor force, by occupation, 1994
executive/administrative/
  managerial 72,000
professional/specialty 78,000
technicians & related support 18,000
sales 78,000
adminstrative support/clerical 75,000
service occupations 95,000
precision production/craft/repair 71,000
machine operators/assemblers 47,000
transportation/material moving 28,000
handlers/helpers/laborers 27,000
farming/forestry/fishing 22,000

Civilian labor force, by industry, 1994
construction 26,000
manufacturing 101,000
transportation/communication 26,000
wholesale/retail trade 126,000
finance/real estate/insurance 27,000
services 131,000
government 80,000
agriculture .... NA

Average annual pay, 1994 (prelim.) $22,389
change in average annual pay,
  1993-1994 .... 1.6%

Hours and earnings of production workers on manufacturing payrolls, 1994
average weekly hours 40.6
average hourly earnings $11.91
average weekly earnings $483.55

Labor union membership, 1994 71,600

Household income (in constant 1993 dollars)
median household income, 1992 .... $30,504
median household income, 1993 .... $27,438

Poverty
persons below poverty level, 1992 .... 13.5%
persons below poverty level, 1993 .... 15.4%

Personal income ($per capita)
1994
  in current dollars 19,663
  in constant (1987) dollars 15,207
1995 (projected)
  in constant (1982) dollars 13,205
2000 (projected)
  in constant (1982) dollars 14,014

Federal income tax returns, 1993
returns filed 548,592
adjusted gross income ($1000) 15,159,536
total income tax paid ($1000) 1,895,543

Maine 7

ECONOMY, BUSINESS, INDUSTRY & AGRICULTURE

Fortune 500 companies, 1994 2

Business incorporations, 1994
total 2,637
change, 1993-94 .... -1.0%

Business failures, 1994
total 334
rate per 10,000 concerns 71
change, 1993-94 .... -12.8%

Business firm ownership
Hispanic owned firms, 1987 139
black owned firms, 1987 131
women owned firms, 1987 23,900
foreign owned firms, 1982 60

Gross state product, 1991 ($mil)
total $23,241
 agriculture services, forestry, fisheries 545
 mining 6
 construction 978
 manufacturing—durable goods 1,868
 manufacturing—nondurable goods 2,351
 transportation, communication &
   public utilities 1,822
 wholesale trade 1,285
 retail trade 2,662
 finance/real estate/insurance 4,242
 services 4,192
 federal, state & local government 3,291

Establishments, by major industry group, 1992
total 34,790
 agriculture 613
 mining 27
 construction 4,084
 manufacturing 2,219
 transportation 1,699
 wholesale trade 1,962
 retail trade 9,448
 finance/real estate/insurance 2,637
 service industries 11,625
 unclassified 476

Payroll, by major industry group, 1992
total ($1,000) $8,563,334
 agriculture 47,715

mining 4,033
construction 451,795
manufacturing 2,436,760
transportation 506,759
wholesale trade 611,027
retail trade 1,265,431
finance/real estate/insurance 681,691
service industries 2,553,734
unclassified 4,389

Agriculture
number of farms, 1994 7,000
farm acreage, 1994 1,000,000
acres per farm, 1994 201
value of farms, 1994 ($mil) 1,535
farm income, 1993 ($mil)
 gross farm income 571
 net farm income 154
 debt/asset ratio 15.0%
farm marketings, 1993 ($mil)
 total $472
 crops 198
 livestock 274
government payments 20
farm marketings in order of marketing
receipts, 1993
  1) Eggs
  2) Potatoes
  3) Dairy products
  4) Aquaculture

Federal economic activity
 ($mil, except per capita)
expenditures, 1994
 total $6,708
 per capita $5,409
 defense $1,502
 non-defense $5,206
defense department, 1994
 contract awards ($mil) $925
 payroll ($mil) $584
 civilian employees (x1,000) 6.0
 military personnel (x1,000) 2.2

Fishing, 1992
catch (millions of pounds) 201
value ($mil) 163

Mining, 1994 ($mil)
total non-fuel mineral production $58

161

Maine 8

principal non-fuel minerals in order of value, 1994
  1) Sand and gravel
  2) Cement
  3) Stone

Construction, 1994 ($mil)
total contracts (including
  non-building) $1,056
    residential 463
    non-residential 297

Manufacturing, 1992
total establishments 2,200
employees, total (x1,000) 91
payroll ($mil) 2,447
production workers (x1,000) 67
value added ($mil) 5,458
value of shipments ($mil) 11,611

Finance
commercial banks, 1994
  number 20
    assets ($bil) 8.7
    deposits ($bil) 6.8
    closed or assisted 0
    deposits ($bil) .... NA
savings and loan associations, 1991
  non-current real estate loans 2.81%
  net income after taxes ($mil) .... -1
  return on assets .... -1.35%

Retail trade, 1992
establishments (x1,000) 9.3
sales ($mil) 10,287
annual payroll ($mil) 1,120
paid employees (x1,000) 90

Wholesale trade, 1992
establishments 1,974
sales ($bil) 6.5
annual payroll ($mil) 541
paid employees (x1,000) 21.9

Service industries, 1992
establishments (x1,000) (non-exempt firms) . 9.0
receipts ($mil) (non-exempt firms) 3,597
annual payroll ($mil) 1,367
paid employees (x1,000) (non-exempt firms) .. 68

COMMUNICATION, ENERGY & TRANSPORTATION

Communication
daily newspapers, 1993 7
broadcast stations, 1990
  radio: commercial, educational 103
  television: commercial, noncommercial 13
cable TV households, 1988 241,000

Energy
consumption estimates, 1992
total (trillion Btu) 370
per capita (million Btu) 299.5
by source of production (trillion Btu)
  coal 22
  natural gas 5
  petroleum 225
  nuclear electric power 57
  hydroelectric power 50
by end-use sector (trillion Btu)
  residential 78
  commercial 53
  industrial 135
  transportation 104
electrical energy
  production, 1993 (billion kWh) 8.1
  net summer capability, 1993 (million kW) .. 2.4
gas utilities, 1993
  customers 19,000
  sales (trillion Btu) 5
  revenues ($mil) 30
nuclear plants, 1993 1

Transportation, 1994
public road & street mileage
total 22,561
  urban 2,605
  rural 19,956
  interstate 366
vehicle miles of travel (mil) 12,469
total motor vehicle registrations 945,744
  automobiles 610,727
licensed drivers 913,597
  per 1,000 driving age population 943
deaths from motor vehicle
  accidents 188

Maryland 1

STATE SUMMARY

Capital City . . . . Annapolis

Governor . . . . Parris Glendening

Address . . . . STATE HOUSE
ANNAPOLIS, MD 21401
410 974-3901

Admitted as a state 1788

Area (square miles) 12,407

Population, 1980 4,216,975

Population, 1990 4,781,468

Population, 1994 (est.) 5,006,000

Persons per square mile, 1994 . . . . 512.1

Largest city . . . . Baltimore
population, 1990 736,000

Personal income per capita, 1994
(in current dollars) $24,933

Gross state product ($mil), 1991 111,874

Leading industries, 1992 (by payroll)
SERVICE INDUSTRIES
MANUFACTURING
RETAIL TRADE

Leading agricultural commodities, 1993
BROILERS
GREENHOUSE
DAIRY PRODUCTS
SOYBEANS

GEOGRAPHY & ENVIRONMENT

Area (square miles)
total 12,407
land 9,775
water (includes territorial water) 2,633

Federally owned land, 1991 . . . . 3.0%

Highest point
name . . . . Backbone Mountain
elevation (feet) 3,360

Lowest point
name . . . . Atlantic Ocean
elevation (feet) .sea level

General coastline (miles) 31

Tidal shoreline (miles) 3,190

Capital city . . . . Annapolis
population, 1990 33,200

Largest city . . . . Baltimore
population, 1990 736,000

Number of cities with over 100,000 population
1980 1

Number of cities with over 100,000 population
1990 1

State parks and Recreation areas, 1991
area (acres) 226,000
number of visitors 7,828,000
revenues $6,320,000

National forest land, 1992 (acres) 0

National park acreage, 1984 39,700

DEMOGRAPHICS & CHARACTERISTICS OF THE POPULATION

Population
1970 3,923,897
1980 4,216,975
1990 4,781,468
1994 (est.) 5,006,000
2000 (revised projection) 5,322,000
2010 (revised projection) 5,782,000

Metropolitan area population
1970 3,668,000
1980 3,920,000
1992 4,563,000

Non-metropolitan area population
1970 255,000
1980 287,000
1992 354,000

Change in population, 1980-90
number 564,493
percent 13.39%

Persons per square mile, 1994 . . . . 512.1

Age distribution, 1980
under 5 years 6.5%
5 to 17 years 21.2%
65 and over 9.4%

Age distribution, 1990
under 5 years 7.5%
5 to 17 years 16.8%
65 and over 10.8%

Maryland 2

Age distribution, 2000 (projected)
under 5 years 5.9%
5 to 17 years 18.0%
65 and over 11.5%

Persons by age, 1990
under 5 years 357,818
5 to 17 years 804,423
65 and over 517,482

Median age, 1990 .... 33.00

Race, 1990
White 3,393,964
Black 1,189,899
American Indian 12,601
Chinese 30,868
Filipino 19,376
Japanese 6,617
Asian Indian 28,330
Korean 30,320
Vietnamese 8,862
all other 60,260

Race, 2010 (projected)
White 3,631,000
Black 1,776,000

Persons of Hispanic origin, 1990
total 125,102
Mexican 18,434
Puerto Rican 17,528
Cuban 6,367
Other Hispanic 82,773

Persons by sex, 1990
male 2,318,671
female 2,462,797

Marital status, 1990
males
15 years & older 1,814,522
single 587,368
married 1,066,185
separated 60,311
widowed 44,219
divorced 116,750
females
15 years & older 1,979,591
single 516,498
married 1,077,126
separated 80,567

widowed 216,413
divorced 169,554

Households & families, 1990
households 1,748,991
persons per household 2.67
families 1,245,814
married couples 948,563
female householder, no husband
present 231,889
one person households 394,572
households, 1994 1,831,000
persons per household, 1994 .... 2.67

Nativity, 1990
number of persons born in state 2,383,427
percent of total residents 49.8%

Immigration & naturalization, 1993
immigrants admitted 16,899
persons naturalized 9,864
refugees granted resident status 1,497

VITAL STATISTICS & HEALTH

Births
1992 76,173
with low birth weight 8.3%
to teenage mothers 9.8%
to unmarried mothers 30.5%
1993 75,526
1994 71,553

Abortions, 1992
total 31,000
rate (per 1,000 women age 15-44) 26.4
rate per 1,000 live births 454

Adoptions, 1986
total 1,400
related 46.2%

Deaths
1992 37,806
1993 43,087
1994 40,600

Infant deaths
1992 675
1993 709
1994 638

164

Average lifetime, 1979-1981
both sexes . . . . 73.32 years
  men . . . . 69.71 years
  women . . . . 76.83 years

Marriages
1992 44,083
1993 42,323
1994 43,385

Divorces
1992 17,570
1993 16,968
1994 17,439

Physicians, 1993
total 16,496
rate (per 1,000 persons) 3.35

Dentists, 1992
total 3,669
rate (per 1,000 persons) 0.75

Hospitals, 1993
number 50
beds (x 1,000) 13.0
average daily census (x 1,000) 9.8
occupancy rate 75.3%
personnel (x 1,000) 60.9
average cost per day to hospital $889
average cost per stay to hospital $5,632

EDUCATION

Educational attainment of all persons
  25 years and older, 1990
less than 9th grade 246,505
high school graduates 878,432
bachelor's degree 486,695
graduate or professional degree 339,469

Public school enrollment, Fall, 1993
total 772,638
  Kindergarten through grade 8 569,497
  grades 9 through 12 203,141

Public School Teachers
total, 1994 44,171
  elementary 25,027
  secondary 19,144
salaries, 1994
  beginning $24,703
  average $39,475

State receipts & expenditures for public
  schools, 1993
receipts ($mil) 4,997
expenditures
  total ($mil) 4,932
    per capita $1,003
    per pupil $6,447

Graduating high school seniors,
  public high schools, 1995 (est) 41,411

SAT scores, 1994
verbal 429
math 479

Institutions of higher education, 1995
total 57
  public 33
  private 24

Enrollment in institutions of higher
  education, Fall, 1993
total 268,005
full-time men 57,985
full-time women 65,487
part-time men 56,519
part-time women 88,014

Minority enrollment in institutions of higher
  education, Fall, 1993
Black, non-Hispanic 53,538
Hispanic 5,503
Asian/Pacific Islander 13,954

Earned degrees conferred, 1993
Bachelor's 20,427
First professional 1,050
Master's 8,006
Doctor's 963

SOCIAL INSURANCE & WELFARE PROGRAMS

Social Security beneficiaries & benefits, 1993
beneficiaries
total 653,000
  retired and dependents 469,000
  survivors 119,000
  disabled & dependents 65,000
annual benefit payments ($mil)
total $4,775
  retired and dependents 3,301
  survivors 1,016
  disabled & dependents 458

Maryland 4

Medicare, 1993
enrollment (x1,000) 578
payments ($mil) 2,470

Medicaid, 1993
recipients (x1,000) 445
payments ($mil) 1,721

Federal public aid, 1993
recipients as a percent of population 5.9%
Aid to Families with Dependent Children
   recipients (x1,000) 215
average monthly payment $319
Supplemental Security Income
   total recipients (x1,000) 74

Food Stamp Program
participants, 1994 (x1,000) 387

HOUSING & CONSTRUCTION

Total housing units, 1990 1,891,917
   year round housing units 1,849,431
   vacant 142,926

New privately owned housing units
   authorized, 1994
number (x1,000) 29.0
value ($mil) 2,395

New privately owned housing units
   started, 1994 (x1,000) 32.5

Existing home sales, 1994 (x1,000) 69.5

GOVERNMENT & ELECTIONS

State officials, 1996
   Governor (name/party/term expires)
   PARRIS GLENDENING
   Democrat - 1999
Lt. Governor .... Kathleen K. Townsend
Sec. of State .... Tyrus Athey
Atty. General .... Joseph Curran
Chf. Justice .... Robert C. Murphy

Governorship
minimum age 30
length of term .... 4 years
number of consecutive
   terms permitted 2
who succeeds .... Lt. Governor

State legislature
name .... Legislature
   upper chamber
      name .... Senate
      number of members 47
      length of term .... 4 years
      party in majority, 1996 .... Democratic
   lower chamber
      name .... House of Delegates
      number of members 141
      length of term .... 4 years
      party in majority, 1996 .... Democratic

State employees October, 1992
total 97,529
October payroll ($1,000) 223,037

Local governments, 1992
total 416
   county 23
   municipal 155
   township 0
   school districts 0
   special districts 237

Voting, November, 1994
voting age population 3,726,000
   registered 62.6%
   voted 46.2%

Vote for president
1988
   Bush 834,202
   Dukakis 793,939
1992
   Clinton 941,978
   Bush 671,609
   Perot 271,198

Federal representation, 1996 (104th Congress)
Senators (name/party/term expires)

PAUL S. SARBANES
Democrat - 2001
BARBARA MIKULSKI
Democrat - 1999

Representatives, total 8
   Democrats 4
   Republicans 4
   other 0

Maryland 5

Women holding public office
U.S. Congress, 1995 2
statewide elected office, 1995 1
state legislature, 1995 54

Black elected officials, 1993
total 140
　US and state legislatures 32
　city/county/regional offices 79
　judicial/law enforcement 23
　education/school boards 6

Hispanic public officials, 1994
total 2
　state executives & legislators 0
　city/county/regional offices 1
　judicial/law enforcement 0
　education/school boards 1

GOVERNMENTAL FINANCE

State & local government revenues, (selected items), 1991-92 ($per capita)
total $4,430.99
　total general revenues 3,774.22
　　from federal government 614.75
　　from own sources 3,159.48
　　from taxes 2,359.49
　　　from property taxes 660.51
　　　from all other taxes 1,536.75
　　from charges & misc. 799.98

State & local government expenditures, (selected items), 1991-92 ($per capita)
total $4,240.71
　total direct general expenditures 3,692.44
　　education 1,287.51
　　libraries 24.92
　　public welfare 558.73
　　health & hospitals 184.51
　　highways 229.19
　　police protection 145.26
　　fire protection 69.21
　　correction 136.69
　　housing & comm. development 89.64
　　natural resources & parks 131.58
　　interest on general debt 218.29

State & local debt, 1992 ($per capita) 3,920.16

Federal aid grants to state & local government, 1994 ($per capita total & selected items)
per capita total 726.61
　compensatory education 18.54
　waste treatment facilities 10.37
　medicaid 237.88
　housing assistance 48.54
　job training 8.69
　highway trust fund 59.54

CRIME, LAW ENFORCEMENT & COURTS

Crime, 1994 (all rates per 100,000 persons)
total crimes 306,496
overall crime rate 6,122.6
　property crimes 259,039
　　burglaries 52,234
　　larcenies 168,608
　　motor vehicle thefts 38,197
　property crime rate 5,174.6
　violent crimes 47,457
　　murders 579
　　forcible rapes 2,035
　　robberies 20,147
　　aggravated assaults 24,696
　violent crime rate 948.0

Number of police agencies, 1994 145

Arrests, 1994
total 273,198
　persons under 18 years of age 48,295

Prisoners under state & federal jurisdiction, 1994
total 20,998
percent change, 1993-94 ....3.6%
　sentenced to more than one year
　total 19,854
　rate per 100,000 residents 395

Persons under sentence of death, 4/20/95 13

State's highest court
name ....Court of Appeals
number of members 7
length of term ....10 years
intermediate appeals court? ....yes

167

Maryland 6

LABOR & INCOME

Civilian labor force, 1994
total 2,691,000
  men 1,399,000
  women 1,292,000
  persons 16-19 years 116,000
  white 1,855,000
  black 733,000

Civilian labor force as a percent of
civilian non-institutional population, 1994
total 70.6%
  men 77.8%
  women 64.2%
  persons 16-19 years 52.6%
  white 69.4%
  black 73.6%

Employment, 1994
total 2,554,000
  men 1,319,000
  women 1,235,000
  persons 16-19 years 98,000
  white 1,789,000
  black 665,000

Full-time/part-time labor force, 1994
full-time labor force 2,256,000
  working part-time for
    ecomonic reasons 20,000
part-time labor force 436,000

Unemployment rate, 1994
total 5.1%
  men 5.7%
  women 4.5%
  persons 16-19 years 15.0%
  white 3.5%
  black 9.2%

Unemployed by reason for unemployment
(as a percent of total unemployment), 1994
job losers or completed temp jobs 45.5%
job leavers 10.9%
reentrants 39.4%
new entrants 4.1%

Civilian labor force, by occupation, 1994
executive/administrative/
  managerial 444,000
professional/specialty 452,000
technicians & related support 98,000
sales 304,000
adminstrative support/clerical 442,000
service occupations 355,000
precision production/craft/repair 260,000
machine operators/assemblers 76,000
transportation/material moving 124,000
handlers/helpers/laborers 88,000
farming/forestry/fishing ....NA

Civilian labor force, by industry, 1994
construction 134,000
manufacturing 233,000
transportation/communication 136,000
wholesale/retail trade 471,000
finance/real estate/insurance 190,000
services 722,000
government 588,000
agriculture ....NA

Average annual pay, 1994 (prelim.) $28,421
change in average annual pay,
  1993-1994 .... 2.7%

Hours and earnings of production workers
on manufacturing payrolls, 1994
average weekly hours 41.5
average hourly earnings $13.15
average weekly earnings $545.73

Labor union membership, 1994 371,700

Household income (in constant 1993 dollars)
median household income, 1992 .... $38,317
median household income, 1993 .... $39,939

Poverty
persons below poverty level, 1992 .... 11.8%
persons below poverty level, 1993 .... 9.7%

Personal income ($per capita)
1994
  in current dollars 24,933
  in constant (1987) dollars 19,283
1995 (projected)
  in constant (1982) dollars 16,804
2000 (projected)
  in constant (1982) dollars 17,665

Federal income tax returns, 1993
returns filed 2,306,649
adjusted gross income ($1000) 86,119,622
total income tax paid ($1000) 11,904,130

ECONOMY, BUSINESS, INDUSTRY & AGRICULTURE

Fortune 500 companies, 1994 6

Business incorporations, 1994
total 17,730
change, 1993-94 .... 3.7%

Business failures, 1994
total 1,614
rate per 10,000 concerns 106
change, 1993-94 .... 4.2%

Business firm ownership
Hispanic owned firms, 1987 2,931
black owned firms, 1987 21,678
women owned firms, 1987 81,900
foreign owned firms, 1982 249

Gross state product, 1991 ($mil)
total $111,874
  agriculture services, forestry, fisheries ... 1,100
  mining 125
  construction 6,698
  manufacturing—durable goods 5,790
  manufacturing—nondurable goods 5,442
  transportation, communication &
    public utilities 9,483
  wholesale trade 6,736
  retail trade 11,176
  finance/real estate/insurance 21,292
  services 24,926
  federal, state & local government 19,106

Establishments, by major industry group, 1992
total 117,644
  agriculture 1,981
  mining 112
  construction 14,110
  manufacturing 4,358
  transportation 4,422
  wholesale trade 7,177
  retail trade 28,982
  finance/real estate/insurance 11,176
  service industries 43,987
  unclassified 1,339

Payroll, by major industry group, 1992
total ($1,000) $42,712,572
  agriculture 231,821

  mining 71,812
  construction 3,543,641
  manufacturing 6,266,794
  transportation 2,979,736
  wholesale trade 3,422,863
  retail trade 5,674,489
  finance/real estate/insurance 4,444,737
  service industries 16,051,814
  unclassified 24,865

Agriculture
number of farms, 1994 15,000
farm acreage, 1994 2,000,000
acres per farm, 1994 152
value of farms, 1994 ($mil) 6,305
farm income, 1993 ($mil)
  gross farm income 1,551
  net farm income 313
  debt/asset ratio 14.7%
farm marketings, 1993 ($mil)
total $1,366
  crops 560
  livestock 806
government payments 26
farm marketings in order of marketing receipts, 1993
    1) Broilers
    2) Greenhouse
    3) Dairy products
    4) Soybeans

Federal economic activity ($mil, except per capita)
expenditures, 1994
  total $36,576
  per capita $7,306
  defense $7,588
  non-defense $28,988
defense department, 1994
  contract awards ($mil) $4,256
  payroll ($mil) $3,308
  civilian employees (x1,000) 37.5
  military personnel (x1,000) 31.8

Fishing, 1992
catch (millions of pounds) 57
value ($mil) 36

Mining, 1994 ($mil)
total non-fuel mineral production $324

Maryland 8

principal non-fuel minerals in order of value, 1994
1) Stone
2) Cement
3) Sand and gravel

Construction, 1994 ($mil)
total contracts (including
  non-building) $6,077
    residential 2,725
    non-residential 1,955

Manufacturing, 1992
total establishments 4,337
employees, total (x1,000) 195
payroll ($mil) 6,291
production workers (x1,000) 114
value added ($mil) 15,588
value of shipments ($mil) 31,047

Finance
commercial banks, 1994
  number 94
    assets ($bil) 52.0
    deposits ($bil) 40.7
    closed or assisted 0
    deposits ($bil) .... NA
savings and loan associations, 1991
  non-current real estate loans 3.94%
  net income after taxes ($mil) .... -62
  return on assets .... -0.29%

Retail trade, 1992
establishments (x1,000) 28.0
sales ($mil) 37,625
annual payroll ($mil) 4,801
paid employees (x1,000) 367

Wholesale trade, 1992
establishments 7,188
sales ($bil) 52.9
annual payroll ($mil) 3,180
paid employees (x1,000) 100.5

Service industries, 1992
establishments (x1,000) (non-exempt firms)   36.8
receipts ($mil) (non-exempt firms) 26,937
annual payroll ($mil) 10,765
paid employees (x1,000) (non-exempt firms) . 419

COMMUNICATION, ENERGY & TRANSPORTATION

Communication
daily newspapers, 1993 15
broadcast stations, 1990
  radio: commercial, educational 113
  television: commercial, noncommercial 16
cable TV households, 1988 657,000

Energy
consumption estimates, 1992
total (trillion Btu) 1,204
per capita (million Btu) 244.8
by source of production (trillion Btu)
  coal 248
  natural gas 186
  petroleum 498
  nuclear electric power 114
  hydroelectric power 19
by end-use sector (trillion Btu)
  residential 321
  commercial 185
  industrial 353
  transportation 344
electrical energy
  production, 1993 (billion kWh) 43.5
  net summer capability, 1993 (million kW) . 10.7
gas utilities, 1993
  customers 869,000
  sales (trillion Btu) 136
  revenues ($mil) 837
nuclear plants, 1993 2

Transportation, 1994
public road & street mileage
total 29,474
  urban 13,758
  rural 15,716
  interstate 482
vehicle miles of travel (mil) 44,165
total motor vehicle registrations 3,640,337
  automobiles 2,731,510
licensed drivers 3,308,006
  per 1,000 driving age population 856
deaths from motor vehicle
  accidents 651

Massachusetts 1

STATE SUMMARY

Capital City ....Boston

Governor ....William Weld

Address ....STATE HOUSE
        BOSTON, MA 02133
        617 727-3600

Admitted as a state 1788

Area (square miles) 10,555

Population, 1980 5,737,037

Population, 1990 6,016,425

Population, 1994 (est.) 6,041,000

Persons per square mile, 1994 .... 770.7

Largest city ....Boston
  population, 1990 574,000

Personal income per capita, 1994
  (in current dollars) $25,616

Gross state product ($mil), 1991 156,090

Leading industries, 1992 (by payroll)
        SERVICE INDUSTRIES
        MANUFACTURING
        FINANCE, REAL ESTATE, &
        INSURANCE

Leading agricultural commodities, 1993
        GREENHOUSE
        CRANBERRIES
        DAIRY PRODUCTS
        EGGS

GEOGRAPHY & ENVIRONMENT

Area (square miles)
total 10,555
  land 7,838
  water (includes territorial water) 2,717

Federally owned land, 1991 .... 1.3%

Highest point
name .... Mt. Greylock
elevation (feet) 3,487

Lowest point
name ....Atlantic Ocean
elevation (feet) ....sea level

General coastline (miles) 192

Tidal shoreline (miles) 1,519

Capital city ....Boston
population, 1990 574,000

Largest city ....Boston
population, 1990 574,000

Number of cities with over 100,000 population
1980 3

Number of cities with over 100,000 population
1990 3

State parks and Recreation areas, 1991
area (acres) 273,000
number of visitors 11,975,000
revenues $10,408,000

National forest land, 1992 (acres) 0

National park acreage, 1984 30,900

DEMOGRAPHICS & CHARACTERISTICS OF THE POPULATION

Population
1970 5,689,170
1980 5,737,037
1990 6,016,425
1994 (est.) 6,041,000
2000 (revised projection) 5,950,000
2010 (revised projection) 6,097,000

Metropolitan area population
1970 5,266,000
1980 5,231,000
1992 5,763,000

Non-metropolitan area population
1970 423,000
1980 506,000
1992 230,000

Change in population, 1980-90
number 279,388
percent 4.87%

Persons per square mile, 1994 .... 770.7

Age distribution, 1980
under 5 years 5.9%
5 to 17 years 20.1%
65 and over 12.7%

Age distribution, 1990
under 5 years 6.9%
5 to 17 years 15.6%
65 and over 13.6%

Massachusetts 2

Age distribution, 2000 (projected)
under 5 years 5.6%
5 to 17 years 16.8%
65 and over 14.0%

Persons by age, 1990
under 5 years 412,473
5 to 17 years 940,602
65 and over 819,284

Median age, 1990 .... *33.60*

Race, 1990
White 5,405,374
Black 300,130
American Indian 11,857
Chinese 53,792
Filipino 6,212
Japanese 8,784
Asian Indian 19,719
Korean 11,744
Vietnamese 15,449
all other 182,980

Race, 2010 (projected)
White 5,387,000
Black 393,000

Persons of Hispanic origin, 1990
total 287,549
Mexican 12,703
Puerto Rican 151,193
Cuban 8,106
Other Hispanic 115,547

Persons by sex, 1990
male............................2,888,745
female 3,127,680

Marital status, 1990
males
15 years & older 2,305,194
single 832,633
married 1,273,184
separated 38,922
widowed 63,724
divorced 135,653
females
15 years & older 2,572,630
single 765,274
married 1,287,900
separated 60,931

widowed 311,956
divorced 207,500

Households & families, 1990
households 2,247,110
persons per household 2.58
families 1,514,746
married couples 1,170,275
female householder, no husband
present 270,923
one person households 580,774
households, 1994 2,265,000
persons per household, 1994 .... 2.57

Nativity, 1990
number of persons born in state 4,134,235
percent of total residents 68.7%

Immigration & naturalization, 1993
immigrants admitted 25,011
persons naturalized 6,574
refugees granted resident status 4,303

VITAL STATISTICS & HEALTH

Births
1992 88,185
with low birth weight 6.0%
to teenage mothers 7.7%
to unmarried mothers 25.9%
1993 86,317
1994 83,449

Abortions, 1992
total 41,000
rate (per 1,000 women age 15-44) 28.4
rate per 1,000 live births 472

Adoptions, 1986
total 2,334
related 50.4%

Deaths
1992 54,292
1993 56,460
1994 54,558

Infant deaths
1992 601
1993 484
1994 473

Massachusetts 3

Average lifetime, 1979-1981
both sexes .... 75.01 years
  men .... 71.27 years
  women .... 78.46 years

Marriages
1992 42,219
1993 37,468
1994 49,695

Divorces
1992 16,650
1993 16,002
1994 14,530

Physicians, 1993
total 21,676
rate (per 1,000 persons) 3.61

Dentists, 1992
total 4,765
rate (per 1,000 persons) 0.80

Hospitals, 1993
number 99
beds (x 1,000) 21.1
average daily census (x 1,000) 15.1
occupancy rate 71.5%
personnel (x 1,000) 107.8
average cost per day to hospital $1,036
average cost per stay to hospital $6,843

EDUCATION

*Educational attainment of all persons
  25 years and older, 1990*
less than 9th grade 317,943
high school graduates 1,178,509
bachelor's degree 657,161
graduate or professional degree 421,838

Public school enrollment, Fall, 1993
total 877,726
  Kindergarten through grade 8 645,518
  grades 9 through 12 232,208

Public School Teachers
total, 1994 58,766
  elementary 21,480
  secondary 29,367
salaries, 1994
  beginning $23,000
  average $38,960

*State receipts & expenditures for public
  schools, 1993*
receipts ($mil) 5,762
expenditures
  total ($mil) 5,470
  per capita $913
  per pupil $6,505

*Graduating high school seniors,
  public high schools, 1995 (est)* 48,259

SAT scores, 1994
verbal 426
math 475

Institutions of higher education, 1995
total 118
  public 32
  private 86

*Enrollment in institutions of higher
  education, Fall, 1993*
total 420,127
full-time men 124,561
full-time women 138,201
part-time men 63,123
part-time women 94,242

*Minority enrollment in institutions of higher
  education, Fall, 1993*
Black, non-Hispanic 21,344
Hispanic 15,810
Asian/Pacific Islander 21,601

Earned degrees conferred, 1993
Bachelor's 42,747
First professional 3,677
Master's 19,215
Doctor's 2,276

SOCIAL INSURANCE &
WELFARE PROGRAMS

Social Security beneficiaries & benefits, 1993
beneficiaries
total 1,027,000
  retired and dependents 744,000
  survivors 155,000
  disabled & dependents 127,000
annual benefit payments ($mil)
total $7,528
  retired and dependents 5,307
  survivors 1,380
  disabled & dependents 841

173

Massachusetts 4

Medicare, 1993
enrollment (x1,000) 911
payments ($mil) 4,487

Medicaid, 1993
recipients (x1,000) 765
payments ($mil) 2,726

Federal public aid, 1993
recipients as a percent of population 7.7%
Aid to Families with Dependent Children
  recipients (x1,000) 313
average monthly payment $549
Supplemental Security Income
  total recipients (x1,000) 149

Food Stamp Program
  participants, 1994 (x1,000) 442

HOUSING & CONSTRUCTION

Total housing units, 1990 2,472,711
  year round housing units 2,382,210
  vacant 225,601

New privately owned housing units authorized, 1994
number (x1,000) 18.1
value ($mil) 2,046

New privately owned housing units started, 1994 (x1,000) 17.8

Existing home sales, 1994 (x1,000) 68.7

GOVERNMENT & ELECTIONS

State officials, 1996
  Governor (name/party/term expires)
      WILLIAM WELD
      Republican - 1999
Lt. Governor . . . . .Paul Cellucci
Sec. of State . . . . .Michael J. Connolly
Atty. General . . . . .Scott Harshberger
Chf. Justice . . . . .Paul Liacos

Governorship
minimum age .not specified
length of term . . . . .4 years
number of consecutive
  terms permitted . . . . .not specified
who succeeds . . . . Lt. Governor

State legislature
name . . . . General Court
  upper chamber
      name . . . . Senate
      number of members 40
      length of term .2 years
      party in majority, 1996 . . . . .Democratic
  lower chamber
      name . . . . House of Representatives
      number of members 160
      length of term .2 years
      party in majority, 1996 . . . . .Democratic

State employees October, 1992
total 101,646
October payroll ($1,000) 223,416

Local governments, 1992
total 851
  county 12
  municipal 39
  township 312
  school districts 86
  special districts 401

Voting, November, 1994
voting age population 4,532,000
  registered 65.6%
  voted 51.6%

Vote for president
1988
  Bush 1,184,323
  Dukakis 1,387,398
1992
  Clinton 1,311,845
  Bush 802,479
  Perot 629,903

Federal representation, 1996 (104th Congress)
Senators (name/party/term expires)

      EDWARD M. KENNEDY
      Democrat - 2001
      JOHN F. KERRY
      Democrat - 1997

Representatives, total 10
  Democrats 8
  Republicans 2
  other 0

Massachusetts 5

Women holding public office
U.S. Congress, 1995 0
statewide elected office, 1995 0
state legislature, 1995 48

Black elected officials, 1993
total 30
  US and state legislatures 8
  city/county/regional offices 18
  judicial/law enforcement 2
  education/school boards 2

Hispanic public officials, 1994
total 1
  state executives & legislators 0
  city/county/regional offices 0
  judicial/law enforcement 0
  education/school boards 1

GOVERNMENTAL FINANCE

State & local government revenues, (selected items), 1991-92 ($per capita)
total $5,018.12
  total general revenues 4,281.93
    from federal government 808.69
    from own sources 3,473.25
    from taxes 2,553.20
      from property taxes 876.15
      from all other taxes 1,541.49
    from charges & misc. 920.04

State & local government expenditures, (selected items), 1991-92 ($per capita)
total $5,107.35
  total direct general expenditures 4,118.58
    education 1,070.03
    libraries 23.45
    public welfare 845.12
    health & hospitals 358.21
    highways 220.00
    police protection 131.23
    fire protection 90.05
    correction 108.01
    housing & comm. development 153.65
    natural resources & parks 51.35
    interest on general debt 289.03

State & local debt, 1992 ($per capita) 5,494.20

Federal aid grants to state & local government, 1994 ($per capita total & selected items)
per capita total 1,038.49
  compensatory education 22.14
  waste treatment facilities 32.26
  medicaid 348.35
  housing assistance 98.90
  job training 15.80
  highway trust fund 159.36

CRIME, LAW ENFORCEMENT & COURTS

Crime, 1994 (all rates per 100,000 persons)
total crimes 268,281
overall crime rate 4,441.0
  property crimes 225,532
    burglaries 53,222
    larcenies 129,962
    motor vehicle thefts 42,348
  property crime rate 3,733.4
  violent crimes 42,749
    murders 214
    forcible rapes 1,825
    robberies 10,160
    aggravated assaults 30,550
  violent crime rate 707.6

Number of police agencies, 1994 186

Arrests, 1994
total 138,524
  persons under 18 years of age 19,530

Prisoners under state & federal jurisdiction, 1994
total 11,282
percent change, 1993-94 ....1.6%
  sentenced to more than one year
    total 10,340
    rate per 100,000 residents 171

Persons under sentence of death, 4/20/95 ....NA

State's highest court
name ....Supreme Court
number of members 7
length of term ....to age 70
intermediate appeals court? ....yes

175

Massachusetts 6

LABOR & INCOME

Civilian labor force, 1994

total	3,179,000
men	1,697,000
women	1,482,000
persons 16-19 years	169,000
white	2,932,000
black	145,000

Civilian labor force as a percent of civilian non-institutional population, 1994

total	67.9%
men	75.7%
women	60.7%
persons 16-19 years	57.9%
white	68.1%
black	67.3%

Employment, 1994

total	2,988,000
men	1,586,000
women	1,402,000
persons 16-19 years	142,000
white	2,767,000
black	127,000

Full-time/part-time labor force, 1994

full-time labor force	2,471,000
working part-time for ecomonic reasons	23,000
part-time labor force	708,000

Unemployment rate, 1994

total	6.0%
men	6.6%
women	5.4%
persons 16-19 years	15.9%
white	5.6%
black	12.8%

Unemployed by reason for unemployment (as a percent of total unemployment), 1994

job losers or completed temp jobs	57.4%
job leavers	7.9%
reentrants	30.2%
new entrants	4.6%

Civilian labor force, by occupation, 1994

executive/administrative/ managerial	478,000
professional/specialty	600,000
technicians & related support	111,000
sales	364,000
adminstrative support/clerical	490,000
service occupations	433,000
precision production/craft/repair	294,000
machine operators/assemblers	160,000
transportation/material moving	97,000
handlers/helpers/laborers	108,000
farming/forestry/fishing	34,000

Civilian labor force, by industry, 1994

construction	137,000
manufacturing	491,000
transportation/communication	143,000
wholesale/retail trade	592,000
finance/real estate/insurance	229,000
services	931,000
government	374,000
agriculture	26,000

Average annual pay, 1994 (prelim.)	$31,024
change in average annual pay, 1993-1994	2.6%

Hours and earnings of production workers on manufacturing payrolls, 1994

average weekly hours	41.7
average hourly earnings	$12.59
average weekly earnings	$525.00

Labor union membership, 1994 419,400

Household income (in constant 1993 dollars)

median household income, 1992	$37,447
median household income, 1993	$37,064

Poverty

persons below poverty level, 1992	10.3%
persons below poverty level, 1993	10.7%

Personal income ($per capita)

1994	
in current dollars	25,616
in constant (1987) dollars	19,811
1995 (projected)	
in constant (1982) dollars	17,861
2000 (projected)	
in constant (1982) dollars	18,694

Federal income tax returns, 1993

returns filed	2,783,535
adjusted gross income ($1000)	101,964,611
total income tax paid ($1000)	15,513,521

ECONOMY, BUSINESS, INDUSTRY & AGRICULTURE

Fortune 500 companies, 1994 17

Business incorporations, 1994
total 14,065
change, 1993-94 .... 9.5%

Business failures, 1994
total 2,097
rate per 10,000 concerns 98
change, 1993-94 .... -22.7%

Business firm ownership
Hispanic owned firms, 1987 2,636
black owned firms, 1987 4,761
women owned firms, 1987 111,400
foreign owned firms, 1982 327

Gross state product, 1991 ($mil)
total $156,090
  agriculture services, forestry, fisheries ... 1,121
  mining 64
  construction 4,767
  manufacturing—durable goods 20,781
  manufacturing—nondurable goods 8,428
  transportation, communication &
    public utilities 11,121
  wholesale trade 10,874
  retail trade 13,196
  finance/real estate/insurance 33,118
  services 38,168
  federal, state & local government 14,453

Establishments, by major industry group, 1992
total 154,574
  agriculture 2,655
  mining 97
  construction 13,902
  manufacturing 10,195
  transportation 5,616
  wholesale trade 10,915
  retail trade 39,362
  finance/real estate/insurance 12,872
  service industries 57,328
  unclassified 1,632

Payroll, by major industry group, 1992
total ($1,000) $71,683,284
  agriculture 217,718

  mining 44,496
  construction 2,583,811
  manufacturing 16,852,851
  transportation 4,045,764
  wholesale trade 5,808,259
  retail trade 7,305,950
  finance/real estate/insurance 8,231,935
  service industries 26,554,030
  unclassified 38,470

Agriculture
number of farms, 1994 6,000
farm acreage, 1994 1,000,000
acres per farm, 1994 102
value of farms, 1994 ($mil) 2,595
farm income, 1993 ($mil)
  gross farm income 560
  net farm income 191
  debt/asset ratio 8.1%
farm marketings, 1993 ($mil)
  total $497
    crops 375
    livestock 122
government payments 4
farm marketings in order of marketing receipts, 1993
    1) Greenhouse
    2) Cranberries
    3) Dairy products
    4) Eggs

Federal economic activity
  ($mil, except per capita)
expenditures, 1994
  total $35,374
  per capita $5,856
  defense $6,251
  non-defense $29,123
defense department, 1994
  contract awards ($mil) $5,106
  payroll ($mil) $1,081
  civilian employees (x1,000) 9.9
  military personnel (x1,000) 6.1

Fishing, 1992
catch (millions of pounds) 274
value ($mil) 280

Mining, 1994 ($mil)
total non-fuel mineral production $157

Massachusetts 8

principal non-fuel minerals in order of value, 1994

    1) Stone
    2) Sand and gravel
    3) Stone

Construction, 1994 ($mil)
total contracts (including
  non-building) $6,366
    residential 2,478
    non-residential 2,597

Manufacturing, 1992
total establishments 10,145
employees, total (x1,000) 480
payroll ($mil) 16,421
production workers (x1,000) 273
value added ($mil) 36,519
value of shipments ($mil) 65,702

Finance
commercial banks, 1994
  number 61
    assets ($bil) 97.7
    deposits ($bil) 70.0
  closed or assisted 2
    deposits ($bil) 0.2
savings and loan associations, 1991
  non-current real estate loans 4.13%
  net income after taxes ($mil) .... -158
  return on assets .... -3.35%

Retail trade, 1992
establishments (x1,000) 38.5
sales ($mil) 47,663
annual payroll ($mil) 5,986
paid employees (x1,000) 470

Wholesale trade, 1992
establishments 10,950
sales ($bil) 86.7
annual payroll ($mil) 5,035
paid employees (x1,000) 141.5

Service industries, 1992
establishments (x1,000) (non-exempt firms) 46.6
receipts ($mil) (non-exempt firms) 38,949
annual payroll ($mil) 15,103
paid employees (x1,000) (non-exempt firms) . 545

COMMUNICATION, ENERGY & TRANSPORTATION

Communication
daily newspapers, 1993 39
broadcast stations, 1990
  radio: commercial, educational 174
  television: commercial, noncommercial 19
cable TV households, 1988 1,376,000

Energy
consumption estimates, 1992
total (trillion Btu) 1,370
per capita (million Btu) 228.5
by source of production (trillion Btu)
  coal 111
  natural gas 306
  petroleum 751
  nuclear electric power 51
  hydroelectric power 20
by end-use sector (trillion Btu)
  residential 407
  commercial 342
  industrial 236
  transportation 386
electrical energy
  production, 1993 (billion kWh) 28.2
  net summer capability, 1993 (million kW) .. 9.5
gas utilities, 1993
  customers 1,266,000
  sales (trillion Btu) 234
  revenues ($mil) 1,594
nuclear plants, 1993 1

Transportation, 1994
public road & street mileage
total 30,599
  urban 19,745
  rural 10,854
  interstate 565
vehicle miles of travel (mil) 46,990
total motor vehicle registrations 4,026,804
  automobiles 3,068,374
licensed drivers 4,471,529
  per 1,000 driving age population 940
deaths from motor vehicle
  accidents 440

Michigan 1

STATE SUMMARY

Capital City . . . . Lansing

Governor . . . . John Engler

Address . . . . STATE CAPITOL
LANSING, MI 48909
517 373-3400

Admitted as a state 1837

Area (square miles) 96,810

Population, 1980 9,262,078

Population, 1990 9,295,297

Population, 1994 (est.) 9,496,000

Persons per square mile, 1994 . . . . 167.2

Largest city . . . . Detroit
population, 1990 1,028,000

Personal income per capita, 1994
(in current dollars) $22,333

Gross state product ($mil), 1991 189,445

Leading industries, 1992 (by payroll)
MANUFACTURING
SERVICE INDUSTRIES
RETAIL TRADE

Leading agricultural commodities, 1993
DAIRY PRODUCTS
CORN
GREENHOUSE
CATTLE

GEOGRAPHY & ENVIRONMENT

Area (square miles)
total 96,810
 land 56,809
 water (includes territorial water) 40,001

Federally owned land, 1991 . . . . 12.6%

Highest point
name . . . . Mt. Avron
elevation (feet) 1,979

Lowest point
name . . . . Lake Erie
elevation (feet) 572

General coastline (miles) 0

Tidal shoreline (miles) 0

Capital city . . . . Lansing
population, 1990 127,000

Largest city . . . . Detroit
population, 1990 1,028,000

Number of cities with over 100,000 population
1980 8

Number of cities with over 100,000 population
1990 7

State parks and Recreation areas, 1991
area (acres) 264,000
number of visitors 25,260,000
revenues $21,383,000

National forest land, 1992 (acres) 4,895,000

National park acreage, 1984 630,200

DEMOGRAPHICS & CHARACTERISTICS OF THE POPULATION

Population
1970 8,881,826
1980 9,262,078
1990 9,295,297
1994 (est.) 9,496,000
2000 (revised projection) 9,759,000
2010 (revised projection) 10,033,000

Metropolitan area population
1970 7,361,000
1980 7,481,000
1992 7,799,000

Non-metropolitan area population
1970 1,521,000
1980 1,782,000
1992 1,635,000

Change in population, 1980-90
number 33,219
percent 0.36%

Persons per square mile, 1994 . . . . 167.2

Age distribution, 1980
under 5 years 7.4%
5 to 17 years 22.3%
65 and over 9.8%

Age distribution, 1990
under 5 years 7.6%
5 to 17 years 18.8%
65 and over 11.9%

Michigan 2

Age distribution, 2000 (projected)
under 5 years 6.3%
5 to 17 years 19.0%
65 and over 12.1%

Persons by age, 1990
under 5 years 702,554
5 to 17 years 1,756,211
65 and over 1,108,461

Median age, 1990 .... 32.60

Race, 1990
White 7,756,086
Black 1,291,706
American Indian 55,131
Chinese 19,145
Filipino 13,786
Japanese 10,681
Asian Indian 23,845
Korean 16,316
Vietnamese 6,117
all other 101,977

Race, 2010 (projected)
White 7,979,000
Black 1,737,000

Persons of Hispanic origin, 1990
total 201,596
Mexican 138,312
Puerto Rican 18,538
Cuban 5,157
Other Hispanic 39,589

Persons by sex, 1990
male 4,512,781
female 4,782,516

Marital status, 1990
males
15 years & older 3,458,188
single 1,078,995
married 2,015,282
separated 57,534
widowed 88,226
divorced 275,685
females
15 years & older 3,775,938
single 931,043
married 2,031,579
separated 82,215

widowed 433,615
divorced 379,701

Households & families, 1990
households 3,419,331
persons per household 2.66
families 2,439,171
married couples 1,883,143
female householder, no husband
present 442,239
one person households 809,449
households, 1994 3,502,000
persons per household, 1994 .... 2.65

Nativity, 1990
number of persons born in state 6,958,717
percent of total residents 74.9%

Immigration & naturalization, 1993
immigrants admitted 14,913
persons naturalized 6,091
refugees granted resident status 2,596

VITAL STATISTICS & HEALTH

Births
1992 138,968
with low birth weight 7.5%
to teenage mothers 13.0%
to unmarried mothers 26.8%
1993 143,576
1994 139,931

Abortions, 1992
total 56,000
rate (per 1,000 women age 15-44) 25.2
rate per 1,000 live births 393

Adoptions, 1986
total 4,115
related 50.4%

Deaths
1992 79,307
1993 82,651
1994 83,312

Infant deaths
1992 1,459
1993 1,338
1994 1,200

Average lifetime, 1979-1981
both sexes .... 73.67 years
  men .... 70.07 years
  women .... 77.29 years

Marriages
1992 70,700
1993 71,222
1994 70,751

Divorces
1992 39,424
1993 39,183
1994 38,727

Physicians, 1993
total 18,513
rate (per 1,000 persons) 1.95

Dentists, 1992
total 5,955
rate (per 1,000 persons) 0.63

Hospitals, 1993
number 167
beds (x 1,000) 30.9
average daily census (x 1,000) 20.0
occupancy rate 64.7%
personnel (x 1,000) 140.9
average cost per day to hospital $902
average cost per stay to hospital $6,147

EDUCATION

*Educational attainment of all persons
  25 years and older, 1990*
less than 9th grade 452,893
high school graduates 1,887,449
bachelor's degree 638,267
graduate or professional degree 375,780

Public school enrollment, Fall, 1993
total 1,599,377
  Kindergarten through grade 8 1,159,968
  grades 9 through 12 439,409

Public School Teachers
total, 1994 80,267
  elementary 34,136
  secondary 36,419
salaries, 1994
  beginning $24,400
  average $45,218

*State receipts & expenditures for public
  schools, 1993*
receipts ($mil) 11,409
expenditures
  total ($mil) 10,896
  per capita $1,155
  per pupil $6,402

*Graduating high school seniors,
  public high schools, 1995 (est)* 88,500

SAT scores, 1994
verbal 472
math 537

Institutions of higher education, 1995
total 109
  public 45
  private 64

*Enrollment in institutions of higher
  education, Fall, 1993*
total 568,210
full-time men 136,177
full-time women 150,788
part-time men 117,085
part-time women 164,160

*Minority enrollment in institutions of higher
  education, Fall, 1993*
Black, non-Hispanic 60,662
Hispanic 10,920
Asian/Pacific Islander 13,672

Earned degrees conferred, 1993
Bachelor's 45,711
First professional 2,581
Master's 14,944
Doctor's 1,513

SOCIAL INSURANCE &
WELFARE PROGRAMS

Social Security beneficiaries & benefits, 1993
beneficiaries
total 1,569,000
  retired and dependents 1,086,000
  survivors 281,000
  disabled & dependents 201,000
annual benefit payments ($mil)
total $12,096
  retired and dependents 8,106
  survivors 2,557
  disabled & dependents 1,434

Michigan 4

Medicare, 1993
enrollment (x1,000) 1,309
payments ($mil) 5,171

Medicaid, 1993
recipients (x1,000) 1,172
payments ($mil) 3,077

Federal public aid, 1993
recipients as a percent of population 9.3%
Aid to Families with Dependent Children
   recipients (x1,000) 676
average monthly payment $438
Supplemental Security Income
   total recipients (x1,000) 192

Food Stamp Program
participants, 1994 (x1,000) 1,031

HOUSING & CONSTRUCTION

Total housing units, 1990 3,847,926
   year round housing units 3,621,305
   vacant 428,595

New privately owned housing units
   authorized, 1994
number (x1,000) 46.5
value ($mil) 4,149

New privately owned housing units
   started, 1994 (x1,000) 48.1

Existing home sales, 1994 (x1,000) 184.2

GOVERNMENT & ELECTIONS

State officials, 1996
   Governor (name/party/term expires)
            JOHN ENGLER
            Republican - 1999
Lt. Governor . . . . Connie Binsfeld
Sec. of State . . . . Candice Miller
Atty. General . . . . Frank J. Kelley
Chf. Justice . . . . Michael F. Cavanagh

Governorship
minimum age 30
length of term . . . . 4 years
number of consecutive
   terms permitted . . . . not specified
who succeeds . . . . Lt. Governor

State legislature
name . . . . Legislature
   upper chamber
      name . . . . Senate
      number of members 38
      length of term . . . . 4 years
      party in majority, 1996 . . . . Republican
   lower chamber
      name . . . . House of Representatives
      number of members 110
      length of term . . . . 2 years
      party in majority, 1996 . . . . Republican

State employees October, 1992
total 172,502
October payroll ($1,000) 401,837

Local governments, 1992
total 2,727
   county 83
   municipal 534
   township 1,242
   school districts 587
   special districts 280

Voting, November, 1994
voting age population 6,921,000
   registered 73.7%
   voted 52.2%

Vote for president
1988
   Bush 1,969,435
   Dukakis 1,673,496
1992
   Clinton 1,860,143
   Bush 1,557,550
   Perot 820,137

Federal representation, 1996 (104th Congress)
Senators (name/party/term expires)

            SPENCER ABRAHAM
            Republican - 2001
            CARL LEVIN
            Democrat - 1997

Representatives, total 16
   Democrats 9
   Republicans 7
   other 0

Michigan 5

Women holding public office
U.S. Congress, 1995 2
statewide elected office, 1995 2
state legislature, 1995 33

Black elected officials, 1993
total 333
   US and state legislatures 17
   city/county/regional offices 133
   judicial/law enforcement 68
   education/school boards 115

Hispanic public officials, 1994
total 8
   state executives & legislators 0
   city/county/regional offices 5
   judicial/law enforcement 1
   education/school boards 2

GOVERNMENTAL FINANCE

State & local government revenues, (selected items), 1991-92 ($per capita)
total $4,520.41
   total general revenues 3,833.87
    from federal government 683.77
    from own sources 3,150.11
    from taxes 2,188.66
     from property taxes 958.90
     from all other taxes 1,109.22
    from charges & misc. 961.45

State & local government expenditures, (selected items), 1991-92 ($per capita)
total $4,419.97
   total direct general expenditures 3,799.04
    education 1,479.05
    libraries 17.66
    public welfare 601.48
    health & hospitals 383.76
    highways 201.74
    police protection 134.54
    fire protection 46.17
    correction 119.59
    housing & comm. development 17.44
    natural resources & parks 77.03
    interest on general debt 144.04

State & local debt, 1992 ($per capita) 2,552.42

Federal aid grants to state & local government, 1994 ($per capita total & selected items)
per capita total 749.48
   compensatory education 29.44
   waste treatment facilities 11.35
   medicaid 306.86
   housing assistance 34.79
   job training 14.77
   highway trust fund 43.90

CRIME, LAW ENFORCEMENT & COURTS

Crime, 1994 (all rates per 100,000 persons)
total crimes 517,076
overall crime rate 5,445.2
   property crimes 444,325
    burglaries 91,849
    larcenies 290,172
    motor vehicle thefts 62,304
   property crime rate 4,679.1
   violent crimes 72,751
    murders 927
    forcible rapes 6,720
    robberies 21,733
    aggravated assaults 43,371
   violent crime rate 766.1

Number of police agencies, 1994 391

Arrests, 1994
total 352,288
   persons under 18 years of age 55,254

Prisoners under state & federal jurisdiction, 1994
total 40,775
percent change, 1993-94 .... 3.7%
   sentenced to more than one year
    total 40,775
    rate per 100,000 residents 428

Persons under sentence of death, 4/20/95 .... NA

State's highest court
name .... Supreme Court
number of members 7
length of term .... 8 years
intermediate appeals court? .... yes

Michigan 6

LABOR & INCOME

Civilian labor force, 1994

total	4,753,000
men	2,572,000
women	2,181,000
persons 16-19 years	311,000
white	4,099,000
black	556,000

Civilian labor force as a percent of civilian non-institutional population, 1994

total	66.6%
men	75.2%
women	58.7%
persons 16-19 years	60.2%
white	68.0%
black	57.7%

Employment, 1994

total	4,473,000
men	2,421,000
women	2,052,000
persons 16-19 years	264,000
white	3,892,000
black	490,000

Full-time/part-time labor force, 1994

full-time labor force	3,761,000
working part-time for ecomonic reasons	43,000
part-time labor force	993,000

Unemployment rate, 1994

total	5.9%
men	5.9%
women	5.9%
persons 16-19 years	15.3%
white	5.1%
black	11.9%

Unemployed by reason for unemployment (as a percent of total unemployment), 1994

job losers or completed temp jobs	45.6%
job leavers	8.8%
reentrants	38.4%
new entrants	7.2%

Civilian labor force, by occupation, 1994

executive/administrative/ managerial	557,000
professional/specialty	650,000
technicians & related support	154,000
sales	566,000
adminstrative support/clerical	656,000
service occupations	676,000
precision production/craft/repair	543,000
machine operators/assemblers	411,000
transportation/material moving	191,000
handlers/helpers/laborers	213,000
farming/forestry/fishing	113,000

Civilian labor force, by industry, 1994

construction	194,000
manufacturing	1,088,000
transportation/communication	196,000
wholesale/retail trade	980,000
finance/real estate/insurance	207,000
services	1,06400
government	609,000
agriculture	97,000

Average annual pay, 1994 (prelim.)	$29,541
change in average annual pay, 1993-1994	4.5%

Hours and earnings of production workers on manufacturing payrolls, 1994

average weekly hours	44.9
average hourly earnings	$16.13
average weekly earnings	$724.24

Labor union membership, 1994	960,600

Household income (in constant 1993 dollars)

median household income, 1992	$33,233
median household income, 1993	$32,662

Poverty

persons below poverty level, 1992	13.6%
persons below poverty level, 1993	15.4%

Personal income ($per capita)
1994

in current dollars	22,333
in constant (1987) dollars	17,272

1995 (projected)

in constant (1982) dollars	14,507

2000 (projected)

in constant (1982) dollars	15,361

Federal income tax returns, 1993

returns filed	4,141,907
adjusted gross income ($1000)	137,426,632
total income tax paid ($1000)	19,234,274

ECONOMY, BUSINESS, INDUSTRY & AGRICULTURE

Fortune 500 companies, 1994 16

Business incorporations, 1994
total 30,374
change, 1993-94 .... 5.5%

Business failures, 1994
total 1,956
rate per 10,000 concerns 66
change, 1993-94 .... -23.4%

Business firm ownership
Hispanic owned firms, 1987 2,654
black owned firms, 1987 13,708
women owned firms, 1987 134,000
foreign owned firms, 1982 318

Gross state product, 1991 ($mil)
total $189,445
  agriculture services, forestry, fisheries ... 2,372
  mining 1,049
  construction 6,552
  manufacturing—durable goods 34,939
  manufacturing—nondurable goods 14,152
  transportation, communication &
    public utilities 13,840
  wholesale trade 12,599
  retail trade 17,839
  finance/real estate/insurance 31,643
  services 33,193
  federal, state & local government 21,267

Establishments, by major industry group, 1992
total 215,567
  agriculture 3,278
  mining 501
  construction 21,034
  manufacturing 16,554
  transportation 7,300
  wholesale trade 15,480
  retail trade 55,565
  finance/real estate/insurance 17,044
  service industries 75,672
  unclassified 3,139

Payroll, by major industry group, 1992
total ($1,000) $87,332,181
  agriculture 300,539

mining 298,501
construction 3,726,800
manufacturing 33,117,166
transportation 5,048,427
wholesale trade 6,414,948
retail trade 9,311,578
finance/real estate/insurance 5,580,645
service industries 23,457,558
unclassified 76,019

Agriculture
number of farms, 1994 52,000
farm acreage, 1994 11,000,000
acres per farm, 1994 206
value of farms, 1994 ($mil) 12,969
farm income, 1993 ($mil)
  gross farm income 4,062
  net farm income 624
  debt/asset ratio 16.3%
farm marketings, 1993 ($mil)
total $3,367
  crops 1,991
  livestock 1,376
government payments 241
farm marketings in order of marketing
receipts, 1993
  1) Dairy products
  2) Corn
  3) Greenhouse
  4) Soybeans

Federal economic activity
($mil, except per capita)
expenditures, 1994
  total $38,975
  per capita $4,104
  defense $2,601
  non-defense $36,374
defense department, 1994
  contract awards ($mil) $1,602
  payroll ($mil) $878
  civilian employees (x1,000) 9.8
  military personnel (x1,000) 3.8

Fishing, 1992
catch (millions of pounds) .... NA
value ($mil) .... NA

Mining, 1994 ($mil)
total non-fuel mineral production $1,621

Michigan 8

principal non-fuel minerals in order of value, 1994
  1) Iron ore
  2) Cement
  3) Sand and gravel

Construction, 1994 ($mil)
total contracts (including
  non-building) $9,592
    residential 4,085
    non-residential 3,378

Manufacturing, 1992
total establishments 16,531
employees, total (x1,000) 917
payroll ($mil) 34,207
production workers (x1,000) 574
value added ($mil) 71,724
value of shipments ($mil) 161,409

Finance
commercial banks, 1994
  number 208
    assets ($bil) 106.0
    deposits ($bil) 81.6
  closed or assisted 0
    deposits ($bil) ....NA
savings and loan associations, 1991
  non-current real estate loans 1.37%
  net income after taxes ($mil) 145
  return on assets .... +0.46%

Retail trade, 1992
establishments (x1,000) 54.5
sales ($mil) 71,523
annual payroll ($mil) 8,187
paid employees (x1,000) 707

Wholesale trade, 1992
establishments 15,517
sales ($bil) 125.7
annual payroll ($mil) 5,960
paid employees (x1,000) 185.2

Service industries, 1992
establishments (x1,000) (non-exempt firms) 61.3
receipts ($mil) (non-exempt firms) 35,124
annual payroll ($mil) 14,203
paid employees (x1,000) (non-exempt firms) . 614

COMMUNICATION, ENERGY & TRANSPORTATION

Communication
daily newspapers, 1993 52
broadcast stations, 1990
    radio: commercial, educational 340
    television: commercial, noncommercial 45
cable TV households, 1988 1,621,000

Energy
consumption estimates, 1992
total (trillion Btu) 2,784
per capita (million Btu) 295.1
by source of production (trillion Btu)
    coal 702
    natural gas 909
    petroleum 914
    nuclear electric power 201
    hydroelectric power 8
by end-use sector (trillion Btu)
    residential 700
    commercial 442
    industrial 943
    transportation 699
electrical energy
    production, 1993 (billion kWh) 92.3
    net summer capability, 1993 (million kW) . 22.4
gas utilities, 1993
    customers 3,021,000
    sales (trillion Btu) 550
    revenues ($mil) 2,518
nuclear plants, 1993 5

Transportation, 1994
public road & street mileage
total 117,671
    urban 28,147
    rural 89,524
    interstate 1,238
vehicle miles of travel (mil) 85,183
total motor vehicle registrations 7,573,593
    automobiles 5,276,953
licensed drivers 6,601,924
    per 1,000 driving age population 912
deaths from motor vehicle
    accidents 1,419

Minnesota 1

STATE SUMMARY

Capital City . . . . St. Paul

Governor . . . . Arne Carlson

Address . . . . STATE CAPITOL
ST. PAUL, MN 55155
612 296-3391

Admitted as a state 1858

Area (square miles) 86,943

Population, 1980 4,075,970

Population, 1990 4,375,099

Population, 1994 (est.) 4,567,000

Persons per square mile, 1994 . . . . 57.4

Largest city . . . . Minneapolis
population, 1990 368,000

Personal income per capita, 1994
(in current dollars) $22,453

Gross state product ($mil), 1991 103,301

Leading industries, 1992 (by payroll)
SERVICE INDUSTRIES
MANUFACTURING
RETAIL TRADE

Leading agricultural commodities, 1993
DAIRY PRODUCTS
CORN
SOYBEANS
CATTLE

GEOGRAPHY & ENVIRONMENT

Area (square miles)
total 86,943
land 79,617
water (includes territorial water) 7,326

Federally owned land, 1991 . . . . 10.5%

Highest point
name . . . . Eagle Mountain
elevation (feet) 2,301

Lowest point
name . . . . Lake Superior
elevation (feet) 602

General coastline (miles) 0

Tidal shoreline (miles) 0

Capital city . . . . St. Paul
population, 1990 272,000

Largest city . . . . Minneapolis
population, 1990 368,000

Number of cities with over 100,000 population
1980 2

Number of cities with over 100,000 population
1990 2

State parks and Recreation areas, 1991
area (acres) 231,000
number of visitors 7,981,000
revenues $7,117,000

National forest land, 1992 (acres) 5,467,000

National park acreage, 1984 138,100

DEMOGRAPHICS & CHARACTERISTICS OF THE POPULATION

Population
1970 3,806,103
1980 4,075,970
1990 4,375,099
1994 (est.) 4,567,000
2000 (revised projection) 4,824,000
2010 (revised projection) 5,127,000

Metropolitan area population
1970 2,434,000
1980 2,621,000
1992 3,096,000

Non-metropolitan area population
1970 1,373,000
1980 1,455,000
1992 1,372,000

Change in population, 1980-90
number 299,129
percent 7.34%

Persons per square mile, 1994 . . . . 57.4

Age distribution, 1980
under 5 years 7.5%
5 to 17 years 21.2%
65 and over 11.8%

Age distribution, 1990
under 5 years 7.7%
5 to 17 years 18.9%
65 and over 12.5%

Minnesota 2

Age distribution, 2000 (projected)
under 5 years 6.4%
5 to 17 years 18.9%
65 and over 12.8%

Persons by age, 1990
under 5 years 336,800
5 to 17 years 829,983
65 and over 546,934

Median age, 1990 .... *32.50*

Race, 1990
White 4,130,395
Black 94,944
American Indian 49,392
Chinese 8,980
Filipino 4,237
Japanese 3,581
Asian Indian........................ 8,234
Korean 11,576
Vietnamese 9,387
all other 53,856

Race, 2010 (projected)
White 4,699,000
Black 122,000

Persons of Hispanic origin, 1990
total 53,884
Mexican 34,691
Puerto Rican 3,286
Cuban 1,539
Other Hispanic 14,368

Persons by sex, 1990
male 2,145,183
female 2,229,916

Marital status, 1990
males
15 years & older 1,635,377
single 504,483
married 985,981
separated 17,429
widowed 36,176
divorced 108,737
females
15 years & older 1,743,785
single 420,836
married 987,634
separated 22,253

widowed 193,619
divorced 141,696

Households & families, 1990
households 1,647,853
persons per household 2.58
families 1,130,683
married couples 942,524
female householder, no husband
present 141,554
one person households 413,531
households, 1994 1,711,000
persons per household, 1994 .... 2.60

Nativity, 1990
number of persons born in state 3,220,512
percent of total residents 73.6%

Immigration & naturalization, 1993
immigrants admitted 7,438
persons naturalized 1,921
refugees granted resident status 2,678

VITAL STATISTICS & HEALTH

Births
1992 65,477
with low birth weight 5.2%
to teenage mothers 8.1%
to unmarried mothers 23.0%
1993 63,761
1994 64,681

Abortions, 1992
total 16,000
rate (per 1,000 women age 15-44) 15.6
rate per 1,000 live births 251

Adoptions, 1986
total 2,100
related 71.4%

Deaths
1992 34,909
1993 36,236
1994 36,417

Infant deaths
1992 458
1993 464
1994 430

Average lifetime, 1979-1981
both sexes .... 76.15 years
   men .... 72.52 years
   women .... 79.82 years

Marriages
1992 32,299
1993 31,444
1994 32,510

Divorces
1992 16,295
1993 16,848
1994 16,217

Physicians, 1993
total 10,476
rate (per 1,000 persons) 2.32

Dentists, 1992
total 2,913
rate (per 1,000 persons) 0.65

Hospitals, 1993
number 145
beds (x 1,000) 18.4
average daily census (x 1,000) 12.1
occupancy rate 66.0%
personnel (x 1,000) 55.0
average cost per day to hospital $652
average cost per stay to hospital $5,867

EDUCATION

*Educational attainment of all persons
25 years and older, 1990*
less than 9th grade 239,322
high school graduates 913,265
bachelor's degree 431,381
graduate or professional degree 173,203

Public school enrollment, Fall, 1993
total 810,233
   Kindergarten through grade 8 576,980
   grades 9 through 12 233,253

Public School Teachers
total, 1994 46,956
   elementary 23,981
   secondary 22,949
salaries, 1994
   beginning $23,408
   average $36,146

*State receipts & expenditures for public
schools, 1993*
receipts ($mil) 5,129
expenditures
   total ($mil) 5,022
   per capita $1,124
   per pupil $5,572

*Graduating high school seniors,
public high schools, 1995 (est)* 50,900

SAT scores, 1994
verbal 495
math 562

Institutions of higher education, 1995
total 109
   public 64
   private 45

*Enrollment in institutions of higher
education, Fall, 1993*
total 268,118
full-time men 75,511
full-time women 80,410
part-time men 44,827
part-time women 67,370

*Minority enrollment in institutions of higher
education, Fall, 1993*
Black, non-Hispanic 6,016
Hispanic 3,275
Asian/Pacific Islander 8,002

Earned degrees conferred, 1993
Bachelor's 24,762
First professional 1,854
Master's 5,217
Doctor's 674

SOCIAL INSURANCE &
WELFARE PROGRAMS

Social Security beneficiaries & benefits, 1993
beneficiaries
total 698,000
   retired and dependents 514,000
   survivors 117,000
   disabled & dependents 67,000
annual benefit payments ($mil)
total $4,956
   retired and dependents 3,502
   survivors 1,010
   disabled & dependents 443

Minnesota 4

Medicare, 1993
enrollment (x1,000) 615
payments ($mil) 2,106

Medicaid, 1993
recipients (x1,000) 425
payments ($mil) 1,930

Federal public aid, 1993
recipients as a percent of population 5.5%
Aid to Families with Dependent Children
recipients (x1,000) 189
average monthly payment $501
Supplemental Security Income
total recipients (x1,000) 55

Food Stamp Program
participants, 1994 (x1,000) 316

HOUSING & CONSTRUCTION

Total housing units, 1990 1,848,445
year round housing units 1,742,786
vacant 200,592

New privately owned housing units authorized, 1994
number (x1,000) 25.6
value ($mil) 2,558

New privately owned housing units started, 1994 (x1,000) 24.5

Existing home sales, 1994 (x1,000) 82.0

GOVERNMENT & ELECTIONS

State officials, 1996
Governor (name/party/term expires)
ARNE CARLSON
Republican - 1999
Lt. Governor .... Joanell Durstad
Sec. of State .... Joan Anderson Growe
Atty. General .... Hubert H. Humphrey, III
Chf. Justice .... Sandy Keith

Governorship
minimum age 25
length of term .... 4 years
number of consecutive
terms permitted .... not specified
who succeeds .... Lt. Governor

State legislature
name .... Legislature
upper chamber
name .... Senate
number of members 67
length of term .... 4 years
party in majority, 1996 .... Democratic
lower chamber
name .... House of Representatives
number of members 134
length of term .... 2 years
party in majority, 1996 .... Democratic

State employees October, 1992
total 83,922
October payroll ($1,000) 190,889

Local governments, 1992
total 3,616
county 87
municipal 854
township 1,804
school districts 477
special districts 393

Voting, November, 1994
voting age population 3,296,000
registered 80.9%
voted 58.4%

Vote for president
1988
Bush 958,199
Dukakis 1,106,975
1992
Clinton 972,403
Bush 727,502
Perot 544,480

Federal representation, 1996 (104th Congress)
Senators (name/party/term expires)

ROD GRAMS
Republican - 2001
PAUL WELLSTONE
Democrat - 1997

Representatives, total 8
Democrats 6
Republicans 2
other 0

Minnesota 5

Women holding public office
U.S. Congress, 1995 0
statewide elected office, 1995 3
state legislature, 1995 50

Black elected officials, 1993
total 16
US and state legislatures 1
city/county/regional offices 2
judicial/law enforcement 10
education/school boards 3

Hispanic public officials, 1994
total 3
state executives & legislators 2
city/county/regional offices 0
judicial/law enforcement 1
education/school boards 0

GOVERNMENTAL FINANCE

State & local government revenues, (selected items), 1991-92 ($per capita)
total $5,331.09
total general revenues 4,422.78
from federal government 705.28
from own sources 3,717.50
from taxes 2,500.26
from property taxes 784.18
from all other taxes 1,549.97
from charges & misc. 1,217.24

State & local government expenditures, (selected items), 1991-92 ($per capita)
total $5,106.26
total direct general expenditures 4,542.71
education 1,511.38
libraries 22.46
public welfare 817.83
health & hospitals 421.91
highways 381.59
police protection 115.05
fire protection 38.48
correction 67.27
housing & comm. development 93.96
natural resources & parks 159.88
interest on general debt 276.64

State & local debt, 1992 ($per capita) 4,376.06

Federal aid grants to state & local government, 1994 ($per capita total & selected items)
per capita total 769.56
compensatory education 17.69
waste treatment facilities 2.13
medicaid 304.25
housing assistance 50.27
job training 10.05
highway trust fund 64.13

CRIME, LAW ENFORCEMENT & COURTS

Crime, 1994 (all rates per 100,000 persons)
total crimes 198,253
overall crime rate 4,341.0
property crimes 181,856
burglaries 36,157
larcenies 131,344
motor vehicle thefts 14,355
property crime rate 3,982.0
violent crimes 16,397
murders 147
forcible rapes 2,725
robberies 5,370
aggravated assaults 8,155
violent crime rate 359.0

Number of police agencies, 1994 279

Arrests, 1994
total 203,786
persons under 18 years of age 58,900

Prisoners under state & federal jurisdiction, 1994
total 4,572
percent change, 1993-94 .... 8.9%
sentenced to more than one year
total 4,572
rate per 100,000 residents 100

Persons under sentence of death, 4/20/95 ....NA

State's highest court
name .... Supreme Court
number of members 9
length of term .... 6 years
intermediate appeals court? .... no

191

Minnesota 6

LABOR & INCOME

Civilian labor force, 1994

total	2,565,000
men	1,353,000
women	1,212,000
persons 16-19 years	162,000
white	2,426,000
black	78,000

Civilian labor force as a percent of civilian non-institutional population, 1994

total	75.6%
men	81.6%
women	69.8%
persons 16-19 years	73.4%
white	75.8%
black	65.6%

Employment, 1994

total	2,462,000
men	1,291,000
women	1,171,000
persons 16-19 years	145,000
white	2,340,000
black	65,000

Full-time/part-time labor force, 1994

full-time labor force	1,972,000
working part-time for ecomonic reasons	30,000
part-time labor force	592,000

Unemployment rate, 1994

total	4.0%
men	4.6%
women	3.4%
persons 16-19 years	10.8%
white	3.5%
black	16.0%

Unemployed by reason for unemployment (as a percent of total unemployment), 1994

job losers or completed temp jobs	53.4%
job leavers	13.5%
reentrants	29.6%
new entrants	3.8%

Civilian labor force, by occupation, 1994

executive/administrative/ managerial	317,000
professional/specialty	344,000
technicians & related support	93,000
sales	296,000
adminstrative support/clerical	417,000
service occupations	377,000
precision production/craft/repair	239,000
machine operators/assemblers	139,000
transportation/material moving	116,000
handlers/helpers/laborers	102,000
farming/forestry/fishing	121,000

Civilian labor force, by industry, 1994

construction	93,000
manufacturing	393,000
transportation/communication	145,000
wholesale/retail trade	512,000
finance/real estate/insurance	153,000
services	595,000
government	356,000
agriculture	117,000

Average annual pay, 1994 (prelim.) $26,425
change in average annual pay, 1993-1994 .... 2.8%

Hours and earnings of production workers on manufacturing payrolls, 1994

average weekly hours	41.6
average hourly earnings	$12.60
average weekly earnings	$524.16

Labor union membership, 1994 413,500

Household income (in constant 1993 dollars)

median household income, 1992	$31,908
median household income, 1993	$33,682

Poverty

persons below poverty level, 1992	13.0%
persons below poverty level, 1993	11.6%

Personal income ($per capita)
1994

in current dollars	22,453
in constant (1987) dollars	17,365

1995 (projected)

in constant (1982) dollars	14,617

2000 (projected)

in constant (1982) dollars	15,508

Federal income tax returns, 1993

returns filed	2,060,951
adjusted gross income ($1000)	69,040,004
total income tax paid ($1000)	9,577,140

ECONOMY, BUSINESS, INDUSTRY & AGRICULTURE

Fortune 500 companies, 1994 16

Business incorporations, 1994
total 11,429
change, 1993-94 .... 5.4%

Business failures, 1994
total 723
rate per 10,000 concerns 48
change, 1993-94 .... -21.2%

Business firm ownership
Hispanic owned firms, 1987 751
black owned firms, 1987 1,448
women owned firms, 1987 88,100
foreign owned firms, 1982 204

Gross state product, 1991 ($mil)
total $103,301
 agriculture services, forestry, fisheries ... 3,295
 mining 611
 construction 4,030
 manufacturing—durable goods 11,410
 manufacturing—nondurable goods 10,376
 transportation, communication &
  public utilities 8,593
 wholesale trade 8,173
 retail trade 9,434
 finance/real estate/insurance 17,894
 services 18,156
 federal, state & local government 11,329

Establishments, by major industry group, 1992
total 117,477
 agriculture 1,543
 mining 157
 construction 10,910
 manufacturing 8,010
 transportation 5,200
 wholesale trade 10,121
 retail trade 28,520
 finance/real estate/insurance 10,645
 service industries 40,727
 unclassified 1,644

Payroll, by major industry group, 1992
total ($1,000) $45,238,189
 agriculture 141,615
 mining 281,503
 construction 2,520,122
 manufacturing 12,648,837
 transportation 3,356,902
 wholesale trade 4,267,008
 retail trade 4,851,698
 finance/real estate/insurance 4,134,625
 service industries 12,999,716
 unclassified 36,163

Agriculture
number of farms, 1994 85,000
farm acreage, 1994 30,000,000
acres per farm, 1994 349
value of farms, 1994 ($mil) 26,722
farm income, 1993 ($mil)
 gross farm income 7,105
 net farm income 193
 debt/asset ratio 19.7%
farm marketings, 1993 ($mil)
total $6,574
 crops 2,800
 livestock 3,774
government payments 823
farm marketings in order of marketing receipts, 1993
 1) Dairy products
 2) Cattle
 3) Hogs
 4) Corn

Federal economic activity ($mil, except per capita)
expenditures, 1994
 total $18,797
 per capita $4,116
 defense $1,585
 non-defense $17,212
defense department, 1994
 contract awards ($mil) $1,137
 payroll ($mil) $403
 civilian employees (x1,000) 2.7
 military personnel (x1,000) 0.9

Fishing, 1992
catch (millions of pounds) ....NA
value ($mil) ....NA

Mining, 1994 ($mil)
total non-fuel mineral production $1,352

Minnesota 8

principal non-fuel minerals in order of value, 1994
1) Iron ore
2) Sand and gravel
3) Stone

Construction, 1994 ($mil)
total contracts (including
non-building) $5,478
   residential 2,598
   non-residential 1,999

Manufacturing, 1992
total establishments 7,934
employees, total (x1,000) 394
payroll ($mil) 12,664
production workers (x1,000) 225
value added ($mil) 27,175
value of shipments ($mil) 57,324

Finance
commercial banks, 1994
   number 573
     assets ($bil) 62.3
     deposits ($bil) 47.9
   closed or assisted 0
     deposits ($bil) ....NA
savings and loan associations, 1991
   non-current real estate loans 0.97%
   net income after taxes ($mil) 27
   return on assets .... +0.39%

Retail trade, 1992
establishments (x1,000) 27.7
sales ($mil) 35,622
annual payroll ($mil) 4,069
paid employees (x1,000) 372

Wholesale trade, 1992
establishments 10,219
sales ($bil) 72.5
annual payroll ($mil) 3,819
paid employees (x1,000) 123.1

Service industries, 1992
establishments (x1,000) (non-exempt firms) 31.0
receipts ($mil) (non-exempt firms) 18,764
annual payroll ($mil) 7,544
paid employees (x1,000) (non-exempt firms) . 349

COMMUNICATION, ENERGY & TRANSPORTATION

Communication
daily newspapers, 1993 25
broadcast stations, 1990
   radio: commercial, educational 240
   television: commercial, noncommercial 26
cable TV households, 1988 701,000

Energy
consumption estimates, 1992
total (trillion Btu) 1,369
per capita (million Btu) 306.4
by source of production (trillion Btu)
   coal 300
   natural gas 312
   petroleum 540
   nuclear electric power 119
   hydroelectric power 60
by end-use sector (trillion Btu)
   residential 307
   commercial 189
   industrial 498
   transportation 376
electrical energy
   production, 1993 (billion kWh) 41.3
   net summer capability, 1993 (million kW) .. 8.9
gas utilities, 1993
   customers 1,149,000
   sales (trillion Btu) 258
   revenues ($mil) 1,193
nuclear plants, 1993 3

Transportation, 1994
public road & street mileage
total 130,198
   urban 15,016
   rural 115,182
   interstate 914
vehicle miles of travel (mil) 43,317
total motor vehicle registrations 4,057,415
   automobiles 2,677,293
licensed drivers 2,705,701
   per 1,000 driving age population 783
deaths from motor vehicle
   accidents 644

Mississippi 1

STATE SUMMARY

Capital City . . . . Jackson

Governor . . . . Kirk Fordice

Address . . . . STATE CAPITOL
JACKSON, MS 39201
601 359-3100

Admitted as a state 1817

Area (square miles) 48,434

Population, 1980 2,520,638

Population, 1990 2,573,216

Population, 1994 (est.) 2,669,000

Persons per square mile, 1994 . . . . 56.9

Largest city . . . . Jackson
population, 1990 197,000

Personal income per capita, 1994
(in current dollars) $15,838

Gross state product ($mil), 1991 41,481

Leading industries, 1992 (by payroll)
MANUFACTURING
SERVICE INDUSTRIES
RETAIL TRADE

Leading agricultural commodities, 1993
COTTON
BROILERS
SOYBEANS
CATTLE

GEOGRAPHY & ENVIRONMENT

Area (square miles)
total 48,434
  land 46,914
  water (includes territorial water) 1,520

Federally owned land, 1991 . . . . 4.3%

Highest point
name . . . . Woodall Mountain
elevation (feet) 806

Lowest point
name . . . . Gulf of Mexico
elevation (feet) . . . . sea level

General coastline (miles) 44

Tidal shoreline (miles) 359

Capital city . . . . Jackson
population, 1990 197,000

Largest city . . . . Jackson
population, 1990 197,000

Number of cities with over 100,000 population
1980 1

Number of cities with over 100,000 population
1990 1

State parks and Recreation areas, 1991
area (acres) 23,000
number of visitors 3,912,000
revenues $4,796,000

National forest land, 1992 (acres) 2,310,000

National park acreage, 1984 107,500

DEMOGRAPHICS & CHARACTERISTICS OF THE POPULATION

Population
1970 2,216,994
1980 2,520,638
1990 2,573,216
1994 (est.) 2,669,000
2000 (revised projection) 2,750,000
2010 (revised projection) 2,918,000

Metropolitan area population
1970 564,000
1980 716,000
1992 803,000

Non-metropolitan area population
1970 1,653,000
1980 1,804,000
1992 1,812,000

Change in population, 1980-90
number 52,578
percent 2.09%

Persons per square mile, 1994 . . . . 56.9

Age distribution, 1980
under 5 years 8.5%
5 to 17 years 23.7%
65 and over 11.5%

Age distribution, 1990
under 5 years 7.6%
5 to 17 years 21.4%
65 and over 12.4%

195

Mississippi 2

Age distribution, 2000 (projected)
under 5 years 7.0%
5 to 17 years 20.4%
65 and over 12.5%

Persons by age, 1990
under 5 years 195,365
5 to 17 years 551,396
65 and over 321,284

Median age, 1990 .... 31.20

Race, 1990
White 1,633,461
Black 915,057
American Indian 8,435
Chinese 2,518
Filipino 1,565
Japanese 700
Asian Indian 1,872
Korean 1,123
Vietnamese 3,815
all other 4,580

Race, 2010 (projected)
White 1,845,000
Black 1,032,000

Persons of Hispanic origin, 1990
total 15,931
Mexican 6,718
Puerto Rican 1,304
Cuban 497
Other Hispanic 7,412

Persons by sex, 1990
male 1,230,617
female 1,342,599

Marital status, 1990
males
15 years & older 913,815
single 275,422
married 545,992
separated 22,646
widowed 27,747
divorced 64,654
females
15 years & older 1,038,813
single 245,289
married 554,540
separated 34,234

widowed 150,004
divorced 88,980

Households & families, 1990
households 911,374
persons per household 2.75
families 674,378
married couples 498,240
female householder, no husband
present 145,221
one person households 212,949
households, 1994 949,000
persons per household, 1994 .... 2.74

Nativity, 1990
number of persons born in state 1,989,265
percent of total residents 77.3%

Immigration & naturalization, 1993
immigrants admitted 906
persons naturalized 426
refugees granted resident status 66

VITAL STATISTICS & HEALTH

Births
1992 43,487
with low birth weight 9.9%
to teenage mothers 21.4%
to unmarried mothers 42.9%
1993 42,160
1994 43,382

Abortions, 1992
total 8,000
rate (per 1,000 women age 15-44) 12.4
rate per 1,000 live births 176

Adoptions, 1986
total 1,468
related 50.4%

Deaths
1992 25,290
1993 26,575
1994 26,934

Infant deaths
1992 505
1993 501
1994 439

Mississippi 3

Average lifetime, 1979-1981
both sexes .... 71.98 years
men .... 67.64 years
women .... 76.39 years

Marriages
1992 22,773
1993 23,654
1994 22,360

Divorces
1992 14,633
1993 13,260
1994 15,212

Physicians, 1993
total 3,401
rate (per 1,000 persons) 1.30

Dentists, 1992
total 1,019
rate (per 1,000 persons) 0.39

Hospitals, 1993
number 97
beds (x 1,000) 12.5
average daily census (x 1,000) 7.4
occupancy rate 59.3%
personnel (x 1,000) 38.3
average cost per day to hospital $555
average cost per stay to hospital $4,053

EDUCATION

*Educational attainment of all persons
25 years and older, 1990*
less than 9th grade 240,267
high school graduates 423,624
bachelor's degree 149,109
graduate or professional degree 77,838

Public school enrollment, Fall, 1993
total 505,907
Kindergarten through grade 8 368,688
grades 9 through 12 137,219

Public School Teachers
total, 1994 28,376
elementary 18,592
secondary 9,184
salaries, 1994
beginning $18,833
average $25,153

*State receipts & expenditures for public
schools, 1993*
receipts ($mil) 1,915
expenditures
total ($mil) 1,769
per capita $676
per pupil $3,390

*Graduating high school seniors,
public high schools, 1995 (est) 23,117*

SAT scores, 1994
verbal 485
math 528

Institutions of higher education, 1995
total 46
public 31
private 15

*Enrollment in institutions of higher
education, Fall, 1993*
total 122,408
full-time men 42,717
full-time women 50,496
part-time men 10,916
part-time women 18,279

*Minority enrollment in institutions of higher
education, Fall, 1993*
Black, non-Hispanic 34,959
Hispanic 523
Asian/Pacific Islander 905

Earned degrees conferred, 1993
Bachelor's 10,673
First professional 466
Master's 2,672
Doctor's 303

SOCIAL INSURANCE &
WELFARE PROGRAMS

Social Security beneficiaries & benefits, 1993
beneficiaries
total 478,000
retired and dependents 286,000
survivors 98,000
disabled & dependents 94,000
annual benefit payments ($mil)
total $2,932
retired and dependents 1,735
survivors 663
disabled & dependents 533

197

Mississippi 4

Medicare, 1993
enrollment (x1,000) 384
payments ($mil) 1,328

Medicaid, 1993
recipients (x1,000) 504
payments ($mil) 896

Federal public aid, 1993
recipients as a percent of population 11.3%
Aid to Families with Dependent Children
   recipients (x1,000) 161
average monthly payment $120
Supplemental Security Income
   total recipients (x1,000) 134

Food Stamp Program
   participants, 1994 (x1,000) 511

HOUSING & CONSTRUCTION

Total housing units, 1990 1,010,423
   year round housing units 994,075
   vacant 99,049

New privately owned housing units authorized, 1994
number (x1,000) 10.9
value ($mil) 660

New privately owned housing units started, 1994 (x1,000) 13.9

Existing home sales, 1994 (x1,000) 43.5

GOVERNMENT & ELECTIONS

State officials, 1996
   Governor (name/party/term expires)
               KIRK FORDICE
               Republican - 2000
Lt. Governor . . . . Ronnie Musgrove
Sec. of State . . . . Eric Clark
Atty. General . . . . Mike Moore
Chf. Justice . . . . Roy Noble Lee

Governorship
minimum age 30
length of term . . . . 4 years
number of consecutive
   terms permitted . . . . not specified
who succeeds . . . . Lt. Governor

State legislature
name . . . . Legislature
   upper chamber
      name . . . . Senate
      number of members 52
      length of term . . . . 4 years
      party in majority, 1996 . . . . Democratic
   lower chamber
      name . . . . House of Representatives
      number of members 122
      length of term . . . . 4 years
      party in majority, 1996 . . . . Democratic

State employees October, 1992
total 55,388
October payroll ($1,000) 93,589

Local governments, 1992
total 898
   county 82
   municipal 294
   township 0
   school districts 176
   special districts 345

Voting, November, 1994
voting age population 1,863,000
   registered 72.6%
   voted 44.3%

Vote for president
1988
   Bush 551,745
   Dukakis 360,892
1992
   Clinton 391,657
   Bush 479,602
   Perot 83,885

Federal representation, 1996 (104th Congress)
Senators (name/party/term expires)

               TRENT LOTT
               Republican - 2001
               THAD COCHRAN
               Republican - 1997

Representatives, total 5
   Democrats 4
   Republicans 1
   other 0

Mississippi 5

Women holding public office
U.S. Congress, 1995 0
statewide elected office, 1995 0
state legislature, 1995 20

Black elected officials, 1993
total 751
  US and state legislatures 42
  city/county/regional offices 495
  judicial/law enforcement 88
  education/school boards 126

Hispanic public officials, 1994
total .... NA
  state executives & legislators .... NA
  city/county/regional offices .... NA
  judicial/law enforcement .... NA
  education/school boards .... NA

GOVERNMENTAL FINANCE

State & local government revenues, (selected items), 1991-92 ($per capita)
total $3,465.77
  total general revenues 2,983.80
    from federal government 841.66
    from own sources 2,142.14
    from taxes 1,334.34
      from property taxes 380.04
      from all other taxes 895.33
    from charges & misc. 807.81

State & local government expenditures, (selected items), 1991-92 ($per capita)
total $3,251.59
  total direct general expenditures 2,893.89
    education 1,028.15
    libraries 6.13
    public welfare 451.30
    health & hospitals 435.55
    highways 277.29
    police protection 72.32
    fire protection 31.25
    correction 39.83
    housing & comm. development 32.72
    natural resources & parks 76.49
    interest on general debt 127.73

State & local debt, 1992 ($per capita) 1,943.50

Federal aid grants to state & local government, 1994 ($per capita total & selected items)
per capita total 939.15
  compensatory education 45.22
  waste treatment facilities 5.27
  medicaid 399.97
  housing assistance 43.46
  job training 15.73
  highway trust fund 64.99

CRIME, LAW ENFORCEMENT & COURTS

Crime, 1994 (all rates per 100,000 persons)
total crimes 129,101
overall crime rate 4,837.1
  property crimes 115,924
    burglaries 34,493
    larcenies 70,621
    motor vehicle thefts 10,810
  property crime rate 4,343.3
  violent crimes 13,177
    murders 409
    forcible rapes 1,212
    robberies 4,336
    aggravated assaults 7,220
  violent crime rate 493.7

Number of police agencies, 1994 48

Arrests, 1994
total 61,676
  persons under 18 years of age 9,225

Prisoners under state & federal jurisdiction, 1994
total 11,274
percent change, 1993-94 .... 11.9%
  sentenced to more than one year
  total 10,950
  rate per 100,000 residents 408

Persons under sentence of death, 4/20/95 55

State's highest court
name .... Supreme Court
number of members 9
length of term .... 6 years
intermediate appeals court? .... no

199

Mississippi 6

LABOR & INCOME

Civilian labor force, 1994
total	1,254,000
men	677,000
women	578,000
persons 16-19 years	72,000
white	830,000
black	415,000

Civilian labor force as a percent of civilian non-institutional population, 1994
total	63.5%
men	72.7%
women	55.2%
persons 16-19 years	41.4%
white	65.5%
black	59.7%

Employment, 1994
total	1,171,000
men	634,000
women	537,000
persons 16-19 years	55,000
white	798,000
black	365,000

Full-time/part-time labor force, 1994
full-time labor force	1,052,000
working part-time for ecomonic reasons	22,000
part-time labor force	203,000

Unemployment rate, 1994
total	6.6%
men	6.3%
women	6.9%
persons 16-19 years	23.4%
white	3.9%
black	12.1%

Unemployed by reason for unemployment (as a percent of total unemployment), 1994
job losers or completed temp jobs	38.4%
job leavers	10.6%
reentrants	40.0%
new entrants	11.0%

Civilian labor force, by occupation, 1994
executive/administrative/managerial	136,000
professional/specialty	146,000
technicians & related support	NA
sales	142,000
adminstrative support/clerical	159,000
service occupations	168,000
precision production/craft/repair	160,000
machine operators/assemblers	115,000
transportation/material moving	69,000
handlers/helpers/laborers	72,000
farming/forestry/fishing	55,000

Civilian labor force, by industry, 1994
construction	63,000
manufacturing	256,000
transportation/communication	68,000
wholesale/retail trade	228,000
finance/real estate/insurance	47,000
services	222,000
government	188,000
agriculture	49,000

Average annual pay, 1994 (prelim.) $20,382
change in average annual pay, 1993-1994	3.5%

Hours and earnings of production workers on manufacturing payrolls, 1994
average weekly hours	41.7
average hourly earnings	$9.40
average weekly earnings	$391.98

Labor union membership, 1994 66,500

Household income (in constant 1993 dollars)
median household income, 1992	$21,186
median household income, 1993	$22,191

Poverty
persons below poverty level, 1992	24.6%
persons below poverty level, 1993	24.7%

Personal income ($per capita)
1994	
in current dollars	15,838
in constant (1987) dollars	12,249
1995 (projected)	
in constant (1982) dollars	9,927
2000 (projected)	
in constant (1982) dollars	10,631

Federal income tax returns, 1993
returns filed	1,056,684
adjusted gross income ($1000)	25,435,785
total income tax paid ($1000)	3,090,173

ECONOMY, BUSINESS, INDUSTRY & AGRICULTURE

Fortune 500 companies, 1994 1

Business incorporations, 1994
total 4,814
change, 1993-94 .... 9.7%

Business failures, 1994
total 253
rate per 10,000 concerns 37
change, 1993-94 .... -21.7%

Business firm ownership
Hispanic owned firms, 1987 308
black owned firms, 1987 9,667
women owned firms, 1987 29,000
foreign owned firms, 1982 117

Gross state product, 1991 ($mil)
total $41,481
  agriculture services, forestry, fisheries ... 1,187
  mining 755
  construction 1,292
  manufacturing—durable goods 5,123
  manufacturing—nondurable goods 5,051
  transportation, communication &
    public utilities 5,215
  wholesale trade 2,137
  retail trade 4,166
  finance/real estate/insurance 5,774
  services 5,032
  federal, state & local government 5,749

*Establishments, by major industry
  group, 1992*
total 54,240
  agriculture 723
  mining 413
  construction 3,994
  manufacturing 3,795
  transportation 3,038
  wholesale trade 3,842
  retail trade 15,492
  finance/real estate/insurance 5,185
  service industries 16,820
  unclassified 938

Payroll, by major industry group, 1992
total ($1,000) $13,824,960
  agriculture 79,790

  mining 125,239
  construction 651,224
  manufacturing 5,047,686
  transportation 1,142,604
  wholesale trade 962,115
  retail trade 1,753,117
  finance/real estate/insurance 853,007
  service industries 3,200,041
  unclassified 10,137

Agriculture
number of farms, 1994 39,000
farm acreage, 1994 13,000,000
acres per farm, 1994 326
value of farms, 1994 ($mil) 10,585
farm income, 1993 ($mil)
  gross farm income 3,230
  net farm income 368
  debt/asset ratio 20.0%
farm marketings, 1993 ($mil)
total $2,605
  crops 1,028
  livestock 1,577
government payments 384
farm marketings in order of marketing
receipts, 1993
    1) Broilers
    2) Cotton
    3) Soybeans
    4) Aquaculture

*Federal economic activity
  ($mil, except per capita)*
expenditures, 1994
    total $14,072
    per capita $5,272
    defense $3,091
    non-defense $10,981
defense department, 1994
    contract awards ($mil) $1,855
    payroll ($mil) $1,246
    civilian employees (x1,000) 10.9
    military personnel (x1,000) 12.6

Fishing, 1992
catch (millions of pounds) 188
value ($mil) 31

Mining, 1994 ($mil)
total non-fuel mineral production $112

Mississippi 8

principal non-fuel minerals in order of value, 1994
1) Sand and gravel
2) Clay
3) Cement

Construction, 1994 ($mil)
total contracts (including
  non-building) $2,546
    residential 885
    non-residential 983

Manufacturing, 1992
total establishments 3,767
employees, total (x1,000) 238
payroll ($mil) 5,030
production workers (x1,000) 188
value added ($mil) 13,988
value of shipments ($mil) 32,655

Finance
commercial banks, 1994
  number 118
    assets ($bil) 24.4
    deposits ($bil) 20.5
    closed or assisted 0
    deposits ($bil) .... NA
savings and loan associations, 1991
  non-current real estate loans 3.05%
  net income after taxes ($mil) .... -31
  return on assets .... -0.97%

Retail trade, 1992
establishments (x1,000) 15.3
sales ($mil) 14,781
annual payroll ($mil) 1,597
paid employees (x1,000) 151

Wholesale trade, 1992
establishments 3,868
sales ($bil) 15.8
annual payroll ($mil) 914
paid employees (x1,000) 39.9

Service industries, 1992
establishments (x1,000) (non-exempt firms) 12.8
receipts ($mil) (non-exempt firms) 5,487
annual payroll ($mil) 1,991
paid employees (x1,000) (non-exempt firms) . 108

COMMUNICATION, ENERGY & TRANSPORTATION

Communication
daily newspapers, 1993 22
broadcast stations, 1990
  radio: commercial, educational 231
  television: commercial, noncommercial 25
cable TV households, 1988 480,000

Energy
consumption estimates, 1992
total (trillion Btu) 968
per capita (million Btu) 370.0
by source of production (trillion Btu)
  coal 87
  natural gas 251
  petroleum 415
  nuclear electric power 87
  hydroelectric power 0
by end-use sector (trillion Btu)
  residential 167
  commercial 102
  industrial 365
  transportation 333
electrical-energy
  production, 1993 (billion kWh) 23.2
  net summer capability, 1993 (million kW) .. 7.0
gas utilities, 1993
  customers 430,000
  sales (trillion Btu) 95
  revenues ($mil) 361
nuclear plants, 1993 1

Transportation, 1994
public road & street mileage
total 72,910
  urban 7,913
  rural 64,997
  interstate 685
vehicle miles of travel (mil) 28,548
total motor vehicle registrations 2,062,967
  automobiles 1,340,513
licensed drivers 1,671,690
  per 1,000 driving age population 836
deaths from motor vehicle
  accidents 791

STATE SUMMARY

Capital City ....Jefferson City

Governor .... Mel Carnahan

Address ....STATE CAPITOL
JEFFERSON CITY, MO 65102
314 751-3222

Admitted as a state 1821

Area (square miles) 69,709

Population, 1980 4,916,686

Population, 1990 5,117,073

Population, 1994 (est.) 5,278,000

Persons per square mile, 1994 .... 76.6

Largest city .... St. Louis
population, 1990 397,000

Personal income per capita, 1994
(in current dollars) $20,717

Gross state product ($mil), 1991 106,214

Leading industries, 1992 (by payroll)
SERVICE INDUSTRIES
MANUFACTURING
RETAIL TRADE

Leading agricultural commodities, 1993
CATTLE
SOYBEANS
HOGS
CORN

GEOGRAPHY & ENVIRONMENT

Area (square miles)
total 69,709
land 68,898
water (includes territorial water) 811

Federally owned land, 1991 .... 4.7%

Highest point
name ....Taum Sauk Mountain
elevation (feet) 1,772

Lowest point
name .... St. Francis River
elevation (feet) 230

General coastline (miles) 0

Tidal shoreline (miles) 0

Capital city ....Jefferson City
population, 1990 35,500

Largest city .... St. Louis
population, 1990 397,000

Number of cities with over 100,000 population
1980 4

Number of cities with over 100,000 population
1990 4

State parks and Recreation areas, 1991
area (acres) 117,000
number of visitors 14,998,000
revenues $3,780,000

National forest land, 1992 (acres) 3,082,000

National park acreage, 1984 62,700

DEMOGRAPHICS & CHARACTERISTICS OF THE POPULATION

Population
1970 4,677,623
1980 4,916,686
1990 5,117,073
1994 (est.) 5,278,000
2000 (revised projection) 5,437,000
2010 (revised projection) 5,760,000

Metropolitan area population
1970 3,170,000
1980 3,226,000
1992 3,543,000

Non-metropolitan area population
1970 1,508,000
1980 1,690,000
1992 1,647,000

Change in population, 1980-90
number 200,387
percent 4.08%

Persons per square mile, 1994 .... 76.6

Age distribution, 1980
under 5 years 7.2%
5 to 17 years 20.5%
65 and over 13.2%

Age distribution, 1990
under 5 years 7.2%
5 to 17 years 18.4%
65 and over 14.0%

Missouri 2

Age distribution, 2000 (projected)
under 5 years 6.2%
5 to 17 years 18.4%
65 and over 14.1%

Persons by age, 1990
under 5 years 369,244
5 to 17 years 945,582
65 and over 717,681

Median age, 1990 .... *33.50*

Race, 1990
White 4,486,228
Black 548,208
American Indian 19,508
Chinese 8,614
Filipino 5,624
Japanese 3,391
Asian Indian 6,111
Korean 5,731
Vietnamese 4,380
all other 28,951

Race, 2010 (projected)
White 4,970,000
Black 664,000

Persons of Hispanic origin, 1990
total 61,702
Mexican 38,274
Puerto Rican 3,959
Cuban 2,108
Other Hispanic 17,361

Persons by sex, 1990
male..............................2,464,315
female 2,652,758

Marital status, 1990
males
15 years & older 1,896,107
single 516,097
married 1,178,576
separated 32,893
widowed 50,859
divorced 150,575
females
15 years & older 2,112,391
single 440,593
married 1,185,687
separated 45,638

widowed 280,906
divorced 205,205

Households & families, 1990
households 1,961,206
persons per household 2.54
families 1,368,334
married couples 1,104,723
female householder, no husband
present 208,175
one person households 510,684
households, 1994 2,008,000
persons per household, 1994 .... 2.56

Nativity, 1990
number of persons born in state 3,563,820
percent of total residents 69.6%

Immigration & naturalization, 1993
immigrants admitted 4,644
persons naturalized 1,379
refugees granted resident status 1,029

VITAL STATISTICS & HEALTH

Births
1992 75,437
with low birth weight 7.3%
to teenage mothers 14.5%
to unmarried mothers 31.5%
1993 77,424
1994 75,366

Abortions, 1992
total 14,000
rate (per 1,000 women age 15-44) 11.6
rate per 1,000 live births 175

Adoptions, 1986
total 2,660
related 66.0%

Deaths
1992 50,447
1993 56,305
1994 55,985

Infant deaths
1992 680
1993 656
1994 607

Missouri 3

Average lifetime, 1979-1981
both sexes . . . . 73.84 years
men . . . . 69.92 years
women . . . . 77.72 years

Marriages
1992 42,428
1993 44,133
1994 44,223

Divorces
1992 25,653
1993 26,582
1994 26,324

Physicians, 1993
total 10,830
rate (per 1,000 persons) 2.07

Dentists, 1992
total 2,756
rate (per 1,000 persons) 0.53

Hospitals, 1993
number 130
beds (x 1,000) 23.6
average daily census (x 1,000) 13.9
occupancy rate 58.9%
personnel (x 1,000) 95.9
average cost per day to hospital $863
average cost per stay to hospital $6,161

EDUCATION

Educational attainment of all persons 25 years and older, 1990
less than 9th grade 380,613
high school graduates 1,090,940
bachelor's degree 383,678
graduate or professional degree 202,083

Public school enrollment, Fall, 1993
total 875,639
Kindergarten through grade 8 631,552
grades 9 through 12 244,087

Public School Teachers
total, 1994 54,543
elementary 28,729
secondary 25,814
salaries, 1994
beginning $21,078
average $30,324

State receipts & expenditures for public schools, 1993
receipts ($mil) 4,646
expenditures
total ($mil) 3,966
per capita $764
per pupil $4,487

Graduating high school seniors, public high schools, 1995 (est) 46,932

SAT scores, 1994
verbal 485
math 537

Institutions of higher education, 1995
total 102
public 30
private 72

Enrollment in institutions of higher education, Fall, 1993
total 297,062
full-time men 81,671
full-time women 87,341
part-time men 51,166
part-time women 76,884

Minority enrollment in institutions of higher education, Fall, 1993
Black, non-Hispanic 25,682
Hispanic 4,212
Asian/Pacific Islander 5,704

Earned degrees conferred, 1993
Bachelor's 26,954
First professional 2,171
Master's 9,303
Doctor's 711

SOCIAL INSURANCE & WELFARE PROGRAMS

Social Security beneficiaries & benefits, 1993
beneficiaries
total 952,000
retired and dependents 664,000
survivors 165,000
disabled & dependents 124,000
annual benefit payments ($mil)
total $6,739
retired and dependents 4,549
survivors 1,382
disabled & dependents 808

Missouri 4

Medicare, 1993
enrollment (x1,000) 814
payments ($mil) 3,122

Medicaid, 1993
recipients (x1,000) 609
payments ($mil) 1,548

Federal public aid, 1993
recipients as a percent of population 6.9%
Aid to Families with Dependent Children
    recipients (x1,000) 264
average monthly payment $261
Supplemental Security Income
    total recipients (x1,000) 105

Food Stamp Program
    participants, 1994 (x1,000) 593

HOUSING & CONSTRUCTION

Total housing units, 1990 2,199,129
    year round housing units 2,143,282
    vacant 237,923

New privately owned housing units authorized, 1994
number (x1,000) 26.4
value ($mil) 2,149

New privately owned housing units started, 1994 (x1,000) 28.1

Existing home sales, 1994 (x1,000) 110.2

GOVERNMENT & ELECTIONS

State officials, 1996
    Governor (name/party/term expires)
        MEL CARNAHAN
        Democrat - 1997
Lt. Governor .... Roger Wilson
Sec. of State .... Judith Moriarity
Atty. General .... Jay Nixon
Chf. Justice .... Ann Covington

Governorship
minimum age 30
length of term .... 4 years
number of consecutive
    terms permitted ..2 max. (not nec. consecutive)
who succeeds .... Lt. Governor

State legislature
name .... Legislature
    upper chamber
        name .... Senate
        number of members 34
        length of term .... 4 years
        party in majority, 1996 .... Democratic
    lower chamber
        name .... House of Representatives
        number of members 163
        length of term .... 2 years
        party in majority, 1996 .... Democratic

State employees October, 1992
total 90,424
October payroll ($1,000) 153,212

Local governments, 1992
total 3,368
    county 114
    municipal 933
    township 324
    school districts 553
    special districts 1,443

Voting, November, 1994
voting age population 3,797,000
    registered 72.3%
    voted 54.5%

Vote for president
1988
    Bush 1,081,163
    Dukakis 1,004,040
1992
    Clinton 1,053,034
    Bush 820,839
    Perot 518,214

Federal representation, 1996 (104th Congress)
Senators (name/party/term expires)

        JOHN ASHCROFT
        Republican - 2001
        KIT BOND
        Republican - 1999

Representatives, total 9
    Democrats 6
    Republicans 3
    other 0

Missouri 5

Women holding public office
U.S. Congress, 1995 2
statewide elected office, 1995 2
state legislature, 1995 39

Black elected officials, 1993
total 185
 US and state legislatures 18
 city/county/regional offices 134
 judicial/law enforcement 14
 education/school boards 19

Hispanic public officials, 1994
total 1
 state executives & legislators 0
 city/county/regional offices 1
 judicial/law enforcement 0
 education/school boards 0

GOVERNMENTAL FINANCE

State & local government revenues, (selected items), 1991-92 ($per capita)
total $3,552.36
 total general revenues 2,995.50
 from federal government 621.48
 from own sources 2,374.02
 from taxes 1,676.24
 from property taxes 404.34
 from all other taxes 1,142.73
 from charges & misc. 697.78

State & local government expenditures, (selected items), 1991-92 ($per capita)
total $3,294.82
 total direct general expenditures 2,903.51
 education 1,072.50
 libraries 13.69
 public welfare 498.50
 health & hospitals 238.76
 highways 247.45
 police protection 102.70
 fire protection 55.24
 correction 54.57
 housing & comm. development 30.31
 natural resources & parks 92.81
 interest on general debt 139.88

State & local debt, 1992 ($per capita) 2,292.45

Federal aid grants to state & local government, 1994 ($per capita total & selected items)
per capita total 752.34
 compensatory education 21.19
 waste treatment facilities 7.81
 medicaid 298.85
 housing assistance 39.73
 job training 12.94
 highway trust fund 83.10

CRIME, LAW ENFORCEMENT & COURTS

Crime, 1994 (all rates per 100,000 persons)
total crimes 280,138
overall crime rate 5,307.7
 property crimes 240,898
 burglaries 55,577
 larcenies 158,283
 motor vehicle thefts 27,038
 property crime rate 4,564.2
 violent crimes 39,240
 murders 554
 forcible rapes 1,955
 robberies 12,178
 aggravated assaults 24,553
 violent crime rate 743.5

Number of police agencies, 1994 178

Arrests, 1994
total 278,583
 persons under 18 years of age 38,141

Prisoners under state & federal jurisdiction, 1994
total 17,898
percent change, 1993-94 . . . . 10.6%
 sentenced to more than one year
 total 17,898
 rate per 100,000 residents 338

Persons under sentence of death, 4/20/95 92

State's highest court
name . . . . Supreme Court
number of members 7
length of term . . . . 12 years
intermediate appeals court? . . . . yes

Missouri 6

LABOR & INCOME

Civilian labor force, 1994

total	2,695,000
men	1,450,000
women	1,244,000
persons 16-19 years	158,000
white	2,416,000
black	247,000

Civilian labor force as a percent of civilian non-institutional population, 1994

total	68.0%
men	75.9%
women	60.6%
persons 16-19 years	60.9%
white	68.7%
black	62.6%

Employment, 1994

total	2,564,000
men	1,379,000
women	1,184,000
persons 16-19 years	133,000
white	2,314,000
black	219,000

Full-time/part-time labor force, 1994

full-time labor force	2,206,000
working part-time for ecomonic reasons	25,000
part-time labor force	489,000

Unemployment rate, 1994

total	4.9%
men	4.9%
women	4.8%
persons 16-19 years	16.0%
white	4.2%
black	11.4%

Unemployed by reason for unemployment (as a percent of total unemployment), 1994

job losers or completed temp jobs	50.3%
job leavers	9.2%
reentrants	35.2%
new entrants	5.6%

Civilian labor force, by occupation, 1994

executive/administrative/ managerial	319,000
professional/specialty	333,000
technicians & related support	100,000
sales	337,000
adminstrative support/clerical	426,000
service occupations	351,000
precision production/craft/repair	293,000
machine operators/assemblers	195,000
transportation/material moving	116,000
handlers/helpers/laborers	107,000
farming/forestry/fishing	111,000

Civilian labor force, by industry, 1994

construction	125,000
manufacturing	468,000
transportation/communication	181,000
wholesale/retail trade	544,000
finance/real estate/insurance	153,000
services	581,000
government	324,000
agriculture	105,000

Average annual pay, 1994 (prelim.)	$24,625
change in average annual pay, 1993-1994	3.0%

Hours and earnings of production workers on manufacturing payrolls, 1994

average weekly hours	42.0
average hourly earnings	$11.78
average weekly earnings	$494.76

Labor union membership, 1994	329,100

Household income (in constant 1993 dollars)

median household income, 1992	$28,180
median household income, 1993	$28,682

Poverty

persons below poverty level, 1992	15.7%
persons below poverty level, 1993	16.1%

Personal income ($per capita)

1994	
in current dollars	20,717
in constant (1987) dollars	16,022
1995 (projected)	
in constant (1982) dollars	13,683
2000 (projected)	
in constant (1982) dollars	14,592

Federal income tax returns, 1993

returns filed	2,283,031
adjusted gross income ($1000)	68,569,150
total income tax paid ($1000)	9,501,307

Missouri 7

ECONOMY, BUSINESS, INDUSTRY & AGRICULTURE

Fortune 500 companies, 1994 12

Business incorporations, 1994
total 11,022
change, 1993-94 .... -4.5%

Business failures, 1994
total 1,064
rate per 10,000 concerns 66
change, 1993-94 .... -13.6%

Business firm ownership
Hispanic owned firms, 1987 1,247
black owned firms, 1987 7,832
women owned firms, 1987 87,700
foreign owned firms, 1982 236

Gross state product, 1991 ($mil)
total $106,214
  agriculture services, forestry, fisheries ... 2,085
  mining 333
  construction 3,967
  manufacturing—durable goods 10,646
  manufacturing—nondurable goods 10,873
  transportation, communication &
    public utilities 12,104
  wholesale trade 7,876
  retail trade 10,638
  finance/real estate/insurance 16,860
  services 19,174
  federal, state & local government 11,656

Establishments, by major industry group, 1992
total 133,494
  agriculture 1,884
  mining 332
  construction 13,193
  manufacturing 7,925
  transportation 6,445
  wholesale trade 11,112
  retail trade 33,114
  finance/real estate/insurance 11,989
  service industries 45,684
  unclassified 1,816

Payroll, by major industry group, 1992
total ($1,000) $45,105,454
  agriculture 149,462

  mining 158,575
  construction 2,446,689
  manufacturing 12,049,720
  transportation 4,092,750
  wholesale trade 3,934,803
  retail trade 5,254,227
  finance/real estate/insurance 3,844,516
  service industries 13,148,464
  unclassified 26,248

Agriculture
number of farms, 1994 104,000
farm acreage, 1994 30,000,000
acres per farm, 1994 288
value of farms, 1994 ($mil) 23,016
farm income, 1993 ($mil)
  gross farm income 4,907
  net farm income 564
  debt/asset ratio 16.2%
farm marketings, 1993 ($mil)
  total $4,053
    crops 1,783
    livestock 2,270
  government payments 455
farm marketings in order of marketing receipts, 1993
  1) Cattle
  2) Soybeans
  3) Hogs
  4) Corn

Federal economic activity
  ($mil, except per capita)
expenditures, 1994
  total $31,766
  per capita $6,019
  defense $7,797
  non-defense $23,968
defense department, 1994
  contract awards ($mil) $6,147
  payroll ($mil) $1,566
  civilian employees (x1,000) 16.6
  military personnel (x1,000) 15.3

Fishing, 1992
catch (millions of pounds) .... NA
value ($mil) .... NA

Mining, 1994 ($mil)
total non-fuel mineral production $1,003

209

Missouri 8

principal non-fuel minerals in order of value, 1994
1) Stone
2) Cement
3) Lead

Construction, 1994 ($mil)
total contracts (including
  non-building) $5,589
  residential 2,622
  non-residential 1,980

Manufacturing, 1992
total establishments 7,846
employees, total (x1,000) 408
payroll ($mil) 11,868
production workers (x1,000) 260
value added ($mil) 33,995
value of shipments ($mil) 73,746

Finance
commercial banks, 1994
  number 490
  assets ($bil) 68.5
  deposits ($bil) 55.7
  closed or assisted 0
  deposits ($bil) .... NA
savings and loan associations, 1991
  non-current real estate loans 6.21%
  net income after taxes ($mil) .... -169
  return on assets .... -0.95%

Retail trade, 1992
establishments (x1,000) 32.2
sales ($mil) 37,918
annual payroll ($mil) 4,411
paid employees (x1,000) 392

Wholesale trade, 1992
establishments 11,236
sales ($bil) 68.4
annual payroll ($mil) 3,553
paid employees (x1,000) 129.6

Service industries, 1992
establishments (x1,000) (non-exempt firms) 36.4
receipts ($mil) (non-exempt firms) 20,339
annual payroll ($mil) 7,699
paid employees (x1,000) (non-exempt firms) .374

COMMUNICATION, ENERGY & TRANSPORTATION

Communication
daily newspapers, 1993 45
broadcast stations, 1990
  radio: commercial, educational 272
  television: commercial, noncommercial 34
cable TV households, 1988 841,000

Energy
consumption estimates, 1992
total (trillion Btu) 1,499
per capita (million Btu) 288.8
by source of production (trillion Btu)
  coal 523
  natural gas 241
  petroleum 648
  nuclear electric power 86
  hydroelectric power 15
by end-use sector (trillion Btu)
  residential 369
  commercial 286
  industrial 353
  transportation 492
electrical energy
  production, 1993 (billion kWh) 53.2
  net summer capability, 1993 (million kW) . 15.4
gas utilities, 1993
  customers 1,382,000
  sales (trillion Btu) 213
  revenues ($mil) 1,050
nuclear plants, 1993 1

Transportation, 1994
public road & street mileage
total 122,311
  urban 16,499
  rural 105,812
  interstate 1,178
vehicle miles of travel (mil) 57,288
total motor vehicle registrations 4,207,930
  automobiles 2,741,383
licensed drivers 3,382,046
  per 1,000 driving age population 836
deaths from motor vehicle
  accidents 1,089

STATE SUMMARY

Capital City . . . . .Helena

Governor . . . . Marc Racicot

Address . . . . STATE CAPITOL
HELENA, MT 59620
406 444-3111

Admitted as a state 1889

Area (square miles) 147,046

Population, 1980 786,690

Population, 1990 799,065

Population, 1994 (est.) 856,000

Persons per square mile, 1994 . . . . 5.9

Largest city . . . . Billings
   population, 1990 81,200

Personal income per capita, 1994
   (in current dollars) $17,865

Gross state product ($mil), 1991 14,419

Leading industries, 1992 (by payroll)
SERVICE INDUSTRIES
RETAIL TRADE
MANUFACTURING

Leading agricultural commodities, 1993
CATTLE
WHEAT
BARLEY
HAY

GEOGRAPHY & ENVIRONMENT

Area (square miles)
total 147,046
   land 145,556
   water (includes territorial water) 1,490

Federally owned land, 1991 . . . . 28.0%

Highest point
name . . . . Granite Peak
elevation (feet) 12,799

Lowest point
name .Kootenal River
elevation (feet) 1,800

General coastline (miles) 0

Tidal shoreline (miles) 0

Capital city . . . . .Helena
population, 1990 24,600

Largest city . . . . Billings
population, 1990 81,200

Number of cities with over 100,000 population
1980 0

Number of cities with over 100,000 population
1990 0

State parks and Recreation areas, 1991
area (acres) 32,000
number of visitors 1,652,000
revenues $1,022,000

National forest land, 1992 (acres) 19,102,000

National park acreage, 1984 1,220,900

DEMOGRAPHICS & CHARACTERISTICS OF THE POPULATION

Population
1970 694,409
1980 786,690
1990 799,065
1994 (est.) 856,000
2000 (revised projection) 920,000
2010 (revised projection) 996,000

Metropolitan area population
1970 169,000
1980 189,000
1992 197,000

Non-metropolitan area population
1970 525,000
1980 598,000
1992 625,000

Change in population, 1980-90
number 12,375
percent 1.57%

Persons per square mile, 1994 . . . . 5.9

Age distribution, 1980
under 5 years 8.2%
5 to 17 years 21.3%
65 and over 10.7%

Age distribution, 1990
under 5 years 7.4%
5 to 17 years 20.3%
65 and over 13.3%

211

Montana 2

Age distribution, 2000 (projected)
under 5 years 6.2%
5 to 17 years 18.6%
65 and over 12.8%

Persons by age, 1990
under 5 years 59,257
5 to 17 years 162,847
65 and over 106,497

Median age, 1990 .... 33.80

Race, 1990
White 741,111
Black 2,381
American Indian 47,524
Chinese 655
Filipino 735
Japanese 829
Asian Indian 248
Korean 668
Vietnamese 159
all other 4,600

Race, 2010 (projected)
White 908,000
Black 3,000

Persons of Hispanic origin, 1990
total 12,174
Mexican 8,362
Puerto Rican 437
Cuban 124
Other Hispanic 3,251

Persons by sex, 1990
male 395,769
female 403,296

Marital status, 1990
males
15 years & older 299,504
single 79,234
married 186,723
separated 3,584
widowed 7,466
divorced 26,081
females
15 years & older 312,028
single 57,335
married 187,117
separated 4,548

widowed 36,750
divorced 30,826

Households & families, 1990
households 306,163
persons per household 2.53
families 211,666
married couples 176,526
female householder, no husband
present 26,397
one person households 80,491
households, 1994 325,000
persons per household, 1994 .... 2.56

Nativity, 1990
number of persons born in state 470,861
percent of total residents 58.9%

Immigration & naturalization, 1993
immigrants admitted 509
persons naturalized 165
refugees granted resident status 61

VITAL STATISTICS & HEALTH

Births
1992 11,551
with low birth weight 6.0%
to teenage mothers 11.9%
to unmarried mothers 26.4%
1993 11,450
1994 11,032

Abortions, 1992
total 3,000
rate (per 1,000 women age 15-44) 18.2
rate per 1,000 live births 298

Adoptions, 1986
total 652
related 50.5%

Deaths
1992 7,151
1993 7,502
1994 7,346

Infant deaths
1992 98
1993 91
1994 91

Average lifetime, 1979-1981
both sexes . . . . 73.93 years
  men . . . . 70.47 years
  women . . . . 77.68 years

Marriages
1992 7,221
1993 7,019
1994 6,895

Divorces
1992 4,258
1993 4,320
1994 4,153

Physicians, 1993
total 1,407
rate (per 1,000 persons) 1.69

Dentists, 1992
total 468
rate (per 1,000 persons) 0.57

Hospitals, 1993
number 52
beds (x 1,000) 4.2
average daily census (x 1,000) 2.7
occupancy rate 64.2%
personnel (x 1,000) 11.9
average cost per day to hospital $481
average cost per stay to hospital $4,953

EDUCATION

*Educational attainment of all persons
  25 years and older, 1990*
less than 9th grade 41,144
high school graduates 170,070
bachelor's degree 71,610
graduate or professional degree 28,911

Public school enrollment, Fall, 1993
total 163,009
  Kindergarten through grade 8 116,668
  grades 9 through 12 46,341

Public School Teachers
total, 1994 9,950
  elementary 6,914
  secondary 3,036
salaries, 1994
  beginning $18,750
  average $28,200

*State receipts & expenditures for public
  schools, 1993*
receipts ($mil) 836
expenditures
  total ($mil) 868
  per capita $1,056
  per pupil $5,348

*Graduating high school seniors,
  public high schools, 1995 (est)* 9,970

SAT scores, 1994
verbal 463
math 523

Institutions of higher education, 1995
total 21
  public 15
  private 6

*Enrollment in institutions of higher
  education, Fall, 1993*
total 39,557
full-time men 14,922
full-time women 15,290
part-time men 3,813
part-time women 5,532

*Minority enrollment in institutions of higher
  education, Fall, 1993*
Black, non-Hispanic 153
Hispanic 394
Asian/Pacific Islander 314

Earned degrees conferred, 1993
Bachelor's 4,194
First professional 68
Master's 756
Doctor's 57

SOCIAL INSURANCE &
WELFARE PROGRAMS

Social Security beneficiaries & benefits, 1993
beneficiaries
total 148,000
  retired and dependents 103,000
  survivors 25,000
  disabled & dependents 21,000
annual benefit payments ($mil)
total $1,028
  retired and dependents 688
  survivors 204
  disabled & dependents 136

Montana 4

Medicare, 1993
enrollment (x1,000) 125
payments ($mil) 370

Medicaid, 1993
recipients (x1,000) 89
payments ($mil) 287

Federal public aid, 1993
recipients as a percent of population 5.6%
Aid to Families with Dependent Children
  recipients (x1,000) 35
average monthly payment $331
Supplemental Security Income
  total recipients (x1,000) 12

Food Stamp Program
  participants, 1994 (x1,000) 71

HOUSING & CONSTRUCTION

Total housing units, 1990 361,155
  year round housing units 340,086
  vacant 54,992

New privately owned housing units
  authorized, 1994
number (x1,000) 3.0
value ($mil) 233

New privately owned housing units
  started, 1994 (x1,000) 3.9

Existing home sales, 1994 (x1,000) 15.6

GOVERNMENT & ELECTIONS

State officials, 1996
  Governor (name/party/term expires)
          MARC RACICOT
          Republican - 1997
Lt. Governor . . . . .Dennis Rehberg
Sec. of State . . . . Mike Cooney
Atty. General . . . . .Joe Mezurek
Chf. Justice . . . . Jean Turnage

Governorship
minimum age 25
length of term . . . . 4 years
number of consecutive
  terms permitted . . . . .not specified
who succeeds . . . . Lt. Governor

State legislature
name . . . . Legislature
  upper chamber
      name . . . . Senate
      number of members 50
      length of term . . . . 4 years
      party in majority, 1996 . . . . Republican
  lower chamber
      name . . . . House of Representatives
      number of members 100
      length of term . . . . 2 years
      party in majority, 1996 . . . . Republican

State employees October, 1992
total 23,693
October payroll ($1,000) 37,577

Local governments, 1992
total 1,305
  county 54
  municipal 128
  township 0
  school districts 544
  special districts 578

Voting, November, 1994
voting age population 619,000
  registered 73.2%
  voted 60.7%

Vote for president
1988
  Bush 189,598
  Dukakis 168,120
1992
  Clinton 153,331
  Bush 143,676
  Perot 106,700

Federal representation, 1996 (104th Congress)
Senators (name/party/term expires)

          CONRAD BURNS
          Republican - 2001
          MAX BAUCUS
          Democrat - 1997

Representatives, total 1
  Democrats 1
  Republicans 0
  other 0

Montana 5

Women holding public office
U.S. Congress, 1995 0
statewide elected office, 1995 1
state legislature, 1995 36

Black elected officials, 1993
total 0
  US and state legislatures 0
  city/county/regional offices 0
  judicial/law enforcement 0
  education/school boards 0

Hispanic public officials, 1994
total 2
  state executives & legislators 0
  city/county/regional offices 0
  judicial/law enforcement 1
  education/school boards 1

GOVERNMENTAL FINANCE

State & local government revenues, (selected items), 1991-92 ($per capita)
total $4,529.38
  total general revenues 3,807.81
    from federal government 956.57
    from own sources 2,851.24
    from taxes 1,800.97
    from property taxes 719.73
    from all other taxes 719.71
    from charges & misc. 1,050.27

State & local government expenditures, (selected items), 1991-92 ($per capita)
total $4,115.63
  total direct general expenditures 3,622.98
    education 1,347.05
    libraries 13.29
    public welfare 442.79
    health & hospitals 210.77
    highways 436.92
    police protection 91.15
    fire protection 29.18
    correction 56.12
    housing & comm. development 52.06
    natural resources & parks 165.93
    interest on general debt 244.60

State & local debt, 1992 ($per capita) 3,635.64

Federal aid grants to state & local government, 1994 ($per capita total & selected items)
per capita total 1,058.73
  compensatory education 29.18
  waste treatment facilities 10.23
  medicaid 288.18
  housing assistance 65.72
  job training 17.16
  highway trust fund 193.28

CRIME, LAW ENFORCEMENT & COURTS

Crime, 1994 (all rates per 100,000 persons)
total crimes 42,961
overall crime rate 5,018.8
  property crimes 41,445
    burglaries 6,178
    larcenies 32,817
    motor vehicle thefts 2,450
  property crime rate 4,841.7
  violent crimes 1,516
    murders 28
    forcible rapes 233
    robberies 280
    aggravated assaults 975
  violent crime rate 177.1

Number of police agencies, 1994 ....NA

Arrests, 1994
total ....NA
  persons under 18 years of age ....NA

Prisoners under state & federal jurisdiction, 1994
total 1,680
percent change, 1993-94 ....9.0%
  sentenced to more than one year
    total 1,680
    rate per 100,000 residents 194

Persons under sentence of death, 4/20/95 8

State's highest court
name .... Supreme Court
number of members 7
length of term ....8 years
intermediate appeals court? ....no

Montana 6

LABOR & INCOME

Civilian labor force, 1994

total 437,000
  men 231,000
  women 205,000
  persons 16-19 years 26,000
  white 416,000
  black . . . . NA

Civilian labor force as a percent of
civilian non-institutional population, 1994

total 68.2%
  men 75.2%
  women 61.8%
  persons 16-19 years 56.8%
  white 68.6%
  black . . . . NA%

Employment, 1994

total 414,000
  men 219,000
  women 195,000
  persons 16-19 years 21,000
  white 396,000
  black . . . . NA

Full-time/part-time labor force, 1994

full-time labor force 333,000
  working part-time for
    ecomonic reasons 5,000
part-time labor force 103,000

Unemployment rate, 1994

total 5.1%
  men 5.3%
  women 4.8%
  persons 16-19 years 17.2%
  white 4.6%
  black . . . . NA%

Unemployed by reason for unemployment
(as a percent of total unemployment), 1994

job losers or completed temp jobs 44.3%
job leavers 13.4%
reentrants 38.8%
new entrants 3.6%

Civilian labor force, by occupation, 1994

executive/administrative/
  managerial 50,000
professional/specialty 59,000
technicians & related support 11,000
sales 49,000
adminstrative support/clerical 64,000
service occupations 68,000
precision production/craft/repair 45,000
machine operators/assemblers 12,000
transportation/material moving 24,000
handlers/helpers/laborers 16,000
farming/forestry/fishing 38,000

Civilian labor force, by industry, 1994

construction 19,000
manufacturing 28,000
transportation/communication 23,000
wholesale/retail trade 89,000
finance/real estate/insurance 17,000
services 83,000
government 80,000
agriculture 37,000

Average annual pay, 1994 (prelim.) $20,219
change in average annual pay,
  1993-1994 . . . . 1.4%

Hours and earnings of production workers
on manufacturing payrolls, 1994

average weekly hours 39.3
average hourly earnings $12.50
average weekly earnings $491.25

Labor union membership, 1994 60,400

Household income (in constant 1993 dollars)
median household income, 1992 . . . . $27,319
median household income, 1993 . . . . $26,470

Poverty
persons below poverty level, 1992 . . . . 13.8%
persons below poverty level, 1993 . . . . 14.9%

Personal income ($per capita)
1994
  in current dollars 17,865
  in constant (1987) dollars 13,817
1995 (projected)
  in constant (1982) dollars 11,654
2000 (projected)
  in constant (1982) dollars 12,474

Federal income tax returns, 1993
returns filed 375,861
adjusted gross income ($1000) 9,593,941
total income tax paid ($1000) 1,242,721

ECONOMY, BUSINESS, INDUSTRY & AGRICULTURE

Fortune 500 companies, 1994 0

Business incorporations, 1994
total 2,177
change, 1993-94 .... -3.7%

Business failures, 1994
total 179
rate per 10,000 concerns 48
change, 1993-94 .... 2.9%

Business firm ownership
Hispanic owned firms, 1987 304
black owned firms, 1987 77
women owned firms, 1987 17,700
foreign owned firms, 1982 39

Gross state product, 1991 ($mil)
total $14,419
   agriculture services, forestry, fisheries ... 1,024
   mining 860
   construction 563
   manufacturing—durable goods 620
   manufacturing—nondurable goods 559
   transportation, communication &
      public utilities 1,847
   wholesale trade 795
   retail trade 1,408
   finance/real estate/insurance 2,324
   services 2,268
   federal, state & local government . 2,152

Establishments, by major industry group, 1992
total 26,735
   agriculture 450
   mining 302
   construction 2,683
   manufacturing 1,397
   transportation 1,570
   wholesale trade 1,812
   retail trade 6,979
   finance/real estate/insurance 2,194
   service industries 8,945
   unclassified 403

Payroll, by major industry group, 1992
total ($1,000) $4,235,529
   agriculture 20,865

   mining 190,412
   construction 313,240
   manufacturing 541,482
   transportation 449,943
   wholesale trade 352,203
   retail trade 756,717
   finance/real estate/insurance ... 318,847
   service industries 1,288,367
   unclassified 3,453

Agriculture
number of farms, 1994 23,000
farm acreage, 1994 60,000,000
acres per farm, 1994 2,584
value of farms, 1994 ($mil) 18,115
farm income, 1993 ($mil)
   gross farm income 2,511
   net farm income 765
   debt/asset ratio 11.8%
farm marketings, 1993 ($mil)
total $1,781
   crops 843
   livestock 938
government payments 338
farm marketings in order of marketing receipts, 1993
   1) Cattle
   2) Wheat
   3) Barley
   4) Hay

Federal economic activity
($mil, except per capita)
expenditures, 1994
   total $4,638
   per capita $5,418
   defense $330
   non-defense $4,307
defense department, 1994
   contract awards ($mil) $63
   payroll ($mil) $258
   civilian employees (x1,000) .. 1.1
   military personnel (x1,000) .. 4.6

Fishing, 1992
catch (millions of pounds) ...... NA
value ($mil) .... NA

Mining, 1994 ($mil)
total non-fuel mineral production .. $492

217

Montana 8

principal non-fuel minerals in order of value, 1994

    1) Gold
    2) Copper
    3) Cement

Construction, 1994 ($mil)
total contracts (including
  non-building) $770
    residential 348
    non-residential 236

Manufacturing, 1992
total establishments 1,375
employees, total (x1,000) 22
payroll ($mil) 544
production workers (x1,000) 16
value added ($mil) 1,421
value of shipments ($mil) 4,137

Finance
commercial banks, 1994
  number 117
    assets ($bil) 7.9
    deposits ($bil) 6.8
  closed or assisted 0
    deposits ($bil) .... NA
savings and loan associations, 1991
  non-current real estate loans 0.67%
  net income after taxes ($mil) 10
  return on assets .... +0.83%

Retail trade, 1992
establishments (x1,000) 6.8
sales ($mil) 6,247
annual payroll ($mil) 697
paid employees (x1,000) 64

Wholesale trade, 1992
establishments 1,853
sales ($bil) 5.9
annual payroll ($mil) 343
paid employees (x1,000) 16.4

Service industries, 1992
establishments (x1,000) (non-exempt firms) . 6.9
receipts ($mil) (non-exempt firms) 2,197
annual payroll ($mil) 722
paid employees (x1,000) (non-exempt firms) .. 44

COMMUNICATION, ENERGY & TRANSPORTATION

Communication
daily newspapers, 1993 11
broadcast stations, 1990
  radio: commercial, educational 108
  television: commercial, noncommercial 16
cable TV households, 1988 168,000

Energy
consumption estimates, 1992
total (trillion Btu) 341
per capita (million Btu) 414.1
by source of production (trillion Btu)
  coal 190
  natural gas 47
  petroleum 149
  nuclear electric power 0
  hydroelectric power 85
by end-use sector (trillion Btu)
  residential 56
  commercial 50
  industrial 145
  transportation 90
electrical energy
  production, 1993 (billion kWh) 23.4
  net summer capability, 1993 (million kW) .. 4.9
gas utilities, 1993
  customers 213,000
  sales (trillion Btu) 40
  revenues ($mil) 174
nuclear plants, 1993 0

Transportation, 1994
public road & street mileage
total 69,346
  urban 2,385
  rural 66,961
  interstate 1,190
vehicle miles of travel (mil) 9,116
total motor vehicle registrations 949,525
  automobiles 512,144
licensed drivers 525,780
  per 1,000 driving age population 814
deaths from motor vehicle
  accidents 202

STATE SUMMARY

Capital City .... Lincoln

Governor ....Ben Nelson

Address ....STATE CAPITOL
LINCOLN, NE 68509
402 471-2244

Admitted as a state 1867

Area (square miles) 77,358

Population, 1980 1,569,825

Population, 1990 1,578,385

Population, 1994 (est.) 1,623,000

Persons per square mile, 1994 .... 21.1

Largest city .... Omaha
population, 1990 336,000

Personal income per capita, 1994
(in current dollars) $20,488

Gross state product ($mil), 1991 35,281

Leading industries, 1992 (by payroll)
SERVICE INDUSTRIES
MANUFACTURING
RETAIL TRADE

Leading agricultural commodities, 1993
CATTLE
CORN
HOGS
SOYBEANS

GEOGRAPHY & ENVIRONMENT

Area (square miles)
total 77,358
land 76,878
water (includes territorial water) 481

Federally owned land, 1991 .... 1.4%

Highest point
name ....Johnson Twp. (Kimball County)
elevation (feet) 5,426

Lowest point
name .... southeast corner of state
elevation (feet) 840

General coastline (miles) 0

Tidal shoreline (miles) 0

Capital city .... Lincoln
population, 1990 192,000

Largest city .... Omaha
population, 1990 336,000

Number of cities with over 100,000 population
1980 2

Number of cities with over 100,000 population
1990 2

State parks and Recreation areas, 1991
area (acres) 142,000
number of visitors 9,215,000
revenues $7,550,000

National forest land, 1992 (acres) 442,000

National park acreage, 1984 5,900

DEMOGRAPHICS & CHARACTERISTICS OF THE POPULATION

Population
1970 1,485,333
1980 1,569,825
1990 1,578,385
1994 (est.) 1,623,000
2000 (revised projection) 1,704,000
2010 (revised projection) 1,793,000

Metropolitan area population
1970 650,000
1980 708,000
1992 809,000

Non-metropolitan area population
1970 835,000
1980 862,000
1992 791,000

Change in population, 1980-90
number 8,560
percent 0.55%

Persons per square mile, 1994 .... 21.1

Age distribution, 1980
under 5 years 7.8%
5 to 17 years 20.6%
65 and over 13.1%

Age distribution, 1990
under 5 years 7.6%
5 to 17 years 19.6%
65 and over 14.1%

219

Nebraska 2

Age distribution, 2000 (projected)
under 5 years 6.5%
5 to 17 years 18.9%
65 and over 14.5%

Persons by age, 1990
under 5 years 119,606
5 to 17 years 309,406
65 and over 223,068

Median age, 1990 .... 33.00

Race, 1990
White 1,480,558
Black 57,404
American Indian 12,344
Chinese 1,775
Filipino 1,377
Japanese 1,574
Asian Indian 1,218
Korean 1,943
Vietnamese 1,806
all other 18,320

Race, 2010 (projected)
White 1,669,000
Black 76,000

Persons of Hispanic origin, 1990
total 36,969
  Mexican 29,665
  Puerto Rican 1,159
  Cuban 480
  Other Hispanic 5,665

Persons by sex, 1990
male 769,439
female 808,946

Marital status, 1990
males
  15 years & older 583,134
    single 162,919
    married 366,215
      separated 5,839
    widowed 14,891
    divorced 39,109
females
  15 years & older 631,861
    single 132,954
    married 366,625
      separated 7,713

widowed 81,161
divorced 51,121

Households & families, 1990
households 602,363
persons per household 2.54
  families 415,427
    married couples 350,514
    female householder, no husband
      present 50,175
    one person households 159,671
households, 1994 614,000
persons per household, 1994 .... 2.56

Nativity, 1990
number of persons born in state 1,107,280
percent of total residents 70.2%

Immigration & naturalization, 1993
immigrants admitted 1,980
persons naturalized 4,411
refugees granted resident status 663

VITAL STATISTICS & HEALTH

Births
1992 23,003
  with low birth weight 5.6%
  to teenage mothers 9.9%
  to unmarried mothers 22.6%
1993 22,847
1994 23,032

Abortions, 1992
total 6,000
rate (per 1,000 women age 15-44) 15.7
rate per 1,000 live births 246

Adoptions, 1986
total 1,009
  related 79.4%

Deaths
1992 14,852
1993 15,401
1994 14,732

Infant deaths
1992 154
1993 202
1994 181

Average lifetime, 1979-1981
both sexes . . . . 75.49 years
men . . . . 71.73 years
women . . . . 79.29 years

Marriages
1992 12,847
1993 12,397
1994 12,347

Divorces
1992 6,566
1993 6,334
1994 6,547

Physicians, 1993
total 3,025
rate (per 1,000 persons) 1.89

Dentists, 1992
total 1,079
rate (per 1,000 persons) 0.68

Hospitals, 1993
number 90
beds (x 1,000) 8.4
average daily census (x 1,000) 4.6
occupancy rate 55.2%
personnel (x 1,000) 25.7
average cost per day to hospital $626
average cost per stay to hospital $6,024

EDUCATION

*Educational attainment of all persons
25 years and older, 1990*
less than 9th grade 79,925
high school graduates 345,778
bachelor's degree 130,172
graduate or professional degree 58,490

Public school enrollment, Fall, 1993
total 285,097
Kindergarten through grade 8 203,426
grades 9 through 12 81,671

Public School Teachers
total, 1994 19,552
elementary 11,180
secondary 8,372
salaries, 1994
beginning $20,804
average $29,564

*State receipts & expenditures for public
schools, 1993*
receipts ($mil) 1,408
expenditures
total ($mil) 1,449
per capita $905
per pupil $4,950

*Graduating high school seniors,
public high schools, 1995 (est)* 19,871

SAT scores, 1994
verbal 482
math 543

Institutions of higher education, 1995
total 35
public 18
private 17

*Enrollment in institutions of higher
education, Fall, 1993*
total 115,523
full-time men 31,939
full-time women 34,103
part-time men 20,687
part-time women 28,794

*Minority enrollment in institutions of higher
education, Fall, 1993*
Black, non-Hispanic 3,322
Hispanic 2,105
Asian/Pacific Islander 1,566

Earned degrees conferred, 1993
Bachelor's 9,522
First professional 806
Master's 2,007
Doctor's 238

SOCIAL INSURANCE &
WELFARE PROGRAMS

Social Security beneficiaries & benefits, 1993
beneficiaries
total 278,000
retired and dependents 204,000
survivors 48,000
disabled & dependents 27,000
annual benefit payments ($mil)
total $1,982
retired and dependents 1,396
survivors 416
disabled & dependents 170

Nebraska 4

Medicare, 1993
enrollment (x1,000) 245
payments ($mil) 689

Medicaid, 1993
recipients (x1,000) 165
payments ($mil) 553

Federal public aid, 1993
recipients as a percent of population 4.2%
Aid to Families with Dependent Children
  recipients (x1,000) 46
average monthly payment $325
Supplemental Security Income
  total recipients (x1,000) 20

Food Stamp Program
participants, 1994 (x1,000) 111

HOUSING & CONSTRUCTION

Total housing units, 1990 660,621
  year round housing units 649,292
  vacant 58,258

New privately owned housing units authorized, 1994
number (x1,000) 7.9
value ($mil) 574

New privately owned housing units started, 1994 (x1,000) 8.9

Existing home sales, 1994 (x1,000) 23.3

GOVERNMENT & ELECTIONS

State officials, 1996
Governor (name/party/term expires)
BEN NELSON
Democrat - 1999
Lt. Governor .... Kim Robak
Sec. of State .... Allen J. Beermann
Atty. General .... Don Stenberg
Chf. Justice .... William C. Hastings

Governorship
minimum age 30
length of term .... 4 years
number of consecutive
  terms permitted 2
who succeeds .... Lt. Governor

State legislature
name .... Unicameral Legislature
  upper chamber
    name .... NA
    number of members 49
    length of term .... 4 year
    party in majority, 1996 .... NA
  lower chamber
    name .... NA
    number of members .... NA
    length of term .... NA
    party in majority, 1996 .... NA

State employees October, 1992
total 34,545
October payroll ($1,000) 59,849

Local governments, 1992
total 2,997
  county 93
  municipal 534
  township 452
  school districts 842
  special districts 1,075

Voting, November, 1994
voting age population 1,156,000
  registered 72.6%
  voted 54.3%

Vote for president
1988
  Bush 389,394
  Dukakis 254,426
1992
  Clinton 214,126
  Bush 338,648
  Perot 171,943

Federal representation, 1996 (104th Congress)
Senators (name/party/term expires)

BOB KERREY
Democrat - 2001
J. JAMES EXON, JR.
Democrat - 1997

Representatives, total 3
  Democrats 0
  Republicans 3
  other 0

Nebraska 5

Women holding public office
U.S. Congress, 1995 0
statewide elected office, 1995 1
state legislature, 1995 12

Black elected officials, 1993
total 6
  US and state legislatures 1
  city/county/regional offices 2
  judicial/law enforcement 0
  education/school boards 3

Hispanic public officials, 1994
total 3
  state executives & legislators 0
  city/county/regional offices 2
  judicial/law enforcement 0
  education/school boards 1

GOVERNMENTAL FINANCE

State & local government revenues, (selected items), 1991-92 ($per capita)
total $4,819.88
  total general revenues 3,630.32
    from federal government 619.71
    from own sources 3,010.61
    from taxes 2,030.82
      from property taxes 732.43
      from all other taxes 1,185.69
    from charges & misc. 979.79

State & local government expenditures, (selected items), 1991-92 ($per capita)
total $4,654.91
  total direct general expenditures 3,470.64
    education 1,412.48
    libraries 14.46
    public welfare 467.22
    health & hospitals 305.98
    highways 353.32
    police protection 88.99
    fire protection 37.63
    correction 66.99
    housing & comm. development 53.04
    natural resources & parks 143.00
    interest on general debt 142.20

State & local debt, 1992 ($per capita) 4,062.30

Federal aid grants to state & local government, 1994 ($per capita total & selected items)
per capita total 686.39
  compensatory education 19.08
  waste treatment facilities 3.95
  medicaid 239.85
  housing assistance 37.53
  job training 5.53
  highway trust fund 92.72

CRIME, LAW ENFORCEMENT & COURTS

Crime, 1994 (all rates per 100,000 persons)
total crimes 72,068
overall crime rate 4,440.4
  property crimes 65,746
    burglaries 10,963
    larcenies 48,547
    motor vehicle thefts 6,236
  property crime rate 4,050.9
  violent crimes 6,322
    murders 51
    forcible rapes 500
    robberies 1,223
    aggravated assaults 4,548
  violent crime rate 389.5

Number of police agencies, 1994 237

Arrests, 1994
total 80,346
  persons under 18 years of age 17,065

Prisoners under state & federal jurisdiction, 1994
total 2,633
percent change, 1993-94 .... 4.6%
  sentenced to more than one year
    total 2,590
    rate per 100,000 residents 159

Persons under sentence of death, 4/20/95 11

State's highest court
name .... Supreme Court
number of members 7
length of term .... 6 years
intermediate appeals court? .... no

Nebraska 6

LABOR & INCOME

Civilian labor force, 1994

total	876,000
men	460,000
women	416,000
persons 16-19 years	66,000
white	832,000
black	31,000

Civilian labor force as a percent of civilian non-institutional population, 1994

total	73.1%
men	79.8%
women	66.9%
persons 16-19 years	69.4%
white	73.5%
black	65.4%

Employment, 1994

total	851,000
men	448,000
women	403,000
persons 16-19 years	60,000
white	811,000
black	28,000

Full-time/part-time labor force, 1994

full-time labor force	689,000
working part-time for ecomonic reasons	7,000
part-time labor force	187,000

Unemployment rate, 1994

total	2.9%
men	2.5%
women	3.3%
persons 16-19 years	8.8%
white	2.5%
black	10.6%

Unemployed by reason for unemployment (as a percent of total unemployment), 1994

job losers or completed temp jobs	39.0%
job leavers	17.1%
reentrants	39.5%
new entrants	4.7%

Civilian labor force, by occupation, 1994

executive/administrative/ managerial	100,000
professional/specialty	110,000
technicians & related support	27,000
sales	105,000
adminstrative support/clerical	129,000
service occupations	128,000
precision production/craft/repair	91,000
machine operators/assemblers	47,000
transportation/material moving	33,000
handlers/helpers/laborers	35,000
farming/forestry/fishing	70,000

Civilian labor force, by industry, 1994

construction	31,000
manufacturing	107,000
transportation/communication	43,000
wholesale/retail trade	188,000
finance/real estate/insurance	52,000
services	191,000
government	127,000
agriculture	71,000

Average annual pay, 1994 (prelim.) $21,500
change in average annual pay, 1993-1994 ...... 3.3%

Hours and earnings of production workers on manufacturing payrolls, 1994

average weekly hours	42.1
average hourly earnings	$10.94
average weekly earnings	$460.57

Labor union membership, 1994 77,500

Household income (in constant 1993 dollars)

median household income, 1992	$30,948
median household income, 1993	$31,008

Poverty

persons below poverty level, 1992	10.6%
persons below poverty level, 1993	10.3%

Personal income ($per capita)

1994
in current dollars	20,488
in constant (1987) dollars	15,845

1995 (projected)
in constant (1982) dollars	13,419

2000 (projected)
in constant (1982) dollars	14,322

Federal income tax returns, 1993

returns filed	740,824
adjusted gross income ($1000)	21,072,721
total income tax paid ($1000)	2,814,450

Nebraska 7

ECONOMY, BUSINESS, INDUSTRY & AGRICULTURE

Fortune 500 companies, 1994 5

Business incorporations, 1994
total 3,447
change, 1993-94 .... -0.3%

Business failures, 1994
total 315
rate per 10,000 concerns 53
change, 1993-94 .... -20.9%

Business firm ownership
Hispanic owned firms, 1987 619
black owned firms, 1987 863
women owned firms, 1987 32,300
foreign owned firms, 1982 84

Gross state product, 1991 ($mil)
total $35,281
   agriculture services, forestry, fisheries ... 3,719
   mining 75
   construction 1,093
   manufacturing—durable goods 2,317
   manufacturing—nondurable goods 2,125
   transportation, communication &
      public utilities 3,680
   wholesale trade 2,687
   retail trade 3,024
   finance/real estate/insurance 5,896
   services 5,387
   federal, state & local government 5,278

Establishments, by major industry group, 1992
total 45,269
   agriculture 910
   mining 162
   construction 4,471
   manufacturing 2,049
   transportation 2,307
   wholesale trade 3,904
   retail trade 11,774
   finance/real estate/insurance 4,331
   service industries 14,787
   unclassified 574

Payroll, by major industry group, 1992
total ($1,000) $12,011,492
   agriculture 61,867

   mining 32,837
   construction 664,547
   manufacturing 2,500,586
   transportation 883,422
   wholesale trade 1,164,529
   retail trade 1,459,615
   finance/real estate/insurance 1,353,303
   service industries 3,883,193
   unclassified 7,593

Agriculture
number of farms, 1994 55,000
farm acreage, 1994 47,000,000
acres per farm, 1994 856
value of farms, 1994 ($mil) 29,894
farm income, 1993 ($mil)
   gross farm income 9,872
   net farm income 2,092
   debt/asset ratio 18.7%
farm marketings, 1993 ($mil)
total $8,909
   crops 3,067
   livestock 5,842
government payments 806
farm marketings in order of marketing receipts, 1993
      1) Cattle
      2) Corn
      3) Hogs
      4) Soybeans

Federal economic activity
   ($mil, except per capita)
expenditures, 1994
   total $7,439
   per capita $4,584
   defense $936
   non-defense $6,504
defense department, 1994
   contract awards ($mil) $310
   payroll ($mil) $612
   civilian employees (x1,000) 3.6
   military personnel (x1,000) 9.7

Fishing, 1992
catch (millions of pounds) .... NA
value ($mil) .... NA

Mining, 1994 ($mil)
total non-fuel mineral production $137

Nebraska 8

principal non-fuel minerals in order of value, 1994

  1) Cement
  2) Stone
  3) Sand and gravel

Construction, 1994 ($mil)
total contracts (including
  non-building) $1,826
    residential 660
    non-residential 663

Manufacturing, 1992
total establishments 2,028
employees, total (x1,000) 100
payroll ($mil) 2,516
production workers (x1,000) 72
value added ($mil) 7,952
value of shipments ($mil) 21,816

Finance
commercial banks, 1994
  number 361
    assets ($bil) 24.1
    deposits ($bil) 20.9
    closed or assisted 0
    deposits ($bil) .... NA
savings and loan associations, 1991
  non-current real estate loans 1.06%
  net income after taxes ($mil) 64
  return on assets .... +0.75%

Retail trade, 1992
establishments (x1,000) 11.4
sales ($mil) 11,522
annual payroll ($mil) 1,308
paid employees (x1,000) 132

Wholesale trade, 1992
establishments 4,035
sales ($bil) 32.5
annual payroll ($mil) 1,076
paid employees (x1,000) 47.1

Service industries, 1992
establishments (x1,000) (non-exempt firms) 11.3
receipts ($mil) (non-exempt firms) 5,828
annual payroll ($mil) 2,290
paid employees (x1,000) (non-exempt firms) . 120

COMMUNICATION, ENERGY & TRANSPORTATION

Communication
daily newspapers, 1993 18
broadcast stations, 1990
  radio: commercial, educational 122
  television: commercial, noncommercial 24
cable TV households, 1988 364,000

Energy
consumption estimates, 1992
total (trillion Btu) 506
per capita (million Btu) 316.0
by source of production (trillion Btu)
  coal 141
  natural gas 105
  petroleum 207
  nuclear electric power 93
  hydroelectric power 11
by end-use sector (trillion Btu)
  residential 116
  commercial 106
  industrial 131
  transportation 152
electrical energy
  production, 1993 (billion kWh) 22.7
  net summer capability, 1993 (million kW) .. 5.5
gas utilities, 1993
  customers 614,000
  sales (trillion Btu) 98
  revenues ($mil) 436
nuclear plants, 1993 2

Transportation, 1994
public road & street mileage
total 92,730
  urban 5,083
  rural 87,647
  interstate 482
vehicle miles of travel (mil) 15,466
total motor vehicle registrations 1,457,584
  automobiles 840,533
licensed drivers 1,146,447
  per 1,000 driving age population 933
deaths from motor vehicle
  accidents 271

Nevada 1

STATE SUMMARY

Capital City .Carson City

Governor . . . . Bob Miller

Address . . . . STATE CAPITOL
CARSON CITY, NV 89710
702 687-5670

Admitted as a state 1864

Area (square miles) 110,567

Population, 1980 800,493

Population, 1990 1,201,833

Population, 1994 (est.) 1,457,000

Persons per square mile, 1994 . . . . 13.3

Largest city . . . . .Las Vegas
population, 1990 258,000

Personal income per capita, 1994
(in current dollars) $24,023

Gross state product ($mil), 1991 33,322

Leading industries, 1992 (by payroll)
SERVICE INDUSTRIES
RETAIL TRADE
CONSTRUCTION

Leading agricultural commodities, 1993
CATTLE
DAIRY PRODUCTS
HAY
POTATOES

GEOGRAPHY & ENVIRONMENT

Area (square miles)
total 110,567
land 109,806
water (includes territorial water) 761

Federally owned land, 1991 . . . . 82.9%

Highest point
name . . . . .Boundary Peak
elevation (feet) 13,140

Lowest point
name . . . . Colorado River
elevation (feet) 470

General coastline (miles) 0

Tidal shoreline (miles) 0

Capital city . . . . .Carson City
population, 1990 40,400

Largest city . . . . .Las Vegas
population, 1990 258,000

Number of cities with over 100,000 population
1980 2

Number of cities with over 100,000 population
1990 3

State parks and Recreation areas, 1991
area (acres) 142,000
number of visitors 2,563,000
revenues $756,000

National forest land, 1992 (acres) 6,275,000

National park acreage, 1984 700,200

DEMOGRAPHICS & CHARACTERISTICS OF THE POPULATION

Population
1970 488,738
1980 800,493
1990 1,201,833
1994 (est.) 1,457,000
2000 (revised projection) 1,691,000
2010 (revised projection) 1,935,000

Metropolitan area population
1970 394,000
1980 657,000
1992 1,134,000

Non-metropolitan area population
1970 94,000
1980 144,000
1992 203,000

Change in population, 1980-90
number 401,340
percent 50.14%

Persons per square mile, 1994 . . . . 13.3

Age distribution, 1980
under 5 years 7.0%
5 to 17 years 20.0%
65 and over 8.2%

Age distribution, 1990
under 5 years 7.7%
5 to 17 years 17.0%
65 and over 10.6%

227

Nevada 2

Age distribution, 2000 (projected)
under 5 years 5.5%
5 to 17 years 16.4%
65 and over 10.7%

Persons by age, 1990
under 5 years 92,217
5 to 17 years 204,731
65 and over 127,631

Median age, 1990 .... 33.30

Race, 1990
White 1,012,695
Black 78,771
American Indian 19,377
Chinese 6,618
Filipino 12,048
Japanese 4,024
Asian Indian 1,825
Korean 4,315
Vietnamese 1,934
all other 59,966

Race, 2010 (projected)
White 1,609,000
Black 144,000

Persons of Hispanic origin, 1990
total 124,419
Mexican 85,287
Puerto Rican 4,272
Cuban 5,988
Other Hispanic 28,872

Persons by sex, 1990
male 611,880
female 589,953

Marital status, 1990
males
15 years & older 481,852
single 135,767
married 268,566
separated 10,990
widowed 11,204
divorced 66,315
females
15 years & older 466,194
single 89,055
married 264,789
separated 12,211

widowed 42,131
divorced 70,219

Households & families, 1990
households 466,297
persons per household 2.53
families 307,400
married couples 239,573
female householder, no husband
present 47,509
one person households 119,627
households, 1994 560,000
persons per household, 1994 .... 2.56

Nativity, 1990
number of persons born in state 261,998
percent of total residents 21.8%

Immigration & naturalization, 1993
immigrants admitted 4,045
persons naturalized 1,518
refugees granted resident status 400

VITAL STATISTICS & HEALTH

Births
1992 22,345
with low birth weight 7.1%
to teenage mothers 12.4%
to unmarried mothers 33.3%
1993 21,129
1994 21,511

Abortions, 1992
total 13,000
rate (per 1,000 women age 15-44) 44.2
rate per 1,000 live births 591

Adoptions, 1986
total 427
related 40.3%

Deaths
1992 10,102
1993 10,886
1994 11,769

Infant deaths
1992 148
1993 140
1994 134

Average lifetime, 1979-1981
both sexes . . . . 72.64 years
  men . . . . 69.26 years
  women . . . . 76.48 years

Marriages
1992 114,223
1993 123,184
1994 140,325

Divorces
1992 . . . . NA
1993 . . . . NA
1994 13,061

Physicians, 1993
total 2,045
rate (per 1,000 persons) 1.48

Dentists, 1992
total 553
rate (per 1,000 persons) 0.42

Hospitals, 1993
number 21
beds (x 1,000) 3.7
average daily census (x 1,000) 2.5
occupancy rate 67.8%
personnel (x 1,000) 12.8
average cost per day to hospital $900
average cost per stay to hospital $6,796

EDUCATION

*Educational attainment of all persons
  25 years and older, 1990*
less than 9th grade 47,771
high school graduates 248,968
bachelor's degree 79,693
graduate or professional degree 40,947

Public school enrollment, Fall, 1993
total 235,800
  Kindergarten through grade 8 175,054
  grades 9 through 12 60,746

Public School Teachers
total, 1994 12,579
  elementary 6,563
  secondary 4,648
salaries, 1994
  beginning $24,155
  average $37,181

*State receipts & expenditures for public
  schools, 1993*
receipts ($mil) 1,197
expenditures
  total ($mil) 1,288
  per capita $964
  per pupil $4,976

*Graduating high school seniors,
  public high schools, 1995 (est)* 9,971

SAT scores, 1994
verbal 429
math 484

Institutions of higher education, 1995
total 10
  public 6
  private 4

*Enrollment in institutions of higher
  education, Fall, 1993*
total 63,947
full-time men 9,734
full-time women 10,460
part-time men 18,437
part-time women 25,316

*Minority enrollment in institutions of higher
  education, Fall, 1993*
Black, non-Hispanic 3,125
Hispanic 3,873
Asian/Pacific Islander 3,207

Earned degrees conferred, 1993
Bachelor's 3,029
First professional 54
Master's 845
Doctor's 39

SOCIAL INSURANCE &
WELFARE PROGRAMS

Social Security beneficiaries & benefits, 1993
beneficiaries
total 205,000
  retired and dependents 152,000
  survivors 28,000
  disabled & dependents 25,000
annual benefit payments ($mil)
total $1,489
  retired and dependents 1,070
  survivors 243
  disabled & dependents 176

Nevada 4

Medicare, 1993
enrollment (x1,000) 170
payments ($mil) 664

Medicaid, 1993
recipients (x1,000) 88
payments ($mil) 301

Federal public aid, 1993
recipients as a percent of population 3.7%
Aid to Families with Dependent Children
   recipients (x1,000) 37
average monthly payment $282
Supplemental Security Income
   total recipients (x1,000) 17

Food Stamp Program
participants, 1994 (x1,000) 97

HOUSING & CONSTRUCTION

Total housing units, 1990 518,858
   year round housing units 507,336
   vacant 52,561

New privately owned housing units
authorized, 1994
number (x1,000) 31.1
value ($mil) 2,185

New privately owned housing units
started, 1994 (x1,000) 29.5

Existing home sales, 1994 (x1,000) 32.9

GOVERNMENT & ELECTIONS

State officials, 1996
   Governor (name/party/term expires)
         BOB MILLER
         Democrat - 1999
Lt. Governor .... Lonnie Hammargren
Sec. of State .... Dean Heller
Atty. General .... Frankie Sue Del Papa
Chf. Justice .... Robert Rose

Governorship
minimum age 25
length of term .... 4 years
number of consecutive
   terms permitted 2
who succeeds .... Lt. Governor

State legislature
name .... Legislature
  upper chamber
    name .... Senate
    number of members 21
    length of term .... 4 years
    party in majority, 1996 .... Republican
  lower chamber
    name .... State Assembly
    number of members 42
    length of term .... 2 years
    party in majority, 1996 .... 50/50

State employees October, 1992
total 20,961
October payroll ($1,000) 49,783

Local governments, 1992
total 212
  county 16
  municipal 18
  township 0
  school districts 17
  special districts 160

Voting, November, 1994
voting age population 1,081,000
  registered 49.5%
  voted 40.1%

Vote for president
1988
  Bush 205,942
  Dukakis 132,716
1992
  Clinton 188,169
  Bush 174,775
  Perot 131,856

Federal representation, 1996 (104th Congress)
Senators (name/party/term expires)

      RICHARD BRYAN
      Democrat - 2001
      HARRY REID
      Democrat - 1999

Representatives, total 2
  Democrats 0
  Republicans 2
  other 0

Nevada 5

Women holding public office
U.S. Congress, 1995 1
statewide elected office, 1995 1
state legislature, 1995 22

Black elected officials, 1993
total 10
  US and state legislatures 3
  city/county/regional offices 4
  judicial/law enforcement 1
  education/school boards 2

Hispanic public officials, 1994
total 4
  state executives & legislators 1
  city/county/regional offices 0
  judicial/law enforcement 1
  education/school boards 2

GOVERNMENTAL FINANCE

State & local government revenues, (selected items), 1991-92 ($per capita)
total $4,771.69
  total general revenues 3,693.84
    from federal government 556.34
    from own sources 3,137.50
    from taxes 2,112.82
      from property taxes 507.99
      from all other taxes 1,312.76
    from charges & misc. 1,024.68

State & local government expenditures, (selected items), 1991-92 ($per capita)
total $4,987.52
  total direct general expenditures 4,131.50
    education 1,246.90
    libraries 33.72
    public welfare 377.86
    health & hospitals 311.79
    highways 338.34
    police protection 197.49
    fire protection 110.00
    correction 181.61
    housing & comm. development 51.18
    natural resources & parks 217.80
    interest on general debt 323.16

State & local debt, 1992 ($per capita) 5,070.59

Federal aid grants to state & local government, 1994 ($per capita total & selected items)
per capita total 546.86
  compensatory education 11.95
  waste treatment facilities 6.74
  medicaid 131.48
  housing assistance 42.98
  job training 9.17
  highway trust fund 86.12

CRIME, LAW ENFORCEMENT & COURTS

Crime, 1994 (all rates per 100,000 persons)
total crimes 97,290
overall crime rate 6,677.4
  property crimes 82,693
    burglaries 19,735
    larcenies 51,893
    motor vehicle thefts 11,065
  property crime rate 5,675.6
  violent crimes 14,597
    murders 170
    forcible rapes 1,001
    robberies 5,134
    aggravated assaults 8,292
  violent crime rate 1,001.9

Number of police agencies, 1994 27

Arrests, 1994
total 106,315
  persons under 18 years of age 18,186

Prisoners under state & federal jurisdiction, 1994
total 7,122
percent change, 1993-94 ....16.0%
sentenced to more than one year
  total 6,877
  rate per 100,000 residents 460

Persons under sentence of death, 4/20/95 72

State's highest court
name .... Supreme Court
number of members 5
length of term ....6 years
intermediate appeals court? ....no

231

Nevada 6

LABOR & INCOME

Civilian labor force, 1994
total 779,000
  men 433,000
  women 345,000
  persons 16-19 years 41,000
  white 688,000
  black 48,000

Civilian labor force as a percent of
  civilian non-institutional population, 1994
total 70.2%
  men 77.8%
  women 62.4%
  persons 16-19 years 60.6%
  white 70.2%
  black 68.1%

Employment, 1994
total 731,000
  men 408,000
  women 323,000
  persons 16-19 years 34,000
  white 648,000
  black 44,000

Full-time/part-time labor force, 1994
full-time labor force 662,000
  working part-time for
    ecomonic reasons 8,000
part-time labor force 115,000

Unemployment rate, 1994
total 6.2%
  men 5.9%
  women 6.5%
  persons 16-19 years 18.9%
  white 5.9%
  black 9.3%

Unemployed by reason for unemployment
  (as a percent of total unemployment), 1994
job losers or completed temp jobs 43.2%
job leavers 15.5%
reentrants 36.0%
new entrants 5.3%

Civilian labor force, by occupation, 1994
executive/administrative/
  managerial 93,000
professional/specialty 71,000
technicians & related support 22,000

sales 102,000
adminstrative support/clerical 113,000
service occupations 191,000
precision production/craft/repair 81,000
machine operators/assemblers 22,000
transportation/material moving 32,000
handlers/helpers/laborers 35,000
farming/forestry/fishing ....NA

Civilian labor force, by industry, 1994
construction 63,000
manufacturing 41,000
transportation/communication 44,000
wholesale/retail trade 148,000
finance/real estate/insurance 36,000
services 285,000
government 90,000
agriculture ....NA

Average annual pay, 1994 (prelim.) $25,700
change in average annual pay,
  1993-1994 .... 0.9%

Hours and earnings of production workers
  on manufacturing payrolls, 1994
average weekly hours 41.1
average hourly earnings $11.83
average weekly earnings $486.21

Labor union membership, 1994 120,900

Household income (in constant 1993 dollars)
median household income, 1992 .... $32,863
median household income, 1993 .... $35,814

Poverty
persons below poverty level, 1992 .... 14.7%
persons below poverty level, 1993 .... 9.8%

Personal income ($per capita)
1994
  in current dollars 24,023
  in constant (1987) dollars 18,579
1995 (projected)
  in constant (1982) dollars 15,058
2000 (projected)
  in constant (1982) dollars 15,855

Federal income tax returns, 1993
returns filed 684,067
adjusted gross income ($1000) 23,589,558
total income tax paid ($1000) 3,831,695

ECONOMY, BUSINESS, INDUSTRY & AGRICULTURE

Fortune 500 companies, 1994 0

Business incorporations, 1994
total 17,023
change, 1993-94 .... 11.8%

Business failures, 1994
total 448
rate per 10,000 concerns 106
change, 1993-94 .... -21.3%

Business firm ownership
Hispanic owned firms, 1987 1,767
black owned firms, 1987 1,002
women owned firms, 1987 18,800
foreign owned firms, 1982 77

Gross state product, 1991 ($mil)
total $33,322
  agriculture services, forestry, fisheries 299
  mining 1,908
  construction 1,843
  manufacturing—durable goods 729
  manufacturing—nondurable goods 443
  transportation, communication &
    public utilities 2,865
  wholesale trade 1,398
  retail trade 3,118
  finance/real estate/insurance 5,405
  services 11,824
  federal, state & local government 3,490

Establishments, by major industry group, 1992
total 32,645
  agriculture 549
  mining 258
  construction 3,360
  manufacturing 1,263
  transportation 1,267
  wholesale trade 2,065
  retail trade 7,821
  finance/real estate/insurance 3,704
  service industries 11,848
  unclassified 510

Payroll, by major industry group, 1992
total ($1,000) $12,247,868
  agriculture 53,609

  mining 454,837
  construction 1,185,316
  manufacturing 788,464
  transportation 863,821
  wholesale trade 665,009
  retail trade 1,589,509
  finance/real estate/insurance 760,095
  service industries 5,877,043
  unclassified 10,165

Agriculture
number of farms, 1994 2,000
farm acreage, 1994 9,000,000
acres per farm, 1994 3,708
value of farms, 1994 ($mil) 2,036
farm income, 1993 ($mil)
  gross farm income 311
  net farm income 80
  debt/asset ratio 9.0%
farm marketings, 1993 ($mil)
  total $289
    crops 102
    livestock 187
  government payments 7
farm marketings in order of marketing receipts, 1993
    1) Cattle
    2) Hay
    3) Dairy products
    4) Potatoes

Federal economic activity
  ($mil, except per capita)
expenditures, 1994
    total $6,104
    per capita $4,189
    defense $917
    non-defense $5,187
defense department, 1994
    contract awards ($mil) $274
    payroll ($mil) $643
    civilian employees (x1,000) 2.2
    military personnel (x1,000) 8.6

Fishing, 1992
catch (millions of pounds) .... NA
value ($mil) .... NA

Mining, 1994 ($mil)
total non-fuel mineral production $2,761

principal non-fuel minerals in order of value, 1994
1) Gold
2) Sand and gravel
3) Diatomite

Construction, 1994 ($mil)
total contracts (including
  non-building) $4,690
  residential 2,285
  non-residential 1,632

Manufacturing, 1992
total establishments 1,249
employees, total (x1,000) 28
payroll ($mil) 744
production workers (x1,000) 18
value added ($mil) 1,720
value of shipments ($mil) 3,288

Finance
commercial banks, 1994
  number 21
  assets ($bil) 18.0
  deposits ($bil) 10.2
  closed or assisted 0
  deposits ($bil) .... NA
savings and loan associations, 1991
  non-current real estate loans 2.47%
  net income after taxes ($mil) .... -70
  return on assets .... -1.65%

Retail trade, 1992
establishments (x1,000) 7.5
sales ($mil) 11,546
annual payroll ($mil) 1,422
paid employees (x1,000) 99

Wholesale trade, 1992
establishments 2,075
sales ($bil) 7.8
annual payroll ($mil) 607
paid employees (x1,000) 21.8

Service industries, 1992
establishments (x1,000) (non-exempt firms) 10.8
receipts ($mil) (non-exempt firms) 16,585
annual payroll ($mil) 5,431
paid employees (x1,000) (non-exempt firms) . 256

COMMUNICATION, ENERGY & TRANSPORTATION

Communication
daily newspapers, 1993 8
broadcast stations, 1990
  radio: commercial, educational 66
  television: commercial, noncommercial 14
cable TV households, 1988 192,000

Energy
consumption estimates, 1992
  total (trillion Btu) 412
  per capita (million Btu) 307.9
by source of production (trillion Btu)
  coal 179
  natural gas 71
  petroleum 176
  nuclear electric power 0
  hydroelectric power 21
by end-use sector (trillion Btu)
  residential 87
  commercial 72
  industrial 112
  transportation 141
electrical energy
  production, 1993 (billion kWh) 19.8
  net summer capability, 1993 (million kW) .. 5.2
gas utilities, 1993
  customers 338,000
  sales (trillion Btu) 40
  revenues ($mil) 195
nuclear plants, 1993 0

Transportation, 1994
public road & street mileage
  total 46,152
  urban 4,590
  rural 41,562
  interstate 560
vehicle miles of travel (mil) 13,019
total motor vehicle registrations 984,696
  automobiles 537,855
licensed drivers 1,007,191
  per 1,000 driving age population 902
deaths from motor vehicle
  accidents 294

STATE SUMMARY

Capital City . . . . Concord

Governor . . . . Steve Merrill

Address . . . . STATE HOUSE
CONCORD, NH 03301
603 271-2121

Admitted as a state 1788

Area (square miles) 9,351

Population, 1980 920,610

Population, 1990 1,109,252

Population, 1994 (est.) 1,137,000

Persons per square mile, 1994 . . . . 126.7

Largest city . . . . .Manchester
population, 1990 99,600

Personal income per capita, 1994
(in current dollars) $23,434

Gross state product ($mil), 1991 24,404

Leading industries, 1992 (by payroll)
SERVICE INDUSTRIES
MANUFACTURING
RETAIL TRADE

Leading agricultural commodities, 1993
DAIRY PRODUCTS
GREENHOUSE
APPLES
HAY

GEOGRAPHY & ENVIRONMENT

Area (square miles)
total 9,351
land 8,969
water (includes territorial water) 382

Federally owned land, 1991 . . . . 12.7%

Highest point
name . . . . .Mt. Washington
elevation (feet) 6,288

Lowest point
name . . . . .Atlantic Ocean
elevation (feet) .sea level

General coastline (miles) 13

Tidal shoreline (miles) 131

Capital city . . . . Concord
population, 1990 36,000

Largest city . . . . .Manchester
population, 1990 99,600

Number of cities with over 100,000 population
1980 0

Number of cities with over 100,000 population
1990 0

State parks and Recreation areas, 1991
area (acres) 31,000
number of visitors 2,815,000
revenues $4,000,000

National forest land, 1992 (acres) 825,000

National park acreage, 1984 8,600

DEMOGRAPHICS & CHARACTERISTICS OF THE POPULATION

Population
1970 737,681
1980 920,610
1990 1,109,252
1994 (est.) 1,137,000
2000 (revised projection) 1,165,000
2010 (revised projection) 1,280,000

Metropolitan area population
1970 404,000
1980 511,000
1992 662,000

Non-metropolitan area population
1970 333,000
1980 410,000
1992 453,000

Change in population, 1980-90
number 188,642
percent 20.49%

Persons per square mile, 1994 . . . . 126.7

Age distribution, 1980
under 5 years 6.8%
5 to 17 years 21.3%
65 and over 11.2%

Age distribution, 1990
under 5 years 7.6%
5 to 17 years 17.5%
65 and over 11.2%

New Hampshire 2

Age distribution, 2000 (projected)
under 5 years 6.1%
5 to 17 years 18.5%
65 and over 11.1%

Persons by age, 1990
under 5 years 84,565
5 to 17 years 194,190
65 and over 125,029

Median age, 1990 .... 32.80

Race, 1990
White 1,087,433
Black 7,198
American Indian 2,075
Chinese 2,314
Filipino 874
Japanese 747
Asian Indian 1,697
Korean 1,501
Vietnamese 553
all other 4,801

Race, 2010 (projected)
White 1,236,000
Black 10,000

Persons of Hispanic origin, 1990
total 11,333
Mexican 2,362
Puerto Rican 3,299
Cuban 578
Other Hispanic 5,094

Persons by sex, 1990
male 543,544
female 565,708

Marital status, 1990
males
15 years & older 422,521
single 120,673
married 260,469
separated 6,023
widowed 9,653
divorced 31,726
females
15 years & older 449,800
single 101,572
married 261,146
separated 7,629

widowed 45,976
divorced 41,106

Households & families, 1990
households 411,186
persons per household 2.62
families 292,601
married couples 245,307
female householder, no husband
present 34,777
one person households 90,364
households, 1994 424,000
persons per household, 1994 .... 2.61

Nativity, 1990
number of persons born in state 488,894
percent of total residents 44.1%

Immigration & naturalization, 1993
immigrants admitted 1,263
persons naturalized 387
refugees granted resident status 155

VITAL STATISTICS & HEALTH

Births
1992 15,719
with low birth weight 5.3%
to teenage mothers 6.7%
to unmarried mothers 19.2%
1993 14,952
1994 14,605

Abortions, 1992
total 4,000
rate (per 1,000 women age 15-44) 14.6
rate per 1,000 live births 269

Adoptions, 1986
total 512
related 67.6%

Deaths
1992 8,555
1993 8,919
1994 8,907

Infant deaths
1992 85
1993 72
1994 96

Average lifetime, 1979-1981
both sexes . . . . 74.98 years
  men . . . . 71.43 years
  women . . . . 78.42 years

Marriages
1992 8,832
1993 9,611
1994 9,818

Divorces
1992 5,520
1993 5,035
1994 5,041

Physicians, 1993
total 2,373
rate (per 1,000 persons) 2.11

Dentists, 1992
total 673
rate (per 1,000 persons) 0.61

Hospitals, 1993
number 28
beds (x 1,000) 3.4
average daily census (x 1,000) 2.1
occupancy rate 63.7%
personnel (x 1,000) 13.8
average cost per day to hospital $976
average cost per stay to hospital $6,964

EDUCATION

*Educational attainment of all persons
  25 years and older, 1990*
less than 9th grade 47,691
high school graduates 226,267
bachelor's degree 117,260
graduate or professional degree 56,681

Public school enrollment, Fall, 1993
total 185,360
  Kindergarten through grade 8 136,211
  grades 9 through 12 49,149

Public School Teachers
total, 1994 11,972
  elementary 8,059
  secondary 3,913
salaries, 1994
  beginning $22,400
  average $34,121

*State receipts & expenditures for public
  schools, 1993*
receipts ($mil) 1,114
expenditures
  total ($mil) 1,021
  per capita $916
  per pupil $5,619

*Graduating high school seniors,
  public high schools, 1995 (est)* 9,274

SAT scores, 1994
verbal 438
math 486

Institutions of higher education, 1995
total 30
  public 12
  private 18

*Enrollment in institutions of higher
  education, Fall, 1993*
total 64,043
full-time men 18,880
full-time women 21,145
part-time men 9,229
part-time women 14,789

*Minority enrollment in institutions of higher
  education, Fall, 1993*
Black, non-Hispanic 939
Hispanic 854
Asian/Pacific Islander 1,022

Earned degrees conferred, 1993
Bachelor's 7,524
First professional 195
Master's 2,267
Doctor's 118

SOCIAL INSURANCE & WELFARE PROGRAMS

Social Security beneficiaries & benefits, 1993
beneficiaries
total 176,000
  retired and dependents 131,000
  survivors 25,000
  disabled & dependents 20,000
annual benefit payments ($mil)
total $1,291
  retired and dependents 934
  survivors 226
  disabled & dependents 131

Medicare, 1993
enrollment (x1,000) 148
payments ($mil) 462

Medicaid, 1993
recipients (x1,000) 79
payments ($mil) 380

Federal public aid, 1993
recipients as a percent of population 3.4%
Aid to Families with Dependent Children
   recipients (x1,000) 30
average monthly payment $433
Supplemental Security Income
   total recipients (x1,000) 9

Food Stamp Program
   participants, 1994 (x1,000) 62

HOUSING & CONSTRUCTION

Total housing units, 1990 503,904
   year round housing units 446,727
   vacant 92,718

New privately owned housing units
   authorized, 1994
number (x1,000) 4.7
value ($mil) 454

New privately owned housing units
   started, 1994 (x1,000) 4.3

Existing home sales, 1994 (x1,000) 16.2

GOVERNMENT & ELECTIONS

State officials, 1996
   Governor (name/party/term expires)
            STEVE MERRILL
            Republican - 1997
Lt. Governor .... (no Lieutenant Governor)
Sec. of State .... William H. Gardener
Atty. General .... Jeffrey Howard
Chf. Justice .... David A. Brock

Governorship
minimum age 30
length of term .... 2 years
number of consecutive
   terms permitted .... not specified
who succeeds .... Pres. of Senate

State legislature
name .... General Court
   upper chamber
      name .... Sentate
      number of members 24
      length of term .... 2 years
      party in majority, 1996 .... Republican
   lower chamber
      name .... House of Representatives
      number of members 400
      length of term .... 2 years
      party in majority, 1996 .... Republican

State employees October, 1992
total 21,328
October payroll ($1,000) 38,410

Local governments, 1992
total 531
   county 10
   municipal 13
   township 221
   school districts 168
   special districts 118

Voting, November, 1994
voting age population 832,000
   registered 64.3%
   voted 41.2%

Vote for president
1988
   Bush 279,770
   Dukakis 162,335
1992
   Clinton 207,264
   Bush 199,623
   Perot 120,029

Federal representation, 1996 (104th Congress)
Senators (name/party/term expires)

            ROBERT SMITH
            Republican - 1997
            JUDD GREGG
            Republican - 1999

Representatives, total 2
   Democrats 0
   Republicans 2
   other 0

Women holding public office
U.S. Congress, 1995 0
statewide elected office, 1995 0
state legislature, 1995 128

Black elected officials, 1993
total 2
  US and state legislatures 2
  city/county/regional offices 0
  judicial/law enforcement 0
  education/school boards 0

Hispanic public officials, 1994
total . . . . NA
  state executives & legislators . . . . NA
  city/county/regional offices . . . . NA
  judicial/law enforcement . . . . NA
  education/school boards . . . . NA

GOVERNMENTAL FINANCE

State & local government revenues, (selected items), 1991-92 ($per capita)
total $4,199.76
  total general revenues 3,763.39
    from federal government 709.81
    from own sources 3,053.58
    from taxes 2,258.02
      from property taxes 1,356.48
      from all other taxes 739.66
    from charges & misc. 795.57

State & local government expenditures, (selected items), 1991-92 ($per capita)
total $4,135.25
  total direct general expenditures 3,697.01
    education 1,182.17
    libraries 16.50
    public welfare 888.13
    health & hospitals 139.30
    highways 256.14
    police protection 115.03
    fire protection 59.85
    correction 64.23
    housing & comm. development 35.77
    natural resources & parks 68.53
    interest on general debt 327.46

State & local debt, 1992 ($per capita) 5,243.02

Federal aid grants to state & local government, 1994 ($per capita total & selected items)
per capita total 840.47
  compensatory education 13.47
  waste treatment facilities 9.24
  medicaid 436.26
  housing assistance 48.00
  job training 13.73
  highway trust fund 60.80

CRIME, LAW ENFORCEMENT & COURTS

Crime, 1994 (all rates per 100,000 persons)
total crimes 31,165
overall crime rate 2,741.0
  property crimes 29,837
    burglaries 5,275
    larcenies 22,260
    motor vehicle thefts 2,302
  property crime rate 2,624.2
  violent crimes 1,328
    murders 16
    forcible rapes 407
    robberies 308
    aggravated assaults 597
  violent crime rate 116.8

Number of police agencies, 1994 72

Arrests, 1994
total 24,625
  persons under 18 years of age 5,951

Prisoners under state & federal jurisdiction, 1994
total 2,021
percent change, 1993-94 . . . . 13.9%
  sentenced to more than one year
    total 2,021
    rate per 100,000 residents 177

Persons under sentence of death, 4/20/95 0

State's highest court
name . . . . Supreme Court
number of members 5
length of term . . . . to age 70
intermediate appeals court? . . . . no

New Hampshire 6

LABOR & INCOME

Civilian labor force, 1994

total 628,000
men 342,000
women 287,000
persons 16-19 years 32,000
white 614,000
black .... NA

Civilian labor force as a percent of civilian non-institutional population, 1994

total 72.2%
men 78.8%
women 65.7%
persons 16-19 years 59.0%
white 72.3%
black .... NA%

Employment, 1994

total 599,000
men 327,000
women 273,000
persons 16-19 years 27,000
white 586,000
black .... NA

Full-time/part-time labor force, 1994

full-time labor force 495,000
working part-time for
ecomonic reasons 7,000
part-time labor force 134,000

Unemployment rate, 1994

total 4.6%
men 4.4%
women 4.8%
persons 16-19 years 14.1%
white 4.5%
black .... NA%

Unemployed by reason for unemployment (as a percent of total unemployment), 1994

job losers or completed temp jobs 54.5%
job leavers 11.4%
reentrants 31.3%
new entrants 2.9%

Civilian labor force, by occupation, 1994

executive/administrative/
managerial 97,000
professional/specialty 92,000
technicians & related support 26,000

sales 82,000
adminstrative support/clerical 82,000
service occupations 74,000
precision production/craft/repair 78,000
machine operators/assemblers 38,000
transportation/material moving 24,000
handlers/helpers/laborers 23,000
farming/forestry/fishing ....NA

Civilian labor force, by industry, 1994

construction 25,000
manufacturing 132,000
transportation/communication 27,000
wholesale/retail trade 126,000
finance/real estate/insurance 30,000
services 137,000
government 75,000
agriculture ....NA

Average annual pay, 1994 (prelim.) $25,555

change in average annual pay,
1993-1994 .... 2.4%

Hours and earnings of production workers on manufacturing payrolls, 1994

average weekly hours 42.3
average hourly earnings $11.73
average weekly earnings $496.18

Labor union membership, 1994 55,100

Household income (in constant 1993 dollars)

median household income, 1992 .... $40,617
median household income, 1993 .... $37,964

Poverty

persons below poverty level, 1992 .... 8.7%
persons below poverty level, 1993 .... 9.9%

Personal income ($per capita)

1994
in current dollars 23,434
in constant (1987) dollars 18,124
1995 (projected)
in constant (1982) dollars 16,536
2000 (projected)
in constant (1982) dollars 17,363

Federal income tax returns, 1993

returns filed 536,568
adjusted gross income ($1000) 18,276,460
total income tax paid ($1000) 2,696,979

240

New Hampshire 7

ECONOMY, BUSINESS, INDUSTRY & AGRICULTURE

Fortune 500 companies, 1994 1

Business incorporations, 1994
total 2,990
change, 1993-94 .... 3.7%

Business failures, 1994
total 410
rate per 10,000 concerns 89
change, 1993-94 .... -34.0%

Business firm ownership
Hispanic owned firms, 1987 244
black owned firms, 1987 229
women owned firms, 1987 22,700
foreign owned firms, 1982 73

Gross state product, 1991 ($mil)
total $24,404
agriculture services, forestry, fisheries 213
mining 28
construction 910
manufacturing—durable goods 3,715
manufacturing—nondurable goods 1,599
transportation, communication &
public utilities 1,936
wholesale trade 1,311
retail trade 2,436
finance/real estate/insurance 5,236
services 4,715
federal, state & local government 2,306

Establishments, by major industry group, 1992
total 32,779
agriculture 542
mining 43
construction 3,402
manufacturing 2,338
transportation 1,147
wholesale trade 2,070
retail trade 8,781
finance/real estate/insurance 2,613
service industries 11,397
unclassified 446

Payroll, by major industry group, 1992
total ($1,000) $9,923,247
agriculture 36,876

mining 11,165
construction 422,331
manufacturing 2,799,174
transportation 615,960
wholesale trade 695,412
retail trade 1,354,498
finance/real estate/insurance 824,824
service industries 3,157,695
unclassified 5,312

Agriculture
number of farms, 1994 3,000
farm acreage, 1994 500,000
acres per farm, 1994 180
value of farms, 1994 ($mil) 1,116
farm income, 1993 ($mil)
gross farm income 201
net farm income 58
debt/asset ratio 5.5%
farm marketings, 1993 ($mil)
total $163
crops 99
livestock 65
government payments 2
farm marketings in order of marketing receipts, 1993
1) Dairy Products
2) Greenhouse
3) Xmas trees
4) Apples

Federal economic activity ($mil, except per capita)
expenditures, 1994
total $4,636
per capita $4,078
defense $607
non-defense $4,029
defense department, 1994
contract awards ($mil) $369
payroll ($mil) $236
civilian employees (x1,000) 1.4
military personnel (x1,000) 0.3

Fishing, 1992
catch (millions of pounds) 10
value ($mil) 12

Mining, 1994 ($mil)
total non-fuel mineral production $40

New Hampshire 8

principal non-fuel minerals in order of value, 1994
  1) Sand and gravel
  2) Stone
  3) Stone

Construction, 1994 ($mil)
total contracts (including
  non-building) $1,092
    residential 483
    non-residential 385

Manufacturing, 1992
total establishments 2,332
employees, total (x1,000) 94
payroll ($mil) 2,820
production workers (x1,000) 60
value added ($mil) 6,493
value of shipments ($mil) 11,260

Finance
commercial banks, 1994
  number 26
    assets ($bil) 7.4
    deposits ($bil) 5.8
    closed or assisted 0
    deposits ($bil) .... NA
savings and loan associations, 1991
  non-current real estate loans 3.57%
  net income after taxes ($mil) .... -28
  return on assets ....-1.54%

Retail trade, 1992
establishments (x1,000) 8.6
sales ($mil) 11,099
annual payroll ($mil) 1,261
paid employees (x1,000) 97

Wholesale trade, 1992
establishments 2,104
sales ($bil) 8.2
annual payroll ($mil) 635
paid employees (x1,000) 20.5

Service industries, 1992
establishments (x1,000) (non-exempt firms) . 9.2
receipts ($mil) (non-exempt firms) 4,612
annual payroll ($mil) 1,840
paid employees (x1,000) (non-exempt firms) .. 83

COMMUNICATION, ENERGY & TRANSPORTATION

Communication
daily newspapers, 1993 11
broadcast stations, 1990
  radio: commercial, educational 62
  television: commercial, noncommercial 9
cable TV households, 1988 244,000

Energy
consumption estimates, 1992
  total (trillion Btu) 244
  per capita (million Btu) 218.9
by source of production (trillion Btu)
  coal 35
  natural gas 17
  petroleum 143
  nuclear electric power 84
  hydroelectric power 21
by end-use sector (trillion Btu)
  residential 71
  commercial 40
  industrial 59
  transportation 74
electrical energy
  production, 1993 (billion kWh) 14.6
  net summer capability, 1993 (million kW) .. 2.5
gas utilities, 1993
  customers 81,000
  sales (trillion Btu) 17
  revenues ($mil) 110
nuclear plants, 1993 1

Transportation, 1994
public road & street mileage
  total 15,022
    urban 2,899
    rural 12,123
    interstate 224
  vehicle miles of travel (mil) 10,501
  total motor vehicle registrations 991,815
    automobiles 643,840
  licensed drivers 877,471
    per 1,000 driving age population 1,004
  deaths from motor vehicle
    accidents 119

242

New Jersey 1

STATE SUMMARY

Capital City . . . . Trenton

Governor . . . . Christie Whitman

Address . . . . STATE HOUSE
TRENTON, NJ 08625
609 292-6000

Admitted as a state 1787

Area (square miles) 8,722

Population, 1980 7,364,823

Population, 1990 7,730,188

Population, 1994 (est.) 7,904,000

Persons per square mile, 1994 . . . . 1,065.4

Largest city . . . . Newark
population, 1990 275,000

Personal income per capita, 1994
(in current dollars) $28,038

Gross state product ($mil), 1991 212,822

Leading industries, 1992 (by payroll)
SERVICE INDUSTRIES
MANUFACTURING
WHOLESALE TRADE

Leading agricultural commodities, 1993
GREENHOUSE
DAIRY PRODUCTS
EGGS
PEACHES

GEOGRAPHY & ENVIRONMENT

Area (square miles)
total 8,722
land 7,419
water (includes territorial water) 1,303

Federally owned land, 1991 . . . . 3.1%

Highest point
name . . . . High Point
elevation (feet) 1,803

Lowest point
name . . . . Atlantic Ocean
elevation (feet) .sea level

General coastline (miles) 130

Tidal shoreline (miles) 1,792

Capital city . . . . .Trenton
population, 1990 88,700

Largest city . . . . Newark
population, 1990 275,000

Number of cities with over 100,000 population
1980 4

Number of cities with over 100,000 population
1990 4

State parks and Recreation areas, 1991
area (acres) 303,000
number of visitors 10,945,000
revenues $6,514,000

National forest land, 1992 (acres) 0

National park acreage, 1984 34,500

DEMOGRAPHICS & CHARACTERISTICS OF THE POPULATION

Population
1970 7,171,112
1980 7,364,823
1990 7,730,188
1994 (est.) 7,904,000
2000 (revised projection) 8,135,000
2010 (revised projection) 8,562,000

Metropolitan area population
1970 7,171,000
1980 7,365,000
1992 7,820,000

Non-metropolitan area population
1970 . . . . .NA
1980 . . . . .NA
1992 . . . . .NA

Change in population, 1980-90
number 365,365
percent 4.96%

Persons per square mile, 1994 . . . . 1,065.4

Age distribution, 1980
under 5 years 6.3%
5 to 17 years 20.8%
65 and over 11.7%

Age distribution, 1990
under 5 years 6.9%
5 to 17 years 16.3%
65 and over 13.3%

243

Age distribution, 2000 (projected)
under 5 years 5.8%
5 to 17 years 17.9%
65 and over 13.7%

Persons by age, 1990
under 5 years 532,637
5 to 17 years 1,266,825
65 and over 1,032,025

Median age, 1990 .... *34.50*

Race, 1990
White 6,130,465
Black 1,036,825
American Indian 14,500
Chinese 59,084
Filipino 53,146
Japanese 17,253
Asian Indian 79,440
Korean 38,540
Vietnamese 7,330
all other 293,135

Race, 2010 (projected)
White 6,526,000
Black 1,434,000

Persons of Hispanic origin, 1990
total 739,861
Mexican 28,759
Puerto Rican 320,133
Cuban 85,378
Other Hispanic 305,591

Persons by sex, 1990
male 3,735,685
female 3,994,503

Marital status, 1990
males
15 years & older 2,964,562
single 970,980
married 1,747,960
separated 65,293
widowed 86,408
divorced 159,214
females
15 years & older 3,258,962
single 842,911
married 1,760,170
separated 94,224

widowed 412,403
divorced 243,478

Households & families, 1990
households 2,794,711
persons per household 2.70
families 2,021,346
married couples 1,578,702
female householder, no husband
present 338,455
one person households 646,171
households, 1994 2,845,000
persons per household, 1994 .... 2.72

Nativity, 1990
number of persons born in state 4,232,369
percent of total residents 54.8%

Immigration & naturalization, 1993
immigrants admitted 50,285
persons naturalized 18,495
refugees granted resident status 3,186

VITAL STATISTICS & HEALTH

Births
1992 119,923
with low birth weight 7.2%
to teenage mothers 8.0%
to unmarried mothers 26.4%
1993 123,020
1994 116,430

Abortions, 1992
total 55,000
rate (per 1,000 women age 15-44) 31.0
rate per 1,000 live births 460

Adoptions, 1986
total 1,631
related 10.9%

Deaths
1992 71,201
1993 72,776
1994 72,391

Infant deaths
1992 1,030
1993 980
1994 923

New Jersey 3

Average lifetime, 1979-1981
both sexes .... 74.00 years
  men .... 70.48 years
  women .... 77.39 years

Marriages
1992 55,181
1993 53,391
1994 52,776

Divorces
1992 25,405
1993 24,784
1994 23,899

Physicians, 1993
total 20,657
rate (per 1,000 persons) 2.63

Dentists, 1992
total 6,418
rate (per 1,000 persons) 0.83

Hospitals, 1993
number 97
beds (x 1,000) 31.1
average daily census (x 1,000) 23.9
occupancy rate 77.0%
personnel (x 1,000) 121.0
average cost per day to hospital $829
average cost per stay to hospital $6,540

EDUCATION

Educational attainment of all persons 25 years and older, 1990
less than 9th grade 486,210
high school graduates 1,606,555
bachelor's degree 826,887
graduate or professional degree 457,130

Public school enrollment, Fall, 1993
total 1,151,307
  Kindergarten through grade 8 843,526
  grades 9 through 12 307,781

Public School Teachers
total, 1994 84,564
  elementary 46,855
  secondary 26,509
salaries, 1994
  beginning $29,346
  average $45,582

State receipts & expenditures for public schools, 1993
receipts ($mil) 10,989
expenditures
  total ($mil) 10,569
  per capita $1,351
  per pupil $9,712

Graduating high school seniors, public high schools, 1995 (est) 65,838

SAT scores, 1994
verbal 418
math 475

Institutions of higher education, 1995
total 61
  public 33
  private 28

Enrollment in institutions of higher education, Fall, 1993
total 343,029
full-time men 83,378
full-time women 90,846
part-time men 67,955
part-time women 100,850

Minority enrollment in institutions of higher education, Fall, 1993
Black, non-Hispanic 38,146
Hispanic 26,955
Asian/Pacific Islander 18,203

Earned degrees conferred, 1993
Bachelor's 25,185
First professional 1,679
Master's 8,110
Doctor's 965

SOCIAL INSURANCE & WELFARE PROGRAMS

Social Security beneficiaries & benefits, 1993
beneficiaries
total 1,286,000
  retired and dependents 955,000
  survivors 202,000
  disabled & dependents 129,000
annual benefit payments ($mil)
total $10,239
  retired and dependents 7,439
  survivors 1,866
  disabled & dependents 934

New Jersey 4

Medicare, 1993
enrollment (x1,000) 1,144
payments ($mil) 4,749

Medicaid, 1993
recipients (x1,000) 794
payments ($mil) 3,485

Federal public aid, 1993
recipients as a percent of population 6.1%
Aid to Families with Dependent Children
  recipients (x1,000) 340
average monthly payment $356
Supplemental Security Income
  total recipients (x1,000) 134

Food Stamp Program
participants, 1994 (x1,000) 545

HOUSING & CONSTRUCTION

Total housing units, 1990 3,075,310
  year round housing units 2,974,452
  vacant 280,599

New privately owned housing units
  authorized, 1994
number (x1,000) 25.4
value ($mil) 2,318

New privately owned housing units
  started, 1994 (x1,000) 29.8

Existing home sales, 1994 (x1,000) 145.4

GOVERNMENT & ELECTIONS

State officials, 1996
Governor (name/party/term expires)
  CHRISTIE WHITMAN
  Democrat - 1998
Lt. Governor ....(no Lieutenant Governor)
Sec. of State .... Dan Dalton
Atty. General .... Deborah Poritz
Chf. Justice .... Robert N. Wilentz

Governorship
minimum age 30
length of term .... 4 years
number of consecutive
  terms permitted 2
who succeeds .... Pres. of Senate

State legislature
name .... Legislature
  upper chamber
    name .... Senate
    number of members 40
    length of term .... 4 years
    party in majority, 1996 .... Republican
  lower chamber
    name .... General Assembly
    number of members 80
    length of term .... 2 years
    party in majority, 1996 .... Republican

State employees October, 1992
total 131,841
October payroll ($1,000) 351,750

Local governments, 1992
total 1,625
  county 21
  municipal 320
  township 247
  school districts 550
  special districts 486

Voting, November, 1994
voting age population 5,918,000
  registered 61.6%
  voted 40.3%

Vote for president
1988
  Bush 1,699,634
  Dukakis 1,275,063
1992
  Clinton 1,375,775
  Bush 1,314,146
  Perot 507,010

Federal representation, 1996 (104th Congress)
Senators (name/party/term expires)

FRANK R. LAUTENBERG
Democrat - 2001
WILLIAM BRADLEY
Democrat - 1997

Representatives, total 13
  Democrats 5
  Republicans 8
  other 0

New Jersey 5

Women holding public office
U.S. Congress, 1995 1
statewide elected office, 1995 1
state legislature, 1995 16

Black elected officials, 1993
total 211
  US and state legislatures 13
  city/county/regional offices 113
  judicial/law enforcement 0
  education/school boards 85

Hispanic public officials, 1994
total 37
  state executives & legislators 2
  city/county/regional offices 17
  judicial/law enforcement 1
  education/school boards 17

GOVERNMENTAL FINANCE

State & local government revenues, (selected items), 1991-92 ($per capita)
total $5,471.65
  total general revenues 4,694.06
   from federal government 692.56
   from own sources 4,001.50
   from taxes 2,948.74
    from property taxes 1,277.55
    from all other taxes 1,541.96
   from charges & misc. 1,052.76

State & local government expenditures, (selected items), 1991-92 ($per capita)
total $5,467.14
  total direct general expenditures 4,711.22
   education 1,590.16
   libraries 24.07
   public welfare 753.54
   health & hospitals 222.78
   highways 324.22
   police protection 170.75
   fire protection 50.84
   correction 119.11
   housing & comm. development 54.35
   natural resources & parks 109.17
   interest on general debt 284.06

State & local debt, 1992 ($per capita) 4,451.13

Federal aid grants to state & local government, 1994 ($per capita total & selected items)
per capita total 779.70
  compensatory education 22.67
  waste treatment facilities 10.33
  medicaid 307.58
  housing assistance 71.74
  job training 10.64
  highway trust fund 64.56

CRIME, LAW ENFORCEMENT & COURTS

Crime, 1994 (all rates per 100,000 persons)
total crimes 368,400
overall crime rate 4,660.9
  property crimes 319,856
   burglaries 72,074
   larcenies 195,618
   motor vehicle thefts 52,164
  property crime rate 4,046.8
  violent crimes 48,544
   murders 396
   forcible rapes 1,972
   robberies 22,762
   aggravated assaults 23,414
  violent crime rate 614.2

Number of police agencies, 1994 542

Arrests, 1994
total 377,146
  persons under 18 years of age 87,875

Prisoners under state & federal jurisdiction, 1994
total 24,632
percent change, 1993-94 ....3.4%
  sentenced to more than one year
   total 24,544
   rate per 100,000 residents 310

Persons under sentence of death, 4/20/95 9

State's highest court
name .... Supreme Court
number of members 7
length of term ....7 years
intermediate appeals court? ....yes

New Jersey 6

LABOR & INCOME

Civilian labor force, 1994
total 3,991,000
 men 2,180,000
 women 1,811,000
 persons 16-19 years 170,000
 white 3,316,000
 black 479,000

Civilian labor force as a percent of
civilian non-institutional population, 1994
total 65.9%
 men 75.1%
 women 57.4%
 persons 16-19 years 43.3%
 white 65.9%
 black 64.3%

Employment, 1994
total 3,719,000
 men 2,031,000
 women 1,688,000
 persons 16-19 years 137,000
 white 3,116,000
 black 420,000

Full-time/part-time labor force, 1994
full-time labor force 3,328,000
 working part-time for
  ecomonic reasons 32,000
part-time labor force 663,000

Unemployment rate, 1994
total 6.8%
 men 6.8%
 women 6.8%
 persons 16-19 years 19.5%
 white 6.0%
 black 12.4%

Unemployed by reason for unemployment
(as a percent of total unemployment), 1994
job losers or completed temp jobs 58.4%
job leavers 7.6%
reentrants 27.4%
new entrants 6.6%

Civilian labor force, by occupation, 1994
executive/administrative/
 managerial 621,000
professional/specialty 607,000
technicians & related support 139,000

sales 478,000
adminstrative support/clerical 686,000
service occupations 481,000
precision production/craft/repair 404,000
machine operators/assemblers 208,000
transportation/material moving 146,000
handlers/helpers/laborers 154,000
farming/forestry/fishing 47,000

Civilian labor force, by industry, 1994
construction 180,000
manufacturing 627,000
transportation/communication 295,000
wholesale/retail trade 745,000
finance/real estate/insurance 301,000
services 982,000
government 548,000
agriculture 42,000

Average annual pay, 1994 (prelim.) $33,439
change in average annual pay,
 1993-1994 . . . . 2.2%

Hours and earnings of production workers
on manufacturing payrolls, 1994
average weekly hours 41.8
average hourly earnings $13.38
average weekly earnings $559.28

Labor union membership, 1994 779,500

Household income (in constant 1993 dollars)
median household income, 1992 . . . . $40,168
median household income, 1993 . . . . $40,500

Poverty
persons below poverty level, 1992 . . . . 10.3%
persons below poverty level, 1993 . . . . 10.9%

Personal income ($per capita)
1994
 in current dollars 28,038
 in constant (1987) dollars 21,684
1995 (projected)
 in constant (1982) dollars 18,985
2000 (projected)
 in constant (1982) dollars 19,932

Federal income tax returns, 1993
returns filed 3,759,633
adjusted gross income ($1000) 151,586,226
total income tax paid ($1000) 23,616,357

ECONOMY, BUSINESS, INDUSTRY & AGRICULTURE

Fortune 500 companies, 1994 24

Business incorporations, 1994
total 30,869
change, 1993-94 .... 4.3%

Business failures, 1994
total 2,182
rate per 10,000 concerns 80
change, 1993-94 .... -23.4%

Business firm ownership
Hispanic owned firms, 1987 12,094
black owned firms, 1987 14,556
women owned firms, 1987 117,400
foreign owned firms, 1982 527

Gross state product, 1991 ($mil)
total $212,822
  agriculture services, forestry, fisheries ... 1,131
  mining 100
  construction 7,896
  manufacturing—durable goods 12,598
  manufacturing—nondurable goods 24,461
  transportation, communication &
    public utilities 20,013
  wholesale trade 18,161
  retail trade 17,167
  finance/real estate/insurance 44,208
  services 44,907
  federal, state & local government 22,182

Establishments, by major industry group, 1992
total 211,264
  agriculture 3,740
  mining 131
  construction 20,024
  manufacturing 13,452
  transportation 9,701
  wholesale trade 18,544
  retail trade 49,676
  finance/real estate/insurance 18,150
  service industries 75,286
  unclassified 2,560

Payroll, by major industry group, 1992
total ($1,000) $90,561,364
  agriculture 292,046

  mining 184,685
  construction 4,094,777
  manufacturing 20,955,253
  transportation 8,990,015
  wholesale trade 10,696,462
  retail trade 9,233,532
  finance/real estate/insurance 8,794,828
  service industries 27,247,207
  unclassified 72,559

Agriculture
number of farms, 1994 9,000
farm acreage, 1994 1,000,000
acres per farm, 1994 101
value of farms, 1994 ($mil) 4,210
farm income, 1993 ($mil)
  gross farm income 813
  net farm income 242
  debt/asset ratio 6.8%
farm marketings, 1993 ($mil)
  total $706
  crops 508
  livestock 199
government payments 7
farm marketings in order of marketing receipts, 1993
  1) Greenhouse
  2) Dairy products
  3) Eggs
  4) Blueberries

Federal economic activity
($mil, except per capita)
expenditures, 1994
  total $37,328
  per capita $4,723
  defense $4,719
  non-defense $32,609
defense department, 1994
  contract awards ($mil) $3,034
  payroll ($mil) $1,524
  civilian employees (x1,000) 22.0
  military personnel (x1,000) 9.1

Fishing, 1992
catch (millions of pounds) 204
value ($mil) 97

Mining, 1994 ($mil)
total non-fuel mineral production $274

New Jersey 8

principal non-fuel minerals in order of value,
1994
1) Stone
2) Sand and gravel
3) Sand and gravel

Construction, 1994 ($mil)
total contracts (including
  non-building) $6,452
    residential 2,252
    non-residential 2,653

Manufacturing, 1992
total establishments 13,281
employees, total (x1,000) 574
payroll ($mil) 20,616
production workers (x1,000) 301
value added ($mil) 46,091
value of shipments ($mil) 86,885

Finance
commercial banks, 1994
  number 99
    assets ($bil) 100.3
    deposits ($bil) 84.4
  closed or assisted 0
    deposits ($bil) . . . . NA
savings and loan associations, 1991
  non-current real estate loans 5.74%
  net income after taxes ($mil) . . . . -387
  return on assets . . . . -0.98%

Retail trade, 1992
establishments (x1,000) 48.6
sales ($mil) 63,109
annual payroll ($mil) 7,613
paid employees (x1,000) 522

Wholesale trade, 1992
establishments 18,444
sales ($bil) 176.0
annual payroll ($mil) 9,629
paid employees (x1,000) 262.7

Service industries, 1992
establishments (x1,000) (non-exempt firms) 65.9
receipts ($mil) (non-exempt firms) 50,242
annual payroll ($mil) 18,485
paid employees (x1,000) (non-exempt firms) . 671

COMMUNICATION, ENERGY & TRANSPORTATION

Communication
daily newspapers, 1993 21
broadcast stations, 1990
  radio: commercial, educational 102
  television: commercial, noncommercial 12
cable TV households, 1988 1,785,000

Energy
consumption estimates, 1992
total (trillion Btu) 2,401
per capita (million Btu) 307.0
by source of production (trillion Btu)
  coal 62
  natural gas 561
  petroleum 1,213
  nuclear electric power 231
  hydroelectric power . . . . -1
by end-use sector (trillion Btu)
  residential 495
  commercial 484
  industrial 614
  transportation 809
electrical energy
  production, 1993 (billion kWh) 34.3
  net summer capability, 1993 (million kW) . 13.9
gas utilities, 1993
  customers 2,278,000
  sales (trillion Btu) 469
  revenues ($mil) 2,499
nuclear plants, 1993 4

Transportation, 1994
public road & street mileage
total 35,432
  urban 24,188
  rural 11,244
  interstate 420
vehicle miles of travel (mil) 60,466
total motor vehicle registrations 5,839,209
  automobiles 4,601,597
licensed drivers 5,433,383
  per 1,000 driving age population 881
deaths from motor vehicle
  accidents 761

STATE SUMMARY
Capital City . . . . Santa Fe

Governor . . . . Gary Johnson

Address . . . . STATE CAPITOL
SANTA FE, NM 87503
505 827-3000

Admitted as a state 1912

Area (square miles) 121,598

Population, 1980 1,302,894

Population, 1990 1,515,069

Population, 1994 (est.) 1,654,000

Persons per square mile, 1994 . . . . 13.6

Largest city . . . . Albuquerque
population, 1990 385,000

Personal income per capita, 1994
(in current dollars) $17,106

Gross state product ($mil), 1991 30,250

Leading industries, 1992 (by payroll)
SERVICE INDUSTRIES
RETAIL TRADE
MANUFACTURING

Leading agricultural commodities, 1993
CATTLE
DAIRY PRODUCTS
HAY
CHILI PEPPERS

GEOGRAPHY & ENVIRONMENT
Area (square miles)
total 121,598
land 121,365
water (includes territorial water) 234

Federally owned land, 1991 . . . . 32.4%

Highest point
name . . . . Wheeler Peak
elevation (feet) 13,161

Lowest point
name . . . . Red Bluff Reservoir
elevation (feet) 2,842

General coastline (miles) 0

Tidal shoreline (miles) 0

Capital city . . . . Santa Fe
population, 1990 55,900

Largest city . . . . Albuquerque
population, 1990 385,000

Number of cities with over 100,000 population
1980 1

Number of cities with over 100,000 population
1990 1

State parks and Recreation areas, 1991
area (acres) 123,000
number of visitors 4,251,000
revenues $2,657,000

National forest land, 1992 (acres) 10,367,000

National park acreage, 1984 250,300

DEMOGRAPHICS & CHARACTERISTICS OF THE POPULATION
Population
1970 1,017,055
1980 1,302,894
1990 1,515,069
1994 (est.) 1,654,000
2000 (revised projection) 1,823,000
2010 (revised projection) 2,082,000

Metropolitan area population
1970 456,000
1980 609,000
1992 886,000

Non-metropolitan area population
1970 562,000
1980 694,000
1992 696,000

Change in population, 1980-90
number 212,175
percent 16.28%

Persons per square mile, 1994 . . . . 13.6

Age distribution, 1980
under 5 years 8.8%
5 to 17 years 23.3%
65 and over 8.9%

Age distribution, 1990
under 5 years 8.3%
5 to 17 years 21.1%
65 and over 10.7%

Age distribution, 2000 (projected)
under 5 years 7.6%
5 to 17 years 17.3%
65 and over 10.3%

Persons by age, 1990
under 5 years 125,878
5 to 17 years 320,863
65 and over 163,062

Median age, 1990 .... *31.30*

Race, 1990
White 1,146,028
Black 30,210
American Indian 134,097
Chinese 2,607
Filipino 2,018
Japanese 1,895
Asian Indian 1,593
Korean 1,464
Vietnamese 1,485
all other 193,414

Race, 2010 (projected)
White 1,760,000
Black 35,000

Persons of Hispanic origin, 1990
total 579,224
  Mexican 328,836
  Puerto Rican 2,635
  Cuban 903
  Other Hispanic 246,850

Persons by sex, 1990
male 745,253
female 769,816

Marital status, 1990
males
  15 years & older 552,408
    single 161,891
    married 327,955
      separated 8,651
      widowed 12,842
      divorced 49,720
females
  15 years & older 584,092
    single 131,144
    married 328,570
      separated 11,879

widowed 58,273
divorced 66,105

Households & families, 1990
households 542,709
persons per household 2.74
  families 391,487
    married couples 303,789
    female householder, no husband
      present 64,555
    one person households 124,883
households, 1994 587,000
persons per household, 1994 .... 2.77

Nativity, 1990
number of persons born in state 783,311
percent of total residents 51.7%

Immigration & naturalization, 1993
immigrants admitted 3,409
persons naturalized 665
refugees granted resident status 215

VITAL STATISTICS & HEALTH

Births
1992 28,463
  with low birth weight 7.2%
  to teenage mothers 17.0%
  to unmarried mothers 39.5%
1993 27,658
1994 27,981

Abortions, 1992
total 6,000
rate (per 1,000 women age 15-44) 17.7
rate per 1,000 live births 228

Adoptions, 1986
total 979
  related 18.1%

Deaths
1992 11,561
1993 11,861
1994 12,305

Infant deaths
1992 235
1993 256
1994 250

Average lifetime, 1979-1981
both sexes . . . . 74.01 years
 men . . . . 69.91 years
 women . . . . 78.34 years

Marriages
1992 12,984
1993 12,618
1994 12,159

Divorces
1992 9,737
1993 9,943
1994 9,882

Physicians, 1993
total 3,049
rate (per 1,000 persons) 1.90

Dentists, 1992
total 662
rate (per 1,000 persons) 0.42

Hospitals, 1993
number 37
beds (x 1,000) 4.1
average daily census (x 1,000) 2.2
occupancy rate 54.0%
personnel (x 1,000) 18.5
average cost per day to hospital $1,046
average cost per stay to hospital $5,600

EDUCATION

*Educational attainment of all persons
 25 years and older, 1990*
less than 9th grade 105,362
high school graduates 264,943
bachelor's degree 111,957
graduate or professional degree 76,379

Public school enrollment, Fall, 1993
total 322,292
 Kindergarten through grade 8 226,287
 grades 9 through 12 96,005

Public School Teachers
total, 1994 18,404
 elementary 10,570
 secondary 4,564
salaries, 1994
 beginning $22,057
 average $27,922

*State receipts & expenditures for public
 schools, 1993*
receipts ($mil) 1,396
expenditures
 total ($mil) 1,453
 per capita $919
 per pupil $4,643

*Graduating high school seniors,
 public high schools, 1995 (est)* 15,146

SAT scores, 1994
verbal 475
math 528

Institutions of higher education, 1995
total 35
 public 24
 private 11

*Enrollment in institutions of higher
 education, Fall, 1993*
total 101,460
full-time men 24,215
full-time women 27,078
part-time men 19,887
part-time women 30,280

*Minority enrollment in institutions of higher
 education, Fall, 1993*
Black, non-Hispanic 2,489
Hispanic 30,069
Asian/Pacific Islander 1,397

Earned degrees conferred, 1993
Bachelor's 5,667
First professional 178
Master's 2,142
Doctor's 243

SOCIAL INSURANCE &
WELFARE PROGRAMS

Social Security beneficiaries & benefits, 1993
beneficiaries
total 244,000
 retired and dependents 162,000
 survivors 45,000
 disabled & dependents 36,000
annual benefit payments ($mil)
total $1,579
 retired and dependents 1,029
 survivors 338
 disabled & dependents 211

Medicare, 1993
enrollment (x1,000) 198
payments ($mil) 557

Medicaid, 1993
recipients (x1,000) 241
payments ($mil) 543

Federal public aid, 1993
recipients as a percent of population 8.3%
Aid to Families with Dependent Children
recipients (x1,000) 101
average monthly payment $324
Supplemental Security Income
total recipients (x1,000) 40

Food Stamp Program
participants, 1994 (x1,000) 244

HOUSING & CONSTRUCTION

Total housing units, 1990 632,058
year round housing units 609,594
vacant 89,349

New privately owned housing units
authorized, 1994
number (x1,000) 11.5
value ($mil) 969

New privately owned housing units
started, 1994 (x1,000) 10.5

Existing home sales, 1994 (x1,000) 30.4

GOVERNMENT & ELECTIONS

State officials, 1996
Governor (name/party/term expires)
GARY JOHNSON
Republican - 1999
Lt. Governor ....Casey Luna
Sec. of State ....Stephanie Gonzales
Atty. General .... Tom Udall
Chf. Justice .... Richard Ransom

Governorship
minimum age 30
length of term ....4 years
number of consecutive
terms permitted ....none
who succeeds .... Lt. Governor

State legislature
name ....Legislature
upper chamber
name ....Senate
number of members 42
length of term ....4 years
party in majority, 1996 ....Democratic
lower chamber
name .... House of Representatives
number of members 70
length of term ....2 years
party in majority, 1996 ....Democratic

State employees October, 1992
total 53,317
October payroll ($1,000) 88,128

Local governments, 1992
total 494
county 33
municipal 99
township 0
school districts 94
special districts 267

Voting, November, 1994
voting age population 1,175,000
registered 58.8%
voted 46.8%

Vote for president
1988
Bush 260,792
Dukakis 236,528
1992
Clinton 257,159
Bush 209,842
Perot 90,750

Federal representation, 1996 (104th Congress)
Senators (name/party/term expires)

JEFF BINGAMAN
Democrat - 2001
PETE V. DOMENICI
Republican - 1997

Representatives, total 3
Democrats 1
Republicans 2
other 0

New Mexico 5

Women holding public office
U.S. Congress, 1995 0
statewide elected office, 1995 2
state legislature, 1995 23

Black elected officials, 1993
total 3
  US and state legislatures 0
  city/county/regional offices 0
  judicial/law enforcement 2
  education/school boards 1

Hispanic public officials, 1994
total 716
  state executives & legislators 50
  city/county/regional offices 410
  judicial/law enforcement 105
  education/school boards 151

GOVERNMENTAL FINANCE

State & local government revenues, (selected items), 1991-92 ($per capita)
total $4,582.95
  total general revenues 3,886.51
   from federal government 799.81
   from own sources 3,086.70
   from taxes 1,627.36
    from property taxes 222.10
    from all other taxes 1,341.56
   from charges & misc. 1,259.34

State & local government expenditures, (selected items), 1991-92 ($per capita)
total $4,256.64
  total direct general expenditures 3,868.47
   education 1,380.76
   libraries 13.40
   public welfare 478.07
   health & hospitals 360.98
   highways 471.78
   police protection 137.62
   fire protection 50.16
   correction 107.03
   housing & comm. development 26.24
   natural resources & parks 138.18
   interest on general debt 182.48

State & local debt, 1992 ($per capita) 2,944.54

Federal aid grants to state & local government, 1994 ($per capita total & selected items)
per capita total 1,038.49
  compensatory education 34.23
  waste treatment facilities 8.89
  medicaid 321.10
  housing assistance 44.01
  job training 13.95
  highway trust fund 89.71

CRIME, LAW ENFORCEMENT & COURTS

Crime, 1994 (all rates per 100,000 persons)
total crimes 102,346
overall crime rate 6,187.8
  property crimes 87,638
   burglaries 21,945
   larcenies 57,343
   motor vehicle thefts 8,350
  property crime rate 5,298.5
  violent crimes 14,708
   murders 177
   forcible rapes 866
   robberies 2,329
   aggravated assaults 11,336
  violent crime rate 889.2

Number of police agencies, 1994 28

Arrests, 1994
total 26,072
  persons under 18 years of age 5,619

Prisoners under state & federal jurisdiction, 1994
total 3,866
percent change, 1993-94 .... 10.5%
  sentenced to more than one year
  total 3,679
  rate per 100,000 residents 220

Persons under sentence of death, 4/20/95 3

State's highest court
name .... Supreme Court
number of members 5
length of term .... 8 years
intermediate appeals court? .... yes

255

New Mexico 6

LABOR & INCOME

Civilian labor force, 1994

total	770,000
men	429,000
women	342,000
persons 16-19 years	48,000
white	688,000
black	NA

*Civilian labor force as a percent of
civilian non-institutional population, 1994*

total	63.8%
men	72.8%
women	55.3%
persons 16-19 years	47.7%
white	64.4%
black	NA%

Employment, 1994

total	722,000
men	398,000
women	324,000
persons 16-19 years	38,000
white	649,000
black	NA

Full-time/part-time labor force, 1994

full-time labor force	602,000
working part-time for ecomonic reasons	10,000
part-time labor force	167,000

Unemployment rate, 1994

total	6.3%
men	7.1%
women	5.3%
persons 16-19 years	20.6%
white	5.8%
black	NA%

*Unemployed by reason for unemployment
(as a percent of total unemployment), 1994*

job losers or completed temp jobs	40.7%
job leavers	10.3%
reentrants	44.9%
new entrants	4.1%

Civilian labor force, by occupation, 1994

executive/administrative/ managerial	99,000
professional/specialty	121,000
technicians & related support	25,000
sales	89,000
adminstrative support/clerical	104,000
service occupations	114,000
precision production/craft/repair	94,000
machine operators/assemblers	23,000
transportation/material moving	39,000
handlers/helpers/laborers	31,000
farming/forestry/fishing	28,000

Civilian labor force, by industry, 1994

construction	45,000
manufacturing	49,000
transportation/communication	35,000
wholesale/retail trade	142,000
finance/real estate/insurance	37,000
services	152,000
government	173,000
agriculture	25,000

Average annual pay, 1994 (prelim.) $22,351
change in average annual pay,
1993-1994 ..... 2.9%

*Hours and earnings of production workers
on manufacturing payrolls, 1994*

average weekly hours	40.9
average hourly earnings	$10.14
average weekly earnings	$414.73

Labor union membership, 1994 56,200

Household income (in constant 1993 dollars)

median household income, 1992	$26,634
median household income, 1993	$26,758

Poverty

persons below poverty level, 1992	21.6%
persons below poverty level, 1993	17.4%

Personal income ($per capita)
1994

in current dollars	17,106
in constant (1987) dollars	13,230

1995 (projected)

in constant (1982) dollars	11,163

2000 (projected)

in constant (1982) dollars	11,949

Federal income tax returns, 1993

returns filed	698,914
adjusted gross income ($1000)	18,363,855
total income tax paid ($1000)	2,313,889

ECONOMY, BUSINESS, INDUSTRY & AGRICULTURE

Fortune 500 companies, 1994 0

Business incorporations, 1994
total 3,088
change, 1993-94 .... -4.5%

Business failures, 1994
total 328
rate per 10,000 concerns 65
change, 1993-94 .... -26.9%

Business firm ownership
Hispanic owned firms, 1987 14,299
black owned firms, 1987 587
women owned firms, 1987 25,400
foreign owned firms, 1982 72

Gross state product, 1991 ($mil)
total $30,250
  agriculture services, forestry, fisheries 754
  mining 2,671
  construction 1,062
  manufacturing—durable goods 3,007
  manufacturing—nondurable goods 863
  transportation, communication &
    public utilities 2,972
  wholesale trade 1,199
  retail trade 2,888
  finance/real estate/insurance 4,256
  services 5,279
  federal, state & local government 5,298

Establishments, by major industry group, 1992
total 37,723
  agriculture 455
  mining 653
  construction 4,118
  manufacturing 1,612
  transportation 1,586
  wholesale trade 2,520
  retail trade 9,589
  finance/real estate/insurance 3,370
  service industries 13,228
  unclassified 592

Payroll, by major industry group, 1992
total ($1,000) $8,815,488
  agriculture 34,934
  mining 569,566
  construction 631,772
  manufacturing 994,166
  transportation 785,972
  wholesale trade 541,604
  retail trade 1,382,963
  finance/real estate/insurance 612,530
  service industries 3,254,215
  unclassified 7,766

Agriculture
number of farms, 1994 14,000
farm acreage, 1994 44,000,000
acres per farm, 1994 3,274
value of farms, 1994 ($mil) 10,630
farm income, 1993 ($mil)
  gross farm income 1,835
  net farm income 565
  debt/asset ratio 9.1%
farm marketings, 1993 ($mil)
total $1,621
  crops 486
  livestock 1,135
government payments 76
farm marketings in order of marketing receipts, 1993
  1) Cattle
  2) Dairy products
  3) Hay
  4) Greenhouse

Federal economic activity ($mil, except per capita)
expenditures, 1994
  total $11,274
  per capita $6,816
  defense $1,764
  non-defense $9,510
defense department, 1994
  contract awards ($mil) $658
  payroll ($mil) $1,056
  civilian employees (x1,000) 8.6
  military personnel (x1,000) 16.2

Fishing, 1992
catch (millions of pounds) ....NA
value ($mil) ....NA

Mining, 1994 ($mil)
total non-fuel mineral production $914

principal non-fuel minerals in order of value, 1994
1) Copper
2) Potash
3) Sand and gravel

Construction, 1994 ($mil)
total contracts (including
  non-building) $1,928
    residential 845
    non-residential 659

Manufacturing, 1992
total establishments 1,594
employees, total (x1,000) 39
payroll ($mil) 965
production workers (x1,000) 27
value added ($mil) 4,946
value of shipments ($mil) 9,492

Finance
commercial banks, 1994
  number 81
    assets ($bil) 12.8
    deposits ($bil) 11.2
  closed or assisted 0
    deposits ($bil) .... NA
savings and loan associations, 1991
  non-current real estate loans 3.25%
  net income after taxes ($mil) 1
  return on assets .... +0.05%

Retail trade, 1992
establishments (x1,000) 9.3
sales ($mil) 11,279
annual payroll ($mil) 1,294
paid employees (x1,000) 112

Wholesale trade, 1992
establishments 2,515
sales ($bil) 6.3
annual payroll ($mil) 513
paid employees (x1,000) 22.6

Service industries, 1992
establishments (x1,000) (non-exempt firms) 10.7
receipts ($mil) (non-exempt firms) 6,191
annual payroll ($mil) 2,332
paid employees (x1,000) (non-exempt firms) . 111

COMMUNICATION, ENERGY & TRANSPORTATION

Communication
daily newspapers, 1993 18
broadcast stations, 1990
  radio: commercial, educational 133
  television: commercial, noncommercial 21
cable TV households, 1988 281,000

Energy
consumption estimates, 1992
total (trillion Btu) 584
per capita (million Btu) 369.4
by source of production (trillion Btu)
  coal 268
  natural gas 211
  petroleum 241
  nuclear electric power 0
  hydroelectric power 3
by end-use sector (trillion Btu)
  residential 78
  commercial 96
  industrial 195
  transportation 215
electrical energy
  production, 1993 (billion kWh) 28.4
  net summer capability, 1993 (million kW) .. 5.1
gas utilities, 1993
  customers 435,000
  sales (trillion Btu) 66
  revenues ($mil) 282
nuclear plants, 1993 0

Transportation, 1994
public road & street mileage
total 61,221
  urban 6,081
  rural 55,140
  interstate 1,000
vehicle miles of travel (mil) 20,480
total motor vehicle registrations 1,422,440
  automobiles 734,634
licensed drivers 1,167,462
  per 1,000 driving age population 966
deaths from motor vehicle
  accidents 447

STATE SUMMARY

Capital City . . . . .Albany

Governor . . . . George Pataki

Address . . . . . . .STATE CAPITOL
ALBANY, NY 12224
518 474-8390

Admitted as a state 1788

Area (square miles) 54,475

Population, 1980 17,558,072

Population, 1990 17,990,455

Population, 1994 (est.) 18,169,000

Persons per square mile, 1994 . . . . 384.7

Largest city . . . . New York
population, 1990 7,323,000

Personal income per capita, 1994
(in current dollars) $25,999

Gross state product ($mil), 1991 475,961

Leading industries, 1992 (by payroll)
SERVICE INDUSTRIES
FINANCE, INSURANCE &
REAL ESTATE
MANUFACTURING

Leading agricultural commodities, 1993
DAIRY PRODUCTS
GREENHOUSE
CATTLE
APPLES

GEOGRAPHY & ENVIRONMENT

Area (square miles)
total 54,475
land 47,224
water (includes territorial water) 7,251

Federally owned land, 1991 . . . . 0.7%

Highest point
name . . . . .Mt. Marcy
elevation (feet) 5,344

Lowest point
name . . . . .Atlantic Ocean
elevation (feet) .sea level

General coastline (miles) 127

Tidal shoreline (miles) 1,850

Capital city . . . . .Albany
population, 1990 101,000

Largest city . . . . New York
population, 1990 7,323,000

Number of cities with over 100,000 population
1980 5

Number of cities with over 100,000 population
1990 5

State parks and Recreation areas, 1991
area (acres) 260,000
number of visitors 60,744,000
revenues $32,914,000

National forest land, 1992 (acres) 13,000

National park acreage, 1984 35,000

DEMOGRAPHICS & CHARACTERISTICS OF THE POPULATION

Population
1970 18,241,391
1980 17,558,072
1990 17,990,455
1994 (est.) 18,169,000
2000 (revised projection) 18,237,000
2010 (revised projection) 18,546,000

Metropolitan area population
1970 16,647,000
1980 15,869,000
1992 16,613,000

Non-metropolitan area population
1970 1,594,000
1980 1,689,000
1992 1,497,000

Change in population, 1980-90
number 432,383
percent 2.46%

Persons per square mile, 1994 . . . . 384.7

Age distribution, 1980
under 5 years 6.5%
5 to 17 years 20.2%
65 and over 12.3%

Age distribution, 1990
under 5 years 7.0%
5 to 17 years 16.7%
65 and over 13.1%

New York 2

Age distribution, 2000 (projected)
under 5 years 5.9%
5 to 17 years 17.2%
65 and over 13.7%

Persons by age, 1990
under 5 years 1,255,764
5 to 17 years 3,003,785
65 and over 2,363,722

Median age, 1990 .... 33.90

Race, 1990
White 13,385,255
Black 2,859,055
American Indian 60,855
Chinese 284,144
Filipino 62,259
Japanese 35,281
Asian Indian 140,985
Korean 95,648
Vietnamese 15,555
all other 1,049,622

Race, 2010 (projected)
White 13,542,000
Black 3,705,000

Persons of Hispanic origin, 1990
total 2,214,026
Mexican 93,244
Puerto Rican 1,086,601
Cuban 74,345
Other Hispanic 959,836

Persons by sex, 1990
male 8,625,673
female 9,364,782

Marital status, 1990
males
15 years & older 6,797,219
single 2,432,069
married 3,804,860
separated 187,868
widowed 199,610
divorced 360,680
females
15 years & older 7,619,289
single 2,200,191
married 3,874,584
separated 302,498

widowed 967,501
divorced 577,013

Households & families, 1990
households 6,639,322
persons per household 2.63
families 4,489,312
married couples 3,315,845
female householder, no husband
present 919,266
one person households 1,806,263
households, 1994 6,669,000
persons per household, 1994 .... 2.64

Nativity, 1990
number of persons born in state 12,147,209
percent of total residents 67.5%

Immigration & naturalization, 1993
immigrants admitted 151,209
persons naturalized 55,519
refugees granted resident status 16,986

VITAL STATISTICS & HEALTH

Births
1992 285,568
with low birth weight 7.6%
to teenage mothers 9.0%
to unmarried mothers 34.8%
1993 278,307
1994 279,187

Abortions, 1992
total 195,000
rate (per 1,000 women age 15-44) 46.2
rate per 1,000 live births 694

Adoptions, 1986
total 7,213
related 50.4%

Deaths
1992 164,869
1993 170,203
1994 167,977

Infant deaths
1992 2,419
1993 2,312
1994 2,366

Average lifetime, 1979-1981
both sexes . . . . 73.70 years
  men . . . . 70.02 years
  women . . . . 77.18 years

Marriages
1992 156,252
1993 151,477
1994 149,615

Divorces
1992 57,038
1993 56,729
1994 59,195

Physicians, 1993
total 60,759
rate (per 1,000 persons) 3.34

Dentists, 1992
total 14,859
rate (per 1,000 persons) 0.82

Hospitals, 1993
number 231
beds (x 1,000) 77.4
average daily census (x 1,000) 64.1
occupancy rate 82.8%
personnel (x 1,000) 328.7
average cost per day to hospital $784
average cost per stay to hospital $7,716

EDUCATION

*Educational attainment of all persons
  25 years and older, 1990*
less than 9th grade 1,200,827
high school graduates 3,485,686
bachelor's degree 1,561,719
graduate or professional degree 1,172,110

Public school enrollment, Fall, 1993
total 2,733,813
  Kindergarten through grade 8 1,920,609
  grades 9 through 12 813,204

Public School Teachers
total, 1994 179,413
  elementary 90,022
  secondary 63,453
salaries, 1994
  beginning $26,903
  average $45,772

*State receipts & expenditures for public
  schools, 1993*
receipts ($mil) 24,504
expenditures
  total ($mil) 22,917
  per capita $1,265
  per pupil $8,525

*Graduating high school seniors,
  public high schools, 1995 (est)* 135,500

SAT scores, 1994
verbal 416
math 472

Institutions of higher education, 1995
total 314
  public 89
  private 225

*Enrollment in institutions of higher
  education, Fall, 1993*
total 1,063,779
full-time men 317,224
full-time women 362,414
part-time men 147,374
part-time women 236,767

*Minority enrollment in institutions of higher
  education, Fall, 1993*
Black, non-Hispanic 131,868
Hispanic 91,251
Asian/Pacific Islander 58,107

Earned degrees conferred, 1993
Bachelor's 97,104
First professional 7,476
Master's 42,539
Doctor's 4,045

SOCIAL INSURANCE &
WELFARE PROGRAMS

Social Security beneficiaries & benefits, 1993
beneficiaries
total 2,937,000
  retired and dependents 2,113,000
  survivors 474,000
  disabled & dependents 351,000
annual benefit payments ($mil)
total $22,670
  retired and dependents 15,962
  survivors 4,202
  disabled & dependents 2,506

New York 4

Medicare, 1993
enrollment (x1,000) 2,594
payments ($mil) 11,448

Medicaid, 1993
recipients (x1,000) 2,742
payments ($mil) 17,557

Federal public aid, 1993
recipients as a percent of population 9.6%
Aid to Families with Dependent Children
  recipients (x1,000) 1,240
average monthly payment $546
Supplemental Security Income
  total recipients (x1,000) 536

Food Stamp Program
  participants, 1994 (x1,000) 2,154

HOUSING & CONSTRUCTION

Total housing units, 1990 7,226,891
  year round housing units 7,013,455
  vacant 587,569

New privately owned housing units authorized, 1994
number (x1,000) 31.1
value ($mil) 2,787

New privately owned housing units started, 1994 (x1,000) 28.3

Existing home sales, 1994 (x1,000) 156.3

GOVERNMENT & ELECTIONS

State officials, 1996
  Governor (name/party/term expires)
    GEORGE PATAKI
    Republican - 1999
Lt. Governor .... Stan Lundine
Sec. of State .... Gail Shaffer
Atty. General .... Dennis Vacco
Chf. Justice .... Judith Kaye

Governorship
minimum age 30
length of term .... 4 years
number of consecutive
  terms permitted .... not specified
who succeeds .... Lt. Governor

State legislature
name .... Legislature
  upper chamber
    name .... Senate
    number of members 61
    length of term .... 2 years
    party in majority, 1996 .... Republican
  lower chamber
    name .... Assembly
    number of members 150
    length of term .... 2 years
    party in majority, 1996 .... Democratic

State employees October, 1992
total 290,433
October payroll ($1,000) 832,608

Local governments, 1992
total 3,319
  county 57
  municipal 620
  township 929
  school districts 714
  special districts 998

Voting, November, 1994
voting age population 13,599,000
  registered 56.8%
  voted 44.6%

Vote for president
1988
  Bush 2,975,276
  Dukakis 3,228,304
1992
  Clinton 3,241,371
  Bush 2,250,676
  Perot 893,774

Federal representation, 1996 (104th Congress)
Senators (name/party/term expires)

    DANIEL P. MOYNIHAN
    Democrat - 2001
    ALFONSO M. D'AMATO
    Republican - 1999

Representatives, total 31
  Democrats 17
  Republicans 14
  other 0

New York 5

Women holding public office
U.S. Congress, 1995 6
statewide elected office, 1995 1
state legislature, 1995 38

Black elected officials, 1993
total 299
   US and state legislatures 30
   city/county/regional offices 63
   judicial/law enforcement 70
   education/school boards 136

Hispanic public officials, 1994
total 83
   state executives & legislators 12
   city/county/regional offices 13
   judicial/law enforcement 11
   education/school boards 47

GOVERNMENTAL FINANCE

State & local government revenues, (selected items), 1991-92 ($per capita)
total $7,009.80
   total general revenues 5,715.60
     from federal government 1,061.09
     from own sources 4,654.51
     from taxes 3,543.78
       from property taxes 1,181.48
       from all other taxes 2,197.76
     from charges & misc. 1,110.73

State & local government expenditures, (selected items), 1991-92 ($per capita)
total $6,888.17
   total direct general expenditures 5,661.46
     education 1,575.07
     libraries 20.93
     public welfare 1,154.93
     health & hospitals 551.95
     highways 282.55
     police protection 205.68
     fire protection 77.47
     correction 191.85
     housing & comm. development 163.79
     natural resources & parks 87.08
     interest on general debt 360.71

State & local debt, 1992 ($per capita) 6,427.15

Federal aid grants to state & local government, 1994 ($per capita total & selected items)
per capita total 1,235.37
   compensatory education 34.57
   waste treatment facilities 6.06
   medicaid 623.21
   housing assistance 80.14
   job training 12.58
   highway trust fund 42.93

CRIME, LAW ENFORCEMENT & COURTS

Crime, 1994 (all rates per 100,000 persons)
total crimes 921,278
overall crime rate 5,070.6
   property crimes 745,845
     burglaries 164,650
     larcenies 452,322
     motor vehicle thefts 128,873
   property crime rate 4,105.0
   violent crimes 175,433
     murders 2,016
     forcible rapes 4,700
     robberies 86,617
     aggravated assaults 82,100
   violent crime rate 965.6

Number of police agencies, 1994 513

Arrests, 1994
total 1,171,999
   persons under 18 years of age 163,723

Prisoners under state & federal jurisdiction, 1994
total 66,750
percent change, 1993-94 .... 3.4%
   sentenced to more than one year
     total 66,750
     rate per 100,000 residents 367

Persons under sentence of death, 4/20/95 0

State's highest court
name .... Court of Appeals
number of members 7
length of term .... 14 years
intermediate appeals court? .... yes

New York 6

LABOR & INCOME

Civilian labor force, 1994
total	8,571,000
men	4,606,000
women	3,965,000
persons 16-19 years	397,000
white	6,878,000
black	1,237,000

Civilian labor force as a percent of civilian non-institutional population, 1994
total	61.3%
men	70.5%
women	53.2%
persons 16-19 years	39.5%
white	61.7%
black	58.3%

Employment, 1994
total	7,978,000
men	4,259,000
women	3,720,000
persons 16-19 years	313,000
white	6,449,000
black	1,108,000

Full-time/part-time labor force, 1994
full-time labor force	6,991,000
working part-time for ecomonic reasons	59,000
part-time labor force	1,580,000

Unemployment rate, 1994
total	6.9%
men	7.5%
women	6.2%
persons 16-19 years	21.2%
white	6.2%
black	10.5%

Unemployed by reason for unemployment (as a percent of total unemployment), 1994
job losers or completed temp jobs	53.3%
job leavers	6.8%
reentrants	31.5%
new entrants	8.4%

Civilian labor force, by occupation, 1994
executive/administrative/managerial	1,111,000
professional/specialty	1,400,000
technicians & related support	262,000
sales	966,000
adminstrative support/clerical	1,413,000
service occupations	1,392,000
precision production/craft/repair	816,000
machine operators/assemblers	417,000
transportation/material moving	327,000
handlers/helpers/laborers	304,000
farming/forestry/fishing	111,000

Civilian labor force, by industry, 1994
construction	341,000
manufacturing	1,143,000
transportation/communication	461,000
wholesale/retail trade	1,468,000
finance/real estate/insurance	647,000
services	2,250,000
government	1,481,000
agriculture	96,000

Average annual pay, 1994 (prelim.)	$33,438
change in average annual pay, 1993-1994	1.6%

Hours and earnings of production workers on manufacturing payrolls, 1994
average weekly hours	41.0
average hourly earnings	$12.19
average weekly earnings	$499.79

Labor union membership, 1994	2,050,000

Household income (in constant 1993 dollars)
median household income, 1992	$31,981
median household income, 1993	$31,697

Poverty
persons below poverty level, 1992	15.7%
persons below poverty level, 1993	16.4%

Personal income ($per capita)
1994	
in current dollars	25,999
in constant (1987) dollars	20,108
1995 (projected)	
in constant (1982) dollars	16,889
2000 (projected)	
in constant (1982) dollars	17,852

Federal income tax returns, 1993
returns filed	7,844,199
adjusted gross income ($1000)	293,196,545
total income tax paid ($1000)	45,164,525

ECONOMY, BUSINESS, INDUSTRY & AGRICULTURE

Fortune 500 companies, 1994 65

Business incorporations, 1994
total 70,689
change, 1993-94 .... 1.2%

Business failures, 1994
total 5,533
rate per 10,000 concerns 87
change, 1993-94 .... -20.1%

Business firm ownership
Hispanic owned firms, 1987 28,254
black owned firms, 1987 36,289
women owned firms, 1987 284,900
foreign owned firms, 1982 779

Gross state product, 1991 ($mil)
total $475,961
  agriculture services, forestry, fisheries ... 2,627
  mining 374
  construction 16,323
  manufacturing—durable goods 35,523
  manufacturing—nondurable goods 31,904
  transportation, communication &
    public utilities 40,142
  wholesale trade 31,638
  retail trade 36,516
  finance/real estate/insurance 119,425
  services 107,369
  federal, state & local government 54,120

Establishments, by major industry group, 1992
total 460,162
  agriculture 5,349
  mining 434
  construction 37,322
  manufacturing 27,097
  transportation 17,240
  wholesale trade 40,898
  retail trade 112,343
  finance/real estate/insurance 53,356
  service industries 160,669
  unclassified 5,454

Payroll, by major industry group, 1992
total ($1,000) $201,426,434
  agriculture 484,901

  mining 320,757
  construction 7,900,055
  manufacturing 35,912,037
  transportation 14,664,025
  wholesale trade 16,929,422
  retail trade 17,359,243
  finance/real estate/insurance 38,839,247
  service industries 68,871,023
  unclassified 145,724

Agriculture
number of farms, 1994 37,000
farm acreage, 1994 8,000,000
acres per farm, 1994 216
value of farms, 1994 ($mil) 10,261
farm income, 1993 ($mil)
  gross farm income 3,051
  net farm income 494
  debt/asset ratio 15.9%
farm marketings, 1993 ($mil)
total $2,817
  crops 930
  livestock 1,888
government payments 72
farm marketings in order of marketing
receipts, 1993
    1) Dairy products
    2) Greenhouse
    3) Cattle
    4) Apples

Federal economic activity
  ($mil, except per capita)
expenditures, 1994
  total $90,346
  per capita $4,973
  defense $5,533
  non-defense $84,813
defense department, 1994
  contract awards ($mil) $3,629
  payroll ($mil) $1,894
  civilian employees (x1,000) 15.5
  military personnel (x1,000) 23.7

Fishing, 1992
catch (millions of pounds) 50
value ($mil) 54

Mining, 1994 ($mil)
total non-fuel mineral production $871

principal non-fuel minerals in order of value, 1994
1) Salt
2) Stone
3) Sand and gravel

Construction, 1994 ($mil)
total contracts (including
  non-building) $13,179
    residential 3,464
    non-residential 5,936

Manufacturing, 1992
total establishments 26,617
employees, total (x1,000) 1,049
payroll ($mil) 35,225
production workers (x1,000) 592
value added ($mil) 86,349
value of shipments ($mil) 154,211

Finance
commercial banks, 1994
  number 175
    assets ($bil) 770.5
    deposits ($bil) 493.9
    closed or assisted 0
    deposits ($bil) .... NA
savings and loan associations, 1991
  non-current real estate loans 5.59%
  net income after taxes ($mil) .... -173
  return on assets .... -0.38%

Retail trade, 1992
establishments (x1,000) 110.8
sales ($mil) 118,886
annual payroll ($mil) 14,867
paid employees (x1,000) 1,088

Wholesale trade, 1992
establishments 40,934
sales ($bil) 287.7
annual payroll ($mil) 15,220
paid employees (x1,000) 433.6

Service industries, 1992
establishments (x1,000) (non-exempt firms) 133.7
receipts ($mil) (non-exempt firms) 103,025
annual payroll ($mil) 38,012
paid employees (x1,000) (non-exempt firms) 1,344

COMMUNICATION, ENERGY & TRANSPORTATION

Communication
daily newspapers, 1993 71
broadcast stations, 1990
  radio: commercial, educational 416
  television: commercial, noncommercial 52
cable TV households, 1988 3,022,000

Energy
consumption estimates, 1992
total (trillion Btu) 3,616
per capita (million Btu) 199.7
by source of production (trillion Btu)
  coal 337
  natural gas 987
  petroleum 1,574
  nuclear electric power 258
  hydroelectric power 306
by end-use sector (trillion Btu)
  residential 995
  commercial 1,021
  industrial 723
  transportation 878
electrical energy
  production, 1993 (billion kWh) 106.3
  net summer capability, 1993 (million kW) . 32.7
gas utilities, 1993
  customers 4,297,000
  sales (trillion Btu) 593
  revenues ($mil) 4,330
nuclear plants, 1993 6

Transportation, 1994
public road & street mileage
total 112,004
  urban 39,907
  rural 72,097
  interstate 1,498
vehicle miles of travel (mil) 112,970
total motor vehicle registrations 10,196,166
  automobiles 7,906,975
licensed drivers 10,376,615
  per 1,000 driving age population 735
deaths from motor vehicle
  accidents 1,658

STATE SUMMARY

Capital City . . . . Raleigh

Governor . . . . Jim Hunt, Jr.

Address . . . . STATE CAPITOL
RALEIGH, NC 27611
919 733-5811

Admitted as a state 1789

Area (square miles) 53,821

Population, 1980 5,881,766

Population, 1990 6,628,637

Population, 1994 (est.) 7,070,000

Persons per square mile, 1994 . . . . 145.1

Largest city . . . . .Charlotte
population, 1990 396,000

Personal income per capita, 1994
(in current dollars) $19,669

Gross state product ($mil), 1991 147,520

Leading industries, 1992 (by payroll)
MANUFACTURING
SERVICE INDUSTRIES
RETAIL TRADE

Leading agricultural commodities, 1993
TOBACCO
BROILERS
HOGS
TURKEYS

GEOGRAPHY & ENVIRONMENT

Area (square miles)
total 53,821
  land 48,718
  water (includes territorial water) 5,103

Federally owned land, 1991 . . . . 6.3%

Highest point
name . . . . Mt. Mitchell
elevation (feet) 6,684

Lowest point
name . . . . .Atlantic Ocean
elevation (feet) .sea level

General coastline (miles) 301

Tidal shoreline (miles) 3,375

Capital city . . . . Raleigh
population, 1990 208,000

Largest city . . . . Charlotte
population, 1990 396,000

Number of cities with over 100,000 population
1980 5

Number of cities with over 100,000 population
1990 5

State parks and Recreation areas, 1991
area (acres) 134,000
number of visitors 9,463,000
revenues $1,700,000

National forest land, 1992 (acres) 3,165,000

National park acreage, 1984 377,800

DEMOGRAPHICS & CHARACTERISTICS OF THE POPULATION

Population
1970 5,088,411
1980 5,881,766
1990 6,628,637
1994 (est.) 7,070,000
2000 (revised projection) 7,617,000
2010 (revised projection) 8,341,000

Metropolitan area population
1970 2,755,000
1980 3,204,000
1992 4,535,000

Non-metropolitan area population
1970 2,330,000
1980 2,678,000
1992 2,301,000

Change in population, 1980-90
number 746,871
percent 12.70%

Persons per square mile, 1994 . . . . 145.1

Age distribution, 1980
under 5 years 6.9%
5 to 17 years 21.3%
65 and over 10.3%

Age distribution, 1990
under 5 years 6.9%
5 to 17 years 17.3%
65 and over 12.1%

Age distribution, 2000 (projected)
under 5 years 5.7%
5 to 17 years 17.2%
65 and over 13.2%

Persons by age, 1990
under 5 years 458,955
5 to 17 years 1,147,194
65 and over 804,341

Median age, 1990 .... 33.10

Race, 1990
White 5,008,491
Black 1,456,323
American Indian 79,825
Chinese 8,859
Filipino 5,332
Japanese 5,040
Asian Indian 9,847
Korean 7,267
Vietnamese 5,211
all other 42,112

Race, 2010 (projected)
White 6,125,000
Black 1,916,000

Persons of Hispanic origin, 1990
total 76,726
    Mexican 32,670
    Puerto Rican 14,620
    Cuban 3,723
    Other Hispanic 25,713

Persons by sex, 1990
male 3,214,290
female 3,414,347

Marital status, 1990
males
    15 years & older 2,532,813
        single 726,858
        married 1,581,394
        separated 78,527
        widowed 61,149
        divorced 163,412
females
    15 years & older 2,760,408
        single 603,374
        married 1,581,108
        separated 103,674

widowed 352,110
divorced 223,816

Households & families, 1990
households 2,517,026
persons per household 2.54
    families 1,812,053
        married couples 1,424,206
        female householder, no husband
            present 309,876
        one person households 596,959
households, 1994 2,679,000
persons per household, 1994 .... 2.55

Nativity, 1990
number of persons born in state 4,668,539
percent of total residents 70.4%

Immigration & naturalization, 1993
immigrants admitted 6,892
persons naturalized 2,397
refugees granted resident status 867

VITAL STATISTICS & HEALTH

Births
1992 103,047
    with low birth weight 8.4%
    to teenage mothers 15.4%
    to unmarried mothers 31.3%
1993 100,597
1994 101,911

Abortions, 1992
total 36,000
rate (per 1,000 women age 15-44) 22.4
rate per 1,000 live births 357

Adoptions, 1986
total 3,535
    related 71.1%

Deaths
1992 59,478
1993 62,580
1994 64,512

Infant deaths
1992 1,052
1993 1,032
1994 1,019

Average lifetime, 1979-1981
both sexes .... 72.96 years
  men .... 68.60 years
  women .... 77.35 years

Marriages
1992 48,202
1993 47,099
1994 51,934

Divorces
1992 36,159
1993 34,927
1994 36,292

Physicians, 1993
total 13,574
rate (per 1,000 persons) 1.98

Dentists, 1992
total 2,895
rate (per 1,000 persons) 0.43

Hospitals, 1993
number 117
beds (x 1,000) 22.7
average daily census (x 1,000) 15.8
occupancy rate 69.6%
personnel (x 1,000) 97.0
average cost per day to hospital $763
average cost per stay to hospital $5,571

EDUCATION

*Educational attainment of all persons
  25 years and older, 1990*
less than 9th grade 539,974
high school graduates 1,232,868
bachelor's degree 510,003
graduate or professional degree 229,046

Public school enrollment, Fall, 1993
total 1,133,231
  Kindergarten through grade 8 828,171
  grades 9 through 12 305,060

Public School Teachers
total, 1994 69,421
  elementary 40,237
  secondary 24,935
salaries, 1994
  beginning $20,002
  average $29,727

*State receipts & expenditures for public
  schools, 1993*
receipts ($mil) 5,697
expenditures
  total ($mil) 5,594
  per capita $818
  per pupil $4,810

*Graduating high school seniors,
  public high schools, 1995 (est)* 59,705

SAT scores, 1994
verbal 405
math 455

Institutions of higher education, 1995
total 123
  public 75
  private 48

*Enrollment in institutions of higher
  education, Fall, 1993*
total 371,280
full-time men 107,253
full-time women 128,415
part-time men 54,978
part-time women 80,634

*Minority enrollment in institutions of higher
  education, Fall, 1993*
Black, non-Hispanic 71,137
Hispanic 3,853
Asian/Pacific Islander 6,299

Earned degrees conferred, 1993
Bachelor's 31,852
First professional 1,709
Master's 6,864
Doctor's 980

SOCIAL INSURANCE &
WELFARE PROGRAMS

Social Security beneficiaries & benefits, 1993
beneficiaries
  total 1,174,000
  retired and dependents 791,000
  survivors 204,000
  disabled & dependents 180,000
annual benefit payments ($mil)
  total $7,909
  retired and dependents 5,237
  survivors 1,530
  disabled & dependents 1,142

North Carolina 4

Medicare, 1993
enrollment (x1,000) 971
payments ($mil) 3,242

Medicaid, 1993
recipients (x1,000) 898
payments ($mil) 2,452

Federal public aid, 1993
recipients as a percent of population 7.3%
Aid to Families with Dependent Children
   recipients (x1,000) 334
average monthly payment $227
Supplemental Security Income
   total recipients (x1,000) 175

Food Stamp Program
   participants, 1994 (x1,000) 630

HOUSING & CONSTRUCTION

Total housing units, 1990 2,818,193
   year round housing units 2,718,050
   vacant 301,167

New privately owned housing units
authorized, 1994
number (x1,000) 62.9
value ($mil) 5,277

New privately owned housing units
started, 1994 (x1,000) 70.0

Existing home sales, 1994 (x1,000) 204.1

GOVERNMENT & ELECTIONS

State officials, 1996
  Governor (name/party/term expires)
               JIM HUNT, JR.
               Democrat - 1997
Lt. Governor .... Dennis Wicker
Sec. of State .... Rufus Edminston
Atty. General .... Michael Easley
Chf. Justice .... James Exum, Jr.

Governorship
minimum age 30
length of term .... 4 years
number of consecutive
   terms permitted ..2 max. (not nec. consecutive)
who succeeds .... Lt. Governor

State legislature
name .... General Assembly
  upper chamber
    name .... Senate
    number of members 50
    length of term .... 2 years
    party in majority, 1996 .... Democratic
  lower chamber
    name .... House of Representatives
    number of members 120
    length of term .... 2 years
    party in majority, 1996 .... Republican

State employees October, 1992
total 127,279
October payroll ($1,000) 257,507

Local governments, 1992
total 954
  county 100
  municipal 518
  township 0
  school districts 0
  special districts 335

Voting, November, 1994
voting age population 5,211,000
  registered 60.8%
  voted 35.7%

Vote for president
1988
  Bush 1,232,132
  Dukakis 890,034
1992
  Clinton 1,099,191
  Bush 1,118,279
  Perot 351,746

Federal representation, 1996 (104th Congress)
Senators (name/party/term expires)

       JESSE A. HELMS
       Republican - 1997
      LAUCH FAIRCLOTH
       Republican - 1999

Representatives, total 12
  Democrats 4
  Republicans 8
  other 0

Women holding public office
U.S. Congress, 1995 2
statewide elected office, 1995 0
state legislature, 1995 27

Black elected officials, 1993
total 468
  US and state legislatures 28
  city/county/regional offices 328
  judicial/law enforcement 31
  education/school boards 81

Hispanic public officials, 1994
total . . . . NA
  state executives & legislators . . . . NA
  city/county/regional offices . . . . NA
  judicial/law enforcement . . . . NA
  education/school boards . . . . NA

GOVERNMENTAL FINANCE

State & local government revenues, (selected items), 1991-92 ($per capita)
total $3,972.85
  total general revenues 3,213.61
    from federal government 610.35
    from own sources 2,603.26
    from taxes 1,840.17
      from property taxes 379.45
      from all other taxes 1,342.34
    from charges & misc. 763.09

State & local government expenditures, (selected items), 1991-92 ($per capita)
total $3,766.38
  total direct general expenditures 3,156.69
    education 1,219.07
    libraries 12.63
    public welfare 443.99
    health & hospitals 382.73
    highways 235.00
    police protection 104.15
    fire protection 38.52
    correction 96.29
    housing & comm. development 43.28
    natural resources & parks 98.97
    interest on general debt 105.60

State & local debt, 1992 ($per capita) 2,559.95

Federal aid grants to state & local government, 1994 ($per capita total & selected items)
per capita total 687.72
  compensatory education 19.93
  waste treatment facilities 5.74
  medicaid 296.77
  housing assistance 35.55
  job training 9.80
  highway trust fund 66.91

CRIME, LAW ENFORCEMENT & COURTS

Crime, 1994 (all rates per 100,000 persons)
total crimes 397,705
overall crime rate 5,625.2
  property crimes 351,397
    burglaries 104,118
    larcenies 225,937
    motor vehicle thefts 21,342
  property crime rate 4,970.3
  violent crimes 46,308
    murders 772
    forcible rapes 2,334
    robberies 12,811
    aggravated assaults 30,391
  violent crime rate 655.0

Number of police agencies, 1994 463

Arrests, 1994
total 437,063
  persons under 18 years of age 49,086

Prisoners under state & federal jurisdiction, 1994
total 23,639
percent change, 1993-94 . . . . 8.0%
  sentenced to more than one year
    total 22,983
    rate per 100,000 residents 322

Persons under sentence of death, 4/20/95 155

State's highest court
name . . . . Supreme Court
number of members 7
length of term . . . . 8 years
intermediate appeals court? . . . . yes

North Carolina 6

LABOR & INCOME

Civilian labor force, 1994

total 3,609,000
  men 1,887,000
  women 1,722,000
  persons 16-19 years 202,000
  white 2,789,000
  black 745,000

Civilian labor force as a percent of
civilian non-institutional population, 1994

total 67.1%
  men 74.6%
  women 60.4%
  persons 16-19 years 54.5%
  white 67.5%
  black 65.2%

Employment, 1994

total 3,451,000
  men 1,812,000
  women 1,639,000
  persons 16-19 years 169,000
  white 2,694,000
  black 687,000

Full-time/part-time labor force, 1994

full-time labor force 3,028,000
  working part-time for
    ecomonic reasons 49,000
part-time labor force 581,000

Unemployment rate, 1994

total 4.4%
  men 4.0%
  women 4.8%
  persons 16-19 years 16.1%
  white 3.4%
  black 7.7%

Unemployed by reason for unemployment
(as a percent of total unemployment), 1994

job losers or completed temp jobs 41.5%
job leavers 14.8%
reentrants 36.4%
new entrants 7.3%

Civilian labor force, by occupation, 1994

executive/administrative/
  managerial 414,000
professional/specialty 458,000
technicians & related support 112,000

sales 416,000
adminstrative support/clerical 466,000
service occupations 447,000
precision production/craft/repair 448,000
machine operators/assemblers 428,000
transportation/material moving 150,000
handlers/helpers/laborers 173,000
farming/forestry/fishing 83,000

Civilian labor force, by industry, 1994

construction 170,000
manufacturing 912,000
transportation/communication 170,000
wholesale/retail trade 659,000
finance/real estate/insurance 152,000
services 677,000
government 503,000
agriculture 75,000

Average annual pay, 1994 (prelim.) $23,449
change in average annual pay,
  1993-1994 .... 3.0%

Hours and earnings of production workers
on manufacturing payrolls, 1994

average weekly hours 41.1
average hourly earnings $10.19
average weekly earnings $418.81

Labor union membership, 1994 158,600

Household income (in constant 1993 dollars)

median household income, 1992 .... $28,602
median household income, 1993 .... $28,820

Poverty

persons below poverty level, 1992 .... 15.8%
persons below poverty level, 1993 .... 14.4%

Personal income ($per capita)

1994
  in current dollars 19,669
  in constant (1987) dollars 15,212
1995 (projected)
  in constant (1982) dollars 12,658
2000 (projected)
  in constant (1982) dollars 13,481

Federal income tax returns, 1993

returns filed 3,165,227
adjusted gross income ($1000) 92,645,247
total income tax paid ($1000) 11,991,677

ECONOMY, BUSINESS, INDUSTRY & AGRICULTURE

Fortune 500 companies, 1994 7

Business incorporations, 1994
total 14,830
change, 1993-94 .... 10.5%

Business failures, 1994
total 1,051
rate per 10,000 concerns 54
change, 1993-94 .... -12.0%

Business firm ownership
Hispanic owned firms, 1987 918
black owned firms, 1987 19,487
women owned firms, 1987 93,500
foreign owned firms, 1982 251

Gross state product, 1991 ($mil)
total $147,520
  agriculture services, forestry, fisheries ... 4,042
  mining 437
  construction 5,290
  manufacturing—durable goods 15,476
  manufacturing—nondurable goods 29,311
  transportation, communication &
    public utilities 12,124
  wholesale trade 9,192
  retail trade 13,958
  finance/real estate/insurance 20,203
  services 19,332
  federal, state & local government 18,154

Establishments, by major industry group, 1992
total 168,488
  agriculture 2,699
  mining 211
  construction 18,898
  manufacturing 11,996
  transportation 6,182
  wholesale trade 13,225
  retail trade 45,240
  finance/real estate/insurance 14,033
  service industries 53,873
  unclassified 2,131

Payroll, by major industry group, 1992
total ($1,000) $56,969,572
  agriculture 231,848
  mining 100,303
  construction 3,009,464
  manufacturing 20,524,503
  transportation 4,480,321
  wholesale trade 4,492,144
  retail trade 6,648,294
  finance/real estate/insurance 3,633,260
  service industries 13,821,733
  unclassified 27,702

Agriculture
number of farms, 1994 58,000
farm acreage, 1994 9,000,000
acres per farm, 1994 160
value of farms, 1994 ($mil) 12,679
farm income, 1993 ($mil)
  gross farm income 6,472
  net farm income 2,490
  debt/asset ratio 17.9%
farm marketings, 1993 ($mil)
  total $5,457
  crops 2,256
  livestock 3,201
government payments 132
farm marketings in order of marketing
receipts, 1993
    1) Tobacco
    2) Broilers
    3) Hogs
    4) Turkeys

Federal economic activity ($mil, except per capita)
expenditures, 1994
  total $28,858
  per capita $4,082
  defense $5,313
  non-defense $23,546
defense department, 1994
  contract awards ($mil) $1,163
  payroll ($mil) $4,186
  civilian employees (x1,000) 17.4
  military personnel (x1,000) 96.2

Fishing, 1992
catch (millions of pounds) 154
value ($mil) 57

Mining, 1994 ($mil)
total non-fuel mineral production $705

North Carolina 8

principal non-fuel minerals in order of value, 1994

   1) Stone
   2) Phosphate rock
   3) Sand and gravel

Construction, 1994 ($mil)
total contracts (including
   non-building) $10,040
      residential 5,384
      non-residential 3,212

Manufacturing, 1992
total establishments 11,877
employees, total (x1,000) 831
payroll ($mil) 20,456
production workers (x1,000) 609
value added ($mil) 65,446
value of shipments ($mil) 128,599

Finance
commercial banks, 1994
   number 71
      assets ($bil) 104.0
      deposits ($bil) 70.3
      closed or assisted 0
      deposits ($bil)- ....NA
savings and loan associations, 1991
   non-current real estate loans 2.02%
   net income after taxes ($mil) 41
   return on assets .... +0.21%

Retail trade, 1992
establishments (x1,000) 44.2
sales ($mil) 49,564
annual payroll ($mil) 5,687
paid employees (x1,000) 508

Wholesale trade, 1992
establishments 13,351
sales ($bil) 76.4
annual payroll ($mil) 4,167
paid employees (x1,000) 151.1

Service industries, 1992
establishments (x1,000) (non-exempt firms) 42.2
receipts ($mil) (non-exempt firms) 22,155
annual payroll ($mil) 8,410
paid employees (x1,000) (non-exempt firms) . 425

COMMUNICATION, ENERGY & TRANSPORTATION

Communication
daily newspapers, 1993 49
broadcast stations, 1990
   radio: commercial, educational 370
   television: commercial, noncommercial 40
cable TV households, 1988 1,196,000

Energy
consumption estimates, 1992
total (trillion Btu) 2,019
per capita (million Btu) 295.3
by source of production (trillion Btu)
   coal 600
   natural gas 186
   petroleum 754
   nuclear electric power 243
   hydroelectric power 60
by end-use sector (trillion Btu)
   residential 468
   commercial 344
   industrial 666
   transportation 541
electrical energy
   production, 1993 (billion kWh) 88.8
   net summer capability, 1993 (million kW) . 20.2
gas utilities, 1993
   customers 683,000
   sales (trillion Btu) 162
   revenues ($mil) 798
nuclear plants, 1993 5

Transportation, 1994
public road & street mileage
total 96,479
   urban 21,899
   rural 74,580
   interstate 970
vehicle miles of travel (mil) 71,928
total motor vehicle registrations 5,442,720
   automobiles 3,525,315
licensed drivers 4,840,104
   per 1,000 driving age population 880
deaths from motor vehicle
   accidents 1,431

STATE SUMMARY

Capital City . . . . .Bismark

Governor . . . . Edward Schafer

Address . . . . STATE CAPITOL
BISMARK, ND 58505
701 328-2200

Admitted as a state 1889

Area (square miles) 70,704

Population, 1980 652,717

Population, 1990 638,800

Population, 1994 (est.) 638,000

Persons per square mile, 1994 . . . . 9.2

Largest city . . . . .Fargo
population, 1990 74,100

Personal income per capita, 1994
(in current dollars) $18,546

Gross state product ($mil), 1991 12,045

Leading industries, 1992 (by payroll)
SERVICE INDUSTRIES
RETAIL TRADE
MANUFACTURING

Leading agricultural commodities, 1993
WHEAT
CATTLE
BARLEY
SUNFLOWERS

GEOGRAPHY & ENVIRONMENT

Area (square miles)
total 70,704
land 68,994
water (includes territorial water) 1,710

Federally owned land, 1991 . . . . 4.2%

Highest point
name . . . . White Butte (Slope County)
elevation (feet) 3,506

Lowest point
name . . . . Red River
elevation (feet) 750

General coastline (miles) 0

Tidal shoreline (miles) 0

Capital city . . . . .Bismark
population, 1990 49,300

Largest city . . . . .Fargo
population, 1990 74,100

Number of cities with over 100,000 population
1980 0

Number of cities with over 100,000 population
1990 0

State parks and Recreation areas, 1991
area (acres) 19,000
number of visitors 954,000
revenues $813,000

National forest land, 1992 (acres) 1,106,000

National park acreage, 1984 71,300

DEMOGRAPHICS & CHARACTERISTICS OF THE POPULATION

Population
1970 617,792
1980 652,717
1990 638,800
1994 (est.) 638,000
2000 (revised projection) 643,000
2010 (revised projection) 676,000

Metropolitan area population
1970 196,000
1980 234,000
1992 263,000

Non-metropolitan area population
1970 422,000
1980 418,000
1992 371,000

Change in population, 1980-90
number . . . .-13,917
percent . . . . -2.13%

Persons per square mile, 1994 . . . . 9.2

Age distribution, 1980
under 5 years 8.4%
5 to 17 years 20.9%
65 and over 12.3%

Age distribution, 1990
under 5 years 7.5%
5 to 17 years 19.9%
65 and over 14.2%

North Dakota 2

Age distribution, 2000 (projected)
under 5 years 6.2%
5 to 17 years 18.7%
65 and over 13.6%

Persons by age, 1990
under 5 years 47,845
5 to 17 years 127,540
65 and over 91,055

Median age, 1990 ....*32.40*

Race, 1990
White 604,142
Black 3,524
American Indian 25,870
Chinese 557
Filipino 708
Japanese 245
Asian Indian 482
Korean 526
Vietnamese 281
all other 2,418

Race, 2010 (projected)
White 622,000
Black 5,000

Persons of Hispanic origin, 1990
total 4,665
Mexican 2,878
Puerto Rican 386
Cuban 63
Other Hispanic 1,338

Persons by sex, 1990
male 318,201
female 320,599

Marital status, 1990
males
15 years & older 241,899
single 74,201
married 148,509
separated 1,653
widowed 5,663
divorced 13,526
females
15 years & older 248,204
single 52,711
married 148,021
separated 2,116

widowed 31,525
divorced 15,947

Households & families, 1990
households 240,878
persons per household 2.55
families 166,270
married couples 142,374
female householder, no husband
present 17,523
one person households 63,953
households, 1994 241,000
persons per household, 1994 .... 2.54

Nativity, 1990
number of persons born in state 467,822
percent of total residents 73.2%

Immigration & naturalization, 1993
immigrants admitted 601
persons naturalized 159
refugees granted resident status 180

VITAL STATISTICS & HEALTH

Births
1992 8,935
with low birth weight 5.1%
to teenage mothers 9.3%
to unmarried mothers 22.6%
1993 8,746
1994 8,639

Abortions, 1992
total 1,000
rate (per 1,000 women age 15-44) 10.7
rate per 1,000 live births 149

Adoptions, 1986
total 484
related 64.3%

Deaths
1992 5,797
1993 5,925
1994 6,107

Infant deaths
1992 70
1993 62
1994 54

North Dakota 3

Average lifetime, 1979-1981
both sexes . . . . 75.71 years
  men . . . . 72.09 years
  women . . . . 79.68 years

Marriages
1992 4,809
1993 4,892
1994 4,791

Divorces
1992 2,305
1993 2,233
1994 2,201

Physicians, 1993
total 1,178
rate (per 1,000 persons) 1.88

Dentists, 1992
total 299
rate (per 1,000 persons) 0.48

Hospitals, 1993
number 45
beds (x 1,000) 4.4
average daily census (x 1,000) 2.8
occupancy rate 64.2%
personnel (x 1,000) 12.2
average cost per day to hospital $507
average cost per stay to hospital $5,403

EDUCATION

Educational attainment of all persons 25 years and older, 1990
less than 9th grade 59,354
high school graduates 111,215
bachelor's degree 53,637
graduate or professional degree 18,002

Public school enrollment, Fall, 1993
total 119,127
  Kindergarten through grade 8 84,127
  grades 9 through 12 35,000

Public School Teachers
total, 1994 7,755
  elementary 5,211
  secondary 2,544
salaries, 1994
  beginning $17,453
  average $25,506

State receipts & expenditures for public schools, 1993
receipts ($mil) 579
expenditures
  total ($mil) 547
  per capita $863
  per pupil $4,404

Graduating high school seniors, public high schools, 1995 (est) 7,522

SAT scores, 1994
verbal 497
math 559

Institutions of higher education, 1995
total 20
  public 15
  private 5

Enrollment in institutions of higher education, Fall, 1993
total 40,316
full-time men 16,722
full-time women 15,417
part-time men 3,550
part-time women 4,627

Minority enrollment in institutions of higher education, Fall, 1993
Black, non-Hispanic 263
Hispanic 229
Asian/Pacific Islander 282

Earned degrees conferred, 1993
Bachelor's 4,555
First professional 142
Master's 649
Doctor's 74

SOCIAL INSURANCE & WELFARE PROGRAMS

Social Security beneficiaries & benefits, 1993
beneficiaries
total 114,000
  retired and dependents 82,000
  survivors 22,000
  disabled & dependents 11,000
annual benefit payments ($mil)
total $769
  retired and dependents 523
  survivors 181
  disabled & dependents 66

North Dakota 4

Medicare, 1993
enrollment (x1,000) 102
payments ($mil) 347

Medicaid, 1993
recipients (x1,000) 62
payments ($mil) 273

Federal public aid, 1993
recipients as a percent of population 4.2%
Aid to Families with Dependent Children
  recipients (x1,000) 17
average monthly payment $365
Supplemental Security Income
  total recipients (x1,000) 9

Food Stamp Program
participants, 1994 (x1,000) 45

HOUSING & CONSTRUCTION

Total housing units, 1990 276,340
  year round housing units 268,594
  vacant 35,462

New privately owned housing units
authorized, 1994
number (x1,000) 3.4
value ($mil) 211

New privately owned housing units
started, 1994 (x1,000) 3.8

Existing home sales, 1994 (x1,000) 10.9

GOVERNMENT & ELECTIONS

State officials, 1996
  Governor (name/party/term expires)
    EDWARD SCHAFER
    Republican - 1996
Lt. Governor .... Rosemarie Myrdal
Sec. of State .... Al Jaeger
Atty. General .... Heidie M.K. Heitkamp
Chf. Justice .... Ralph J. Erickstad

Governorship
minimum age 30
length of term .... 4 years
number of consecutive
  terms permitted .... not specified
who succeeds .... Lt. Governor

State legislature
name .... Legislative Assembly
  upper chamber
    name .... Senate
    number of members 53
    length of term .... 4 years
    party in majority, 1996 .... Republican
  lower chamber
    name .... House of Representatives
    number of members 106
    length of term .... 2 years
    party in majority, 1996 .... Republican

State employees October, 1992
total 21,964
October payroll ($1,000) 33,979

Local governments, 1992
total 2,795
  county 53
  municipal 366
  township 1,351
  school districts 284
  special districts 740

Voting, November, 1994
voting age population 441,000
  registered 93.3%
  voted 61.1%

Vote for president
1988
  Bush 165,517
  Dukakis 127,081
1992
  Clinton 98,928
  Bush 135,498
  Perot 70,703

Federal representation, 1996 (104th Congress)
Senators (name/party/term expires)

KENT CONRAD
Democrat - 2001
BYRON DORGAN
Democrat - 1999

Representatives, total 1
  Democrats 1
  Republicans 0
  other 0

278

North Dakota 5

Women holding public office
U.S. Congress, 1995 0
statewide elected office, 1995 5
state legislature, 1995 22

Black elected officials, 1993
total 0
  US and state legislatures 0
  city/county/regional offices 0
  judicial/law enforcement 0
  education/school boards 0

Hispanic public officials, 1994
total . . . . NA
  state executives & legislators . . . . NA
  city/county/regional offices . . . . NA
  judicial/law enforcement . . . . NA
  education/school boards . . . . NA

GOVERNMENTAL FINANCE

State & local government revenues, (selected items), 1991-92 ($per capita)
total $4,302.92
  total general revenues 3,799.40
    from federal government 951.10
    from own sources 2,848.29
    from taxes 1,701.18
      from property taxes 532.39
      from all other taxes 929.58
    from charges & misc. 1,147.11

State & local government expenditures, (selected items), 1991-92 ($per capita)
total $4,251.34
  total direct general expenditures 3,904.04
    education 1,484.94
    libraries 10.46
    public welfare 574.56
    health & hospitals 134.28
    highways 439.43
    police protection 66.76
    fire protection 24.32
    correction 42.37
    housing & comm. development 58.05
    natural resources & parks 233.71
    interest on general debt 215.57

State & local debt, 1992 ($per capita) 3,076.32

Federal aid grants to state & local government, 1994 ($per capita total & selected items)
per capita total 1,100.32
  compensatory education 26.31
  waste treatment facilities 11.29
  medicaid 314.87
  housing assistance 57.65
  job training 14.36
  highway trust fund 164.88

CRIME, LAW ENFORCEMENT & COURTS

Crime, 1994 (all rates per 100,000 persons)
total crimes 17,455
overall crime rate 2,735.9
  property crimes 16,933
    burglaries 2,070
    larcenies 13,899
    motor vehicle thefts 964
  property crime rate 2,654.1
  violent crimes 522
    murders 1
    forcible rapes 149
    robberies 71
    aggravated assaults 301
  violent crime rate 81.8

Number of police agencies, 1994 57

Arrests, 1994
total 25,296
  persons under 18 years of age 7,569

Prisoners under state & federal jurisdiction, 1994
total 536
percent change, 1993-94 . . . . 7.6%
  sentenced to more than one year
    total 501
    rate per 100,000 residents 78

Persons under sentence of death, 4/20/95 . . . . NA

State's highest court
name . . . . Supreme Court
number of members 5
length of term . . . . 10 years
intermediate appeals court? . . . . no

North Dakota 6

LABOR & INCOME

Civilian labor force, 1994
total 338,000
  men 179,000
  women 158,000
  persons 16-19 years 24,000
  white 325,000
  black .... NA

Civilian labor force as a percent of
civilian non-institutional population, 1994
total 71.6%
  men 77.9%
  women 65.6%
  persons 16-19 years 62.8%
  white 72.0%
  black .... NA%

Employment, 1994
total 324,000
  men 171,000
  women 153,000
  persons 16-19 years 22,000
  white 314,000
  black .... NA

Full-time/part-time labor force, 1994
full-time labor force 254,000
  working part-time for
    ecomonic reasons 4,000
part-time labor force 83,000

Unemployment rate, 1994
total 3.9%
  men 4.4%
  women 3.3%
  persons 16-19 years 10.5%
  white 3.4%
  black .... NA%

Unemployed by reason for unemployment
(as a percent of total unemployment), 1994
job losers or completed temp jobs 47.1%
job leavers 11.4%
reentrants 36.5%
new entrants 5.0%

Civilian labor force, by occupation, 1994
executive/administrative/
  managerial 33,000
professional/specialty 45,000
technicians & related support ....NA

sales 40,000
adminstrative support/clerical 42,000
service occupations 58,000
precision production/craft/repair 31,000
machine operators/assemblers 11,000
transportation/material moving 15,000
handlers/helpers/laborers 12,000
farming/forestry/fishing 42,000

Civilian labor force, by industry, 1994
construction 16,000
manufacturing 20,000
transportation/communication 14,000
wholesale/retail trade 70,000
finance/real estate/insurance 12,000
services 72,000
government 63,000
agriculture 44,000

Average annual pay, 1994 (prelim.) $19,893
change in average annual pay,
  1993-1994 .... 2.6%

Hours and earnings of production workers
on manufacturing payrolls, 1994
average weekly hours 42.4
average hourly earnings $10.19
average weekly earnings $432.06

Labor union membership, 1994 24,300

Household income (in constant 1993 dollars)
median household income, 1992 .... $27,766
median household income, 1993 .... $28,118

Poverty
persons below poverty level, 1992 .... 12.1%
persons below poverty level, 1993 .... 11.2%

Personal income ($per capita)
1994
  in current dollars 18,546
  in constant (1987) dollars 14,343
1995 (projected)
  in constant (1982) dollars 11,663
2000 (projected)
  in constant (1982) dollars 12,461

Federal income tax returns, 1993
returns filed 283,759
adjusted gross income ($1000) 7,599,759
total income tax paid ($1000) 1,029,510

North Dakota 7

ECONOMY, BUSINESS, INDUSTRY & AGRICULTURE

Fortune 500 companies, 1994 0

Business incorporations, 1994
total 1,042
change, 1993-94 .... 11.8%

Business failures, 1994
total 89
rate per 10,000 concerns 35
change, 1993-94 .... -38.6%

Business firm ownership
Hispanic owned firms, 1987 88
black owned firms, 1987 57
women owned firms, 1987 12,700
foreign owned firms, 1982 34

Gross state product, 1991 ($mil)
total $12,045
  agriculture services, forestry, fisheries ... 1,154
  mining 769
  construction 417
  manufacturing—durable goods 385
  manufacturing—nondurable goods 445
  transportation, communication &
    public utilities 1,123
  wholesale trade 957
  retail trade 1,193
  finance/real estate/insurance 1,881
  services 1,844
  federal, state & local government 1,876

Establishments, by major industry group, 1992
total 19,394
  agriculture 297
  mining 238
  construction 1,733
  manufacturing 678
  transportation 1,308
  wholesale trade 2,007
  retail trade 4,944
  finance/real estate/insurance 1,857
  service industries 6,077
  unclassified 255

Payroll, by major industry group, 1992
total ($1,000) $3,780,407
  agriculture 14,290

  mining 164,874
  construction 262,312
  manufacturing 442,398
  transportation 363,850
  wholesale trade 412,917
  retail trade 550,271
  finance/real estate/insurance 284,195
  service industries 1,283,571
  unclassified 1,729

Agriculture
number of farms, 1994 32,000
farm acreage, 1994 40,000,000
acres per farm, 1994 1,263
value of farms, 1994 ($mil) 16,541
farm income, 1993 ($mil)
  gross farm income 3,540
  net farm income 690
  debt/asset ratio 14.8%
farm marketings, 1993 ($mil)
total $2,933
  crops 2,227
  livestock 707
government payments 565
farm marketings in order of marketing receipts, 1993
  1) Wheat
  2) Cattle
  3) Barley
  4) Sugar beets

*Federal economic activity
($mil, except per capita)*
expenditures, 1994
  total $3,909
  per capita $6,127
  defense $473
  non-defense $3,436
defense department, 1994
  contract awards ($mil) $120
  payroll ($mil) $340
  civilian employees (x1,000) 1.7
  military personnel (x1,000) 9.8

Fishing, 1992
catch (millions of pounds) .... NA
value ($mil) .... NA

Mining, 1994 ($mil)
total non-fuel mineral production $26

281

North Dakota 8

principal non-fuel minerals in order of value, 1994
- 1) Sand and gravel
- 2) Lime
- 3) Sand and gravel

Construction, 1994 ($mil)
total contracts (including
  non-building) $850
    residential 226
    non-residential 326

Manufacturing, 1992
total establishments 666
employees, total (x1,000) 19
payroll ($mil) 438
production workers (x1,000) 13
value added ($mil) 1,423
value of shipments ($mil) 3,678

Finance
commercial banks, 1994
  number 141
    assets ($bil) 8.1
    deposits ($bil) 7.1
    closed or assisted 0
    deposits ($bil) .... NA
savings and loan associations, 1991
    non-current real estate loans 2.16%
    net income after taxes ($mil) 62
    return on assets .... +1.18%

Retail trade, 1992
establishments (x1,000) 4.8
sales ($mil) 4,697
annual payroll ($mil) 514
paid employees (x1,000) 52

Wholesale trade, 1992
establishments 2,086
sales ($bil) 7.6
annual payroll ($mil) 406
paid employees (x1,000) 18.5

Service industries, 1992
establishments (x1,000) (non-exempt firms) . 4.2
receipts ($mil) (non-exempt firms) 1,576
annual payroll ($mil) 616
paid employees (x1,000) (non-exempt firms) .. 33

COMMUNICATION, ENERGY & TRANSPORTATION

Communication
daily newspapers, 1993 10
broadcast stations, 1990
    radio: commercial, educational 67
    television: commercial, noncommercial 21
cable TV households, 1988 143,000

Energy
consumption estimates, 1992
  total (trillion Btu) 327
  per capita (million Btu) 516.1
  by source of production (trillion Btu)
    coal 399
    natural gas 38
    petroleum 118
    nuclear electric power 0
    hydroelectric power 25
  by end-use sector (trillion Btu)
    residential 51
    commercial 38
    industrial 169
    transportation 70
electrical energy
  production, 1993 (billion kWh) 28.5
  net summer capability, 1993 (million kW) .. 4.5
gas utilities, 1993
    customers 104,000
    sales (trillion Btu) 21
    revenues ($mil) 98
nuclear plants, 1993 0

Transportation, 1994
public road & street mileage
  total 86,731
    urban 1,819
    rural 84,912
    interstate 571
vehicle miles of travel (mil) 6,338
total motor vehicle registrations 684,640
    automobiles 373,106
licensed drivers 439,330
    per 1,000 driving age population 904
deaths from motor vehicle
    accidents 88

282

Ohio 1

STATE SUMMARY

Capital City . . . . Columbus

Governor . . . . George Voinvovich

Address . . . . STATE HOUSE
COLUMBUS, OH 43215
614 466-2000

Admitted as a state 1803

Area (square miles) 44,828

Population, 1980 10,797,630

Population, 1990 10,847,115

Population, 1994 (est.) 11,102,000

Persons per square mile, 1994 . . . . 271.1

Largest city . . . . Columbus
population, 1990 633,000

Personal income per capita, 1994
(in current dollars) $20,928

Gross state product ($mil), 1991 228,109

Leading industries, 1992 (by payroll)
MANUFACTURING
SERVICE INDUSTRIES
RETAIL TRADE

Leading agricultural commodities, 1993
SOYBEANS
CORN
DAIRY PRODUCTS
GREENHOUSE

GEOGRAPHY & ENVIRONMENT

Area (square miles)
total 44,828
 land 40,953
 water (includes territorial water) 3,875

Federally owned land, 1991 . . . . 1.3%

Highest point
name . . . . .Campbell Hill
elevation (feet) 1,549

Lowest point
name . . . . Ohio River
elevation (feet) 455

General coastline (miles) 0

Tidal shoreline (miles) 0

Capital city . . . . Columbus
population, 1990 633,000

Largest city . . . . Columbus
population, 1990 633,000

Number of cities with over 100,000 population
1980 7

Number of cities with over 100,000 population
1990 6

State parks and Recreation areas, 1991
area (acres) 208,000
number of visitors 67,222,000
revenues $12,082,000

National forest land, 1992 (acres) 833,000

National park acreage, 1984 14,600

DEMOGRAPHICS & CHARACTERISTICS OF THE POPULATION

Population
1970 10,657,423
1980 10,797,630
1990 10,847,115
1994 (est.) 11,102,000
2000 (revised projection) 11,453,000
2010 (revised projection) 11,659,000

Metropolitan area population
1970 8,565,000
1980 8,521,000
1992 8,966,000

Non-metropolitan area population
1970 2,092,000
1980 2,277,000
1992 2,056,000

Change in population, 1980-90
number 49,485
percent 0.46%

Persons per square mile, 1994 . . . . 271.1

Age distribution, 1980
under 5 years 7.3%
5 to 17 years 21.3%
65 and over 10.8%

Age distribution, 1990
under 5 years 7.2%
5 to 17 years 18.5%
65 and over 12.9%

Ohio 2

Age distribution, 2000 (projected)
under 5 years 6.3%
5 to 17 years 18.4%
65 and over 13.5%

Persons by age, 1990
under 5 years 785,149
5 to 17 years 2,014,595
65 and over 1,406,961

Median age, 1990 .... *33.30*

Race, 1990
White 9,521,756
Black 1,154,826
American Indian 19,859
Chinese 19,447
Filipino 10,268
Japanese 10,485
Asian Indian 20,848
Korean 11,237
Vietnamese 4,964
all other 72,926

Race, 2010 (projected)
White 9,948,000
Black 1,483,000

Persons of Hispanic origin, 1990
total 139,696
  Mexican 57,815
  Puerto Rican 45,853
  Cuban 3,559
  Other Hispanic 32,469

Persons by sex, 1990
male 5,226,340
female 5,620,775

Marital status, 1990
males
  15 years & older : 4,024,476
    single 1,156,250
    married 2,436,833
      separated 58,248
    widowed 109,520
    divorced 321,873
females
  15 years & older 4,475,533
    single 1,013,457
    married 2,452,698
      separated 82,065

widowed 556,165
divorced 453,213

Households & families, 1990
households 4,087,546
persons per household 2.59
  families 2,895,223
    married couples 2,294,111
    female householder, no husband
      present 478,070
    one person households 1,020,450
households, 1994 4,190,000
persons per household, 1994 .... 2.59

Nativity, 1990
number of persons born in state 8,038,140
percent of total residents 74.1%

Immigration & naturalization, 1993
immigrants admitted 10,703
persons naturalized 3,362
refugees granted resident status 2,378

VITAL STATISTICS & HEALTH

Births
1992 169,067
  with low birth weight 7.4%
  to teenage mothers 13.6%
  to unmarried mothers 31.6%
1993 156,748
1994 162,059

Abortions, 1992
total 50,000
rate (per 1,000 women age 15-44) 19.5
rate per 1,000 live births 294

Adoptions, 1986
total 1,898
  related 17.3%

Deaths
1992 99,601
1993 100,678
1994 105,603

Infant deaths
1992 1,474
1993 1,386
1994 1,435

Average lifetime, 1979-1981
both sexes .... 73.49 years
  men .... 69.85 years
  women .... 77.06 years

Marriages
1992 92,156
1993 88,864
1994 92,797

Divorces
1992 53,535
1993 51,243
1994 49,968

Physicians, 1993
total 22,928
rate (per 1,000 persons) 2.07

Dentists, 1992
total 6,090
rate (per 1,000 persons) 0.55

Hospitals, 1993
number 192
beds (x 1,000) 41.1
average daily census (x 1,000) 24.9
occupancy rate 60.5%
personnel (x 1,000) 176.2
average cost per day to hospital $940
average cost per stay to hospital $5,923

EDUCATION

*Educational attainment of all persons
  25 years and older, 1990*
less than 9th grade 546,954
high school graduates 2,515,987
bachelor's degree 767,845
graduate or professional degree 407,491

Public school enrollment, Fall, 1993
total 1,807,319
  Kindergarten through grade 8 1,290,197
  grades 9 through 12 517,122

Public School Teachers
total, 1994 107,444
  elementary 71,186
  secondary 36,103
salaries, 1994
  beginning $19,553
  average $35,912

*State receipts & expenditures for public
  schools, 1993*
receipts ($mil) 11,355
expenditures
  total ($mil) 11,289
  per capita $1,024
  per pupil $5,963

*Graduating high school seniors,
public high schools, 1995 (est)* 110,070

SAT scores, 1994
verbal 456
math 510

Institutions of higher education, 1995
total 157
  public 61
  private 96

*Enrollment in institutions of higher
education, Fall, 1993*
total 562,402
full-time men 164,434
full-time women 182,990
part-time men 91,593
part-time women 123,385

*Minority enrollment in institutions of higher
education, Fall, 1993*
Black, non-Hispanic 49,922
Hispanic 7,743
Asian/Pacific Islander 10,055

Earned degrees conferred, 1993
Bachelor's 51,487
First professional 3,225
Master's 14,613
Doctor's 1,973

SOCIAL INSURANCE &
WELFARE PROGRAMS

Social Security beneficiaries & benefits, 1993
beneficiaries
total 1,882,000
  retired and dependents 1,300,000
  survivors 357,000
  disabled & dependents 225,000
annual benefit payments ($mil)
total $13,951
  retired and dependents 9,213
  survivors 3,191
  disabled & dependents 1,546

Ohio 4

Medicare, 1993
enrollment (x1,000) 1,626
payments ($mil) 6,086

Medicaid, 1993
recipients (x1,000) 1,491
payments ($mil) 4,667

Federal public aid, 1993
recipients as a percent of population 8.3%
Aid to Families with Dependent Children
    recipients (x1,000) 694
    average monthly payment $317
Supplemental Security Income
    total recipients (x1,000) 214

Food Stamp Program
    participants, 1994 (x1,000) 1,245

HOUSING & CONSTRUCTION

Total housing units, 1990 4,371,945
    year round housing units 4,334,164
    vacant 284,399

New privately owned housing units
    authorized, 1994
number (x1,000) 47.2
value ($mil) 4,799

New privately owned housing units
    started, 1994 (x1,000) 54.3

Existing home sales, 1994 (x1,000) 186.4

GOVERNMENT & ELECTIONS

State officials, 1996
Governor (name/party/term expires)
        GEORGE VOINVOVICH
            Republican - 1999
Lt. Governor .... Michael DeWine
Sec. of State .... Robert Taft II
Atty. General .... Betty Dee Montgomery
Chf. Justice .... Thomas Moyer

Governorship
minimum age .... not specified
length of term .... 4 years
number of consecutive
    terms permitted 2
who succeeds .... Lt. Governor

State legislature
name .... General Assembly
    upper chamber
        name .... Senate
        number of members 33
        length of term .... 4 years
        party in majority, 1996 .... Republican
lower chamber
        name .... House of Representatives
        number of members 99
        length of term .... 2 years
        party in majority, 1996 .... Republican

State employees October, 1992
total 176,781
October payroll ($1,000) 352,935

Local governments, 1992
total 3,534
    county 88
    municipal 942
    township 1,317
    school districts 665
    special districts 521

Voting, November, 1994
voting age population 8,152,000
    registered 64.6%
    voted 46.6%

Vote for president
1988
    Bush 2,411,719
    Dukakis 1,934,922
1992
    Clinton 1,965,155
    Bush 1,875,664
    Perot 1,024,479

Federal representation, 1996 (104th Congress)
Senators (name/party/term expires)

        MIKE DEWINE
        Republican - 2001
        JOHN GLENN
        Democrat - 1999

Representatives, total 19
    Democrats 6
    Republicans 13
    other 0

Women holding public office
U.S. Congress, 1995 2
statewide elected office, 1995 2
state legislature, 1995 32

Black elected officials, 1993
total 219
  US and state legislatures 16
  city/county/regional offices 124
  judicial/law enforcement 30
  education/school boards 49

Hispanic public officials, 1994
total 4
  state executives & legislators 0
  city/county/regional offices 1
  judicial/law enforcement 2
  education/school boards 1

GOVERNMENTAL FINANCE

State & local government revenues, (selected items), 1991-92 ($per capita)
total $4,683.37
  total general revenues 3,411.51
    from federal government 647.50
    from own sources 2,764.00
    from taxes 1,950.50
      from property taxes 571.67
      from all other taxes 1,259.03
    from charges & misc. 813.50

State & local government expenditures, (selected items), 1991-92 ($per capita)
total $4,166.30
  total direct general expenditures 3,426.32
    education 1,209.66
    libraries 17.59
    public welfare 638.05
    health & hospitals 292.39
    highways 249.14
    police protection 121.76
    fire protection 60.67
    correction 82.23
    housing & comm. development 57.33
    natural resources & parks 69.44
    interest on general debt 152.81

State & local debt, 1992 ($per capita) 2,354.38

Federal aid grants to state & local government, 1994 ($per capita total & selected items)
per capita total 753.58
  compensatory education 23.53
  waste treatment facilities 11.13
  medicaid 315.59
  housing assistance 53.48
  job training 10.57
  highway trust fund 63.46

CRIME, LAW ENFORCEMENT & COURTS

Crime, 1994 (all rates per 100,000 persons)
total crimes 495,310
overall crime rate 4,461.4
  property crimes 441,380
    burglaries 96,175
    larcenies 297,792
    motor vehicle thefts 47,413
  property crime rate 3,975.7
  violent crimes 53,930
    murders 662
    forcible rapes 5,231
    robberies 20,821
    aggravated assaults 27,216
  violent crime rate 485.8

Number of police agencies, 1994 257

Arrests, 1994
total 369,112
  persons under 18 years of age 76,423

Prisoners under state & federal jurisdiction, 1994
total 41,913
percent change, 1993-94 .... 3.1%
  sentenced to more than one year
    total 41,913
    rate per 100,000 residents 377

Persons under sentence of death, 4/20/95 142

State's highest court
name .... Supreme Court
number of members 7
length of term .... 6 years
intermediate appeals court? .... yes

Ohio 6

LABOR & INCOME

Civilian labor force, 1994
total 5,537,000
  men 2,975,000
  women 2,562,000
  persons 16-19 years 335,000
  white 4,959,000
  black 507,000

*Civilian labor force as a percent of
civilian non-institutional population, 1994*
total 65.8%
  men 75.0%
  women 57.6%
  persons 16-19 years 55.6%
  white 66.5%
  black 59.4%

Employment, 1994
total 5,231,000
  men 2,807,000
  women 2,424,000
  persons 16-19 years 281,000
  white 4,730,000
  black 432,000

Full-time/part-time labor force, 1994
full-time labor force 4,433,000
  working part-time for
    ecomonic reasons 48,000
part-time labor force 1,104,000

Unemployment rate, 1994
total 5.5%
  men 5.6%
  women 5.4%
  persons 16-19 years 16.1%
  white 4.6%
  black 14.8%

*Unemployed by reason for unemployment
(as a percent of total unemployment), 1994*
job losers or completed temp jobs 45.6%
job leavers 10.5%
reentrants 36.5%
new entrants 7.5%

Civilian labor force, by occupation, 1994
executive/administrative/
  managerial 664,000
professional/specialty 747,000
technicians & related support 166,000

sales 621,000
adminstrative support/clerical 791,000
service occupations 757,000
precision production/craft/repair 641,000
machine operators/assemblers 495,000
transportation/material moving 234,000
handlers/helpers/laborers 272,000
farming/forestry/fishing 124,000

Civilian labor force, by industry, 1994
construction 231,000
manufacturing 1,210,000
transportation/communication 256,000
wholesale/retail trade 1,143,000
finance/real estate/insurance 283,000
services 1,198,000
government 707,000
agriculture 108,000

Average annual pay, 1994 (prelim.) $26,133
change in average annual pay,
  1993-1994 . . . . 3.1%

*Hours and earnings of production workers
on manufacturing payrolls, 1994*
average weekly hours 43.8
average hourly earnings $14.38
average weekly earnings $629.84

Labor union membership, 1994 896,600

Household income (in constant 1993 dollars)
median household income, 1992 . . . . $32,344
median household income, 1993 . . . . $31,285

Poverty
persons below poverty level, 1992 . . . . 12.5%
persons below poverty level, 1993 . . . . 13.0%

Personal income ($per capita)
1994
  in current dollars 20,928
  in constant (1987) dollars 16,186
1995 (projected)
  in constant (1982) dollars 13,679
2000 (projected)
  in constant (1982) dollars 14,531

Federal income tax returns, 1993
returns filed 5,101,148
adjusted gross income ($1000) 153,216,681
total income tax paid ($1000) 20,993,250

ECONOMY, BUSINESS, INDUSTRY & AGRICULTURE

Fortune 500 companies, 1994 30

Business incorporations, 1994
total 20,013
change, 1993-94 .... -0.3%

Business failures, 1994
total 1,988
rate per 10,000 concerns 64
change, 1993-94 .... -6.7%

Business firm ownership
Hispanic owned firms, 1987 1,989
black owned firms, 1987 15,983
women owned firms, 1987 154,100
foreign owned firms, 1982 350

Gross state product, 1991 ($mil)
total $228,109
   agriculture services, forestry, fisheries ... 2,756
   mining 1,158
   construction 8,263
   manufacturing—durable goods 37,826
   manufacturing—nondurable goods 22,349
   transportation, communication &
      public utilities 19,733
   wholesale trade 15,252
   retail trade 21,800
   finance/real estate/insurance 36,397
   services 39,100
   federal, state & local government 23,476

Establishments, by major industry group, 1992
total 253,956
   agriculture 3,871
   mining 989
   construction 23,709
   manufacturing 18,470
   transportation 9,209
   wholesale trade 19,243
   retail trade 65,231
   finance/real estate/insurance 22,378
   service industries 88,256
   unclassified 2,600

Payroll, by major industry group, 1992
total ($1,000) $100,769,422
   agriculture 449,442

   mining 586,344
   construction 5,135,499
   manufacturing 35,069,758
   transportation 6,390,335
   wholesale trade 8,328,444
   retail trade 11,084,619
   finance/real estate/insurance 7,001,691
   service industries 26,672,461
   unclassified 50,829

Agriculture
number of farms, 1994 75,000
farm acreage, 1994 15,000,000
acres per farm, 1994 203
value of farms, 1994 ($mil) 21,067
farm income, 1993 ($mil)
   gross farm income 5,139
   net farm income 1,183
   debt/asset ratio 12.7%
farm marketings, 1993 ($mil)
total $4,393
   crops 2,720
   livestock 1,673
government payments 265
farm marketings in order of marketing
receipts, 1993
   1) Soybeans
   2) Corn
   3) Dairy products
   4) Greenhouse

Federal economic activity
   ($mil, except per capita)
expenditures, 1994
   total $48,023
   per capita $4,326
   defense $5,198
   non-defense $42,825
defense department, 1994
   contract awards ($mil) $2,966
   payroll ($mil) $2,215
   civilian employees (x1,000) 31.9
   military personnel (x1,000) 9.6

Fishing, 1992
catch (millions of pounds) ....NA
value ($mil) ....NA

Mining, 1994 ($mil)
total non-fuel mineral production $893

Ohio 8

principal non-fuel minerals in order of value, 1994
1) Stone
2) Sand and gravel
3) Salt

Construction, 1994 ($mil)
total contracts (including
  non-building) $11,935
    residential 5,147
    non-residential 4,349

Manufacturing, 1992
total establishments 18,292
employees, total (x1,000) 1,046
payroll ($mil) 34,904
production workers (x1,000) 681
value added ($mil) 86,161
value of shipments ($mil) 184,637

Finance
commercial banks, 1994
  number 263
    assets ($bil) 132.9
    deposits ($bil) 96.5
    closed or assisted 0
    deposits ($bil) .... NA
savings and loan associations, 1991
  non-current real estate loans 1.77%
  net income after taxes ($mil) 90
  return on assets .... +0.20%

Retail trade, 1992
establishments (x1,000) 63.7
sales ($mil) 79,031
annual payroll ($mil) 9,257
paid employees (x1,000) 838

Wholesale trade, 1992
establishments 19,305
sales ($bil) 127.3
annual payroll ($mil) 7,283
paid employees (x1,000) 260.1

Service industries, 1992
establishments (x1,000) (non-exempt firms) 69.9
receipts ($mil) (non-exempt firms) 40,844
annual payroll ($mil) 16,137
paid employees (x1,000) (non-exempt firms) . 758

COMMUNICATION, ENERGY & TRANSPORTATION

Communication
daily newspapers, 1993 84
broadcast stations, 1990
    radio: commercial, educational 355
    television: commercial, noncommercial 50
cable TV households, 1988 2,206,000

Energy
consumption estimates, 1992
  total (trillion Btu) 3,733
  per capita (million Btu) 338.7
  by source of production (trillion Btu)
    coal 1,419
    natural gas 839
    petroleum 1,137
    nuclear electric power 158
    hydroelectric power 3
  by end-use sector (trillion Btu)
    residential 822
    commercial 579
    industrial 1,551
    transportation 780
electrical energy
  production, 1993 (billion kWh) 133.7
  net summer capability, 1993 (million kW) . 27.2
gas utilities, 1993
  customers 3,095,000
  sales (trillion Btu) 547
  revenues ($mil) 2,896
nuclear plants, 1993 2

Transportation, 1994
public road & street mileage
  total 114,464
    urban 33,085
    rural 81,379
    interstate 1,572
vehicle miles of travel (mil) 98,200
total motor vehicle registrations 9,663,727
    automobiles 7,177,441
licensed drivers 7,142,173
    per 1,000 driving age population 834
deaths from motor vehicle
    accidents 1,371

Oklahoma 1

STATE SUMMARY

Capital City .... Oklahoma City

Governor .... Frank Keating

Address .... STATE CAPITOL
　　　　　　OKLAHOMA, CITY 73105
　　　　　　405 521-2342

Admitted as a state 1907

Area (square miles) 69,903

Population, 1980 3,025,290

Population, 1990 3,145,585

Population, 1994 (est.) 3,258,000

Persons per square mile, 1994 .... 47.4

Largest city .... Oklahoma City
　population, 1990 445,000

Personal income per capita, 1994
　(in current dollars) $17,744

Gross state product ($mil), 1991 57,914

Leading industries, 1992 (by payroll)
　　　　　SERVICE INDUSTRIES
　　　　　MANUFACTURING
　　　　　RETAIL TRADE

Leading agricultural commodities, 1993
　　　　　CATTLE
　　　　　WHEAT
　　　　　GREENHOUSE
　　　　　BROILERS

GEOGRAPHY & ENVIRONMENT

Area (square miles)
total 69,903
　land 68,679
　water (includes territorial water) 1,224

Federally owned land, 1991 .... 1.6%

Highest point
name .... Black Mesa
elevation (feet) 4,973

Lowest point
name .... Little River
elevation (feet) 289

General coastline (miles) 0

Tidal shoreline (miles) 0

Capital city .... Oklahoma City
population, 1990 445,000

Largest city .... Oklahoma City
population, 1990 445,000

Number of cities with over 100,000 population
　1980 2

Number of cities with over 100,000 population
　1990 2

State parks and Recreation areas, 1991
area (acres) 77,000
number of visitors 16,031,000
revenues $15,320,000

National forest land, 1992 (acres) 465,000

National park acreage, 1984 9,500

DEMOGRAPHICS & CHARACTERISTICS OF THE POPULATION

Population
1970 2,559,463
1980 3,025,290
1990 3,145,585
1994 (est.) 3,258,000
2000 (revised projection) 3,382,000
2010 (revised projection) 3,683,000

Metropolitan area population
1970 1,432,000
1980 1,724,000
1992 1,927,000

Non-metropolitan area population
1970 1,127,000
1980 1,301,000
1992 1,278,000

Change in population, 1980-90
number 120,295
percent 3.98%

Persons per square mile, 1994 .... 47.4

Age distribution, 1980
under 5 years 7.7%
5 to 17 years 20.6%
65 and over 12.4%

Age distribution, 1990
under 5 years 7.2%
5 to 17 years 19.4%
65 and over 13.4%

Oklahoma 2

Age distribution, 2000 (projected)
under 5 years 6.2%
5 to 17 years 18.5%
65 and over 13.3%

Persons by age, 1990
under 5 years 226,523
5 to 17 years 610,484
65 and over 424,213

Median age, 1990 .... 33.20

Race, 1990
White 2,583,512
Black 233,801
American Indian 252,089
Chinese 5,193
Filipino 3,024
Japanese 2,385
Asian Indian 4,546
Korean 4,717
Vietnamese 7,320
all other 48,667

Race, 2010 (projected)
White 2,979,000
Black 269,000

Persons of Hispanic origin, 1990
total 86,160
Mexican 63,226
Puerto Rican 4,693
Cuban 1,043
Other Hispanic 17,198

Persons by sex, 1990
male 1,530,819
female 1,614,766

Marital status, 1990
males
15 years & older 1,170,478
single 291,237
married 744,454
separated 17,573
widowed 29,341
divorced 105,446
females
15 years & older 1,272,570
single 220,159
married 744,704
separated 23,955

widowed 165,735
divorced 141,972

Households & families, 1990
households 1,206,135
persons per household 2.53
families 855,321
married couples 695,961
female householder, no husband
present 125,469
one person households 309,369
households, 1994 1,236,000
persons per household, 1994 .... 2.56

Nativity, 1990
number of persons born in state 1,996,579
percent of total residents 63.5%

Immigration & naturalization, 1993
immigrants admitted 2,942
persons naturalized 1,092
refugees granted resident status 258

VITAL STATISTICS & HEALTH

Births
1992 47,850
with low birth weight 6.7%
to teenage mothers 16.8%
to unmarried mothers 28.4%
1993 46,711
1994 45,682

Abortions, 1992
total 9,000
rate (per 1,000 women age 15-44) 12.5
rate per 1,000 live births 193

Adoptions, 1986
total 2,350
related 50.0%

Deaths
1992 30,626
1993 32,574
1994 32,452

Infant deaths
1992 438
1993 430
1994 430

Oklahoma 3

Average lifetime, 1979-1981
both sexes . . . . 73.67 years
men . . . . 69.63 years
women . . . . 77.81 years

Marriages
1992 31,783
1993 30,495
1994 29,297

Divorces
1992 23,447
1993 22,784
1994 21,855

Physicians, 1993
total 4,897
rate (per 1,000 persons) 1.53

Dentists, 1992
total 1,556
rate (per 1,000 persons) 0.49

Hospitals, 1993
number 110
beds (x 1,000) 11.7
average daily census (x 1,000) 6.4
occupancy rate 54.5%
personnel (x 1,000) 44.4
average cost per day to hospital $797
average cost per stay to hospital $5,093

EDUCATION

*Educational attainment of all persons
  25 years and older, 1990*
less than 9th grade 195,015
high school graduates 607,903
bachelor's degree 236,112
graduate or professional degree 118,857

Public school enrollment, Fall, 1993
total 604,076
Kindergarten through grade 8 441,094
grades 9 through 12 162,982

Public School Teachers
total, 1994 39,031
elementary 18,735
secondary 16,180
salaries, 1994
beginning $22,181
average $27,612

*State receipts & expenditures for public
  schools, 1993*
receipts ($mil) 2,813
expenditures
total ($mil) 2,726
per capita $850
per pupil $4,085

*Graduating high school seniors,
  public high schools, 1995 (est)* 31,299

SAT scores, 1994
verbal 482
math 537

Institutions of higher education, 1995
total 46
public 29
private 17

*Enrollment in institutions of higher
  education, Fall, 1993*
total 183,342
full-time men 52,795
full-time women 56,202
part-time men 30,484
part-time women 43,861

*Minority enrollment in institutions of higher
  education, Fall, 1993*
Black, non-Hispanic 13,022
Hispanic 3,592
Asian/Pacific Islander 3,563

Earned degrees conferred, 1993
Bachelor's 15,002
First professional 928
Master's 4,457
Doctor's 416

SOCIAL INSURANCE & WELFARE PROGRAMS

Social Security beneficiaries & benefits, 1993
beneficiaries
total 562,000
retired and dependents 389,000
survivors 104,000
disabled & dependents 69,000
annual benefit payments ($mil)
total $3,849
retired and dependents 2,571
survivors 844
disabled & dependents 434

Oklahoma 4

Medicare, 1993
enrollment (x1,000) 473
payments ($mil) 1,547

Medicaid, 1993
recipients (x1,000) 387
payments ($mil) 1,043

Federal public aid, 1993
recipients as a percent of population 6.2%
Aid to Families with Dependent Children
  recipients (x1,000) 132
average monthly payment $297
Supplemental Security Income
  total recipients (x1,000) 70

Food Stamp Program
  participants, 1994 (x1,000) 376

HOUSING & CONSTRUCTION

Total housing units, 1990 1,406,499
  year round housing units 1,380,952
  vacant 200,364

New privately owned housing units authorized, 1994
number (x1,000) 9.5
value ($mil) 903

New privately owned housing units started, 1994 (x1,000) 14.1

Existing home sales, 1994 (x1,000) 59.7

GOVERNMENT & ELECTIONS

State officials, 1996
  Governor (name/party/term expires)
      FRANK KEATING
      Republican - 1999
Lt. Governor .... Mary Fallin
Sec. of State .... John Kennedy
Atty. General .... Drew Edmondson
Chf. Justice .... Marion Opala

Governorship
minimum age 31
length of term .... 4 years
number of consecutive
  terms permitted 2
who succeeds .... Lt. Governor

State legislature
name .... Legislature
  upper chamber
      name .... Senate
      number of members 48
      length of term .... 4 years
      party in majority, 1996 .... Democratic
  lower chamber
      name .... House of Representatives
      number of members 101
      length of term .... 2 years
      party in majority, 1996 .... Democratic

State employees October, 1992
total 79,346
October payroll ($1,000) 133,413

Local governments, 1992
total 1,822
  county 77
  municipal 589
  township 0
  school districts 614
  special districts 541

Voting, November, 1994
voting age population 2,325,000
  registered 65.8%
  voted 46.8%

Vote for president
1988
  Bush 678,244
  Dukakis 483,373
1992
  Clinton 473,066
  Bush 592,929
  Perot 319,978

Federal representation, 1996 (104th Congress)
Senators (name/party/term expires)

      JAMES INHOFE
      Republican - 2001
      DON NICKLES
      Republican - 1999

Representatives, total 6
  Democrats 1
  Republicans 5
  other 0

Oklahoma 5

Women holding public office
U.S. Congress, 1995 0
statewide elected office, 1995 3
state legislature, 1995 16

Black elected officials, 1993
total 123
  US and state legislatures 6
  city/county/regional offices 95
  judicial/law enforcement 1
  education/school boards 21

Hispanic public officials, 1994
total 1
  state executives & legislators 0
  city/county/regional offices 1
  judicial/law enforcement 0
  education/school boards 0

GOVERNMENTAL FINANCE

State & local government revenues, (selected items), 1991-92 ($per capita)
total $3,730.26
  total general revenues 3,119.68
    from federal government 595.92
    from own sources 2,523.77
    from taxes 1,650.58
      from property taxes 245.28
      from all other taxes 1,138.45
    from charges & misc. 873.18

State & local government expenditures, (selected items), 1991-92 ($per capita)
total $3,673.23
  total direct general expenditures 3,161.54
    education 1,174.77
    libraries 9.78
    public welfare 471.25
    health & hospitals 355.36
    highways 296.35
    police protection 92.22
    fire protection 47.10
    correction 68.48
    housing & comm. development 36.76
    natural resources & parks 81.13
    interest on general debt 149.88

State & local debt, 1992 ($per capita) 2,905.97

Federal aid grants to state & local government, 1994 ($per capita total & selected items)
per capita total 723.97
  compensatory education 24.06
  waste treatment facilities 4.30
  medicaid 239.89
  housing assistance 50.12
  job training 13.89
  highway trust fund 76.39

CRIME, LAW ENFORCEMENT & COURTS

Crime, 1994 (all rates per 100,000 persons)
total crimes 181,475
overall crime rate 5,570.1
  property crimes 160,250
    burglaries 40,764
    larcenies 104,025
    motor vehicle thefts 15,461
  property crime rate 4,918.7
  violent crimes 21,225
    murders 226
    forcible rapes 1,616
    robberies 4,174
    aggravated assaults 15,209
  violent crime rate 651.5

Number of police agencies, 1994 280

Arrests, 1994
total 148,542
  persons under 18 years of age 27,632

Prisoners under state & federal jurisdiction, 1994
total 16,631
percent change, 1993-94 .... 1.4%
  sentenced to more than one year
    total 16,631
    rate per 100,000 residents 508

Persons under sentence of death, 4/20/95 128

State's highest court
name .... Supreme Court*
number of members 9
length of term .... 6 years
intermediate appeals court? .... yes

Oklahoma 6

LABOR & INCOME

Civilian labor force, 1994

total	1,540,000
men	848,000
women	693,000
persons 16-19 years	103,000
white	1,335,000
black	98,000

Civilian labor force as a percent of
civilian non-institutional population, 1994

total	63.6%
men	73.4%
women	54.7%
persons 16-19 years	54.5%
white	64.1%
black	56.6%

Employment, 1994

total	1,451,000
men	795,000
women	655,000
persons 16-19 years	88,000
white	1,268,000
black	87,000

Full-time/part-time labor force, 1994

full-time labor force	1,247,000
working part-time for ecomonic reasons	19,000
part-time labor force	293,000

Unemployment rate, 1994

total	5.8%
men	6.2%
women	5.4%
persons 16-19 years	14.5%
white	5.0%
black	11.4%

Unemployed by reason for unemployment
(as a percent of total unemployment), 1994

job losers or completed temp jobs	41.7%
job leavers	15.5%
reentrants	38.4%
new entrants	4.4%

Civilian labor force, by occupation, 1994

executive/administrative/ managerial	183,000
professional/specialty	210,000
technicians & related support	46,000
sales	205,000
adminstrative support/clerical	201,000
service occupations	213,000
precision production/craft/repair	174,000
machine operators/assemblers	103,000
transportation/material moving	67,000
handlers/helpers/laborers	52,000
farming/forestry/fishing	80,000

Civilian labor force, by industry, 1994

construction	61,000
manufacturing	210,000
transportation/communication	77,000
wholesale/retail trade	306,000
finance/real estate/insurance	71,000
services	311,000
government	257,000
agriculture	72,000

Average annual pay, 1994 (prelim.)	$22,292
change in average annual pay, 1993-1994	1.3%

Hours and earnings of production workers
on manufacturing payrolls, 1994

average weekly hours	43.1
average hourly earnings	$11.41
average weekly earnings	$491.77

Labor union membership, 1994 110,700

Household income (in constant 1993 dollars)

median household income, 1992	$26,041
median household income, 1993	$26,260

Poverty

persons below poverty level, 1992	18.6%
persons below poverty level, 1993	19.9%

Personal income ($per capita)

1994	
in current dollars	17,744
in constant (1987) dollars	13,723
1995 (projected)	
in constant (1982) dollars	12,010
2000 (projected)	
in constant (1982) dollars	12,937

Federal income tax returns, 1993

returns filed	1,328,928
adjusted gross income ($1000)	36,052,176
total income tax paid ($1000)	4,701,419

ECONOMY, BUSINESS, INDUSTRY & AGRICULTURE

Fortune 500 companies, 1994 5

Business incorporations, 1994
total 7,633
change, 1993-94 .... -2.5%

Business failures, 1994
total 1,166
rate per 10,000 concerns 104
change, 1993-94 .... -19.2%

Business firm ownership
Hispanic owned firms, 1987 1,516
black owned firms, 1987 3,461
women owned firms, 1987 63,700
foreign owned firms, 1982 143

Gross state product, 1991 ($mil)
total $57,914
  agriculture services, forestry, fisheries ... 1,723
  mining 3,669
  construction 1,683
  manufacturing — durable goods 5,334
  manufacturing — nondurable goods 3,825
  transportation, communication &
    public utilities 6,071
  wholesale trade 3,415
  retail trade 5,896
  finance/real estate/insurance 8,672
  services 8,890
  federal, state & local government 8,735

Establishments, by major industry group, 1992
total 77,584
  agriculture 1,048
  mining 2,628
  construction 5,777
  manufacturing 4,116
  transportation 3,333
  wholesale trade 5,916
  retail trade 19,855
  finance/real estate/insurance 7,159
  service industries 26,710
  unclassified 1,042

Payroll, by major industry group, 1992
total ($1,000) $20,435,492
  agriculture 76,261

  mining 1,686,494
  construction 951,649
  manufacturing 4,288,493
  transportation 2,038,426
  wholesale trade 1,655,762
  retail trade 2,541,214
  finance/real estate/insurance 1,548,395
  service industries 5,632,984
  unclassified 15,814

Agriculture
number of farms, 1994 70,000
farm acreage, 1994 34,000,000
acres per farm, 1994 486
value of farms, 1994 ($mil) 18,143
farm income, 1993 ($mil)
  gross farm income 4,666
  net farm income 1,250
  debt/asset ratio 16.8%
farm marketings, 1993 ($mil)
  total $3,869
    crops 1,108
    livestock 2,762
  government payments 324
farm marketings in order of marketing
receipts, 1993
    1) Cattle
    2) Wheat
    3) Greenhouse
    4) Broilers

Federal economic activity
  ($mil, except per capita)
expenditures, 1994
    total $15,718
    per capita $4,824
    defense $2,796
    non-defense $12,922
defense department, 1994
    contract awards ($mil) $759
    payroll ($mil) $2,015
    civilian employees (x1,000) 19.6
    military personnel (x1,000) 28.3

Fishing, 1992
catch (millions of pounds) ....NA
value ($mil) ....NA

Mining, 1994 ($mil)
total non-fuel mineral production $338

Oklahoma 8

principal non-fuel minerals in order of value,
1994
1) Stone
2) Cement
3) Sand and gravel

Construction, 1994 ($mil)
total contracts (including
  non-building) $2,990
    residential 1,265
    non-residential 999

Manufacturing, 1992
total establishments 4,064
employees, total (x1,000) 157
payroll ($mil) 4,282
production workers (x1,000) 109
value added ($mil) 13,808
value of shipments ($mil) 30,287

Finance
commercial banks, 1994
  number 371
    assets ($bil) 31.0
    deposits ($bil) 27.0
  closed or assisted 0
    deposits ($bil) .... NA
savings and loan associations, 1991
  non-current real estate loans 4.39%
  net income after taxes ($mil) 24
  return on assets .... +0.34%

Retail trade, 1992
establishments (x1,000) 19.4
sales ($mil) 21,213
annual payroll ($mil) 2,305
paid employees (x1,000) 211

Wholesale trade, 1992
establishments 5,993
sales ($bil) 26.4
annual payroll ($mil) 1,398
paid employees (x1,000) 57.9

Service industries, 1992
establishments (x1,000) (non-exempt firms) 21.2
receipts ($mil) (non-exempt firms) 9,607
annual payroll ($mil) 3,641
paid employees (x1,000) (non-exempt firms) . 196

COMMUNICATION, ENERGY & TRANSPORTATION

Communication
daily newspapers, 1993 46
broadcast stations, 1990
  radio: commercial, educational 172
  television: commercial, noncommercial 24
cable TV households, 1988 701,000

Energy
consumption estimates, 1992
total (trillion Btu) 1,302
per capita (million Btu) 406.2
by source of production (trillion Btu)
  coal 307
  natural gas 558
  petroleum 473
  nuclear electric power 0
  hydroelectric power 33
by end-use sector (trillion Btu)
  residential 224
  commercial 173
  industrial 529
  transportation 377
electrical energy
  production, 1993 (billion kWh) 48.8
  net summer capability, 1993 (million kW) . 12.9
gas utilities, 1993
  customers 932,000
  sales (trillion Btu) 188
  revenues ($mil) 699
nuclear plants, 1993 0

Transportation, 1994
public road & street mileage
total 112,467
  urban 12,794
  rural 99,673
  interstate 929
vehicle miles of travel (mil) 36,980
total motor vehicle registrations 2,805,750
  automobiles 1,559,306
licensed drivers 2,343,555
  per 1,000 driving age population 947
deaths from motor vehicle
  accidents 687

STATE SUMMARY

Capital City . . . . .Salem

Governor . . . . John Kitzhaber

Address . . . . STATE CAPITOL
SALEM, OR 97310
503 378-3111

Admitted as a state 1859

Area (square miles) 98,386

Population, 1980 2,633,105

Population, 1990 2,842,321

Population, 1994 (est.) 3,086,000

Persons per square mile, 1994 . . . . 32.1

Largest city . . . . Portland
population, 1990 437,000

Personal income per capita, 1994
(in current dollars) $20,419

Gross state product ($mil), 1991 58,799

Leading industries, 1992 (by payroll)
SERVICE INDUSTRIES
MANUFACTURING
RETAIL TRADE

Leading agricultural commodities, 1993
CATTLE
GREENHOUSE
DAIRY PRODUCTS
WHEAT

GEOGRAPHY & ENVIRONMENT

Area (square miles)
total 98,386
  land 96,003
  water (includes territorial water) 2,383

Federally owned land, 1991 . . . . 52.4%

Highest point
name . . . . Mt. Hood
elevation (feet) 11,239

Lowest point
name . . . . Pacific Ocean
elevation (feet) . . . . .sea level

General coastline (miles) 26

Tidal shoreline (miles) 1,410

Capital city . . . . .Salem
population, 1990 107,800

Largest city . . . . Portland
population, 1990 437,000

Number of cities with over 100,000 population
1980 2

Number of cities with over 100,000 population
1990 3

State parks and Recreation areas, 1991
area (acres) 90,000
number of visitors 39,479,000
revenues $7,682,000

National forest land, 1992 (acres) 17,504,000

National park acreage, 1984 194,600

DEMOGRAPHICS & CHARACTERISTICS OF THE POPULATION

Population
1970 2,091,533
1980 2,633,105
1990 2,842,321
1994 (est.) 3,086,000
2000 (revised projection) 3,404,000
2010 (revised projection) 3,876,000

Metropolitan area population
1970 1,415,000
1980 1,763,000
1992 2,081,000

Non-metropolitan area population
1970 676,000
1980 870,000
1992 890,000

Change in population, 1980-90
number 209,216
percent 7.95%

Persons per square mile, 1994 . . . . 32.1

Age distribution, 1980
under 5 years 7.5%
5 to 17 years 19.9%
65 and over 11.5%

Age distribution, 1990
under 5 years 7.1%
5 to 17 years 18.3%
65 and over 13.7%

Oregon 2

Age distribution, 2000 (projected)
under 5 years 5.9%
5 to 17 years 17.6%
65 and over 12.9%

Persons by age, 1990
under 5 years 201,421
5 to 17 years 522,709
65 and over 391,324

Median age, 1990 .... 34.50

Race, 1990
White 2,636,787
Black 46,178
American Indian 37,443
Chinese 13,652
Filipino 7,411
Japanese 11,796
Asian Indian 3,508
Korean 8,668
Vietnamese 9,088
all other 66,737

Race, 2010 (projected)
White 3,508,000
Black 70,000

Persons of Hispanic origin, 1990
total 112,707
Mexican 85,632
Puerto Rican 2,764
Cuban 1,333
Other Hispanic 22,978

Persons by sex, 1990
male 1,397,073
female 1,445,248

Marital status, 1990
males
15 years & older 1,083,101
single 292,169
married 660,657
separated 18,665
widowed 25,266
divorced 105,009
females
15 years & older 1,146,659
single 222,695
married 660,289
separated 23,687

widowed 127,945
divorced 135,730

Households & families, 1990
households 1,103,313
persons per household 2.52
families 750,844
married couples 613,297
female householder, no husband
present 101,762
one person households 278,716
households, 1994 1,195,000
persons per household, 1994 .... 2.53

Nativity, 1990
number of persons born in state 1,324,179
percent of total residents 46.6%

Immigration & naturalization, 1993
immigrants admitted 7,250
persons naturalized 2,146
refugees granted resident status 2,619

VITAL STATISTICS & HEALTH

Births
1992 41,606
with low birth weight 5.2%
to teenage mothers 12.4%
to unmarried mothers 27.0%
1993 42,195
1994 42,276

Abortions, 1992
total 16,000
rate (per 1,000 women age 15-44) 23.9
rate per 1,000 live births 372

Adoptions, 1986
total 1,161
related 10.8%

Deaths
1992 25,862
1993 27,275
1994 27,303

Infant deaths
1992 306
1993 282
1994 294

Oregon 3

Average lifetime, 1979-1981
both sexes .... 74.99 years
  men .... 71.35 years
  women .... 78.77 years

Marriages
1992 24,299
1993 24,322
1994 25,186

Divorces
1992 15,905
1993 15,970
1994 16,307

Physicians, 1993
total 6,354
rate (per 1,000 persons) 2.10

Dentists, 1992
total 2,050
rate (per 1,000 persons) 0.69

Hospitals, 1993
number 63
beds (x 1,000) 7.4
average daily census (x 1,000) 4.1
occupancy rate 54.7%
personnel (x 1,000) 33.1
average cost per day to hospital $1,053
average cost per stay to hospital $5,309

EDUCATION

Educational attainment of all persons
25 years and older, 1990
less than 9th grade 114,724
high school graduates 536,687
bachelor's degree 252,626
graduate or professional degree 129,545

Public school enrollment, Fall, 1993
total 516,611
  Kindergarten through grade 8 368,141
  grades 9 through 12 148,470

Public School Teachers
total, 1994 26,488
  elementary 14,386
  secondary 8,716
salaries, 1994
  beginning $23,186
  average $37,589

State receipts & expenditures for public
schools, 1993
receipts ($mil) 3,201
expenditures
  total ($mil) 3,382
  per capita $1,138
  per pupil $6,240

Graduating high school seniors,
public high schools, 1995 (est) 27,500

SAT scores, 1994
verbal 436
math 491

Institutions of higher education, 1995
total 44
  public 21
  private 23

Enrollment in institutions of higher
education, Fall, 1993
total 165,834
full-time men 46,585
full-time women 46,506
part-time men 31,818
part-time women 40,925

Minority enrollment in institutions of higher
education, Fall, 1993
Black, non-Hispanic 2,711
Hispanic 4,943
Asian/Pacific Islander 8,539

Earned degrees conferred, 1993
Bachelor's 13,139
First professional 988
Master's 3,650
Doctor's 535

SOCIAL INSURANCE & WELFARE PROGRAMS

Social Security beneficiaries & benefits, 1993
beneficiaries
total 530,000
  retired and dependents 395,000
  survivors 79,000
  disabled & dependents 56,000
annual benefit payments ($mil)
total $3,878
  retired and dependents 2,804
  survivors 695
  disabled & dependents 379

Oregon 4

Medicare, 1993
enrollment (x1,000) 452
payments ($mil) 1,444

Medicaid, 1993
recipients (x1,000) 325
payments ($mil) 831

Federal public aid, 1993
recipients as a percent of population 5.3%
Aid to Families with Dependent Children
  recipients (x1,000) 115
average monthly payment $395
Supplemental Security Income
  total recipients (x1,000) 43

Food Stamp Program
participants, 1994 (x1,000) 286

HOUSING & CONSTRUCTION

Total housing units, 1990 1,193,567
  year round housing units 1,161,888
  vacant 90,254

New privately owned housing units authorized, 1994
number (x1,000) 24.1
value ($mil) 2,276

New privately owned housing units started, 1994 (x1,000) 24.8

Existing home sales, 1994 (x1,000) 58.1

GOVERNMENT & ELECTIONS

State officials, 1996
  Governor (name/party/term expires)
        JOHN KITZHABER
        Democrat - 1999
Lt. Governor .... (no Lieutenant Governor)
Sec. of State .... Phil Keisling
Atty. General .... Ted Kulongoski
Chf. Justice .... Wally Carson

Governorship
  minimum age 30
  length of term .... 4 years
  number of consecutive
    terms permitted 2
  who succeeds .... Sec. of State

State legislature
name .... Legislature Assembly
  upper chamber
    name .... Senate
    number of members 30
    length of term .... 4 years
    party in majority, 1996 .... Republican
  lower chamber
    name .... House of Representatives
    number of members 60
    length of term .... 2 years
    party in majority, 1996 .... Republican

State employees October, 1992
total 63,229
October payroll ($1,000) 130,410

Local governments, 1992
total 1,487
  county 36
  municipal 240
  township 0
  school districts 340
  special districts 870

Voting, November, 1994
voting age population 2,309,000
  registered 72.7%
  voted 60.9%

Vote for president
1988
  Bush 517,731
  Dukakis 575,071
1992
  Clinton 538,793
  Bush 404,301
  Perot 316,334

Federal representation, 1996 (104th Congress)
Senators (name/party/term expires)

        MARK HATFIELD
        Republican - 1997
        (Vacant)

Representatives, total 5
  Democrats 3
  Republicans 2
  other 0

302

Oregon 5

Women holding public office
U.S. Congress, 1995 1
statewide elected office, 1995 1
state legislature, 1995 24

Black elected officials, 1993
total 10
  US and state legislatures 4
  city/county/regional offices 2
  judicial/law enforcement 4
  education/school boards 0

Hispanic public officials, 1994
total 5
  state executives & legislators 0
  city/county/regional offices 3
  judicial/law enforcement 1
  education/school boards 1

GOVERNMENTAL FINANCE

State & local government revenues, (selected items), 1991-92 ($per capita)
total $5,255.90
  total general revenues 4,114.44
    from federal government 826.85
    from own sources 3,287.59
    from taxes 2,134.80
      from property taxes 878.98
      from all other taxes 1,000.30
    from charges & misc. 1,152.79

State & local government expenditures, (selected items), 1991-92 ($per capita)
total $4,703.89
  total direct general expenditures 4,033.67
    education 1,423.93
    libraries 20.40
    public welfare 463.89
    health & hospitals 307.64
    highways 270.19
    police protection 122.81
    fire protection 72.79
    correction 103.67
    housing & comm. development 70.85
    natural resources & parks 151.47
    interest on general debt 340.97

State & local debt, 1992 ($per capita) 3,545.45

Federal aid grants to state & local government, 1994 ($per capita total & selected items)
per capita total 763.07
  compensatory education 22.15
  waste treatment facilities 7.15
  medicaid 244.58
  housing assistance 41.28
  job training 12.33
  highway trust fund 65.68

CRIME, LAW ENFORCEMENT & COURTS

Crime, 1994 (all rates per 100,000 persons)
total crimes 194,307
overall crime rate 6,296.4
  property crimes 178,240
    burglaries 33,970
    larcenies 122,506
    motor vehicle thefts 21,764
  property crime rate 5,775.8
  violent crimes 16,067
    murders 150
    forcible rapes 1,333
    robberies 4,264
    aggravated assaults 10,320
  violent crime rate 520.6

Number of police agencies, 1994 192

Arrests, 1994
total 157,775
  persons under 18 years of age 44,750

Prisoners under state & federal jurisdiction, 1994
total 6,936
percent change, 1993-94 . . . . 5.8%
  sentenced to more than one year
    total 5,458
    rate per 100,000 residents 175

Persons under sentence of death, 4/20/95 14

State's highest court
name . . . . Supreme Court
number of members 7
length of term . . . . 6 years
intermediate appeals court? . . . . yes

Oregon 6

LABOR & INCOME

Civilian labor force, 1994

total	1,643,000
men	904,000
women	739,000
persons 16-19 years	91,000
white	1,556,000
black	NA

*Civilian labor force as a percent of
civilian non-institutional population, 1994*

total	68.9%
men	75.4%
women	62.2%
persons 16-19 years	56.1%
white	69.0%
black	NA%

Employment, 1994

total	1,553,000
men	851,000
women	702,000
persons 16-19 years	73,000
white	1,475,000
black	NA

Full-time/part-time labor force, 1994

full-time labor force	1,296,000
working part-time for ecomonic reasons	20,000
part-time labor force	347,000

Unemployment rate, 1994

total	5.4%
men	5.8%
women	5.0%
persons 16-19 years	19.3%
white	5.2%
black	NA%

*Unemployed by reason for unemployment
(as a percent of total unemployment), 1994*

job losers or completed temp jobs	48.6%
job leavers	9.6%
reentrants	35.9%
new entrants	5.8%

Civilian labor force, by occupation, 1994

executive/administrative/ managerial	245,000
professional/specialty	231,000
technicians & related support	42,000
sales	216,000
adminstrative support/clerical	230,000
service occupations	201,000
precision production/craft/repair	170,000
machine operators/assemblers	92,000
transportation/material moving	62,000
handlers/helpers/laborers	77,000
farming/forestry/fishing	72,000

Civilian labor force, by industry, 1994

construction	71,000
manufacturing	249,000
transportation/communication	77,000
wholesale/retail trade	347,000
finance/real estate/insurance	80,000
services	321,000
government	247,000
agriculture	62,000

Average annual pay, 1994 (prelim.) $24,780
change in average annual pay,
    1993-1994 ..... 2.9%

*Hours and earnings of production workers
on manufacturing payrolls, 1994*

average weekly hours	40.3
average hourly earnings	$12.31
average weekly earnings	$496.09

Labor union membership, 1994 275,300

Household income (in constant 1993 dollars)
median household income, 1992 ..... $32,883
median household income, 1993 ..... $33,138

Poverty
persons below poverty level, 1992 ..... 11.4%
persons below poverty level, 1993 ..... 11.8%

Personal income ($per capita)
1994
    in current dollars 20,419
    in constant (1987) dollars 15,792
1995 (projected)
    in constant (1982) dollars 13,091
2000 (projected)
    in constant (1982) dollars 13,908

Federal income tax returns, 1993
returns filed 1,357,284
adjusted gross income ($1000) 41,830,525
total income tax paid ($1000) 5,584,004

ECONOMY, BUSINESS, INDUSTRY & AGRICULTURE

Fortune 500 companies, 1994 0

Business incorporations, 1994
total 10,015
change, 1993-94 . . . . 1.4%

Business failures, 1994
total 1,025
rate per 10,000 concerns 87
change, 1993-94 . . . . 5.8%

Business firm ownership
Hispanic owned firms, 1987 1,598
black owned firms, 1987 848
women owned firms, 1987 58,900
foreign owned firms, 1982 176

Gross state product, 1991 ($mil)
total $58,799
  agriculture services, forestry, fisheries . . . 2,104
  mining 83
  construction 2,473
  manufacturing—durable goods 7,763
  manufacturing—nondurable goods 3,186
  transportation, communication &
    public utilities 5,328
  wholesale trade 4,382
  retail trade 5,692
  finance/real estate/insurance 10,138
  services 10,305
  federal, state & local government 7,344

Establishments, by major industry group, 1992
total 85,377
  agriculture 1,779
  mining 151
  construction 8,967
  manufacturing 6,950
  transportation 3,811
  wholesale trade 6,388
  retail trade 20,076
  finance/real estate/insurance 7,409
  service industries 28,693
  unclassified 1,153

Payroll, by major industry group, 1992
total ($1,000) $23,359,032
  agriculture 180,668

  mining 64,585
  construction 1,406,427
  manufacturing 5,834,269
  transportation 1,976,751
  wholesale trade 2,306,334
  retail trade 3,339,071
  finance/real estate/insurance 1,850,498
  service industries 6,386,603
  unclassified 13,826

Agriculture
number of farms, 1994 38,000
farm acreage, 1994 18,000,000
acres per farm, 1994 467
value of farms, 1994 ($mil) 12,956
farm income, 1993 ($mil)
  gross farm income 3,389
  net farm income 908
  debt/asset ratio 15.1%
farm marketings, 1993 ($mil)
  total $2,476
    crops 1,737
    livestock 739
  government payments 93
farm marketings in order of marketing receipts, 1993
    1) Cattle
    2) Greenhouse
    3) Dairy products
    4) Wheat

Federal economic activity
($mil, except per capita)
expenditures, 1994
  total $13,057
  per capita $4,231
  defense $643
  non-defense $12,415
defense department, 1994
  contract awards ($mil) $131
  payroll ($mil) $496
  civilian employees (x1,000) 3.0
  military personnel (x1,000) 1.0

Fishing, 1992
catch (millions of pounds) 257
value ($mil) 76

Mining, 1994 ($mil)
total non-fuel mineral production $253

Oregon 8

principal non-fuel minerals in order of value, 1994

    1) Stone
    2) Sand and gravel
    3) Cement

Construction, 1994 ($mil)
total contracts (including
    non-building) $4,137
        residential 2,114
        non-residential 962

Manufacturing, 1992
total establishments 6,865
employees, total (x1,000) 213
payroll ($mil) 6,076
production workers (x1,000) 144
value added ($mil) 14,444
value of shipments ($mil) 32,215

Finance
commercial banks, 1994
    number 45
        assets ($bil) 27.4
        deposits ($bil) 21.4
    closed or assisted 0
        deposits ($bil) ....NA
savings and loan associations, 1991
    non-current real estate loans 2.49%
    net income after taxes ($mil) .... -51
    return on assets ....-1.26%

Retail trade, 1992
establishments (x1,000) 19.6
sales ($mil) 24,170
annual payroll ($mil) 2,872
paid employees (x1,000) 227

Wholesale trade, 1992
establishments 6,455
sales ($bil) 42.4
annual payroll ($mil) 2,021
paid employees (x1,000) 72.1

Service industries, 1992
establishments (x1,000) (non-exempt firms) 23.3
receipts ($mil) (non-exempt firms) 10,663
annual payroll ($mil) 3,963
paid employees (x1,000) (non-exempt firms) . 195

COMMUNICATION, ENERGY & TRANSPORTATION

Communication
daily newspapers, 1993 19
broadcast stations, 1990
    radio: commercial, educational 178
    television: commercial, noncommercial 24
cable TV households, 1988 572,000

Energy
consumption estimates, 1992
total (trillion Btu) 942
per capita (million Btu) 317.1
by source of production (trillion Btu)
    coal 41
    natural gas 127
    petroleum 369
    nuclear electric power 49
    hydroelectric power 388
by end-use sector (trillion Btu)
    residential 194
    commercial 162
    industrial 284
    transportation 302
electrical energy
    production, 1993 (billion kWh) 40.7
    net summer capability, 1993 (million kW) . 10.1
gas utilities, 1993
    customers ....NA
    sales (trillion Btu) ....NA
    revenues ($mil) ....NA
nuclear plants, 1993 0

Transportation, 1994
public road & street mileage
total 84,029
    urban 10,148
    rural 73,881
    interstate 727
vehicle miles of travel (mil) 29,453
total motor vehicle registrations 2,752,569
    automobiles 1,530,070
licensed drivers 2,542,681
    per 1,000 driving age population 1,064
deaths from motor vehicle
    accidents 490

Pennsylvania 1

STATE SUMMARY

Capital City . . . . Harrisburg

Governor . . . . Tom Ridge

Address . . . . STATE CAPITOL
HARRISBURG, PA 17120
717 787-2500

Admitted as a state 1787

Area (square miles) 46,058

Population, 1980 11,863,895

Population, 1990 11,881,643

Population, 1994 (est.) 12,052,000

Persons per square mile, 1994 . . . . 268.9

Largest city . . . . Philadelphia
population, 1990 1,586,000

Personal income per capita, 1994
(in current dollars) $22,324

Gross state product ($mil), 1991 254,528

Leading industries, 1992 (by payroll)
SERVICE INDUSTRIES
MANUFACTURING
RETAIL TRADE

Leading agricultural commodities, 1993
DAIRY PRODUCTS
CATTLE
GREENHOUSE
MUSHROOMS

GEOGRAPHY & ENVIRONMENT

Area (square miles)
total 46,058
land 44,820
water (includes territorial water) 1,239

Federally owned land, 1991 . . . . 2.1%

Highest point
name . . . . Mt. Davis
elevation (feet) 3,213

Lowest point
name . . . . Delaware River
elevation (feet) .sea level

General coastline (miles) 0

Tidal shoreline (miles) 83

Capital city . . . . Harrisburg
population, 1990 52,400

Largest city . . . . Philadelphia
population, 1990 1,586,000

Number of cities with over 100,000 population
1980 4

Number of cities with over 100,000 population
1990 4

State parks and Recreation areas, 1991
area (acres) 277,000
number of visitors 36,311,000
revenues $7,150,000

National forest land, 1992 (acres) 744,000

National park acreage, 1984 40,900

DEMOGRAPHICS & CHARACTERISTICS OF THE POPULATION

Population
1970 11,800,766
1980 11,863,895
1990 11,881,643
1994 (est.) 12,052,000
2000 (revised projection) 12,296,000
2010 (revised projection) 12,438,000

Metropolitan area population
1970 10,102,000
1980 10,038,000
1992 10,170,000

Non-metropolitan area population
1970 1,698,000
1980 1,826,000
1992 1,825,000

Change in population, 1980-90
number 17,748
percent 0.15%

Persons per square mile, 1994 . . . . 268.9

Age distribution, 1980
under 5 years 6.3%
5 to 17 years 20.0%
65 and over 12.9%

Age distribution, 1990
under 5 years 6.7%
5 to 17 years 16.8%
65 and over 15.3%

Pennsylvania 2

Age distribution, 2000 (projected)
under 5 years 5.4%
5 to 17 years 17.1%
65 and over 15.8%

Persons by age, 1990
under 5 years 797,058
5 to 17 years 1,997,752
65 and over 1,829,106

Median age, 1990 .... *35.00*

Race, 1990
White 10,520,201
Black 1,089,795
American Indian 14,210
Chinese 29,562
Filipino 12,160
Japanese 6,613
Asian Indian 28,396
Korean 26,787
Vietnamese 15,887
all other 137,509

Race, 2010 (projected)
White 10,792,000
Black 1,318,000

Persons of Hispanic origin, 1990
total 232,262
Mexican 24,220
Puerto Rican 148,988
Cuban 7,485
Other Hispanic 51,569

Persons by sex, 1990
male 5,694,265
female 6,187,378

Marital status, 1990
males
15 years & older 4,494,327
single 1,376,014
married 2,707,088
separated 99,588
widowed 147,096
divorced 264,129
females
15 years & older 5,046,796
single 1,232,919
married 2,727,635
separated 134,770

widowed 716,548
divorced 369,694

Households & families, 1990
households 4,495,966
persons per household 2.57
families 3,155,989
married couples 2,502,072
female householder, no husband
present 507,008
one person households 1,150,694
households, 1994 4,551,000
persons per household, 1994 .... 2.57

Nativity, 1990
number of persons born in state 9,527,402
percent of total residents 80.2%

Immigration & naturalization, 1993
immigrants admitted 16,964
persons naturalized 7,236
refugees granted resident status 3,748

VITAL STATISTICS & HEALTH

Births
1992 165,206
with low birth weight 7.2%
to teenage mothers 10.5%
to unmarried mothers 31.6%
1993 159,189
1994 157,060

Abortions, 1992
total 50,000
rate (per 1,000 women age 15-44) 18.6
rate per 1,000 live births 302

Adoptions, 1986
total 4,105
related 50.4%

Deaths
1992 123,325
1993 126,977
1994 128,164

Infant deaths
1992 1,428
1993 1,381
1994 1,198

Pennsylvania 3

Average lifetime, 1979-1981
both sexes .... 73.58 years
  men .... 69.90 years
  women .... 77.16 years

Marriages
1992 80,424
1993 76,679
1994 75,512

Divorces
1992 39,864
1993 39,839
1994 40,040

Physicians, 1993
total 30,640
rate (per 1,000 persons) 2.54

Dentists, 1992
total 8,097
rate (per 1,000 persons) 0.67

Hospitals, 1993
number 233
beds (x 1,000) 53.4
average daily census (x 1,000) 38.7
occupancy rate 72.6%
personnel (x 1,000) 230.3
average cost per day to hospital $861
average cost per stay to hospital $6,564

EDUCATION

Educational attainment of all persons 25 years and older, 1990
less than 9th grade 741,167
high school graduates 3,035,080
bachelor's degree 890,660
graduate or professional degree 522,086

Public school enrollment, Fall, 1993
total 1,744,082
  Kindergarten through grade 8 1,233,113
  grades 9 through 12 510,969

Public School Teachers
total, 1994 101,301
  elementary 45,974
  secondary 43,358
salaries, 1994
  beginning $28,231
  average $42,411

State receipts & expenditures for public schools, 1993
receipts ($mil) 15,728
expenditures
  total ($mil) 13,148
  per capita $1,096
  per pupil $7,748

Graduating high school seniors, public high schools, 1995 (est) 107,230

SAT scores, 1994
verbal 417
math 462

Institutions of higher education, 1995
total 218
  public 65
  private 153

Enrollment in institutions of higher education, Fall, 1993
total 621,228
full-time men 190,522
full-time women 198,637
part-time men 92,270
part-time women 139,799

Minority enrollment in institutions of higher education, Fall, 1993
Black, non-Hispanic 46,315
Hispanic 9,671
Asian/Pacific Islander 18,335

Earned degrees conferred, 1993
Bachelor's 65,073
First professional 3,774
Master's 17,649
Doctor's 2,267

SOCIAL INSURANCE & WELFARE PROGRAMS

Social Security beneficiaries & benefits, 1993
beneficiaries
total 2,314,000
  retired and dependents 1,690,000
  survivors 410,000
  disabled & dependents 214,000
annual benefit payments ($mil)
total $17,420
  retired and dependents 12,199
  survivors 3,716
  disabled & dependents 1,504

Pennsylvania 4

Medicare, 1993
enrollment (x1,000) 2,039
payments ($mil) 9,271

Medicaid, 1993
recipients (x1,000) 1,223
payments ($mil) 3,886

Federal public aid, 1993
recipients as a percent of population 7.0%
Aid to Families with Dependent Children
    recipients (x1,000) 614
average monthly payment $371
Supplemental Security Income
    total recipients (x1,000) 236

Food Stamp Program
    participants, 1994 (x1,000) 1,208

HOUSING & CONSTRUCTION

Total housing units, 1990 4,938,140
    year round housing units 4,793,569
    vacant 442,174

*New privately owned housing units
    authorized, 1994*
number (x1,000) 40.2
value ($mil) 3,728

*New privately owned housing units
    started, 1994 (x1,000)* 36.6

Existing home sales, 1994 (x1,000) 216.4

GOVERNMENT & ELECTIONS

State officials, 1996
    Governor (name/party/term expires)
            TOM RIDGE
        Republican - 1999
Lt. Governor .... Mark Singel
Sec. of State .... Brenda Mitchell
Atty. General .... Ernie Preate
Chf. Justice .... Robert N.C. Nix, Jr.

Governorship
minimum age 30
length of term .... 4 years
number of consecutive
    terms permitted 2
who succeeds .... Lt. Governor

State legislature
name .... General Assembly
    upper chamber
        name .... Senate
        number of members 50
        length of term .... 4 years
        party in majority, 1996 .... Republican
    lower chamber
        name .... House of Representatives
        number of members 203
        length of term .... 2 years
        party in majority, 1996 .... Democratic

State employees October, 1992
total 173,030
October payroll ($1,000) 400,895

Local governments, 1992
total 5,397
    county 66
    municipal 1,022
    township 1,548
    school districts 516
    special districts 2,244

Voting, November, 1994
voting age population 9,004,000
    registered 58.9%
    voted 42.7%

Vote for president
1988
    Bush 2,291,297
    Dukakis 2,183,928
1992
    Clinton 2,225,905
    Bush 1,779,627
    Perot 896,734

Federal representation, 1996 (104th Congress)
Senators (name/party/term expires)

            RICK SANTORUM
        Republican - 2001
            ARLEN SPECTER
        Republican - 1999

Representatives, total 21
    Democrats 11
    Republicans 10
    other 0

Pennsylvania 5

Women holding public office
U.S. Congress, 1995 0
statewide elected office, 1995 2
state legislature, 1995 30

Black elected officials, 1993
total 158
  US and state legislatures 18
  city/county/regional offices 55
  judicial/law enforcement 52
  education/school boards 33

Hispanic public officials, 1994
total 8
  state executives & legislators 1
  city/county/regional offices 3
  judicial/law enforcement 1
  education/school boards 3

GOVERNMENTAL FINANCE

State & local government revenues, (selected items), 1991-92 ($per capita)
total $4,526.64
  total general revenues 3,815.81
    from federal government 735.63
    from own sources 3,080.18
    from taxes 2,196.18
      from property taxes 610.36
      from all other taxes 1,299.23
    from charges & misc. 884.01

State & local government expenditures, (selected items), 1991-92 ($per capita)
total $4,424.66
  total direct general expenditures 3,773.17
    education 1,329.90
    libraries 9.18
    public welfare 772.10
    health & hospitals 220.69
    highways 223.08
    police protection 102.97
    fire protection 28.07
    correction 87.12
    housing & comm. development 58.77
    natural resources & parks 65.62
    interest on general debt 281.90

State & local debt, 1992 ($per capita) 3,964.01

Federal aid grants to state & local government, 1994 ($per capita total & selected items)
per capita total 805.26
  compensatory education 25.52
  waste treatment facilities 5.55
  medicaid 331.75
  housing assistance 59.05
  job training 11.14
  highway trust fund 62.84

CRIME, LAW ENFORCEMENT & COURTS

Crime, 1994 (all rates per 100,000 persons)
total crimes 394,326
overall crime rate 3,271.9
  property crimes 342,901
    burglaries 66,468
    larcenies 222,280
    motor vehicle thefts 54,153
  property crime rate 2,845.2
  violent crimes 51,425
    murders 712
    forcible rapes 3,145
    robberies 22,497
    aggravated assaults 25,071
  violent crime rate 426.7

Number of police agencies, 1994 687

Arrests, 1994
total 347,930
  persons under 18 years of age 87,748

Prisoners under state & federal jurisdiction, 1994
total 28,302
percent change, 1993-94 .... 8.6%
  sentenced to more than one year
  total 28,301
  rate per 100,000 residents 235

Persons under sentence of death, 4/20/95 186

State's highest court
name .... Supreme Court
number of members 7
length of term .... 10 years
intermediate appeals court? .... yes

311

Pennsylvania 6

LABOR & INCOME

Civilian labor force, 1994
total	5,829,000
men	3,189,000
women	2,639,000
persons 16-19 years	327,000
white	5,278,000
black	441,000

Civilian labor force as a percent of civilian non-institutional population, 1994
total	62.8%
men	71.7%
women	54.6%
persons 16-19 years	54.3%
white	63.4%
black	56.6%

Employment, 1994
total	5,468,000
men	2,982,000
women	2,486,000
persons 16-19 years	275,000
white	4,984,000
black	385,000

Full-time/part-time labor force, 1994
full-time labor force	4,653,000
working part-time for ecomonic reasons	57,000
part-time labor force	1,175,000

Unemployment rate, 1994
total	6.2%
men	6.5%
women	5.8%
persons 16-19 years	15.8%
white	5.6%
black	12.8%

Unemployed by reason for unemployment (as a percent of total unemployment), 1994
job losers or completed temp jobs	50.1%
job leavers	8.2%
reentrants	34.9%
new entrants	6.7%

Civilian labor force, by occupation, 1994
executive/administrative/managerial	655,000
professional/specialty	825,000
technicians & related support	186,000
sales	680,000
adminstrative support/clerical	875,000
service occupations	797,000
precision production/craft/repair	667,000
machine operators/assemblers	421,000
transportation/material moving	264,000
handlers/helpers/laborers	306,000
farming/forestry/fishing	125,000

Civilian labor force, by industry, 1994
construction	266,000
manufacturing	1,015,000
transportation/communication	319,000
wholesale/retail trade	1,164,000
finance/real estate/insurance	317,000
services	1,505,000
government	653,000
agriculture	115,00

Average annual pay, 1994 (prelim.) $26,950
change in average annual pay, 1993-1994 ...... 2.6%

Hours and earnings of production workers on manufacturing payrolls, 1994
average weekly hours	41.6
average hourly earnings	$12.49
average weekly earnings	$519.58

Labor union membership, 1994 962,300

Household income (in constant 1993 dollars)
median household income, 1992	$30,777
median household income, 1993	$30,995

Poverty
persons below poverty level, 1992	11.9%
persons below poverty level, 1993	13.2%

Personal income ($per capita)
1994
in current dollars	22,324
in constant (1987) dollars	17,265

1995 (projected)
in constant (1982) dollars	14,287

2000 (projected)
in constant (1982) dollars	15,173

Federal income tax returns, 1993
returns filed	5,378,327
adjusted gross income ($1000)	171,311,334
total income tax paid ($1000)	24,176,133

ECONOMY, BUSINESS, INDUSTRY & AGRICULTURE

Fortune 500 companies, 1994 33

Business incorporations, 1994
total 17,394
change, 1993-94 .... 3.0%

Business failures, 1994
total 2,743
rate per 10,000 concerns 73
change, 1993-94 .... -12.4%

Business firm ownership
Hispanic owned firms, 1987 2,650
black owned firms, 1987 11,728
women owned firms, 1987 167,400
foreign owned firms, 1982 402

Gross state product, 1991 ($mil)
total $254,528
  agriculture services, forestry, fisheries ... 2,592
  mining 1,598
  construction 10,184
  manufacturing—durable goods 27,470
  manufacturing—nondurable goods 24,355
  transportation, communication &
    public utilities 24,275
  wholesale trade 15,615
  retail trade 23,077
  finance/real estate/insurance 46,888
  services 52,542
  federal, state & local government 25,933

Establishments, by major industry group, 1992
total 281,343
  agriculture 3,884
  mining 1,172
  construction 26,779
  manufacturing 18,311
  transportation 10,583
  wholesale trade 20,246
  retail trade 73,224
  finance/real estate/insurance 23,600
  service industries 101,000
  unclassified 2,544

Payroll, by major industry group, 1992
total ($1,000) $108,801,892
  agriculture 399,269

  mining 863,312
  construction 5,799,021
  manufacturing 28,977,177
  transportation 8,175,257
  wholesale trade 8,154,184
  retail trade 11,507,612
  finance/real estate/insurance 9,289,898
  service industries 35,570,989
  unclassified 65,173

Agriculture
number of farms, 1994 51,000
farm acreage, 1994 8,000,000
acres per farm, 1994 153
value of farms, 1994 ($mil) 15,088
farm income, 1993 ($mil)
  gross farm income 4,039
  net farm income 816
  debt/asset ratio 13.5%
farm marketings, 1993 ($mil)
total $3,712
  crops 1,091
  livestock 2,622
government payments 45
farm marketings in order of marketing receipts, 1993
  1) Dairy products
  2) Cattle
  3) Greenhouse
  4) Mushrooms

Federal economic activity ($mil, except per capita)
expenditures, 1994
  total $61,025
  per capita $5,064
  defense $5,348
  non-defense $55,677
defense department, 1994
  contract awards ($mil) $2,760
  payroll ($mil) $2,646
  civilian employees (x1,000) 40.1
  military personnel (x1,000) 5.3

Fishing, 1992
catch (millions of pounds) .... NA
value ($mil) .... NA

Mining, 1994 ($mil)
total non-fuel mineral production $964

Pennsylvania 8

principal non-fuel minerals in order of value, 1994

1) Stone
2) Cement
3) Lime

Construction, 1994 ($mil)
total contracts (including
  non-building) $9,620
    residential 3,746
    non-residential 3,828

Manufacturing, 1992
total establishments 18,102
employees, total (x1,000) 952
payroll ($mil) 29,230
production workers (x1,000) 609
value added ($mil) 69,733
value of shipments ($mil) 139,251

Finance
commercial banks, 1994
  number 261
    assets ($bil) 190.4
    deposits ($bil) 140.1
  closed or assisted 0
    deposits ($bil) .... NA
savings and loan associations, 1991
  non-current real estate loans 3.80%
  net income after taxes ($mil) .... -170
  return on assets .... -0.51%

Retail trade, 1992
establishments (x1,000) 71.7
sales ($mil) 87,788
annual payroll ($mil) 10,043
paid employees (x1,000) 862

Wholesale trade, 1992
establishments 20,230
sales ($bil) 126.4
annual payroll ($mil) 7,485
paid employees (x1,000) 254.4

Service industries, 1992
establishments (x1,000) (non-exempt firms) 77.8
receipts ($mil) (non-exempt firms) 49,383
annual payroll ($mil) 18,741
paid employees (x1,000) (non-exempt firms) . 797

COMMUNICATION, ENERGY & TRANSPORTATION

Communication
daily newspapers, 1993 89
broadcast stations, 1990
  radio: commercial, educational 420
  television: commercial, noncommercial 42
cable TV households, 1988 2,587,000

Energy
consumption estimates, 1992
total (trillion Btu) 3,597
per capita (million Btu) 299.9
by source of production (trillion Btu)
  coal 1,408
  natural gas 707
  petroleum 1,268
  nuclear electric power 642
  hydroelectric power 13
by end-use sector (trillion Btu)
  residential 838
  commercial 542
  industrial 1,357
  transportation 860
electrical energy
  production, 1993 (billion kWh) 166.2
  net summer capability, 1993 (million kW) . 33.4
gas utilities, 1993
  customers 2,572,000
  sales (trillion Btu) 455
  revenues ($mil) 2,695
nuclear plants, 1993 9

Transportation, 1994
public road & street mileage
total 118,445
  urban 33,233
  rural 85,212
  interstate 1,589
vehicle miles of travel (mil) 92,347
total motor vehicle registrations 8,482,387
  automobiles 6,026,443
licensed drivers 8,115,074
  per 1,000 driving age population 857
deaths from motor vehicle
  accidents 1,441

Rhode Island 1

STATE SUMMARY

Capital City .... Providence

Governor .... Lincoln Almond

Address .... STATE HOUSE
PROVIDENCE, RI 02903
401 277-2080

Admitted as a state 1790

Area (square miles) 1,545

Population, 1980 947,154

Population, 1990 1,003,464

Population, 1994 (est.) 997,000

Persons per square mile, 1994 .... 953.8

Largest city .... Providence
population, 1990 161,000

Personal income per capita, 1994
(in current dollars) $22,251

Gross state product ($mil), 1991 20,657

Leading industries, 1992 (by payroll)
SERVICE INDUSTRIES
MANUFACTURING
RETAIL TRADE

Leading agricultural commodities, 1993
GREENHOUSE
DAIRY PRODUCTS
EGGS
POTATOES

GEOGRAPHY & ENVIRONMENT

Area (square miles)
total 1,545
 land 1,045
 water (includes territorial water) 500

Federally owned land, 1991 .... 0.3%

Highest point
name .... Jerimoth Hill
elevation (feet) 812

Lowest point
name .... Atlantic Ocean
elevation (feet) .... sea level

General coastline (miles) 40

Tidal shoreline (miles) 384

Capital city .... Providence
population, 1990 161,000

Largest city .... Providence
population, 1990 161,000

Number of cities with over 100,000 population
1980 1

Number of cities with over 100,000 population
1990 1

State parks and Recreation areas, 1991
area (acres) 9,000
number of visitors 5,075,000
revenues $2,854,000

National forest land, 1992 (acres) 0

National park acreage, 1984 .... NA

DEMOGRAPHICS & CHARACTERISTICS OF THE POPULATION

Population
1970 949,723
1980 947,154
1990 1,003,464
1994 (est.) 997,000
2000 (revised projection) 998,000
2010 (revised projection) 1,034,000

Metropolitan area population
1970 868,000
1980 878,000
1992 937,000

Non-metropolitan area population
1970 82,000
1980 69,000
1992 64,000

Change in population, 1980-90
number 56,310
percent 5.95%

Persons per square mile, 1994 .... 953.8

Age distribution, 1980
under 5 years 6.0%
5 to 17 years 19.7%
65 and over 13.4%

Age distribution, 1990
under 5 years 6.7%
5 to 17 years 15.8%
65 and over 15.0%

Rhode Island 2

Age distribution, 2000 (projected)
under 5 years	5.6%
5 to 17 years	16.8%
65 and over	14.4%

Persons by age, 1990
under 5 years	66,969
5 to 17 years	158,721
65 and over	150,547

Median age, 1990 .... *34.00*

Race, 1990
White	917,375
Black	38,861
American Indian	3,987
Chinese	3,170
Filipino	1,836
Japanese	750
Asian Indian	1,975
Korean	1,294
Vietnamese	772
all other	33,360

Race, 2010 (projected)
White	933,000
Black	51,000

Persons of Hispanic origin, 1990
total	45,752
Mexican	2,437
Puerto Rican	13,016
Cuban	840
Other Hispanic	29,459

Persons by sex, 1990
male	481,496
female	521,968

Marital status, 1990
males
15 years & older	383,935
single	127,464
married	219,614
separated	5,483
widowed	11,712
divorced	25,145
females
15 years & older	429,423
single	113,671
married	220,490
separated	8,668
widowed	57,244
divorced	38,018

Households & families, 1990
households	377,977
persons per household	2.55
families	258,886
married couples	202,283
female householder, no husband present	44,342
one person households	99,111
households, 1994	374,000
persons per household, 1994	2.57

Nativity, 1990
number of persons born in state	636,222
percent of total residents	63.4%

Immigration & naturalization, 1993
immigrants admitted	3,168
persons naturalized	1,720
refugees granted resident status	385

VITAL STATISTICS & HEALTH

Births
1992	14,789
with low birth weight	6.3%
to teenage mothers	9.8%
to unmarried mothers	29.6%
1993	14,275
1994	13,440

Abortions, 1992
total	7,000
rate (per 1,000 women age 15-44)	30.0
rate per 1,000 live births	461

Adoptions, 1986
total	493
related	63.5%

Deaths
1992	9,444
1993	9,709
1994	9,333

Infant deaths
1992	117
1993	121
1994	81

Rhode Island 3

Average lifetime, 1979-1981
both sexes .... 74.76 years
   men .... 70.96 years
   women .... 78.33 years

Marriages
1992 7,287
1993 7,123
1994 6,976

Divorces
1992 3,591
1993 3,361
1994 3,231

Physicians, 1993
total 2,695
rate (per 1,000 persons) 2.71

Dentists, 1992
total 556
rate (per 1,000 persons) 0.56

Hospitals, 1993
number 11
beds (x 1,000) 3.0
average daily census (x 1,000) 2.2
occupancy rate 73.3%
personnel (x 1,000) 14.7
average cost per day to hospital $885
average cost per stay to hospital $5,672

EDUCATION

*Educational attainment of all persons
25 years and older, 1990*
less than 9th grade 72,842
high school graduates 194,064
bachelor's degree 88,634
graduate or professional degree 51,526

Public school enrollment, Fall, 1993
total 145,676
   Kindergarten through grade 8 107,047
   grades 9 through 12 38,629

Public School Teachers
total, 1994 9,823
   elementary 4,404
   secondary 4,103
salaries, 1994
   beginning $23,365
   average $39,261

*State receipts & expenditures for public
schools, 1993*
receipts ($mil) 904
expenditures
   total ($mil) 904
   per capita $903
   per pupil $6,649

*Graduating high school seniors,
public high schools, 1995 (est) 7,770*

SAT scores, 1994
verbal 420
math 462

Institutions of higher education, 1995
total 13
   public 3
   private 10

*Enrollment in institutions of higher
education, Fall, 1993*
total 77,407
full-time men 23,936
full-time women 24,740
part-time men 11,007
part-time women 17,724

*Minority enrollment in institutions of higher
education, Fall, 1993*
Black, non-Hispanic 3,057
Hispanic 2,441
Asian/Pacific Islander 2,492

Earned degrees conferred, 1993
Bachelor's 9,341
First professional 81
Master's 2,070
Doctor's 269

SOCIAL INSURANCE &
WELFARE PROGRAMS

Social Security beneficiaries & benefits, 1993
beneficiaries
total 187,000
   retired and dependents 139,000
   survivors 27,000
   disabled & dependents 21,000
annual benefit payments ($mil)
total $1,370
   retired and dependents 1,002
   survivors 230
   disabled & dependents 137

Rhode Island 4

Medicare, 1993
enrollment (x1,000) 165
payments ($mil) 628

Medicaid, 1993
recipients (x1,000) 191
payments ($mil) 710

Federal public aid, 1993
recipients as a percent of population 8.3%
Aid to Families with Dependent Children
    recipients (x1,000) 63
average monthly payment $506
Supplemental Security Income
    total recipients (x1,000) 21

Food Stamp Program
    participants, 1994 (x1,000) 93

HOUSING & CONSTRUCTION

Total housing units, 1990 414,572
    year round housing units 402,519
    vacant 36,595

*New privately owned housing units
    authorized, 1994*
number (x1,000) 2.5
value ($mil) 233

*New privately owned housing units
    started, 1994 (x1,000)* 2.6

Existing home sales, 1994 (x1,000) 11.6

GOVERNMENT & ELECTIONS

State officials, 1996
Governor (name/party/term expires)
        LINCOLN ALMOND
        Republican - 1999
Lt. Governor .... Robert Weygand
Sec. of State .... Barbara Leonard
Atty. General .... Jeffrey Pine
Chf. Justice .... J. Weisberger (actg)

Governorship
minimum age .... not specified
length of term .... 4 years
number of consecutive
    terms permitted .... not specified
who succeeds .... Lt. Governor

State legislature
name .... General Assembly
    upper chamber
        name .... Senate
        number of members 50
        length of term .... 2 years
        party in majority, 1996 .... Democratic
    lower chamber
        name .... House of Representatives
        number of members 100
        length of term .... 2 years
        party in majority, 1996 .... Democratic

State employees October, 1992
total 24,225
October payroll ($1,000) 54,871

Local governments, 1992
total 128
    county 0
    municipal 8
    township 31
    school districts 4
    special districts 84

Voting, November, 1994
voting age population 729,000
    registered 64.2%
    voted 50.6%

Vote for president
1988
    Bush 169,730
    Dukakis 216,668
1992
    Clinton 198,877
    Bush 121,864
    Perot 94,717

Federal representation, 1996 (104th Congress)
Senators (name/party/term expires)

        JOHN H. CHAFEE
        Republican - 2001
        CLAIBORNE PELL
        Democrat - 1997

Representatives, total 2
    Democrats 2
    Republicans 0
    other 0

Rhode Island 5

Women holding public office
U.S. Congress, 1995 0
statewide elected office, 1995 1
state legislature, 1995 36

Black elected officials, 1993
total 12
  US and state legislatures 9
  city/county/regional offices 3
  judicial/law enforcement 0
  education/school boards 0

Hispanic public officials, 1994
total 1
  state executives & legislators 1
  city/county/regional offices 0
  judicial/law enforcement 0
  education/school boards 0

GOVERNMENTAL FINANCE

State & local government revenues, (selected items), 1991-92 ($per capita)
total $4,822.49
  total general revenues 3,969.21
    from federal government 1,008.67
    from own sources 2,960.54
    from taxes 2,235.93
      from property taxes 940.42
      from all other taxes 1,190.31
      from charges & misc. 724.62

State & local government expenditures, (selected items), 1991-92 ($per capita)
total $5,125.39
  total direct general expenditures 4,379.90
  education 1,256.00
  libraries 17.89
  public welfare 749.06
  health & hospitals 251.89
  highways 226.09
  police protection 128.71
  fire protection 104.51
  correction 100.62
  housing & comm. development 97.35
  natural resources & parks 138.47
  interest on general debt 343.07

State & local debt, 1992 ($per capita) 5,907.70

Federal aid grants to state & local government, 1994 ($per capita total & selected items)
per capita total 1,103.27
  compensatory education 22.14
  waste treatment facilities 6.71
  medicaid 446.38
  housing assistance 128.11
  job training 14.86
  highway trust fund 136.90

CRIME, LAW ENFORCEMENT & COURTS

Crime, 1994 (all rates per 100,000 persons)
total crimes 41,067
overall crime rate 4,119.1
  property crimes 37,323
    burglaries 9,101
    larcenies 23,039
    motor vehicle thefts 5,183
  property crime rate 3,743.5
  violent crimes 3,744
    murders 41
    forcible rapes 273
    robberies 870
    aggravated assaults 2,560
  violent crime rate 375.5

Number of police agencies, 1994 44

Arrests, 1994
total 41,135
  persons under 18 years of age 9,664

Prisoners under state & federal jurisdiction, 1994
total 2,919
percent change, 1993-94 ....4.9%
  sentenced to more than one year
    total 1,853
    rate per 100,000 residents 186

Persons under sentence of death, 4/20/95 ....NA

State's highest court
name .... Supreme Court
number of members 5
length of term ....life
intermediate appeals court? ....no

Rhode Island 6

LABOR & INCOME

Civilian labor force, 1994
total 505,000
men 262,000
women 244,000
persons 16-19 years 29,000
white 472,000
black 18,000

Civilian labor force as a percent of
civilian non-institutional population, 1994
total 65.9%
men 73.5%
women 59.3%
persons 16-19 years 56.9%
white 65.9%
black 66.1%

Employment, 1994
total 470,000
men 242,000
women 228,000
persons 16-19 years 23,000
white 442,000
black 15,000

Full-time/part-time labor force, 1994
full-time labor force 398,000
working part-time for
ecomonic reasons 6,000
part-time labor force 107,000

Unemployment rate, 1994
total 7.1%
men 7.6%
women 6.5%
persons 16-19 years 18.6%
white 6.3%
black 18.0%

Unemployed by reason for unemployment
(as a percent of total unemployment), 1994
job losers or completed temp jobs 59.0%
job leavers 7.6%
reentrants 26.8%
new entrants 6.6%

Civilian labor force, by occupation, 1994
executive/administrative/
managerial 65,000
professional/specialty 80,000
technicians & related support 14,000

sales 54,000
adminstrative support/clerical 70,000
service occupations 76,000
precision production/craft/repair .,...... 55,000
machine operators/assemblers 48,000
transportation/material moving 16,000
handlers/helpers/laborers 17,000
farming/forestry/fishing ....NA

Civilian labor force, by industry, 1994
construction 21,000
manufacturing 108,000
transportation/communication 17,000
wholesale/retail trade 96,000
finance/real estate/insurance 28,000
services 139,000
government 57,000
agriculture ....NA

Average annual pay, 1994 (prelim.) $25,454
change in average annual pay,
1993-1994 .... 2.3%

Hours and earnings of production workers
on manufacturing payrolls, 1994
average weekly hours 40.3
average hourly earnings $10.35
average weekly earnings $417.11

Labor union membership, 1994 66,700

Household income (in constant 1993 dollars)
median household income, 1992 .... $31,343
median household income, 1993 .... $33,509

Poverty
persons below poverty level, 1992 .... 12.4%
persons below poverty level, 1993 .... 11.2%

Personal income ($per capita)
1994
in current dollars 22,251
in constant (1987) dollars 17,209
1995 (projected)
in constant (1982) dollars 14,746
2000 (projected)
in constant (1982) dollars 15,555

Federal income tax returns, 1993
returns filed 446,625
adjusted gross income ($1000) 14,341,042
total income tax paid ($1000) 1,974,642

320

ECONOMY, BUSINESS, INDUSTRY & AGRICULTURE

Fortune 500 companies, 1994 3

Business incorporations, 1994
total 2,503
change, 1993-94 . . . . -7.2%

Business failures, 1994
total 212
rate per 10,000 concerns 60
change, 1993-94 . . . . -38.7%

Business firm ownership
Hispanic owned firms, 1987 426
black owned firms, 1987 489
women owned firms, 1987 14,500
foreign owned firms, 1982 64

Gross state product, 1991 ($mil)
total $20,657
  agriculture services, forestry, fisheries 192
  mining 6
  construction 615
  manufacturing—durable goods 3,168
  manufacturing—nondurable goods 1,155
  transportation, communication &
    public utilities 1,233
  wholesale trade 1,045
  retail trade 1,885
  finance/real estate/insurance 4,645
  services 4,355
  federal, state & local government 2,357

*Establishments, by major industry
group, 1992*
total 26,802
  agriculture 482
  mining 20
  construction 2,858
  manufacturing 2,680
  transportation 815
  wholesale trade 1,724
  retail trade 6,574
  finance/real estate/insurance 1,939
  service industries 9,397
  unclassified 313

Payroll, by major industry group, 1992
total ($1,000) $8,440,813
  agriculture 32,348

mining 5,339
construction 348,581
manufacturing 2,426,171
transportation 390,487
wholesale trade 551,893
retail trade 950,380
finance/real estate/insurance 827,920
service industries 2,900,182
unclassified 7,512

Agriculture
number of farms, 1994 1,000
farm acreage, 1994 500,000
acres per farm, 1994 87
value of farms, 1994 ($mil) 336
farm income, 1993 ($mil)
  gross farm income 87
  net farm income 40
  debt/asset ratio 9.2%
farm marketings, 1993 ($mil)
  total $79
    crops 67
    livestock 12
  government payments 0.5
farm marketings in order of marketing
receipts, 1993
    1) Greenhouse
    2) Eggs
    3) Dairy products
    4) Potatoes

*Federal economic activity
  ($mil, except per capita)*
expenditures, 1994
  total $5,473
  per capita $5,489
  defense $845
  non-defense $4,628
defense department, 1994
  contract awards ($mil) $422
  payroll ($mil) $436
  civilian employees (x1,000) 4.0
  military personnel (x1,000) 3.6

Fishing, 1992
catch (millions of pounds) 142
value ($mil) 86

Mining, 1994 ($mil)
total non-fuel mineral production $27

Rhode Island 8

principal non-fuel minerals in order of value, 1994
1) Sand and gravel
2) Stone
3) Sand and gravel

Construction, 1994 ($mil)
total contracts (including
non-building) $673
   residential 278
   non-residential 235

Manufacturing, 1992
total establishments 2,664
employees, total (x1,000) 88
payroll ($mil) 2,403
production workers (x1,000) 59
value added ($mil) 5,166
value of shipments ($mil) 9,578

Finance
commercial banks, 1994
  number 10
   assets ($bil) 13.5
   deposits ($bil) 10.0
   closed or assisted 0
   deposits ($bil) .... NA
savings and loan associations, 1991
  non-current real estate loans 8.00%
  net income after taxes ($mil) .... -136
  return on assets .... -5.18%

Retail trade, 1992
establishments (x1,000) 6.4
sales ($mil) 6,734
annual payroll ($mil) 839
paid employees (x1,000) 67

Wholesale trade, 1992
establishments 1,771
sales ($bil) 6.6
annual payroll ($mil) 551
paid employees (x1,000) 19.5

Service industries, 1992
establishments (x1,000) (non-exempt firms) . 7.6
receipts ($mil) (non-exempt firms) 3,664
annual payroll ($mil) 1,413
paid employees (x1,000) (non-exempt firms) .. 64

COMMUNICATION, ENERGY & TRANSPORTATION

Communication
daily newspapers, 1993 6
broadcast stations, 1990
  radio: commercial, educational 30
  television: commercial, noncommercial 4
cable TV households, 1988 211,000

Energy
consumption estimates, 1992
  total (trillion Btu) 247
  per capita (million Btu) 246.5
by source of production (trillion Btu)
  coal .... NA
  natural gas 79
  petroleum 101
  nuclear electric power 0
  hydroelectric power 10
by end-use sector (trillion Btu)
  residential 66
  commercial 45
  industrial 79
  transportation 57
electrical energy
  production, 1993 (billion kWh) 0.1
  net summer capability, 1993 (million kW) .. 0.2
gas utilities, 1993
  customers 217,000
  sales (trillion Btu) 35
  revenues ($mil) 263
nuclear plants, 1993 0

Transportation, 1994
public road & street mileage
  total 5,973
   urban 4,613
   rural 1,360
   interstate 70
vehicle miles of travel (mil) 7,095
total motor vehicle registrations 699,093
  automobiles 545,194
licensed drivers 688,399
  per 1,000 driving age population 882
deaths from motor vehicle
  accidents 63

STATE SUMMARY

Capital City .... Columbia

Governor .... David Beasley

Address ....STATE HOUSE
COLUMBIA, SC 29211
803 734-2170

Admitted as a state 1788

Area (square miles) 32,007

Population, 1980 3,121,820

Population, 1990 3,486,703

Population, 1994 (est.) 3,664,000

Persons per square mile, 1994 .... 121.7

Largest city .... Columbia
population, 1990 98,100

Personal income per capita, 1994
(in current dollars) $17,695

Gross state product ($mil), 1991 66,408

Leading industries, 1992 (by payroll)
MANUFACTURING
SERVICE INDUSTRIES
RETAIL TRADE

Leading agricultural commodities, 1993
TOBACCO
BROILERS
CATTLE
SOYBEANS

GEOGRAPHY & ENVIRONMENT

Area (square miles)
total 32,007
  land 30,111
  water (includes territorial water) 1,896

Federally owned land, 1991 .... 3.7%

Highest point
name ....Sassafras Mountain
elevation (feet) 3,560

Lowest point
name ....Atlantic Ocean
elevation (feet) ....sea level

General coastline (miles) 187

Tidal shoreline (miles) 2,876

Capital city .... Columbia
population, 1990 98,100

Largest city .... Columbia
population, 1990 98,100

Number of cities with over 100,000 population
1980 0

Number of cities with over 100,000 population
1990 0

State parks and Recreation areas, 1991
area (acres) 80,000
number of visitors 7,970,000
revenues $10,587,000

National forest land, 1992 (acres) 1,376,000

National park acreage, 1984 21,000

DEMOGRAPHICS & CHARACTERISTICS OF THE POPULATION

Population
1970 2,590,713
1980 3,121,820
1990 3,486,703
1994 (est.) 3,664,000
2000 (revised projection) 3,932,000
2010 (revised projection) 4,311,000

Metropolitan area population
1970 1,504,000
1980 1,865,000
1992 2,514,000

Non-metropolitan area population
1970 1,087,000
1980 1,256,000
1992 1,089,000

Change in population, 1980-90
number 364,883
percent 11.69%

Persons per square mile, 1994 .... 121.7

Age distribution, 1980
under 5 years 7.6%
5 to 17 years 22.6%
65 and over 9.2%

Age distribution, 1990
under 5 years 7.4%
5 to 17 years 19.0%
65 and over 11.3%

South Carolina 2

Age distribution, 2000 (projected)
under 5 years 6.3%
5 to 17 years 18.4%
65 and over 11.9%

Persons by age, 1990
under 5 years 256,337
5 to 17 years 663,870
65 and over 396,935

Median age, 1990 .... 32.00

Race, 1990
White 2,406,974
Black 1,039,884
American Indian 8,049
Chinese 3,039
Filipino 5,521
Japanese 1,885
Asian Indian 3,900
Korean 2,577
Vietnamese 1,752
all other 12,925

Race, 2010 (projected)
White 2,902,000
Black 1,344,000

Persons of Hispanic origin, 1990
total 30,551
Mexican 11,028
Puerto Rican 6,423
Cuban 1,652
Other Hispanic 11,448

Persons by sex, 1990
male 1,688,510
female 1,798,193

Marital status, 1990
males
15 years & older 1,298,504
single 386,819
married 793,839
separated 39,238
widowed 32,582
divorced 85,264
females
15 years & older 1,422,067
single 330,381
married 798,571
separated 56,261

widowed 181,673
divorced 111,442

Households & families, 1990
households 1,258,044
persons per household 2.68
families 928,206
married couples 710,089
female householder, no husband
present 176,204
one person households 281,347
households, 1994 1,337,000
persons per household, 1994 .... 2.66

Nativity, 1990
number of persons born in state 2,385,744
percent of total residents 68.4%

Immigration & naturalization, 1993
immigrants admitted 2,195
persons naturalized 675
refugees granted resident status 150

VITAL STATISTICS & HEALTH

Births
1992 56,635
with low birth weight 9.0%
to teenage mothers 16.6%
to unmarried mothers 35.5%
1993 53,997
1994 50,907

Abortions, 1992
total 12,000
rate (per 1,000 women age 15-44) 14.2
rate per 1,000 live births 229

Adoptions, 1986
total 1,569
related 59.3%

Deaths
1992 30,609
1993 31,404
1994 31,570

Infant deaths
1992 592
1993 510
1994 453

324

Average lifetime, 1979-1981
both sexes .... 71.85 years
  men .... 67.56 years
  women .... 76.12 years

Marriages
1992 53,304
1993 52,547
1994 50,872

Divorces
1992 15,920
1993 15,110
1994 15,301

Physicians, 1993
total 6,205
rate (per 1,000 persons) 1.73

Dentists, 1992
total 1,521
rate (per 1,000 persons) 0.43

Hospitals, 1993
number 68
beds (x 1,000) 11.4
average daily census (x 1,000) 7.7
occupancy rate 67.3%
personnel (x 1,000) 45.9
average cost per day to hospital $838
average cost per stay to hospital $5,955

EDUCATION

Educational attainment of all persons 25 years and older, 1990
less than 9th grade 295,167
high school graduates 639,358
bachelor's degree 243,161
graduate or professional degree 117,672

Public school enrollment, Fall, 1993
total 643,859
  Kindergarten through grade 8 467,114
  grades 9 through 12 176,745

Public School Teachers
total, 1994 38,620
  elementary 26,252
  secondary 12,368
salaries, 1994
  beginning $20,533
  average $29,414

State receipts & expenditures for public schools, 1993
receipts ($mil) 3,300
expenditures
  total ($mil) 3,055
  per capita $848
  per pupil $4,573

Graduating high school seniors, public high schools, 1995 (est) 33,900

SAT scores, 1994
verbal 395
math 443

Institutions of higher education, 1995
total 59
  public 33
  private 26

Enrollment in institutions of higher education, Fall, 1993
total 174,302
full-time men 49,955
full-time women 58,119
part-time men 24,544
part-time women 41,684

Minority enrollment in institutions of higher education, Fall, 1993
Black, non-Hispanic 36,933
Hispanic 1,297
Asian/Pacific Islander 1,990

Earned degrees conferred, 1993
Bachelor's 15,254
First professional 604
Master's 4,245
Doctor's 408

SOCIAL INSURANCE & WELFARE PROGRAMS

Social Security beneficiaries & benefits, 1993
beneficiaries
total 591,000
  retired and dependents 387,000
  survivors 107,000
  disabled & dependents 97,000
annual benefit payments ($mil)
total $3,949
  retired and dependents 2,552
  survivors 775
  disabled & dependents 623

South Carolina 4

Medicare, 1993
enrollment (x1,000) 481
payments ($mil) 1,440

Medicaid, 1993
recipients (x1,000) 470
payments ($mil) 1,249

Federal public aid, 1993
recipients as a percent of population 6.8%
Aid to Families with Dependent Children
recipients (x1,000) 142
average monthly payment $184
Supplemental Security Income
total recipients (x1,000) 104

Food Stamp Program
participants, 1994 (x1,000) 385

HOUSING & CONSTRUCTION

Total housing units, 1990 1,424,155
year round housing units 1,373,952
vacant 166,111

New privately owned housing units authorized, 1994
number (x1,000) 24.6
value ($mil) 2,019

New privately owned housing units started, 1994 (x1,000) 27.7

Existing home sales, 1994 (x1,000) 67.3

GOVERNMENT & ELECTIONS

State officials, 1996
Governor (name/party/term expires)
DAVID BEASLEY
Republican - 1999
Lt. Governor .... Bob Peeler
Sec. of State .... James Miles
Atty. General ....Charles Condon
Chf. Justice .... David W. Harwell

Governorship
minimum age 30
length of term .... 4 years
number of consecutive
terms permitted 2
who succeeds .... Lt. Governor

State legislature
name .... General Assembly
upper chamber
name .... Senate
number of members 46
length of term .... 4 years
party in majority, 1996 ....Democratic
lower chamber
name .... House of Representatives
number of members 124
length of term .... 2 years
party in majority, 1996 ....Democratic

State employees October, 1992
total 90,504
October payroll ($1,000) 157,742

Local governments, 1992
total 705
county 46
municipal 270
township 0
school districts 91
special districts 297

Voting, November, 1994
voting age population 2,681,000
registered 60.8%
voted 45.2%

Vote for president
1988
Bush 599,871
Dukakis 367,511
1992
Clinton 476,631
Bush 574,120
Perot 138,135

Federal representation, 1996 (104th Congress)
Senators (name/party/term expires)

STROM THURMOND
Republican - 1997
ERNEST F. HOLLINGS
Democrat - 1999

Representatives, total 6
Democrats 2
Republicans 4
other 0

South Carolina 5

Women holding public office
U.S. Congress, 1995 0
statewide elected office, 1995 1
state legislature, 1995 21

Black elected officials, 1993
total 450
  US and state legislatures 26
  city/county/regional offices 269
  judicial/law enforcement 15
  education/school boards 140

Hispanic public officials, 1994
total . . . . NA
  state executives & legislators . . . . NA
  city/county/regional offices . . . . NA
  judicial/law enforcement . . . . NA
  education/school boards . . . . NA

GOVERNMENTAL FINANCE

State & local government revenues, (selected items), 1991-92 ($per capita)
total $3,970.67
  total general revenues 3,199.13
    from federal government 710.61
    from own sources 2,488.52
    from taxes 1,603.07
    from property taxes 456.17
    from all other taxes 1,029.16
    from charges & misc. 885.45

State & local government expenditures, (selected items), 1991-92 ($per capita)
total $3,997.28
  total direct general expenditures 3,353.14
    education 1,212.26
    libraries 16.00
    public welfare 533.07
    health & hospitals 510.52
    highways 176.52
    police protection 92.34
    fire protection 35.36
    correction 116.93
    housing & comm. development 30.93
    natural resources & parks 79.88
    interest on general debt 144.29

State & local debt, 1992 ($per capita) 3,198.20

Federal aid grants to state & local government, 1994 ($per capita total & selected items)
per capita total 744.10
  compensatory education 24.62
  waste treatment facilities 6.35
  medicaid 362.63
  housing assistance 35.55
  job training 9.94
  highway trust fund 63.28

CRIME, LAW ENFORCEMENT & COURTS

Crime, 1994 (all rates per 100,000 persons)
total crimes 219,870
overall crime rate 6,000.8
  property crimes 182,114
    burglaries 46,678
    larcenies 122,252
    motor vehicle thefts 13,184
  property crime rate 4,970.4
  violent crimes 37,756
    murders 353
    forcible rapes 1,991
    robberies 6,817
    aggravated assaults 28,595
  violent crime rate 1,030.5

Number of police agencies, 1994 284

Arrests, 1994
total 202,609
  persons under 18 years of age 26,381

Prisoners under state & federal jurisdiction, 1994
total 18,999
percent change, 1993-94 . . . . 1.6%
sentenced to more than one year
  total 18,168
  rate per 100,000 residents 494

Persons under sentence of death, 4/20/95 59

State's highest court
name . . . . Supreme Court
number of members 5
length of term . . . . 10 years
intermediate appeals court? . . . . yes

South Carolina 6

LABOR & INCOME

Civilian labor force, 1994
total	1,828,000
men	955,000
women	873,000
persons 16-19 years	101,000
white	1,317,000
black	498,000

*Civilian labor force as a percent of
civilian non-institutional population, 1994*
total	66.2%
men	74.2%
women	59.1%
persons 16-19 years	47.3%
white	68.2%
black	61.4%

Employment, 1994
total	1,713,000
men	901,000
women	812,000
persons 16-19 years	77,000
white	1,262,000
black	439,000

Full-time/part-time labor force, 1994
full-time labor force	1,521,000
working part-time for ecomonic reasons	24,000
part-time labor force	308,000

Unemployment rate, 1994
total	6.3%
men	5.6%
women	7.0%
persons 16-19 years	23.3%
white	4.2%
black	11.9%

*Unemployed by reason for unemployment
(as a percent of total unemployment), 1994*
job losers or completed temp jobs	42.5%
job leavers	10.5%
reentrants	33.8%
new entrants	13.2%

Civilian labor force, by occupation, 1994
executive/administrative/ managerial	201,000
professional/specialty	209,000
technicians & related support	53,000
sales	228,000
adminstrative support/clerical	235,000
service occupations	219,000
precision production/craft/repair	224,000
machine operators/assemblers	227,000
transportation/material moving	73,000
handlers/helpers/laborers	101,000
farming/forestry/fishing	42,000

Civilian labor force, by industry, 1994
construction	91,000
manufacturing	457,000
transportation/communication	75,000
wholesale/retail trade	368,000
finance/real estate/insurance	88,000
services	321,000
government	259,000
agriculture	38,000

Average annual pay, 1994 (prelim.) $22,477
change in average annual pay,
1993-1994 ...... 2.5%

*Hours and earnings of production workers
on manufacturing payrolls, 1994*
average weekly hours	41.8
average hourly earnings	$9.99
average weekly earnings	$417.58

Labor union membership, 1994 59,300

Household income (in constant 1993 dollars)
median household income, 1992	$28,404
median household income, 1993	$26,053

Poverty
persons below poverty level, 1992	19.0%
persons below poverty level, 1993	18.7%

Personal income ($per capita)
1994
in current dollars	17,695
in constant (1987) dollars	13,685

1995 (projected)
in constant (1982) dollars	11,513

2000 (projected)
in constant (1982) dollars	12,304

Federal income tax returns, 1993
returns filed	1,581,259
adjusted gross income ($1000)	43,494,090
total income tax paid ($1000)	5,326,897

South Carolina 7

ECONOMY, BUSINESS, INDUSTRY & AGRICULTURE

Fortune 500 companies, 1994 2

Business incorporations, 1994
total 7,374
change, 1993-94 .... 13.7%

Business failures, 1994
total 499
rate per 10,000 concerns 53
change, 1993-94 .... 25.7%

Business firm ownership
Hispanic owned firms, 1987 393
black owned firms, 1987 12,815
women owned firms, 1987 42,600
foreign owned firms, 1982 144

Gross state product, 1991 ($mil)
total $66,408
agriculture services, forestry, fisheries 949
mining 138
construction 3,370
manufacturing—durable goods 5,982
manufacturing—nondurable goods 11,258
transportation, communication &
public utilities 5,877
wholesale trade 3,196
retail trade 6,946
finance/real estate/insurance 8,977
services 8,949
federal, state & local government 10,768

Establishments, by major industry group, 1992
total 82,239
agriculture 1,340
mining 93
construction 8,617
manufacturing 4,881
transportation 2,913
wholesale trade 5,385
retail trade 23,392
finance/real estate/insurance 7,165
service industries 26,968
unclassified 1,485

Payroll, by major industry group, 1992
total ($1,000) $26,133,689
agriculture 128,945

mining 50,135
construction 1,818,994
manufacturing 9,529,533
transportation 1,751,792
wholesale trade 1,540,481
retail trade 3,315,385
finance/real estate/insurance 1,556,395
service industries 6,419,717
unclassified 22,312

Agriculture
number of farms, 1994 24,000
farm acreage, 1994 5,000,000
acres per farm, 1994 213
value of farms, 1994 ($mil) 4,751
farm income, 1993 ($mil)
gross farm income 1,418
net farm income 288
debt/asset ratio 14.5%
farm marketings, 1993 ($mil)
total $1,221
crops 618
livestock 603
government payments 103
farm marketings in order of marketing receipts, 1993
1) Tobacco
2) Broilers
3) Cattle
4) Greenhouse

Federal economic activity ($mil, except per capita)
expenditures, 1994
total $17,097
per capita $4,666
defense $3,494
non-defense $13,603
defense department, 1994
contract awards ($mil) $998
payroll ($mil) $2,529
civilian employees (x1,000) 14.5
military personnel (x1,000) 39.0

Fishing, 1992
catch (millions of pounds) 19
value ($mil) 26

Mining, 1994 ($mil)
total non-fuel mineral production $415

329

South Carolina 8

principal non-fuel minerals in order of value, 1994
1) Stone
2) Cement
3) Gold

Construction, 1994 ($mil)
total contracts (including
   non-building) $4,182
     residential 2,223
     non-residential 1,341

Manufacturing, 1992
total establishments 4,839
employees, total (x1,000) 367
payroll ($mil) 9,425
production workers (x1,000) 272
value added ($mil) 24,725
value of shipments ($mil) 51,996

Finance
commercial banks, 1994
   number 78
     assets ($bil) 27.7
     deposits ($bil) 20.6
     closed or assisted 0
     deposits ($bil) .... NA
savings and loan associations, 1991
   non-current real estate loans 2.08%
   net income after taxes ($mil) 43
   return on assets .... +0.39%

Retail trade, 1992
establishments (x1,000) 22.8
sales ($mil) 24,743
annual payroll ($mil) 2,845
paid employees (x1,000) 264

Wholesale trade, 1992
establishments 5,564
sales ($bil) 21.3
annual payroll ($mil) 1,457
paid employees (x1,000) 56.7

Service industries, 1992
establishments (x1,000) (non-exempt firms) 21.5
receipts ($mil) (non-exempt firms) 10,930
annual payroll ($mil) 4,349
paid employees (x1,000) (non-exempt firms) . 233

COMMUNICATION, ENERGY & TRANSPORTATION

Communication
daily newspapers, 1993 16
broadcast stations, 1990
   radio: commercial, educational 212
   television: commercial, noncommercial 27
cable TV households, 1988 593,000

Energy
consumption estimates, 1992
total (trillion Btu) 1,224
per capita (million Btu) 339.8
by source of production (trillion Btu)
   coal 288
   natural gas 142
   petroleum 405
   nuclear electric power 486
   hydroelectric power 28
by end-use sector (trillion Btu)
   residential 240
   commercial 165
   industrial 513
   transportation 307
electrical energy
   production, 1993 (billion kWh) 75.6
   net summer capability, 1993 (million kW) . 16.1
gas utilities, 1993
   customers 422,000
   sales (trillion Btu) 111
   revenues ($mil) 507
nuclear plants, 1993 7

Transportation, 1994
public road & street mileage
total 64,253
   urban 10,518
   rural 53,735
   interstate 810
vehicle miles of travel (mil) 37,245
total motor vehicle registrations 2,742,813
   automobiles 1,816,606
licensed drivers 2,492,019
   per 1,000 driving age population 885
deaths from motor vehicle
   accidents 847

South Dakota 1

STATE SUMMARY

Capital City . . . . .Pierre

Governor . . . . William Janklow

Address . . . . STATE CAPITOL
         PIERRE, SD 57501
         605 773-3212

Admitted as a state 1889

Area (square miles) 77,121

Population, 1980 690,768

Population, 1990 696,004

Population, 1994 (est.) 721,000

Persons per square mile, 1994 . . . . 9.5

Largest city . . . . Sioux Falls
   population, 1990 100,800

Personal income per capita, 1994
   (in current dollars) $19,577

Gross state product ($mil), 1991 13,712

Leading industries, 1992 (by payroll)
        SERVICE INDUSTRIES
        MANUFACTURING
        RETAIL TRADE .

Leading agricultural commodities, 1993
        CATTLE
        WHEAT
        HOGS
        CORN

GEOGRAPHY & ENVIRONMENT

Area (square miles)
total 77,121
   land 75,898
   water (includes territorial water) 1,224

Federally owned land, 1991 . . . . 5.7%

Highest point
name . . . . .Henry Peak
elevation (feet) 7,242

Lowest point
name . . . . Big Stone Lake
elevation (feet) 966

General coastline (miles) 0

Tidal shoreline (miles) 0

Capital city . . . . Pierre
population, 1990 12,900

Largest city . . . . Sioux Falls
population, 1990 100,800

Number of cities with over 100,000 population
   1980 0

Number of cities with over 100,000 population
   1990 0

State parks and Recreation areas, 1991
area (acres) 92,000
number of visitors 5,894,000
revenues $3,810,000

National forest land, 1992 (acres) 2,352,000

National park acreage, 1984 183,300

DEMOGRAPHICS & CHARACTERISTICS OF THE POPULATION

Population
1970 666,257
1980 690,768
1990 696,004
1994 (est.) 721,000
2000 (revised projection) 770,000
2010 (revised projection) 815,000

Metropolitan area population
1970 155,000
1980 180,000
1992 231,000

Non-metropolitan area population
1970 512,000
1980 511,000
1992 478,000

Change in population, 1980-90
number 5,236
percent 0.76%

Persons per square mile, 1994 . . . . 9.5

Age distribution, 1980
under 5 years 8.5%
5 to 17 years 21.3%
65 and over 13.2%

Age distribution, 1990
under 5 years 7.8%
5 to 17 years 20.6%
65 and over 14.7%

South Dakota 2

Age distribution, 2000 (projected)
under 5 years 7.0%
5 to 17 years 20.0%
65 and over 14.2%

Persons by age, 1990
under 5 years 54,504
5 to 17 years 143,958
65 and over 102,331

Median age, 1990 .... *32.50*

Race, 1990
White 637,515
Black 3,258
American Indian 50,501
Chinese 385
Filipino 531
Japanese 286
Asian Indian 287
Korean 525
Vietnamese 268
all other 2,374

Race, 2010 (projected)
White 702,000
Black 4,000

Persons of Hispanic origin, 1990
total 5,252
  Mexican 3,438
  Puerto Rican 377
  Cuban 44
  Other Hispanic 1,393

Persons by sex, 1990
male 342,498
female 353,506

Marital status, 1990
males
  15 years & older 256,241
    single 73,080
    married 159,641
      separated 2,346
      widowed 6,744
      divorced 16,776
females
  15 years & older 271,027
    single 55,668
    married 159,462
      separated 2,811

widowed 36,326
divorced 19,571

Households & families, 1990
households 259,034
persons per household 2.59
  families 180,306
    married couples 152,519
    female householder, no husband
      present 20,711
    one person households 68,308
households, 1994 265,000
persons per household, 1994 .... 2.63

Nativity, 1990
number of persons born in state 488,514
percent of total residents 70.2%

Immigration & naturalization, 1993
immigrants admitted 543
persons naturalized 85
refugees granted resident status 213

VITAL STATISTICS & HEALTH

Births
1992 11,281
  with low birth weight 5.2%
  to teenage mothers 11.4%
  to unmarried mothers 26.6%
1993 10,830
1994 10,615

Abortions, 1992
total 1,000
rate (per 1,000 women age 15-44) 6.8
rate per 1,000 live births 92

Adoptions, 1986
total 482
  related 51.2%

Deaths
1992 6,927
1993 6,863
1994 6,851

Infant deaths
1992 113
1993 114
1994 125

South Dakota 3

Average lifetime, 1979-1981
both sexes .... 74.97 years
  men .... 71.03 years
  women .... 79.21 years

Marriages
1992 7,559
1993 7,427
1994 7,451

Divorces
1992 2,926
1993 2,890
1994 3,022

Physicians, 1993
total 1,108
rate (per 1,000 persons) 1.56

Dentists, 1992
total 308
rate (per 1,000 persons) 0.44

Hospitals, 1993
number 51
beds (x 1,000) 4.3
average daily census (x 1,000) 2.6
occupancy rate 60.6%
personnel (x 1,000) 11.4
average cost per day to hospital $506
average cost per stay to hospital $5,052

EDUCATION

*Educational attainment of all persons
  25 years and older, 1990*
less than 9th grade 57,707
high school graduates 144,990
bachelor's degree 52,773
graduate or professional degree 21,118

Public school enrollment, Fall, 1993
total 142,825
  Kindergarten through grade 8 102,281
  grades 9 through 12 40,544

Public School Teachers
total, 1994 9,557
  elementary 5,897
  secondary 2,589
salaries, 1994
  beginning $18,935
  average $25,259

*State receipts & expenditures for public
  schools, 1993*
receipts ($mil) 638
expenditures
  total ($mil) 627
  per capita $885
  per pupil $4,359

*Graduating high school seniors,
  public high schools, 1995 (est)* 8,578

SAT scores, 1994
verbal 483
math 548

Institutions of higher education, 1995
total 21
  public 9
  private 12

*Enrollment in institutions of higher
  education, Fall, 1993*
total 38,166
full-time men 13,243
full-time women 14,545
part-time men 3,742
part-time women 6,636

*Minority enrollment in institutions of higher
  education, Fall, 1993*
Black, non-Hispanic 312
Hispanic 191
Asian/Pacific Islander 331

Earned degrees conferred, 1993
Bachelor's 4,252
First professional 130
Master's 913
Doctor's 52

SOCIAL INSURANCE & WELFARE PROGRAMS

Social Security beneficiaries & benefits, 1993
beneficiaries
total 134,000
  retired and dependents 95,000
  survivors 25,000
  disabled & dependents 14,000
annual benefit payments ($mil)
total $883
  retired and dependents 605
  survivors 194
  disabled & dependents 84

South Dakota 4

Medicare, 1993
enrollment (x1,000) 115
payments ($mil) 331

Medicaid, 1993
recipients (x1,000) 70
payments ($mil) 264

Federal public aid, 1993
recipients as a percent of population 4.5%
Aid to Families with Dependent Children
  recipients (x1,000) 19
average monthly payment $291
Supplemental Security Income
  total recipients (x1,000) 13

Food Stamp Program
participants, 1994 (x1,000) 53

HOUSING & CONSTRUCTION

Total housing units, 1990 292,436
  year round housing units 283,952
  vacant 33,402

New privately owned housing units
authorized, 1994
number (x1,000) 4.6
value ($mil) 288

New privately owned housing units
started, 1994 (x1,000) 4.7

Existing home sales, 1994 (x1,000) 13.2

GOVERNMENT & ELECTIONS

State officials, 1996
Governor (name/party/term expires)
    WILLIAM JANKLOW
    Republican - 1999
Lt. Governor .... Steve Kirby
Sec. of State .... Joyce Hazeltine
Atty. General .... Mark Barnett
Chf. Justice .... Robert Miller

Governorship
minimum age .... not specified
length of term .... 4 years
number of consecutive
  terms permitted 2
who succeeds .... Lt. Governor

State legislature
name .... Legislature
upper chamber
  name .... Senate
  number of members 35
  length of term .... 2 years
  party in majority, 1996 .... Republican
lower chamber
  name .... House of Representatives
  number of members 70
  length of term .... 2 years
  party in majority, 1996 .... Republican

State employees October, 1992
total 17,631
October payroll ($1,000) 28,512

Local governments, 1992
total 1,803
  county 64
  municipal 310
  township 971
  school districts 184
  special districts 273

Voting, November, 1994
voting age population 495,000
  registered 75.4%
  voted 63.9%

Vote for president
1988
  Bush 165,516
  Dukakis 145,632
1992
  Clinton 124,861
  Bush 136,670
  Perot 73,296

Federal representation, 1996 (104th Congress)
Senators (name/party/term expires)

    LARRY PRESSLER
    Republican - 1997
    TOM DASCHLE
    Democrat - 1999

Representatives, total 1
  Democrats 1
  Republicans 0
  other 0

Women holding public office
U.S. Congress, 1995 0
statewide elected office, 1995 3
state legislature, 1995 19

Black elected officials, 1993
total 3
   US and state legislatures 1
   city/county/regional offices 2
   judicial/law enforcement 0
   education/school boards 0

Hispanic public officials, 1994
total ....NA
   state executives & legislators ....NA
   city/county/regional offices ....NA
   judicial/law enforcement ....NA
   education/school boards ....NA

GOVERNMENTAL FINANCE

State & local government revenues, (selected items), 1991-92 ($per capita)
total $3,777.63
   total general revenues 3,267.38
     from federal government 852.21
     from own sources 2,415.18
     from taxes 1,576.33
      from property taxes 616.51
      from all other taxes 817.06
     from charges & misc. 838.85

State & local government expenditures, (selected items), 1991-92 ($per capita)
total $3,485.43
   total direct general expenditures 3,215.08
     education 1,141.72
     libraries 15.72
     public welfare 427.06
     health & hospitals 165.40
     highways 437.91
     police protection 79.99
     fire protection 27.36
     correction 55.33
     housing & comm. development 34.63
     natural resources & parks 160.62
     interest on general debt 233.30

State & local debt, 1992 ($per capita) 3,420.45

Federal aid grants to state & local government, 1994 ($per capita total & selected items)
per capita total 1,004.46
   compensatory education 27.88
   waste treatment facilities 13.52
   medicaid 285.66
   housing assistance 77.02
   job training 15.10
   highway trust fund 185.82

CRIME, LAW ENFORCEMENT & COURTS

Crime, 1994 (all rates per 100,000 persons)
total crimes 22,367
overall crime rate 3,102.2
   property crimes 20,726
     burglaries 3,938
     larcenies 15,916
     motor vehicle thefts 872
   property crime rate 2,874.6
   violent crimes 1,641
     murders 10
     forcible rapes 303
     robberies 135
     aggravated assaults 1,193
   violent crime rate 227.6

Number of police agencies, 1994 37

Arrests, 1994
total 29,766
   persons under 18 years of age 8,959

Prisoners under state & federal jurisdiction, 1994
total 1,734
percent change, 1993-94 ....11.7%
   sentenced to more than one year
   total 1,734
   rate per 100,000 residents 240

Persons under sentence of death, 4/20/95 2

State's highest court
name .... Supreme Court
number of members 5
length of term ....8 years
intermediate appeals court? ....no

South Dakota 6

LABOR & INCOME

Civilian labor force, 1994

total 374,000
 men 199,000
 women 175,000
 persons 16-19 years 31,000
 white 355,000
 black .... NA

Civilian labor force as a percent of civilian non-institutional population, 1994

total 71.8%
 men 78.2%
 women 65.7%
 persons 16-19 years 70.1%
 white 72.0%
 black .... NA%

Employment, 1994

total 362,000
 men 193,000
 women 169,000
 persons 16-19 years 29,000
 white 345,000
 black .... NA

Full-time/part-time labor force, 1994

full-time labor force 293,000
 working part-time for
  ecomonic reasons 3,000
part-time labor force 81,000

Unemployment rate, 1994

total 3.3%
 men 3.1%
 women 3.6%
 persons 16-19 years 8.2%
 white 2.9%
 black .... NA%

Unemployed by reason for unemployment (as a percent of total unemployment), 1994

job losers or completed temp jobs 31.0%
job leavers 15.1%
reentrants 48.2%
new entrants 5.7%

Civilian labor force, by occupation, 1994

executive/administrative/
 managerial 38,000
professional/specialty 41,000
technicians & related support 11,000

sales 43,000
adminstrative support/clerical 49,000
service occupations 61,000
precision production/craft/repair 41,000
machine operators/assemblers 20,000
transportation/material moving 16,000
handlers/helpers/laborers 15,000
farming/forestry/fishing 39,000

Civilian labor force, by industry, 1994

construction 15,000
manufacturing 41,000
transportation/communication 15,000
wholesale/retail trade 77,000
finance/real estate/insurance 16,000
services 71,000
government 62,000
agriculture 41,000

Average annual pay, 1994 (prelim.) $19,255
change in average annual pay,
 1993-1994 .... 3.5%

Hours and earnings of production workers on manufacturing payrolls, 1994

average weekly hours 41.9
average hourly earnings $9.19
average weekly earnings $385.06

Labor union membership, 1994 23,400

Household income (in constant 1993 dollars)

median household income, 1992 .... $27,045
median household income, 1993 .... $27,737

Poverty

persons below poverty level, 1992 .... 15.1%
persons below poverty level, 1993 .... 14.2%

Personal income ($per capita)

1994
 in current dollars 19,577
 in constant (1987) dollars 15,141
1995 (projected)
 in constant (1982) dollars 11,518
2000 (projected)
 in constant (1982) dollars 12,330

Federal income tax returns, 1993

returns filed 320,834
adjusted gross income ($1000) 8,546,334
total income tax paid ($1000) 1,230,568

ECONOMY, BUSINESS, INDUSTRY & AGRICULTURE

Fortune 500 companies, 1994 1

Business incorporations, 1994
total 1,349
change, 1993-94 . . . . 0.9%

Business failures, 1994
total 168
rate per 10,000 concerns 57
change, 1993-94 . . . . -3.4%

Business firm ownership
Hispanic owned firms, 1987 109
black owned firms, 1987 63
women owned firms, 1987 13,400
foreign owned firms, 1982 29

Gross state product, 1991 ($mil)
total $13,712
  agriculture services, forestry, fisheries . . . 1,716
  mining 185
  construction 428
  manufacturing—durable goods 778
  manufacturing—nondurable goods 431
  transportation, communication &
    public utilities 1,078
  wholesale trade 857
  retail trade 1,437
  finance/real estate/insurance 2,971
  services 2,002
  federal, state & local government 1,829

Establishments, by major industry group, 1992
total 21,387
  agriculture 370
  mining 56
  construction 2,050
  manufacturing 904
  transportation 1,379
  wholesale trade 1,754
  retail trade 5,739
  finance/real estate/insurance 2,025
  service industries 6,811
  unclassified 299

Payroll, by major industry group, 1992
total ($1,000) $4,065,011
  agriculture 19,412

  mining 77,055
  construction 260,402
  manufacturing 717,778
  transportation 332,355
  wholesale trade 362,502
  retail trade 662,042
  finance/real estate/insurance 363,003
  service industries 1,268,550
  unclassified 1,912

Agriculture
number of farms, 1994 34,000
farm acreage, 1994 44,000,000
acres per farm, 1994 1,300
value of farms, 1994 ($mil) 17,139
farm income, 1993 ($mil)
  gross farm income 3,909
  net farm income 1,179
  debt/asset ratio 15.8%
farm marketings, 1993 ($mil)
total $3,320
  crops 1,147
  livestock 2,173
government payments 432
farm marketings in order of marketing
receipts, 1993
    1) Cattle
    2) Wheat
    3) Hogs
    4) Corn

Federal economic activity
  ($mil, except per capita)
expenditures, 1994
  total $3,814
  per capita $5,289
  defense $331
  non-defense $3,483
defense department, 1994
  contract awards ($mil) $75
  payroll ($mil) $251
  civilian employees (x1,000) 1.3
  military personnel (x1,000) 5.0

Fishing, 1992
catch (millions of pounds) . . . . NA
value ($mil) . . . . NA

Mining, 1994 ($mil)
total non-fuel mineral production $322

South Dakota 8

principal non-fuel minerals in order of value, 1994
1) Gold
2) Cement
3) Sand and gravel

Construction, 1994 ($mil)
total contracts (including
non-building) $851
residential 267
non-residential 298

Manufacturing, 1992
total establishments 889
employees, total (x1,000) 35
payroll ($mil) 739
production workers (x1,000) 25
value added ($mil) 2,267
value of shipments ($mil) 5,956

Finance
commercial banks, 1994
number 121
assets ($bil) 19.2
deposits ($bil) 11.0
closed or assisted 0
deposits ($bil) .... NA
savings and loan associations, 1991
non-current real estate loans 3.32%
net income after taxes ($mil) .... -3
return on assets .... -0.27%

Retail trade, 1992
establishments (x1,000) 5.6
sales ($mil) 5,108
annual payroll ($mil) 576
paid employees (x1,000) 57

Wholesale trade, 1992
establishments 1,809
sales ($bil) 6.5
annual payroll ($mil) 335
paid employees (x1,000) 16.4

Service industries, 1992
establishments (x1,000) (non-exempt firms) . 4.8
receipts ($mil) (non-exempt firms) 1,790
annual payroll ($mil) 592
paid employees (x1,000) (non-exempt firms) .. 34

COMMUNICATION, ENERGY & TRANSPORTATION

Communication
daily newspapers, 1993 11
broadcast stations, 1990
radio: commercial, educational 86
television: commercial, noncommercial 22
cable TV households, 1988 140,000

Energy
consumption estimates, 1992
total (trillion Btu) 205
per capita (million Btu) 289.2
by source of production (trillion Btu)
coal 34
natural gas 27
petroleum 104
nuclear electric power 0
hydroelectric power 41
by end-use sector (trillion Btu)
residential 48
commercial 32
industrial 53
transportation 72
electrical energy
production, 1993 (billion kWh) 5.3
net summer capability, 1993 (million kW) .. 2.7
gas utilities, 1993
customers 145,000
sales (trillion Btu) 26
revenues ($mil) 117
nuclear plants, 1993 0

Transportation, 1994
public road & street mileage
total 83,317
urban 1,907
rural 81,410
interstate 678
vehicle miles of travel (mil) 7,631
total motor vehicle registrations 769,386
automobiles 468,678
licensed drivers 508,076
per 1,000 driving age population 948
deaths from motor vehicle
accidents 154

338

Tennessee 1

STATE SUMMARY

Capital City . . . . Nashville

Governor . . . . Don Sundquist

Address . . . . STATE CAPITOL
NASHVILLE, TN 37219
615 741-2001

Admitted as a state 1796

Area (square miles) 42,146

Population, 1980 4,591,120

Population, 1990 4,877,185

Population, 1994 (est.) 5,175,000

Persons per square mile, 1994 . . . . 125.6

Largest city . . . . Memphis
population, 1990 610,000

Personal income per capita, 1994
(in current dollars) $19,482

Gross state product ($mil), 1991 100,804

Leading industries, 1992 (by payroll)
MANUFACTURING
SERVICE INDUSTRIES
RETAIL TRADE

Leading agricultural commodities, 1993
CATTLE
DAIRY PRODUCTS
COTTON
TOBACCO

GEOGRAPHY & ENVIRONMENT

Area (square miles)
total 42,146
land 41,220
water (includes territorial water) 926

Federally owned land, 1991 . . . . 3.7%

Highest point
name . . . . Clingmans Dome
elevation (feet) 6,643

Lowest point
name . . . . Mississippi River
elevation (feet) 178

General coastline (miles) 0

Tidal shoreline (miles) 0

Capital city . . . . Nashville
population, 1990 488,000

Largest city . . . . Memphis
population, 1990 610,000

Number of cities with over 100,000 population
1980 4

Number of cities with over 100,000 population
1990 4

State parks and Recreation areas, 1991
area (acres) 133,000
number of visitors 26,974,000
revenues $19,737,000

National forest land, 1992 (acres) 1,212,000

National park acreage, 1984 266,400

DEMOGRAPHICS & CHARACTERISTICS OF THE POPULATION

Population
1970 3,926,018
1980 4,591,120
1990 4,877,185
1994 (est.) 5,175,000
2000 (revised projection) 5,538,000
2010 (revised projection) 6,007,000

Metropolitan area population
1970 2,630,000
1980 3,048,000
1992 3,404,000

Non-metropolitan area population
1970 1,296,000
1980 1,543,000
1992 1,621,000

Change in population, 1980-90
number 286,065
percent 6.23%

Persons per square mile, 1994 . . . . 125.6

Age distribution, 1980
under 5 years 7.1%
5 to 17 years 21.2%
65 and over 11.3%

Age distribution, 1990
under 5 years 6.8%
5 to 17 years 18.1%
65 and over 12.6%

Tennessee 2

Age distribution, 2000 (projected)
under 5 years 6.0%
5 to 17 years 18.1%
65 and over 14.2%

Persons by age, 1990
under 5 years 333,415
5 to 17 years 883,189
65 and over 618,818

Median age, 1990 .... 33.60

Race, 1990
White 4,048,068
Black 778,035
American Indian 9,859
Chinese 5,653
Filipino 3,032
Japanese 3,440
Asian Indian 5,911
Korean 4,508
Vietnamese 2,062
all other 16,437

Race, 2010 (projected)
White 4,899,000
Black 1,014,000

Persons of Hispanic origin, 1990
total 32,741
Mexican 13,879
Puerto Rican 4,292
Cuban 2,012
Other Hispanic 12,558

Persons by sex, 1990
male 2,348,928
female 2,528,257

Marital status, 1990
males
15 years & older 1,831,058
single 488,843
married 1,141,001
separated 33,320
widowed 45,612
divorced 155,602
females
15 years & older 2,036,246
single 409,983
married 1,148,469
separated 48,119

widowed 266,366
divorced 211,428

Households & families, 1990
households 1,853,725
persons per household 2.56
families 1,348,019
married couples 1,059,569
female householder, no husband
present 232,699
one person households 442,129
households, 1994 1,966,000
persons per household, 1994 .... 2.57

Nativity, 1990
number of persons born in state 3,373,365
percent of total residents 69.2%

Immigration & naturalization, 1993
immigrants admitted 4,287
persons naturalized 1,039
refugees granted resident status 869

VITAL STATISTICS & HEALTH

Births
1992 74,048
with low birth weight 8.5%
to teenage mothers 16.9%
to unmarried mothers 32.7%
1993 73,613
1994 75,688

Abortions, 1992
total 19,000
rate (per 1,000 women age 15-44) 16.2
rate per 1,000 live births 243

Adoptions, 1986
total 2,058
related 60.7%

Deaths
1992 47,149
1993 49,628
1994 49,645

Infant deaths
1992 705
1993 726
1994 668

Average lifetime, 1979-1981
both sexes .... 73.30 years
   men .... 69.15 years
   women .... 77.47 years

Marriages
1992 70,905
1993 73,052
1994 80,030

Divorces
1992 33,939
1993 33,199
1994 34,167

Physicians, 1993
total 10,685
rate (per 1,000 persons) 2.10

Dentists, 1992
total 2,767
rate (per 1,000 persons) 0.55

Hospitals, 1993
number 130
beds (x 1,000) 22.8
average daily census (x 1,000) 13.9
occupancy rate 60.8%
personnel (x 1,000) 86.1
average cost per day to hospital $859
average cost per stay to hospital $5,798

EDUCATION

Educational attainment of all persons
  25 years and older, 1990
less than 9th grade 500,929
high school graduates 942,865
bachelor's degree 330,742
graduate or professional degree 170,249

Public school enrollment, Fall, 1993
total 866,991
  Kindergarten through grade 8 630,449
  grades 9 through 12 236,542

Public School Teachers
total, 1994 46,066
  elementary 32,072
  secondary 12,398
salaries, 1994
  beginning $19,625
  average $30,514

State receipts & expenditures for public
  schools, 1993
receipts ($mil) 3,489
expenditures
  total ($mil) 3,333
  per capita $663
  per pupil $4,033

Graduating high school seniors,
  public high schools, 1995 (est) 45,388

SAT scores, 1994
verbal 488
math 535

Institutions of higher education, 1995
total 78
  public 25
  private 53

Enrollment in institutions of higher
  education, Fall, 1993
total 244,936
full-time men 73,381
full-time women 82,828
part-time men 36,459
part-time women 52,268

Minority enrollment in institutions of higher
  education, Fall, 1993
Black, non-Hispanic 35,843
Hispanic 2,124
Asian/Pacific Islander 3,061

Earned degrees conferred, 1993
Bachelor's 20,371
First professional 1,341
Master's 5,016
Doctor's 721

SOCIAL INSURANCE & WELFARE PROGRAMS

Social Security beneficiaries & benefits, 1993
beneficiaries
total 891,000
  retired and dependents 575,000
  survivors 169,000
  disabled & dependents 147,000
annual benefit payments ($mil)
total $5,957
  retired and dependents 3,752
  survivors 1,301
  disabled & dependents 904

Tennessee 4

Medicare, 1993
enrollment (x1,000) 738
payments ($mil) 3,252

Medicaid, 1993
recipients (x1,000) 909
payments ($mil) 1,977

Federal public aid, 1993
recipients as a percent of population 9.4%
Aid to Families with Dependent Children
   recipients (x1,000) 301
average monthly payment $168
Supplemental Security Income
   total recipients (x1,000) 168

Food Stamp Program
   participants, 1994 (x1,000) 735

HOUSING & CONSTRUCTION

Total housing units, 1990 2,026,067
   year round housing units 2,002,378
   vacant 172,342

New privately owned housing units
   authorized, 1994
number (x1,000) 31.9
value ($mil) 2,539

New privately owned housing units
   started, 1994 (x1,000) 37.2

Existing home sales, 1994 (x1,000) 129.8

GOVERNMENT & ELECTIONS

State officials, 1996
   Governor (name/party/term expires)
         DON SUNDQUIST
         Republican - 1999
Lt. Governor .... John S. Wilder
Sec. of State .... Riley Darnell
Atty. General .... Charles Burson
Chf. Justice .... Lyle Reid

Governorship
minimum age 30
length of term .... 4 years
number of consecutive
   terms permitted 2
who succeeds .... Lt. Governor

State legislature
name .... General Assembly
   upper chamber
         name .... Senate
         number of members 33
         length of term .... 4 years
         party in majority, 1996 .... Democratic
   lower chamber
         name .... House of Representatives
         number of members 99
         length of term .... 2 years
         party in majority, 1996 .... Democratic

State employees October, 1992
total 90,593
October payroll ($1,000) 160,337

Local governments, 1992
total 960
   county 93
   municipal 339
   township 0
   school districts 14
   special districts 513

Voting, November, 1994
voting age population 3,856,000
   registered 63.7%
   voted 43.0%

Vote for president
1988
   Bush 939,434
   Dukakis 677,715
1992
   Clinton 931,910
   Bush 838,977
   Perot 199,314

Federal representation, 1996 (104th Congress)
Senators (name/party/term expires)

         BILL FIRST
         Republican - 2001
         FRED THOMPSON
         Republican - 1997

Representatives, total 9
   Democrats 4
   Republicans 5
   other 0

342

Tennessee 5

Women holding public office
U.S. Congress, 1995 0
statewide elected office, 1995 1
state legislature, 1995 18

Black elected officials, 1993
total 168
  US and state legislatures 16
  city/county/regional offices 104
  judicial/law enforcement 24
  education/school boards 24

Hispanic public officials, 1994
total .... NA
  state executives & legislators .... NA
  city/county/regional offices .... NA
  judicial/law enforcement .... NA
  education/school boards .... NA

GOVERNMENTAL FINANCE

State & local government revenues, (selected items), 1991-92 ($per capita)
total $4,245.88
  total general revenues 3,131.28
    from federal government 744.99
    from own sources 2,386.29
    from taxes 1,559.89
      from property taxes 352.86
      from all other taxes 1,049.80
    from charges & misc. 826.40

State & local government expenditures, (selected items), 1991-92 ($per capita)
total $3,987.51
  total direct general expenditures 3,048.44
  education 955.75
  libraries 8.94
  public welfare 530.46
  health & hospitals 372.30
  highways 266.22
  police protection 94.81
  fire protection 44.32
  correction 92.11
  housing & comm. development 49.24
  natural resources & parks 85.66
  interest on general debt 143.27

State & local debt, 1992 ($per capita) 2,498.81

Federal aid grants to state & local government, 1994 ($per capita total & selected items)
per capita total 761.26
  compensatory education 23.52
  waste treatment facilities 6.74
  medicaid 348.38
  housing assistance 40.42
  job training 9.87
  highway trust fund 54.88

CRIME, LAW ENFORCEMENT & COURTS

Crime, 1994 (all rates per 100,000 persons)
total crimes 264,952
  overall crime rate 5,119.8
  property crimes 226,247
    burglaries 59,080
    larcenies 138,173
    motor vehicle thefts 28,994
  property crime rate 4,371.9
  violent crimes 38,705
    murders 482
    forcible rapes 2,545
    robberies 10,735
    aggravated assaults 24,943
  violent crime rate 747.9

Number of police agencies, 1994 93

Arrests, 1994
total 138,239
  persons under 18 years of age 19,923

Prisoners under state & federal jurisdiction, 1994
total 14,474
percent change, 1993-94 .... 12.9%
  sentenced to more than one year
  total 14,474
  rate per 100,000 residents 277

Persons under sentence of death, 4/20/95 102

State's highest court
name .... Supreme Court
number of members 5
length of term .... 8 years
intermediate appeals court? .... yes

Tennessee 6

LABOR & INCOME

Civilian labor force, 1994
total	2,664,000
men	1,398,000
women	1,267,000
persons 16-19 years	144,000
white	2,172,000
black	459,000

Civilian labor force as a percent of civilian non-institutional population, 1994
total	66.9%
men	74.4%
women	60.2%
persons 16-19 years	54.2%
white	67.2%
black	65.1%

Employment, 1994
total	2,537,000
men	1,336,000
women	1,201,000
persons 16-19 years	126,000
white	2,087,000
black	419,000

Full-time/part-time labor force, 1994
full-time labor force	2,240,000
working part-time for ecomonic reasons	26,000
part-time labor force	425,000

Unemployment rate, 1994
total	4.8%
men	4.4%
women	5.2%
persons 16-19 years	13.1%
white	4.0%
black	8.6%

Unemployed by reason for unemployment (as a percent of total unemployment), 1994
job losers or completed temp jobs	47.3%
job leavers	14.0%
reentrants	32.5%
new entrants	6.3%

Civilian labor force, by occupation, 1994
executive/administrative/ managerial	285,000
professional/specialty	306,000
technicians & related support	82,000
sales	302,000
adminstrative support/clerical	372,000
service occupations	348,000
precision production/craft/repair	314,000
machine operators/assemblers	323,000
transportation/material moving	133,000
handlers/helpers/laborers	122,000
farming/forestry/fishing	69,000

Civilian labor force, by industry, 1994
construction	113,000
manufacturing	573,000
transportation/communication	155,000
wholesale/retail trade	537,000
finance/real estate/insurance	101000
services	578,000
government	333,000
agriculture	65,000

Average annual pay, 1994 (prelim.) $24,106
change in average annual pay, 1993-1994 .... 3.2%

Hours and earnings of production workers on manufacturing payrolls, 1994
average weekly hours	40.9
average hourly earnings	$10.51
average weekly earnings	$429.86

Labor union membership, 1994 265,300

Household income (in constant 1993 dollars)
median household income, 1992	$25,046
median household income, 1993	$25,102

Poverty
persons below poverty level, 1992	17.0%
persons below poverty level, 1993	19.6%

Personal income ($per capita)
1994
in current dollars	19,482
in constant (1987) dollars	15,067

1995 (projected)
in constant (1982) dollars	12,370

2000 (projected)
in constant (1982) dollars	13,192

Federal income tax returns, 1993
returns filed	2,253,718
adjusted gross income ($1000)	65,753,820
total income tax paid ($1000)	9,344,233

Tennessee 7

ECONOMY, BUSINESS, INDUSTRY & AGRICULTURE

Fortune 500 companies, 1994 6

Business incorporations, 1994
total 10,073
change, 1993-94 .... 13.7%

Business failures, 1994
total 957
rate per 10,000 concerns 70
change, 1993-94 .... -20.9%

Business firm ownership
Hispanic owned firms, 1987 554
black owned firms, 1987 10,423
women owned firms, 1987 67,400
foreign owned firms, 1982 222

Gross state product, 1991 ($mil)
total $100,804
  agriculture services, forestry, fisheries ... 1,558
  mining 310
  construction 3,587
  manufacturing—durable goods 11,269
  manufacturing—nondurable goods 12,409
  transportation, communication &
    public utilities 7,638
  wholesale trade 7,209
  retail trade 11,351
  finance/real estate/insurance 14,519
  services 18,096
  federal, state & local government 12,857

Establishments, by major industry group, 1992
total 116,573
  agriculture 1,356
  mining 279
  construction 9,514
  manufacturing 7,682
  transportation 4,862
  wholesale trade 9,251
  retail trade 31,440
  finance/real estate/insurance 10,277
  service industries 40,375
  unclassified 1,537

Payroll, by major industry group, 1992
total ($1,000) $41,737,733
  agriculture 110,767
  mining 128,483
  construction 1,930,549
  manufacturing 12,676,578
  transportation 3,303,573
  wholesale trade 3,305,948
  retail trade 4,968,415
  finance/real estate/insurance 2,961,408
  service industries 12,317,446
  unclassified 34,566

Agriculture
number of farms, 1994 84,000
farm acreage, 1994 12,000,000
acres per farm, 1994 146
value of farms, 1994 ($mil) 13,066
farm income, 1993 ($mil)
  gross farm income 2,659
  net farm income 549
  debt/asset ratio 12.8%
farm marketings, 1993 ($mil)
total $2,039
  crops 1,027
  livestock 1,012
government payments 161
farm marketings in order of marketing receipts, 1993
    1) Cattle
    2) Dairy products
    3) Tobacco
    4) Soybeans

Federal economic activity ($mil, except per capita)
expenditures, 1994
  total $25,056
  per capita $4,842
  defense $2,272
  non-defense $22,784
defense department, 1994
  contract awards ($mil) $1,173
  payroll ($mil) $1,068
  civilian employees (x1,000) 6.3
  military personnel (x1,000) 7.3

Fishing, 1992
catch (millions of pounds) .... NA
value ($mil) .... NA

Mining, 1994 ($mil)
total non-fuel mineral production $577

345

Tennessee 8

principal non-fuel minerals in order of value, 1994
1) Stone
2) Zinc
3) Cement

Construction, 1994 ($mil)
total contracts (including
  non-building) $6,314
    residential 3,181
    non-residential 2,140

Manufacturing, 1992
total establishments 7,610
employees, total (x1,000) 504
payroll ($mil) 12,618
production workers (x1,000) 370
value added ($mil) 35,799
value of shipments ($mil) 76,209

Finance
commercial banks, 1994
  number 250
    assets ($bil) 57.0
    deposits ($bil) 46.6
  closed or assisted 0
    deposits ($bil) ....NA
savings and loan associations, 1991
  non-current real estate loans 3.94%
  net income after taxes ($mil) 1
  return on assets .... +0.01%

Retail trade, 1992
establishments (x1,000) 30.6
sales ($mil) 37,508
annual payroll ($mil) 4,231
paid employees (x1,000) 368

Wholesale trade, 1992
establishments 9,341
sales ($bil) 59.7
annual payroll ($mil) 3,064
paid employees (x1,000) 115.4

Service industries, 1992
establishments (x1,000) (non-exempt firms)   32.0
receipts ($mil) (non-exempt firms) 20,410
annual payroll ($mil) 7,581
paid employees (x1,000) (non-exempt firms) . 362

COMMUNICATION, ENERGY & TRANSPORTATION

Communication
daily newspapers, 1993 27
broadcast stations, 1990
  radio: commercial, educational 328
  television: commercial, noncommercial 34
cable TV households, 1988 878,000

Energy
consumption estimates, 1992
total (trillion Btu) 1,793
per capita (million Btu) 356.7
by source of production (trillion Btu)
  coal 591
  natural gas 249
  petroleum 608
  nuclear electric power 167
  hydroelectric power 99
by end-use sector (trillion Btu)
  residential 382
  commercial 140
  industrial 810
  transportation 461
electrical energy
  production, 1993 (billion kWh) 71.6
  net summer capability, 1993 (million kW) . 16.2
gas utilities, 1993
  customers 815,000
  sales (trillion Btu) 169
  revenues ($mil) 808
nuclear plants, 1993 2

Transportation, 1994
public road & street mileage
total 85,527
  urban 16,826
  rural 68,701
  interstate 1,062
vehicle miles of travel (mil) 54,524
total motor vehicle registrations 5,058,653
  automobiles 3,712,180
licensed drivers 3,825,671
  per 1,000 driving age population 951
deaths from motor vehicle
  accidents 1,214

STATE SUMMARY

Capital City . . . . Austin

Governor . . . . George Bush

Address . . . . STATE CAPITOL
AUSTIN, TX 78711
512 463-2000

Admitted as a state 1845

Area (square miles) 268,601

Population, 1980 14,229,191

Population, 1990 16,986,510

Population, 1994 (est.) 18,378,000

Persons per square mile, 1994 . . . . 70.2

Largest city . . . . Houston
population, 1990 1,631,000

Personal income per capita, 1994
(in current dollars) $19,857

Gross state product ($mil), 1991 395,673

Leading industries, 1992 (by payroll)
SERVICE INDUSTRIES
MANUFACTURING
RETAIL TRADE

Leading agricultural commodities, 1993
CATTLE
COTTON
DAIRY PRODUCTS
GREENHOUSE

GEOGRAPHY & ENVIRONMENT

Area (square miles)
total 268,601
land 261,914
water (includes territorial water) 6,687

Federally owned land, 1991 . . . . 1.3%

Highest point
name . . . . Gaudalupe Peak
elevation (feet) 8,749

Lowest point
name . . . . Gulf of Mexico
elevation (feet) . . . . .sea level

General coastline (miles) 367

Tidal shoreline (miles) 3,359

Capital city . . . . Austin
population, 1990 466,000

Largest city . . . . Houston
population, 1990 1,631,000

Number of cities with over 100,000 population
1980 16

Number of cities with over 100,000 population
1990 17

State parks and Recreation areas, 1991
area (acres) 499,000
number of visitors 23,957,000
revenues $12,722,000

National forest land, 1992 (acres) 1,994,000

National park acreage, 1984 1,098,700

DEMOGRAPHICS & CHARACTERISTICS OF THE POPULATION

Population
1970 11,198,655
1980 14,229,191
1990 16,986,510
1994 (est.) 18,378,000
2000 (revised projection) 20,039,000
2010 (revised projection) 22,850,000

Metropolitan area population
1970 8,716,000
1980 11,307,000
1992 14,840,000

Non-metropolitan area population
1970 2,483,000
1980 2,922,000
1992 2,842,000

Change in population, 1980-90
number 2,757,319
percent 19.38%

Persons per square mile, 1994 . . . . 70.2

Age distribution, 1980
under 5 years 8.2%
5 to 17 years 22.1%
65 and over 9.6%

Age distribution, 1990
under 5 years 8.2%
5 to 17 years 20.2%
65 and over 10.1%

Texas 2

Age distribution, 2000 (projected)
under 5 years 7.2%
5 to 17 years 19.5%
65 and over 10.5%

Persons by age, 1990
under 5 years 1,390,054
5 to 17 years 3,445,785
65 and over 1,716,576

Median age, 1990 .... 30.80

Race, 1990
White 12,774,762
Black 2,021,632
American Indian 64,349
Chinese 63,232
Filipino 34,350
Japanese 14,795
Asian Indian 55,795
Korean 31,775
Vietnamese 69,634
all other 1,854,658

Race, 2010 (projected)
White 19,130,000
Black 2,817,000

Persons of Hispanic origin, 1990
total 4,339,905
Mexican 3,890,820
Puerto Rican 42,981
Cuban 18,195
Other Hispanic 387,909

Persons by sex, 1990
male 8,365,963
female 8,620,547

Marital status, 1990
males
15 years & older 6,279,064
single 1,822,173
married 3,830,591
separated 144,206
widowed 132,379
divorced 493,921
females
15 years & older 6,626,866
single 1,421,299
married 3,819,716
separated 202,639

widowed 705,759
divorced 680,092

Households & families, 1990
households 6,070,937
persons per household 2.73
families 4,343,878
married couples 3,435,540
female householder, no husband
present 701,826
one person households 1,452,936
households, 1994 6,539,000
persons per household, 1994 .... 2.75

Nativity, 1990
number of persons born in state 10,994,794
percent of total residents 64.7%

Immigration & naturalization, 1993
immigrants admitted 67,380
persons naturalized 26,403
refugees granted resident status 4,862

VITAL STATISTICS & HEALTH

Births
1992 324,861
with low birth weight 7.0%
to teenage mothers 15.9%
to unmarried mothers 17.5%
1993 330,596
1994 322,268

Abortions, 1992
total 97,000
rate (per 1,000 women age 15-44) 23.1
rate per 1,000 live births 297

Adoptions, 1986
total 8,998
related 50.0%

Deaths
1992 130,947
1993 135,603
1994 137,638

Infant deaths
1992 2,506
1993 2,510
1994 2,314

Texas 3

Average lifetime, 1979-1981
both sexes .... 73.64 years
   men .... 69.70 years
   women .... 77.67 years

Marriages
1992 182,997
1993 185,642
1994 190,272

Divorces
1992 98,960
1993 98,650
1994 99,073

Physicians, 1993
total 31,699
rate (per 1,000 persons) 1.77

Dentists, 1992
total 8,688
rate (per 1,000 persons) 0.50

Hospitals, 1993
number 414
beds (x 1,000) 58.5
average daily census (x 1,000) 32.5
occupancy rate 55.5%
personnel (x 1,000) 228.5
average cost per day to hospital $1,010
average cost per stay to hospital $6,021

EDUCATION

*Educational attainment of all persons
   25 years and older, 1990*
less than 9th grade 1,387,528
high school graduates 2,640,162
bachelor's degree 1,428,031
graduate or professional degree 666,874

Public school enrollment, Fall, 1993
total 3,608,262
   Kindergarten through grade 8 2,681,053
   grades 9 through 12 927,209

Public School Teachers
total, 1994 224,830
   elementary 113,630
   secondary 82,139
salaries, 1994
   beginning $21,806
   average $30,519

*State receipts & expenditures for public
   schools, 1993*
receipts ($mil) 19,621
expenditures
   total ($mil) 18,555
   per capita $1,049
   per pupil $4,933

*Graduating high school seniors,
   public high schools, 1995 (est) 162,385*

SAT scores, 1994
verbal 412
math 474

Institutions of higher education, 1995
total 178
   public 105
   private 73

*Enrollment in institutions of higher
   education, Fall, 1993*
total 942,178
full-time men 251,344
full-time women 259,172
part-time men 185,881
part-time women 245,781

*Minority enrollment in institutions of higher
   education, Fall, 1993*
Black, non-Hispanic 89,307
Hispanic 175,973
Asian/Pacific Islander 36,505

Earned degrees conferred, 1993
Bachelor's 67,598
First professional 4,882
Master's 20,887
Doctor's 2,546

SOCIAL INSURANCE & WELFARE PROGRAMS

Social Security beneficiaries & benefits, 1993
beneficiaries
   total 2,377,000
   retired and dependents 1,604,000
   survivors 484,000
   disabled & dependents 289,000
annual benefit payments ($mil)
   total $16,287
   retired and dependents 10,623
   survivors 3,870
   disabled & dependents 1,794

Texas 4

Medicare, 1993
enrollment (x1,000) 1,973
payments ($mil) 8,007

Medicaid, 1993
recipients (x1,000) 2,308
payments ($mil) 5,575

Federal public aid, 1993
recipients as a percent of population 6.3%
Aid to Families with Dependent Children
  recipients (x1,000) 799
average monthly payment $159
Supplemental Security Income
  total recipients (x1,000) 371

Food Stamp Program
  participants, 1994 (x1,000) 2,730

HOUSING & CONSTRUCTION

Total housing units, 1990 7,008,999
  year round housing units 6,851,350
  vacant 938,062

New privately owned housing units
  authorized, 1994
number (x1,000) 102.6
value ($mil) 8,098

New privately owned housing units
  started, 1994 (x1,000) 109.1

Existing home sales, 1994 (x1,000) 266.9

GOVERNMENT & ELECTIONS

State officials, 1996
  Governor (name/party/term expires)
        GEORGE BUSH
        Republican - 1999
Lt. Governor .... Bob Bullock
Sec. of State .... John Hannah
Atty. General .... Dan Morales
Chf. Justice .... Tom Phillips

Governorship
minimum age 30
length of term .... 4 years
number of consecutive
  terms permitted .... not specified
who succeeds .... Lt. Governor

State legislature
name .... Legislature
  upper chamber
        name .... Senate
        number of members 31
        length of term .... 4 years
        party in majority, 1996 .... Democratic
  lower chamber
        name .... House of Representatives
        number of members 150
        length of term .... 2 years
        party in majority, 1996 .... Democratic

State employees October, 1992
total 278,281
October payroll ($1,000) 552,537

Local governments, 1992
total 4,919
  county 254
  municipal 1,171
  township 0
  school districts 1,101
  special districts 2,392

Voting, November, 1994
voting age population 13,134,000
  registered 58.2%
  voted 37.6%

Vote for president
1988
  Bush 3,014,007
  Dukakis 2,331,286
1992
  Clinton 2,264,070
  Bush 2,445,866
  Perot 1,345,576

Federal representation, 1996 (104th Congress)
Senators (name/party/term expires)

        KAY BAILEY HUTCHISON
        Republican - 2001
        PHIL GRAMM
        Republican - 1997

Representatives, total 30
  Democrats 19
  Republicans 11
  other 0

Women holding public office
U.S. Congress, 1995 3
statewide elected office, 1995 2
state legislature, 1995 33

Black elected officials, 1993
total 472
  US and state legislatures 18
  city/county/regional offices 323
  judicial/law enforcement 40
  education/school boards 91

Hispanic public officials, 1994
total 2,215
  state executives & legislators 41
  city/county/regional offices 1,022
  judicial/law enforcement 389
  education/school boards 763

GOVERNMENTAL FINANCE

State & local government revenues, (selected items), 1991-92 ($per capita)
total $3,846.22
  total general revenues 3,267.33
    from federal government 541.55
    from own sources 2,725.77
    from taxes 1,892.46
      from property taxes 743.96
      from all other taxes 933.29
    from charges & misc. 833.31

State & local government expenditures, (selected items), 1991-92 ($per capita)
total $3,742.37
  total direct general expenditures 3,206.39
    education 1,260.56
    libraries 10.07
    public welfare 423.57
    health & hospitals 298.73
    highways 226.78
    police protection 112.12
    fire protection 44.24
    correction 105.41
    housing & comm. development 25.51
    natural resources & parks 77.12
    interest on general debt 206.18

State & local debt, 1992 ($per capita) 3,852.64

Federal aid grants to state & local government, 1994 ($per capita total & selected items)
per capita total 889.35
  compensatory education 31.46
  waste treatment facilities 7.46
  medicaid 293.08
  housing assistance 31.30
  job training 12.06
  highway trust fund 58.27

CRIME, LAW ENFORCEMENT & COURTS

Crime, 1994 (all rates per 100,000 persons)
total crimes 1,079,225
overall crime rate 5,872.4
  property crimes 949,387
    burglaries 214,687
    larcenies 623,947
    motor vehicle thefts 110,753
  property crime rate 5,165.9
  violent crimes 129,838
    murders 2,022
    forcible rapes 9,102
    robberies 37,643
    aggravated assaults 81,071
  violent crime rate 706.5

Number of police agencies, 1994 826

Arrests, 1994
total 1,035,601
  persons under 18 years of age 212,326

Prisoners under state & federal jurisdiction, 1994
total 118,195
percent change, 1993-94 .... 28.5%
  sentenced to more than one year
  total 118,094
  rate per 100,000 residents 636

Persons under sentence of death, 4/20/95 398

State's highest court
name .... Supreme Court
number of members 9
length of term .... 6 years
intermediate appeals court? .... yes

Texas 6

LABOR & INCOME

Civilian labor force, 1994
total 9,385,000
  men 5,218,000
  women 4,166,000
  persons 16-19 years 552,000
  white 7,941,000
  black 1,099,000

Civilian labor force as a percent of
civilian non-institutional population, 1994
total 69.3%
  men 78.9%
  women 60.1%
  persons 16-19 years 50.4%
  white 69.3%
  black 69.5%

Employment, 1994
total 8,780,000
  men 4,889,000
  women 3,891,000
  persons 16-19 years 437,000
  white 7,505,000
  black 961,000

Full-time/part-time labor force, 1994
full-time labor force 7,844,000
  working part-time for
    ecomonic reasons 109,000
part-time labor force 1,540,000

Unemployment rate, 1994
total 6.4%
  men 6.3%
  women 6.6%
  persons 16-19 years 20.8%
  white 5.5%
  black 12.5%

Unemployed by reason for unemployment
(as a percent of total unemployment), 1994
job losers or completed temp jobs 44.1%
job leavers 10.6%
reentrants 36.9%
new entrants 8.4%

Civilian labor force, by occupation, 1994
executive/administrative/
  managerial 1,162,000
professional/specialty 1,210,000
technicians & related support 282,000

sales 1,175,000
adminstrative support/clerical 1,407,000
service occupations 1,358,000
precision production/craft/repair 1,068,000
machine operators/assemblers 458,000
transportation/material moving 454,000
handlers/helpers/laborers 437,000
farming/forestry/fishing 321,000

Civilian labor force, by industry, 1994
construction 513,000
manufacturing 1,199,000
transportation/communication 581,000
wholesale/retail trade 1,895,000
finance/real estate/insurance 482,000
services 1,871,000
government 1,451,000
agriculture 321,000

Average annual pay, 1994 (prelim.) $25,959
change in average annual pay,
  1993-1994 .... 1.7%

Hours and earnings of production workers
on manufacturing payrolls, 1994
average weekly hours 43.1
average hourly earnings $11.14
average weekly earnings $480.13

Labor union membership, 1994 543,000

Household income (in constant 1993 dollars)
median houschold income, 1992 .... $28,790
median household income, 1993 .... $28,727

Poverty
persons below poverty level, 1992 .... 18.3%
persons below poverty level, 1993 .... 17.4%

Personal income ($per capita)
1994
  in current dollars 19,857
  in constant (1987) dollars 15,357
1995 (projected)
  in constant (1982) dollars 12,951
2000 (projected)
  in constant (1982) dollars 13,851

Federal income tax returns, 1993
returns filed 7,715,165
adjusted gross income ($1000) 233,252,699
total income tax paid ($1000) 35,014,627

ECONOMY, BUSINESS, INDUSTRY & AGRICULTURE

Fortune 500 companies, 1994 36

Business incorporations, 1994
total 37,362
change, 1993-94 .... 7.0%

Business failures, 1994
total 5,838
rate per 10,000 concerns 100
change, 1993-94 .... -17.7%

Business firm ownership
Hispanic owned firms, 1987 94,754
black owned firms, 1987 35,725
women owned firms, 1987 298,100
foreign owned firms, 1982 643

Gross state product, 1991 ($mil)
total $395,673
   agriculture services, forestry, fisheries ... 6,948
   mining 26,623
   construction 14,560
   manufacturing—durable goods 28,976
   manufacturing—nondurable goods 35,487
   transportation, communication &
      public utilities 43,422
   wholesale trade 27,414
   retail trade 37,359
   finance/real estate/insurance 61,165
   services 69,257
   federal, state & local government 44,461

Establishments, by major industry group, 1992
total 412,326
   agriculture 5,887
   mining 7,344
   construction 30,342
   manufacturing 21,984
   transportation 18,038
   wholesale trade 36,377
   retail trade 101,600
   finance/real estate/insurance 38,733
   service industries 145,588
   unclassified 6,433

Payroll, by major industry group, 1992
total ($1,000) $145,635,718
   agriculture 580,256

   mining 6,919,282
   construction 8,276,318
   manufacturing 29,934,267
   transportation 12,456,479
   wholesale trade 13,135,453
   retail trade 17,547,304
   finance/real estate/insurance 12,615,245
   service industries 44,035,232
   unclassified 135,882

Agriculture
number of farms, 1994 185,000
farm acreage, 1994 129,000,000
acres per farm, 1994 699
value of farms, 1994 ($mil) 64,146
farm income, 1993 ($mil)
   gross farm income 15,725
   net farm income 4,098
   debt/asset ratio 12.7%
farm marketings, 1993 ($mil)
   total $12,617
      crops 4,275
      livestock 8,342
government payments 1,421
farm marketings in order of marketing
receipts, 1993
   1) Cattle
   2) Cotton
   3) Dairy products
   4) Greenhouse

Federal economic activity
($mil, except per capita)
expenditures, 1994
   total $79,308
   per capita $4,315
   defense $15,538
   non-defense $63,770
defense department, 1994
   contract awards ($mil) $8,145
   payroll ($mil) $7,201
   civilian employees (x1,000) 54.3
   military personnel (x1,000) 102.5

Fishing, 1992
catch (millions of pounds) 96
value ($mil) 181

Mining, 1994 ($mil)
total non-fuel mineral production $1,409

Texas 8

principal non-fuel minerals in order of value, 1994

  1) Cement
  2) Stone
  3) Magnesium metal

Construction, 1994 ($mil)
total contracts (including
  non-building) $20,713
    residential 9,704
    non-residential 6,981

Manufacturing, 1992
total establishments 21,678
employees, total (x1,000) 957
payroll ($mil) 29,451
production workers (x1,000) 584
value added ($mil) 82,532
value of shipments ($mil) 211,648

Finance
commercial banks, 1994
  number 1,011
    assets ($bil) 184.0
    deposits ($bil) 151.2
    closed or assisted 0
    deposits ($bil) .... NA
savings and loan associations, 1991
    non-current real estate loans 4.53%
    net income after taxes ($mil) .... -935
    return on assets .... -1.49%

Retail trade, 1992
establishments (x1,000) 98.4
sales ($mil) 130,686
annual payroll ($mil) 14,676
paid employees (x1,000) 1,230

Wholesale trade, 1992
establishments 36,611
sales ($bil) 281.3
annual payroll ($mil) 11,800
paid employees (x1,000) 408.9

Service industries, 1992
establishments (x1,000) (non-exempt firms) 123.6
receipts ($mil) (non-exempt firms) 84,763
annual payroll ($mil) 32,402
paid employees (x1,000) (non-exempt firms) 1,430

COMMUNICATION, ENERGY & TRANSPORTATION

Communication
daily newspapers, 1993 92
broadcast stations, 1990
    radio: commercial, educational 689
    television: commercial, noncommercial 108
cable TV households, 1988 3,072,000

Energy
consumption estimates, 1992
  total (trillion Btu) 9,915
  per capita (million Btu) 560.7
  by source of production (trillion Btu)
    coal 1,324
    natural gas 3,626
    petroleum 4,665
    nuclear electric power 262
    hydroelectric power 17
  by end-use sector (trillion Btu)
    residential 1,114
    commercial 993
    industrial 5,614
    transportation 2,194
electrical energy
    production, 1993 (billion kWh) 248.2
    net summer capability, 1993 (million kW) . 63.9
gas utilities, 1993
    customers 3,662,000
    sales (trillion Btu) 1,015
    revenues ($mil) 4,766
nuclear plants, 1993 4

Transportation, 1994
public road & street mileage
  total 294,491
    urban 80,903
    rural 213,588
    interstate 3,234
vehicle miles of travel (mil) 178,348
total motor vehicle registrations 13,625,865
    automobiles 8,698,528
licensed drivers 12,109,960
    per 1,000 driving age population 889
deaths from motor vehicle
    accidents 3,186

354

STATE SUMMARY

Capital City ....Salt Lake City

Governor ....Mike Leavitt

Address ....STATE CAPITOL
SALT LAKE CITY, UT 84114
801 538-1000

Admitted as a state 1896

Area (square miles) 84,904

Population, 1980 1,461,037

Population, 1990 1,722,850

Population, 1994 (est.) 1,908,000

Persons per square mile, 1994 ....23.2

Largest city ....Salt Lake City
population, 1990 160,000

Personal income per capita, 1994
(in current dollars) $17,043

Gross state product ($mil), 1991 33,078

Leading industries, 1992 (by payroll)
SERVICE INDUSTRIES
MANUFACTURING
RETAIL TRADE

Leading agricultural commodities, 1993
CATTLE
DAIRY PRODUCTS
HAY
TURKEYS

GEOGRAPHY & ENVIRONMENT

Area (square miles)
total 84,904
land 82,168
water (includes territorial water) 2,736

Federally owned land, 1991 ....63.9%

Highest point
name .... Kings Peak
elevation (feet) 13,528

Lowest point
name .... Beaverdam Creek
elevation (feet) 2,000

General coastline (miles) 0

Tidal shoreline (miles) 0

Capital city ....Salt Lake City
population, 1990 160,000

Largest city ....Salt Lake City
population, 1990 160,000

Number of cities with over 100,000 population
1980 1

Number of cities with over 100,000 population
1990 1

State parks and Recreation areas, 1991
area (acres) 97,000
number of visitors 4,940,000
revenues $2,970,000

National forest land, 1992 (acres) 9,186,000

National park acreage, 1984 2,022,700

DEMOGRAPHICS & CHARACTERISTICS OF THE POPULATION

Population
1970 1,059,273
1980 1,461,037
1990 1,722,850
1994 (est.) 1,908,000
2000 (revised projection) 2,148,000
2010 (revised projection) 2,462,000

Metropolitan area population
1970 822,000
1980 1,128,000
1992 1,403,000

Non-metropolitan area population
1970 238,000
1980 333,000
1992 408,000

Change in population, 1980-90
number 261,813
percent 17.92%

Persons per square mile, 1994 .... 23.2

Age distribution, 1980
under 5 years 13.0%
5 to 17 years 24.0%
65 and over 7.5%

Age distribution, 1990
under 5 years 9.9%
5 to 17 years 26.5%
65 and over 8.7%

Utah 2

Age distribution, 2000 (projected)
under 5 years 10.5%
5 to 17 years 25.3%
65 and over 8.2%

Persons by age, 1990
under 5 years 169,633
5 to 17 years 457,811
65 and over 149,958

Median age, 1990 .... 26.20

Race, 1990
White 1,615,845
Black 11,576
American Indian 24,093
Chinese 5,322
Filipino 1,905
Japanese 6,500
Asian Indian 1,557
Korean 2,629
Vietnamese 2,797
all other 50,436

Race, 2010 (projected)
White 2,272,000
Black 18,000

Persons of Hispanic origin, 1990
total 84,597
  Mexican 56,842
  Puerto Rican 2,181
  Cuban 456
  Other Hispanic 25,118

Persons by sex, 1990
male 855,759
female 867,091

Marital status, 1990
males
  15 years & older 580,050
  single 165,764
  married 366,139
    separated 6,288
    widowed 9,074
    divorced 39,073
females
  15 years & older 605,647
  single 136,825
  married 367,263
    separated 8,478
    widowed 48,925
    divorced 52,634

Households & families, 1990
households 537,273
persons per household 3.15
  families 410,862
    married couples 348,029
    female householder, no husband
      present 49,077
    one person households 101,640
households, 1994 599,000
persons per household, 1994 .... 3.13

Nativity, 1990
number of persons born in state 1,157,744
percent of total residents 67.2%

Immigration & naturalization, 1993
immigrants admitted 3,266
persons naturalized 950
refugees granted resident status 441

VITAL STATISTICS & HEALTH

Births
1992 37,411
  with low birth weight 5.6%
  to teenage mothers 10.5%
  to unmarried mothers 15.1%
1993 36,462
1994 38,808

Abortions, 1992
total 4,000
rate (per 1,000 women age 15-44) 9.3
rate per 1,000 live births 104

Adoptions, 1986
total 1,261
  related 62.0%

Deaths
1992 9,904
1993 10,193
1994 10,545

Infant deaths
1992 233
1993 217
1994 233

Utah 3

Average lifetime, 1979-1981
both sexes .... 75.76 years
  men .... 72.38 years
  women .... 79.18 years

Marriages
1992 19,895
1993 20,588
1994 20,325

Divorces
1992 9,685
1993 8,888
1994 8,999

Physicians, 1993
total 3,463
rate (per 1,000 persons) 1.87

Dentists, 1992
total 1,167
rate (per 1,000 persons) 0.65

Hospitals, 1993
number 42
beds (x 1,000) 4.4
average daily census (x 1,000) 2.3
occupancy rate 53.4%
personnel (x 1,000) 20.7
average cost per day to hospital $1,081
average cost per stay to hospital $5,314

EDUCATION

Educational attainment of all persons
  25 years and older, 1990
less than 9th grade 30,379
high school graduates 244,132
bachelor's degree 138,534
graduate or professional degree 61,219

Public school enrollment, Fall, 1993
total 471,365
  Kindergarten through grade 8 329,926
  grades 9 through 12 141,439

Public School Teachers
total, 1994 19,053
  elementary 8,918
  secondary 7,780
salaries, 1994
  beginning $18,787
  average $28,056

State receipts & expenditures for public
  schools, 1993
receipts ($mil) 1,832
expenditures
  total ($mil) 1,510
  per capita $834
  per pupil $3,218

Graduating high school seniors,
  public high schools, 1995 (est) 29,177

SAT scores, 1994
verbal 509
math 558

Institutions of higher education, 1995
total 16
  public 9
  private 7

Enrollment in institutions of higher
  education, Fall, 1993
total 138,139
full-time men 47,405
full-time women 46,397
part-time men 21,967
part-time women 22,370

Minority enrollment in institutions of higher
  education, Fall, 1993
Black, non-Hispanic 988
Hispanic 3,513
Asian/Pacific Islander 2,784

Earned degrees conferred, 1993
Bachelor's 12,901
First professional 388
Master's 2,868
Doctor's 376

SOCIAL INSURANCE & WELFARE PROGRAMS

Social Security beneficiaries & benefits, 1993
beneficiaries
total 213,000
  retired and dependents 153,000
  survivors 34,000
  disabled & dependents 26,000
annual benefit payments ($mil)
total $1,495
  retired and dependents 1,056
  survivors 285
  disabled & dependents 154

Utah 4

Medicare, 1993
enrollment (x1,000) 177
payments ($mil) 591

Medicaid, 1993
recipients (x1,000) 148
payments ($mil) 408

Federal public aid, 1993
recipients as a percent of population 3.7%
Aid to Families with Dependent Children
   recipients (x1,000) 50
average monthly payment $354
Supplemental Security Income
   total recipients (x1,000) 18

Food Stamp Program
  participants, 1994 (x1,000) 128

HOUSING & CONSTRUCTION

Total housing units, 1990 598,388
  year round housing units 577,185
  vacant 61,115

New privately owned housing units
  authorized, 1994
number (x1,000) 18.6
value ($mil) 1,717

New privately owned housing units
  started, 1994 (x1,000) 20.0

Existing home sales, 1994 (x1,000) 32.4

GOVERNMENT & ELECTIONS

State officials, 1996
  Governor (name/party/term expires)
        MIKE LEAVITT
        Republican - 1996
Lt. Governor ....Olene Walker
Sec. of State .... (no Secretary of State)
Atty. General .... Jan Graham
Chf. Justice .... Gordon R. Hall

Governorship
minimum age 30
length of term .... 4 years
number of consecutive
  terms permitted .... not specified
who succeeds .... Lt. Governor

State legislature
name .... Legislature
  upper chamber
    name .... Senate
    number of members 29
    length of term .... 4 years
    party in majority, 1996 .... Republican
  lower chamber
    name .... House of Representatives
    number of members 75
    length of term .... 2 years
    party in majority, 1996 .... Republican

State employees October, 1992
total 46,491
October payroll ($1,000) 80,955

Local governments, 1992
total 635
  county 29
  municipal 228
  township 0
  school districts 40
  special districts 337

Voting, November, 1994
voting age population 1,231,000
  registered 59.4%
  voted 44.1%

Vote for president
1988
  Bush 426,858
  Dukakis 206,853
1992
  Clinton 182,850
  Bush 320,950
  Perot 202,823

Federal representation, 1996 (104th Congress)
Senators (name/party/term expires)

      ORRIN G. HATCH
      Republican - 2001
     ROBERT BENNETT
      Republican - 1999

Representatives, total 3
  Democrats 1
  Republicans 2
  other 0

Utah 5

Women holding public office
U.S. Congress, 1995 1
statewide elected office, 1995 2
state legislature, 1995 15

Black elected officials, 1993
total 0
  US and state legislatures 0
  city/county/regional offices 0
  judicial/law enforcement 0
  education/school boards 0

Hispanic public officials, 1994
total 1
  state executives & legislators 1
  city/county/regional offices 0
  judicial/law enforcement 0
  education/school boards 0

GOVERNMENTAL FINANCE

State & local government revenues, (selected items), 1991-92 ($per capita)
total $4,344.91
  total general revenues 3,361.77
   from federal government 671.15
   from own sources 2,690.62
   from taxes 1,740.56
   from property taxes 471.52
   from all other taxes 1,190.26
   from charges & misc. 850.06

State & local government expenditures, (selected items), 1991-92 ($per capita)
total $4,106.00
  total direct general expenditures 3,280.33
  education 1,399.07
  libraries 18.45
  public welfare 383.33
  health & hospitals 227.88
  highways 233.77
  police protection 98.70
  fire protection 88.67
  correction 76.31
  housing & comm. development 60.84
  natural resources & parks 124.06
  interest on general debt 176.20

State & local debt, 1992 ($per capita) 5,860.69

Federal aid grants to state & local government, 1994 ($per capita total & selected items)
per capita total 633.51
  compensatory education 16.03
  waste treatment facilities 7.78
  medicaid 212.61
  housing assistance 21.77
  job training 6.69
  highway trust fund 57.78

CRIME, LAW ENFORCEMENT & COURTS

Crime, 1994 (all rates per 100,000 persons)
total crimes 101,142
overall crime rate 5,300.9
  property crimes 95,332
   burglaries 15,089
   larcenies 74,554
   motor vehicle thefts 5,689
  property crime rate 4,996.4
  violent crimes 5,810
   murders 56
   forcible rapes 806
   robberies 1,213
   aggravated assaults 3,735
  violent crime rate 304.5

Number of police agencies, 1994 95

Arrests, 1994
total 112,226
  persons under 18 years of age 38,697

Prisoners under state & federal jurisdiction, 1994
total 3,016
percent change, 1993-94 .... 4.4%
  sentenced to more than one year
  total 2,997
  rate per 100,000 residents 155

Persons under sentence of death, 4/20/95 11

State's highest court
name .... Supreme Court
number of members 5
length of term .... 10 years
intermediate appeals court? .... no

359

Utah 6

LABOR & INCOME

Civilian labor force, 1994

total	975,000
men	539,000
women	435,000
persons 16-19 years	100,000
white	944,000
black	NA

Civilian labor force as a percent of civilian non-institutional population, 1994

total	74.3%
men	83.3%
women	65.5%
persons 16-19 years	68.3%
white	74.4%
black	NA%

Employment, 1994

total	938,000
men	521,000
women	417,000
persons 16-19 years	90,000
white	909,000
black	NA

Full-time/part-time labor force, 1994

full-time labor force	720,000
working part-time for ecomonic reasons	9,000
part-time labor force	256,000

Unemployment rate, 1994

total	3.7%
men	3.4%
women	4.2%
persons 16-19 years	10.3%
white	3.7%
black	NA%

Unemployed by reason for unemployment (as a percent of total unemployment), 1994

job losers or completed temp jobs	31.8%
job leavers	22.0%
reentrants	37.6%
new entrants	8.6%

Civilian labor force, by occupation, 1994

executive/administrative/ managerial	136,000
professional/specialty	138,000
technicians & related support	34,000
sales	115,000
adminstrative support/clerical	148,000
service occupations	126,000
precision production/craft/repair	111,000
machine operators/assemblers	54,000
transportation/material moving	37,000
handlers/helpers/laborers	45,000
farming/forestry/fishing	27,000

Civilian labor force, by industry, 1994

construction	55,000
manufacturing	134,000
transportation/communication	55,000
wholesale/retail trade	186,000
finance/real estate/insurance	46,000
services	212,000
government	174,000
agriculture	NA

Average annual pay, 1994 (prelim.) $22,811
change in average annual pay, 1993-1994 ...... 2.5%

Hours and earnings of production workers on manufacturing payrolls, 1994

average weekly hours	40.6
average hourly earnings	$11.26
average weekly earnings	$457.16

Labor union membership, 1994 79,800

Household income (in constant 1993 dollars)

median household income, 1992	$35,276
median household income, 1993	$35,786

Poverty

persons below poverty level, 1992	9.4%
persons below poverty level, 1993	10.7%

Personal income ($per capita)

1994
in current dollars	17,043
in constant (1987) dollars	13,181

1995 (projected)
in constant (1982) dollars	10,827

2000 (projected)
in constant (1982) dollars	11,605

Federal income tax returns, 1993

returns filed	747,636
adjusted gross income ($1000)	22,500,133
total income tax paid ($1000)	2,787,878

ECONOMY, BUSINESS, INDUSTRY & AGRICULTURE

Fortune 500 companies, 1994 2

Business incorporations, 1994
total 5,560
change, 1993-94 .... 5.5%

Business failures, 1994
total 261
rate per 10,000 concerns 51
change, 1993-94 .... -26.7%

Business firm ownership
Hispanic owned firms, 1987 1,300
black owned firms, 1987 202
women owned firms, 1987 29,800
foreign owned firms, 1982 97

Gross state product, 1991 ($mil)
total $33,078
  agriculture services, forestry, fisheries 495
  mining 1,334
  construction 1,322
  manufacturing – durable goods 3,360
  manufacturing – nondurable goods 1,762
  transportation, communication &
    public utilities 3,298
  wholesale trade 2,086
  retail trade 3,058
  finance/real estate/insurance 5,019
  services 6,134
  federal, state & local government 5,210

Establishments, by major industry group, 1992
total 39,779
  agriculture 509
  mining 340
  construction 4,463
  manufacturing 2,555
  transportation 1,565
  wholesale trade 3,224
  retail trade 9,521
  finance/real estate/insurance 3,669
  service industries 13,328
  unclassified 605

Payroll, by major industry group, 1992
total ($1,000) $13,098,682
  agriculture 39,249
  mining 342,419
  construction 775,194
  manufacturing 2,793,407
  transportation 1,287,367
  wholesale trade 1,038,634
  retail trade 1,653,326
  finance/real estate/insurance 845,528
  service industries 4,312,574
  unclassified 10,984

Agriculture
number of farms, 1994 13,000
farm acreage, 1994 11,000,000
acres per farm, 1994 854
value of farms, 1994 ($mil) 5,685
farm income, 1993 ($mil)
  gross farm income 946
  net farm income 291
  debt/asset ratio 10.7%
farm marketings, 1993 ($mil)
total $804
  crops 177
  livestock 626
government payments 37
farm marketings in order of marketing receipts, 1993
  1) Cattle
  2) Dairy products
  3) Hay
  4) Turkeys

Federal economic activity ($mil, except per capita)
expenditures, 1994
  total $7,594
  per capita $3,980
  defense $1,452
  non-defense $6,141
defense department, 1994
  contract awards ($mil) $521
  payroll ($mil) $906
  civilian employees (x1,000) 15.5
  military personnel (x1,000) 5.7

Fishing, 1992
catch (millions of pounds) .... NA
value ($mil) .... NA

Mining, 1994 ($mil)
total non-fuel mineral production $1,428

Utah 8

principal non-fuel minerals in order of value, 1994
1) Copper
2) Gold
3) Magnesium metal

Construction, 1994 ($mil)
total contracts (including
  non-building) $3,364
    residential 1,684
    non-residential 1,199

Manufacturing, 1992
total establishments 2,525
employees, total (x1,000) 106
payroll ($mil) 2,860
production workers (x1,000) 68
value added ($mil) 7,271
value of shipments ($mil) 15,750

Finance
commercial banks, 1994
  number 48
    assets ($bil) 15.4
    deposits ($bil) 11.2
    closed or assisted 0
    deposits ($bil) .... NA
savings and loan associations, 1991
  non-current real estate loans 5.19%
  net income after taxes ($mil) 20
  return on assets .... +0.58%

Retail trade, 1992
establishments (x1,000) 9.2
sales ($mil) 12,373
annual payroll ($mil) 1,385
paid employees (x1,000) 126

Wholesale trade, 1992
establishments 3,231
sales ($bil) 15.3
annual payroll ($mil) 1,005
paid employees (x1,000) 39.6

Service industries, 1992
establishments (x1,000) (non-exempt firms) 11.7
receipts ($mil) (non-exempt firms) 7,491
annual payroll ($mil) 2,667
paid employees (x1,000) (non-exempt firms) . 139

COMMUNICATION, ENERGY & TRANSPORTATION

Communication
daily newspapers, 1993 6
broadcast stations, 1990
  radio: commercial, educational 89
  television: commercial, noncommercial 10
cable TV households, 1988 202,000

Energy
consumption estimates, 1992
total (trillion Btu) 557
per capita (million Btu) 307.4
by source of production (trillion Btu)
  coal 363
  natural gas 132
  petroleum 208
  nuclear electric power 0
  hydroelectric power 6
by end-use sector (trillion Btu)
  residential 100
  commercial 87
  industrial 210
  transportation 159
electrical energy
  production, 1993 (billion kWh) 33.5
  net summer capability, 1993 (million kW) .. 4.8
gas utilities, 1993
  customers 522,000
  sales (trillion Btu) 83
  revenues ($mil) 368
nuclear plants, 1993 0

Transportation, 1994
public road & street mileage
total 40,842
  urban 6,201
  rural 34,641
  interstate 940
vehicle miles of travel (mil) 18,078
total motor vehicle registrations 1,414,668
  automobiles 808,372
licensed drivers 1,245,205
  per 1,000 driving age population 947
deaths from motor vehicle
  accidents 342

Vermont 1

STATE SUMMARY

Capital City .... Montpelier

Governor ....Howard Dean

Address .... STATE CAPITOL
MONTPELIER, VT 05602
802 828-3333

Admitted as a state 1791

Area (square miles) 9,615

Population, 1980 511,456

Population, 1990 562,758

Population, 1994 (est.) 580,000

Persons per square mile, 1994 .... 62.7

Largest city .... Burlington
population, 1990 39,100

Personal income per capita, 1994
(in current dollars) $20,224

Gross state product ($mil), 1991 11,198

Leading industries, 1992 (by payroll)
MANUFACTURING
SERVICE INDUSTRIES
RETAIL TRADE

Leading agricultural commodities, 1993
DAIRY PRODUCTS
CATTLE
GREENHOUSE
HAY

GEOGRAPHY & ENVIRONMENT

Area (square miles)
total 9,615
land 9,249
water (includes territorial water) 366

Federally owned land, 1991 .... 6.0%

Highest point
name ....Mt. Mansfield
elevation (feet) 4,393

Lowest point
name .... Lake Champlain
elevation (feet) 95

General coastline (miles) 0

Tidal shoreline (miles) 0

Capital city .... Montpelier
population, 1990 8,200

Largest city .... Burlington
population, 1990 39,100

Number of cities with over 100,000 population
1980 0

Number of cities with over 100,000 population
1990 0

State parks and Recreation areas, 1991
area (acres) 90,000
number of visitors 982,000
revenues $4,402,000

National forest land, 1992 (acres) 816,000

National park acreage, 1984 4,100

DEMOGRAPHICS & CHARACTERISTICS OF THE POPULATION

Population
1970 444,732
1980 511,456
1990 562,758
1994 (est.) 580,000
2000 (revised projection) 592,000
2010 (revised projection) 623,000

Metropolitan area population
1970 99,000
1980 115,000
1992 154,000

Non-metropolitan area population
1970 346,000
1980 396,000
1992 417,000

Change in population, 1980-90
number 51,302
percent 10.03%

Persons per square mile, 1994 .... 62.7

Age distribution, 1980
under 5 years 7.0%
5 to 17 years 21.4%
65 and over 11.4%

Age distribution, 1990
under 5 years 7.3%
5 to 17 years 18.0%
65 and over 11.7%

Vermont 2

Age distribution, 2000 (projected)
under 5 years 6.4%
5 to 17 years 18.9%
65 and over 11.8%

Persons by age, 1990
under 5 years 41,261
5 to 17 years 101,822
65 and over 66,163

Median age, 1990 .... 33.00

Race, 1990
White 555,088
Black 1,951
American Indian 1,650
Chinese 679
Filipino 253
Japanese 373
Asian Indian 529
Korean 563
Vietnamese 236
all other 1,390

Race, 2010 (projected)
White 609,000
Black 4,000

Persons of Hispanic origin, 1990
total 3,661
Mexican 725
Puerto Rican 659
Cuban 168
Other Hispanic 2,109

Persons by sex, 1990
male 275,492
female 287,266

Marital status, 1990
males
15 years & older 213,331
single 66,171
married 125,887
separated 3,166
widowed 5,039
divorced 16,234
females
15 years & older 228,387
single 55,531
married 126,511
separated 4,003

widowed 25,054
divorced 21,291

Households & families, 1990
households 210,650
persons per household 2.57
families 144,895
married couples 118,905
female householder, no husband
present 19,360
one person households 49,366
households, 1994 220,000
persons per household, 1994 .... 2.54

Nativity, 1990
number of persons born in state 321,704
percent of total residents 57.2%

Immigration & naturalization, 1993
immigrants admitted 709
persons naturalized 221
refugees granted resident status 67

VITAL STATISTICS & HEALTH

Births
1992 7,625
with low birth weight 5.6%
to teenage mothers 8.5%
to unmarried mothers 23.4%
1993 7,286
1994 7,158

Abortions, 1992
total 3,000
rate (per 1,000 women age 15-44) 21.2
rate per 1,000 live births 393

Adoptions, 1986
total 333
related 61.0%

Deaths
1992 4,732
1993 4,868
1994 4,573

Infant deaths
1992 52
1993 36
1994 48

Vermont 3

Average lifetime, 1979-1981
both sexes . . . . 74.79 years
  men . . . . 71.06 years
  women . . . . 78.49 years

Marriages
1992 5,901
1993 6,027
1994 5,831

Divorces
1992 2,955
1993 2,766
1994 2,316

Physicians, 1993
total 1,492
rate (per 1,000 persons) 2.59

Dentists, 1992
total 326
rate (per 1,000 persons) 0.57

Hospitals, 1993
number 15
beds (x 1,000) 1.9
average daily census (x 1,000) 1.2
occupancy rate 64.2%
personnel (x 1,000) 7.0
average cost per day to hospital $676
average cost per stay to hospital $5,241

EDUCATION

*Educational attainment of all persons
25 years and older, 1990*
less than 9th grade 30,945
high school graduates 123,430
bachelor's degree 55,120
graduate or professional degree 31,734

Public school enrollment, Fall, 1993
total 102,755
  Kindergarten through grade 8 74,828
  grades 9 through 12 27,927

Public School Teachers
total, 1994 8,102
  elementary 3,371
  secondary 3,140
salaries, 1994
  beginning $22,982
  average $34,517

*State receipts & expenditures for public
schools, 1993*
receipts ($mil) 697
expenditures
  total ($mil) 684
  per capita $1,197
  per pupil $7,172

*Graduating high school seniors,
public high schools, 1995 (est)* 5,676

SAT scores, 1994
verbal 427
math 472

Institutions of higher education, 1995
total 22
  public 6
  private 16

*Enrollment in institutions of higher
education, Fall, 1993*
total 36,415
full-time men 11,834
full-time women 12,477
part-time men 3,787
part-time women 8,317

*Minority enrollment in institutions of higher
education, Fall, 1993*
Black, non-Hispanic 355
Hispanic 417
Asian/Pacific Islander 471

Earned degrees conferred, 1993
Bachelor's 4,707
First professional 96
Master's 1,103
Doctor's 53

SOCIAL INSURANCE & WELFARE PROGRAMS

Social Security beneficiaries & benefits, 1993
beneficiaries
total 95,000
  retired and dependents 66,000
  survivors 15,000
  disabled & dependents 14,000
annual benefit payments ($mil)
total $664
  retired and dependents 454
  survivors 126
  disabled & dependents 84

Vermont 4

Medicare, 1993
enrollment (x1,000) 79
payments ($mil) 228

Medicaid, 1993
recipients (x1,000) 81
payments ($mil) 235

Federal public aid, 1993
recipients as a percent of population 7.0%
Aid to Families with Dependent Children
  recipients (x1,000) 28
average monthly payment $543
Supplemental Security Income
  total recipients (x1,000) 12

Food Stamp Program
  participants, 1994 (x1,000) 65

HOUSING & CONSTRUCTION

Total housing units, 1990 271,214
  year round housing units 225,771
  vacant 60,564

New privately owned housing units
  authorized, 1994
number (x1,000) 2.4
value ($mil) 220

New privately owned housing units
  started, 1994 (x1,000) 2.2

Existing home sales, 1994 (x1,000) 10.9

GOVERNMENT & ELECTIONS

State officials, 1996
  Governor (name/party/term expires)
        HOWARD DEAN
        Democrat - 1997
Lt. Governor .... Barbara Snelling
Sec. of State .... Don Hooper
Atty. General .... Jeff Amestoy
Chf. Justice .... F. W. Allen

Governorship
minimum age .... not specified
length of term .... 2 years
number of consecutive
  terms permitted .... not specified
who succeeds .... Lt. Governor

State legislature
name .... General Assembly
  upper chamber
    name .... Senate
    number of members 30
    length of term .... 2 years
    party in majority, 1996 .... Republican
  lower chamber
    name .... House of Representatives
    number of members 150
    length of term .... 2 years
    party in majority, 1996 .... Democratic

State employees October, 1992
total 14,474
October payroll ($1,000) 31,270

Local governments, 1992
total 690
  county 14
  municipal 50
  township 237
  school districts 278
  special districts 110

Voting, November, 1994
voting age population 432,000
  registered 70.7%
  voted 48.8%

Vote for president
1988
  Bush 123,166
  Dukakis 116,419
1992
  Clinton 125,803
  Bush 85,512
  Perot 61,510

Federal representation, 1996 (104th Congress)
Senators (name/party/term expires)

        JIM JEFFORDS
        Republican - 2001
        PATRICK J. LEAHY
        Democrat - 1999

Representatives, total 1
  Democrats 0
  Republicans 0
  other 1

Vermont 5

Women holding public office
U.S. Congress, 1995 0
statewide elected office, 1995 1
state legislature, 1995 53

Black elected officials, 1993
total 2
  US and state legislatures 2
  city/county/regional offices 0
  judicial/law enforcement 0
  education/school boards 0

Hispanic public officials, 1994
total .... NA
  state executives & legislators .... NA
  city/county/regional offices .... NA
  judicial/law enforcement .... NA
  education/school boards .... NA

GOVERNMENTAL FINANCE

State & local government revenues, (selected items), 1991-92 ($per capita)
total $4,678.96
  total general revenues 4,143.86
    from federal government 913.50
    from own sources 3,230.36
    from taxes 2,303.31
      from property taxes 960.96
      from all other taxes 1,185.48
    from charges & misc. 927.04

State & local government expenditures, (selected items), 1991-92 ($per capita)
total $4,570.46
  total direct general expenditures 4,098.44
    education 1,702.70
    libraries 12.11
    public welfare 653.04
    health & hospitals 118.85
    highways 425.34
    police protection 96.62
    fire protection 32.21
    correction 59.52
    housing & comm. development 79.40
    natural resources & parks 108.73
    interest on general debt 225.22

State & local debt, 1992 ($per capita) 3,550.92

Federal aid grants to state & local government, 1994 ($per capita total & selected items)
per capita total 942.11
  compensatory education 28.08
  waste treatment facilities 7.22
  medicaid 322.48
  housing assistance 58.28
  job training 12.47
  highway trust fund 83.27

CRIME, LAW ENFORCEMENT & COURTS

Crime, 1994 (all rates per 100,000 persons)
total crimes 18,852
overall crime rate 3,250.3
  property crimes 18,290
    burglaries 4,274
    larcenies 13,154
    motor vehicle thefts 862
  property crime rate 3,153.4
  violent crimes 562
    murders 6
    forcible rapes 160
    robberies 71
    aggravated assaults 325
  violent crime rate 96.9

Number of police agencies, 1994 18

Arrests, 1994
total 3,702
  persons under 18 years of age 467

Prisoners under state & federal jurisdiction, 1994
total 1,301
percent change, 1993-94 .... 6.4%
sentenced to more than one year
  total 981
  rate per 100,000 residents 168

Persons under sentence of death, 4/20/95 .... NA

State's highest court
name .... Supreme Court
number of members 5
length of term .... 6 years
intermediate appeals court? .... no

367

Vermont 6

LABOR & INCOME

Civilian labor force, 1994
total 321,000
men 166,000
women 155,000
persons 16-19 years 15,000
white 317,000
black .... NA

Civilian labor force as a percent of civilian non-institutional population, 1994
total 71.1%
men 77.5%
women 65.3%
persons 16-19 years 59.8%
white 71.1%
black .... NA%

Employment, 1994
total 306,000
men 158,000
women 148,000
persons 16-19 years 14,000
white 302,000
black .... NA

Full-time/part-time labor force, 1994
full-time labor force 250,000
working part-time for
ecomonic reasons 4,000
part-time labor force 70,000

Unemployment rate, 1994
total 4.7%
men 5.0%
women 4.4%
persons 16-19 years 9.6%
white 4.7%
black .... NA%

Unemployed by reason for unemployment (as a percent of total unemployment), 1994
job losers or completed temp jobs 57.3%
job leavers 8.5%
reentrants 32.1%
new entrants 2.3%

Civilian labor force, by occupation, 1994
executive/administrative/
managerial 44,000
professional/specialty 52,000
technicians & related support 12,000
sales 38,000
adminstrative support/clerical 44,000
service occupations 42,000
precision production/craft/repair 35,000
machine operators/assemblers 18,000
transportation/material moving 11,000
handlers/helpers/laborers 9,000
farming/forestry/fishing 14,000

Civilian labor force, by industry, 1994
construction 15,000
manufacturing 52,000
transportation/communication 12,000
wholesale/retail trade 53,000
finance/real estate/insurance 15,000
services 80,000
government 37,000
agriculture 12,000

Average annual pay, 1994 (prelim.) $22,964
change in average annual pay,
1993-1994 .... 1.1%

Hours and earnings of production workers on manufacturing payrolls, 1994
average weekly hours 40.9
average hourly earnings $11.97
average weekly earnings $489.57

Labor union membership, 1994 22,700

Household income (in constant 1993 dollars)
median household income, 1992 .... $33,736
median household income, 1993 .... $31,065

Poverty
persons below poverty level, 1992 .... 10.5%
persons below poverty level, 1993 .... 10.0%

Personal income ($per capita)
1994
in current dollars 20,224
in constant (1987) dollars 15,641
1995 (projected)
in constant (1982) dollars 13,393
2000 (projected)
in constant (1982) dollars 14,193

Federal income tax returns, 1993
returns filed 264,347
adjusted gross income ($1000) 7,630,597
total income tax paid ($1000) 987,530

368

Vermont 7

ECONOMY, BUSINESS, INDUSTRY & AGRICULTURE

Fortune 500 companies, 1994 0

Business incorporations, 1994
total 1,599
change, 1993-94 .... -1.1%

Business failures, 1994
total 131
rate per 10,000 concerns 54
change, 1993-94 .... -24.7%

Business firm ownership
Hispanic owned firms, 1987 118
black owned firms, 1987 98
women owned firms, 1987 13,800
foreign owned firms, 1982 34

Gross state product, 1991 ($mil)
total $11,198
  agriculture services, forestry, fisheries 287
  mining 28
  construction 535
  manufacturing—durable goods 1,600
  manufacturing—nondurable goods 587
  transportation, communication &
    public utilities 790
  wholesale trade 611
  retail trade 1,210
  finance/real estate/insurance 2,060
  services 2,183
  federal, state & local government 1,308

Establishments, by major industry group, 1992
total 19,824
  agriculture 356
  mining 60
  construction 2,580
  manufacturing 1,338
  transportation 828
  wholesale trade 1,082
  retail trade 5,263
  finance/real estate/insurance 1,496
  service industries 6,588
  unclassified 233

Payroll, by major industry group, 1992
total ($1,000) $4,336,460
  agriculture 26,090

  mining 21,429
  construction 253,068
  manufacturing 1,278,195
  transportation 271,829
  wholesale trade 306,001
  retail trade 602,915
  finance/real estate/insurance 344,337
  service industries 1,230,816
  unclassified 1,780

Agriculture
number of farms, 1994 6,000
farm acreage, 1994 1,000,000
acres per farm, 1994 230
value of farms, 1994 ($mil) 1,906
farm income, 1993 ($mil)
  gross farm income 517
  net farm income 114
  debt/asset ratio 13.6%
farm marketings, 1993 ($mil)
  total $484
    crops 81
    livestock 403
  government payments 3
farm marketings in order of marketing receipts, 1993
  1) Dairy products
  2) Cattle
  3) Greenhouse
  4) Xmas trees

Federal economic activity
($mil, except per capita)
expenditures, 1994
  total $2,411
  per capita $4,157
  defense $155
  non-defense $2,256
defense department, 1994
  contract awards ($mil) $57
  payroll ($mil) $94
  civilian employees (x1,000) 0.6
  military personnel (x1,000) 0.2

Fishing, 1992
catch (millions of pounds) .... NA
value ($mil) .... NA

Mining, 1994 ($mil)
total non-fuel mineral production $48

369

Vermont 8

principal non-fuel minerals in order of value, 1994
1) Stone
2) Stone
3) Sand and gravel

Construction, 1994 ($mil)
total contracts (including
 non-building) $553
  residential 255
  non-residential 208

Manufacturing, 1992
total establishments 1,343
employees, total (x1,000) 45
payroll ($mil) 1,289
production workers (x1,000) 30
value added ($mil) 3,379
value of shipments ($mil) 6,386

Finance
commercial banks, 1994
 number 20
  assets ($bil) 5.8
  deposits ($bil) 4.8
 closed or assisted 0
  deposits ($bil) .... NA
savings and loan associations, 1991
 non-current real estate loans 3.52%
 net income after taxes ($mil) .... -10
 return on assets .... -0.22%

Retail trade, 1992
establishments (x1,000) 5.2
sales ($mil) 4,735
annual payroll ($mil) 564
paid employees (x1,000) 46

Wholesale trade, 1992
establishments 1,112
sales ($bil) 4.5
annual payroll ($mil) 307
paid employees (x1,000) 11.4

Service industries, 1992
establishments (x1,000) (non-exempt firms) . 5.0
receipts ($mil) (non-exempt firms) 1,946
annual payroll ($mil) 633
paid employees (x1,000) (non-exempt firms) .. 37

COMMUNICATION, ENERGY & TRANSPORTATION

Communication
daily newspapers, 1993 8
broadcast stations, 1990
 radio: commercial, educational 56
 television: commercial, noncommercial 7
cable TV households, 1988 110,000

Energy
consumption estimates, 1992
total (trillion Btu) 140
per capita (million Btu) 244.9
by source of production (trillion Btu)
 coal 1
 natural gas 8
 petroleum 79
 nuclear electric power 40
 hydroelectric power 24
by end-use sector (trillion Btu)
 residential 42
 commercial 26
 industrial 27
 transportation 45
electrical energy
 production, 1993 (billion kWh) 4.3
 net summer capability, 1993 (million kW) .. 1.1
gas utilities, 1993
 customers 29,000
 sales (trillion Btu) 8
 revenues ($mil) 40
nuclear plants, 1993 1

Transportation, 1994
public road & street mileage
total 14,180
 urban 1,333
 rural 12,847
 interstate 320
vehicle miles of travel (mil) 6,152
total motor vehicle registrations 489,436
 automobiles 315,054
licensed drivers 445,576
 per 1,000 driving age population 990
deaths from motor vehicle
 accidents 77

STATE SUMMARY

Capital City .... Richmond

Governor .... George Allen

Address .... STATE CAPITOL
RICHMOND, VA 23219
804 786-2211

Admitted as a state 1788

Area (square miles) 42,769

Population, 1980 5,346,818

Population, 1990 6,187,358

Population, 1994 (est.) 6,552,000

Persons per square mile, 1994 .... 165.5

Largest city .... Virginia Beach
population, 1990 393,000

Personal income per capita, 1994
(in current dollars) $22,594

Gross state product ($mil), 1991 145,189

Leading industries, 1992 (by payroll)
SERVICE INDUSTRIES
MANUFACTURING
RETAIL TRADE

Leading agricultural commodities, 1993
CATTLE
BROILERS
DAIRY PRODUCTS
TOBACCO

GEOGRAPHY & ENVIRONMENT

Area (square miles)
total 42,769
land 39,598
water (includes territorial water) 3,171

Federally owned land, 1991 .... 6.3%

Highest point
name .... Mt. Rogers
elevation (feet) 5,729

Lowest point
name .... Atlantic Ocean
elevation (feet) .... sea level

General coastline (miles) 112

Tidal shoreline (miles) 3,315

Capital city .... Richmond
population, 1990 203,000

Largest city .... Virginia Beach
population, 1990 393,000

Number of cities with over 100,000 population
1980 9

Number of cities with over 100,000 population
1990 8

State parks and Recreation areas, 1991
area (acres) 59,000
number of visitors 3,862,000
revenues $2,686,000

National forest land, 1992 (acres) 3,223,000

National park acreage, 1984 309,600

DEMOGRAPHICS & CHARACTERISTICS OF THE POPULATION

Population
1970 4,651,448
1980 5,346,818
1990 6,187,358
1994 (est.) 6,552,000
2000 (revised projection) 7,048,000
2010 (revised projection) 7,728,000

Metropolitan area population
1970 3,279,000
1980 3,745,000
1992 4,954,000

Non-metropolitan area population
1970 1,373,000
1980 1,601,000
1992 1,440,000

Change in population, 1980-90
number 840,540
percent 15.72%

Persons per square mile, 1994 .... 165.5

Age distribution, 1980
under 5 years 6.7%
5 to 17 years 20.8%
65 and over 9.5%

Age distribution, 1990
under 5 years 7.2%
5 to 17 years 17.1%
65 and over 10.7%

Virginia 2

Age distribution, 2000 (projected)
under 5 years 5.8%
5 to 17 years 18.3%
65 and over 11.4%

Persons by age, 1990
under 5 years 443,155
5 to 17 years 1,061,583
65 and over 664,470

Median age, 1990 .... *32.60*

Race, 1990
White 4,791,739
Black 1,162,994
American Indian 14,893
Chinese 21,238
Filipino 35,067
Japanese 7,931
Asian Indian 20,494
Korean 30,164
Vietnamese 20,693
all other 81,756

Race, 2010 (projected)
White 5,743,000
Black 1,592,000

Persons of Hispanic origin, 1990
total 160,288
Mexican 33,044
Puerto Rican 23,698
Cuban 6,268
Other Hispanic 97,278

Persons by sex, 1990
male 3,033,974
female 3,153,384

Marital status, 1990
males
15 years & older 2,386,768
single 733,040
married 1,447,219
separated 67,405
widowed 52,018
divorced 154,491
females
15 years & older 2,534,543
single 598,188
married 1,445,038
separated 85,886

widowed 280,192
divorced 211,125

Households & families, 1990
households 2,291,830
persons per household 2.61
families 1,629,490
married couples 1,302,219
female householder, no husband
present 255,106
one person households 523,770
households, 1994 2,439,000
persons per household, 1994 .... 2.60

Nativity, 1990
number of persons born in state 3,356,594
percent of total residents 54.2%

Immigration & naturalization, 1993
immigrants admitted 16,451
persons naturalized 7,141
refugees granted resident status 1,786

VITAL STATISTICS & HEALTH

Births
1992 97,600
with low birth weight 7.4%
to teenage mothers 11.0%
to unmarried mothers 28.3%
1993 95,161
1994 95,865

Abortions, 1992
total 35,000
rate (per 1,000 women age 15-44) 22.7
rate per 1,000 live births 373

Adoptions, 1986
total 2,348
related 65.6%

Deaths
1992 49,541
1993 51,773
1994 53,829

Infant deaths
1992 917
1993 812
1994 766

Average lifetime, 1979-1981
both sexes .... 73.43 years
   men .... 69.60 years
   women .... 77.27 years

Marriages
1992 69,694
1993 68,411
1994 69,256

Divorces
1992 29,655
1993 29,463
1994 30,016

Physicians, 1993
total 13,567
rate (per 1,000 persons) 2.15

Dentists, 1992
total 3,502
rate (per 1,000 persons) 0.57

Hospitals, 1993
number 96
beds (x 1,000) 19.5
average daily census (x 1,000) 12.5
occupancy rate 64.2%
personnel (x 1,000) 76.4
average cost per day to hospital $830
average cost per stay to hospital $5,504

EDUCATION

*Educational attainment of all persons
25 years and older, 1990*
less than 9th grade 443,668
high school graduates 1,059,199
bachelor's degree 612,679
graduate or professional degree 360,215

Public school enrollment, Fall, 1993
total 1,045,471
   Kindergarten through grade 8 767,347
   grades 9 through 12 278,124

Public School Teachers
total, 1994 70,220
   elementary 42,205
   secondary 28,015
salaries, 1994
   beginning $23,273
   average $33,472

*State receipts & expenditures for public
schools, 1993*
receipts ($mil) 5,641
expenditures
   total ($mil) 6,014
   per capita $940
   per pupil $5,517

*Graduating high school seniors,
public high schools, 1995 (est)* 58,526

SAT scores, 1994
verbal 424
math 469

Institutions of higher education, 1995
total 93
   public 39
   private 54

*Enrollment in institutions of higher
education, Fall, 1993*
total 348,535
full-time men 91,543
full-time women 105,504
part-time men 62,481
part-time women 89,007

*Minority enrollment in institutions of higher
education, Fall, 1993*
Black, non-Hispanic 53,682
Hispanic 6,483
Asian/Pacific Islander 15,228

Earned degrees conferred, 1993
Bachelor's 30,858
First professional 1,811
Master's 9,325
Doctor's 998

SOCIAL INSURANCE & WELFARE PROGRAMS

Social Security beneficiaries & benefits, 1993
beneficiaries
total 901,000
   retired and dependents 618,000
   survivors 163,000
   disabled & dependents 121,000
annual benefit payments ($mil)
total $6,192
   retired and dependents 4,105
   survivors 1,302
   disabled & dependents 786

Virginia 4

Medicare, 1993
enrollment (x1,000) 779
payments ($mil) 2,420

Medicaid, 1993
recipients (x1,000) 576
payments ($mil) 1,623

Federal public aid, 1993
recipients as a percent of population 4.8%
Aid to Families with Dependent Children
recipients (x1,000) 195
average monthly payment $262
Supplemental Security Income
total recipients (x1,000) 118

Food Stamp Program
participants, 1994 (x1,000) 547

HOUSING & CONSTRUCTION

Total housing units, 1990 2,496,334
year round housing units 2,454,125
vacant 204,504

New privately owned housing units authorized, 1994
number (x1,000) 46.8
value ($mil) 3,965

New privately owned housing units started, 1994 (x1,000) 50.0

Existing home sales, 1994 (x1,000) 99.5

GOVERNMENT & ELECTIONS

State officials, 1996
Governor (name/party/term expires)
GEORGE ALLEN
Republican - 1998
Lt. Governor . . . . Donald S. Beyer
Sec. of State . . . . Elizabeth Beamer
Atty. General . . . . James Gilmore
Chf. Justice . . . . Harry Lee Carrico

Governorship
minimum age 30
length of term . . . . 4 years
number of consecutive
terms permitted . . . . none
who succeeds . . . . Lt. Governor

State legislature
name . . . . General Assembly
upper chamber
name . . . . Senate
number of members 40
length of term . . . . 4 years
party in majority, 1996 . . . . Democratic
lower chamber
name . . . . House of Delegates
number of members 100
length of term . . . . 2 years
party in majority, 1996 . . . . Democratic

State employees October, 1992
total 141,664
October payroll ($1,000) 252,987

Local governments, 1992
total 461
county 95
municipal 230
township 0
school districts 0
special districts 135

Voting, November, 1994
voting age population 4,760,000
registered 60.0%
voted 45.7%

Vote for president
1988
Bush 1,305,131
Dukakis 860,767
1992
Clinton 1,006,730
Bush 1,120,811
Perot 338,924

Federal representation, 1996 (104th Congress)
Senators (name/party/term expires)

CHARLES ROBB
Democrat - 2001
JOHN W. WARNER
Republican - 1997

Representatives, total 11
Democrats 6
Republicans 5
other 0

Virginia 5

Women holding public office
U.S. Congress, 1995 0
statewide elected office, 1995 0
state legislature, 1995 16

Black elected officials, 1993
total 155
  US and state legislatures 14
  city/county/regional offices 126
  judicial/law enforcement 15
  education/school boards 0

Hispanic public officials, 1994
total ....NA
  state executives & legislators ....NA
  city/county/regional offices ....NA
  judicial/law enforcement ....NA
  education/school boards ....NA

GOVERNMENTAL FINANCE

State & local government revenues, (selected items), 1991-92 ($per capita)
total $3,927.69
  total general revenues 3,882.54
  from federal government 470.04
  from own sources 2,912.50
  from taxes 2,017.84
    from property taxes 659.07
    from all other taxes 1,188.84
  from charges & misc. 894.66

State & local government expenditures, (selected items), 1991-92 ($per capita)
total $3,742.86
  total direct general expenditures 3,358.81
  education 1,258.72
  libraries 24.34
  public welfare 370.23
  health & hospitals 295.40
  highways 279.83
  police protection 116.76
  fire protection 60.19
  correction 106.82
  housing & comm. development 64.29
  natural resources & parks 81.57
  interest on general debt 185.11

State & local debt, 1992 ($per capita) 3,221.77

Federal aid grants to state & local government, 1994 ($per capita total & selected items)
per capita total 485.41
  compensatory education 16.81
  waste treatment facilities 7.38
  medicaid 153.51
  housing assistance 36.10
  job training 8.84
  highway trust fund 46.82

CRIME, LAW ENFORCEMENT & COURTS

Crime, 1994 (all rates per 100,000 persons)
total crimes 265,200
overall crime rate 4,047.6
  property crimes 241,763
    burglaries 41,855
    larcenies 181,619
    motor vehicle thefts 18,289
  property crime rate 3,689.9
  violent crimes 23,437
    murders 571
    forcible rapes 1,868
    robberies 8,704
    aggravated assaults 12,294
  violent crime rate 357.7

Number of police agencies, 1994 362

Arrests, 1994
total 387,065
  persons under 18 years of age 53,533

Prisoners under state & federal jurisdiction, 1994
total 26,192
percent change, 1993-94 .... 14.6%
sentenced to more than one year
  total 26,016
  rate per 100,000 residents 395

Persons under sentence of death, 4/20/95 56

State's highest court
name .... Supreme Court
number of members 7
length of term .... 12 years
intermediate appeals court? ....no

Virginia 6

LABOR & INCOME

Civilian labor force, 1994
total 3,422,000
  men 1,800,000
  women 1,622,000
  persons 16-19 years 203,000
  white 2,682,000
  black 631,000

Civilian labor force as a percent of
civilian non-institutional population, 1994
total 69.4%
  men 76.4%
  women 63.0%
  persons 16-19 years 52.9%
  white 69.8%
  black 67.5%

Employment, 1994
total 3,255,000
  men 1,716,000
  women 1,539,000
  persons 16-19 years 166,000
  white 2,572,000
  black 582,000

Full-time/part-time labor force, 1994
full-time labor force 2,815,000
  working part-time for
    ecomonic reasons 33,000
part-time labor force 607,000

Unemployment rate, 1994
total 4.9%
  men 4.7%
  women 5.1%
  persons 16-19 years 18.5%
  white 4.1%
  black 7.7%

Unemployed by reason for unemployment
(as a percent of total unemployment), 1994
job losers or completed temp jobs 39.4%
job leavers 14.6%
reentrants 35.0%
new entrants 11.0%

Civilian labor force, by occupation, 1994
executive/administrative/
  managerial 504,000
professional/specialty 494,000
technicians & related support 111,000

sales 409,000
adminstrative support/clerical 507,000
service occupations 449,000
precision production/craft/repair 377,000
machine operators/assemblers 206,000
transportation/material moving 127,000
handlers/helpers/laborers 128,000
farming/forestry/fishing 88,000

Civilian labor force, by industry, 1994
construction 174,000
manufacturing 454,000
transportation/communication 177,000
wholesale/retail trade 618,000
finance/real estate/insurance 186,000
services 820,000
government 622,000
agriculture 89,000

Average annual pay, 1994 (prelim.) $26,031
change in average annual pay,
  1993-1994 .... 2.1%

Hours and earnings of production workers
on manufacturing payrolls, 1994
average weekly hours 41.7
average hourly earnings $11.25
average weekly earnings $469.13

Labor union membership, 1994 210,700

Household income (in constant 1993 dollars)
median household income, 1992 .... $39,341
median household income, 1993 .... $36,433

Poverty
persons below poverty level, 1992 .... 9.5%
persons below poverty level, 1993 .... 9.7%

Personal income ($per capita)
1994
  in current dollars 22,594
  in constant (1987) dollars 17,474
1995 (projected)
  in constant (1982) dollars 15,448
2000 (projected)
  in constant (1982) dollars 16,345

Federal income tax returns, 1993
returns filed 2,940,159
adjusted gross income ($1000) 101,990,433
total income tax paid ($1000) 14,150,558

Virginia 7

ECONOMY, BUSINESS, INDUSTRY & AGRICULTURE

Fortune 500 companies, 1994 13

Business incorporations, 1994
total 19,150
change, 1993-94 .... 11.3%

Business failures, 1994
total 1,455
rate per 10,000 concerns 86
change, 1993-94 .... -16.4%

Business firm ownership
Hispanic owned firms, 1987 2,716
black owned firms, 1987 18,781
women owned firms, 1987 94,400
foreign owned firms, 1982 240

Gross state product, 1991 ($mil)
total $145,189
  agriculture services, forestry, fisheries ... 1,845
  mining 971
  construction 6,477
  manufacturing — durable goods 9,130
  manufacturing — nondurable goods 14,277
  transportation, communication &
    public utilities 12,698
  wholesale trade 7,988
  retail trade 13,213
  finance/real estate/insurance 23,628
  services 26,627
  federal, state & local government 28,334

Establishments, by major industry group, 1992
total 152,780
  agriculture 2,365
  mining 552
  construction 17,661
  manufacturing 6,569
  transportation 6,035
  wholesale trade 9,209
  retail trade 38,312
  finance/real estate/insurance 14,544
  service industries 55,721
  unclassified 1,812

Payroll, by major industry group, 1992
total ($1,000) $53,156,355
  agriculture 252,501

  mining 584,263
  construction 3,235,739
  manufacturing 11,463,525
  transportation 4,483,367
  wholesale trade 3,601,313
  retail trade 6,575,334
  finance/real estate/insurance 4,580,449
  service industries 18,346,527
  unclassified 33,337

Agriculture
number of farms, 1994 43,000
farm acreage, 1994 9,000,000
acres per farm, 1994 200
value of farms, 1994 ($mil) 11,506
farm income, 1993 ($mil)
  gross farm income 2,373
  net farm income 465
  debt/asset ratio 14.1%
farm marketings, 1993 ($mil)
total $2,068
  crops 683
  livestock 1,385
government payments 46
farm marketings in order of marketing receipts, 1993
    1) Broilers
    2) Cattle
    3) Dairy products
    4) Tobacco

Federal economic activity
  ($mil, except per capita)
expenditures, 1994
  total $45,890
  per capita $7,004
  defense $19,023
  non-defense $26,867
defense department, 1994
  contract awards ($mil) $8,017
  payroll ($mil) $11,483
  civilian employees (x1,000) 98.8
  military personnel (x1,000) 90.0

Fishing, 1992
catch (millions of pounds) 631
value ($mil) 91

Mining, 1994 ($mil)
total non-fuel mineral production $514

377

Virginia 8

principal non-fuel minerals in order of value, 1994
1) Stone
2) Cement
3) Lime

Construction, 1994 ($mil)
total contracts (including
non-building) $8,459
   residential 4,126
   non-residential 2,413

Manufacturing, 1992
total establishments 6,521
employees, total (x1,000) 408
payroll ($mil) 11,265
production workers (x1,000) 283
value added ($mil) 35,933
value of shipments ($mil) 65,860

Finance
commercial banks, 1994
   number 165
      assets ($bil) 74.4
      deposits ($bil) 57.5
   closed or assisted 0
      deposits ($bil) . . . . NA
savings and loan associations, 1991
   non-current real estate loans 7.90%
   net income after taxes ($mil) . . . . -401
   return on assets . . . . -1.57%

Retail trade, 1992
establishments (x1,000) 37.4
sales ($mil) 48,049
annual payroll ($mil) 5,753
paid employees (x1,000) 475

Wholesale trade, 1992
establishments 9,290
sales ($bil) 51.5
annual payroll ($mil) 3,268
paid employees (x1,000) 115.8

Service industries, 1992
establishments (x1,000) (non-exempt firms) 45.9
receipts ($mil) (non-exempt firms) 33,606
annual payroll ($mil) 13,138
paid employees (x1,000) (non-exempt firms) . 526

COMMUNICATION, ENERGY & TRANSPORTATION

Communication
daily newspapers, 1993 28
broadcast stations, 1990
   radio: commercial, educational 274
   television: commercial, noncommercial 30
cable TV households, 1988 1,148,000

Energy
consumption estimates, 1992
total (trillion Btu) 1,853
per capita (million Btu) 289.8
by source of production (trillion Btu)
   coal 344
   natural gas 208
   petroleum 732
   nuclear electric power 249
   hydroelectric power 4
by end-use sector (trillion Btu)
   residential 429
   commercial 392
   industrial 468
   transportation 565
electrical energy
   production, 1993 (billion kWh) 52.2
   net summer capability, 1993 (million kW) . 14.1
gas utilities, 1993
   customers 754,000
   sales (trillion Btu) 135
   revenues ($mil) 806
nuclear plants, 1993 4

Transportation, 1994
public road & street mileage
total 68,943
   urban 18,196
   rural 50,747
   interstate 1,106
vehicle miles of travel (mil) 67,609
total motor vehicle registrations 5,507,060
   automobiles 3,920,576
licensed drivers 4,601,235
   per 1,000 driving age population 900
deaths from motor vehicle
   accidents 930

Washington 1

STATE SUMMARY

Capital City . . . . Olympia

Governor . . . . Mike Lowry

Address . . . . STATE CAPITOL
OLYMPIA, WA 98504
206 753-6780

Admitted as a state 1889

Area (square miles) 71,303

Population, 1980 4,132,156

Population, 1990 4,866,692

Population, 1994 (est.) 5,343,000

Persons per square mile, 1994 . . . . 80.2

Largest city . . . . Seattle
population, 1990 516,000

Personal income per capita, 1994
(in current dollars) $22,610

Gross state product ($mil), 1991 118,997

Leading industries, 1992 (by payroll)
SERVICE INDUSTRIES
MANUFACTURING
RETAIL TRADE

Leading agricultural commodities, 1993
APPLES
CATTLE
DAIRY PRODUCTS
WHEAT

GEOGRAPHY & ENVIRONMENT

Area (square miles)
total 71,303
land 66,582
water (includes territorial water) 4,721

Federally owned land, 1991 . . . . 28.3%

Highest point
name . . . . Mt. Rainier
elevation (feet) 14,410

Lowest point
name . . . . Pacific Ocean
elevation (feet) . . . . .sea level

General coastline (miles) 157

Tidal shoreline (miles) 3,026

Capital city . . . . Olympia
population, 1990 33,800

Largest city . . . . Seattle
population, 1990 516,000

Number of cities with over 100,000 population
1980 3

Number of cities with over 100,000 population
1990 3

State parks and Recreation areas, 1991
area (acres) 241,000
number of visitors 46,813,000
revenues $6,292,000

National forest land, 1992 (acres) 10,061,000

National park acreage, 1984 1,912,700

DEMOGRAPHICS & CHARACTERISTICS OF THE POPULATION

Population
1970 3,413,244
1980 4,132,156
1990 4,866,692
1994 (est.) 5,343,000
2000 (revised projection) 6,070,000
2010 (revised projection) 7,025,000

Metropolitan area population
1970 2,752,000
1980 3,322,000
1992 4,270,000

Non-metropolitan area population
1970 661,000
1980 810,000
1992 873,000

Change in population, 1980-90
number 734,536
percent 17.78%

Persons per square mile, 1994 . . . . 80.2

Age distribution, 1980
under 5 years 7.4%
5 to 17 years 20.2%
65 and over 10.4%

Age distribution, 1990
under 5 years 7.5%
5 to 17 years 18.3%
65 and over 11.8%

Washington 2

Age distribution, 2000 (projected)
under 5 years 5.8%
5 to 17 years 17.4%
65 and over 11.9%

Persons by age, 1990
under 5 years 366,780
5 to 17 years 894,607
65 and over 575,288

Median age, 1990 .... *33.10*

Race, 1990
White 4,308,937
Black 149,801
American Indian 77,627
Chinese 33,962
Filipino 43,799
Japanese 34,366
Asian Indian 8,205
Korean 29,697
Vietnamese 18,696
all other 157,746

Race, 2010 (projected)
White 6,071,000
Black 187,000

Persons of Hispanic origin, 1990
total 214,570
  Mexican 155,864
  Puerto Rican 9,345
  Cuban 2,281
  Other Hispanic 47,080

Persons by sex, 1990
male 2,413,747
female 2,452,945

Marital status, 1990
males
  15 years & older 1,862,291
  single 539,893
  married 1,109,090
    separated 30,865
  widowed 38,826
  divorced 174,482
females
  15 years & older 1,928,866
  single 402,111
  married 1,109,215
    separated 40,404

widowed 190,605
divorced 226,935

Households & families, 1990
households 1,872,431
persons per household 2.53
  families 1,264,934
    married couples 1,029,267
    female householder, no husband
      present 175,522
    one person households 476,320
households, 1994 2,042,000
persons per household, 1994 .... 2.56

Nativity, 1990
number of persons born in state 2,344,187
percent of total residents 48.2%

Immigration & naturalization, 1993
immigrants admitted 17,147
persons naturalized 5,741
refugees granted resident status 6,018

VITAL STATISTICS & HEALTH

Births
1992 79,300
  with low birth weight 5.3%
  to teenage mothers 10.6%
  to unmarried mothers 25.3%
1993 71,437
1994 79,296

Abortions, 1992
total 33,000
rate (per 1,000 women age 15-44) 27.7
rate per 1,000 live births 447

Adoptions, 1986
total 2,133
  related 54.8%

Deaths
1992 37,272
1993 41,986
1994 39,648

Infant deaths
1992 493
1993 494
1994 432

Average lifetime, 1979-1981
both sexes .... 75.13 years
  men .... 71.74 years
  women .... 78.57 years

Marriages
1992 45,144
1993 43,393
1994 43,557

Divorces
1992 23,398
1993 27,415
1994 29,976

Physicians, 1993
total 11,457
rate (per 1,000 persons) 2.20

Dentists, 1992
total 3,179
rate (per 1,000 persons) 0.63

Hospitals, 1993
number 90
beds (x 1,000) 12.0
average daily census (x 1,000) 6.9
occupancy rate 57.6%
personnel (x 1,000) 53.2
average cost per day to hospital $1,143
average cost per stay to hospital $5,792

EDUCATION

*Educational attainment of all persons
  25 years and older, 1990*
less than 9th grade 171,311
high school graduates 873,150
bachelor's degree 496,866
graduate or professional degree 220,103

Public school enrollment, Fall, 1993
total 915,952
  Kindergarten through grade 8 660,424
  grades 9 through 12 255,528

Public School Teachers
total, 1994 45,524
  elementary 24,232
  secondary 17,533
salaries, 1994
  beginning $23,183
  average $35,860

*State receipts & expenditures for public
  schools, 1993*
receipts ($mil) 5,861
expenditures
  total ($mil) 5,816
  per capita $1,131
  per pupil $5,528

*Graduating high school seniors,
  public high schools, 1995 (est)* 49,559

SAT scores, 1994
verbal 434
math 488

Institutions of higher education, 1995
total 62
  public 36
  private 26

*Enrollment in institutions of higher
  education, Fall, 1993*
total 279,845
full-time men 78,096
full-time women 86,050
part-time men 47,007
part-time women 68,692

*Minority enrollment in institutions of higher
  education, Fall, 1993*
Black, non-Hispanic 9,902
Hispanic 8,487
Asian/Pacific Islander 20,020

Earned degrees conferred, 1993
Bachelor's 20,829
First professional 920
Master's 6,745
Doctor's 618

SOCIAL INSURANCE &
WELFARE PROGRAMS

Social Security beneficiaries & benefits, 1993
beneficiaries
total 762,000
  retired and dependents 562,000
  survivors 115,000
  disabled & dependents 85,000
annual benefit payments ($mil)
total $5,696
  retired and dependents 4,068
  survivors 1,032
  disabled & dependents 595

Washington 4

Medicare, 1993
enrollment (x1,000) 658
payments ($mil) 2,167

Medicaid, 1993
recipients (x1,000) 633
payments ($mil) 1,537

Federal public aid, 1993
recipients as a percent of population 7.1%
Aid to Families with Dependent Children
   recipients (x1,000) 290
average monthly payment $498
Supplemental Security Income
   total recipients (x1,000) 82

Food Stamp Program
   participants, 1994 (x1,000) 468

HOUSING & CONSTRUCTION

Total housing units, 1990 2,032,378
   year round housing units 1,974,036
   vacant 159,947

New privately owned housing units
authorized, 1994
number (x1,000) 44.0
value ($mil) 4,018

New privately owned housing units
started, 1994 (x1,000) 45.1

Existing home sales, 1994 (x1,000) 101.2

GOVERNMENT & ELECTIONS

State officials, 1996
  Governor (name/party/term expires)
        MIKE LOWRY
        Democrat - 1997
Lt. Governor .... Joel Pritchard
Sec. of State .... Ralph Munro
Atty. General .... Kenneth O. Eikenberry
Chf. Justice .... Fred Dore

Governorship
minimum age 18
length of term .... 4 years
number of consecutive
   terms permitted .... not specified
who succeeds .... Lt. Governor

State legislature
name .... Legislature
  upper chamber
     name .... Senate
     number of members 49
     length of term .... 4 years
     party in majority, 1996 .... Democratic
  lower chamber
     name .... House of Representatives
     number of members 98
     length of term .... 2 years
     party in majority, 1996 .... Republican

State employees October, 1992
total 120,368
October payroll ($1,000) 249,095

Local governments, 1992
total 1,796
  county 39
  municipal 268
  township 0
  school districts 296
  special districts 1,192

Voting, November, 1994
voting age population 3,924,000
  registered 66.8%
  voted 46.3%

Vote for president
1988
  Bush 800,182
  Dukakis 844,554
1992
  Clinton 856,056
  Bush 610,166
  Perot 470,491

Federal representation, 1996 (104th Congress)
Senators (name/party/term expires)

       SLADE GORTON
       Republican - 2001
       PATTY MURRAY
       Democrat - 1999

Representatives, total 10
  Democrats 2
  Republicans 8
  other 0

Washington 5

Women holding public office
U.S. Congress, 1995 3
statewide elected office, 1995 4
state legislature, 1995 58

Black elected officials, 1993
total 19
  US and state legislatures 2
  city/county/regional offices 9
  judicial/law enforcement 5
  education/school boards 3

Hispanic public officials, 1994
total 14
  state executives & legislators 2
  city/county/regional offices 4
  judicial/law enforcement 2
  education/school boards 6

GOVERNMENTAL FINANCE

State & local government revenues, (selected items), 1991-92 ($per capita)
total $5,416.26
  total general revenues 4,024.32
    from federal government 663.94
    from own sources 3,360.39
    from taxes 2,380.28
      from property taxes 697.07
      from all other taxes 1,465.13
    from charges & misc. 980.11

State & local government expenditures, (selected items), 1991-92 ($per capita)
total $5,520.59
  total direct general expenditures 4,309.60
    education 1,547.28
    libraries 31.14
    public welfare 553.25
    health & hospitals 392.99
    highways 277.08
    police protection 124.96
    fire protection 60.78
    correction 145.61
    housing & comm. development 54.83
    natural resources & parks 212.20
    interest on general debt 182.29

State & local debt, 1992 ($per capita) 5,589.30

Federal aid grants to state & local government, 1994 ($per capita total & selected items)
per capita total 734.47
  compensatory education 18.35
  waste treatment facilities 7.43
  medicaid 269.77
  housing assistance 41.80
  job training 11.43
  highway trust fund 86.39

CRIME, LAW ENFORCEMENT & COURTS

Crime, 1994 (all rates per 100,000 persons)
total crimes 322,051
overall crime rate 6,027.5
  property crimes 294,734
    burglaries 55,793
    larcenies 212,198
    motor vehicle thefts 26,743
  property crime rate 5,516.3
  violent crimes 27,317
    murders 294
    forcible rapes 3,230
    robberies 7,464
    aggravated assaults 16,329
  violent crime rate 511.3

Number of police agencies, 1994 200

Arrests, 1994
total 230,280
  persons under 18 years of age 52,993

Prisoners under state & federal jurisdiction, 1994
total 10,833
percent change, 1993-94 .... 4.0%
  sentenced to more than one year
    total 10,833
    rate per 100,000 residents 201

Persons under sentence of death, 4/20/95 13

State's highest court
name .... Supreme Court
number of members 9
length of term .... 6 years
intermediate appeals court? .... yes

Washington 6

LABOR & INCOME

Civilian labor force, 1994
total 2,708,000
  men 1,478,000
  women 1,229,000
  persons 16-19 years 153,000
  white 2,513,000
  black .... NA

Civilian labor force as a percent of
* civilian non-institutional population, 1994*
total 67.3%
  men 75.0%
  women 59.9%
  persons 16-19 years 58.4%
  white 67.9%
  black .... NA%

Employment, 1994
total 2,534,000
  men 1,383,000
  women 1,151,000
  persons 16-19 years 128,000
  white 2,355,000
  black .... NA

Full-time/part-time labor force, 1994
full-time labor force 2,114,000
  working part-time for
    ecomonic reasons 40,000
part-time labor force 594,000

Unemployment rate, 1994
total 6.4%
  men 6.5%
  women 6.3%
  persons 16-19 years 15.9%
  white 6.3%
  black .... NA%

Unemployed by reason for unemployment
* (as a percent of total unemployment), 1994*
job losers or completed temp jobs 50.9%
job leavers 12.2%
reentrants 31.4%
new entrants 5.4%

Civilian labor force, by occupation, 1994
executive/administrative/
  managerial 365,000
professional/specialty 414,000
technicians & related support 92,000

sales 343,000
adminstrative support/clerical 381,000
service occupations 383,000
precision production/craft/repair 295,000
machine operators/assemblers 114,000
transportation/material moving 104,000
handlers/helpers/laborers 115,000
farming/forestry/fishing 89,000

Civilian labor force, by industry, 1994
construction 132,000
manufacturing 335,000
transportation/communication 141,000
wholesale/retail trade 558,000
finance/real estate/insurance 175,000
services 556,000
government 446,000
agriculture 76,000

Average annual pay, 1994 (prelim.) $26,362
change in average annual pay,
  1993-1994 .... 2.3%

Hours and earnings of production workers
* on manufacturing payrolls, 1994*
average weekly hours 40.6
average hourly earnings $14.42
average weekly earnings $585.45

Labor union membership, 1994 486,900

Household income (in constant 1993 dollars)
median household income, 1992 .... $34,915
median household income, 1993 .... $35,655

Poverty
persons below poverty level, 1992 .... 11.2%
persons below poverty level, 1993 .... 12.1%

Personal income ($per capita)
1994
  in current dollars 22,610
  in constant (1987) dollars 17,486
1995 (projected)
  in constant (1982) dollars 14,447
2000 (projected)
  in constant (1982) dollars 15,316

Federal income tax returns, 1993
returns filed 2,401,163
adjusted gross income ($1000) 82,319,993
total income tax paid ($1000) 12,132,328

Washington 7

ECONOMY, BUSINESS, INDUSTRY & AGRICULTURE

Fortune 500 companies, 1994 7

Business incorporations, 1994
total 14,444
change, 1993-94 .... 7.4%

Business failures, 1994
total 2,000
rate per 10,000 concerns 114
change, 1993-94 .... -1.6%

Business firm ownership
Hispanic owned firms, 1987 2,686
black owned firms, 1987 2,583
women owned firms, 1987 90,300
foreign owned firms, 1982 265

Gross state product, 1991 ($mil)
total $118,997
 agriculture services, forestry, fisheries ... 3,779
 mining 304
 construction 5,824
 manufacturing—durable goods 14,487
 manufacturing—nondurable goods 5,901
 transportation, communication &
  public utilities 9,114
 wholesale trade 8,456
 retail trade 12,258
 finance/real estate/insurance 20,031
 services 21,811
 federal, state & local government 17,032

Establishments, by major industry group, 1992
total 142,069
 agriculture 3,068
 mining 179
 construction 17,734
 manufacturing 8,640
 transportation 5,884
 wholesale trade 10,624
 retail trade 32,207
 finance/real estate/insurance 13,177
 service industries 48,371
 unclassified 2,185

Payroll, by major industry group, 1992
total ($1,000) $46,210,269
 agriculture 553,164

 mining 167,945
 construction 3,462,782
 manufacturing 11,697,767
 transportation 3,553,004
 wholesale trade 4,797,489
 retail trade 5,780,992
 finance/real estate/insurance 3,646,961
 service industries 12,516,803
 unclassified 33,362

Agriculture
number of farms, 1994 36,000
farm acreage, 1994 16,000,000
acres per farm, 1994 445
value of farms, 1994 ($mil) 14,370
farm income, 1993 ($mil)
 gross farm income 5,568
 net farm income 1,572
 debt/asset ratio 17.3%
farm marketings, 1993 ($mil)
 total $4,574
  crops 3,013
  livestock 1,561
government payments 207
farm marketings in order of marketing
receipts, 1993
  1) Cattle
  2) Apples
  3) Dairy products
  4) Wheat

Federal economic activity
 ($mil, except per capita)
expenditures, 1994
 total $26,644
 per capita $4,987
 defense $5,028
 non-defense $21,615
defense department, 1994
 contract awards ($mil) $1,861
 payroll ($mil) $3,416
 civilian employees (x1,000) 27.0
 military personnel (x1,000) 35.8

Fishing, 1992
catch (millions of pounds) 122
value ($mil) 105

Mining, 1994 ($mil)
total non-fuel mineral production $556

385

Washington 8

principal non-fuel minerals in order of value, 1994

1) Sand and gravel
2) Magnesium metal
3) Stone

Construction, 1994 ($mil)
total contracts (including
  non-building) $7,823
    residential 3,790
    non-residential 2,506

Manufacturing, 1992
total establishments 8,521
employees, total (x1,000) 342
payroll ($mil) 11,612
production workers (x1,000) 200
value added ($mil) 27,765
value of shipments ($mil) 72,800

Finance
commercial banks, 1994
  number 87
    assets ($bil) 41.4
    deposits ($bil) 34.5
    closed or assisted 0
    deposits ($bil) .... NA
savings and loan associations, 1991
  non-current real estate loans 2.29%
  net income after taxes ($mil) 147
  return on assets .... +0.91%

Retail trade, 1992
establishments (x1,000) 31.7
sales ($mil) 40,910
annual payroll ($mil) 5,081
paid employees (x1,000) 381

Wholesale trade, 1992
establishments 10,732
sales ($bil) 62.5
annual payroll ($mil) 3,628
paid employees (x1,000) 122.5

Service industries, 1992
establishments (x1,000) (non-exempt firms) 39.5
receipts ($mil) (non-exempt firms) 21,448
annual payroll ($mil) 8,091
paid employees (x1,000) (non-exempt firms) . 355

COMMUNICATION, ENERGY & TRANSPORTATION

Communication
daily newspapers, 1993 24
broadcast stations, 1990
  radio: commercial, educational 211
  television: commercial, noncommercial 29
cable TV households, 1988 993,000

Energy
consumption estimates, 1992
total (trillion Btu) 1,991
per capita (million Btu) 387.2
by source of production (trillion Btu)
  coal 106
  natural gas 175
  petroleum 860
  nuclear electric power 61
  hydroelectric power 697
by end-use sector (trillion Btu)
  residential 363
  commercial 288
  industrial 698
  transportation 642
electrical energy
  production, 1993 (billion kWh) 83.8
  net summer capability, 1993 (million kW) . 24.3
gas utilities, 1993
  customers .... NA
  sales (trillion Btu) .... NA
  revenues ($mil) .... NA
nuclear plants, 1993 1

Transportation, 1994
public road & street mileage
total 79,799
  urban 17,501
  rural 62,298
  interstate 763
vehicle miles of travel (mil) 47,428
total motor vehicle registrations 4,465,069
  automobiles 2,882,261
licensed drivers 3,775,019
  per 1,000 driving age population 925
deaths from motor vehicle
  accidents 638

STATE SUMMARY

Capital City .... Charleston

Governor ....Gaston Caperton

Address ....STATE CAPITOL
CHARLESTON, WV 25305
304 558-2000

Admitted as a state 1863

Area (square miles) 24,231

Population, 1980 1,949,644

Population, 1990 1,793,477

Population, 1994 (est.) 1,822,000

Persons per square mile, 1994 .... 75.6

Largest city .... Charleston
population, 1990 57,300

Personal income per capita, 1994
(in current dollars) $17,208

Gross state product ($mil), 1991 29,014

Leading industries, 1992 (by payroll)
SERVICE INDUSTRIES
MANUFACTURING
RETAIL TRADE

Leading agricultural commodities, 1993
CATTLE
BROILERS
DAIRY PRODUCTS
TURKEYS

GEOGRAPHY & ENVIRONMENT

Area (square miles)
total 24,231
land 24,087
water (includes territorial water) 145

Federally owned land, 1991 .... 6.7%

Highest point
name ....Spruce Knob
elevation (feet) 4,861

Lowest point
name ....Potomac River
elevation (feet) 240

General coastline (miles) 0

Tidal shoreline (miles) 0

Capital city .... Charleston
population, 1990 57,300

Largest city .... Charleston
population, 1990 57,300

Number of cities with over 100,000 population
1980 0

Number of cities with over 100,000 population
1990 0

State parks and Recreation areas, 1991
area (acres) 202,000
number of visitors 8,278,000
revenues $12,973,000

National forest land, 1992 (acres) 1,863,000

National park acreage, 1984 3,200

DEMOGRAPHICS & CHARACTERISTICS OF THE POPULATION

Population
1970 1,744,237
1980 1,949,644
1990 1,793,477
1994 (est.) 1,822,000
2000 (revised projection) 1,840,000
2010 (revised projection) 1,842,000

Metropolitan area population
1970 683,000
1980 718,000
1992 756,000

Non-metropolitan area population
1970 1,061,000
1980 1,232,000
1992 1,053,000

Change in population, 1980-90
number ....-156,167
percent ....-8.01%

Persons per square mile, 1994 .... 75.6

Age distribution, 1980
under 5 years 7.5%
5 to 17 years 21.3%
65 and over 12.2%

Age distribution, 1990
under 5 years 6.0%
5 to 17 years 18.7%
65 and over 14.9%

West Virginia 2

Age distribution, 2000 (projected)
under 5 years 5.8%
5 to 17 years 17.4%
65 and over 14.8%

Persons by age, 1990
under 5 years 106,659
5 to 17 years 336,918
65 and over 268,897

Median age, 1990 .... 35.40

Race, 1990
White 1,725,523
Black 56,295
American Indian 2,385
Chinese 1,170
Filipino 1,606
Japanese 780
Asian Indian 1,981
Korean 777
Vietnamese 184
all other 2,703

Race, 2010 (projected)
White 1,768,000
Black 50,000

Persons of Hispanic origin, 1990
total 8,489
Mexican 2,810
Puerto Rican 897
Cuban 261
Other Hispanic 4,521

Persons by sex, 1990
male 861,536
female 931,941

Marital status, 1990
males
15 years & older 675,682
single 174,280
married 429,780
separated 8,422
widowed 21,012
divorced 50,610
females
15 years & older 756,449
single 143,058
married 431,831
separated 11,458

widowed 116,043
divorced 65,517

Households & families, 1990
households 688,557
persons per household 2.55
families 500,259
married couples 406,105
female householder, no husband
present 73,527
one person households 168,735
households, 1994 705,000
persons per household, 1994 .... 2.53

Nativity, 1990
number of persons born in state 1,386,139
percent of total residents 77.3%

Immigration & naturalization, 1993
immigrants admitted 689
persons naturalized 206
refugees granted resident status 6

VITAL STATISTICS & HEALTH

Births
1992 22,123
with low birth weight 7.2%
to teenage mothers 17.2%
to unmarried mothers 27.7%
1993 22,044
1994 21,554

Abortions, 1992
total 3,000
rate (per 1,000 women age 15-44) 7.7
rate per 1,000 live births 134

Adoptions, 1986
total 1,254
related 78.3%

Deaths
1992 20,107
1993 19,929
1994 20,221

Infant deaths
1992 202
1993 204
1994 146

West Virginia 3

Average lifetime, 1979-1981
both sexes . . . . 72.84 years
  men . . . . 68.86 years
  women . . . . 76.93 years

Marriages
1992 12,264
1993 13,056
1994 10,986

Divorces
1992 9,867
1993 9,690
1994 9,179

Physicians, 1993
total 3,311
rate (per 1,000 persons) 1.82

Dentists, 1992
total 867
rate (per 1,000 persons) 0.48

Hospitals, 1993
number 58
beds (x 1,000) 8.3
average daily census (x 1,000) 5.2
occupancy rate 61.9%
personnel (x 1,000) 30.4
average cost per day to hospital $701
average cost per stay to hospital $4,712

EDUCATION

Educational attainment of all persons
  25 years and older, 1990
less than 9th grade 196,319
high school graduates 429,123
bachelor's degree 88,136
graduate or professional degree 56,382

Public school enrollment, Fall, 1993
total 314,383
  Kindergarten through grade 8 215,784
  grades 9 through 12 98,599

Public School Teachers
total, 1994 21,029
  elementary 10,070
  secondary 7,394
salaries, 1994
  beginning $21,450
  average $30,549

State receipts & expenditures for public
  schools, 1993
receipts ($mil) 1,926
expenditures
  total ($mil) 1,890
  per capita $1,045
  per pupil $5,689

Graduating high school seniors,
  public high schools, 1995 (est) 20,800

SAT scores, 1994
verbal 439
math 482

Institutions of higher education, 1995
total 28
  public 16
  private 12

Enrollment in institutions of higher
  education, Fall, 1993
total 88,852
full-time men 29,701
full-time women 30,733
part-time men 9,733
part-time women 18,685

Minority enrollment in institutions of higher
  education, Fall, 1993
Black, non-Hispanic 3,433
Hispanic 433
Asian/Pacific Islander 870

Earned degrees conferred, 1993
Bachelor's 8,606
First professional 320
Master's 1,916
Doctor's 99

SOCIAL INSURANCE & WELFARE PROGRAMS

Social Security beneficiaries & benefits, 1993
beneficiaries
total 380,000
  retired and dependents 231,000
  survivors 82,000
  disabled & dependents 66,000
annual benefit payments ($mil)
total $2,669
  retired and dependents 1,551
  survivors 678
  disabled & dependents 440

389

West Virginia 4

Medicare, 1993
enrollment (x1,000) 322
payments ($mil) 1,017

Medicaid, 1993
recipients (x1,000) 347
payments ($mil) 1,056

Federal public aid, 1993
recipients as a percent of population 9.6%
Aid to Families with Dependent Children
　recipients (x1,000) 116
average monthly payment $246
Supplemental Security Income
　total recipients (x1,000) 60

Food Stamp Program
　participants, 1994 (x1,000) 321

HOUSING & CONSTRUCTION

Total housing units, 1990 781,295
　year round housing units 758,769
　vacant 92,738

New privately owned housing units
authorized, 1994
number (x1,000) 3.9
value ($mil) 283

New privately owned housing units
started, 1994 (x1,000) 5.5

Existing home sales, 1994 (x1,000) 45.8

GOVERNMENT & ELECTIONS

State officials, 1996
　Governor (name/party/term expires)
　　GASTON CAPERTON
　　Democrat - 1997
Lt. Governor .... (no Lieutenant Governor)
Sec. of State .... Ken Hechler
Atty. General .... Darrell McGraw
Chf. Justice .... W.T. Brotherton, Jr.

Governorship
minimum age 30
length of term .... 4 years
number of consecutive
　terms permitted 2
who succeeds .... Pres. of Senate

State legislature
name .... Legislature
　upper chamber
　　name .... Senate
　　number of members 34
　　length of term .... 4 years
　　party in majority, 1996 .... Democratic
　lower chamber
　　name .... House of Delegates
　　number of members 100
　　length of term .... 2 years
　　party in majority, 1996 .... Democratic

State employees October, 1992
total 40,280
October payroll ($1,000) 64,883

Local governments, 1992
total 708
　county 55
　municipal 231
　township 0
　school districts 55
　special districts 366

Voting, November, 1994
voting age population 1,396,000
　registered 60.8%
　voted 33.9%

Vote for president
1988
　Bush 307,824
　Dukakis 339,112
1992
　Clinton 327,054
　Bush 238,918
　Perot 106,488

Federal representation, 1996 (104th Congress)
Senators (name/party/term expires)

ROBERT C. BYRD
Democrat - 2001
JAY ROCKEFELLER
Democrat - 1997

Representatives, total 3
　Democrats 3
　Republicans 0
　other 0

West Virginia 5

Women holding public office
U.S. Congress, 1995 0
statewide elected office, 1995 0
state legislature, 1995 20

Black elected officials, 1993
total 21
  US and state legislatures 1
  city/county/regional offices 17
  judicial/law enforcement 3
  education/school boards 0

Hispanic public officials, 1994
total ....NA
  state executives & legislators ....NA
  city/county/regional offices ....NA
  judicial/law enforcement ....NA
  education/school boards ....NA

GOVERNMENTAL FINANCE

State & local government revenues, (selected items), 1991-92 ($per capita)
total $3,857.86
  total general revenues 3,302.76
    from federal government 854.39
    from own sources 2,448.37
    from taxes 1,667.51
      from property taxes 295.23
      from all other taxes 1,133.59
    from charges & misc. 780.86

State & local government expenditures, (selected items), 1991-92 ($per capita)
total $3,788.01
  total direct general expenditures 3,232.56
  education 1,241.56
  libraries 8.82
  public welfare 607.86
  health & hospitals 225.02
  highways 303.03
  police protection 51.63
  fire protection 19.23
  correction 31.95
  housing & comm. development 30.12
  natural resources & parks 95.97
  interest on general debt 233.03

State & local debt, 1992 ($per capita) 3,500.26

Federal aid grants to state & local government, 1994 ($per capita total & selected items)
per capita total 1,188.69
  compensatory education 33.59
  waste treatment facilities 14.29
  medicaid 542.72
  housing assistance 55.27
  job training 20.78
  highway trust fund 94.47

CRIME, LAW ENFORCEMENT & COURTS

Crime, 1994 (all rates per 100,000 persons)
total crimes 46,067
overall crime rate 2,528.4
  property crimes 42,136
    burglaries 10,673
    larcenies 28,189
    motor vehicle thefts 3,274
  property crime rate 2,312.6
  violent crimes 3,931
    murders 99
    forcible rapes 370
    robberies 772
    aggravated assaults 2,690
  violent crime rate 215.8

Number of police agencies, 1994 297

Arrests, 1994
total 59,828
  persons under 18 years of age 6,869

Prisoners under state & federal jurisdiction, 1994
total 1,930
percent change, 1993-94 .... 6.9%
  sentenced to more than one year
  total 1,930
  rate per 100,000 residents 106

Persons under sentence of death, 4/20/95 ....NA

State's highest court
name .... Supreme Court of Appeals
number of members 5
length of term .... 12 years
intermediate appeals court? ....no

West Virginia 6

LABOR & INCOME

Civilian labor force, 1994
total 788,000
  men 435,000
  women 353,000
  persons 16-19 years 40,000
  white 760,000
  black 24,000

Civilian labor force as a percent of
civilian non-institutional population, 1994
total 54.6%
  men 63.5%
  women 46.6%
  persons 16-19 years 39.6%
  white 54.6%
  black 54.5%

Employment, 1994
total 717,000
  men 391,000
  women 326,000
  persons 16-19 years 28,000
  white 695,000
  black 20,000

Full-time/part-time labor force, 1994
full-time labor force 633,000
  working part-time for
    ecomonic reasons 9,000
part-time labor force 155,000

Unemployment rate, 1994
total 8.9%
  men 10.1%
  women 7.5%
  persons 16-19 years 31.2%
  white 8.6%
  black 17.7%

Unemployed by reason for unemployment
(as a percent of total unemployment), 1994
job losers or completed temp jobs 45.9%
job leavers 11.9%
reentrants 33.2%
new entrants 9.0%

Civilian labor force, by occupation, 1994
executive/administrative/
  managerial 63,000
professional/specialty 94,000
technicians & related support 26,000

sales 94,000
adminstrative support/clerical 104,000
service occupations 128,000
precision production/craft/repair 108,000
machine operators/assemblers 44,000
transportation/material moving 55,000
handlers/helpers/laborers 42,000
farming/forestry/fishing 23,000

Civilian labor force, by industry, 1994
construction 41,000
manufacturing 995,000
transportation/communication 47,000
wholesale/retail trade 160,000
finance/real estate/insurance 29,000
services 156,000
government 135,000
agriculture ....NA

Average annual pay, 1994 (prelim.) $22,959
change in average annual pay,
  1993-1994 .... 2.6%

Hours and earnings of production workers
on manufacturing payrolls, 1994
average weekly hours 41.3
average hourly earnings $12.60
average weekly earnings $520.38

Labor union membership, 1994 113,100

Household income (in constant 1993 dollars)
median household income, 1992 .... $20,878
median household income, 1993 .... $22,421

Poverty
persons below poverty level, 1992 .... 22.3%
persons below poverty level, 1993 .... 22.2%

Personal income ($per capita)
1994
  in current dollars 17,208
  in constant (1987) dollars 13,309
1995 (projected)
  in constant (1982) dollars 10,300
2000 (projected)
  in constant (1982) dollars 10,921

Federal income tax returns, 1993
returns filed 695,300
adjusted gross income ($1000) 18,543,327
total income tax paid ($1000) 2,327,956

ECONOMY, BUSINESS, INDUSTRY & AGRICULTURE

Fortune 500 companies, 1994 0

Business incorporations, 1994
total 2,327
change, 1993-94 . . . . -3.3%

Business failures, 1994
total 297
rate per 10,000 concerns 71
change, 1993-94 . . . . -6.0%

Business firm ownership
Hispanic owned firms, 1987 177
black owned firms, 1987 727
women owned firms, 1987 22,500
foreign owned firms, 1982 81

Gross state product, 1991 ($mil)
total $29,014
  agriculture services, forestry, fisheries 306
  mining 3,105
  construction 1,158
  manufacturing—durable goods 2,110
  manufacturing—nondurable goods 2,463
  transportation, communication &
    public utilities 3,881
  wholesale trade 1,519
  retail trade 2,573
  finance/real estate/insurance 4,106
  services 4,275
  federal, state & local government 3,518

Establishments, by major industry group, 1992
total 38,714
  agriculture 341
  mining 1,110
  construction 3,709
  manufacturing 1,809
  transportation 2,017
  wholesale trade 2,465
  retail trade 10,729
  finance/real estate/insurance 3,089
  service industries 13,013
  unclassified 432

Payroll, by major industry group, 1992
total ($1,000) $10,419,210
  agriculture 30,557

  mining 1,263,783
  construction 551,083
  manufacturing 2,384,177
  transportation 897,890
  wholesale trade 654,857
  retail trade 1,295,484
  finance/real estate/insurance 524,961
  service industries 2,811,388
  unclassified 5,030

Agriculture
number of farms, 1994 20,000
farm acreage, 1994 4,000,000
acres per farm, 1994 185
value of farms, 1994 ($mil) 2,638
farm income, 1993 ($mil)
  gross farm income 514
  net farm income 105
  debt/asset ratio 13.6%
farm marketings, 1993 ($mil)
  total $405
  crops 77
  livestock 328
government payments 6
farm marketings in order of marketing receipts, 1993
    1) Cattle
    2) Broilers
    3) Dairy products
    4) Turkeys

Federal economic activity ($mil, except per capita)
expenditures, 1994
  total $9,550
  per capita $5,242
  defense $416
  non-defense $9,134
defense department, 1994
  contract awards ($mil) $176
  payroll ($mil) $224
  civilian employees (x1,000) 1.5
  military personnel (x1,000) 0.6

Fishing, 1992
catch (millions of pounds) . . . . NA
value ($mil) . . . . NA

Mining, 1994 ($mil)
total non-fuel mineral production $176

West Virginia 8

principal non-fuel minerals in order of value, 1994
1) Stone
2) Cement
3) Sand and gravel

Construction, 1994 ($mil)
total contracts (including
   non-building) $1,205
     residential 244
     non-residential 513

Manufacturing, 1992
total establishments 1,786
employees, total (x1,000) 78
payroll ($mil) 2,337
production workers (x1,000) 56
value added ($mil) 6,511
value of shipments ($mil) 13,217

Finance
commercial banks, 1994
   number 148
     assets ($bil) 19.9
     deposits ($bil) 16.6
   closed or assisted 0
     deposits ($bil) ....NA
savings and loan associations, 1991
   non-current real estate loans 1.60%
   net income after taxes ($mil) 4
   return on assets .... +0.21%

Retail trade, 1992
establishments (x1,000) 10.5
sales ($mil) 11,194
annual payroll ($mil) 1,208
paid employees (x1,000) 112

Wholesale trade, 1992
establishments 2,427
sales ($bil) 7.8
annual payroll ($mil) 575
paid employees (x1,000) 24.5

Service industries, 1992
establishments (x1,000) (non-exempt firms) . 9.5
receipts ($mil) (non-exempt firms) 4,466
annual payroll ($mil) 1,575
paid employees (x1,000) (non-exempt firms) ..84

COMMUNICATION, ENERGY & TRANSPORTATION

Communication
daily newspapers, 1993 23
broadcast stations, 1990
   radio: commercial, educational 147
   television: commercial, noncommercial 14
cable TV households, 1988 470,000

Energy
consumption estimates, 1992
   total (trillion Btu) 794
   per capita (million Btu) 439.1
by source of production (trillion Btu)
   coal 805
   natural gas 137
   petroleum 295
   nuclear electric power 0
   hydroelectric power 12
by end-use sector (trillion Btu)
   residential 131
   commercial 88
   industrial 416
   transportation 159
electrical energy
   production, 1993 (billion kWh) 71.1
   net summer capability, 1993 (million kW) . 14.4
gas utilities, 1993
   customers 393,000
   sales (trillion Btu) 78
   revenues ($mil) 384
nuclear plants, 1993 0

Transportation, 1994
public road & street mileage
   total 34,822
   urban 3,151
   rural 31,671
   interstate 549
vehicle miles of travel (mil) 17,112
total motor vehicle registrations 1,462,328
   automobiles 879,205
licensed drivers 1,298,478
   per 1,000 driving age population 896
deaths from motor vehicle
   accidents 356

Wisconsin 1

STATE SUMMARY

Capital City . . . . Madison

Governor . . . . Tommy Thompson

Address . . . . STATE CAPITOL
MADISON, WI 53702
608 266-1212

Admitted as a state 1848

Area (square miles) 65,503

Population, 1980 4,705,767

Population, 1990 4,891,769

Population, 1994 (est.) 5,082,000

Persons per square mile, 1994 . . . . 93.6

Largest city . . . . Milwaukee
population, 1990 628,000

Personal income per capita, 1994
(in current dollars) $21,019

Gross state product ($mil), 1991 102,729

Leading industries, 1992 (by payroll)
MANUFACTURING
SERVICE INDUSTRIES
RETAIL TRADE

Leading agricultural commodities, 1993
DAIRY PRODUCTS
CATTLE
CORN
HOGS

GEOGRAPHY & ENVIRONMENT

Area (square miles)
total 65,503
land 54,314
water (includes territorial water) 11,190

Federally owned land, 1991 . . . . 10.1%

Highest point
name . . . . .Timms Hil
elevation (feet) 1,951

Lowest point
name . . . . .Lake Michigan
elevation (feet) 581

General coastline (miles) 0

Tidal shoreline (miles) 0

Capital city . . . . Madison
population, 1990 191,000

Largest city . . . . Milwaukee
population, 1990 628,000

Number of cities with over 100,000 population
1980 2

Number of cities with over 100,000 population
1990 2

State parks and Recreation areas, 1991
area (acres) 139,000
number of visitors 12,252,000
revenues $5,221,000

National forest land, 1992 (acres) 2,023,000

National park acreage, 1984 66,400

DEMOGRAPHICS & CHARACTERISTICS OF THE POPULATION

Population
1970 4,417,821
1980 4,705,767
1990 4,891,769
1994 (est.) 5,082,000
2000 (revised projection) 5,381,000
2010 (revised projection) 5,629,000

Metropolitan area population
1970 3,019,000
1980 3,145,000
1992 3,402,000

Non-metropolitan area population
1970 1,399,000
1980 1,561,000
1992 1,591,000

Change in population, 1980-90
number 186,002
percent 3.95%

Persons per square mile, 1994 . . . . 93.6

Age distribution, 1980
under 5 years 7.4%
5 to 17 years 21.5%
65 and over 12.0%

Age distribution, 1990
under 5 years 7.4%
5 to 17 years 18.9%
65 and over 13.3%

Wisconsin 2

Age distribution, 2000 (projected)
under 5 years 6.2%
5 to 17 years 18.9%
65 and over 13.7%

Persons by age, 1990
under 5 years 360,730
5 to 17 years 928,252
65 and over 651,221

Median age, 1990 .... *32.90*

Race, 1990
White 4,512,523
Black 244,539
American Indian 38,986
Chinese 7,354
Filipino 3,690
Japanese 2,765
Asian Indian 6,914
Korean 5,618
Vietnamese 2,494
all other 66,485

Race, 2010 (projected)
White 5,035,000
Black 396,000

Persons of Hispanic origin, 1990
total 93,194
Mexican 57,615
Puerto Rican 19,116
Cuban 1,679
Other Hispanic 14,784

Persons by sex, 1990
male 2,392,935
female 2,498,834

Marital status, 1990
males
15 years & older 1,833,873
single 560,190
married 1,101,329
separated 21,613
widowed 47,121
divorced 125,233
females
15 years & older 1,967,276
single 469,094
married 1,105,905
separated 29,411

widowed 233,268
divorced 159,009

Households & families, 1990
households 1,822,118
persons per household 2.61
families 1,275,172
married couples 1,048,010
female householder, no husband
present 174,530
one person households 443,673
households, 1994 1,890,000
persons per household, 1994 .... 2.62

Nativity, 1990
number of persons born in state 3,737,602
percent of total residents 76.4%

Immigration & naturalization, 1993
immigrants admitted 5,168
persons naturalized 6
refugees granted resident status 1,868

VITAL STATISTICS & HEALTH

Births
1992 69,878
with low birth weight 5.9%
to teenage mothers 10.2%
to unmarried mothers 26.1%
1993 69,289
1994 68,800

Abortions, 1992
total 15,000
rate (per 1,000 women age 15-44) 13.6
rate per 1,000 live births 223

Adoptions, 1986
total 1,984
related 56.6%

Deaths
1992 41,807
1993 44,033
1994 44,746

Infant deaths
1992 496
1993 557
1994 531

Wisconsin 3

Average lifetime, 1979-1981
both sexes .... 75.35 years
　men .... 71.86 years
　women .... 78.87 years

Marriages
1992 37,138
1993 36,506
1994 36,368

Divorces
1992 18,344
1993 17,861
1994 17,478

Physicians, 1993
total 9,982
rate (per 1,000 persons) 1.98

Dentists, 1992
total 3,101
rate (per 1,000 persons) 0.62

Hospitals, 1993
number 127
beds (x 1,000) 17.7
average daily census (x 1,000) 11.2
occupancy rate 63.4%
personnel (x 1,000) 65.5
average cost per day to hospital $744
average cost per stay to hospital $5,348

EDUCATION

*Educational attainment of all persons
　25 years and older, 1990*
less than 9th grade 294,862
high school graduates 1,147,697
bachelor's degree 375,603
graduate or professional degree 173,367

Public school enrollment, Fall, 1993
total 844,001
　Kindergarten through grade 8 595,717
　grades 9 through 12 248,284

Public School Teachers
total, 1994 52,822
　elementary 35,585
　secondary 17,237
salaries, 1994
　beginning $23,677
　average $36,644

*State receipts & expenditures for public
　schools, 1993*
receipts ($mil) 6,036
expenditures
　total ($mil) 5,609
　per capita $1,123
　per pupil $6,500

*Graduating high school seniors,
　public high schools, 1995 (est)* 53,495

SAT scores, 1994
verbal 487
math 557

Institutions of higher education, 1995
total 65
　public 30
　private 35

*Enrollment in institutions of higher
　education, Fall, 1993*
total 309,036
full-time men 88,106
full-time women 98,766
part-time men 49,879
part-time women 72,285

*Minority enrollment in institutions of higher
　education, Fall, 1993*
Black, non-Hispanic 12,853
Hispanic 5,818
Asian/Pacific Islander 6,472

Earned degrees conferred, 1993
Bachelor's 27,709
First professional 971
Master's 6,340
Doctor's 851

SOCIAL INSURANCE & WELFARE PROGRAMS

Social Security beneficiaries & benefits, 1993
beneficiaries
total 870,000
　retired and dependents 634,000
　survivors 139,000
　disabled & dependents 96,000
annual benefit payments ($mil)
total $6,464
　retired and dependents 4,563
　survivors 1,254
　disabled & dependents 646

397

Wisconsin 4

Medicare, 1993
enrollment (x1,000) 745
payments ($mil) 2,305

Medicaid, 1993
recipients (x1,000) 471
payments ($mil) 1,786

Federal public aid, 1993
recipients as a percent of population 6.7%
Aid to Families with Dependent Children
    recipients (x1,000) 228
average monthly payment $460
Supplemental Security Income
    total recipients (x1,000) 106

Food Stamp Program
    participants, 1994 (x1,000) 330

HOUSING & CONSTRUCTION

Total housing units, 1990 2,055,774
    year round housing units 1,905,013
    vacant 233,656

New privately owned housing units
    authorized, 1994
number (x1,000) 34.6
value ($mil) 2,917

New privately owned housing units
    started, 1994 (x1,000) 33.4

Existing home sales, 1994 (x1,000) 94.3

GOVERNMENT & ELECTIONS

State officials, 1996
    Governor (name/party/term expires)
        TOMMY THOMPSON
        Republican - 1999
Lt. Governor .... Scott McCallum
Sec. of State .... Douglas LaFollette
Atty. General .... James Doyle
Chf. Justice .... Nathan S. Heffernan

Governorship
minimum age .... not specified
length of term .... 4 years
number of consecutive
    terms permitted .... not specified
who succeeds .... Lt. Governor

State legislature
name .... Legislature
    upper chamber
        name .... Senate
        number of members 33
        length of term .... 4 years
        party in majority, 1996 .... Republican
    lower chamber
        name .... Assembly
        number of members 99
        length of term .... 2 years
        party in majority, 1996 .... Republican

State employees October, 1992
total 96,533
October payroll ($1,000) 210,669

Local governments, 1992
total 2,752
    county 72
    municipal 583
    township 1,267
    school districts 430
    special districts 399

Voting, November, 1994
voting age population 3,638,000
    registered 77.2%
    voted 49.6%

Vote for president
1988
    Bush 1,043,584
    Dukakis 1,122,090
1992
    Clinton 1,036,316
    Bush 926,646
    Perot 542,470

Federal representation, 1996 (104th Congress)
Senators (name/party/term expires)

HERBERT KOHL
Democrat - 2001
RUSSELL FEINGOLD
Democrat - 1999

Representatives, total 9
    Democrats 3
    Republicans 6
    other 0

Wisconsin 5

Women holding public office
U.S. Congress, 1995 0
statewide elected office, 1995 0
state legislature, 1995 32

Black elected officials, 1993
total 30
  US and state legislatures 8
  city/county/regional offices 15
  judicial/law enforcement 4
  education/school boards 3

Hispanic public officials, 1994
total 2
  state executives & legislators 0
  city/county/regional offices 2
  judicial/law enforcement 0
  education/school boards 0

GOVERNMENTAL FINANCE

State & local government revenues, (selected items), 1991-92 ($per capita)
total $5,029.77
  total general revenues 3,859.40
    from federal government 648.20
    from own sources 3,211.20
    from taxes 2,343.02
    from property taxes 828.08
    from all other taxes 1,398.45
    from charges & misc. 868.18

State & local government expenditures, (selected items), 1991-92 ($per capita)
total $4,449.39
  total direct general expenditures 4,005.48
  education 1,516.88
  libraries 23.69
  public welfare 667.16
  health & hospitals 252.81
  highways 306.48
  police protection 140.53
  fire protection 61.79
  correction 97.81
  housing & comm. development 44.28
  natural resources & parks 128.66
  interest on general debt 193.05

State & local debt, 1992 ($per capita) 3,021.69

Federal aid grants to state & local government, 1994 ($per capita total & selected items)
per capita total 678.82
  compensatory education 21.70
  waste treatment facilities 11.92
  medicaid 280.72
  housing assistance 37.31
  job training 8.11
  highway trust fund 66.87

CRIME, LAW ENFORCEMENT & COURTS

Crime, 1994 (all rates per 100,000 persons)
total crimes 200,452
overall crime rate 3,944.4
  property crimes 186,704
    burglaries 32,824
    larcenies 135,559
    motor vehicle thefts 18,321
  property crime rate 3,673.8
  violent crimes 13,748
    murders 227
    forcible rapes 1,192
    robberies 5,739
    aggravated assaults 6,590
  violent crime rate 270.5

Number of police agencies, 1994 321

Arrests, 1994
total 420,676
  persons under 18 years of age 134,941

Prisoners under state & federal jurisdiction, 1994
total 10,020
percent change, 1993-94 .... 14.1%
sentenced to more than one year
  total 9,519
  rate per 100,000 residents 187

Persons under sentence of death, 4/20/95 .... NA

State's highest court
name .... Supreme Court
number of members 7
length of term .... 10 years
intermediate appeals court? .... yes

Wisconsin 6

LABOR & INCOME

Civilian labor force, 1994
total	2,795,000
men	1,497,000
women	1,299,000
persons 16-19 years	187,000
white	2,640,000
black	109,000

Civilian labor force as a percent of civilian non-institutional population, 1994
total	73.2%
men	79.2%
women	67.3%
persons 16-19 years	64.3%
white	74.1%
black	58.5%

Employment, 1994
total	2,663,000
men	1,419,000
women	1,244,000
persons 16-19 years	163,000
white	2,529,000
black	95,000

Full-time/part-time labor force, 1994
full-time labor force	2,194,000
working part-time for ecomonic reasons	27,000
part-time labor force	602,000

Unemployment rate, 1994
total	4.7%
men	5.2%
women	4.2%
persons 16-19 years	12.9%
white	4.2%
black	12.8%

Unemployed by reason for unemployment (as a percent of total unemployment), 1994
job losers or completed temp jobs	44.3%
job leavers	15.6%
reentrants	36.3%
new entrants	4.1%

Civilian labor force, by occupation, 1994
executive/administrative/managerial	305,000
professional/specialty	371,000
technicians & related support	74,000
sales	276,000
adminstrative support/clerical	380,000
service occupations	414,000
precision production/craft/repair	312,000
machine operators/assemblers	284,000
transportation/material moving	106000
handlers/helpers/laborers	128,000
farming/forestry/fishing	141,000

Civilian labor force, by industry, 1994
construction	136,000
manufacturing	632,000
transportation/communication	110,000
wholesale/retail trade	532,000
finance/real estate/insurance	152,000
services	558,000
government	364,000
agriculture	128,000

Average annual pay, 1994 (prelim.) $24,324
change in average annual pay, 1993-1994	3.0%

Hours and earnings of production workers on manufacturing payrolls, 1994
average weekly hours	42.7
average hourly earnings	$12.41
average weekly earnings	$529.91

Labor union membership, 1994 430,600

Household income (in constant 1993 dollars)
median household income, 1992	$34,305
median household income, 1993	$31,766

Poverty
persons below poverty level, 1992	10.9%
persons below poverty level, 1993	12.6%

Personal income ($per capita)
1994
in current dollars	21,019
in constant (1987) dollars	16,256

1995 (projected)
in constant (1982) dollars	13,709

2000 (projected)
in constant (1982) dollars	14,575

Federal income tax returns, 1993
returns filed	2,294,126
adjusted gross income ($1000)	72,199,663
total income tax paid ($1000)	9,625,114

Wisconsin 7

ECONOMY, BUSINESS, INDUSTRY & AGRICULTURE

Fortune 500 companies, 1994 51

Business incorporations, 1994
total 8,107
change, 1993-94 .... 2.9%

Business failures, 1994
total 1,171
rate per 10,000 concerns 72
change, 1993-94 .... -4.2%

Business firm ownership
Hispanic owned firms, 1987 894
black owned firms, 1987 2,381
women owned firms, 1987 69,200
foreign owned firms, 1982 186

Gross state product, 1991 ($mil)
total $102,729
 agriculture services, forestry, fisheries ... 3,151
 mining 138
 construction 3,996
 manufacturing—durable goods 15,948
 manufacturing—nondurable goods 11,996
 transportation, communication &
  public utilities 7,896
 wholesale trade 6,289
 retail trade 9,234
 finance/real estate/insurance 17,516
 services 15,760
 federal, state & local government 10,805

Establishments, by major industry group, 1992
total 127,457
 agriculture 1,749
 mining 163
 construction 13,079
 manufacturing 10,175
 transportation 6,301
 wholesale trade 9,311
 retail trade 32,638
 finance/real estate/insurance 11,195
 service industries 41,311
 unclassified 1,535

Payroll, by major industry group, 1992
total ($1,000) $45,290,724
 agriculture 199,867

 mining 80,373
 construction 2,719,502
 manufacturing 16,164,725
 transportation 2,911,288
 wholesale trade 3,359,512
 retail trade 4,802,587
 finance/real estate/insurance 3,777,469
 service industries 11,250,911
 unclassified 24,490

Agriculture
number of farms, 1994 78,000
farm acreage, 1994 17,000,000
acres per farm, 1994 217
value of farms, 1994 ($mil) 16,678
farm income, 1993 ($mil)
 gross farm income 5,778
 net farm income 474
 debt/asset ratio 20.1%
farm marketings, 1993 ($mil)
total $5,250
 crops 1,086
 livestock 4,164
government payments 310
farm marketings in order of marketing receipts, 1993
 1) Dairy products
 2) Cattle
 3) Corn
 4) Hogs

Federal economic activity ($mil, except per capita)
expenditures, 1994
 total $19,670
 per capita $3,870
 defense $1,227
 non-defense $18,443
defense department, 1994
 contract awards ($mil) $774
 payroll ($mil) $420
 civilian employees (x1,000) 3.3
 military personnel (x1,000) 0.8

Fishing, 1992
catch (millions of pounds) .... NA
value ($mil) .... NA

Mining, 1994 ($mil)
total non-fuel mineral production $344

Wisconsin 8

principal non-fuel minerals in order of value, 1994

1) Stone
2) Sand and gravel
3) Copper

Construction, 1994 ($mil)
total contracts (including
  non-building) $5,442
    residential 2,565
    non-residential 1,875

Manufacturing, 1992
total establishments 10,087
employees, total (x1,000) 546
payroll ($mil) 16,083
production workers (x1,000) 368
value added ($mil) 41,174
value of shipments ($mil) 88,067

Finance
commercial banks, 1994
  number 436
    assets ($bil) 54.2
    deposits ($bil) 44.4
  closed or assisted 0
    deposits ($bil) ....NA
savings and loan associations, 1991
  non-current real estate loans 0.79%
  net income after taxes ($mil) 92
  return on assets .... +0.52%

Retail trade, 1992
establishments (x1,000) 32.0
sales ($mil) 38,351
annual payroll ($mil) 4,350
paid employees (x1,000) 405

Wholesale trade, 1992
establishments 9,383
sales ($bil) 47.6
annual payroll ($mil) 3,223
paid employees (x1,000) 117.6

Service industries, 1992
establishments (x1,000) (non-exempt firms) 32.0
receipts ($mil) (non-exempt firms) 15,577
annual payroll ($mil) 6,295
paid employees (x1,000) (non-exempt firms) . 317

COMMUNICATION, ENERGY & TRANSPORTATION

Communication
daily newspapers, 1993 36
broadcast stations, 1990
  radio: commercial, educational 264
  television: commercial, noncommercial 35
cable TV households, 1988 836,000

Energy
consumption estimates, 1992
total (trillion Btu) 1,404
per capita (million Btu) 281.3
by source of production (trillion Btu)
  coal 399
  natural gas 335
  petroleum 481
  nuclear electric power 120
  hydroelectric power 35
by end-use sector (trillion Btu)
  residential 348
  commercial 236
  industrial 473
  transportation 348
electrical energy
  production, 1993 (billion kWh) 47.8
  net summer capability, 1993 (million kW) . 10.9
gas utilities, 1993
  customers 1,572,000
  sales (trillion Btu) 263
  revenues ($mil) 1,393
nuclear plants, 1993 3

Transportation, 1994
public road & street mileage
total 110,923
  urban 15,725
  rural 95,198
  interstate 638
vehicle miles of travel (mil) 50,273
total motor vehicle registrations 3,925,788
  automobiles 2,460,931
licensed drivers 3,554,003
  per 1,000 driving age population 915
deaths from motor vehicle
  accidents 712

Wyoming 1

STATE SUMMARY

Capital City . . . . Cheyenne

Governor . . . . Jim Geringer

Address . . . . STATE CAPITOL
CHEYENNE, WY 82002
307 777-7434

Admitted as a state 1890

Area (square miles) 97,818

Population, 1980 469,557

Population, 1990 453,588

Population, 1994 (est.) 476,000

Persons per square mile, 1994 . . . . 4.9

Largest city . . . . Cheyenne
population, 1990 50,000

Personal income per capita, 1994
(in current dollars) $20,436

Gross state product ($mil), 1991 12,931

Leading industries, 1992 (by payroll)
MINING
SERVICE INDUSTRIES
RETAIL TRADE

Leading agricultural commodities, 1993
CATTLE
SUGAR BEETS
HAY
SHEEP

GEOGRAPHY & ENVIRONMENT

Area (square miles)
total 97,818
land 97,105
water (includes territorial water) 714

Federally owned land, 1991 . . . . 48.9%

Highest point
name . . . . Gannett Peak
elevation (feet) 13,804

Lowest point
name . . . . Belle Fourche River
elevation (feet) 3,009

General coastline (miles) 0

Tidal shoreline (miles) 0

Capital city . . . . Cheyenne
population, 1990 50,000

Largest city . . . . Cheyenne
population, 1990 50,000

Number of cities with over 100,000 population
1980 0

Number of cities with over 100,000 population
1990 0

State parks and Recreation areas, 1991
area (acres) 120,000
number of visitors 2,018,000
revenues $247,000

National forest land, 1992 (acres) 9,704,000

National park acreage, 1984 2,392,400

DEMOGRAPHICS & CHARACTERISTICS OF THE POPULATION

Population
1970 332,416
1980 469,557
1990 453,588
1994 (est.) 476,000
2000 (revised projection) 522,000
2010 (revised projection) 596,000

Metropolitan area population
1970 108,000
1980 141,000
1992 138,000

Non-metropolitan area population
1970 225,000
1980 329,000
1992 327,000

Change in population, 1980-90
number . . . . -15,969
percent . . . . -3.40%

Persons per square mile, 1994 . . . . 4.9

Age distribution, 1980
under 5 years 9.6%
5 to 17 years 21.4%
65 and over 7.9%

Age distribution, 1990
under 5 years 7.7%
5 to 17 years 22.2%
65 and over 10.4%

Wyoming 2

Age distribution, 2000 (projected)
under 5 years 7.5%
5 to 17 years 20.4%
65 and over 8.3%

Persons by age, 1990
under 5 years 34,780
5 to 17 years 100,745
65 and over 47,195

Median age, 1990 .... 32.00

Race, 1990
White 427,061
Black 3,606
American Indian 9,426
Chinese 554
Filipino 408
Japanese 583
Asian Indian 240
Korean 402
Vietnamese 124
all other 11,131

Race, 2010 (projected)
White 564,000
Black 5,000

Persons of Hispanic origin, 1990
total 25,751
   Mexican 18,730
   Puerto Rican 325
   Cuban 63
   Other Hispanic 6,633

Persons by sex, 1990
male 227,007
female 226,581

Marital status, 1990
males
  15 years & older 168,395
   single 43,086
   married 105,963
    separated 1,700
   widowed 3,533
   divorced 15,813
females
  15 years & older 170,879
   single 30,469
   married 105,665
    separated 2,109

widowed 17,013
divorced 17,732

Households & families, 1990
households 168,839
persons per household 2.63
  families 119,825
   married couples 100,800
   female householder, no husband
    present 13,990
   one person households 41,287
households, 1994 178,000
persons per household, 1994 .... 2.62

Nativity, 1990
number of persons born in state 193,436
percent of total residents 42.6%

Immigration & naturalization, 1993
immigrants admitted 263
persons naturalized 43
refugees granted resident status 1

VITAL STATISTICS & HEALTH

Births
1992 6,823
  with low birth weight 7.3%
  to teenage mothers 13.2%
  to unmarried mothers 24.0%
1993 6,662
1994 6,385

Abortions, 1992
total ....
rate (per 1,000 women age 15-44) 4.3
rate per 1,000 live births 74

Adoptions, 1986
total 232
  related 50.4%

Deaths
1992 3,333
1993 3,544
1994 3,512

Infant deaths
1992 60
1993 54
1994 51

Wyoming 3

Average lifetime, 1979-1981
both sexes .... 73.85 years
   men .... 69.95 years
   women .... 78.20 years

Marriages
1992 4,900
1993 4,603
1994 4,825

Divorces
1992 3,227
1993 3,065
1994 3,071

Physicians, 1993
total 640
rate (per 1,000 persons) 1.37

Dentists, 1992
total 240
rate (per 1,000 persons) 0.52

Hospitals, 1993
number 25
beds (x 1,000) 2.2
average daily census (x 1,000) 1.1
occupancy rate 48.4%
personnel (x 1,000) 8.7
average cost per day to hospital $537
average cost per stay to hospital $4,706

EDUCATION

Educational attainment of all persons
25 years and older, 1990
less than 9th grade 15,919
high school graduates 92,081
bachelor's degree 36,354
graduate or professional degree 15,841

Public school enrollment, Fall, 1993
total 100,899
   Kindergarten through grade 8 71,402
   grades 9 through 12 29,497

Public School Teachers
total, 1994 6,537
   elementary 3,215
   secondary 3,322
salaries, 1994
   beginning $20,416
   average $30,954

State receipts & expenditures for public
schools, 1993
receipts ($mil) 625
expenditures
   total ($mil) 621
   per capita $1,336
   per pupil $5,932

Graduating high school seniors,
public high schools, 1995 (est) 6,254

SAT scores, 1994
verbal 459
math 521

Institutions of higher education, 1995
total 9
   public 8
   private 1

Enrollment in institutions of higher
education, Fall, 1993
total 30,702
full-time men 8,715
full-time women 8,724
part-time men 4,688
part-time women 8,575

Minority enrollment in institutions of higher
education, Fall, 1993
Black, non-Hispanic 277
Hispanic 1,056
Asian/Pacific Islander 240

Earned degrees conferred, 1993
Bachelor's 1,856
First professional 69
Master's 342
Doctor's 50

SOCIAL INSURANCE & WELFARE PROGRAMS

Social Security beneficiaries & benefits, 1993
beneficiaries
total 68,000
   retired and dependents 49,000
   survivors 11,000
   disabled & dependents 8,000
annual benefit payments ($mil)
total $485
   retired and dependents 338
   survivors 95
   disabled & dependents 53

Wyoming 4

Medicare, 1993
enrollment (x1,000) 57
payments ($mil) 139

Medicaid, 1993
recipients (x1,000) 46
payments ($mil) 125

Federal public aid, 1993
recipients as a percent of population 5.0%
Aid to Families with Dependent Children
   recipients (x1,000) 17
average monthly payment $332
Supplemental Security Income
   total recipients (x1,000) 5

Food Stamp Program
  participants, 1994 (x1,000) 34

HOUSING & CONSTRUCTION

Total housing units, 1990 203,411
  year round housing units 193,434
  vacant 34,572

New privately owned housing units
authorized, 1994
number (x1,000) 2.0
value ($mil) 210

New privately owned housing units
started, 1994 (x1,000) 2.8

Existing home sales, 1994 (x1,000) 11.0

GOVERNMENT & ELECTIONS

State officials, 1996
  Governor (name/party/term expires)
          JIM GERINGER
          Republican - 1999
Lt. Governor .... (no Lieutenant Governor)
Sec. of State .... Diana Ohmans
Atty. General .... Joseph Meyer
Chf. Justice .... Richard Macy

Governorship
minimum age 30
length of term .... 4 years
number of consecutive
  terms permitted .... not specified
who succeeds .... Sec. of State

State legislature
name .... Legislature
  upper chamber
    name .... Senate
    number of members 30
    length of term .... 4 years
    party in majority, 1996 .... Republican
  lower chamber
    name .... House of Representatives
    number of members 64
    length of term .... 2 years
    party in majority, 1996 .... Republican

State employees October, 1992
total 13,154
October payroll ($1,000) 22,149

Local governments, 1992
total 576
  county 23
  municipal 97
  township 0
  school districts 56
  special districts 399

Voting, November, 1994
voting age population 333,000
  registered 69.0%
  voted 63.5%

Vote for president
1988
  Bush 106,814
  Dukakis 67,077
1992
  Clinton 67,858
  Bush 79,515
  Perot 51,182

Federal representation, 1996 (104th Congress)
Senators (name/party/term expires)

       CRAIG THOMAS
       Republican - 2001
      ALAN K. SIMPSON
       Republican - 1997

Representatives, total 1
  Democrats 0
  Republicans 1
  other 0

406

Wyoming 5

GOVERNMENTAL FINANCE

State & local government revenues, (selected items), 1991-92 ($per capita)
total $6,305.78
  total general revenues 5,507.42
    from federal government 1,471.66
    from own sources 4,035.76
    from taxes 2,360.37
      from property taxes 1,002.32
      from all other taxes 643.12
    from charges & misc. 1,675.38

State & local government expenditures, (selected items), 1991-92 ($per capita)
total $5,938.61
  total direct general expenditures 5,350.83
    education 1,948.15
    libraries 25.36
    public welfare 423.97
    health & hospitals 593.10
    highways 754.78
    police protection 149.62
    fire protection 47.33
    correction 91.25
    housing & comm. development 34.20
    natural resources & parks 297.74
    interest on general debt 331.72

State & local debt, 1992 ($per capita) 4,477.62

Federal aid grants to state & local government, 1994 ($per capita total & selected items)
per capita total 1,500.61
  compensatory education 23.56
  waste treatment facilities 10.31
  medicaid 206.74
  housing assistance 37.91
  job training 14.45
  highway trust fund 240.23

CRIME, LAW ENFORCEMENT & COURTS

Crime, 1994 (all rates per 100,000 persons)
total crimes 20,419
overall crime rate 4,289.7
  property crimes 19,122
    burglaries 3,097
    larcenies 15,254
    motor vehicle thefts 771
  property crime rate 4,017.2
  violent crimes 1,297
    murders 16
    forcible rapes 160
    robberies 79
    aggravated assaults 1,042
  violent crime rate 272.5

Number of police agencies, 1994 63

Arrests, 1994
total 29,527
  persons under 18 years of age 6,710

Prisoners under state & federal jurisdiction, 1994
total 1,217
percent change, 1993-94 . . . . 7.8%
  sentenced to more than one year
    total 1,217
    rate per 100,000 residents 254

Persons under sentence of death, 4/20/95 0

State's highest court
name . . . . Supreme Court
number of members 5
length of term . . . . 8 years
intermediate appeals court? . . . . no

Wyoming 6

LABOR & INCOME

Civilian labor force, 1994
total 249,000
  men 135,000
  women 114,000
  persons 16-19 years 20,000
  white 243,000
  black .... NA

Civilian labor force as a percent of
civilian non-institutional population, 1994
total 71.3%
  men 78.8%
  women 64.1%
  persons 16-19 years 65.3%
  white 71.3%
  black .... NA%

Employment, 1994
total 236,000
  men 128,000
  women 108,000
  persons 16-19 years 16,000
  white 230,000
  black .... NA

Full-time/part-time labor force, 1994
full-time labor force 193,000
  working part-time for
    ecomonic reasons 3,000
part-time labor force 56,000

Unemployment rate, 1994
total 5.3%
  men 5.4%
  women 5.2%
  persons 16-19 years 17.2%
  white 5.2%
  black .... NA%

Unemployed by reason for unemployment
(as a percent of total unemployment), 1994
job losers or completed temp jobs 41.5%
job leavers 10.8%
reentrants 44.2%
new entrants 3.5%

Civilian labor force, by occupation, 1994
executive/administrative/
  managerial 26,000
professional/specialty 31,000
technicians & related support .... NA

sales 27,000
adminstrative support/clerical 33,000
service occupations 42,000
precision production/craft/repair 32,000
machine operators/assemblers .... NA
transportation/material moving 15,000
handlers/helpers/laborers 10,000
farming/forestry/fishing 20,000

Civilian labor force, by industry, 1994
construction 15,000
manufacturing 12,000
transportation/communication 13,000
wholesale/retail trade 50,000
finance/real estate/insurance 8,000
services 42,000
government 49,000
agriculture 20,000

Average annual pay, 1994 (prelim.) $22,054
change in average annual pay,
  1993-1994 .... 1.4%

Hours and earnings of production workers
on manufacturing payrolls, 1994
average weekly hours 39.9
average hourly earnings $11.81
average weekly earnings $471.22

Labor union membership, 1994 22,200

Household income (in constant 1993 dollars)
median household income, 1992 .... $31,113
median household income, 1993 .... $29,442

Poverty
persons below poverty level, 1992 .... 10.3%
persons below poverty level, 1993 .... 13.3%

Personal income ($per capita)
1994
  in current dollars 20,436
  in constant (1987) dollars 15,805
1995 (projected)
  in constant (1982) dollars 12,059
2000 (projected)
  in constant (1982) dollars 12,898

Federal income tax returns, 1993
returns filed 214,119
adjusted gross income ($1000) 6,483,405
total income tax paid ($1000) 967,596

Wyoming 7

ECONOMY, BUSINESS, INDUSTRY & AGRICULTURE

Fortune 500 companies, 1994 0

Business incorporations, 1994
total 1,934
change, 1993-94 .... 10.7%

Business failures, 1994
total 84
rate per 10,000 concerns 42
change, 1993-94 .... -6.7%

Business firm ownership
Hispanic owned firms, 1987 584
black owned firms, 1987 81
women owned firms, 1987 10,800
foreign owned firms, 1982 45

Gross state product, 1991 ($mil)
total $12,931
    agriculture services, forestry, fisheries 474
    mining 3,572
    construction 473
    manufacturing—durable goods 165
    manufacturing—nondurable goods 464
    transportation, communication &
        public utilities 2,192
    wholesale trade 377
    retail trade 964
    finance/real estate/insurance 1,525
    services 1,103
    federal, state & local government 1,623

*Establishments, by major industry
    group, 1992*
total 15,536
    agriculture 236
    mining 620
    construction 1,707
    manufacturing 581
    transportation 851
    wholesale trade 988
    retail trade 3,804
    finance/real estate/insurance 1,195
    service industries 5,190
    unclassified 364

Payroll, by major industry group, 1992
total ($1,000) $2,854,675
    agriculture 13,367

mining 664,115
construction 240,488
manufacturing 230,123
transportation 317,213
wholesale trade 166,481
retail trade 436,427
finance/real estate/insurance 152,699
service industries 629,603
unclassified 4,159

Agriculture
number of farms, 1994 9,000
farm acreage, 1994 35,000,000
acres per farm, 1994 3,772
value of farms, 1994 ($mil)............... 5,871
farm income, 1993 ($mil)
    gross farm income 1,002
    net farm income 262
    debt/asset ratio 12.4%
farm marketings, 1993 ($mil)
    total $817
        crops................................160
        livestock 657
government payments 43
farm marketings in order of marketing
receipts, 1993
    1) Cattle
    2) Sugar beets
    3) Hay
    4) Sheep

*Federal economic activity
    ($mil, except per capita)*
expenditures, 1994
    total $2,344
    per capita $4,924
    defense $249
    non-defense $2,095
defense department, 1994
    contract awards ($mil) $56
    payroll ($mil) $189
    civilian employees (x1,000) 1.0
    military personnel (x1,000) 3.9

Fishing, 1992
catch (millions of pounds) ....NA
value ($mil) ....NA

Mining, 1994 ($mil)
total non-fuel mineral production $781

409

Wyoming 8

principal non-fuel minerals in order of value, 1994

1) Soda ash
2) Clay
3) Helium

Construction, 1994 ($mil)
total contracts (including
    non-building) $560
      residential 174
      non-residential 118

Manufacturing, 1992
total establishments 577
employees, total (x1,000) 9
payroll ($mil) 225
production workers (x1,000) 6
value added ($mil) 856
value of shipments ($mil) 2,385

Finance
commercial banks, 1994
  number 55
    assets ($bil) 5.2
    deposits ($bil) 4.5
  closed or assisted 0
    deposits ($bil) .... NA
savings and loan associations, 1991
  non-current real estate loans 3.83%
  net income after taxes ($mil) 4
  return on assets .... +0.46%

Retail trade, 1992
establishments (x1,000) 3.7
sales ($mil) 3,554
annual payroll ($mil) 413
paid employees (x1,000) 37

Wholesale trade, 1992
establishments 987
sales ($bil) 2.5
annual payroll ($mil) 165
paid employees (x1,000) 7.0

Service industries, 1992
establishments (x1,000) (non-exempt firms) . 4.1
receipts ($mil) (non-exempt firms) 1,384
annual payroll ($mil) 436
paid employees (x1,000) (non-exempt firms) .. 26

COMMUNICATION, ENERGY & TRANSPORTATION

Communication
daily newspapers, 1993 9
broadcast stations, 1990
  radio: commercial, educational 68
  television: commercial, noncommercial 12
cable TV households, 1988 130,000

Energy
consumption estimates, 1992
  total (trillion Btu) 422
  per capita (million Btu) 908.7
by source of production (trillion Btu)
  coal 491
  natural gas 131
  petroleum 120
  nuclear electric power 0
  hydroelectric power 7
by end-use sector (trillion Btu)
  residential 33
  commercial 38
  industrial 268
  transportation 82
electrical energy
  production, 1993 (billion kWh) 40.2
  net summer capability, 1993 (million kW) .. 5.9
gas utilities, 1993
  customers 137,000
  sales (trillion Btu) 29
  revenues ($mil) 114
nuclear plants, 1993 0

Transportation, 1994
public road & street mileage
  total 36,520
    urban 2,309
    rural 34,211
    interstate 914
vehicle miles of travel (mil) 6,689
total motor vehicle registrations 509,170
  automobiles 268,606
licensed drivers 341,706
  per 1,000 driving age population 963
deaths from motor vehicle
  accidents 144

US Summary 1

STATE SUMMARY

Capital City .... Washington, DC

Governor ....

Address ....

Admitted as a state ....

Area (square miles) 3,787,425

Population, 1980 226,546,000

Population, 1990 248,709,873

Population, 1994 (est.) 260,341,000

Persons per square mile, 1994 .... 73.6

Largest city .... New York
   population, 1990 7,323,000

Personal income per capita, 1994
   (in current dollars) $21,809

Gross state product ($mil), 1991 5,690,865

Leading industries, 1992 (by payroll)
      SERVICE INDUSTRIES
      MANUFACTURING
      RETAIL TRADE

Leading agricultural commodities, 1993
      CATTLE
      DAIRY PRODUCTS
      CORN
      SOYBEANS

GEOGRAPHY & ENVIRONMENT

Area (square miles)

total 3,787,425

   land 3,536,342

   water (includes territorial water) 251,083

Federally owned land, 1991 .... 28.6%

Highest point

name .... Mt. McKinley

elevation (feet) 20,320

Lowest point

name .... Death Valley

elevation (feet) .... -282

General coastline (miles) 12,383

Tidal shoreline (miles) 88,633

Capital city .... Washington, DC
population, 1990 607,000

Largest city .... New York
population, 1990 7,323,000

Number of cities with over 100,000 population
1980 172

Number of cities with over 100,000 population
1990 190

State parks and Recreation areas, 1991
area (acres) 11,148,000
number of visitors 736,897,000
revenues $454,248,000

National forest land, 1992 (acres) 231,502,000

National park acreage, 1984 74,897,800

DEMOGRAPHICS & CHARACTERISTICS OF THE POPULATION

Population

1970 203,320,000

1980 226,546,000

1990 248,709,873

1994 (est.) 260,341,000

2000 (revised projection) 276,242,000

2010 (revised projection) 300,430,000

Metropolitan area population

1970 155,832,000

1980 172,335,000

1992 203,172,000

Non-metropolitan area population

1970 47,470,000

1980 54,211,000

1992 51,905,000

Change in population, 1980-90

number 22,163,873

percent 9.78%

Persons per square mile, 1994 .... 73.6

Age distribution, 1980

under 5 years 7.2%

5 to 17 years 21.0%

65 and over 11.3%

Age distribution, 1990

under 5 years 7.4%

5 to 17 years 18.1%

65 and over 12.5%

US Summary 2

Age distribution, 2000 (projected)
under 5 years 6.3%
5 to 17 years 18.2%
65 and over 13.0%

Persons by age, 1990
under 5 years 18,354,443
5 to 17 years 45,249,989
65 and over 31,241,831

Median age, 1990 . . . . *32.90*

Race, 1990
White 199,686,070
Black 29,986,060
American Indian 1,878,285
Chinese 1,645,472
Filipino 1,406,770
Japanese 847,562
Asian Indian 815,447
Korean 798,849
Vietnamese 614,547
all other 10,949,862

Race, 2010 (projected)
White 240,293,000
Black 40,227,000

Persons of Hispanic origin, 1990
total 22,354,059
Mexican 13,495,938
Puerto Rican 2,727,754
Cuban 1,043,932
Other Hispanic 5,086,435

Persons by sex, 1990
male 121,239,418
female 127,470,455

Marital status, 1990
males
15 years & older 93,817,315
single 28,804,618
married 55,677,642
separated 1,896,397
widowed 2,377,589
divorced 6,957,466
females
15 years & older 101,324,687
single 23,755,235
married 55,820,936
separated 2,676,840

widowed 12,121,939
divorced 9,626,577

Households & families, 1990
households 91,947,410
persons per household 2.63
families 64,517,947
married couples 50,708,322
female householder, no husband
present 10,666,043
one person households 22,580,420
households, 1994 95,946,000
persons per household, 1994 . . . . 2.64

Nativity, 1990
number of persons born in state 153,684,685
percent of total residents 61.8%

Immigration & naturalization, 1993
immigrants admitted 904,292
persons naturalized 314,681
refugees granted resident status 127,343

VITAL STATISTICS & HEALTH

Births
1992 4,084,000
with low birth weight 7.1%
to teenage mothers 12.7%
to unmarried mothers 30.1%
1993 4,039,000
1994 3,980,000

Abortions, 1992
total 1,529,000
rate (per 1,000 women age 15-44) 25.9
rate per 1,000 live births 379

Adoptions, 1986
total 104,088
related 50.9%

Deaths
1992 2,177,000
1993 2,268,000
1994 2,285,000

Infant deaths
1992 34,400
1993 33,300
1994 31,300

US Summary 3

Average lifetime, 1979-1981
both sexes . . . . 73.88 years
 men . . . . 70.11 years
 women . . . . 77.62 years

Marriages
1992 2,362,000
1993 2,334,000
1994 2,363,000

Divorces
1992 1,215,000
1993 1,187,000
1994 1,191,000

Physicians, 1993
total 576,771
rate (per 1,000 persons) 2.25

Dentists, 1992
total 155,058
rate (per 1,000 persons) 0.61

Hospitals, 1993
number 5,261
beds (x 1,000) 916.2
average daily census (x 1,000) 591.7
occupancy rate 64.6%
personnel (x 1,000) 3,676.6
average cost per day to hospital $881
average cost per stay to hospital $6,132

EDUCATION

Educational attainment of all persons 25 years and older, 1990
less than 9th grade 16,502,211
high school graduates 47,642,763
bachelor's degree 20,832,567
graduate or professional degree 11,477,686

Public school enrollment, Fall, 1993
total 43,476,268
 Kindergarten through grade 8 31,515,485
 grades 9 through 12 11,960,783

Public School Teachers
total, 1994 2,505,074
 elementary 1,397,802
 secondary 894,550
salaries, 1994
 beginning $23,258
 average $35,813

State receipts & expenditures for public schools, 1993
receipts ($mil) 262,966
expenditures
 total ($mil) 251,706
 per capita $987
 per pupil $5,574

Graduating high school seniors, public high schools, 1995 (est) 2,299,695

SAT scores, 1994
verbal 423
math 479

Institutions of higher education, 1995
total 3,688
 public 1,641
 private 2,047

Enrollment in institutions of higher education, Fall, 1993
total 14,305,658
full-time men 3,890,603
full-time women 4,237,137
part-time men 2,537,113
part-time women 3,640,805

Minority enrollment in institutions of higher education, Fall, 1993
Black, non-Hispanic 1,410,300
Hispanic 988,960
Asian/Pacific Islander 724,124

Earned degrees conferred, 1993
Bachelor's 1,165,178
First professional 75,387
Master's 369,585
Doctor's 42,132

SOCIAL INSURANCE & WELFARE PROGRAMS

Social Security beneficiaries & benefits, 1993
beneficiaries
total 41,230,000
 retired and dependents 29,033,000
 survivors 7,117,000
 disabled & dependents 5,085,000
annual benefit payments ($mil)
total $297,824
 retired and dependents 203,837
 survivors 60,225
 disabled & dependents 33,763

US Summary 4

Medicare, 1993
enrollment (x1,000) 35,497
payments ($mil) 142,211

Medicaid, 1993
recipients (x1,000) 32,664
payments ($mil) 101,547

Federal public aid, 1993
recipients as a percent of population 7.7%
Aid to Families with Dependent Children
  recipients (x1,000) 14,061
  average monthly payment $381
Supplemental Security Income
  total recipients (x1,000) 5,984

Food Stamp Program
  participants, 1994 (x1,000) 27,440

HOUSING & CONSTRUCTION

Total housing units, 1990 102,263,678
  year round housing units 99,146,811
  vacant 10,316,268

New privately owned housing units authorized, 1994
number (x1,000) 1,371.6
value ($mil) 123,278

New privately owned housing units started, 1994 (x1,000) 1,457.0

Existing home sales, 1994 (x1,000) 3.946

GOVERNMENT & ELECTIONS

State officials, 1996
  Governor (name/party/term expires)

Lt. Governor ....
Sec. of State ....
Atty. General ....
Chf. Justice ....

Governorship
minimum age ....
length of term ....
number of consecutive
  terms permitted ....
who succeeds ....

State legislature
name ....
  upper chamber
    name ....
    number of members ....
    length of term ....
    party in majority, 1996...................
  lower chamber
    name ....
    number of members ....
    length of term ....
    party in majority, 1996...................

State employees October, 1992
total 4,594,635
October payroll ($1,000) 9,828,247

Local governments, 1992
total 86,743
  county 3,043
  municipal 19,296
  township 16,666
  school districts 14,556
  special districts 33,131

Voting, November, 1994
voting age population 190,267,000
  registered 62.0%
  voted 44.6%

Vote for president
1988
  Bush 47,946,422
  Dukakis 41,016,429
1992
  Clinton 43,688,671
  Bush 38,109,410
  Perot 19,089,432

Federal representation, 1996 (104th Congress)
Senators (name/party/term expires)

Representatives, total 435
  Democrats 208
  Republicans 226
  other 1

US Summary 5

Women holding public office
U.S. Congress, 1995 47
statewide elected office, 1995 84
state legislature, 1995 1,535

Black elected officials, 1993
total 7,984
  US and state legislatures 561
  city/county/regional offices 4,819
  judicial/law enforcement 922
  education/school boards 1,682

Hispanic public officials, 1994
total 5,459
  state executives & legislators 199
  city/county/regional offices 2,197
  judicial/law enforcement 651
  education/school boards 2,412

GOVERNMENTAL FINANCE

State & local government revenues, (selected items), 1991-92 ($per capita)
total $4,641.08
  total general revenues 3,815.84
    from federal government 702.57
    from own sources 3,113.27
    from taxes 2,181.27
    from property taxes 699.44
    from all other taxes 1,316.49
    from charges & misc. 937.99

State & local government expenditures, (selected items), 1991-92 ($per capita)
total $4,511.20
  total direct general expenditures 3,812.31
    education 1,279.99
    libraries 17.68
    public welfare 606.26
    health & hospitals 345.43
    highways 261.45
    police protection 135.43
    fire protection 56.29
    correction 112.52
    housing & comm. development 66.91
    natural resources & parks 112.82
    interest on general debt 216.62

State & local debt, 1992 ($per capita) 3,848.33

Federal aid grants to state & local government, 1994 ($per capita total & selected items)
per capita total 810.84
  compensatory education 25.81
  waste treatment facilities 7.46
  medicaid 310.48
  housing assistance 50.21
  job training 12.50
  highway trust fund 70.48

CRIME, LAW ENFORCEMENT & COURTS

Crime, 1994 (all rates per 100,000 persons)
total crimes 13,991,675
overall crime rate 5,374.4
  property crimes 12,127,507
    burglaries 2,712,156
    larcenies 7,876,254
    motor vehicle thefts 1,539,097
  property crime rate 4,658.3
  violent crimes 1,864,168
    murders 23,305
    forcible rapes 102,096
    robberies 618,817
    aggravated assaults 1,119,950
  violent crime rate 716.0

Number of police agencies, 1994 10,654

Arrests, 1994
total 14,648,700
  persons under 18 years of age ....NA

Prisoners under state & federal jurisdiction, 1994
total 1,053,738
percent change, 1993-94 .... 8.6%
  sentenced to more than one year
    total 1,012,463
    rate per 100,000 residents 387

Persons under sentence of death, 4/20/95 .. 3,009

State's highest court
name ....
number of members ....
length of term ....
intermediate appeals court? ....

415

US Summary 6

LABOR & INCOME

Civilian labor force, 1994
total 131,056,000
  men 70,817,000
  women 60,239,000
  persons 16-19 years 7,481,000
  white 111,082,000
  black 14,502,000

Civilian labor force as a percent of
civilian non-institutional population, 1994
total 66.6%
  men 75.1%
  women 58.8%
  persons 16-19 years 52.7%
  white 67.1%
  black 63.4%

Employment, 1994
total 123,060,000
  men 66,450,000
  women 56,610,000
  persons 16-19 years 6,161,000
  white 105,190,000
  black 12,835,000

Full-time/part-time labor force, 1994
full-time labor force 106,248,000
  working part-time for
    ecomonic reasons 1,393,000
part-time labor force 24,761,000

Unemployment rate, 1994
total 6.1%
  men 6.2%
  women 6.0%
  persons 16-19 years 17.6%
  white 5.3%
  black 11.5%

Unemployed by reason for unemployment
(as a percent of total unemployment), 1994
job losers or completed temp jobs 47.7%
job leavers 9.9%
reentrants 34.9%
new entrants 7.5%

Civilian labor force, by occupation, 1994
executive/administrative/
  managerial 16,759,000
professional/specialty 17,979,000
technicians & related support 3,993,000

sales 15,719,000
adminstrative support/clerical 19,540,000
service occupations 18,376,000
precision production/craft/repair 14,395,000
machine operators/assemblers 8,424,000
transportation/material moving 5,499,000
handlers/helpers/laborers 5,708,000
farming/forestry/fishing 3,962,000

Civilian labor force, by industry, 1994
construction 6,149,000
manufacturing 20,765,000
transportation/communication 7,016,000
wholesale/retail trade 25,547,000
finance/real estate/insurance 7,537,000
services 29,626,000
government .... NA
agriculture .... NA

Average annual pay, 1994 (prelim.) $26,939
change in average annual pay,
  1993-1994 .... 2.2%

Hours and earnings of production workers
on manufacturing payrolls, 1994
average weekly hours 42.0
average hourly earnings $12.06
average weekly earnings $506.52

Labor union membership, 1994 16,740,300

Household income (in constant 1993 dollars)
median household income, 1992 .... $31,553
median household income, 1993 .... $31,241

Poverty
persons below poverty level, 1992 .... 14.8%
persons below poverty level, 1993 .... 15.1%

Personal income ($per capita)
1994
  in current dollars 21,809
  in constant (1987) dollars 16,867
1995 (projected)
  in constant (1982) dollars 14,469
2000 (projected)
  in constant (1982) dollars 15,345

Federal income tax returns, 1993
returns filed 115,060,797
adjusted gross income ($1000) 3,720,610,776
total income tax paid ($1000) 532,213,236

416

US Summary 7

ECONOMY, BUSINESS, INDUSTRY & AGRICULTURE

Fortune 500 companies, 1994 500

Business incorporations, 1994
total 741,657
change, 1993-94 .... 5.0%

Business failures, 1994
total 71,520
rate per 10,000 concerns 86
change, 1993-94 .... -17.0%

Business firm ownership
Hispanic owned firms, 1987 422,373
black owned firms, 1987 424,165
women owned firms, 1987 4,114,800
foreign owned firms, 1982 1,661

Gross state product, 1991 ($mil)
total $5,690,865
  agriculture services, forestry, fisheries . 108,630
  mining 91,841
  construction 223,394
  manufacturing—durable goods 551,423
  manufacturing—nondurable goods 474,759
  transportation, communication &
    public utilities 506,017
  wholesale trade 375,133
  retail trade 532,075
  finance/real estate/insurance 1,039,707
  services 1,089,816
  federal, state & local government 698,070

Establishments, by major industry group, 1992
total 6,317,690
  agriculture 97,245
  mining 29,130
  construction 588,667
  manufacturing 386,629
  transportation 258,500
  wholesale trade 492,095
  retail trade 1,564,245
  finance/real estate/insurance 596,888
  service industries 2,217,677
  unclassified 86,614

Payroll, by major industry group, 1992
total ($1,000) $2,271,962,391
  agriculture 10,040,725
  mining 25,605,273
  construction 122,089,076
  manufacturing 563,073,835
  transportation 175,450,694
  wholesale trade 190,840,514
  retail trade 258,566,355
  finance/real estate/insurance 221,022,396
  service industries 703,596,685
  unclassified 1,676,838

Agriculture
number of farms, 1994 2,040,000
farm acreage, 1994 975,000,000
acres per farm, 1994 478
value of farms, 1994 ($mil) 725,711
farm income, 1993 ($mil)
  gross farm income 201,431
  net farm income 43,401
  debt/asset ratio 16.0%
farm marketings, 1993 ($mil)
  total $175,052
  crops 84,497
  livestock 90,555
government payments 13,402
farm marketings in order of marketing receipts, 1993
  1) Cattle
  2) Dairy products
  3) Corn
  4) Soybeans

Federal economic activity
($mil, except per capita)
expenditures, 1994
  total $1,320,132
  per capita $4,996
  defense $227,525
  non-defense $1,092,607
defense department, 1994
  contract awards ($mil) $110,316
  payroll ($mil) $99,822
  civilian employees (x1,000) 810.2
  military personnel (x1,000) 1,130.7

Fishing, 1992
catch (millions of pounds) 9,637
value ($mil) 3,678

Mining, 1994 ($mil)
total non-fuel mineral production $34,209

417

US Summary 8

principal non-fuel minerals in order of value, 1994

1) NA
2) NA
3) NA

Construction, 1994 ($mil)
total contracts (including
  non-building) $293,757
    residential 133,030
    non-residential 99,784

Manufacturing, 1992
total establishments 381,870
employees, total (x1,000) 18,253
payroll ($mil) 560,485
production workers (x1,000) 11,654
value added ($mil) 1,428,707
value of shipments ($mil) 3,006,275

Finance
commercial banks, 1994
  number 10,941
    assets ($bil) 3,683.7
    deposits ($bil) 2,737.5
    closed or assisted 13
    deposits ($bil) 1.2
savings and loan associations, 1991
  non-current real estate loans .... NA%
  net income after taxes ($mil) .... -2,473
  return on assets .... -0.24%

Retail trade, 1992
establishments (x1,000) 1,526.2
sales ($mil) 1,894,880
annual payroll ($mil) 222,868
paid employees (x1,000) 18,407

Wholesale trade, 1992
establishments 495,457
sales ($bil) 3.249.9
annual payroll ($mil) 173,272
paid employees (x1,000) 5,791.4

Service industries, 1992
establishments (x1,000) (non-exempt firms)1,825.4
receipts ($mil) (non-exempt firms) 1,202,613
annual payroll ($mil) 452,697
paid employees (x1,000) (non-exempt firms)19,290

COMMUNICATION, ENERGY & TRANSPORTATION

Communication
daily newspapers, 1993 1,556
broadcast stations, 1990
  radio: commercial, educational 10,578
  television: commercial, noncommercial .. 1,419
cable TV households, 1988 47,042,000

Energy
consumption estimates, 1992
total (trillion Btu) 82,128
per capita (million Btu) 322.0
by source of production (trillion Btu)
  coal 18,846
  natural gas 20,139
  petroleum 33,525
  nuclear electric power 6,607
  hydroelectric power 2,793
by end-use sector (trillion Btu)
  residential 16,193
  commercial 12,875
  industrial 30,597
  transportation 22,464
electrical energy
  production, 1993 (billion kWh) 2,882.5
  net summer capability, 1993 (million kW) 700.0
gas utilities, 1993
  customers 57,759,000
  sales (trillion Btu) 10,415
  revenues ($mil) 51,787
nuclear plants, 1993 109

Transportation, 1994
public road & street mileage
total 3,906,544
  urban 813,591
  rural 3,092,953
  interstate 45,583
vehicle miles of travel (mil) 2,359,984
total motor vehicle registrations 198,045,365
  automobiles 133,929,662
licensed drivers 175,403,465
  per 1,000 driving age population 880
deaths from motor vehicle
  accidents 40,676

Comparative Tables

1. Total Area (square miles)

* UNITED STATES	3,787,425
1. Alaska	656,424
2. Texas	268,601
3. California	163,707
4. Montana	147,046
5. New Mexico	121,598
6. Arizona	114,006
7. Nevada	110,567
8. Colorado	104,100
9. Oregon	98,386
10. Wyoming	97,818
11. Michigan	96,810
12. Minnesota	86,943
13. Utah	84,904
14. Idaho	83,574
15. Kansas	82,282
16. Nebraska	77,358
17. South Dakota	77,121
18. Washington	71,303
19. North Dakota	70,704
20. Oklahoma	69,903
21. Missouri	69,709
22. Florida	65,758
23. Wisconsin	65,503
24. Georgia	59,441
25. Illinois	57,918
26. Iowa	56,276
27. New York	54,475
28. North Carolina	53,821
29. Arkansas	53,182
30. Alabama	52,423
31. Louisiana	51,843
32. Mississippi	48,434
33. Pennsylvania	46,058
34. Ohio	44,828
35. Virginia	42,769
36. Tennessee	42,146
37. Kentucky	40,411
38. Indiana	36,420
39. Maine	35,387
40. South Carolina	32,007
41. West Virginia	24,231
42. Maryland	12,407
43. Hawaii	10,932
44. Massachusetts	10,555
45. Vermont	9,615
46. New Hampshire	9,351
47. New Jersey	8,722
48. Connecticut	5,544
49. Delaware	2,489
50. Rhode Island	1,545
51. District of Columbia	68

2. Federally Owned Land, 1991

1. Nevada	82.9%
2. Alaska	67.9
3. Utah	63.9
4. Idaho	61.7
5. Oregon	52.4
6. Wyoming	48.9
7. Arizona	47.2
8. California	44.6
9. Colorado	36.3
10. New Mexico	32.4
* UNITED STATES	28.6
11. Washington	28.3
12. Montana	28.0
13. District of Columbia	26.1
14. Hawaii	15.5
15. New Hampshire	12.7
16. Michigan	12.6
17. Minnesota	10.5
18. Wisconsin	10.1
19. Florida	9.0
20. Arkansas	8.2
21. West Virginia	6.7
22. Virginia	6.3
23. North Carolina	6.3
24. Vermont	6.0
25. South Dakota	5.7
26. Missouri	4.7
27. Mississippi	4.3
28. North Dakota	4.2
29. Kentucky	4.2
30. Georgia	4.0
31. Tennessee	3.7
32. South Carolina	3.7
33. Alabama	3.3
34. New Jersey	3.1
35. Maryland	3.0
36. Illinois	2.7
37. Louisiana	2.6
38. Delaware	2.2
39. Pennsylvania	2.1
40. Indiana	1.7
41. Oklahoma	1.6
42. Nebraska	1.4
43. Texas	1.3
44. Ohio	1.3
45. Massachusetts	1.3
46. Iowa	0.9
47. Maine	0.8
48. Kansas	0.8
49. New York	0.7
50. Rhode Island	0.3
51. Connecticut	0.2

3. Cities with over 100,000 Population, 1990		4. 1970 Population	
* UNITED STATES	190	* UNITED STATES	203,320,000
1. California	43	1. California	19,971,069
2. Texas	17	2. New York	18,241,391
3. Florida	9	3. Pennsylvania	11,800,766
4. Virginia	8	4. Texas	11,198,655
5. Michigan	7	5. Illinois	11,110,285
6. Ohio	6	6. Ohio	10,657,423
7. Arizona	6	7. Michigan	8,881,826
8. North Carolina	5	8. New Jersey	7,171,112
9. New York	5	9. Florida	6,791,418
10. Indiana	5	10. Massachusetts	5,689,170
11. Connecticut	5	11. Indiana	5,195,392
12. Tennessee	4	12. North Carolina	5,088,411
13. Pennsylvania	4	13. Missouri	4,677,623
14. New Jersey	4	14. Virginia	4,651,448
15. Missouri	4	15. Georgia	4,587,930
16. Louisiana	4	16. Wisconsin	4,417,821
17. Kansas	4	17. Tennessee	3,926,018
18. Illinois	4	18. Maryland	3,923,897
19. Georgia	4	19. Minnesota	3,806,103
20. Colorado	4	20. Louisiana	3,644,637
21. Alabama	4	21. Alabama	3,444,354
22. Washington	3	22. Washington	3,413,244
23. Oregon	3	23. Kentucky	3,220,711
24. Nevada	3	24. Connecticut	3,032,217
25. Massachusetts	3	25. Iowa	2,825,368
26. Wisconsin	2	26. South Carolina	2,590,713
27. Oklahoma	2	27. Oklahoma	2,559,463
28. Nebraska	2	28. Kansas	2,249,071
29. Minnesota	2	29. Mississippi	2,216,994
30. Kentucky	2	30. Colorado	2,209,596
31. Iowa	2	31. Oregon	2,091,533
32. Utah	1	32. Arkansas	1,923,322
33. Rhode Island	1	33. Arizona	1,775,399
34. New Mexico	1	34. West Virginia	1,744,237
35. Mississippi	1	35. Nebraska	1,485,333
36. Maryland	1	36. Utah	1,059,273
37. Idaho	1	37. New Mexico	1,017,055
38. Hawaii	1	38. Maine	993,722
39. Arkansas	1	39. Rhode Island	949,723
40. Alaska	1	40. Hawaii	769,913
41. Wyoming	0	41. District of Columbia	756,668
42. West Virginia	0	42. New Hampshire	737,681
43. Vermont	0	43. Idaho	713,015
44. South Dakota	0	44. Montana	694,409
45. South Carolina	0	45. South Dakota	666,257
46. North Dakota	0	46. North Dakota	617,792
47. New Hampshire	0	47. Delaware	548,107
48. Montana	0	48. Nevada	488,738
49. Maine	0	49. Vermont	444,732
50. District of Columbia	0	50. Wyoming	332,416
51. Delaware	0	51. Alaska	302,583

5. 1980 Population

*UNITED STATES	226,546,000
1. California	23,667,902
2. New York	17,558,072
3. Texas	14,229,191
4. Pennsylvania	11,863,895
5. Illinois	11,426,518
6. Ohio	10,797,630
7. Florida	9,746,324
8. Michigan	9,262,078
9. New Jersey	7,364,823
10. North Carolina	5,881,766
11. Massachusetts	5,737,037
12. Indiana	5,490,224
13. Georgia	5,463,105
14. Virginia	5,346,818
15. Missouri	4,916,686
16. Wisconsin	4,705,767
17. Tennessee	4,591,120
18. Maryland	4,216,975
19. Louisiana	4,205,900
20. Washington	4,132,156
21. Minnesota	4,075,970
22. Alabama	3,893,800
23. Kentucky	3,660,777
24. South Carolina	3,121,820
25. Connecticut	3,107,576
26. Oklahoma	3,025,290
27. Iowa	2,913,808
28. Colorado	2,889,964
29. Arizona	2,718,215
30. Oregon	2,633,105
31. Mississippi	2,520,638
32. Kansas	2,363,679
33. Arkansas	2,286,435
34. West Virginia	1,949,644
35. Nebraska	1,569,825
36. Utah	1,461,037
37. New Mexico	1,302,894
38. Maine	1,124,660
39. Hawaii	964,691
40. Rhode Island	947,154
41. Idaho	943,935
42. New Hampshire	920,610
43. Nevada	800,493
44. Montana	786,690
45. South Dakota	690,768
46. North Dakota	652,717
47. District of Columbia	638,333
48. Delaware	594,338
49. Vermont	511,456
50. Wyoming	469,557
51. Alaska	401,851

6. 1990 Population

*UNITED STATES	248,709,873
1. California	29,760,021
2. New York	17,990,455
3. Texas	16,986,510
4. Florida	12,937,926
5. Pennsylvania	11,881,643
6. Illinois	11,430,602
7. Ohio	10,847,115
8. Michigan	9,295,297
9. New Jersey	7,730,188
10. North Carolina	6,628,637
11. Georgia	6,478,216
12. Virginia	6,187,358
13. Massachusetts	6,016,425
14. Indiana	5,544,159
15. Missouri	5,117,073
16. Wisconsin	4,891,769
17. Tennessee	4,877,185
18. Washington	4,866,692
19. Maryland	4,781,468
20. Minnesota	4,375,099
21. Louisiana	4,219,973
22. Alabama	4,040,587
23. Kentucky	3,685,296
24. Arizona	3,665,228
25. South Carolina	3,486,703
26. Colorado	3,294,394
27. Connecticut	3,287,116
28. Oklahoma	3,145,585
29. Oregon	2,842,321
30. Iowa	2,776,755
31. Mississippi	2,573,216
32. Kansas	2,477,574
33. Arkansas	2,350,725
34. West Virginia	1,793,477
35. Utah	1,722,850
36. Nebraska	1,578,385
37. New Mexico	1,515,069
38. Maine	1,227,928
39. Nevada	1,201,833
40. New Hampshire	1,109,252
41. Hawaii	1,108,229
42. Idaho	1,006,749
43. Rhode Island	1,003,464
44. Montana	799,065
45. South Dakota	696,004
46. Delaware	666,168
47. North Dakota	638,800
48. District of Columbia	606,900
49. Vermont	562,758
50. Alaska	550,043
51. Wyoming	453,588

7. 2000 Projected Population

* UNITED STATES	276,242,000
1. California	34,888,000
2. Texas	20,039,000
3. New York	18,237,000
4. Florida	15,313,000
5. Pennsylvania	12,296,000
6. Illinois	12,168,000
7. Ohio	11,453,000
8. Michigan	9,759,000
9. New Jersey	8,135,000
10. Georgia	7,637,000
11. North Carolina	7,617,000
12. Virginia	7,048,000
13. Washington	6,070,000
14. Indiana	6,045,000
15. Massachusetts	5,950,000
16. Tennessee	5,538,000
17. Missouri	5,437,000
18. Wisconsin	5,381,000
19. Maryland	5,322,000
20. Minnesota	4,824,000
21. Alabama	4,485,000
22. Louisiana	4,478,000
23. Arizona	4,437,000
24. Colorado	4,059,000
25. Kentucky	3,989,000
26. South Carolina	3,932,000
27. Oregon	3,404,000
28. Oklahoma	3,382,000
29. Connecticut	3,271,000
30. Iowa	2,930,000
31. Mississippi	2,750,000
32. Kansas	2,722,000
33. Arkansas	2,578,000
34. Utah	2,148,000
35. West Virginia	1,840,000
36. New Mexico	1,823,000
37. Nebraska	1,704,000
38. Nevada	1,691,000
39. Hawaii	1,327,000
40. Idaho	1,290,000
41. Maine	1,240,000
42. New Hampshire	1,165,000
43. Rhode Island	998,000
44. Montana	920,000
45. South Dakota	770,000
46. Delaware	759,000
47. Alaska	699,000
48. North Dakota	643,000
49. Vermont	592,000
50. District of Columbia	537,000
51. Wyoming	522,000

8. 2010 Projected Population

* UNITED STATES	300,430,000
1. California	41,085,000
2. Texas	22,850,000
3. New York	18,546,000
4. Florida	17,372,000
5. Illinois	12,652,000
6. Pennsylvania	12,438,000
7. Ohio	11,659,000
8. Michigan	10,033,000
9. New Jersey	8,562,000
10. Georgia	8,553,000
11. North Carolina	8,341,000
12. Virginia	7,728,000
13. Washington	7,025,000
14. Indiana	6,286,000
15. Massachusetts	6,097,000
16. Tennessee	6,007,000
17. Maryland	5,782,000
18. Missouri	5,760,000
19. Wisconsin	5,629,000
20. Minnesota	5,127,000
21. Arizona	5,074,000
22. Alabama	4,856,000
23. Louisiana	4,808,000
24. Colorado	4,494,000
25. South Carolina	4,311,000
26. Kentucky	4,160,000
27. Oregon	3,876,000
28. Oklahoma	3,683,000
29. Connecticut	3,412,000
30. Iowa	2,981,000
31. Kansas	2,922,000
32. Mississippi	2,918,000
33. Arkansas	2,782,000
34. Utah	2,462,000
35. New Mexico	2,082,000
36. Nevada	1,935,000
37. West Virginia	1,842,000
38. Nebraska	1,793,000
39. Hawaii	1,551,000
40. Idaho	1,454,000
41. Maine	1,309,000
42. New Hampshire	1,280,000
43. Rhode Island	1,034,000
44. Montana	996,000
45. South Dakota	815,000
46. Delaware	815,000
47. Alaska	781,000
48. North Dakota	676,000
49. Vermont	623,000
50. Wyoming	596,000
51. District of Columbia	577,000

9. Metropolitan Area Population, 1992

* UNITED STATES	203,172,000
1. California	29,875,000
2. New York	16,613,000
3. Texas	14,840,000
4. Florida	12,532,000
5. Pennsylvania	10,170,000
6. Illinois	9,757,000
7. Ohio	8,966,000
8. New Jersey	7,820,000
9. Michigan	7,799,000
10. Massachusetts	5,763,000
11. Virginia	4,954,000
12. Georgia	4,587,000
13. Maryland	4,563,000
14. North Carolina	4,535,000
15. Washington	4,270,000
16. Indiana	4,052,000
17. Missouri	3,543,000
18. Tennessee	3,404,000
19. Wisconsin	3,402,000
20. Arizona	3,244,000
21. Louisiana	3,210,000
22. Connecticut	3,138,000
23. Minnesota	3,096,000
24. Colorado	2,832,000
25. Alabama	2,788,000
26. South Carolina	2,514,000
27. Oregon	2,081,000
28. Oklahoma	1,927,000
29. Kentucky	1,820,000
30. Utah	1,403,000
31. Kansas	1,374,000
32. Iowa	1,228,000
33. Nevada	1,134,000
34. Arkansas	1,071,000
35. Rhode Island	937,000
36. New Mexico	886,000
37. Hawaii	863,000
38. Nebraska	809,000
39. Mississippi	803,000
40. West Virginia	756,000
41. New Hampshire	662,000
42. District of Columbia	585,000
43. Delaware	571,000
44. Maine	441,000
45. Idaho	320,000
46. North Dakota	263,000
47. Alaska	246,000
48. South Dakota	231,000
49. Montana	197,000
50. Vermont	154,000
51. Wyoming	138,000

10. Non-Metropolitan Population, 1992

* UNITED STATES	51,905,000
1. Texas	2,842,000
2. North Carolina	2,301,000
3. Georgia	2,186,000
4. Ohio	2,056,000
5. Kentucky	1,934,000
6. Illinois	1,856,000
7. Pennsylvania	1,825,000
8. Mississippi	1,812,000
9. Missouri	1,647,000
10. Michigan	1,635,000
11. Tennessee	1,621,000
12. Indiana	1,606,000
13. Wisconsin	1,591,000
14. Iowa	1,575,000
15. New York	1,497,000
16. Virginia	1,440,000
17. Minnesota	1,372,000
18. Alabama	1,349,000
19. Arkansas	1,323,000
20. Oklahoma	1,278,000
21. Kansas	1,141,000
22. South Carolina	1,089,000
23. Louisiana	1,069,000
24. West Virginia	1,053,000
25. California	1,021,000
26. Florida	950,000
27. Oregon	890,000
28. Washington	873,000
29. Maine	795,000
30. Nebraska	791,000
31. Idaho	746,000
32. New Mexico	696,000
33. Colorado	632,000
34. Montana	625,000
35. Arizona	588,000
36. South Dakota	478,000
37. New Hampshire	453,000
38. Vermont	417,000
39. Utah	408,000
40. North Dakota	371,000
41. Maryland	354,000
42. Alaska	342,000
43. Wyoming	327,000
44. Hawaii	293,000
45. Massachusetts	230,000
46. Nevada	203,000
47. Connecticut	141,000
48. Delaware	120,000
49. Rhode Island	64,000
50. New Jersey	0
51. District of Columbia	0

11. Change in Population, 1980-1990

1. Nevada	50.14%
2. Alaska	36.88
3. Arizona	34.84
4. Florida	32.75
5. California	25.74
6. New Hampshire	20.49
7. Texas	19.38
8. Georgia	18.58
9. Utah	17.92
10. Washington	17.78
11. New Mexico	16.28
12. Virginia	15.72
13. Hawaii	14.88
14. Colorado	13.99
15. Maryland	13.39
16. North Carolina	12.70
17. Delaware	12.09
18. South Carolina	11.69
19. Vermont	10.03
* UNITED STATES	9.78
20. Maine	9.18
21. Oregon	7.95
22. Minnesota	7.34
23. Idaho	6.65
24. Tennessee	6.23
25. Rhode Island	5.95
26. Connecticut	5.78
27. New Jersey	4.96
28. Massachusetts	4.87
29. Kansas	4.82
30. Missouri	4.08
31. Oklahoma	3.98
32. Wisconsin	3.95
33. Alabama	3.77
34. Arkansas	2.81
35. New York	2.46
36. Mississippi	2.09
37. Montana	1.57
38. Indiana	0.98
39. South Dakota	0.76
40. Kentucky	0.67
41. Nebraska	0.55
42. Ohio	0.46
43. Michigan	0.36
44. Louisiana	0.33
45. Pennsylvania	0.15
46. Illinois	0.04
47. North Dakota	-2.13
48. Wyoming	-3.40
49. Iowa	-4.70
50. District of Columbia	-4.92
51. West Virginia	-8.01

12. Persons per Square Mile, 1994

1. District of Columbia	9,347.1
2. New Jersey	1,065.4
3. Rhode Island	953.8
4. Massachusetts	770.7
5. Connecticut	676.0
6. Maryland	512.1
7. New York	384.7
8. Delaware	361.3
9. Ohio	271.1
10. Pennsylvania	268.9
11. Florida	258.4
12. Illinois	211.4
13. California	201.5
14. Hawaii	183.5
15. Michigan	167.2
16. Virginia	165.5
17. Indiana	160.4
18. North Carolina	145.1
19. New Hampshire	126.7
20. Tennessee	125.6
21. Georgia	121.8
22. South Carolina	121.7
23. Louisiana	99.0
24. Kentucky	96.3
25. Wisconsin	93.6
26. Alabama	83.1
27. Washington	80.2
28. Missouri	76.6
29. West Virginia	75.6
* UNITED STATES	73.6
30. Texas	70.2
31. Vermont	62.7
32. Minnesota	57.4
33. Mississippi	56.9
34. Iowa	50.6
35. Oklahoma	47.4
36. Arkansas	47.1
37. Maine	40.2
38. Arizona	35.9
39. Colorado	35.2
40. Oregon	32.1
41. Kansas	31.2
42. Utah	23.2
43. Nebraska	21.1
44. Idaho	13.7
45. New Mexico	13.6
46. Nevada	13.3
47. South Dakota	9.5
48. North Dakota	9.2
49. Montana	5.9
50. Wyoming	4.9
51. Alaska	1.1

13. Households, 1990

* UNITED STATES	91,947,410
1. California	10,381,206
2. New York	6,639,322
3. Texas	6,070,937
4. Florida	5,134,869
5. Pennsylvania	4,495,966
6. Illinois	4,202,240
7. Ohio	4,087,546
8. Michigan	3,419,331
9. New Jersey	2,794,711
10. North Carolina	2,517,026
11. Georgia	2,366,615
12. Virginia	2,291,830
13. Massachusetts	2,247,110
14. Indiana	2,065,355
15. Missouri	1,961,206
16. Washington	1,872,431
17. Tennessee	1,853,725
18. Wisconsin	1,822,118
19. Maryland	1,748,991
20. Minnesota	1,647,853
21. Alabama	1,506,790
22. Louisiana	1,499,269
23. Kentucky	1,379,782
24. Arizona	1,368,843
25. Colorado	1,282,489
26. South Carolina	1,258,044
27. Connecticut	1,230,479
28. Oklahoma	1,206,135
29. Oregon	1,103,313
30. Iowa	1,064,325
31. Kansas	944,726
32. Mississippi	911,374
33. Arkansas	891,179
34. West Virginia	688,557
35. Nebraska	602,363
36. New Mexico	542,709
37. Utah	537,273
38. Nevada	466,297
39. Maine	465,312
40. New Hampshire	411,186
41. Rhode Island	377,977
42. Idaho	360,723
43. Hawaii	356,267
44. Montana	306,163
45. South Dakota	259,034
46. District of Columbia	249,634
47. Delaware	247,497
48. North Dakota	240,878
49. Vermont	210,650
50. Alaska	188,915
51. Wyoming	168,839

14. Households, 1994

* UNITED STATES	95,946,000
1. California	10,850,000
2. New York	6,669,000
3. Texas	6,539,000
4. Florida	5,456,000
5. Pennsylvania	4,551,000
6. Illinois	4,308,000
7. Ohio	4,190,000
8. Michigan	3,502,000
9. New Jersey	2,845,000
10. North Carolina	2,679,000
11. Georgia	2,581,000
12. Virginia	2,439,000
13. Massachusetts	2,265,000
14. Indiana	2,161,000
15. Washington	2,042,000
16. Missouri	2,008,000
17. Tennessee	1,966,000
18. Wisconsin	1,890,000
19. Maryland	1,831,000
20. Minnesota	1,711,000
21. Alabama	1,583,000
22. Louisiana	1,543,000
23. Arizona	1,503,000
24. Kentucky	1,440,000
25. Colorado	1,417,000
26. South Carolina	1,337,000
27. Oklahoma	1,236,000
28. Connecticut	1,222,000
29. Oregon	1,195,000
30. Iowa	1,082,000
31. Kansas	966,000
32. Mississippi	949,000
33. Arkansas	927,000
34. West Virginia	705,000
35. Nebraska	614,000
36. Utah	599,000
37. New Mexico	587,000
38. Nevada	560,000
39. Maine	474,000
40. New Hampshire	424,000
41. Idaho	405,000
42. Hawaii	381,000
43. Rhode Island	374,000
44. Montana	325,000
45. South Dakota	265,000
46. Delaware	264,000
47. North Dakota	241,000
48. District of Columbia	237,000
49. Vermont	220,000
50. Alaska	208,000
51. Wyoming	178,000

15. Persons Born in State of Residence, 1990		16. Physicians per 1,000 persons, 1993	
1. Pennsylvania	80.2%	1. District of Columbia	6.67
2. Louisiana	79.0	2. Massachusetts	3.61
3. Iowa	77.6	3. Maryland	3.35
4. Kentucky	77.4	4. New York	3.34
5. West Virginia	77.3	5. Connecticut	3.21
6. Mississippi	77.3	6. Rhode Island	2.71
7. Wisconsin	76.4	7. New Jersey	2.63
8. Alabama	75.9	8. Vermont	2.59
9. Michigan	74.9	9. Pennsylvania	2.54
10. Ohio	74.1	10. Hawaii	2.44
11. Minnesota	73.6	11. California	2.40
12. North Dakota	73.2	12. Minnesota	2.32
13. Indiana	71.1	13. Illinois	2.30
14. North Carolina	70.4	* UNITED STATES	2.25
15. South Dakota	70.2	14. Colorado	2.22
16. Nebraska	70.2	15. Washington	2.20
17. Missouri	69.6	16. Virginia	2.15
18. Tennessee	69.2	17. Florida	2.15
19. Illinois	69.1	18. New Hampshire	2.11
20. Massachusetts	68.7	19. Tennessee	2.10
21. Maine	68.5	20. Oregon	2.10
22. South Carolina	68.4	21. Delaware	2.09
23. New York	67.5	22. Ohio	2.07
24. Utah	67.2	23. Missouri	2.07
25. Arkansas	67.1	24. Louisiana	2.01
26. Texas	64.7	25. Wisconsin	1.98
27. Georgia	64.5	26. North Carolina	1.98
28. Oklahoma	63.5	27. Michigan	1.95
29. Rhode Island	63.4	28. Arizona	1.94
* UNITED STATES	61.8	29. Maine	1.92
30. Kansas	61.3	30. New Mexico	1.90
31. Montana	58.9	31. Nebraska	1.89
32. Vermont	57.2	32. North Dakota	1.88
33. Connecticut	57.0	33. Utah	1.87
34. Hawaii	56.1	34. Kansas	1.85
35. New Jersey	54.8	35. West Virginia	1.82
36. Virginia	54.2	36. Georgia	1.82
37. New Mexico	51.7	37. Kentucky	1.79
38. Idaho	50.6	38. Texas	1.77
39. Delaware	50.2	39. South Carolina	1.73
40. Maryland	49.8	40. Alabama	1.70
41. Washington	48.2	41. Montana	1.69
42. Oregon	46.6	42. Indiana	1.68
43. California	46.4	43. Arkansas	1.62
44. New Hampshire	44.1	44. Iowa	1.59
45. Colorado	43.3	45. South Dakota	1.56
46. Wyoming	42.6	46. Oklahoma	1.53
47. District of Columbia	39.3	47. Nevada	1.48
48. Arizona	34.2	48. Alaska	1.42
49. Alaska	34.0	49. Wyoming	1.37
50. Florida	30.5	50. Idaho	1.31
51. Nevada	21.8	51. Mississippi	1.30

17. Dentists per 1,000 persons, 1992

1. District of Columbia	1.29
2. New Jersey	0.83
3. Hawaii	0.83
4. New York	0.82
5. Connecticut	0.81
6. Massachusetts	0.80
7. Maryland	0.75
8. Colorado	0.71
9. Illinois	0.70
10. Oregon	0.69
11. Nebraska	0.68
12. California	0.68
13. Pennsylvania	0.67
14. Utah	0.65
15. Minnesota	0.65
16. Washington	0.63
17. Michigan	0.63
18. Wisconsin	0.62
* UNITED STATES	0.61
19. New Hampshire	0.61
20. Virginia	0.57
21. Vermont	0.57
22. Montana	0.57
23. Kentucky	0.57
24. Rhode Island	0.56
25. Alaska	0.56
26. Tennessee	0.55
27. Ohio	0.55
28. Iowa	0.54
29. Missouri	0.53
30. Kansas	0.53
31. Idaho	0.53
32. Florida	0.53
33. Wyoming	0.52
34. Texas	0.50
35. Arizona	0.50
36. Oklahoma	0.49
37. Indiana	0.49
38. West Virginia	0.48
39. North Dakota	0.48
40. Maine	0.48
41. Louisiana	0.47
42. Georgia	0.47
43. Delaware	0.47
44. South Dakota	0.44
45. South Carolina	0.43
46. North Carolina	0.43
47. Alabama	0.43
48. New Mexico	0.42
49. Nevada	0.42
50. Arkansas	0.41
51. Mississippi	0.39

18. Hospitals-Average Cost per Day, 1993 (to hospital)

1. California	$1,221
2. District of Columbia	1,201
3. Washington	1,143
4. Alaska	1,136
5. Arizona	1,091
6. Utah	1,081
7. Connecticut	1,058
8. Oregon	1,053
9. New Mexico	1,046
10. Massachusetts	1,036
11. Delaware	1,028
12. Texas	1,010
13. New Hampshire	976
14. Colorado	961
15. Ohio	940
16. Florida	940
17. Illinois	912
18. Michigan	902
19. Nevada	900
20. Indiana	898
21. Maryland	889
22. Rhode Island	885
* UNITED STATES	881
23. Louisiana	875
24. Missouri	863
25. Pennsylvania	861
26. Tennessee	859
27. South Carolina	838
28. Virginia	830
29. New Jersey	829
30. Hawaii	823
31. Oklahoma	797
32. New York	784
33. Georgia	775
34. Alabama	775
35. North Carolina	763
36. Wisconsin	744
37. Maine	738
38. Kentucky	703
39. West Virginia	701
40. Arkansas	678
41. Vermont	676
42. Kansas	666
43. Idaho	659
44. Minnesota	652
45. Nebraska	626
46. Iowa	612
47. Mississippi	555
48. Wyoming	537
49. North Dakota	507
50. South Dakota	506
51. Montana	481

19. Hospitals-Average Cost per Stay, 1993 (to hospital)

1. District of Columbia	$8,594
2. New York	7,716
3. Hawaii	7,633
4. Alaska	7,594
5. Connecticut	7,478
6. Delaware	7,307
7. New Hampshire	6,964
8. California	6,918
9. Massachusetts	6,843
10. Nevada	6,796
11. Pennsylvania	6,564
12. New Jersey	6,540
13. Illinois	6,318
14. Colorado	6,212
15. Florida	6,169
16. Missouri	6,161
17. Michigan	6,147
* UNITED STATES	6,132
18. Nebraska	6,024
19. Texas	6,021
20. South Carolina	5,955
21. Ohio	5,923
22. Minnesota	5,867
23. Tennessee	5,798
24. Washington	5,792
25. Louisiana	5,781
26. Indiana	5,677
27. Rhode Island	5,672
28. Maryland	5,632
29. New Mexico	5,600
30. North Carolina	5,571
31. Georgia	5,554
32. Maine	5,543
33. Arizona	5,528
34. Virginia	5,504
35. North Dakota	5,403
36. Wisconsin	5,348
37. Utah	5,314
38. Oregon	5,309
39. Vermont	5,241
40. Alabama	5,229
41. Kansas	5,108
42. Oklahoma	5,093
43. South Dakota	5,052
44. Iowa	4,980
45. Montana	4,953
46. Kentucky	4,749
47. West Virginia	4,712
48. Wyoming	4,706
49. Idaho	4,635
50. Arkansas	4,585
51. Mississippi	4,053

20. Persons with Less Than 9 Years of School, 1990

* UNITED STATES	16,502,211
1. California	2,085,905
2. Texas	1,387,528
3. New York	1,200,827
4. Florida	842,811
5. Illinois	750,932
6. Pennsylvania	741,167
7. Ohio	546,954
8. North Carolina	539,974
9. Tennessee	500,929
10. New Jersey	486,210
11. Georgia	483,755
12. Michigan	452,893
13. Virginia	443,668
14. Kentucky	442,579
15. Missouri	380,613
16. Louisiana	372,913
17. Alabama	348,848
18. Massachusetts	317,943
19. Indiana	297,423
20. South Carolina	295,167
21. Wisconsin	294,862
22. Maryland	246,505
23. Mississippi	240,267
24. Minnesota	239,322
25. Arkansas	227,633
26. Arizona	207,509
27. West Virginia	196,319
28. Oklahoma	195,015
29. Connecticut	185,213
30. Washington	171,311
31. Iowa	163,335
32. Kansas	120,951
33. Colorado	118,252
34. Oregon	114,724
35. New Mexico	105,362
36. Nebraska	79,925
37. Rhode Island	72,842
38. Hawaii	71,806
39. Maine	70,153
40. North Dakota	59,354
41. South Dakota	57,707
42. Nevada	47,771
43. New Hampshire	47,691
44. Idaho	44,219
45. Montana	41,144
46. District of Columbia	39,107
47. Delaware	31,009
48. Vermont	30,945
49. Utah	30,379
50. Alaska	16,621
51. Wyoming	15,919

21. High School Graduates, 1990*	
* UNITED STATES	47,642,763
1. California	4,167,897
2. New York	3,485,686
3. Pennsylvania	3,035,080
4. Florida	2,679,285
5. Texas	2,640,162
6. Ohio	2,515,987
7. Illinois	2,187,342
8. Michigan	1,887,449
9. New Jersey	1,606,555
10. Indiana	1,333,093
11. North Carolina	1,232,868
12. Georgia	1,192,935
13. Massachusetts	1,178,509
14. Wisconsin	1,147,697
15. Missouri	1,090,940
16. Virginia	1,059,199
17. Tennessee	942,865
18. Minnesota	913,265
19. Maryland	878,432
20. Washington	873,150
21. Louisiana	803,328
22. Alabama	749,591
23. Kentucky	741,012
24. Iowa	684,368
25. Connecticut	648,366
26. South Carolina	639,358
27. Oklahoma	607,903
28. Arizona	601,440
29. Colorado	558,312
30. Oregon	536,687
31. Kansas	514,177
32. Arkansas	489,570
33. West Virginia	429,123
34. Mississippi	423,624
35. Nebraska	345,778
36. Maine	295,074
37. New Mexico	264,943
38. Nevada	248,968
39. Utah	244,132
40. New Hampshire	226,267
41. Hawaii	203,893
42. Rhode Island	194,064
43. Idaho	182,892
44. Montana	170,070
45. South Dakota	144,990
46. Delaware	140,030
47. Vermont	123,430
48. North Dakota	111,215
49. Alaska	92,925
50. Wyoming	92,081
51. District of Columbia	86,756

*Persons 25 years and older with high school diplomas

22. Persons Holding Bachelor's Degree, 1990	
* UNITED STATES	20,832,567
1. California	2,858,107
2. New York	1,561,719
3. Texas	1,428,031
4. Florida	1,062,649
5. Illinois	989,808
6. Pennsylvania	890,660
7. New Jersey	826,887
8. Ohio	767,845
9. Massachusetts	657,161
10. Michigan	638,267
11. Virginia	612,679
12. Georgia	519,613
13. North Carolina	510,003
14. Washington	496,866
15. Maryland	486,695
16. Minnesota	431,381
17. Missouri	383,678
18. Colorado	379,150
19. Wisconsin	375,603
20. Connecticut	356,289
21. Tennessee	330,742
22. Indiana	321,278
23. Arizona	306,554
24. Louisiana	267,055
25. Alabama	258,231
26. Oregon	252,626
27. South Carolina	243,161
28. Oklahoma	236,112
29. Kansas	221,016
30. Iowa	207,269
31. Kentucky	189,539
32. Mississippi	149,109
33. Utah	138,534
34. Arkansas	132,712
35. Nebraska	130,172
36. New Hampshire	117,260
37. New Mexico	111,957
38. Hawaii	111,837
39. Maine	100,788
40. Rhode Island	88,634
41. West Virginia	88,136
42. Nevada	79,693
43. Idaho	74,443
44. Montana	71,610
45. District of Columbia	65,892
46. Delaware	58,615
47. Vermont	55,120
48. North Dakota	53,637
49. South Dakota	52,773
50. Alaska	48,617
51. Wyoming	36,354

23. Average Teachers' Salaries, 1994

1. Connecticut	$50,389
2. Alaska	47,902
3. New York	45,772
4. New Jersey	45,582
5. Michigan	45,218
6. District of Columbia	43,014
7. Pennsylvania	42,411
8. California	40,636
9. Maryland	39,475
10. Illinois	39,416
11. Rhode Island	39,261
12. Massachusetts	38,960
13. Oregon	37,589
14. Delaware	37,469
15. Nevada	37,181
16. Wisconsin	36,644
17. Hawaii	36,564
18. Minnesota	36,146
19. Ohio	35,912
20. Washington	35,860
* UNITED STATES	35,813
21. Indiana	35,741
22. Vermont	34,517
23. New Hampshire	34,121
24. Colorado	33,826
25. Virginia	33,472
26. Florida	31,944
27. Arizona	31,825
28. Kansas	31,700
29. Kentucky	31,639
30. Maine	30,996
31. Wyoming	30,954
32. Iowa	30,760
33. West Virginia	30,549
34. Texas	30,519
35. Tennessee	30,514
36. Missouri	30,324
37. North Carolina	29,727
38. Nebraska	29,564
39. South Carolina	29,414
40. Georgia	29,214
41. Alabama	28,659
42. Arkansas	28,312
43. Montana	28,200
44. Utah	28,056
45. New Mexico	27,922
46. Idaho	27,756
47. Oklahoma	27,612
48. Louisiana	26,243
49. North Dakota	25,506
50. South Dakota	25,259
51. Mississippi	25,153

24. Expenditures for Public Schools, per capita, 1993

1. Alaska	$1,800
2. New Jersey	1,351
3. Wyoming	1,336
4. New York	1,265
5. Connecticut	1,252
6. Vermont	1,197
7. Michigan	1,155
8. Oregon	1,138
9. Washington	1,131
10. Minnesota	1,124
11. Wisconsin	1,123
12. Maine	1,098
13. Pennsylvania	1,096
14. District of Columbia	1,061
15. Montana	1,056
16. Texas	1,049
17. West Virginia	1,045
18. Indiana	1,029
19. Ohio	1,024
20. Kansas	1,024
21. Maryland	1,003
* UNITED STATES	987
22. Delaware	974
23. Colorado	974
24. Nevada	964
25. Iowa	943
26. Virginia	940
27. Hawaii	932
28. New Mexico	919
29. California	919
30. New Hampshire	916
31. Arizona	915
32. Massachusetts	913
33. Nebraska	905
34. Rhode Island	903
35. Idaho	898
36. South Dakota	885
37. Illinois	865
38. Florida	864
39. North Dakota	863
40. Oklahoma	850
41. South Carolina	848
42. Kentucky	841
43. Utah	834
44. Georgia	834
45. North Carolina	818
46. Louisiana	804
47. Missouri	764
48. Arkansas	762
49. Alabama	692
50. Mississippi	676
51. Tennessee	663

25. Expenditures for Public Schools, per pupil, 1993

1. New Jersey	$9,712
2. Alaska	9,290
3. New York	8,525
4. Connecticut	8,188
5. District of Columbia	7,998
6. Pennsylvania	7,748
7. Vermont	7,172
8. Rhode Island	6,649
9. Massachusetts	6,505
10. Wisconsin	6,500
11. Maryland	6,447
12. Delaware	6,420
13. Michigan	6,402
14. Oregon	6,240
15. Maine	6,162
16. Ohio	5,963
17. Wyoming	5,932
18. Hawaii	5,806
19. West Virginia	5,689
20. Indiana	5,641
21. New Hampshire	5,619
* UNITED STATES	5,574
22. Minnesota	5,572
23. Washington	5,528
24. Virginia	5,517
25. Kansas	5,459
26. Montana	5,348
27. Florida	5,303
28. Iowa	5,297
29. Illinois	5,191
30. Nevada	4,976
31. Colorado	4,969
32. Nebraska	4,950
33. Kentucky	4,942
34. Texas	4,933
35. North Carolina	4,810
36. New Mexico	4,643
37. California	4,608
38. South Carolina	4,573
39. Georgia	4,544
40. Missouri	4,487
41. North Dakota	4,404
42. South Dakota	4,359
43. Louisiana	4,352
44. Arizona	4,140
45. Oklahoma	4,085
46. Tennessee	4,033
47. Idaho	4,025
48. Arkansas	3,838
49. Alabama	3,779
50. Mississippi	3,390
51. Utah	3,218

26. Social Security Beneficiaries, 1993

* UNITED STATES	41,230,000
1. California	3,891,000
2. New York	2,937,000
3. Florida	2,866,000
4. Texas	2,377,000
5. Pennsylvania	2,314,000
6. Ohio	1,882,000
7. Illinois	1,815,000
8. Michigan	1,569,000
9. New Jersey	1,286,000
10. North Carolina	1,174,000
11. Massachusetts	1,027,000
12. Georgia	964,000
13. Missouri	952,000
14. Indiana	951,000
15. Virginia	901,000
16. Tennessee	891,000
17. Wisconsin	870,000
18. Washington	762,000
19. Alabama	752,000
20. Minnesota	698,000
21. Louisiana	689,000
22. Kentucky	687,000
23. Arizona	658,000
24. Maryland	653,000
25. South Carolina	591,000
26. Oklahoma	562,000
27. Connecticut	553,000
28. Iowa	535,000
29. Oregon	530,000
30. Arkansas	489,000
31. Mississippi	478,000
32. Colorado	469,000
33. Kansas	426,000
34. West Virginia	380,000
35. Nebraska	278,000
36. New Mexico	244,000
37. Maine	228,000
38. Utah	213,000
39. Nevada	205,000
40. Rhode Island	187,000
41. New Hampshire	176,000
42. Idaho	170,000
43. Hawaii	158,000
44. Montana	148,000
45. South Dakota	134,000
46. Delaware	115,000
47. North Dakota	114,000
48. Vermont	95,000
49. District of Columbia	79,000
50. Wyoming	68,000
51. Alaska	39,000

27. Medicare Enrollment, 1993*

* UNITED STATES	35,497
1. California	3,504
2. New York	2,594
3. Florida	2,494
4. Pennsylvania	2,039
5. Texas	1,973
6. Ohio	1,626
7. Illinois	1,593
8. Michigan	1,309
9. New Jersey	1,144
10. North Carolina	971
11. Massachusetts	911
12. Missouri	814
13. Indiana	803
14. Georgia	791
15. Virginia	779
16. Wisconsin	745
17. Tennessee	738
18. Washington	658
19. Alabama	618
20. Minnesota	615
21. Maryland	578
22. Kentucky	565
23. Louisiana	563
24. Arizona	554
25. Connecticut	491
26. South Carolina	481
27. Oklahoma	473
28. Iowa	469
29. Oregon	452
30. Arkansas	410
31. Colorado	396
32. Mississippi	384
33. Kansas	376
34. West Virginia	322
35. Nebraska	245
36. New Mexico	198
37. Maine	194
38. Utah	177
39. Nevada	170
40. Rhode Island	165
41. New Hampshire	148
42. Idaho	142
43. Hawaii	141
44. Montana	125
45. South Dakota	115
46. North Dakota	102
47. Delaware	96
48. Vermont	79
49. District of Columbia	78
50. Wyoming	57
51. Alaska	30

* x1,000

28. Medicaid Recipients, 1993*

* UNITED STATES	32,664
1. California	4,834
2. New York	2,742
3. Texas	2,308
4. Florida	1,745
5. Ohio	1,491
6. Illinois	1,396
7. Pennsylvania	1,223
8. Michigan	1,172
9. Georgia	955
10. Tennessee	909
11. North Carolina	898
12. New Jersey	794
13. Massachusetts	765
14. Louisiana	751
15. Washington	633
16. Kentucky	618
17. Missouri	609
18. Virginia	576
19. Indiana	565
20. Alabama	522
21. Mississippi	504
22. Wisconsin	471
23. South Carolina	470
24. Maryland	445
25. Minnesota	425
26. Arizona	404
27. Oklahoma	387
28. West Virginia	347
29. Arkansas	339
30. Connecticut	334
31. Oregon	325
32. Iowa	289
33. Colorado	281
34. Kansas	243
35. New Mexico	241
36. Rhode Island	191
37. Maine	169
38. Nebraska	165
39. Utah	148
40. District of Columbia	120
41. Hawaii	110
42. Idaho	100
43. Montana	89
44. Nevada	88
45. Vermont	81
46. New Hampshire	79
47. South Dakota	70
48. Delaware	69
49. Alaska	65
50. North Dakota	62
51. Wyoming	46

* x1,000

29. Public Aid Recipients, as percent of population, 1993

1. District of Columbia	15.0%
2. Mississippi	11.3
3. California	11.2
4. Louisiana	9.9
5. West Virginia	9.6
6. New York	9.6
7. Kentucky	9.5
8. Tennessee	9.4
9. Michigan	9.3
10. Georgia	8.4
11. Rhode Island	8.3
12. Ohio	8.3
13. New Mexico	8.3
14. Illinois	7.9
15. Massachusetts	7.7
* UNITED STATES	7.7
16. Maine	7.6
17. North Carolina	7.3
18. Alaska	7.2
19. Washington	7.1
20. Vermont	7.0
21. Pennsylvania	7.0
22. Florida	7.0
23. Alabama	7.0
24. Missouri	6.9
25. South Carolina	6.8
26. Wisconsin	6.7
27. Arkansas	6.6
28. Arizona	6.5
29. Texas	6.3
30. Hawaii	6.3
31. Oklahoma	6.2
32. Connecticut	6.2
33. New Jersey	6.1
34. Maryland	5.9
35. Montana	5.6
36. Minnesota	5.5
37. Oregon	5.3
38. Delaware	5.3
39. Indiana	5.1
40. Wyoming	5.0
41. Iowa	4.9
42. Virginia	4.8
43. Colorado	4.8
44. Kansas	4.7
45. South Dakota	4.5
46. North Dakota	4.2
47. Nebraska	4.2
48. Utah	3.7
49. Nevada	3.7
50. New Hampshire	3.4
51. Idaho	3.2

30. Federal Aid to State & Local Government, per capita, 1994

1. District of Columbia	$3,897.85
2. Alaska	1,754.71
3. Wyoming	1,500.61
4. New York	1,235.37
5. Louisiana	1,212.68
6. West Virginia	1,188.69
7. Rhode Island	1,103.27
8. North Dakota	1,100.32
9. Montana	1,058.73
10. New Mexico	1,038.49
11. Massachusetts	1,038.49
12. Maine	1,023.44
13. South Dakota	1,004.46
14. Vermont	942.11
15. Mississippi	939.15
16. Connecticut	924.48
17. Hawaii	922.82
18. Texas	889.35
19. New Hampshire	840.47
20. California	834.17
* UNITED STATES	810.84
21. Kentucky	809.03
22. Pennsylvania	805.26
23. Arkansas	801.60
24. New Jersey	779.70
25. Minnesota	769.56
26. Oregon	763.07
27. Tennessee	761.26
28. Alabama	760.70
29. Ohio	753.58
30. Missouri	752.34
31. Michigan	749.48
32. South Carolina	744.10
33. Arizona	735.14
34. Washington	734.47
35. Maryland	726.61
36. Oklahoma	723.97
37. Illinois	723.75
38. Georgia	712.74
39. Iowa	712.36
40. North Carolina	687.72
41. Idaho	686.46
42. Nebraska	686.39
43. Wisconsin	678.82
44. Delaware	668.77
45. Kansas	652.48
46. Utah	633.51
47. Indiana	617.74
48. Colorado	575.08
49. Florida	574.65
50. Nevada	546.86
51. Virginia	485.41

31. Crime Rate, per 100,000 persons, 1994

1. District of Columbia	11,085.3
2. Florida	8,250.0
3. Arizona	7,924.6
4. Hawaii	6,680.5
5. Nevada	6,677.4
6. Louisiana	6,671.1
7. Oregon	6,296.4
8. New Mexico	6,187.8
9. California	6,173.8
10. Maryland	6,122.6
11. Washington	6,027.5
12. Georgia	6,010.3
13. South Carolina	6,000.8
14. Texas	5,872.4
15. Alaska	5,708.1
16. Illinois	5,625.9
17. North Carolina	5,625.2
18. Oklahoma	5,570.1
19. Michigan	5,445.2
* UNITED STATES	5,374.4
20. Colorado	5,318.4
21. Missouri	5,307.7
22. Utah	5,300.9
23. Tennessee	5,119.8
24. New York	5,070.6
25. Montana	5,018.8
26. Alabama	4,903.0
27. Kansas	4,893.8
28. Mississippi	4,837.1
29. Arkansas	4,798.7
30. New Jersey	4,660.9
31. Indiana	4,592.8
32. Connecticut	4,548.0
33. Ohio	4,461.4
34. Massachusetts	4,441.0
35. Nebraska	4,440.4
36. Minnesota	4,341.0
37. Wyoming	4,289.7
38. Delaware	4,147.6
39. Rhode Island	4,119.1
40. Idaho	4,077.0
41. Virginia	4,047.6
42. Wisconsin	3,944.4
43. Iowa	3,654.6
44. Kentucky	3,498.6
45. Maine	3,272.7
46. Pennsylvania	3,271.9
47. Vermont	3,250.3
48. South Dakota	3,102.2
49. New Hampshire	2,741.0
50. North Dakota	2,735.9
51. West Virginia	2,528.4

32. Violent Crime Rate, per 100,000 persons, 1994

1. District of Columbia	2,622.6
2. Florida	1,146.8
3. South Carolina	1,030.5
4. California	1,013.0
5. Nevada	1,001.9
6. Louisiana	981.9
7. New York	965.6
8. Illinois	960.9
9. Maryland	948.0
10. New Mexico	889.2
11. Alaska	766.3
12. Michigan	766.1
13. Tennessee	747.9
14. Missouri	743.5
* UNITED STATES	716.0
15. Massachusetts	707.6
16. Texas	706.5
17. Arizona	703.1
18. Alabama	683.7
19. Georgia	667.7
20. North Carolina	655.0
21. Oklahoma	651.5
22. New Jersey	614.2
23. Kentucky	605.3
24. Arkansas	595.1
25. Delaware	561.0
26. Indiana	525.1
27. Oregon	520.6
28. Washington	511.3
29. Colorado	509.6
30. Mississippi	493.7
31. Ohio	485.8
32. Kansas	478.7
33. Connecticut	455.5
34. Pennsylvania	426.7
35. Nebraska	389.5
36. Rhode Island	375.5
37. Minnesota	359.0
38. Virginia	357.7
39. Iowa	315.1
40. Utah	304.5
41. Idaho	285.8
42. Wyoming	272.5
43. Wisconsin	270.5
44. Hawaii	262.2
45. South Dakota	227.6
46. West Virginia	215.8
47. Montana	177.1
48. Maine	129.9
49. New Hampshire	116.8
50. Vermont	96.9
51. North Dakota	81.8

33. Incarceration Rate, 1994*

1. District of Columbia	1,583
2. Texas	636
3. Louisiana	530
4. Oklahoma	508
5. South Carolina	494
6. Nevada	460
7. Arizona	459
8. Georgia	456
9. Alabama	450
10. Michigan	428
11. Mississippi	408
12. Florida	406
13. Virginia	395
14. Maryland	395
15. Delaware	393
* UNITED STATES	387
16. California	384
17. Ohio	377
18. New York	367
19. Arkansas	353
20. Missouri	338
21. North Carolina	322
22. Connecticut	321
23. Alaska	317
24. New Jersey	310
25. Illinois	310
26. Colorado	289
27. Kentucky	288
28. Tennessee	277
29. Indiana	258
30. Idaho	258
31. Wyoming	254
32. Kansas	249
33. South Dakota	240
34. Pennsylvania	235
35. New Mexico	220
36. Hawaii	202
37. Washington	201
38. Montana	194
39. Iowa	192
40. Wisconsin	187
41. Rhode Island	186
42. New Hampshire	177
43. Oregon	175
44. Massachusetts	171
45. Vermont	168
46. Nebraska	159
47. Utah	155
48. Maine	118
49. West Virginia	106
50. Minnesota	100
51. North Dakota	78

The number of prisoners sentenced to more than one year, per 100,000 residents

34. Civilian Labor Force, 1994

* UNITED STATES	131,056,000
1. California	15,471,000
2. Texas	9,385,000
3. New York	8,571,000
4. Florida	6,824,000
5. Illinois	6,000,000
6. Pennsylvania	5,829,000
7. Ohio	5,537,000
8. Michigan	4,753,000
9. New Jersey	3,991,000
10. North Carolina	3,609,000
11. Georgia	3,566,000
12. Virginia	3,422,000
13. Massachusetts	3,179,000
14. Indiana	3,056,000
15. Wisconsin	2,795,000
16. Washington	2,708,000
17. Missouri	2,695,000
18. Maryland	2,691,000
19. Tennessee	2,664,000
20. Minnesota	2,565,000
21. Alabama	2,031,000
22. Colorado	1,996,000
23. Arizona	1,988,000
24. Louisiana	1,939,000
25. South Carolina	1,828,000
26. Kentucky	1,825,000
27. Connecticut	1,726,000
28. Oregon	1,643,000
29. Iowa	1,565,000
30. Oklahoma	1,540,000
31. Kansas	1,331,000
32. Mississippi	1,254,000
33. Arkansas	1,207,000
34. Utah	975,000
35. Nebraska	876,000
36. West Virginia	788,000
37. Nevada	779,000
38. New Mexico	770,000
39. New Hampshire	628,000
40. Maine	613,000
41. Idaho	591,000
42. Hawaii	583,000
43. Rhode Island	505,000
44. Montana	437,000
45. Delaware	384,000
46. South Dakota	374,000
47. North Dakota	338,000
48. Vermont	321,000
49. District of Columbia	314,000
50. Alaska	305,000
51. Wyoming	249,000

35. Unemployment Rate, 1994

1. West Virginia		8.9
2. California		8.6
3. District of Columbia		8.2
4. Louisiana		8.0
5. Alaska		7.8
6. Maine		7.4
7. Rhode Island		7.1
8. New York		6.9
9. New Jersey		6.8
10. Mississippi		6.6
11. Florida		6.6
12. Washington		6.4
13. Texas		6.4
14. Arizona		6.4
15. South Carolina		6.3
16. New Mexico		6.3
17. Pennsylvania		6.2
18. Nevada		6.2
19. Hawaii		6.1
* UNITED STATES		6.1
20. Massachusetts		6.0
21. Alabama		6.0
22. Michigan		5.9
23. Oklahoma		5.8
24. Illinois		5.7
25. Idaho		5.6
26. Connecticut		5.6
27. Ohio		5.5
28. Oregon		5.4
29. Kentucky		5.4
30. Wyoming		5.3
31. Kansas		5.3
32. Arkansas		5.3
33. Georgia		5.2
34. Montana		5.1
35. Maryland		5.1
36. Virginia		4.9
37. Missouri		4.9
38. Indiana		4.9
39. Delaware		4.9
40. Tennessee		4.8
41. Wisconsin		4.7
42. Vermont		4.7
43. New Hampshire		4.6
44. North Carolina		4.4
45. Colorado		4.2
46. Minnesota		4.0
47. North Dakota		3.9
48. Utah		3.7
49. Iowa		3.7
50. South Dakota		3.3
51. Nebraska		2.9

36. Average Annual Pay, 1994

1. District of Columbia		$40,919
2. Connecticut		33,811
3. New Jersey		33,439
4. New York		33,438
5. Alaska		32,657
6. Massachusetts		31,024
7. California		29,878
8. Michigan		29,541
9. Illinois		29,105
10. Maryland		28,421
11. Delaware		27,950
12. Pennsylvania		26,950
* UNITED STATES		26,939
13. Hawaii		26,746
14. Minnesota		26,425
15. Washington		26,362
16. Colorado		26,164
17. Ohio		26,133
18. Virginia		26,031
19. Texas		25,959
20. Nevada		25,700
21. New Hampshire		25,555
22. Rhode Island		25,454
23. Georgia		25,306
24. Indiana		24,908
25. Oregon		24,780
26. Missouri		24,625
27. Wisconsin		24,324
28. Arizona		24,276
29. Tennessee		24,106
30. Florida		23,925
31. Alabama		23,616
32. North Carolina		23,449
33. Louisiana		23,176
34. Vermont		22,964
35. West Virginia		22,959
36. Kansas		22,900
37. Utah		22,811
38. Kentucky		22,747
39. South Carolina		22,477
40. Maine		22,389
41. New Mexico		22,351
42. Oklahoma		22,292
43. Iowa		22,187
44. Wyoming		22,054
45. Idaho		21,938
46. Nebraska		21,500
47. Arkansas		20,898
48. Mississippi		20,382
49. Montana		20,219
50. North Dakota		19,893
51. South Dakota		19,255

438

37. Average Hourly Earnings of Production Workers, 1994

1. Michigan	$16.13
2. Washington	14.42
3. Ohio	14.38
4. Delaware	13.90
5. Indiana	13.56
6. Connecticut	13.53
7. District of Columbia	13.46
8. New Jersey	13.38
9. Maryland	13.15
10. Louisiana	13.13
11. West Virginia	12.60
12. Minnesota	12.60
13. Massachusetts	12.59
14. Montana	12.50
15. Pennsylvania	12.49
16. Iowa	12.47
17. California	12.44
18. Wisconsin	12.41
19. Oregon	12.31
20. Colorado	12.27
21. Illinois	12.26
22. Hawaii	12.22
23. New York	12.19
24. Kansas	12.14
* UNITED STATES	12.06
25. Vermont	11.97
26. Maine	11.91
27. Idaho	11.88
28. Nevada	11.83
29. Kentucky	11.82
30. Wyoming	11.81
31. Missouri	11.78
32. New Hampshire	11.73
33. Oklahoma	11.41
34. Utah	11.26
35. Virginia	11.25
36. Arizona	11.17
37. Texas	11.14
38. Alaska	10.96
39. Nebraska	10.94
40. Alabama	10.75
41. Tennessee	10.51
42. Rhode Island	10.35
43. Georgia	10.35
44. North Dakota	10.19
45. North Carolina	10.19
46. New Mexico	10.14
47. South Carolina	9.99
48. Florida	9.97
49. Arkansas	9.65
50. Mississippi	9.40
51. South Dakota	9.19

38. Average Weekly Earnings of Production Workers, 1994

1. Michigan	$724.24
2. Ohio	629.84
3. Delaware	594.92
4. Indiana	585.79
5. Washington	585.45
6. Connecticut	579.08
7. Louisiana	569.84
8. New Jersey	559.28
9. Maryland	545.73
10. District of Columbia	534.36
11. Wisconsin	529.91
12. Iowa	528.73
13. Massachusetts	525.00
14. Minnesota	524.16
15. West Virginia	520.38
16. Pennsylvania	519.58
17. Alaska	519.50
18. California	515.02
19. Illinois	513.69
20. Colorado	506.75
* UNITED STATES	506.52
21. Kansas	505.02
22. New York	499.79
23. New Hampshire	496.18
24. Oregon	496.09
25. Missouri	494.76
26. Oklahoma	491.77
27. Montana	491.25
28. Vermont	489.57
29. Kentucky	488.17
30. Nevada	486.21
31. Maine	483.55
32. Texas	480.13
33. Idaho	475.20
34. Arizona	471.37
35. Wyoming	471.22
36. Virginia	469.13
37. Hawaii	468.03
38. Nebraska	460.57
39. Utah	457.16
40. Alabama	450.43
41. Georgia	438.84
42. North Dakota	432.06
43. Tennessee	429.86
44. North Carolina	418.81
45. South Carolina	417.58
46. Rhode Island	417.11
47. New Mexico	414.73
48. Florida	412.76
49. Arkansas	403.37
50. Mississippi	391.98
51. South Dakota	385.06

39. Median Household Income, 1993

1. Alaska	$42,931
2. Hawaii	42,662
3. New Jersey	40,500
4. Maryland	39,939
5. Connecticut	39,516
6. New Hampshire	37,964
7. Massachusetts	37,064
8. Virginia	36,433
9. Delaware	36,064
10. Nevada	35,814
11. Utah	35,786
12. Washington	35,655
13. Colorado	34,488
14. California	34,073
15. Minnesota	33,682
16. Rhode Island	33,509
17. Oregon	33,138
18. Illinois	32,857
19. Michigan	32,662
20. Wisconsin	31,766
21. New York	31,697
22. Georgia	31,663
23. Ohio	31,285
* UNITED STATES	31,241
24. Vermont	31,065
25. Idaho	31,010
26. Nebraska	31,008
27. Pennsylvania	30,995
28. Arizona	30,510
29. Kansas	29,770
30. Indiana	29,475
31. Wyoming	29,442
32. North Carolina	28,820
33. Texas	28,727
34. Missouri	28,682
35. Iowa	28,663
36. Florida	28,550
37. North Dakota	28,118
38. South Dakota	27,737
39. Maine	27,438
40. District of Columbia	27,304
41. New Mexico	26,758
42. Montana	26,470
43. Louisiana	26,312
44. Oklahoma	26,260
45. South Carolina	26,053
46. Tennessee	25,102
47. Alabama	25,082
48. Kentucky	24,376
49. Arkansas	23,039
50. West Virginia	22,421
51. Mississippi	22,191

40. Persons Below Poverty Level, 1993

1. Louisiana	26.4%
2. District of Columbia	26.4
3. Mississippi	24.7
4. West Virginia	22.2
5. Kentucky	20.4
6. Arkansas	20.0
7. Oklahoma	19.9
8. Tennessee	19.6
9. South Carolina	18.7
10. California	18.2
11. Florida	17.8
12. Texas	17.4
13. New Mexico	17.4
14. Alabama	17.4
15. New York	16.4
16. Missouri	16.1
17. Michigan	15.4
18. Maine	15.4
19. Arizona	15.4
* UNITED STATES	15.1
20. Montana	14.9
21. North Carolina	14.4
22. South Dakota	14.2
23. Illinois	13.6
24. Georgia	13.5
25. Wyoming	13.3
26. Pennsylvania	13.2
27. Kansas	13.1
28. Idaho	13.1
29. Ohio	13.0
30. Wisconsin	12.6
31. Indiana	12.2
32. Washington	12.1
33. Oregon	11.8
34. Minnesota	11.6
35. Rhode Island	11.2
36. North Dakota	11.2
37. New Jersey	10.9
38. Utah	10.7
39. Massachusetts	10.7
40. Nebraska	10.3
41. Iowa	10.3
42. Delaware	10.2
43. Vermont	10.0
44. New Hampshire	9.9
45. Colorado	9.9
46. Nevada	9.8
47. Virginia	9.7
48. Maryland	9.7
49. Alaska	9.1
50. Connecticut	8.5
51. Hawaii	8.0

41. Personal Income, per capita, in current dollars, 1994	
1. District of Columbia	$31,136
2. Connecticut	29,402
3. New Jersey	28,038
4. New York	25,999
5. Massachusetts	25,616
6. Maryland	24,933
7. Hawaii	24,057
8. Nevada	24,023
9. Alaska	23,788
10. Illinois	23,784
11. New Hampshire	23,434
12. Delaware	22,828
13. Washington	22,610
14. Virginia	22,594
15. California	22,493
16. Minnesota	22,453
17. Michigan	22,333
18. Colorado	22,333
19. Pennsylvania	22,324
20. Rhode Island	22,251
* UNITED STATES	21,809
21. Florida	21,677
22. Wisconsin	21,019
23. Ohio	20,928
24. Kansas	20,896
25. Missouri	20,717
26. Nebraska	20,488
27. Wyoming	20,436
28. Oregon	20,419
29. Indiana	20,378
30. Iowa	20,265
31. Georgia	20,251
32. Vermont	20,224
33. Texas	19,857
34. North Carolina	19,669
35. Maine	19,663
36. South Dakota	19,577
37. Tennessee	19,482
38. Arizona	19,001
39. North Dakota	18,546
40. Idaho	18,231
41. Alabama	18,010
42. Montana	17,865
43. Kentucky	17,807
44. Oklahoma	17,744
45. South Carolina	17,695
46. Louisiana	17,651
47. West Virginia	17,208
48. New Mexico	17,106
49. Utah	17,043
50. Arkansas	16,898
51. Mississippi	15,838

42. Personal Income, per capita: Projections for the Year 2000*	
1. Connecticut	$20,503
2. New Jersey	19,932
3. District of Columbia	19,823
4. Massachusetts	18,694
5. New York	17,852
6. Maryland	17,665
7. New Hampshire	17,363
8. California	17,113
9. Alaska	16,765
10. Virginia	16,345
11. Illinois	16,131
12. Nevada	15,855
13. Delaware	15,747
14. Rhode Island	15,555
15. Minnesota	15,508
16. Florida	15,496
17. Michigan	15,361
* UNITED STATES	15,345
18. Washington	15,316
19. Colorado	15,311
20. Hawaii	15,219
21. Pennsylvania	15,173
22. Kansas	14,986
23. Missouri	14,592
24. Wisconsin	14,575
25. Ohio	14,531
26. Nebraska	14,322
27. Georgia	14,297
28. Vermont	14,193
29. Indiana	14,031
30. Maine	14,014
31. Arizona	13,926
32. Oregon	13,908
33. Texas	13,851
34. Iowa	13,849
35. North Carolina	13,481
36. Tennessee	13,192
37. Oklahoma	12,937
38. Wyoming	12,898
39. Montana	12,474
40. North Dakota	12,461
41. South Dakota	12,330
42. South Carolina	12,304
43. Alabama	12,247
44. Idaho	12,181
45. Kentucky	12,178
46. New Mexico	11,949
47. Louisiana	11,680
48. Utah	11,605
49. Arkansas	11,594
50. West Virginia	10,921
51. Mississippi	10,631

*in constant 1982 dollars

441

43. Average Federal Income Tax Paid, 1992

1. Connecticut	$7,872
2. New Jersey	6,941
3. New York	6,506
4. Nevada	6,398
5. District of Columbia	6,363
6. Illinois	6,100
7. Massachusetts	6,011
8. California	5,956
9. Washington	5,902
10. Maryland	5,755
11. Florida	5,626
12. Texas	5,620
13. New Hampshire	5,539
14. Virginia	5,417
15. Delaware	5,412
* UNITED STATES	5,405
16. Colorado	5,351
17. Michigan	5,243
18. Wyoming	5,204
19. Minnesota	5,188
20. Pennsylvania	5,148
21. Hawaii	5,117
22. Georgia	5,014
23. Kansas	4,972
24. Tennessee	4,941
25. Rhode Island	4,933
26. Indiana	4,858
27. Missouri	4,854
28. Alaska	4,757
29. Wisconsin	4,713
30. Louisiana	4,712
31. Oregon	4,705
32. Arizona	4,695
33. Ohio	4,632
34. Alabama	4,566
35. North Carolina	4,442
36. Nebraska	4,383
37. South Dakota	4,366
38. Oklahoma	4,354
39. Kentucky	4,316
40. Utah	4,301
41. Idaho	4,300
42. Vermont	4,266
43. Iowa	4,244
44. West Virginia	4,114
45. New Mexico	4,106
46. South Carolina	4,105
47. North Dakota	4,062
48. Arkansas	4,046
49. Maine	4,015
50. Montana	3,950
51. Mississippi	3,832

44. Fortune 500 Companies, 1994

* UNITED STATES	500
1. New York	65
2. Wisconsin	51
3. California	51
4. Illinois	40
5. Texas	36
6. Pennsylvania	33
7. Ohio	30
8. New Jersey	24
9. Connecticut	23
10. Massachusetts	17
11. Minnesota	16
12. Michigan	16
13. Georgia	15
14. Virginia	13
15. Missouri	12
16. Florida	12
17. Washington	7
18. North Carolina	7
19. Tennessee	6
20. Maryland	6
21. Indiana	6
22. Oklahoma	5
23. Nebraska	5
24. District of Columbia	5
25. Arkansas	5
26. Colorado	4
27. Rhode Island	3
28. Kentucky	3
29. Idaho	3
30. Delaware	3
31. Arizona	3
32. Utah	2
33. South Carolina	2
34. Maine	2
35. Kansas	2
36. Iowa	2
37. South Dakota	1
38. New Hampshire	1
39. Mississippi	1
40. Louisiana	1
41. Alabama	1
42. Wyoming	0
43. West Virginia	0
44. Vermont	0
45. Oregon	0
46. North Dakota	0
47. New Mexico	0
48. Nevada	0
49. Montana	0
50. Hawaii	0
51. Alaska	0

<table>
<tr><th colspan="2">45. Gross State Product, 1991*</th></tr>
</table>

45. Gross State Product, 1991*

* UNITED STATES	$5,690,865
1. California	763,577
2. New York	475,961
3. Texas	395,673
4. Illinois	279,283
5. Florida	255,129
6. Pennsylvania	254,528
7. Ohio	228,109
8. New Jersey	212,822
9. Michigan	189,445
10. Massachusetts	156,090
11. North Carolina	147,520
12. Virginia	145,189
13. Georgia	143,643
14. Washington	118,997
15. Indiana	114,211
16. Maryland	111,874
17. Missouri	106,214
18. Minnesota	103,301
19. Wisconsin	102,729
20. Tennessee	100,804
21. Connecticut	96,384
22. Louisiana	95,377
23. Colorado	76,921
24. Alabama	73,956
25. Kentucky	69,839
26. Arizona	69,767
27. South Carolina	66,408
28. Oregon	58,799
29. Oklahoma	57,914
30. Iowa	56,032
31. Kansas	53,281
32. Mississippi	41,481
33. Arkansas	40,561
34. District of Columbia	38,160
35. Nebraska	35,281
36. Nevada	33,322
37. Utah	33,078
38. Hawaii	30,802
39. New Mexico	30,250
40. West Virginia	29,014
41. Alaska	26,212
42. New Hampshire	24,404
43. Maine	23,241
44. Delaware	21,274
45. Rhode Island	20,657
46. Idaho	19,047
47. Montana	14,419
48. South Dakota	13,712
49. Wyoming	12,931
50. North Dakota	12,045
51. Vermont	11,198

*millions of dollars

46. Number of Farms, 1994

* UNITED STATES	2,040,000
1. Texas	185,000
2. Missouri	104,000
3. Iowa	100,000
4. Kentucky	89,000
5. Minnesota	85,000
6. Tennessee	84,000
7. Wisconsin	78,000
8. Illinois	77,000
9. California	76,000
10. Ohio	75,000
11. Oklahoma	70,000
12. Kansas	65,000
13. Indiana	63,000
14. North Carolina	58,000
15. Nebraska	55,000
16. Michigan	52,000
17. Pennsylvania	51,000
18. Alabama	46,000
19. Arkansas	44,000
20. Virginia	43,000
21. Georgia	43,000
22. Mississippi	39,000
23. Florida	39,000
24. Oregon	38,000
25. New York	37,000
26. Washington	36,000
27. South Dakota	34,000
28. North Dakota	32,000
29. Louisiana	28,000
30. Colorado	25,000
31. South Carolina	24,000
32. Montana	23,000
33. Idaho	21,000
34. West Virginia	20,000
35. Maryland	15,000
36. New Mexico	14,000
37. Utah	13,000
38. Wyoming	9,000
39. New Jersey	9,000
40. Arizona	8,000
41. Maine	7,000
42. Vermont	6,000
43. Massachusetts	6,000
44. Hawaii	4,000
45. Connecticut	4,000
46. New Hampshire	3,000
47. Delaware	3,000
48. Nevada	2,000
49. Rhode Island	1,000
50. Alaska	1,000
51. District of Columbia	0

47. Value of Farms, 1994*

* UNITED STATES	$725,711
1. Texas	64,146
2. California	51,153
3. Illinois	46,544
4. Iowa	43,838
5. Nebraska	29,894
6. Minnesota	26,722
7. Kansas	25,647
8. Indiana	23,569
9. Missouri	23,016
10. Florida	22,709
11. Ohio	21,067
12. Oklahoma	18,143
13. Montana	18,115
14. South Dakota	17,139
15. Wisconsin	16,678
16. North Dakota	16,541
17. Kentucky	16,127
18. Pennsylvania	15,088
19. Washington	14,370
20. Colorado	14,104
21. Tennessee	13,066
22. Michigan	12,969
23. Oregon	12,956
24. North Carolina	12,679
25. Arkansas	12,312
26. Georgia	11,893
27. Virginia	11,506
28. Arizona	11,295
29. New Mexico	10,630
30. Idaho	10,587
31. Mississippi	10,585
32. New York	10,261
33. Alabama	9,637
34. Louisiana	8,366
35. Maryland	6,305
36. Wyoming	5,871
37. Utah	5,685
38. South Carolina	4,751
39. New Jersey	4,210
40. West Virginia	2,638
41. Massachusetts	2,595
42. Nevada	2,036
43. Connecticut	1,921
44. Vermont	1,906
45. Maine	1,535
46. Delaware	1,452
47. New Hampshire	1,116
48. Rhode Island	336
49. District of Columbia	0

*millions of dollars
Note: No data for Alaska or Hawaii

48. Net Farm Income, 1993*

* UNITED STATES	$43,401
1. California	5,235
2. Texas	4,098
3. North Carolina	2,490
4. Florida	2,224
5. Nebraska	2,092
6. Kansas	1,623
7. Washington	1,572
8. Georgia	1,532
9. Illinois	1,342
10. Oklahoma	1,250
11. Ohio	1,183
12. South Dakota	1,179
13. Kentucky	1,135
14. Alabama	1,093
15. Idaho	1,072
16. Arkansas	1,051
17. Colorado	996
18. Oregon	908
19. Indiana	832
20. Pennsylvania	816
21. Montana	765
22. North Dakota	690
23. Arizona	638
24. Michigan	624
25. New Mexico	565
26. Missouri	564
27. Tennessee	549
28. New York	494
29. Wisconsin	474
30. Virginia	465
31. Iowa	462
32. Mississippi	368
33. Louisiana	335
34. Maryland	313
35. Utah	291
36. South Carolina	288
37. Wyoming	262
38. New Jersey	242
39. Connecticut	216
40. Minnesota	193
41. Massachusetts	191
42. Maine	154
43. Vermont	114
44. Delaware	107
45. West Virginia	105
46. Nevada	80
47. New Hampshire	58
48. Rhode Island	40
49. Hawaii	29
50. Alaska	7
51. District of Columbia	0

* millions of dollars

49. Farm Marketings, 1993*

* UNITED STATES	$175,052
1. California	19,850
2. Texas	12,617
3. Iowa	10,001
4. Nebraska	8,909
5. Illinois	8,082
6. Kansas	7,363
7. Minnesota	6,574
8. Florida	5,750
9. North Carolina	5,457
10. Wisconsin	5,250
11. Indiana	5,118
12. Washington	4,574
13. Ohio	4,393
14. Arkansas	4,382
15. Georgia	4,211
16. Colorado	4,083
17. Missouri	4,053
18. Oklahoma	3,869
19. Pennsylvania	3,712
20. Kentucky	3,376
21. Michigan	3,367
22. South Dakota	3,320
23. North Dakota	2,933
24. Alabama	2,910
25. Idaho	2,847
26. New York	2,817
27. Mississippi	2,605
28. Oregon	2,476
29. Virginia	2,068
30. Tennessee	2,039
31. Arizona	1,922
32. Montana	1,781
33. Louisiana	1,757
34. New Mexico	1,621
35. Maryland	1,366
36. South Carolina	1,221
37. Wyoming	817
38. Utah	804
39. New Jersey	706
40. Delaware	622
41. Connecticut	521
42. Massachusetts	497
43. Hawaii	492
44. Vermont	484
45. Maine	472
46. West Virginia	405
47. Nevada	289
48. New Hampshire	163
49. Rhode Island	79
50. Alaska	27
51. District of Columbia	0

* millions of dollars

50. Total Non-fuel Mineral Production, 1994*

* UNITED STATES	$34,209
1. Arizona	3,323
2. Nevada	2,761
3. California	2,497
4. Michigan	1,621
5. Georgia	1,535
6. Florida	1,468
7. Utah	1,428
8. Texas	1,409
9. Minnesota	1,352
10. Missouri	1,003
11. Pennsylvania	964
12. New Mexico	914
13. Ohio	893
14. New York	871
15. Wyoming	781
16. Illinois	770
17. North Carolina	705
18. Tennessee	577
19. Alabama	576
20. Washington	556
21. Indiana	517
22. Virginia	514
23. Kansas	495
24. Montana	492
25. Colorado	440
26. Kentucky	431
27. Alaska	429
28. Iowa	426
29. South Carolina	415
30. Arkansas	392
31. Wisconsin	344
32. Idaho	343
33. Oklahoma	338
34. Louisiana	328
35. Maryland	324
36. South Dakota	322
37. New Jersey	274
38. Oregon	253
39. West Virginia	176
40. Massachusetts	157
41. Nebraska	137
42. Hawaii	137
43. Mississippi	112
44. Connecticut	97
45. Maine	58
46. Vermont	48
47. New Hampshire	40
48. Rhode Island	27
49. North Dakota	26
50. Delaware	9
51. District of Columbia	0

* millions of dollars

51. Value of Manufacturing Shipments, 1992*		52. Percent of US Manufacturing Employment, 1986	
* UNITED STATES	$3,006,275	* UNITED STATES	100.00%
1. California	305,805	1. California	10.74
2. Texas	211,648	2. New York	6.90
3. Ohio	184,637	3. Ohio	5.92
4. Michigan	161,409	4. Pennsylvania	5.67
5. Illinois	158,129	5. Illinois	5.38
6. New York	154,211	6. Michigan	5.13
7. Pennsylvania	139,251	7. Texas	4.94
8. North Carolina	128,599	8. North Carolina	4.37
9. Indiana	104,871	9. New Jersey	3.70
10. Georgia	90,999	10. Massachusetts	3.35
11. Wisconsin	88,067	11. Indiana	3.13
12. New Jersey	86,885	12. Georgia	2.96
13. Tennessee	76,209	13. Wisconsin	2.64
14. Missouri	73,746	14. Florida	2.61
15. Washington	72,800	15. Connecticut	2.60
16. Virginia	65,860	16. Tennessee	2.54
17. Massachusetts	65,702	17. Missouri	2.22
18. Florida	64,320	18. Virginia	2.21
19. Louisiana	60,940	19. Minnesota	1.95
20. Kentucky	60,029	20. South Carolina	1.92
21. Minnesota	57,324	21. Alabama	1.79
22. Alabama	52,708	22. Washington	1.52
23. South Carolina	51,996	23. Kentucky	1.30
24. Iowa	46,432	24. Maryland	1.18
25. Connecticut	40,778	25. Mississippi	1.11
26. Kansas	36,095	26. Iowa	1.05
27. Arkansas	34,050	27. Arkansas	1.05
28. Mississippi	32,655	28. Oregon	1.02
29. Oregon	32,215	29. Kansas	1.02
30. Maryland	31,047	30. Colorado	0.99
31. Oklahoma	30,287	31. Arizona	0.90
32. Colorado	29,220	32. Oklahoma	0.87
33. Arizona	25,767	33. Louisiana	0.86
34. Nebraska	21,816	34. Rhode Island	0.59
35. Utah	15,750	35. New Hampshire	0.56
36. West Virginia	13,217	36. Maine	0.55
37. Delaware	13,000	37. Utah	0.50
38. Maine	11,611	38. Nebraska	0.48
39. New Hampshire	11,260	39. West Virginia	0.47
40. Idaho	10,557	40. Delaware	0.35
41. Rhode Island	9,578	41. Idaho	0.27
42. New Mexico	9,492	42. Vermont	0.23
43. Vermont	6,386	43. New Mexico	0.18
44. South Dakota	5,956	44. South Dakota	0.14
45. Montana	4,137	45. Hawaii	0.13
46. Hawaii	3,790	46. Nevada	0.11
47. North Dakota	3,678	47. Montana	0.11
48. Alaska	3,678	48. District of Columbia	0.09
49. Nevada	3,288	49. North Dakota	0.08
50. Wyoming	2,385	50. Alaska	0.05
51. District of Columbia	2,008	51. Wyoming	0.04

* millions of dollars

53. Commercial Bank Deposits, 1994*

*UNITED STATES	$2,737.5
1. New York	493.9
2. California	267.0
3. Illinois	161.2
4. Texas	151.2
5. Pennsylvania	140.1
6. Florida	123.4
7. Ohio	96.5
8. New Jersey	84.4
9. Michigan	81.6
10. North Carolina	70.3
11. Massachusetts	70.0
12. Georgia	63.3
13. Virginia	57.5
14. Missouri	55.7
15. Indiana	49.5
16. Minnesota	47.9
17. Tennessee	46.6
18. Wisconsin	44.4
19. Maryland	40.7
20. Alabama	37.4
21. Kentucky	35.1
22. Delaware	34.9
23. Washington	34.5
24. Louisiana	34.0
25. Iowa	32.0
26. Colorado	30.0
27. Arizona	29.7
28. Oklahoma	27.0
29. Kansas	25.5
30. Connecticut	23.6
31. Arkansas	22.8
32. Oregon	21.4
33. Nebraska	20.9
34. South Carolina	20.6
35. Mississippi	20.5
36. West Virginia	16.6
37. Hawaii	14.3
38. Utah	11.2
39. New Mexico	11.2
40. South Dakota	11.0
41. Nevada	10.2
42. Rhode Island	10.0
43. District of Columbia	9.8
44. Idaho	8.3
45. North Dakota	7.1
46. Montana	6.8
47. Maine	6.8
48. New Hampshire	5.8
49. Vermont	4.8
50. Wyoming	4.5
51. Alaska	3.8

* billions of dollars

54. Energy Consumption, 1992*

*UNITED STATES	82,128
1. Texas	9,915
2. California	7,092
3. Ohio	3,733
4. New York	3,616
5. Pennsylvania	3,597
6. Louisiana	3,558
7. Illinois	3,487
8. Florida	3,066
9. Michigan	2,784
10. Indiana	2,408
11. New Jersey	2,401
12. Georgia	2,095
13. North Carolina	2,019
14. Washington	1,991
15. Virginia	1,853
16. Tennessee	1,793
17. Alabama	1,653
18. Kentucky	1,532
19. Missouri	1,499
20. Wisconsin	1,404
21. Massachusetts	1,370
22. Minnesota	1,369
23. Oklahoma	1,302
24. South Carolina	1,224
25. Maryland	1,204
26. Kansas	1,014
27. Mississippi	968
28. Colorado	959
29. Arizona	945
30. Oregon	942
31. Iowa	927
32. Arkansas	796
33. West Virginia	794
34. Connecticut	762
35. Alaska	612
36. New Mexico	584
37. Utah	557
38. Nebraska	506
39. Wyoming	422
40. Nevada	412
41. Idaho	387
42. Maine	370
43. Montana	341
44. North Dakota	327
45. Hawaii	263
46. Rhode Island	247
47. New Hampshire	244
48. Delaware	241
49. South Dakota	205
50. District of Columbia	174
51. Vermont	140

* trillion btu

Comparative Tables